French Philosophy Since 1945

THE NEW PRESS POSTWAR FRENCH THOUGHT SERIES

Ramona Naddaff, Series Editor

Arthur Goldhammer, Translator

Histories: French Constructions of the Past: Postwar French Thought, Volume I
Edited by Jacques Revel and Lynn Hunt

Literary Debate: Texts and Contexts: Postwar French Thought, Volume II
Edited by Denis Hollier and Jeffrey Mehlman

Antiquities: Postwar French Thought, Volume III
Edited by Nicole Loraux, Gregory Nagy, and Laura Slatkin

French Philosophy Since 1945

Problems, Concepts, Inventions

Postwar French Thought, Volume IV

EDITED BY

ETIENNE BALIBAR

AND

JOHN RAJCHMAN

WITH

ANNE BOYMAN

THE NEW PRESS

NEW YORK

LONDON

The New Press is pleased to acknowledge the Florence Gould Foundation for its support of the Postwar French Thought Series.

Published in the United States by The New Press, New York, 2010
Distributed by Perseus Distribution

ISBN 978-1-56584-882-5 (hc.)
CIP data available

The New Press was established in 1990 as a not-for-profit alternative to the large, commercial publishing houses currently dominating the book publishing industry. The New Press operates in the public interest rather than for private gain, and is committed to publishing, in innovative ways, works of educational, cultural, and community value that are often deemed insufficiently profitable.

www.thenewpress.com

Printed in the United States of America

2 4 6 8 10 9 7 5 3 1

Contents

Postwar French Thought Series Preface

French Philosophy Since 1945 is the final volume in The New Press's Postwar French Thought Series. The series began in conversation with André Schiffrin in the early 1990s, when he was establishing The New Press as an alternative model and practice for publishing. At the same time, certain political events—especially in Eastern Europe and in the former Soviet Union—had reshaped the political and global landscape. Our hope, then, was that the conjuncture of these two moments would open up intellectual borders previously censored, bowdlerized, and untranslated authors could now cross. Our aspirations were also domestic. This series was, and is, as I have written before, the realization of a concrete desire to generate, from the unique Franco-American teams selecting texts, a new history of ideas proper to each discipline.

Our ambitions have, of course, been thwarted: not only by political events but also by specific academic and cultural agendas that have not ceased to blame "French" thought for humanism's demise and ruin. Such disciplinary and professional attachments have forsaken recognition of particularities and particular histories, equating "French" postwar thought with an empty and dangerous postmodernism that fails to follow the rules of logic, sense, truth, and reality. This judgment has become a tired and repetitive one. Indeed, these very volumes expose another way of thinking in France, which, as John Rajchman and Etienne Balibar write, "took off on rich and complex paths, which would lead . . . into many new areas in a dramatic history of movements, schools and personalities. . . . [N]ew problems were formulated or reformulated, new ideas and concepts advanced, new styles invented." While this description is intended to capture the trajectory of philosophy in postwar France, it exposes also the evolution of history, classics, literary criticism, and the many other fields whose histories remain to be constructed.

Each volume in the series has had a different style and time of conceptualization, composition, collaboration, and production. *French Philosophy Since 1945* does not differ in this. The volume is organized around seven themes: "In Search of a New Critique," "Histories of Truth," "Questions of Difference," "Event," "The Subject," "Institution and Insurrection," and "Thinking in Art." Each section is preceded by an introduction explaining context and text. New translations have been commissioned. And, finally, an expansive and breathtaking chronology of works and events, dated from 1937 to 2005, has been included to frame the multiple texts collected by the editors.

I wish, once again, to thank the many people who have been involved in the Postwar French Thought Series and who have been acknowledged in prior volumes. Some names must be repeated and new ones added: André Schiffrin, Sarah Fan, Arthur Goldhammer, Etienne Balibar, John Rajchman, and Anne Boyman. It provokes great sadness that, since the inception of this series, we have lost so many beloved colleagues, friends, and scholars whose work forged the various "rich and complex" paths the series has attempted to represent.

May the many pages of these volumes together create unanticipated connections and relations and allow their work to carry and live on.

Ramona Naddaff
Berkeley, California
May 2010

Permissions

Every effort has been made to contact all rights holders of copyrighted material. If notified, The New Press would be pleased to rectify an omission in future editions.

Louis Althusser, "Marxism and Humanism": From *For Marx* by Louis Althusser, translated by Ben Brewster. © François Maspero 1965. Translation © Ben Brewster 1969. This edition published by Verso 2005. Used by permission of Verso.

Louis Althusser and Etienne Balibar, "The Errors of Classical Economics: Outline of a Concept of Historical Time": From *Reading Capital* by Louis Althusser and Etienne Balibar, translated by Ben Brewster. © 1968, Librairie François Maspero. This translation © NLB 1970. This edition published by Verso 2009. Used by permission of Verso.

Alain Badiou, "Veracity and Truth from the Standpoint of the Faithful Procedure: Forcing": From *Being and Event* by Alain Badiou, translated by Oliver Feltham (Continuum, 2006). © Editions du Seuil, 1988. This English-language translation © Continuum 2005. Used by kind permission of Continuum International Publishing Group.

Georges Bataille, "Sovereignty": From *La souveraineté*, in *Oeuvres completes* by Georges Bataille, vol. 8, edited by Denis Hollier. Copyright © 1976 Editions Gallimard, Paris. Used by permission of Editions Gallimard.

Simone de Beauvoir, "The Second Sex": From *The Second Sex* by Simone de Beauvoir, translated by Constance Borde and Sheila Malovny-Chevallier, translation copyright © 2009 by Constance Borde and Sheila Malovny-Chevallier. Used by permission of Alfred A. Knopf, a division of Random House, Inc.

Maurice Blanchot, "The Absence of the Book": From *The Infinite Conversation* by Maurice Blanchot, translated by Susan Hanson (University of Minnesota Press, 1992). English-language edition copyright © 1993 by the Regents of the University of Minnesota Press. Original French-language edition copyright © 1969 by Editions Gallimard. Used by permission of the University of Minnesota Press.

Jacques Bouveresse, "The Myth of Interiority": From *Le mythe de l'intériorité* by Jacques Bouveresse. Copyright © 1976 by Editions de Minuit. Reprinted by permission of Georges Borchardt, Inc., for Editions de Minuit.

Georges Canguilhem, "What Is Psychology?": From "Qu'est-ce que la psychologie?" translated by Howard Davies, in *Etudes d'histoire et de philosophie des sciences* by Georges Canguilhem. © Librairie Philosophique J. Vrin, Paris, 1968. Used by permission of Librairie Philosophique J. Vrin, http://www.vrin.fr.

Jean Cavaillès and Albert Lautman, "Mathematical Thought": From Jean Cavaillès and Albert Lautman, "La pensée mathématique," *Bulletin de la société française de philosophie* 40, no. 1 (1946). © Librairie Philosophique J. Vrin, Paris, 1946. Used by permission of Librairie Philosophique J. Vrin, http://www.vrin.fr.

Gilles Deleuze, "Bergson's Conception of Difference": From *Desert Islands and Other Texts, 1953–1974* by Gilles Deleuze, edited by David Lapoujade and translated by Michael Taormina. Copyright © 2004 Semiotext(e). Copyright © 2002 Les Editions de Minuit. Used by permission of Semiotext(e).

Gilles Deleuze, "Difference and Repetition": From *Difference and Repetition* by Gilles Deleuze, translated by Paul Patton. Copyright © 1995 Columbia University Press. Reprinted by permission of the publisher.

Gilles Deleuze, "Immanence: A Life": From *Pure Immanence* by Gilles Deleuze, translated by Anne Boyman (New York: Zone Books, 2001). © 2001 Urzone, Inc. Used by permission of Zone Books.

Gilles Deleuze, "The Logic of Sense": From *The Logic of Sense* by Gilles Deleuze, edited by Constantin V. Boundas and translated by Mark Lester with Charles Stivale. Copyright © 1990 Columbia University Press. Reprinted by permission of the publisher.

Gilles Deleuze, "On Four Poetic Formulas That Might Summarize Kantian Philosophy": From *Essays Critical and Clinical* by Gilles Deleuze, translated by Daniel W. Smith and Michael A. Greco (University of Minnesota Press, 1997). Copyright © 1997 by the Regents of the University of Minnesota. Originally published as *Critique et clinique*, copyright © 1993 Les Editions de Minuit, Paris. Used by permission of the University of Minnesota Press.

Gilles Deleuze, "The Powers of the False": From *Cinema 2: The Time-Image* by Gilles Deleuze, translated by Hugh Tomlinson and Robert Galeta (University of Minnesota Press, 1989). Copyright © 1989 The Athlone Press. Copyright © 1985 Les Editions de Minuit, Paris. Used by permission of the University of Minnesota Press.

Gilles Deleuze, "Preface to *The Savage Anomaly*": From *Two Regimes of Madness: Texts and Interviews 1975–1995* by Gilles Deleuze, edited by David Lapoujade and translated by Ames Hodges and Mike Taormina. Copyright © 2006 Semiotext(e). Used by permission of Semiotext(e).

Gilles Deleuze, "What Is a *Dispositif?*": From *Two Regimes of Madness: Texts and Interviews 1975–1995* by Gilles Deleuze, edited by David Lapoujade and translated by Ames Hodges and Mike Taormina. Copyright © 2006 Semiotext(e). Used by permission of Semiotext(e).

Gilles Deleuze and Félix Guattari, "A Thousand Plateaus": From *A Thousand Plateaus: Capitalism and Schizophrenia* by Gilles Deleuze and Félix Guattari, translated by Brian Massumi (University of Minnesota Press, 1987). Copyright © 1987 by the University of Minnesota Press. Originally published as *Mille plateaux*, volume 2 of *Capitalisme et schizophrénie* © 1980 by Les Editions de Minuit, Paris. Used by permission of the University of Minnesota Press.

Jacques Derrida, "As If It Were Possible, 'Within Such Limits'": From *Paper Machine* by Jacques Derrida, translated by Rachel Bowlby. Copyright © 2005 by the Board of Trustees of the Leland Stanford Jr. University. All rights reserved. Used with the permission of Stanford University Press, www.sup.org.

Jacques Derrida, "Différance": From *Margins of Philosophy* by Jacques Derrida, translated by Alan Bass. © 1982 by the University of Chicago. © 1972 by Les Editions de Minuit. Used by permission of the University of Chicago Press.

Jacques Derrida, "'Eating Well,' or the Calculation of the Subject: An Interview with Jacques Derrida": From *Who Comes After the Subject?* edited by Eduardo Cadava, Peter Connor, and Jean-Luc Nancy and translated by Peter Connor and Avital Ronell. Originally published in French as "'Il faut bien manger' ou le calcul du sujet: Entretien (avec J.-L. Nancy)," *Cahiers confrontations*, n° 20 © Aubier, 1989. Used by permission of Flammarion Groupe. Translation used by permission of Peter Connor and Avital Ronell.

Jacques Derrida, "Economimesis": From Jacques Derrida and R. Klein, "Economimesis," *Diacritics* 11:2 (1981), 3–12, 19–21. © 1981 The Johns Hopkins University Press. Reprinted with permission of The Johns Hopkins University Press.

Jacques Derrida, "Edmund Husserl's Origin of Geometry: An Introduction": Reprinted from *Edmund Husserl's Origin of Geometry: An Introduction* by Jacques Derrida, translated by John P. Leavey Jr., by permission of the University of Nebraska Press. Copyright © 1962 by the Presses Universitaires de France. Translation copyright © 1978 by John P. Leavey Jr.

Jacques Derrida, "The Ends of Man": From *Margins of Philosophy* by Jacques Derrida, translated by Alan Bass. © 1982 by the University of Chicago. © 1972 by Les Editions de Minuit. Used by permission of the University of Chicago Press.

Jacques Derrida, "Of Grammatology": From *Of Grammatology* by Jacques Derrida, translated by Gayatri Chakravorty Spivak, pp. 20–21. © 1998 The Johns Hopkins University Press. Reprinted with permission of The Johns Hopkins University Press.

Jacques Derrida, "Politics of Friendship": From *Politics of Friendship* by Jacques Derrida, translated by George Collins. © Editions Galilée 1994. Translation © George Collins 1997. This edition published by Verso 2005. Used by permission of Verso.

Jacques Derrida, "Psyche: Inventions of the Other": From "Psyche: Inventions of the Other" by Jacques Derrida, translated by Catherine Porter, in *Reading de Man Reading*, edited by Lindsay Waters and Wlad Godzich (University of Minnesota Press, 1989). Copyright © 1989 by the University of Minnesota. Used by permission of the University of Minnesota Press.

Maurice Florence, "Foucault": From *Aesthetics, Method, and Epistemology* by Michel Foucault, edited by James D. Faubion and translated by Robert Hurley and others. Compilation, introduction, and new translations © 1998 by The New Press. Originally published in French in *Dictionnaire des philosophes*, edited by Denis Huisman, pp. 942–44. © Presses Universitaires de France, 1984. Used by permission of Presses Universitaires de France.

Michel Foucault, "Alexandre Koyré: The Astronomical Revolution, Copernicus, Kepler, Borelli": From "Alexandre Koyré: La révolution astronomique, Copernic, Kepler, Borelli," in *Dits et écrits, tome I: 1954–1975* by Michel Foucault, edited by Daniel Defert and François Ewald with the assistance of Jacques Lagrange. Copyright © 1994 Editions Gallimard, Paris. Used by permission of Editions Gallimard.

Michel Foucault, "Elements for a History of Truth": From "Lecture of 23 January 1974," in *Psychiatric Power: Lectures at the Collège de France, 1973–1974* by Michel Foucault, edited by Jacques Lagrange and translated by Graham Burchell. Copyright © 2003 by Editions du Seuil/Gallimard. Translation © 2006 by Graham Burchell. Used by permission of Palgrave Macmillan.

Michel Foucault, "Eventalization": From "Questions of Method," in *Power* by Michel Foucault, edited by James D. Faubion and translated by Robert Hurley. Originally published in French in *Dits et écrits, 1954–1984*, edited by Daniel Defert and François Ewald with the assistance of Jacques Lagrange. Copyright © 1994 by Editions Gallimard, Paris. Reprinted by permission of Georges Borchardt, Inc., on behalf of Editions Gallimard.

Michel Foucault, "The History of Sexuality: An Introduction": From *The History of Sexuality* by Michel Foucault. Originally published in French as *La volonté du savoir*. Copyright © 1976 by Editions Gallimard, Paris. Reprinted by permission of Georges Borchardt, Inc., for Editions Gallimard.

Michel Foucault, "Introduction to Kant's Anthropology": From *Introduction to Kant's Anthropology* by Michel Foucault, edited by Roberto Nigro and translated by Roberto Nigro and Kate Briggs. Copyright © 2008 Semiotext(e). Copyright © 2008 Librairie Philosophique J. Vrin. Used by permission of Semiotext(e).

Michel Foucault, "Of Other Spaces": From Michel Foucault, "Of Other Spaces," translated by Jay Miskowiec, *Diacritics* 16:1 (1986), 22–7. © 1986 The Johns Hopkins University Press. Reprinted with permission of The Johns Hopkins University Press.

Michel Foucault, "What Is Critique?": From *The Politics of Truth* by Michel Foucault, edited by Sylvère Lotringer and translated by Lysa Hochroth and Catherine Porter. Copyright © 1997, 2007 Semiotext(e). Used by permission of Semiotext(e).

Michel Foucault, "Words and Images": From "Les mots et les images," in *Dits et écrits, tome I: 1954–1975*, by Michel Foucault, edited by Daniel Defert and François Ewald with the assistance of Jacques Lagrange. Copyright © 1994 Editions Gallimard, Paris. Used by permission of Editions Gallimard.

Marcel Gauchet, "The Revolution of the Rights of Man": From *La révolution des droits de l'homme* by Marcel Gauchet. Copyright © 1989 Editions Gallimard, Paris. Used by permission of Editions Gallimard.

Victor Goldschmidt, "The Stoic System and the Idea of Time": From *Le système stoïcien et l'idée du temps* by Victor Goldschmidt. © Librairie Philosophique J. Vrin, Paris, 1953. Used by permission of Librairie Philosophique J. Vrin, http://www.vrin.fr.

Claude Imbert, "For a History of Logic": From *Pour une histoire de la logique: Un héritage platonicien* by Claude Imbert. © Presses Universitaires de France, 1999. Used by permission of Presses Universitaires de France.

Luce Irigaray, "Love Between Us": From *Who Comes After the Subject?* edited by Eduardo Cadava, Peter Connor, and Jean-Luc Nancy and translated by Jeffrey Lomonaco. Originally published in French as "Pour introduire: l'amour entre nous," in *J'aime à toi* by Luce Irigaray. © Editions Grasset & Fasquelle, 1992. Used by permission of Editions Grasset & Fasquelle.

Sarah Kofman, "Respect for Women": From *Le respect des femmes* by Sarah Kofman. Copyright © 1982 Editions Galilée. Used by permission of Editions Galilée.

Julia Kristeva, "The True-Real": From *The Kristeva Reader* by Julia Kristeva, edited by Toril Moi. Copyright © 1986 Columbia University Press. Reprinted by permission of the publisher.

Jacques Lacan, "Intervention on Transference": From *Feminine Sexuality* by Jacques Lacan, edited by Juliet Mitchell & Jacqueline Rose, translated by Jacqueline Rose. Copyright © 1982 by Jacqueline Rose. Copyright © 1966, 1968, 1975 by Editions du Seuil. Copyright © 1975 by Le Graphe. Used by permission of W.W. Norton & Company, Inc.

Jacques Lacan, "Responses to Students of Philosophy Concerning the Object of Psychoanalysis": Used by permission of Jacques-Alain Miller. Translation used by permission of Jeffrey Mehlman.

Claude Lefort, "Disincorporation and Reincorporation of Power" and "Voluntary Servitude": From *Complications: Communism and the Dilemmas of Democracy* by Claude Lefort, translated by Julian Bourg. Copyright © 1999 Columbia University Press. Reprinted with permission of the publisher.

Claude Lévi-Strauss, "Introduction to the Work of Marcel Mauss": From *Introduction to the Work of Marcel Mauss* by Claude Lévi-Strauss, translated by Felicity Baker. © Presses Universitaires de France 1950. This translation © Felicity Baker 1987. This translation first published in 1987 by Routledge & Kegan Paul Ltd. Reproduced by permission of Taylor & Francis Books UK.

Emmanuel Levinas, "Outside the Subject": From *Outside the Subject* by Emmanuel Levinas, translated by Michael B. Smith. Copyright © 1993 Athlone Press. All rights reserved. Used with the permission of Stanford University Press, www.sup.org.

Jean-François Lyotard, "The Differend: Phrases in Dispute": From *The Differend: Phrases in Dispute* by Jean-François Lyotard, translated by Georges Van Den Abbeele (University of Minnesota Press, 1988). Originally published in France as *Le différend*, copyright © 1983 by Les Editions de Minuit. English translation copyright © 1988 by the University of Minnesota. Used by permission of the University of Minnesota Press.

Jean-François Lyotard, "Discourse, Figure": From *Discours, figure* by Jean-François Lyotard. Copyright © 1971 by Klincksieck, Paris. Used by permission of Klincksieck.

Maurice Merleau-Ponty, "Eye and Mind": From *The Primacy of Perception and Other Essays on Phenomenological Psychology, the Philosophy of Art, History and Politics*. Translation copyright © 1964 by Northwestern University Press. Used by permission of Northwestern University Press.

Maurice Merleau-Ponty, "In Praise of Philosophy": From *In Praise of Philosophy* by Maurice Merleau-Ponty, translated by John Wild and James M. Edie. Originally published by Librairie

Gallimard, Paris, in 1953. Translation copyright © 1963 by Northwestern University Press. Used by permission of Northwestern University Press.

Maurice Merleau-Ponty, "A Note on Machiavelli": From *Signs* by Maurice Merleau-Ponty, translated by Richard C. McCleary. Originally published by Librairie Gallimard, Paris, in 1960. Translation copyright © 1964 by Northwestern University Press. Used by permission of Northwestern University Press.

Jean-Claude Milner, "Indistinct Names": From *Les noms indistincts* by Jean-Claude Milner. Copyright © 1983 by Editions du Seuil. Reprinted by permission of Georges Borchardt, Inc., for Editions du Seuil.

Pierre-François Moreau, "Image, Idea": From *Spinoza* by Pierre-François Moreau. © Presses Universitaires de France, 2009. Used by permission of Presses Universitaires de France.

Jean-Luc Nancy, "Being Singular Plural": From *Being Singular Plural* by Jean-Luc Nancy, translated by Robert D. Richardson and Anne E. O'Byrne. Copyright © 2000 by the Board of Trustees of the Leland Stanford Jr. University; 1996 Editions Galilée. All rights reserved. Used with the permission of Stanford University Press, www.sup.org.

Jacques Rancière, "The Community of Equals": From *On the Shores of Politics* by Jacques Rancière, translated by Liz Heron. First published as *Aux bords du politique* © Editions Osiris 1992. This edition © Verso 1995. Translation © Liz Heron 1995. Used by permission of Verso.

Jacques Rancière, "Disagreement: Politics and Philosophy": From *Disagreement: Politics and Philosophy* by Jacques Rancière, translated by Julie Rose (University of Minnesota Press, 1999). Originally published as *La mésentente: Politique et philosophie*, copyright © 1995 Editions Galilée. English translation copyright © 1999 by the Regents of the University of Minnesota. Used by permission of the University of Minnesota Press.

Jacques Rancière, "The Politics of Aesthetics: The Distribution of the Sensible": From *The Politics of Aesthetics: The Distribution of the Sensible* by Jacques Rancière, translated by Gabriel Rockhill (Continuum, 2004). © La Fabrique-Éditions, 2000. © Gabriel Rockhill, 2004. Used by kind permission of Continuum International Publishing Group.

Paul Ricoeur, "Freud and Philosophy: An Essay on Interpretation": From *Freud and Philosophy: An Essay on Interpretation* by Paul Ricoeur, translated by Denis Savage. Copyright © 1970 by Yale University. Used by permission of Yale University Press.

Jean-Paul Sartre, *Search for a Method*: From *Search for a Method* by Jean-Paul Sartre, translated by Hazel Barnes, translation copyright © 1963 by Alfred A. Knopf, a division of Random House, Inc. Used by permission of Alfred A. Knopf, a division of Random House, Inc.

Jules Vuillemin, "The Kantian Heritage and the Copernican Revolution": From *L'héritage kantien et la révolution copernicienne* by Jules Vuillemin. Copyright © Presses Universitaires de France, 1954. Used by permission of Presses Universitaires de France.

Introduction

In the aftermath of World War II, French philosophy took off on a rich and complex path, which would lead it into many new areas in a dramatic history of movements, schools, and personalities. Many new problems were formulated or reformulated, new ideas and concepts advanced, new styles invented. It was a singular episode not simply in postwar French culture but also in the tumultuous untold history of philosophies in the twentieth century; translated into many languages, it remains a key philosophical inheritance and resource for the twenty-first. It was not only a matter of the academic discipline of philosophy. It was the sort of philosophy that would exert an often transformative influence in many other fields, sometimes assuming an ongoing role within them; no area would remain unaffected. It is hard to imagine, for example, what the current study of humanities or social sciences in English-speaking countries would be without it. French philosophy since 1945 is thus today a sprawling, multifaceted field, found in many areas and languages. In this anthology, we have tried to offer a way into it, its history, and its possibilities. We have tried to construct a kind of sourcebook or manual that reflects its peculiar nature.

For this new or "contemporary" philosophy, engaged with many fields, and based in a city at a peculiar moment in its history, one prewar precedent might be found in the Vienna of Wittgenstein and Freud. In fact, philosophy after 1945 in Paris itself goes back to earlier debates in the 1930s, tied up with each of those two Viennese figures, Jacques Lacan for psychoanalysis and Jean Cavaillès for mathematical logic, each of whom would later help displace the centrality of Husserl in the philosophy of the immediate *après-guerre* in France. In the case of both European cities, at these different moments, we find not only find a peculiar overlap of philosophy with many activities in sciences and in arts, forming part of a larger atmosphere of thought; but, tied up with the history of the war and the displacements to which it gave rise, in both cases a singular role would be played by the translation, at once linguistic and intellectual, of this work into English. Of course we would eventually oppose these two great "translated philosophies" as analytic and Continental. One result is that "French philosophy" would work through disciplines outside the academic field of philosophy (itself formed in larger measure through the immigration of analytic-minded German and Viennese philosophers), thus preserving something of the larger cultural sense and impact of the work of philosophy itself. In this anthology, we have tried to keep this sense of the larger field in which French philosophy emerged and so have included many figures who, while trained in philosophy, worked in other fields, often changing them in turn: figures such as Claude Lévi-Strauss, Jacques Lacan, Georges Canguilhem, and Georges Bataille. Working outside the academic discipline of philosophy, they helped pose in new ways the question of the relation of philosophy to the nonphilosophical fields of which it has need and to which it is addressed.

What, then, were the central frameworks within which a new French philosophy arose after 1945? No doubt many interpretive strategies are possible. In this volume, we eventually settled on a fresh starting point and related approach. In an early book on the topic, Vincent Descombes had stressed the question of self and other, derived from Alexandre Kojève's influential reading of Hegel, although he himself would later adopt a more critical stance, influenced by analytic philosophy.[1] This path into French philosophy since 1945 has the drawback of leaving out or marginalizing the kind of anti-Hegelian movement Gilles Deleuze would diagnose in 1968, found in another form in Jacques Derrida's way out of Husserl and his long questioning engagement with Heidegger. The role of Heidegger in French philosophy is now a topic in its own right, studied in detail by Dominique Janicaud; in a short book accompanying his study, he offers a suggestive thesis about the peculiar fate of phenomenology in France, surrounding what he calls the "theological turn" to be found in the work of Emmanuel Levinas, among others.[2] For his part, Levinas, who played a key role in the translation and interpretation of phenomenology in French, would later express regrets about the enthusiastic support he had given to Heidegger in the dramatic debate in Davos in 1929, in which Heidegger had taken on the great "humanist" neo-Kantian philosopher Ernst Cassirer; Levinas's response in turn forms part of the larger question of critical philosophy and the role of humanism in it in French philosophy after the war.[3] The problem, at once political and intellectual, of the destiny of Heidegger's philosophy is in many ways tied up with new kinds of divisions and movements in philosophy on both sides of the Rhine.

On the French side, there would at the same time arise another formation, irreducible to either the French readings of Hegel or to phenomenology and the analytic opposition to them—what would be called structuralism (and its aftermath, poststructuralism). In the 1960s, structuralism would become the key transformative force, drawing not simply on the implications of Saussurian linguistics, which Merleau-Ponty helped introduce into philosophical discussion, but also on "structural" features in Annales-School historiography, the new historically minded epistemology of Canguilhem and Bachelard, and the invention of the New Novel and New Wave cinema, and the critical discussions to which they gave rise. There are many sources of this structuralist moment, linking it with the larger formation to the history of formalisms in the twentieth century. Claude Lévi-Strauss, a central figure in this new configuration, had in fact come across Saussure thanks to an encounter with the great Prague Circle linguist Roman Jakobson in New York during the war, bringing back the results to France. In looking back at the structuralist "constellation" in a recent study, the linguist and philosopher Jean-Claude Milner stresses as well the role of the distinguished linguist Emile Benveniste and his structural analysis of "the formal apparatus of enunciation" in the key question of "the subject" in language or in discourse, suggesting new ways of posing the whole question of self and other.[4]

All of these developments, emerging and confronting one another before 1968, would in turn assume new forms after it, leading to further intersections with Continental philosophies and, in part through a debate with Habermas, with the fate of critical theory in postwar Germany. They would also complicate the relation of French philosophy to analytic traditions. Jacques Bouveresse, initially writing about Wittgenstein in France in a dissident spirit, has helped to raise this question.[5] A less polemical approach has been elaborated by Claude Imbert, starting from the peculiar ways the Husserl-Frege divide was taken up and transformed in France. She tries to work out a new "history of logic," associated in France in the 1930s with two great mathematician-philosophers who were to perish in the Resistance, Jean Cavaillès and Albert Lautman; in this new history, Merleau-Ponty along with Wittgenstein play key transformative roles.[6] French philosophical discussions of mathematics, still active in France in the postwar period, would continue to matter for Alain Badiou as well as Deleuze, albeit in quite different ways.

But if all these various starting points, each connected with a particular history, don't fit into a single monolithic story, they were in turn tied up with a distinguished French scholarly tradition in the history of philosophy, and many new readings, and styles of reading, in the history of philosophy would accompany and amplify the debates and problems of the day. Thus we find a "new" Nietzsche, a new Spinoza, a new Bergson, Marx, Freud, Machiavelli, even a new Kant, themselves brought together in ways that departed from Hegel's or Heidegger's great narratives of a history of spirit or history of metaphysics. We find not only Jacques Derrida's distinctive ongoing "deconstructive questioning" of the entire tradition, but also particular contributions, such as Victor Goldschmidt's account of the problem of event and destiny in Stoicism, which suggested new departures, new concepts. The peculiar way French philosophy—and idea of philosophy—fits within the larger history of "modern" philosophy and the specific forms it had assumed in the nineteenth century, as well as the nature of its relations to ancient philosophy and Jewish traditions, became inseparable with new scholarship and debate. But if such diversity in sources and approaches in French philosophy since 1945 raises the question of its larger consistency, if not unity, it has nevertheless often seemed of a piece, particularly when looked at from the outside, notably from the standpoint of its English-language discussions and uses. Perhaps one could speak of the invention of what Pierre Macherey has called a "French style" in philosophy.[7]

In this anthology, we have tried to devise a method that, while respecting this larger diversity, would offer a useful way into its problems, concepts, and inventions. We decided to take as a starting point a short text by Michel Foucault, itself written in a last restless period in his own work, in which he looks back at the formation of "modern" or "contemporary" philosophies in France and tries to situate them with respect to corresponding traditions in English-speaking and German-speaking philosophy in a history that goes back to Kant and his invention of critical philosophy. In the course of developing this conjecture, Foucault points to a general dividing line in postwar French philosophy first posed by Jean Cavaillès's objections to Husserl in the 1930s. He would repeat this analysis with subtle variations in the last seven years of his work, and to introduce our anthology we have selected the version that served as an introduction to the work of his own great teacher and supporter, Georges Canguilhem. It would be Foucault's last, some say testamentary, writing. From it we retain two basic principles: the search for a new critique in postwar French philosophy and the idea of bifurcations and related "points d'hérésie" in the larger picture of the development and the transformation of philosophy itself. In counterpoint to Foucault's essay, we also include Canguilhem's original review of Foucault's *The Order of Things* from 1967, in which the problem of the "exhaustion of the cogito" is connected to the transcendental idea of the subject that Kant had introduced into the heart of critical philosophy. In these juxtaposed texts the reader can already start to discern the larger idea of divergences and bifurcations that runs throughout the volume.

Foucault dates what he calls "contemporary philosophy" in France from the lectures Edmund Husserl gave in Paris in 1929, called Cartesian Meditations, published through the work of Levinas, which would give rise to two "contested readings," one offered by Cavaillès and leading to a "philosophy of the concept," the other by Jean-Paul Sartre, leading to a "philosophy of the subject." The war would then interrupt and affect the fork dividing the two lines in philosophy that would result from these readings. Cavaillès, citing Spinoza, would join the Resistance, playing a dramatic role, and eventually be put to death—thus, Foucault suggests, finding a more direct engagement than Sartre, the philosopher of engagement. But this early point of bifurcation was later to assume a particular force in "those strange years, the '60s," when, in association with what was called structuralism, it was taken up again by a new generation of philosophers, in particular by the students of Canguilhem, who himself had developed Cavaillès's "philosophy of the concept" in a more historically minded form, focused in the life sciences. The search for a new critique in Foucault's own work in those years would then be associated with the larger problem of "humanism" or philosophical "anthropologism" as it was found in Heidegger or in Marx or with respect to new methods in linguistics, criticism, or the social sciences.

Our anthology thus starts by posing this problem of a new kind of critique in French philosophy after 1945, in relation to Kant and, for Foucault, to Nietzsche, but also, at the same time, in terms of the Marxist as well as the literary or aesthetic senses of the term "critique." But in expanding the field in this way we are now able to distinguish further lines or forks, which then multiply the simple division between concept and subject Foucault introduced, complicating his own picture in turn. Moreover, those lines recur in the series of questions we have tried to present and formulate in the volume. In providing for this more complex picture, we then drew on the second of the two principles we adopted from Foucault—the principle of "points of heresy," or the idea of dividing or turning points in the history of thought, and so of philosophy. Thus for each of the interlocking questions or problems we tried to explore—histories of truth, problems of difference, the concept of event, processes of subjectivization, questions of conflict and community, and the role of thinking in the arts—we went on to identify clusters of discussion or constellations of discourse, each with its points or lines of divergence, and related inventions and concepts. In adopting this method of presentation, we thus tried to suggest something of the larger image of critical thought distinctive of French philosophy in this period.

In an interview conducted about the same time as he was introducing his picture of philosophy in France, Foucault himself offers us this picture of questions and related lines of divergence.[8] In contrast to Habermas's tripartite division of the interest of reason, he declares that reason or philosophy never stops bifurcating, the points of bifurcation being "critical" for new forms of thinking. Allowing for variations and idioms, this idea seemed to us to fit best with the larger search for a new image or "style" of thought in France after the war. In any case, it seemed to offer us a way, in presenting this philosophy, to keep open the question of the nature of philosophy itself: its manners of writing, its functions, and its relations to other fields. What new idea of thought and its ongoing history follows from this principle of constant and uneliminable points of divergence, as distinct from simple contradictions or oppositions, associated with particular questions such as "the question of the subject" or "the question of the concept"? How then are such questions reiterated or reformulated in new configurations—as for example, in Foucault's case, the manner in which Kant's question "What is Enlightenment?" would be itself taken up in various traditions, and eventually within contemporary French philosophy? Could we then construct an anthology not of schools or movements, nor of individual authors, governing methodologies, or even institutions, but of such questions, their points of heresy, and related constellations? Could we see French philosophy itself as exemplifying as well as helping to formulate this new picture of philosophy?

In each section, we thus present a cluster of writings surrounding a particular question, and in the overlap from one section to the next the reader is invited to see a further elaboration or implication of one question or problem in and for another. In each of these sections we offer new translations together with better-known writings or authors not simply in order to draw attention to them but also to offer a better picture of the points from which particular questions or distinctive divisions arose. Unfortunately, including this material along with the rich archive of already published works obliged us to reluctantly have recourse to presenting material in excerpts. According to their particular interests, readers may then wish to turn to the full text and context of each entry, pursuing the historical and philosophical problems they pose. With all this in mind, if we then look back to the 1930s, when, according to Foucault, "contemporary" philosophy began in France, we find not simply Husserl's lectures and the readings of Cavaillès and Sartre but also Bataille and Lacan, who, along with Levinas, would complicate the question of "mutual recognition" (and so the question of the subject) Kojève had emphasized in his influential reading of Hegel's *Phenomenology of Spirit*. On the other hand, we find an "impersonal" element in Sartre's *Transcendence of the Ego*, which Deleuze would take up in opposition to Husserl, associating it instead with a new Bergson, thus providing another path into the question of the subject. As we started to look at this "prehistory" of the 1930s, we came to think it would be useful to provide a chronology offering the reader a sense of the larger historical field. In particular, this chronology might offer a sense of the complex question of the impact of the war (and the occupation of France) not directly mentioned in Foucault's own "archeological" hypothesis, though arguably presupposed by it, and by the new paths taken up by French philosophers after the liberation of France in 1945. Following the war, we then distinguish six "moments," which, inseparable from cultural and political events, crystallize around problematizations of "common sense" and related "processes of subjectivization," leading to the formulation of new philosophical questions or the creation of new concepts. While each moment thus serves to redistribute the lines of battle or the very terms of argument and discussion, they overlap and often have unanticipated aftereffects, as in the case of the line Foucault draws before the war between Cavaillès and Husserl. There are three more programmatic moments of new approaches and ideas—existentialist, structuralist, and what we are calling im-political—and then three minor ones, in which those programs are themselves opened to questions, divisions, or transformations. At the same time, these six moments may be regarded as turning points for the changing relations of French philosophy with philosophies in other languages or traditions. Thus, for example, Foucault's own preoccupation with the critical or enlightenment question and its destiny in German-, English-, and French-language traditions, came at a larger moment of debate and transformation in the relations among the three and their understandings of "modernity" or of democratic politics. The last moment, then, opens onto current debates about universality, translation, and transnationality in our now global condition.

One aspect of these last debates was the issue of nationality and national languages in philosophy and its history or "geography," and the related problems of what Derrida calls "idioms" and Deleuze calls "minorities." In the twenty years that have followed the fourth moment in our chronology, it is perhaps suggestive to look back at this aspect of the problem. If, as Foucault suggests, contemporary French philosophy arose (in a manner punctuated by the war) from a complex departure from nineteenth-century Europe and the role of "critical philosophy" in it, in the twenty-first century, we are perhaps confronted with a new situation in which this great postwar French philosophical *dérive* will be taken up in new ways in other circumstances and in other languages. It is from the perspective of this as yet unwritten global history that the project of a kind of sourcebook or manual of problems, concepts, and inventions might play a useful role, opening up new uses in other places.

The editors would like to give special thanks to Susan Thompson for her invaluable assistance as well as to Chessia Kelley and Stewart Campbell for their work in the preparation of this volume.

Notes

[1] Vincent Descombes, *Modern French Philosophy*, trans. L. Scott-Fox and J.M. Harding (New York: Cambridge University Press, 1980).

[2] Dominique Janicaud et al., *Phenomenology and the "Theological Turn": The French Debate* (New York: Fordham University Press, 2000).

[3] Present at Davos, Levinas staged a farcical replay of the fateful debate playing the role of Cassirer himself to the amusement of all the participants. For his regrets and the role the episode played in the development of his own "humanism of the other," see Richard A. Cohen, "Introduction," Emmanuel Levinas, *Humanism of the Other* (Chicago University Press: 2006), pp. viiff. For a detailed account of the debate itself see Pierre Auberque, *Débat sur le kantisme et la philosophie* (Paris: Editions Beauchesne, 1997).

[4] Jean-Claude Milner, *Le périple structural: Figures et paradigms* (Paris: Editions du Seuil, 2002).

[5] "Why I am so very unFrench" in *Philosophy in France Today,* ed. Alan Montefiore (Cambridge University Press: 1983), pp. 9–13.

[6] Claude Imbert, *Pour une histoire de la logique: Un héritage platonicien* (Paris: Presses Universitaires de France, 1999).

[7] Pierre Macherey, "Y a-t-il une philosophie francaise," in *Histoires de dinosaure: Faire de la philosophie, 1965–1997* (Paris: PUF, 1999), pp. 313ff.

[8] "Structuralism and Post-Structuralism" (interview with Gerard Raulet), in Michel Foucault, *Aesthetics, Method and Epistemology: Essential Works Volume Two*, ed. James D. Fauben (New York: The New Press, 1997), p. 442: "I would not speak about *one* bifurcation of reason but more about an endless, multiple bifurcation . . ."

PART I

In Search of a New Critique

Foucault's fork, dividing a philosophy of subject from a philosophy of concept, goes back to Kant, the idea of critique, and the ways it would be taken up in French philosophy after the war. Foucault's 1962 thesis diagnoses what was original in the French appropriations and reformulations of critical philosophy: the problem of man or finitude. What would new critique be, when freed from the "anthropological slumbers" in which it still seemed mired? When Foucault inserted this problem at the heart of critical thought in *The Order of Things* four years later, he hit upon a neuralgic or heretical point in the philosophies of the day. Althusser elaborated his antihumanist Marx in 1965. In 1968 Derrida would proclaim "the ends of man" as the defining feature of French philosophy. But to awaken from Kant's own anthropological slumbers (as Hume had awoken Kant himself from his dogmatic idealist ones) was not at all to abandon critique. On the contrary, it was the start of a search for a new kind of critique.

This complex search was thus not anti-Kantian, even though it was at odds with a more official French sociological or Republican idea of Kantian philosophy. It was rather a search for a kind of "fourth critique" that would be more historically minded, and closer to the rich relations French philosophy had developed with anthropology, thus displacing the sociological question of modernity with the problem of the codes or structures of a culture and hence the new question of what exists outside them. Thus, for example, Lévi-Strauss's idea of a "symbolic order" of culture was said to pose the question of a transcendence without a subject, while his account of "symbolic effectiveness" suggested a new relation of the subject in this order, developed by Jacques Lacan. These ideas helped encourage a search for structures in culture or art, which, following Lévi-Strauss, would draw on the early linguistic models of Ferdinand de Saussure. At the same time, in Louis Althusser's new reading of Marx, the question of ideology and critique seemed to take a similar Kantian turn, as though ideology were a kind of "transcendental illusion" constitutive of a given mode of production. When Foucault identified the problem of anthropologism in Kant, he thus seemed to capture the larger philosophical question at issue in a range of new disciplines and to formulate the philosophical problem it posed: how to invent a new critique no longer based in either God or man.

The Sartre-Cavaillès division between subject and concept thus matched the development of divergent kinds of critical philosophy. On one hand, there was a search, following Husserl, for a kind of "concrete a priori," rooted in a bodily life-world and relations with the other, in which sensibilia or *le sensible* would find a new philosophical and aesthetic role. On the other hand, Foucault would advance what he called a "historical a priori," rooted in changing forms of knowledge and the particular ideas of the subject within them. Armed with Canguilhem's critical essay on the history of psychologies, which itself pursued Cavalliès's own antipsychologism in a new historical direction, Foucault would reject any unifying or founding notion of subjective experience outside these changing bodies of knowledge. Is the subject then constitutive of knowledge? Or, on the contrary, are our ideas of the subject themselves constituted through evolving forms of discourse, themselves anonymous or irreducible to any single subjective (or even intersubjective) origin? The problem of finitude seemed to lie at the heart of this new division. For it concerned not only the question of anthropology in Kant, but also the new forms it would assume in the dramatic Cassirer-Heidegger debate of 1929 over the fate of Kantian philosophy, in which Levinas actively participated and which Jules Vuillemin would help introduce into the study of philosophy in postwar France. To invent a new critique no longer based in man thus seemed to involve not simply, as with Cassirer, man as the locus of cognitive symbolic structures but also more pointedly, with Heidegger, the question of a constitutive finitude—the idea that our "being-there," "thrown into the world" in the finite interval between birth and death, is constitutive of who we are and can become. In particular, in these years Foucault took on what would become an important theme in French philosophy: the peculiar role of death or mortality in this notion of finitude. To the search for concrete a priori structures of *le vécu* (the lived) Foucault would oppose what Canguilhem called *le vivant* (the living being) or the changing concepts of "life" in the life sciences; it is then in Bichat and with the modern clinic that Foucault would find the source of the idea of life and death in this "analytic of finitude." Thus Canguilhem, the strict historian of the concept, would rejoin Nietzsche, the mad philosopher of a new critique "after man," both concerned with the vital role of error in the growth of knowledge. In this odd marriage, a key role was played by the influential translation of Heidegger's own lecture course on Nietzsche and on his attempt to put the idea of "living being" in the place of the classical idea of the subject. The problem of life and death would thus acquire a distinctive role in the larger search for a critique that would no longer suppose either God's infinite understanding (or its hermeneutic or philological substitutes) or a phenomenological analysis of our finite being-in-the-world. That is then how the question became: how to invent a critique based neither in God nor in man, *ni homme ni Dieu*?

The search for a new critique thus involved a redrawing of the map of modern philosophies, which Kant had helped to program when, awakening from his own slumbers, he presented empiricism and idealism as the two opposing lines that would be brought together in a critique capable of determining the conditions of possibility at once for experience and ideas, sensibility and understanding, and the relations between the two. To awaken in turn from Kant's anthropological slumbers required redrawing those lines, posing the question of the sensible and the intelligible in terms of the new bifurcation between concept and subject. Thus, in the nineteenth century after Kant, there emerged the trio of Marx, Freud, and Nietzsche, what Paul Ricoeur called the "philosophers of suspicion," while in the classical period before him, there would be Spinoza and Leibniz, what Deleuze called the "philosophers of expression." As for empiricism, in his study first of Hume, then of Bergson and Nietzsche, Deleuze sought a kind of experimental route out of transcendental or critical philosophy and its assumption of a grounding urdoxa.

The problem of a critique "after man" thus became a complex theme within French philosophy. As Derrida stressed in his own essay on how to get out of philosophical anthropology, or "the ends of man," a central influence would be Heidegger's own "Letter on Humanism" of 1946. With Derrida and Levinas we find another development of the Kantian critique, centered on the problem of the law, the path Janicaud associates with the "theological turn" in French phenomenology, in which there is the postulation of a kind of hyperlaw and corresponding responsibility. For Levinas, that would become the principle of a "humanism of the other." In Derrida, the attempt to free the idea of transcendence from all "presence-to-self" would lead to the "quasi-transcendental" status of "conditions of impossibility," and the corresponding passage of the idea of critique to "responsibility for aporias" in all forms of thought. In Derrida, the law becomes "messianic" at the same time as critical thought becomes a questioning of presence or proper sense in all forms and institutions of thought. Critique becomes "deconstructive questioning."

Increasingly suspicious in turn of the postulation of any such hyperlaw, Deleuze moved in another direction. He tried to elaborate instead a new empiricism, more akin to the radical empiricism of William James, as well as to Bergson and Whitehead—what he would call a "transcendental empiricism." In his own early readings of Kant, Deleuze elaborates the problem as "common sense" (logical, moral, and aesthetic), from which he imagined Kant himself would break in his last years, with the question of the sublime or the undoing of the faculties in the *Opus Posthumum*. For Deleuze, what mattered was the undoing of the very idea of a tribunal or a court of reason in favor of a kind of experimental play with the conditions of thought—a new way of playing the game of thought—which he found first in Hume, then Nietzsche. In the place of the tribunal, starting with Hume's idea of convention, Deleuze tried to develop a whole new jurisprudence in and of philosophy. He attacked the problem of the law in his study of Masoch, which itself had taken off from Lacan's treatment of the question in his essay "Kant with Sade"; it would be the start of a larger project he called "*critique et clinique*." In Deleuze, the critical question thus became inseparable from the problem of experimentation and invention of new ways of talking, seeing, living—new possibilities of life. No longer tied to a fixed law of transcendental limits any more than prior truth and error, critique thus becomes "clinical," a matter of invention and experimentation with the sensible conditions for new ideas, new styles of thought. The search for a new critique after Kant would thus be pursued along the two divergent lines of a hyperlaw and an indeterminate life.

At the same time, the search for such new or transformed critique intersected with (indeed seemed inseparable from) two other areas traditionally associated with the word "critique" in the new sense Kant gave to it: literary or art "criticism" and "critique" in the political sense of the term. "Anthropologism" or "humanism," concept and subject, were also being raised and debated at the same time in these two areas. In literature, there was a search for a *nouvelle critique*, to use Barthes's term, which broke away from the traditional practices of philology and text interpretation and introduced a whole set of new questions. As Barthes would put it, the problem was to invent critique without a metalanguage, in which writers and critics would find not simply a new relation with one another, but also with the new image of thought that was being developed at the same time in philosophy. The new critique simultaneously involved a search for a new function of the literary intellectual not only with Sartre but also with the new current of thinking represented by Maurice Blanchot. After the war and in response to it, Blanchot tried to develop, in part through his friendship with Levinas, a new picture of the sense in which writing and thinking were related to one another, based in the ideas of impossibility, neutrality, and dispossessing events. With the Algerian War, and then with 1968, Blanchot went on to elaborate the implications of this question for the ideas of community and politics.

The political sense of the term "critique" of course goes back to Marx and the "critique of ideology." But, as Jacques Rancière would point out in his essay on the topic in *Lire le Capital* in 1965, the problem of exactly what Marx meant by the term was itself a matter of debate in the postwar period. In particular, there arose the contrast Rancière developed between Althussser's structuralist view and a more humanist picture rooted in Feuerbach and the themes of alienation and reification of the "species-being" of laboring humanity to be found in Marx's own early writings. A central problem was the very idea of ideology itself, for which Althusser, drawing on Lacan, tried to present as a kind of structural or transcendental illusion, required for the reproduction of the social relations (and related subject-positions) of a given mode of production. But, in a certain sense, Althusser's reading of Marx would lead to an undoing if not a deconstruction of Marxism, and with it a further elaboration of the sense of critique, leading not simply to Pierre Bourdieu's new sociological sense, rooted in the notions of habitus and practice. As with Foucault's own attempt to substitute a critique of "discourse" and "power" for the traditional violence-ideology division that would be extrinsic to knowledge and power, the complex theme of critique would thus become tied up with the break with Kantian common sense and involved with issues of dissensus and problematization in the very idea and function of critical practices.

JULES VUILLEMIN

The Kantian Heritage and the Copernican Revolution

1954

Modern Philosophy and the Copernican Rejection of Originary Time

In the final analysis, the splitting of the Self—a theme central to all philosophies stemming from Kantianism, whether in the form of the opposition between the Absolute Self and the Self opposed to the Non-Self, or of the "I think" and internal meaning, or, finally, of the existent and the subject—can therefore be explained by the fact that the Copernican Revolution sacrifices the world to finitude and time only to draw philosophy back into the eternity that engenders time but is itself atemporal. The history of conceptual shifts in the interpretation of Kantianism can therefore be used freely to illustrate the various ways in which modern philosophy has turned attention away from the idea of originary time, that is, from the history of humanity, so as to bury it in a derived time, conceptualized as in Fichte at the level of the idea, in Cohen at the level of principle, or in Heidegger at the level of intuition. These reflections will also help to reveal the threefold significance of time in Kantianism and its threefold inadequacy to the program of originarity contained in the Copernican Revolution.

For an interpretation that starts from the *Dialectic of Pure Reason*, as Fichte's does, time can only measure the distance that necessarily arises between Ought-to-Be and Being, between theoretical requirement and practical reality, between intellectual intuition and actual self-consciousness. Hence time nicely exemplifies the fall from the Absolute into the Relative. Although it originally points toward the effort whereby the finite, in its finite genesis itself, constitutes the divine infinite of aspiration, this point of view, specific to knowing, soon goes over into the opposite, realist point of view of being, in which only the descending movement of grace seems capable both of extracting such an effort from the illusions of the *for-itself* and of bestowing a kind of effectivity on the

From *L'héritage kantien et la révolution copernicienne* (Paris: Presses Universitaires de France, 1954), pp. 303–6; trans. Arthur Goldhammer.

moral consciousness of self. In Kant this shift found expression in the ambiguous concept of intelligible time, of the moral time of conversion, wherein the human and finite appearance of succession inevitably points to the elimination of such appearance in the immobility of the divine.

For an interpretation that starts with the *Analytic of Pure Reason*, as Cohen's does, time flows from the gap between thought (*la pensée*) and knowledge (*la connaissance*), between the noumenon and the phenomenon, between the whole and the part. Here again it marks the fall from the divine into the positive. In the beginning the claim was that it was the condition of the possibility of phenomena, inasmuch as phenomena acquire their transcendental status only in and through internal meaning, but since genesis can acquire nothing that has not already been created, the principle of intensive magnitudes teaches us that time, which surely conditions, does not determine, and that the category, the only plenary source of determination, brings it forth as "negative condition" and restriction at the moment the category becomes a positive principle of knowledge. Time then indicates only the impossibility of ascending to total knowledge; it plays exactly the same role in the realm of knowledge that it played earlier in the realm of morality. It is the mark of a divergence that divine and total thought, the necessary but unknown foundation of partial human knowledge, ignores in the peace of its omnipotent possession.

Thus far, time is nothing but the symbol of these displacements. Everything seems to change, however, when we move to the interpretation that begins with intuition, that of Heidegger. In fact, doesn't time in *The Transcendental Aesthetics* appear to exclude any displacement a priori, since it no longer measures a problematic gap between the absolute and the real but rather defines the intrinsic structure of that finite-absolute, the existent? Doesn't being-toward-death illustrate the absolute totality in which the originary ontological horizon is constituted? Now, the privilege of the formalism inverts this appearance, because this originary temporality is temporal in name only: in effect, it constitutes, in an eternal act that posits existence, the ecstatic horizon in which the events of time come to be located. It is the form; they are the substance. This time is indifferent to the objects it traverses and to history! But doesn't the implicit image of the empty receptacle already indicate a reference to space? What is this originary time that constitutes the possibility of historical experience only by secreting anguish, only by producing the nothingness of objects and therefore history as well? And isn't this temporality that teaches us the nothingness of history—which is to say, indifference to events—yet another eternity? Doesn't true existential time emerge where existentialism has ceased to expect it, at the juncture of temporality and history, of subjective existence and collective becoming, where the destiny of the divinized individual is placed within humanity and recognizes that it derives its being from humanity? And don't we once again find the same shift from the absolute to the relative, from the existential to the "*existentiel*" that is characteristic of all Copernican efforts?

If the Fichtean displacement made explicit the difficulty of intelligible time in Kant and in moral life in general as well as the problem of the difference between sanctity and obligation, the displacement in Cohen laid bare the contradiction implicit in Kantian physics and in the critical conception of knowledge. A total thought would make time disappear, reducing it to nothing more than a necessary correlate of the finitude of knowledge. Physical time, whether as principle of affection by the external object or, by contrast, a result of the autoaffection by means of which one passes from thought to knowledge, is thus torn between the Aesthetic and the Analytic, now making the Copernican Revolution unfaithful to its own premises, now reconciling it with itself only by veering toward an absolute idealism. This ambiguity of physical time in Kant also applies to psychological time in the existentialist interpretation. Isn't the internal meaning in fact at once the succession of phenomena in which the ego apprehends itself and the act of self-positing of the "I think?" Isn't it now the eternal act of the *cogito* as concentrated within itself, and now its expansion and alienation in an element wherein it can nevertheless find no foreign datum?

Note that in this threefold moment of the transcendental construction of time, originary temporality is in each case ignored in favor of derived time. In the moral time born of the gap between what is and what ought to be, time does not in fact emerge from the immanence of the "I think," here identified with intellectual intuition. It expresses only the movement from intellectual intuition to sensible intuition. Although Kant in certain texts pertaining to the philosophy of history comes close to an originary conception of time, the time at which the transcendental dialectic and its interpretation arrive therefore always remains equally derivative or secondary, that is, external to the purity of the "I think," the only true motor of the transcendental genesis. Moral time is thus not the source of being, since it is in being, whereas the source of being is by definition found only in atemporal intellectual intuition. Similarly, if one defines the "I think" in terms of the principle of intensive magnitudes, time is not constituting but constituted. It epitomizes the system of negative conditions, but only the category exercises the positive act of determination. Finally, if existentialism identifies transcendental apperception and temporalization, it is only to the extent that the latter leads philosophy out of ontic alienation into the ontological eternity of existentialist constitution. As for the empirical history of man, it is once again abandoned to the alienated and constituted being, outside the "I think" and among objects to be conceived.

In the classical era, philosophy presented itself as a complement of theology. Modern philosophy thinks it is suppressing religion when in reality it wants to be a substitute for religion, for while it discovers finitude, it also reveals the eternal essence of that finitude. All things are immersed in time, but philosophy establishes its own eternal status. And the philosopher takes the place of God to support that fragile edifice, the world. Now we can understand why neither Kant nor his interpreters, all of whom sensed the true problem of time in one form or another, nevertheless failed to free themselves from the postulate of the *philosophia perennis*, which is in fact merely a consequence of the Copernican Revolution. Wasn't what Fichte, Cohen, and Heidegger sought in Kant perhaps not the content of his philosophy but the eternal method of philosophizing for which he provided a model? To be sure, they all tell us repeatedly that Kant discovered finitude, but on condition that we except Kant himself—the eternal Kant of philosophy—from that finitude. Thus formalism takes over the infinite, which modern ontology originally wanted to eliminate from philosophy. God no longer exists, but the philosophy that proclaims the nonexistence of God also represents the new divinity. The absence of the sacred is pronounced with the very rites of the sacred. And anguish, the negation of revelation, nevertheless takes the place of revelation. So the Copernican Revolution is inconceivable without inspired philosophers, the heirs of the high priests in the religions of death.

This conceptual shift originates in the very contradiction of philosophical historiography, when historical interpretation pretends to recover the meaning of a *philosophia perennis*, when philosophy, if only to proclaim atheism and finitude, becomes inconceivable without some form of revelation. The existentialist "regression" of course proclaimed a revelation without content, but it was still a revelation. In the blue shade of St. Mark, the priests of Byzantium think they can see both the glory of the classical mosaics and the luminous bodies of Tintoretto, when the resurrection, which to our pleasure and despair liberated them from their divine annihilation, suddenly reminds us that their sacred is also ours and that in order to understand them we have had to leave the Reconciliation for the Collapse.[1]

Note

[1] Jules Vuillemin, "La signification de l'humanisme athée chez Feuerbach et l'idée de nature," *Deucalion* 4: "Le diurne et le nocturne: Etre et penser" (Neuchâtel, 1953), pp. 17–46.

MICHEL FOUCAULT

Introduction to Kant's Anthropology

1961

It is now time to return to the problem we began with—how the critical enterprise was accompanied by the lectures on anthropology, that unchanging counterpoint in relation to which Kant redoubled the effort of transcendental reflection through the constant accumulation of empirical knowledge of man. That Kant taught anthropology for twenty-five years stems from something more than the demands of university life; this persistence is linked to the very structure of the Kantian problem: How to think, analyse, justify, and ground finitude in a thinking which does not take the path of an ontology of the infinite and does not find its justification in a philosophy of the absolute? The question is effectively at work in the *Anthropology* but, because it cannot be thought for itself in the context of an empirical enquiry, it cannot assume its true dimensions there. Hence the *marginal* character of anthropology with regard to the Kantian enterprise: it is at once essential and inessential—a border that is peripheral to the center, but which never stops referring to and interrogating it. One could say that the critical movement *broke away from* the anthropological structure, both because the latter gives it its outline, and because the critical movement acquires its value only by breaking free of anthropology, by turning against it, and, in so doing, by grounding it. The epistemological configuration proper to anthropology mimicks that of the *Critique*; but it was a question of how to avoid getting caught up in the prestige that this affords, and how to reinstate the rational order of this resemblance. That order used to consist in making the *Anthropology* gravitate around the *Critique*. And that order reinstated was, for anthropology, the authentic form of its liberation—the revelation of its true meaning: the *Anthropology* could now emerge as that in which the transition from the a priori to the fundamental, from critical thought to transcendental philosophy, is announced.

We see what web of confusion and illusion anthropology and contemporary philosophy are tangled up in. One aim has been to make the *Anthropology* count

From *Introduction to Kant's Anthropology*, ed. Roberto Nigro and trans. Roberto Nigro and Kate Briggs (Los Angeles, CA: Semiotext[e], 2008), pp. 120–24 [*Introduction à l'anthropologie de Kant* (Paris: Librairie Philosophique J. Vrin, 2008)].

as a *Critique*, as a critique liberated from the prejudices and the dead weight of the a priori, overlooking the fact that it can give access to the realm of the fundamental only if remains under the sway of critical thought. Another (which is just another version of the same oversight) has been to turn anthropology into a positive field which would serve as the basis for and the possibility of all the human sciences, whereas in fact it can only speak the language of the limit and of negativity: its sole purpose is to convey, from the vigour of critical thought to the transcendental foundation, the precedence of finitude.

In the name of what is—that is to say what ought to be on the basis of its essence—anthropology within the field of philosophy as a whole, we challenge all those "philosophical anthropologies" that present themselves as the natural access to the fundamental, as well as all those philosophies which define their starting point and their scope through a certain kind of anthropological reflection on man. In both, we find the play of an "illusion" proper to Western philosophy since Kant. In its anthropological form, it serves as the counterpoint to the transcendental illusion harboured by pre-Kantian metaphysics. It will be by way of symmetry and taking the latter as our guiding thread that we will come to an understanding of what the anthropological illusion consists in.

For the one effectively derives historically from the other—or, rather, it is thanks to a shift in the meaning given to the transcendental illusion in Kantian critique that the anthropological illusion could emerge. The necessary character of the emergence of the trancendental is frequently interpreted, not as a structure of truth, phenomenon and experience, but as one of the concrete marks of finitude. But what Kant had ambiguously designated as "natural" in that emergence had been forgotten as a fundamental form of the relationship to the object and resurrected as the "nature" in human nature. As a result, instead of being defined by the movement that criticized it in the context of a reflection of knowledge, the illusion was submitted to an anterior level where it reemerged as both divided and grounded: it had become the truth of truth—henceforth, truth would be always present and yet never given; thus the illusion had become both the raison d'etre and the source of critical thinking, the origin of that movement by which man loses sight of and is incessantly recalled to truth. The illusion henceforth defined as finitude would become above all else the *retreat* of truth: that in which truth hides and in which truth can always be found.

It is in this way that, from a structural point of view, the anthropological illusion looks like the reverse, the mirror image of the transcendental illusion. The latter consisted in the application of the principles of understanding beyond the limits of experience, and thus in admitting an actual infinite to the field of possible knowledge through a kind of spontaneous transgression. The anthropological illusion resides in a reflexive regression which has to answer for that transgression. Finitude is only gone beyond if it is something other than itself, if it rests on a shortfall in which it finds its source; it falls short, it is itself, but withdrawn from the field of experience where it is encountered and introduced into the realm of the originary in which it is grounded. The problem of finitude goes from interrogating the limit and transgression to interrogating the return to the self; from a problematic of truth to a problematic of the same and other. It has entered into the domain of alienation.

And the paradox is this: freeing itself from a preliminary critique of knowledge and an initial interrogation of the relationship to the object, philosophy did not manage to free itself from subjectivity as the fundamental thesis and starting point of its enquiry. On the contrary, it locked itself into subjectivity by conceiving of it as thickened, essentialized, enclosed in the impassable structure of "*menschliches Wesen*," in which that extenuated truth which is the truth of truth keeps vigil and gathers itself.

We can now see why, in a single movement, characteristic of the thinking of our time, all knowledge of man is presented as either dialecticized from the start or fully dialecticizable—as always invested with a meaning which has to do with the return to the origin, to the authentic, to the founding activity, to the reason why there is meaning in the world. We can also see why all philosophy presents itself as capable of communicating directly with the sciences of man or empirical studies of man without having to take a detour through a critique, an epistemology, or a theory of knowledge. Anthropology is the secret path which, orientated toward the foundations of our knowledge, connects, in the form of an unthought mediation, man's experience with philosophy. The values implicit in the question *Was ist der Mensch?* are responsible for this homogenous, de-structured and infinitely reversible field in which man presents his truth as the soul of truth. The polymorphous notions of "meaning," "structure," and "genesis"—whatever value they might have, and which a rigorous reflection ought to restore to them—here indicate only the confusion of the domain in which they assume their communicative roles. That these notions circulate indiscriminately throughout the human sciences and philosophy does not justify us in thinking this or that, as if in unison, this or that; it merely points up our incapacity to undertake a veritable *critique* of the anthropological illusion.

And yet, the model for just such a critique was given to us more than fifty years ago. The Nietzschian enterprise can be understood as at last bringing that proliferation of the questioning of man to an end. For is not the death of God in effect manifested in a doubly murderous gesture which, by putting an end to the absolute, is at the same time the cause of the death of man himself? For man, in his finitude, is not distinguishable from the infinite of which he is both the negation and the harbinger; it is in the death of man that the death of God is realized. Is it not possible to conceive of a critique of finitude which would be as liberating with regard to man as it would be with regard to the infinite, and which would show that finitude is not an end but rather that camber and knot in time when the end is in fact a beginning?

The trajectory of the question *Was ist der Mensch?* in the field of philosophy reaches its end in the response which both challenges and disarms it: *der übermensch*.[1]

Notes

[1] My italics. See Friedrich Nietzsche, *The Gay Science*, edited by Bernard Williams, Cambridge University Press, Cambridge, 2001: "New battles. [. . .] God is dead; but given the way people are, there may still for millenia be caves in which they show his shadow" (Book three, § 108, p. 109); "The greatest recent events—that 'God is dead'; that the belief in the Christian God has become unbelievable—is already starting to cast its first shadow over Europe" (Book Five, § 343, p. 199). Id., *Thus Spoke Zarathustra: A Book for All and None*, edited by Adrian Del Caro and Robert B. Pippin, translated by Adrian Del Caro, Cambridge and New York, Cambridge University Press, 2006: "*I teach you the Overman*. Human being is something that must be overcome. What have you done to overcome him" ("Zarathustra's Prologue," p. 3). See also Michel Foucault, *The Order of Things. An Archaeology of the Human Sciences*, London, Routledge, 2001, Chapter VIII, § 2, p. 286 and ch. X, § 5, p. 417 and ff.

PAUL RICOEUR

Freud and Philosophy: An Essay on Interpretation

1965

A general theory of interpretation would thus have to account not only for the opposition between two interpretations of interpretation, the one as recollection of meaning, the other as reduction of the illusions and lies of consciousness; but also for the division and scattering of each of these two great "schools" of interpretation into "theories" that differ from one another and are even foreign to one another. This is no doubt truer of the school of supicion than of the school of reminiscence. Three masters, seemingly mutually exclusive, dominate the school of suspicion: Marx, Nietzsche, and Freud. It is easier to show their common opposition to a phenomenology of the sacred, understood as a propaedeutic to the "revelation" of meaning, than their interrelationship within a single method of demystification. It is relatively easy to note that these three figures all contest the primacy of the object in our representation of the sacred, as well as the fulfilling of the intention of the sacred by a type of analogy of being that would engraft us onto being through the power of an assimilating intention. It is also easy to recognize that this contesting is an exercise of suspicion in three different ways; "truth as lying" would be the negative heading under which one might place these three exercises of suspicion. But we are still far from having assimilated the positive meaning of the enterprises of these three thinkers. We are still too attentive to their differences and to the limitations that the prejudices of their times impose upon their successors even more than upon themselves. Thus Marx is relegated to economics and the absurd theory of the reflex consciousness; Nietzsche is drawn toward biologism and a perspectivism incapable of expressing itself without contradiction; Freud is restricted to psychiatry and decked out with a simplistic pansexualism.

If we go back to the intention they had in common, we find in it the decision to look upon the whole of consciousness primarily as "false" consciousness.

From *Freud and Philosophy: An Essay on Interpretation*, trans. Denis Savage (New Haven, CT: Yale University Press, 1970), pp. 32–36 [*De l'interprétation: Essai sur Freud* (Paris: Editions du Seuil, 1965)].

They thereby take up again, each in a different manner, the problem of the Cartesian doubt, to carry it to the very heart of the Cartesian stronghold. The philosopher trained in the school of Descartes knows that things are doubtful, that they are not such as they appear; but he does not doubt that consciousness is such as it appears to itself; in consciousness, meaning and conciousness of meaning coincide. Since Marx, Nietzsche, and Freud, this too has become doubtful. After the doubt about things, we have started to doubt consciousness.

These three masters of suspicion are not to be misunderstood, however, as three masters of skepticism. They are, assuredly, three great "destroyers." But that of itself should not mislead us; destruction, Heidegger says in *Sein und Zeit*, is a moment of every new foundation, including the destruction of religion, insofar as religion is, in Nietzsche's phrase, a "Platonism for the people." It is beyond destruction that the question is posed as to what thought, reason, and even faith still signify.

All three clear the horizon for a more authentic word, for a new reign of Truth, not only by means of a "destructive" critique, but by the invention of an art of *interpreting*. Descartes triumphed over the doubt as to things by the evidence of consciousness; they triumph over the doubt as to consciousness by an exegesis of meaning. Beginning with them, understanding is hermeneutics: hence-forward, to seek meaning is no longer to spell out the consciousness of meaning, but to *decipher its expressions*. What must be faced, therefore, is not only a threefold suspicion, but a threefold guile. If consciousness is not what it thinks it is, a new relation must be instituted between the patent and the latent; this new relation would correspond to the one that consciousness had instituted between appearances and the reality of things. For Marx, Nietzsche, and Freud, the fundamental category of consciousness is the relation hidden-shown or, if you prefer, simulated-manifested. That the Marxists are stubbornly insistent on the "reflex" theory, that Nietzsche contradicts himself in dogmatizing about the "perspectivism" of the will to power, that Freud mythologizes with his "censorship," "watchman," and "disguises"— still, what is essential does not lie in these encumbrances and impasses. What is essential is that all three create with the means at hand, with and against the prejudices of their times, a mediate *science* of meaning, irreducible to the immediate *consciousness* of meaning. What all three attempted, in different ways, was to make their "conscious" methods of deciphering coincide with the "unconscious" *work* of ciphering which they attributed to the will to power, to social being, to the unconscious psychism. *Guile will be met by double guile.*

Thus the distinguishing characteristic of Marx, Freud, and Nietzsche is the general hypothesis concerning both the process of false consciousness and the method of deciphering. The two go together, since the man of suspicion carries out in reverse the work of falsification of the man of guile. Freud entered the problem of false consciousness via the double road of dreams and neurotic symptoms; his working hypothesis has the same limits as his angle of attack, which was, as we shall state fully in the sequel, an economics of instincts. Marx attacks the problem of ideologies from within the limits of economic alienation, now in the sense of political economy. Nietzsche, focusing on the problem of "value"—of evaluation and transvaluation—looks for the key to lying and masks on the side of the "force" and "weakness" of the will to power.

Fundamentally, the *Genealogy of Morals* in Nietzsche's sense, the theory of ideologies in the Marxist sense, and the theory of ideals and illusions in Freud's sense represent three convergent procedures of demystification.

Yet there is perhaps something they have even more in common, an underlying relationship that goes even deeper. All three begin with suspicion concerning the illusions of consciousness, and then proceed to employ the stratagem of deciphering; all three, however, far from being detractors of "consciousness," aim at extending it. What Marx wants is to liberate *praxis* by the understanding of necessity; but this liberation is inseparable from a "conscious insight" which victoriously counterattacks the mystification of false consciousness. What Nietzsche wants is the increase of man's power, the restoration of his force; but the meaning of the will to power must be recaptured by meditating on the ciphers "superman," "eternal return," and "Dionysus," without which the power in question would be but worldly violence. What Freud desires is that the one who is analyzed, by making his own the meaning that was foreign to him, enlarge his field of consciousness, live better, and finally be a little freer and, if possible, a little happier. One of the earliest homages paid to psychoanalysis speaks of "healing through consciousness." The phrase is exact—if one means thereby that analysis wishes to substitute for an immediate and dissimulating consciousness a mediate consciousness taught by the reality principle. Thus the same doubter who depicts the ego as a "poor creature" in subjection to three masters, the id, the superego, and reality or necessity, is also the exegete who rediscovers the logic of the illogical kingdom and who dares, with unparalleled modesty and discretion, to terminate his essay on *The Future of an Illusion* by invoking the god Logos, soft of voice but indefatigable, in no wise omnipotent, but efficacious in the long run.

This last reference to Freud's "reality principle" and to its equivalents in Nietzsche and Marx—eternal return in the former, understood necessity in the latter—brings out the positive benefit of the ascesis required by a reductive and destructive interpretation: confrontation with bare reality, the discipline of Ananke, of necessity.

While finding their positive convergence, our three masters of suspicion also present the most radically contrary stance to the phenomenology of the sacred and to any hermeneutics understood as the recollection of meaning and as the reminiscence of being.

At issue in this controversy is the fate of what I shall call, for the sake of brevity, the mytho-poetic core of imagination. Over against illusion and the fable-making function, demystifying hermeneutics sets up the rude discipline of necessity. It is the lesson of Spinoza: one first finds himself a slave, he understands his slavery, he rediscovers himself free within understood necessity. The *Ethics* is the first model of the ascesis that must be undergone by the libido, the will to power, the imperialism of the dominant class. But, in return, does not this discipline of the real, this ascesis of the necessary lack the grace of imagination, the upsurge of the possible? And does not this grace of imagination have something to do with the Word as Revelation?

This is what is at issue in the debate. Our question now is to determine to what extent such a debate can still be arbitrated within the limits of a philosophy of reflection.

LOUIS ALTHUSSER

Marxism and Humanism

1967

To see beyond this event, to understand it, to know the meaning of socialist humanism, it is not enough just to register the event, nor to record the concepts (humanism, socialism) in which the event itself thinks itself. The theoretical claims of the concepts must be tested to ensure that they really do provide us with a truly scientific knowledge of the event.

But precisely in the couple "humanism-socialism" there is a striking theoretical unevenness: in the framework of the Marxist conception, the concept "socialism" is indeed a scientific concept, but the concept "humanism" is no more than an *ideological* one.

Note that my purpose is not to dispute the reality that the concept of socialist humanism is supposed to designate, but to define the *theoretical* value of the concept. When I say that the concept of humanism is an ideological concept (not a scientific one), I mean that while it really does designate a set of existing relations, unlike a scientific conept, it does not provide us with a means of knowing them. In a particular (ideological) mode, it designates some existents, but it does not give use their essences. If we were to confuse these two orders we should cut ourselves off from all knowledge, uphold a confusion and risk falling into error.

To show this clearly, I shall briefly invoke Marx's own experience, for he only arrived at a scientific theory of history at the price of a radical critique of the philosophy of man that had served as his theoretical basis during the years of his youth (1840–45). I use the words "theoretical basis" in their strict sense. For the young Marx, "Man" was not just a cry denouncing poverty and slavery. It was the theoretical principle of his world outlook and of his practical attitude. The "Essence of Man" (whether freedom-reason or community) was the basis both for a rigorous theory of history and for a consistent political practice.

This can be seen in the two stages of Marx's humanist period.

The First Stage was dominated by a liberal-rationalist humanism closer to Kant and Fichte than to Hegel. In his conflict with censorship, Rhenish feudal

From *For Marx*, trans. Ben Brewster (1969; New York: Verso, 2005), pp. 223–31 ["Marxisme et humanisme," in *Pour Marx* (Paris: Editions Maspero, 1967)].

laws, Prussian despotism, Marx's political struggle and the theory of history sustaining it were based theoretically on a philosophy of man. Only the essence of man makes history, and this essence is freedom and reason. *Freedom*: it is the essence of man just as weight is the essence of bodies. Man is destined to freedom, it is his very being. Whether he rejects it or negates it, he remains in it for ever: "*So much is freedom the essence of Man that even its adversaries are realizing it when they fight against its reality. . . . So freedom has always existed, in one way or another, sometimes only as a particular privilege, sometimes as a general right.*"[1] This distinction illuminates the whole of history: thus, feudalism is freedom, but in the "non-rational" form of privilege; the modern State is freedom, but in the rational form of a universal right. *Reason*: man is only freedom as reason. Human freedom is neither caprice, nor the determinism of interest, but, as Kant and Fichte meant it, autonomy, obedience to the inner law of reason. This reason, which has "*always existed though not always in a rational form*"[2] (e.g., feudalism), in modern times does at least exist in the form of reason in the State, the State of law and right. "*Philosophy regards the State as the great organism in which legal, moral and political freedom should find their realization and in which the individual citizen, when he obeys the State's laws, is only obeying the natural laws of his own reason, of human reason.*"[3] Hence the task of philosophy: "*Philosophy demands that the State be the State of human nature.*"[4] This injunction is addressed to the State itself: if it would recognize its essence it would become reason, the true freedom of man, through its own reform of itself. Therefore, politico-philosophical criticism (which reminds the State of its duty to itself) sums up the whole of politics: the free Press, the free reason of humanity, becomes politics itself. This political practice—summed up in *public theoretical criticism*, that is, in public criticism by way of the Press—which demands as its absolute precondition the *freedom of the Press* is the one Marx adopted in the *Rheinische Zeitung*. Marx's development of his theory of history was the basis and justification for his own *practice*: the journalist's public criticism that he saw as political action *par excellence*. This Enlightenment Philosophy was completely rigorous.

The Second Stage (1842–5) was dominated by a new form of humanism: Feuerbach's "communalist" humanism. The Reason-State had remained deaf to reason: there was no reform of the Prussian State. History itself delivered this judgment on the illusions of the humanism of reason: the young German radicals had been expecting that when he was King the heir to the throne would keep the liberal promises he had made before his coronation. But the throne soon changed the liberal into a despot—the State, which should at last have become reason, since it was in itself reason, gave birth merely to unreason once again. From this enormous disappointment, lived by the young radicals as a true historical and theoretical crisis, Marx drew the conclusion: "*The political State . . . encapsulates the demands of reason precisely in its modern forms. But it does not stop there. Everywhere it presupposes realized reason. But everywhere it also slides into the contradiction between its theoretical definition and its real hypotheses.*" A decisive step had been taken: the State's abuses were no longer conceived as misappropriations of the State *vis-à-vis* its essence, but as a real contradiction between its essence (reason) and its existence (unreason). Feuerbach's humanism made it possible to think just this contradiction by showing in unreason the alienation of reason, and in this alienation the history of man, that is, his realization.[5]

Marx still professes a philosophy of man: "To be radical is to grasp things by the root; but for man the root is man himself" (1843). But then man is only freedom-reason because he is first of all "*Gemeinwesen*," "communal being," a being that is only consummated theoretically (science) and practically (politics) in universal human relations, with men and with his objects (external nature "humanized" by labor). Here also the essence of man is the basis for history and politics.

History is the alienation and production of reason in unreason, of the true man in the alienated man. Without knowing it, man realizes the essence of man in the alienated products of his labour (commodities, State, religion). The loss of man that produces history and man must presuppose a definite pre-existing essence. At the end of history, this man, having become inhuman objectivity, has merely to re-grasp as subject his own essence alienated in property, religion and the State to become total man, true man.

This new theory of man is the basis for a new type of political action: the politics of *practical* reappropriation. The appeal to the simple reason of the State disappears. Politics is no longer simply theoretical criticism, the enlightenment of reason through the free Press, but man's practical reappropriation of his essence. For the State, like religion, may well be man, but man dispossessed: man is split into citizen (State) and civil man, two abstractions. In the heaven of the State, in "the citizen's rights," man lives in imagination the human community he is deprived of on the earth of the "rights of man." So the revolution must no longer be merely *political* (rational liberal reform of the State), but "*human*" ("communist"), if man is to be restored his nature, alienated in the fantastic forms of money, power and gods. From this point on, this practical revolution must be the common work of philosophy and of the proletariat, for, in philosophy, man is theoretically affirmed; in the proletariat he is practically negated. The penetration of philosophy into the proletariat will be the conscious revolt of the affirmation against its own negation, the revolt of man against his inhuman conditions. Then the proletariat will negate its own negation and take possession of itself in communism. The revolution is the very *practice* of the logic immanent in alienation: it is the moment in which criticism, hitherto unarmed, recognizes its arms in the proletariat. It gives the proletariat the theory of what it is; in return, the proletariat gives it its armed force, a single unique force in which no one is allied except to himself. So the revolutionary alliance of the proletariat and of philosophy is once again sealed in the essence of man.

In 1845, Marx broke radically with every theory that based history and politics on an essence of man. This unique rupture contained three indissociable elements.

(1) The formation of a theory of history and politics based on radically new concepts: the concepts of social formation, productive forces, relations of production, superstructure, ideologies, determination in the last instance by the economy, specific determination of the other levels, etc.

(2) A radical critique of the *theoretical* pretensions of every philosophical humanism.

(3) The definition of humanism as an *ideology*.

This new conception is completely rigorous as well, but it is a new rigor: the essence criticized (2) is defined as an ideology (3), a category belonging to the new theory of society and history (1).

This rupture with every *philosophical* anthropology or humanism is no secondary detail; it is Marx's scientific discovery.

It means that Marx rejected the problematic of the earlier philosophy and adopted a new problematic in one and the same act. The earlier idealist ("bourgeois") philosophy depended in all its domains and arguments (its "theory of knowledge," its conception of history, its political economy, its ethics, its aesthetics, etc.) on a problematic of *human nature* (or the essence of man). For centuries, this problematic had been transparency itself, and no one had thought of questioning it even in its internal modifications.

This problematic was neither vague nor loose; on the contrary, it was constituted by a coherent system of precise concepts tightly articulated together. When Marx confronted it, it implied the two complementary postulates he defined in the Sixth Thesis on Feuerbach:

(1) that there is a universal essence of man;

(2) that this essence is the attribute of "*each single individual*" who is its real subject.

These two postulates are complementary and indissociable. But their existence and their unity presuppose a whole empiricist-idealist world outlook. If the essence of man is to be a universal attribute, it is essential that *concrete subjects* exist as absolute givens; this implies an *empiricism of the subject*. If these empirical individuals are to be men, it is essential that each carries in himself the whole human essence, if not in fact, at least in principle; this implies an *idealism of the essence*. So empiricism of the subject implies idealism of the essence and vice versa. This relation can be inverted into its "opposite"—empiricism of the concept/idealism of the subject. But the inversion respects the basic structure of the problematic, which remains fixed.

In this type-structure it is possible to recognize not only the principle of theories of society (from Hobbes to Rousseau), of political economy (from Petty to Ricardo), of ethics (from Descartes to Kant), but also the very principle of the (pre-Marxist) idealist and materialist "theory of knowledge" (from Locke to Feuerbach, via Kant). The content of the human essence or of the empirical subjects may vary (as can be seen from Descartes to Feuerbach); the subject may change from empiricism to idealism (as can be seen from Locke to Kant): the terms presented and their relations only vary within the invariant type-structure which constitutes this very problematic: *an empiricism of the subject always corresponds to an idealism of the essence* (*or an empiricism of the essence to an idealism of the subject*).

By rejecting the essence of man as his theoretical basis, Marx rejected the whole of this organic system of postulates. He drove the philosophical categories of the *subject*, of *empiricism*, of the *ideal essence*, etc., from all the domains in which they had been supreme. Not only from political economy (rejection of the myth of *homo economicus*, that is, of the individual with definite faculties and needs as the *subject* of the classical economy); not just from history (rejection of social atomism and ethico-political idealism); not just from ethics (rejection of the Kantian ethical idea); but also from philosophy itself: for Marx's materialism excludes the empiricism of the subject (and its inverse: the transcendental subject) and the idealism of the concept (and its inverse: the empricism of the concept).

This total theoretical revolution was only empowered to reject the old concepts because it replaced them by new concepts. In fact Marx established a new problematic, a new systematic way of asking questions of the world, new principles and a new method. This discovery is immediately contained in the theory of historical materialism, in which Marx did not only propose a new theory of the history of societies, but at the same time implicitly, but necessarily, a new "philosophy," infinite in its implications. Thus, when Marx replaced the old couple individuals/human essence in the theory of history by new concepts (forces of production, relations of production, etc.), he was, in fact, simultaneously proposing a new conception of "philosophy." He replaced the old postulates (empiricism/idealism of the subject, empiricism/idealism of the essence), which were the basis not only for idealism but also for pre-Marxist materialism, by a historico-dialectical materialism of *praxis*: that is, by a theory of the different specific *levels of human practice* (economic practice, political practice, ideological practice, scientific practice) in their characteristic articulations, based on the specific articulations of the unity of human society. In a word, Marx substituted for the "ideological" and universal concept of Feuerbachian "practice" a concrete conception of the specific differences that enables us to situate each particular practice in the specific differences of the social structure.

So, to understand what was radically new in Marx's contribution, we must become aware not only of the novelty of the concepts of historical materialism, but also of the depth of the theoretical revolution they imply and inaugurate. On this condition it is possible to define humanism's status, and reject its *theoretical* pretensions while recognizing its practical function as an ideology.

Strictly in respect to theory, therefore, one can and must speak openly of *Marx's theoretical anti-humanism*, and see in this *theoretical anti-humanism* the absolute (negative) precondition of the (positive) knowledge of the human world itself, and of its practical transformation. It is impossible to *know* anything about men except on the absolute precondition that the philosophical (theoretical) myth of man is reduced to ashes. So any thought that appeals to Marx for any kind of restoration of a theoretical anthropology or humanism is no more than ashes, *theoretically*. But in practice it could pile up a monument of pre-Marxist ideology that would weigh down on real history and threaten to lead it into blind alleys.

For the corollary of theoretical Marxist anti-humanism is the recognition and knowledge of humanism itself: as an *ideology*. Marx never fell into the idealist illusion of believing that the knowledge of an object might ultimately replace the object or dissipate its existence. Cartesians, knowing that the sun was two thousand leagues away, were astonished that this distance only looked like two hundred paces: they could not even find enough of God to fill in this gap. Marx never believed that a knowledge of the nature of *money* (a social relation) could destroy its *appearance*, its form of existence—a thing, for this appearance was its very being, as necessary as the existing mode of production.[6] Marx never believed that an ideology might be dissipated by a knowledge of it: for the knowledge of this ideology, as the knowledge of its conditions of possibility, of its structure, of its specific logic and of its practical role, within a given society, is simultaneously knowledge of the conditions of its necessity. So Marx's theoretical *anti-humanism* does not suppress anything in the historical *existence* of humanism. In the real world philosophies of man are found after Marx as often as before, and today even some Marxists are tempted to develop the themes of a new theoretical humanism. Furthermore, Marx's theoretical anti-humanism, by relating it to its conditions of existence, recognizes a necessity for humanism as an *ideology*, a conditional necessity. The recognition of this necessity is not purely speculative. On it alone can Marxism base a policy in relation to the existing ideological forms, of every kind: religion, ethics, art, philosophy, law—and in the very front rank, humanism. When (eventually) a Marxist policy of humanist ideology, that is, a political attitude to humanism, is achieved—a policy which may be either a rejection or a critique, or a use, or a support, or a development, or a humanist renewal of contemporary forms of ideology in the *ethico-political* domain—this policy will only have been possible on the absolute condition that it is based on Marxist philosophy, and a precondition for this is theoretical *anti-humanism*.

Notes

[1] *Die Rheinische Zeitung*, "The Freedom of the Press," 12 May 1842.

[2] Letter to Ruge, September 1843—an admirable formulation, the key to Marx's early philosophy.

[3] *Die Rheinische Zeitung*, "On the leading article in no. 179 of the *Kölnische Zeitung*," 14 July 1842.

[4] Ibid.

[5] This confluence of Feuerbach and the theoretical crisis in which history had thrown the young German radicals explains their enthusiasm for the author of the *Provisional Theses*, of the *Essence of Christianity* and of the *Principles of the Philosophy of the Future*. Indeed, Feuerbach represented the *theoretical* solution to the young intellectuals' theoretical crisis. In his humanism of alienation, he gave them the theoretical concepts that enabled them to think the alienation of the human essence as an indispensable moment in the realization of the human essence, unreason (the irrational *reality* of the State) as a necessary moment in the realization of reason (the idea of the State). It thus enabled them to *think* what they would otherwise have suffered as irrationality itself: the necessary *connection* between reason and unreason. Of course, this relation remained trapped in a philosophical anthropology, its basis, with this theoretical proviso: the remanipulation of the concept of man, indispensable to think the historical relation between historical reason and unreason. Man ceases to be defined by reason and freedom: he becomes, in his very principle, "communalist," concrete inter-subjectivity, love, fraternity, "species being."

[6] The whole, fashionable, theory of "reification" depends on a projection of the theory of alienation found in the early texts, particularly the *1844 Manuscripts*, on to the theory of "fetishism" in *Capital*. In the *1844 Manuscripts*, the objectification of the human essence is claimed as the indispensable preliminary to the reappropriation of the human essence by man. Throughout the process of objectification, man only exists in the form of an objectivity in which he meets his own essence in the appearance of a foreign, non-human, essence. This "objectification" is not called "reification" even though it is called *inhuman*. Inhumanity is not represented *par excellence* by the model of a "thing": but sometimes by the model of animality (or even of pre-animality—the man who no longer even has simple animal relations with nature), sometimes by the model of the omnipotence and fascination of transcendence (God, the State) and of money, which is, of course, a "thing." In *Capital* the only social relation that is presented in the form of a *thing* (this piece of metal) is *money*. But the conception of money as a *thing* (that is, the confusion of value with use-value in money) does not correspond to the reality of this "thing": it is not the brutality of a simple "thing" that man is faced with when he is in direct relation with money; it is a *power* (or a *lack* of it) over things and men. An ideology of reification that sees "things" everywhere in human relations confuses in this category "thing" (a category more foreign to Marx cannot be imagined) every social relation, conceived according to the model of a money-thing ideology.

JACQUES DERRIDA

The Ends of Man

1972

Humanism or Metaphysics

Thus the transition will be made quite naturally between the preamble and the theme of this communication, as it was imposed upon me, rather than as I chose it.

Where is France, as concerns man?

The question "of man" is being asked in very current fashion in France, along highly significant lines, and in an original historico-philosophical structure. What I will call "France," then, on the basis of several indices and for the time of this exposition, will be the nonempirical site of a movement, a structure and an articulation of the question "of man." Following this it would be possible, and doubtless necessary—but then only—rigorously to relate this site with every other instance defining something like "France."

Where then is France, as concerns man?

After the war, under the name of Christian or atheist existentialism, and in conjunction with a fundamentally Christian personalism, the thought that dominated France presented itself essentially as humanist. Even if one does not wish to summarize Sartre's thought under the slogan "existentialism is a humanism," it must be recognized that in *Being and Nothingness, The Sketch of a Theory of the Emotions*, etc., the major concept, the theme of the last analysis, the irreducible horizon and origin is what was then called "human-reality." As is well known, this is a translation of Heideggerian *Dasein*. A monstrous translation in many respects, but so much the more significant. That this translation proposed by Corbin was adopted at the time, and that by means of Sartre's authority it reigned, gives us much to think about the reading or the nonreading of Heidegger during this period, and about what was at stake in reading or not reading him in this way.

Certainly the notion of "human-reality" translated the project of thinking the meaning of man, the humanity of man, on a new basis, if you will. If the

From *Margins of Philosophy*, trans. Alan Bass (Chicago: University of Chicago Press, 1982), pp. 114–23 ["Les fins de l'homme," in *Marges de la philosophie* (Paris: Editions de Minuit, 1972)].

neutral and undetermined notion of "human reality" was substituted for the notion of man, with all its metaphysical heritage and the substantialist motif or temptation inscribed in it, it was also in order to suspend all the presuppositions which had always constituted the concept of the unity of man. Thus, it was also a reaction against a certain intellectualist or spiritualist humanism which had dominated French philosophy (Brunschvig, Alain, Bergson, etc.). And this neutralization of every metaphysical or speculative thesis as concerns the unity of the anthropos could be considered in some respects as the faithful inheritance of Husserl's transcendental phenomenology and of the fundamental ontology in *Sein und Zeit* (the only partially known work of Heidegger's at the time, along with *What Is Metaphysics?* and *Kant and the Problem of Metaphysics*). And yet, despite this alleged neutralization of metaphysical presuppositions,[1] it must be recognized that the unity of man is never examined in and of itself. Not only is existentialism a humanism, but the ground and horizon of what Sartre then called his "phenomenological ontology" (the subtitle of *Being and Nothingness*) remains the unity of human-reality. To the extent that it describes the structures of human-reality, phenomenological ontology is a philosophical anthropology. Whatever the breaks marked by this Hegelian-Husserlian-Heideggerian anthropology as concerns the classical anthropologies, there is an uninterrupted metaphysical familiarity with that which, so naturally, links the *we* of the philosopher to "we men," to the *we* in the horizon of humanity. Although the theme of history is quite present in the discourse of the period, there is little practice of the history of concepts. For example, the history of the concept of man is never examined. Everything occurs as if the sign "man" had no origin, no historical, cultural, or linguistic limit. At the end of *Being and Nothingness*, when Sartre in programmatic fashion asks the question of the unity of Being (which in this context means the totality of beings), and when he confers upon this question the rubric "metaphysical" in order to distinguish it from phenomenological ontology, which described the essential specificity of regions, it goes without saying that this metaphysical unity of Being, as the totality of the in-itself and the for-itself, is precisely the unity of human-reality in its project. Being in-itself and Being for-itself were *of Being*; and this totality of beings, in which they were affected, itself was linked up to itself, relating and appearing to itself, by means of the essential project of human-reality.[2] What was named in this way, in an allegedly neutral and undetermined way, was nothing other than the metaphysical unity of man and God, and relation of man to God, the project of becoming God as the project constituting human-reality. Atheism changes nothing in this fundamental structure. The example of the Sartrean project remarkably verifies Heidegger's proposition according to which "every humanism remains metaphysical," metaphysics being the other name of ontotheology.

Thus defined, humanism or anthropologism, during this period, was the common ground of Christian or atheist existentialisms, of the philosophy of values (spiritualist or not), of personalisms of the right or the left, of Marxism in the classical style. And if one takes one's bearings from the terrain of political ideologies, anthropologism was the unperceived and uncontested common ground of Marxism and of Social-Democratic or Christian-Democratic discourse. This profound concordance was authorized, in its philosophical expression, by the *anthropologistic* readings of Hegel (interest in the *Phenomenology of Spirit* as it was read by Kojève), of Marx (the privilege accorded the *Manuscripts of 1844*), of Husserl (whose descriptive and regional work is emphasized, but whose transcendental questions are ignored), and of Heidegger, whose projects for a philosophical anthropology or an existential analytic only were known or retained (*Sein und Zeit*). Of course, here I am picking out the dominant traits of a period. The period itself is not exhausted by these dominant traits. Nor can one say in absolutely rigorous fashion that this period started after the war, and even less that it is over today. Nevertheless, I believe that the empiricism of this cross-section is justifiable here only insofar as it permits the reading of a *dominant* motif and insofar as it takes its authority from indices which are unarguable for anyone approaching such a period. Further, the cross-section is provisional, and in an instant we will reinscribe this sequence in the time and space of a larger totality.

In order to mark in boldface the traits that opposed this period to the following one, the one in which we are, and which too is probably undergoing a mutation, we must recall that during the decade that followed the war we did not yet see the reign of the all-powerful motif of what we call today, more and more, and even exclusively, the "so-called *human* sciences," the expression itself marking a certain distance, but a still respectful distance. On the contrary, the current questioning of humanism is contemporary with the dominating and spellbinding extension of the "human sciences" within the philosophical field.

The *Relève* of Humanism

The anthropologistic reading of Hegel, Husserl, and Heidegger was a mistake in one entire respect, perhaps the most serious mistake. And it is this reading which furnished the best conceptual resources to postwar French thought.

First of all, the *Phenomenology of Spirit*, which had only been read for a short time in France, does not have to do with something one might simply call man. As the science of the experience of consciousness, the science of the structures of the phenomenality of the spirit itself relating to itself, it is rigorously distinguished from anthropology. In the *Encyclopedia*, the section entitled "Phenomenology of Spirit" comes after the "Anthropology," and quite explicitly exceeds its limits. What is true of the *Phenomenology* is a fortiori true of the system of the *Logic*.

Similarly, in the second place, the critique of anthropologism was one of the inaugural motifs of Husserl's transcendental phenomenology. This is an explicit critique, and it calls anthropologism by its name from the *Prolegomena to Pure Logic* on.[3] Later this critique will have as its target not only empirical anthropologism, but also transcendental anthropologism.[4] The transcendental structures described after the phenomenological reduction are not those of the intrawordly being called "man." Nor are they essentially linked to man's society, culture, language, or even to his "soul" or "psyche." Just as, according to Husserl, one may imagine a consciousness without soul (*seelenlos*),[5] similarly—and a fortiori—one may imagine a consciousness without man.

Therefore it is astonishing and highly significant that at the moment when the authority of Husserlian thought was asserted and then established in postwar France, even becoming a kind of philosophical mode, the critique of anthropologism remained totally unnoticed, or in any event without effect. One of the most paradoxical pathways of this motivated misconstruing passes through a reductive reading of Heidegger. Because one has interpreted the analytic of Dasein in strictly anthropological terms, occasionally one limits or criticizes Husserl on the basis of Heidegger, dropping all the aspects of phenomenology that do not serve anthropological description. This pathway is quite paradoxical because it follows the itinerary of a reading of Heidegger that was also Husserl's. In effect, Husserl precipitously interpreted *Sein und Zeit* as an anthropologistic deviation from transcendental phenomenology.[6]

In the third place, immediately following the war and after the appearance of *Being and Nothingness*, Heidegger, in his *Letter on Humanism*, recalled—for all those who did not yet know, and who had not even taken into account the very first sections of *Sein und Zeit*—that anthropology and humanism were not the milieu of his thought and the horizon of his questions. The "destruction" of metaphysics or of classical ontology was even directed against humanism.[7] After the tide of humanism and anthropologism that had covered French philosophy, one might have thought that the antihumanist and antianthropologist ebb that followed, and in which we are now, would rediscover the heritage of the systems of thought that had been disfigured, or in which, rather, the figure of man too quickly had been discerned.

Nothing of the sort has happened, and it is the significance of such a phenomenon that I now wish to examine. The critique of humanism and anthropologism, which is one of the dominant and guiding motifs of current French thought, far from seeking its sources or warranties in the Hegelian, Husserlian, or Heideggerian critiques of the same humanism or the same anthropologism, on the contrary seem, by means of a gesture sometimes more implicit than systematically articulated, to *amalgamate* Hegel, Husserl, and—in a more diffuse and ambiguous fashion—Heidegger with the old metaphysical humanism. I am purposely using the word "amalgam," which in its usage unites references to alchemy, which is the primary one here, with a strategic or tactical reference to the domain of political ideology.

Before attempting to interpret this phenomenon of paradoxical demeanor, we must take several precautions. First of all, this amalgam does not exclude that some progress has been made in France in the reading of Hegel, Husserl, or Heidegger, nor that this progress has led to requestioning the humanist insistence. But this progress and requestioning do not occupy center stage, and this must be significant. Conversely and symmetrically, among those who do practice the amalgamation, the schemas of the anthropologistic misinterpretation from Sartre's time are still at work, and occasionally it is these very schemas which govern the rejection of Hegel, Husserl, and Heidegger into the shadows of humanist metaphysics. Very often, *in fact*, those who denounce humanism at the same time as metaphysics have remained at the stage of this "first reading" of Hegel, Husserl, and Heidegger, and one could locate more than one sign of this in numerous recent texts. Which leads us to think that in certain respects, and at least to this extent, we are still on the same shore.

But no matter, as concerns the question I would like to ask, that such and such an author has read such and such a text poorly, or simply not at all, or that he remains, as concerns systems of thought he believes he has surpassed or overturned, in a state of great ingenuousness. This is why we shall not concern ourselves here with any given author's name or with the title of any given work. What must hold our interest, beyond the justifications which, as a matter of fact, are most often insufficient, is the kind of profound justification, whose necessity is subterranean, which makes the Hegelian, Husserlian, and Heideggerian critiques or *de-limitations* of metaphysical humanism appear to belong to the very sphere of that which they criticize or de-limit. In a word, whether this has been made explicit or not, and whether it has been articulated or not (and more than one index leads us to believe that it has not), what authorizes us today to consider as essentially *anthropic* or anthropocentric everything in metaphysics, or at the limits of metaphysics, that believed itself to be a critique or delimitation of anthropologism? What is the *relève* of man in the thought of Hegel, Husserl, and Heidegger?

The Near End of Man

Let us reconsider, first of all, within the order of Hegelian discourse, which still holds together the language of our era by so many threads, the relations between anthropology on the one hand and phenomenology and logic on the other.[8] Once the confusion of a purely anthropological reading of the *Phenomenology of Spirit* has been rigorously avoided, it must be recognized that according to Hegel the relations between anthropology and phenomenology are not simply external ones. The Hegelian concepts of truth, negativity, and *Aufhebung*, with all their results, prevent this from being so. In the third part of the *Encyclopedia*, which treats the "Philosophy of Spirit," the first section ("Philosophy of Spirit") inscribes the *Phenomenology of Spirit* between the "Anthropology" and the "Psychology." The *Phenomenology of Spirit* succeeds the Anthropology and precedes the Psychology. The Anthropology treats the spirit—which is the "truth of nature"—as soul or as natural-spirit (*Seele* or *Naturgeist*). The development of the soul, such as it is retraced by the anthropology, passes through the natural soul (*natürliche Seele*), through the sensible soul (*fühlende Seele*), and through the real or effective soul (*wirkliche Seele*). This development accomplishes and completes itself, and then opens onto consciousness. The last section of the Anthropology[9] defines the general form of consciousness, the very one from which the *Phenomenology of Spirit* will depart, in the first chapter on "Sensuous Certitude."[10] Consciousness, i.e., the phenomenological, therefore, is the *truth* of the soul, that is, precisely the truth of that which was the object of the anthropolgy. Consciousness is the truth of man, phenomenology is the truth of anthropology. "Truth," here, must be understood in a rigorously Hegelian sense. In this Hegelian sense, the metaphysical essence of truth, the truth of the truth, is achieved. Truth is here the presence or presentation of essence as *Gewesenheit*, of *Wesen* as having-been. Consciousness is the truth of man to the extent that man appears to himself in consciousness in his Being-past, in his to-have-been, in his past surpassed and conserved, retained, interiorized (*erinnert*) and *relevé*. *Aufheben* is *relever*, in the sense in which *relever* can combine to relieve, to displace, to elevate, to replace and to promote, in one and the same movement. Consciousness is the *Aufhebung* of the soul or of man, phenomenology is the *relève* of anthropology. It is *no longer*, but it is *still* a science of man. In this sense, all the structures described by the phenomenology of spirit—like everything which articulates them with the Logic—are the structures of that which has *relevé* man. In them, man remains in relief. His essence rests in *Phenomenology*. This equivocal relationship of *relief* doubtless marks the end of man, man past, but by the same token it also marks the achievement of man, the appropriation of his essence. *It is the end of finite man* [*C'est la fin de l'homme fini*]. The end of the finitude of man, the unity of the finite and the infinite, the finite as the surpassing of the self—these essential themes of Hegel's are to be recognized at the end of the Anthropology when consciousness is finally designated as the "infinite relationship to self." The *relève* or *relevance* of man is his *telos* or *eskhaton*. The unity of these two *ends* of man, the unity of his death, his completion, his accomplishment, is enveloped in the Greek thinking of *telos*, in the discourse on *telos*, which is also a discourse on *eidos*, on *ousia*, and on *aletheia*. Such a discourse, in Hegel as in the entirety of metaphysics, indissociably coordinates teleology with an eschatology, a theology, and an ontology. *The thinking of the end of man, therefore, is always already prescribed in metaphysics, in the thinking of the truth of man.* What is difficult to think today is an end of man which would not be organized by a dialectics of truth and negativity, an end of man which would not be a teleology in the first person plural. The *we*, which articulates natural and philosophical consciousness with each other in the *Phenomenology of Spirit*, assures the proximity to itself of the fixed and central being for which this circular reappropriation is produced. The *we* is the unity of absolute knowledge and anthropology, of God and man, of onto-theo-teleology and humanism. "*Being*" and language—the group of languages—that the *we* governs or opens: such is the name of that which assures the transition between metaphysics and humanism via the *we*.[11]

We have just perceived the necessity which links the thinking of the *phainesthai* to the thinking of the *telos*. The teleology which governs Husserl's transcendental phenomenology can be read in the same opening. Despite the critique of anthropologism, "humanity," here, is still the name of the being to which the transcendental *telos*—determined as Idea (in the Kantian sense) or even as Reason—is announced. It is man as *animal rationnel* who, in his most classical metaphysical determination, designates the site of teleological reason's unfolding, that is, history. For Husserl as for Hegel, reason is history, and there is no history but of reason. The latter "functions in every man, the *animal rationnel*, no matter how primitive he is . . ." Every kind of humanity and human sociality has "a root in the essential structure of what is generally human, through which a teleological reason running throughout all historicity announces itself. With this is revealed a set of problems in its own right related to the totality of history and to the full meaning which ultimately gives it its unity."[12] Transcendental phenomenology is in this sense the ultimate achievement of the teleology of reason that traverses humanity.[13] Thus, under the jurisdiction of the founding concepts of metaphysics, which Husserl revives and restores (if necessary affecting them with phenomenological brackets or indices), the critique of empirical anthropologism is only the affirmation of a transcendental humanism. And, among these metaphysical concepts which form the essential resource of Husserl's discourse, the concept of *end* or of *telos* plays a decisive role. It could be shown that at each stage of phenomenology, and notably each time that a recourse to the "Idea in the Kantian sense" is necessary, the infinity of the *telos*, the infinity of the end regulates phenomenology's capabilities. The end of man (as a factual anthropological limit) is announced to thought from the vantage of the end of man (as a determined opening or the infinity of a *telos*). Man is that which is in relation to his end, in the fundamentally equivocal sense of the world. Since always. The transcendental end can appear to itself and be unfolded only on the condition of mortality, of a relation to finitude as the origin of ideality. The name of man has always been inscribed in metaphysics between these two ends. It has meaning only in this eschato-teleological situation.

Notes

[1] The humanism which marks Sartre's philosophical discourse in its depths, however, is very surely and very ironically taken apart in *Nausea*: in the caricature of the Autodidact, for example, the same figure reassembles the theological project of absolute knowledge and the humanist ethic, in the form of the encyclopedic epistemophilia which leads the Autodidact to undertake the reading of the world library (which is really the Western library, and definitely the municipal library) in alphabetical order by author's name, and in areas where he is able to love Man ("There is an aim, sir, there is an aim . . . there are men . . . one must love them, one must love them") in the representation of men, preferably young men. It is in the dialogue with the Autodidact that Roquentin levels the worst charges against humanism, against all humanist styles; and at the moment when nausea is slowly rising in him, he says to himself, for example, "I don't want to be integrated, I don't want my good red blood to go and fatten this lymphatic beast: I will not be fool enough to call myself 'anti-humanist.' I *am not* a humanist, that's all there is to it." *Nausea*, trans. Lloyd Alexander (New York: New Directions, 1959), p. 160.

[2] "Each human reality is at the same time a direct project to metamorphose its own For-itself in an In-itself-For-itself and a project of the appropriation of the world as a totality of being-in-itself, in the form of a fundamental quality. Every human reality is a passion in that it projects losing itself so as to found being and by the same stroke to constitute the In-itself which escapes contingency by being its own foundation, the *Ens causa sui*, which religions call God. Thus the passion of man is the reverse of that of Christ, for man loses himself as man in order that God may be born. But the idea of God is contradictory and we lose ourselves in vain. Man is a useless passion." *Being and Nothingness*, trans. Hazel Barnes (New York: Pocket Books, 1966), p. 784. This synthetic unity is determined as *lack*: lack of totality in beings, lack *of* God that is soon transformed into a lack *in* God. Human-reality is a *failed* God: "Also the *ens causa sui* remains as the *lacked* . . ." (p. 789); ". . . the for-itself determines its being as *a lack* . . ." (p. 795). As concerns the meaning of the Being of this totality of beings, as concerns the history of this concept of negativity as a relationship to God, the meaning and origin of the concept of (human) reality, and the reality of the real, no questions are asked. In this respect, what is true of *Being and Nothingness* is even more so of the *Critique of Dialectical Reason*. The concept of *lack*, linked to the non-self identity of the subject (as consciousness) and to the desire and agency of the Other in the dialectic of the master and the slave, was then beginning to dominate the French ideological scene.

[3] Chapter 7, "Psychologism as Sceptical Relativism," sec. 39, "Anthropologism in Sigwart's Logic," sec. 40, "Anthropologism in Erdmann's Logic."

[4] *Ideas I*, see, e.g., secs. 49 and 54.

[5] Ibid.

[6] See the Afterword to *Ideas*, and the marginal notes in the copy of *Sein und Zeit* (Husserl Archives, Louvain).

[7] "Every humanism is either grounded in a metaphysics or is itself made to be the ground of one. Every determination of the essence of man that already presupposes an interpretation of being without asking about the truth of Being, whether knowingly or not, is metaphysical. The result is that what is peculiar to all metaphysics, specifically with respect to the way the essence of man is determined, is that it is 'humanistic.' Accordingly, every humanism remains metaphysical." "Letter on Humanism," in *Basic Writings*, ed. David Farrell Krell (New York: Harper and Row, 1977), p. 202.

[8] Without neglecting the complexity of the relations between the *Logic* and the *Phenomenology of Spirit*, the question we are asking authorizes us to consider them *together* at the point of opening where Absolute Knowledge articulates them one with the other.

9 "The actual soul with its sensation and its concrete self-feeling turned into habit, has implicitly realised the 'ideality' of its qualities; in this externality it has recollected and inwardized (*errinert*) itself, and is infinite self-relation. This free universality thus made explicit shows the soul awaking to the higher stage of the ego, or abstract universality, in so far as it is *for* the abstract universality. In this way it gains the position of thinker and subject—specially a subject of the judgment in which the ego excludes from itself the sum total of its merely natural features as an object, a world external to it—but with such respect to that object that in it it is immediately reflected into itself. Thus soul rises to become *Consciousness*. (Die wirkliche Seele in der *Gewohnheit* des Empfindens und ihres *konkreten* Selbst gefühlt ist an sich die für sich seiende *Idealität* ihrer Bestimmtheiten, in ihrer Ausserlichkeit *erinnert* in sich und unendliche Beziehung an sich. Die Fürsichsein der freien Allgemeinheit ist das höhere Erwachen der Seele zum *Ich*, der abstrakten Allgemeinheit, insofern sie für die abstrakte Allgemeinheit ist, welche so *Denken* und *Subjekt* für sich und zwar bestimmt Subjekt seines Urteils ist, in welchem es die natürliche Totalität seiner Bestimmungen als ein Objekt, eine ihm *äussere* Welt, von sich ausschliesst und sich darauf bezieht, so dass es in derselben unmittelbar in sich reflektiert ist, das *Bewusstsein*.)" *Philosophy of Mind*, trans. William Wallace (Oxford: Oxford University Press, 1971), sec. 412, p. 151.

10 That is, objectivity in general, the relation of an "I" in general with a being-object in general.

11 We could verify the necessity of the framework of this ambiguity or *relevance*, which is accomplished in Hegelian metaphysics and persists wherever metaphysics—that is, our language—maintains its authority, not only in our immediate vicinity, but already in all pre-Hegelian systems. In Kant, the figure of finitude organizes the capacity to know from the very emergence of the anthropological limit.

A. *On the one hand*, it is precisely when Kant wishes to think something like the *end*, the pure *end*, the *end* in itself, that he must criticize anthropologism, in the *Metaphysics of Morals*. One cannot deduce the principles of morality on the basis of a knowledge of the nature of a particular being named *man*: "But a completely isolated metaphysics of morals, mixed with no anthropology, no theology, no physics or hyperphysics, and even less with occult qualities (which might be called hypophysical), is not only an indispensable substrate of all theoretically sound and definite knowledge of duties; it is also a desideratum of the highest importance to the actual fulfillment of its precepts" ("Foundations of the Metaphysics of Morals," in *The Critique of Practical Reason* . . . , p. 70). "Furthermore, it is evident that it is not only of the greatest necessity in a theoretical point of view when it is a question of speculation but also of the utmost practical importance to derive the concepts and laws of morals from pure reason and to present them pure and unmixed, and to determine the scope of this entire practical but pure rational knowledge (the entire faculty of pure practical reason) without making the principles depend upon the particular nature of human reason, as speculative philosophy may permit and even sometimes find necessary. But since moral laws should hold for every rational being as such, the principles must be derived from the universal concept of a rational being generally. In this manner all morals, which need ahtropology for their application to men, must be completely developed first as pure philosophy, i.e. metaphysics, independently of anthropology" (ibid., p. 71). "With a view to attaining this, it is extremely important to remember that we must not let ourselves think that the reality of this principle can be derived from the *particular constitution of human nature* (*ous der besondern Eigenschaft der menschlichen Natur*). For duty is practical unconditional necessity of action; it must, therefore, hold for all rational beings (to which alone an imperative can apply), and *only for that reason* can it be a law for all human wills" (ibid., p. 83). We see in these three passages that what is always of the "greatest importance" (*von der höchsten Wichtigkeit . . . von der grössten praktischen Wichtigkeit . . . von der äussersten Wichtigkeit*) is to determine the end in itself (as an unconditioned principle of morality), independently of any anthropological givens. One cannot think the purity of the end of the basis of man.

B. But, *on the other hand*, and inversely, man's specificity, man's essence as a rational being, as the rational animal (*zoon logan ekhon*), announces itself to itself only on the basis of thinking the end in itself; it announces itself to itself *as* the end in itself; that is, equally, as an infinite end, since the thinking of the unconditioned is also the thinking which raises itself above experience, that is, above finitude. Thus is explained the fact that despite the critique of anthropologism, of which we have just given a few indices, man is the *only example*, the only case of a rational being that can ever be cited at the very moment when by all rights one distinguishes the universal concept of a rational being from the concept of the human being. It is through the offices of this *fact* that anthropology remains all its contested authority. This is the point at which the philosopher says "we," and at which in Kant's discourse "rational being" and "humanity" are always associated by the conjunction "and" or *vel*. For example "Now, I say, man *and in general* (*und überhaupt*) every rational being, *exists* as an end in himself, and not merely as a means" (*Foundations* . . . , p. 86). [Note that this phrase is from the passage that serves as the first epigraph to this text. The deconstruction of the end and of man takes place on the *margins* of philosophy: in titles and footnotes.] "This principle of humanity and of every rational creature as an end in itself" (ibid., pp. 88–89).

[12] "The Origin of Geometry," in *The Crisis of European Sciences and Transcendental Phenomenology*, trans. David Carr (Evanston: Northwestern University Press, 1970), p. 378.

[13] In a brief fragment from 1934 (*Stufen der Geschichtlichkeit. Erste Geschichtlichkeit,* Beilage XXVI, in *Die Krisis der europäischen Wissenschaften und die transzendentale Phänomenologie* [The Hague: Martinus Nijhoff, 1954], pp. 502–3) Husserl distinguishes between three levels and three stages of historicity: culture and tradition as human sociality in general; European culture and the theoretical project (science and philosophy); "the conversion of philosophy into phenomenology."

MICHEL FOUCAULT

What Is Critique?

1978

Actually, the question about which I wanted to speak and about which I still want to speak is: *What is critique?* It might be worth trying out a few ideas on this project that keeps taking shape, being extended and reborn on the outer limits of philosophy, very close to it, up against it, at its expense, in the direction of a future philosophy and in lieu, perhaps, of all possible philosophy. And it seems that between the high Kantian enterprise and the little polemical professional activities that are called critique, it seems to me that there has been in the modern Western world (dating, more or less, empirically from the 15th to the 16th centuries) a certain way of thinking, speaking and acting, a certain relationship to society, to culture and also a relationship to others that we could call, let's say, the critical attitude. Of course, you will be surprised to hear that there is something like a critical attitude that would be specific to modern civilization, since there have been so many critiques, polemics, etc. and since even Kant's problems presumably have origins which go back way before the 15th and 16th centuries. One will be surprised to see that one tries to find a unity in this critique, although by its very nature, by its function, I was going to say, by its profession, it seems to be condemned to dispersion, dependency and pure heteronomy. After all, critique only exists in relation to something other than itself: it is an instrument, a means for a future or a truth that it will not know nor happen to be, it oversees a domain it would want to police and is unable to regulate. All this means that it is a function which is subordinated in relation to what philosophy, science, politics, ethics, law, literature, etc., positively constitute. And at the same time, whatever the pleasures or compensations accompanying this curious activity of critique, it seems that it rather regularly, almost always, brings not only some stiff bit of utility it claims to have, but also that it is supported by some kind of more general imperative—more general still than that of eradicating errors. There is some-

From *The Politics of Truth*, ed. Sylvère Lotringer and trans. Lysa Hochroth and Catherine Porter (Los Angeles: Semiotext[e], 1997), pp. 41–47 ["Qu'est-ce que la critique?" is the text of a lecture given to the French Society of Philosophy on May 27, 1978, and published in *Bulletin de la Société française de philosophie* 84, no. 2 (1990)].

thing in critique which is akin to virtue. And in a certain way, what I wanted to speak to you about is this critical attitude as virtue in general.

There are several routes one could take to discuss the history of the critical attitude. I would simply like to suggest this one to you, which is one possible route, again, among many others. I will suggest the following variation: the Christian pastoral, or the Christian church inasmuch as it acted in a precisely and specifically pastoral way, developed this idea—singular and, I believe, quite foreign to ancient culture—that each individual, whatever his age or status, from the beginning to the end of his life and in his every action, had to be governed and had to let himself be governed, that is to say directed towards his salvation, by someone to whom he was bound by a total, meticulous, detailed relationship of obedience. And this salvation-oriented operation in a relationship of obedience to someone has to be made in a triple relationship to the truth: truth understood as dogma, truth also to the degree where this orientation implies a special and individualizing knowledge of individuals; and finally, in that this direction is deployed like a reflective technique comprising general rules, particular knowledge, precepts, methods of examination, confessions, interviews, etc. After all, we must not forget what, for centuries, the Greek church called *technè technôn* and what the Latin Roman church called *ars artium*. It was precisely the direction of conscience; the art of governing men. Of course, this art of governing for a long time was linked to relatively limited practices, even in medieval society, to monastic life and especially to the practice of relatively restricted spiritual groups. But I believe that from the 15th century on and before the Reformation, one can say that there was a veritable explosion of the art of governing men. There was an explosion in two ways: first, by displacement in relation to the religious center, let's say if you will, secularization, the expansion in civil society of this theme of the art of governing men and the methods of doing it; and then, second, the proliferation of this art of governing into a variety of areas—how to govern children, how to govern the poor and beggars, how to govern a family, a house, how to govern armies, different groups, cities, states and also how to govern one's own body and mind. *How to govern* was, I believe, one of the fundamental questions about what was happening in the 15th or 16th centuries. It is a fundamental question which was answered by the multiplication of all the arts of governing—the art of pedagogy, the art of politics, the art of economics, if you will—and of all the institutions of government, in the wider sense the term government had at the time.

So, this governmentalization, which seems to me to be rather characteristic of these societies in Western Europe in the 16th century, cannot apparently be dissociated from the question "How not to be governed?" I do not mean by that that governmentalization would be opposed in a kind of face-off by the opposite affirmation, "we do not want to be governed and we do not want to be governed at all." I mean that, in this great preoccupation about the way to govern and the search for the ways to govern, we identify a perpetual question which would be: "how not to be governed *like that*, by that, in the name of those principles, with such and such an objective in mind and by means of such procedures, not like that, not for that, not by them." And if we accord this movement of governmentalization of both society and individuals the historic dimension and breadth which I believe it has had, it seems that one could approximately locate therein what we could call the critical attitude. Facing them head on and as compensation, or rather, as both partner and adversary to the arts of governing, as an act of defiance, as a challenge, as a way of limiting these arts of governing and sizing them up, transforming them, of finding a way to escape from them or, in any case, a way to displace them, with a basic distrust, but also and by the same token, as a line of development of the arts of governing, there would have been something born in Europe at that time, a kind of general cultural form, both a political and moral attitude, a way of thinking, etc. and which I would very simply call the art of not being governed or better, the art of not being governed like that and at that cost. I would therefore propose, as a very first definition of critique, this general characterization: the art of not being governed quite so much.

You will tell me that this definition is both very general and very vague or fluid. Well, of course it is! But I still believe that it may allow us to identify some precise points inherent to what I try to call the critical attitude. These are historical anchoring points, of course, which we can determine as follows:

1. First anchoring point: during a period of time when governing men was essentially a spiritual art, or an essentially religious practice linked to the authority of a Church, to the prescription of a Scripture, not to want to be governed like that essentially meant finding another function for the Scriptures unrelated to the teaching of God. Not wanting to be governed was a certain way of refusing, challenging, limiting (say it as you like) ecclesiastical rule. It meant returning to the Scriptures, seeking out what was authentic in them, what was really written in the Scriptures. It meant questioning what sort of truth the Scriptures told, gaining access to this truth of the Scriptures in the Scriptures and maybe in spite of what was written, to the point of finally raising the very simple question: were the Scriptures true? And, in short, from Wycliffe to Pierre Bayle, critique develped in part, for the most part, but not exclusively, of course, in relation to the Scriptures. Let us say that critique is biblical, historically.

2. Not to want to be governed, this is the second anchoring point. Not to want to be governed like that also means not wanting to accept these

laws because they are unjust because, by virtue of their antiquity or the more or less threatening ascendancy given them by today's sovereign, they hide a fundamental illegitimacy. Therefore, from this perspective, confronted with government and the obedience it stipulates, critique means putting forth universal and indefeasible rights to which every government, whatever it may be, whether a monarch, a magistrate, an educator or a pater familias, will have to submit. In brief, if you like, we find here again the problem of natural law.

Natural law is certainly not an invention of the Renaissance, but from the 16th century on, it took on a critical function that it still maintains to this day. To the question "How not to be governed?" it answers by saying "What are the limits of the right to govern?" Let us say that here critique is basically a legal issue.

3. And finally "to not to want to be governed" is of course *not* accepting as true—here I will move along quickly—what an authority tells you is true, or at least not accepting it because an authority tells you that it is true, but rather accepting it only if one considers valid the reasons for doing so. And this time, critique finds its anchoring point in the problem of certainty in its confrontation with authority. The Bible, jurisprudence, science, writing, nature, the relationship to oneself; the sovereign, the law, the authority of dogmatism. One sees how the interplay of governmentalization and critique has brought about phenomena which are, I believe, of capital importance in the history of Western culture whether in the development of philological sciences, philosophical thought, legal analysis or methodological reflections. However, above all, one sees that the core of critique is basically made of the bundle of relationships that are tied to one another, or one to the two others, power, truth and the subject. And if governmentalization is indeed this movement through which individuals are subjugated in the reality of a social practice through mechanisms of power that adhere to a truth, well, then! I will say that critique is the movement by which the subject gives himself the right to question truth on its effects of power and question power on its discourses of truth. Well, then! Critique will be the art of voluntary insubordination, that of reflected intractability. Critique would essentially insure the desubjugation of the subject in the context of what we could call, in a word, the politics of truth.

GILLES DELEUZE

On Four Poetic Formulas That Might Summarize Kantian Philosophy

1993

The time is out of joint.
—Shakespeare[1]

Time out of joint, time is unhinged.[2] The hinges are the axis on which the door turns. The hinge, *Cardo*, indicates the subordination of time to precise cardinal points, through which the periodic movements it measures pass. As long as time remains on its hinges, it is subordinated to extensive movement, it is the measure of movement, its interval or number. This characteristic of ancient philosophy has often been emphasized: the subordination of time to the circular movement of the world as the turning Door, a revolving door, a labyrinth opening onto its eternal origin. It will entail an entire hierarchization of movements according to their proximity to the Eternal, according to their necessity, their perfection, their uniformity, their rotation, their composite spirals, their particular axes and doors, and the numbers of Time that correspond to them. Time no doubt tends to free itself when the movement it measures itself becomes increasingly *aberrant* or *derived* [*dérivé*], marked by material, meteorological, and terrestrial contingencies: but this is a downward tendency that still depends on the adventures of movement.[3] Time thus remains subordinate to what, in movement, is both originary *and* derived.

Time *out of joint*, the door off its hinges, signifies the first great Kantian reversal: movement is now subordinated to time. Time is no longer related to the movement it measures, but rather movement to the time that conditions it. Moreover, movement is no longer the determination of objects, but the description of a space, a space we must set aside in order to discover time as the condition of ac-

From *Essays Critical and Clinical*, trans. Daniel W. Smith and Michael A. Greco (Minneapolis: University of Minnesota Press, 1997), pp. 27–35 ["Sur quatre formules poétiques qui pourraient résumer l'ensemble de la philosophie kantienne," in *Critique et clinique* (Paris: Les Editions de Minuit, 1993)].

tion. Time thus becomes unilinear and rectilinear, no longer in the sense that it would measure a derived movement, but in and through itself, insofar as it imposes the succession of its determination on every possible movement. This is a rectification of time. Time ceases to be curved by a God who makes it depend on movement. It ceases to be cardinal and becomes ordinal, the order of an empty time. In time, there is no longer anything either originary or derived that depends on movement. The labyrinth takes on a new look—neither a circle nor a spiral, but a thread, a pure straight line, all the more mysterious in that it is simple, inexorable, terrible—"the labyrinth made of a single straight line which is indivisible, incessant."[4] Hölderlin portrayed Oedipus as having already entered into this strict march of the slow death, following an order of time that had ceased to "rhyme."[5] Nietzsche, in a similar sense, considered it to be the most Semitic of the Greek tragedies. It is Hamlet, rather, who completes the emanicipation of time. He truly brings about the reversal because his own movement results from nothing other than the succession of the determination. Hamlet is the first hero who truly needed time in order to act, whereas earlier heroes were subject to time as the consequence of an original movement (Aeschylus) or an aberrant action (Sophocles). The *Critique of Pure Reason* is the book of Hamlet, the prince of the north. Kant's historical situation allowed him to grasp the implications of this reversal. Time is no longer the cosmic time of an original celestial movement, nor is it the rural time of derived meteorological movements. It has become the time of the city and nothing other, the pure order of time.

It is not succession that defines time, but time that defines the parts of movement as successive inasmuch as they are determined within it. If time itself were succession, it would have to succeed in another time, to infinity. Things succeed each other in diverse times, but they are also simultaneous in the same time, and they subsist in an indeterminate time [*un temps quelconque*]. It is no longer a question of defining time by succession, nor space by simultaneity, nor permanence by eternity. Permanence, succession, and simultaneity are modes or relations of time (*duration, series, set*). They are the fragments [*éclats*] of time. Consequently, just as time can no longer be defined by succession, space can no longer be defined by coexistence or simultaneity. Each of them, space and time, will have to find completely new determinations. Everything that moves and changes is in time, but time itself does not change or move, any more than it is eternal. It is the form of everything that changes and moves, but it is an immutable form that does not change—not an eternal form, but precisely the form of what is *not* eternal, the immutable form of change and movement. Such an autonomous form seems to point to a profound mystery: it requires a new definition of time [and space].

I is an other.

—Rimband[6]

The ancients also conceived of time in another way, as a mode of thought or an intensive movement of the soul, a kind of spiritual or monastic time. Descartes brought about its secularization or laicization with the *cogito*: the *I think* is an act of instantaneous determination, which implies an undetermined existence (*I am*) and determines this existence as that of a thinking substance (I am *a thing that thinks*). But how can the determination apply to the undetermined if we cannot say under what form it is "determinable?" This Kantian objection could lead to no other result than the following: our undetermined existence is determinable only in time, under the form of time. Hence the "I think" affects time, and only determines the existence of a "self" [*moi*] that changes in time and presents a certain degree of consciousness at every moment. Time as the form of determinability therefore does not depend upon the intensive movement of the soul; on the contrary, the intensive production of a degree of consciousness at every moment depends on time. Kant brings about a second emancipation of time, and completes its laicization.

The Self is in time and is constantly changing: it is a passive, or rather receptive, "self" that experiences changes in time. The *I* is an act (I think) that actively determines my existence (I am), but can only determine it in time, as the existence of a passive, receptive, and changing *self*, which only represents to itself the activity of *its own* thought. The I and the Self are thus separated by the line of time, which relates them to each other only under the condition of a fundamental difference. My existence can never be determined as that of an active and spontaneous being, but as a passive "self" that represents to itself the "I"—that is, the spontaneity of the determination—as an Other that affects it ("the paradox of inner sense"). Oedipus, according to Nietzsche, is defined by a purely passive attitude, but one that is related to an activity that continues after his death.[7] For all the more reason, Hamlet displays his eminently Kantian character whenever he appears as a passive existence, who, like an actor or sleeper, receives the activity of his own thought as an Other, which is nonetheless capable of giving him a dangerous power that defies pure reason. In Beckett, it is Murphy's "metabulia."[8] Hamlet is not a man of skepticism or doubt, but the man of the Critique. I am separated from myself by the form of time and yet I am one, because the I necessarily affects this form by bringing about its synthesis—not only of successive parts to each other, but at every moment—and because the Self is necessarily affected by the I as the content of this form. The form of the determinable makes the determined Self represent the determination to itself as an Other. In short, the madness of the subject corresponds to the time out of joint. There is, as it were, a doubt derivation of the I and the Self in time, and it is the derivation that links or stitches them together. Such is the thread of time.

In a certain sense, Kant goes further than Rimbaud. For Rimbaud's great formula takes on its full force only by appealing to recollections from school. Rimbaud gives his formula an Aristotelian interpretation: "So much the worse for the wood that finds itself a violin! . . . If the copper wakes up a bugle, that is not its fault . . ." This is like a concept-object relation in which the concept is an active form, and the object a merely potential matter. It is a mold, a process of molding. For Kant, by contrast, the I is no longer a concept but the representation that accompanies every concept, and the Self is not an object, but that to which all objects are related as to the continuous variation of its own successive states, and to the infinite modulation of its degrees at each instant. The concept-object relation subsists in Kant, but it is doubled by the I-Self relation, which constitutes *a modulation, and no longer a mold*. In this sense, the compartmentalized distinction between forms as concepts (violin-bugle) and matters as objects (wood-copper) gives way to the continuity of a one-way linear development that requires the establishment of new formal relations (time) and the disposition of a new type of matter (phenomenon). It is as if, in Kant, one could already hear Beethoven, and soon Wagner's continuous variation.

If the I determines our existence as a passive self changing in time, time is the formal relation through which the mind affects itself, or the way we are internally affected by ourselves. Time can thus be defined as the Affect of the self by itself, or at least as the formal possibility of being affected by oneself. It is in this sense that time as an immutable form, which can no longer be defined by simple succession, appears as the *form of interiority* (inner sense), whereas space, which can no longer be defined by coexistence or simultaneity, appears for its part as the form of exteriority, the formal possibility of being affected by something else as an exterior object. "Form of interiority" does not simply mean that time is interior to the mind, because space is no less so. Nor does "form of exteriority" mean that space presupposes "something else," since it is space, on the contrary, that makes possible every representation of objects as other or exterior. But this amounts to saying that exteriority entails as much immanence (because space remains interior to my mind) as interiority entails transcendence (because in relation to time my mind is represented as other than myself). It is not time that is interior to us, or at least it is not specifically interior to us; it is we who are interior to time, and for this reason time always separates us from what determines us by affecting it. Interiority constantly hollows us out, splits us in two, doubles us, even though our unity subsists. But because time has no end, this doubling never reaches its limit: *time is constituted by a vertigo or oscillation*, just as unlimited space is constituted by a sliding or floating.

> *It is an extremely painful thing to be ruled by laws that one does not know; . . . For the essence of such laws in this way necessitates the secret of their content.*
>
> —Kafka[9]

Which amounts to saying *the* Law, since one can hardly distinguish between laws one does not know. The conscience of antiquity speaks of laws because, under certain conditions, they give us knowledge of the Good or the Best; laws express the Good from which they are derived. Laws are a "second resort," a representative of the Good in a world deserted by the gods. When the true Politics is absent, it leaves behind general directives that men need to know in order to act correctly. From the point of view of knowledge, laws are like the imitation of the Good in a given case.

In the *Critique of Practical Reason*, by contrast, Kant reverses the relationship between the law and the Good, and thereby raises the law to the level of a pure and empty uniqueness. The good is what the Law says it is—it is the good that depends on the law, and not vice versa. As first principle, the law has neither interiority nor content, since any content would refer it back to a Good of which it would be the imitation. It is a pure form that has no object, whether sensible or intelligible. It does not tell us what we must do, but what subjective rule we must obey no matter what our action. Any action whose maxim can be *thought* without contradiction as universal, and whose motive has no object other than this maxim, will be moral (lying, for example, cannot be thought as universal, since it at least implies people who believe it and who, in believing it, are not lying). The law is thus defined as the pure form of universality. It does not tell us what aim the will must pursue to be good, but what form it must take to be moral. It does not tell us what we must do, it simply tells us "You must!" leaving us to deduce from it the good, that is, the aims of the pure imperative. The law is not known because there is nothing in it to know: it is the object of the purely *practical* determination, and not a theoretical or speculative one.

The law is undistinguishable from its sentence, and the sentence is indistinguishable from its implementation or execution. If the law is primary, it no longer has any way of distinguishing between the "accusation," the "defense," and the "verdict."[10] The law coincides with its imprint on our heart and in our flesh. But it does not thereby even give us a final knowledge of our faults, for what its needle writes on us is *Act through duty* (and not merely in conformity with duty) . . . it writes nothing else. Freud showed that, if duty in this sense presupposes a renunciation of interests and inclinations, the law will exert itself all the more strongly and rigorously the deeper our renunciation. Thus, the more we observe the law with exactitude, the more severe it becomes. Even the most holy are not spared.[11] *It never acquits us*, neither of our virtues nor of our vices or our faults: at every moment there is only an apparent acquittal, and the moral conscience, far from appeasing itself, is intensified by all our renunciations and pricks us even more strongly. This is not Hamlet, but Brutus. How could the law reveal its secret without making the renunciation on which it feeds impossible? An acquittal can only be hoped for, "which makes up for the impotence of speculative reason," no longer at a given moment, but from the viewpoint of a progress that continues to infinity in its ever increasing conformity with the law (sanctification as the consciousness of perseverance in moral progress). This path, which exceeds the limits of our life and requires the soul's immortality, follows the straight line of time, inexorable and incessant, upon which we remain in constant contact with the law. But this indefinite prolongation, rather than leading us to a paradise above, already installs us in a hell here below. Rather than announcing immortality, it distills a "slow death," and continuously *defers the judgment of the law*. When time is out of joint, we have to renounce the ancient cycle of faults and expiations in order to follow the infinite route of the slow death, the deferred judgment, or the infinite debt. Time leaves us no other juridical options than those of Kafka in *The Trial*: either an "apparent acquittal" or an "unlimited postponement."

> *To attain the unknown by disorganizing all the senses . . . a long, boundless, and systematized disorganization of all the senses.*
>
> —Rimbaud[12]

Or rather, an unregulated exercise of all the faculties. This would be the fourth formula of a profoundly romantic Kant in the *Critique of Judgment*. This is because, in the first two Critiques, the various subjective faculties entered into relationships with each other, but these relationships were rigorously regulated, since there was always a dominant or determining fundamental faculty that imposed its rule upon the others. There were numerous faculties: outer sense, inner sense, the imagination, the understanding, reason, each of which was well defined. But in the *Critique of Pure Reason*, it was the understanding that dominated, because it determined inner sense through the intermediary of a synthesis of the imagination, and even reason submitted to the role the understanding assigned to it. In the *Critique of Practical Reason*, the fundamental faculty was reason, because reason constitutes the pure form of the universality of law, the other faculties following as they might (the understanding applied the law, the imagination received the sentence, inner sense experienced the consequences or the sanction). But now we see Kant, at an age when great authors rarely have anything new to say, confronting a problem that will lead him into an extraordinary undertaking; if the faculties can thus enter into variable relationships in which each faculty is in turn regulated by one of the others, it must follow that, taken together they are capable of free and unregulated relationships in which each faculty goes to its own limit, and yet in this way shows the possibility of its entering into an *indeterminate* [*quelconque*] harmony with the others. This will be the *Critique of Judgment* as the foundation of romanticism.

This is no longer the aesthetic of the *Critique of Pure Reason*, which considered the sensible as a quality that could be related to an object in space and time; nor is it a logic of the sensible, nor even a new logos that would be time. It is an aesthetic of the Beautiful and the Sublime, in which the sensible takes on an autonomous value for itself and is deployed in a pathos beyond all logic, and which will grasp time as it bursts forth [*dans son jaillissement*], at the very origin of its thread and its vertigo. This is no longer the Affect of the *Critique of Pure Reason*, which linked the Self to the I in a relationship that was still regulated by the order of time; it is a Pathos that lets them evolve freely in order to form strange combinations as source of time, "arbitrary forms of possible intuitions." It is no longer the determination of an I, which must be joined to the determinability of the Self in order to constitute knowledge: it is now the undetermined unity of all the faculties (the Soul), which makes us enter the unknown.

What is in question in the *Critique of Judgment* is how certain phenomena, which will define the beautiful, give to the inner sense of time an autonomous supplementary dimension to the imagination, a power [*pouvoir*] of free reflection: and to the understanding an infinite conceptual capacity [*puissance*]. The various faculties enter into a spontaneous accord that is no longer determined by any one of them, which is all the more profound in that it no longer has any role, and which demonstrates a spontaneous accord of the Self and the I under the conditions of a beautiful Nature. The Sublime goes even further in this direction: it brings the various faculties into play in such a manner that they struggle against each other like wrestlers, with one faculty pushing another to its maximum or limit, to which the second faculty reacts by pushing the first toward an inspiration it would not have had on its own. One faculty pushes another to a limit, but they each make the one go beyond the limits of the other. The faculty enter into relationship at their deepest level, where they are most foreign to each other. They interact at the point where the distance between them is at its greatest. There is a terrible struggle between the imagination and reason, but also between the understanding and inner sense, a battle whose episodes will be the two forms of the Sublime and the Genius. There is a tempest in the chasm opened up inside the subject. In the first two Critiques, the dominant or fundamental faculty was able to make the other faculties enter into the closest possible harmonics with itself. But now, in an exercise of limits, the various faculties mutually produce the most remote harmonies in each other, so that they form essentially dissonant accords. The emancipation of dissonance, the discordant accord, is the great discovery of the *Critique of Judgment*, the final Kantian reversal. The separation that joins was the first of Kant's themes in the *Critique of Pure Reason*. But in the end, he discovers the discord that produces an accord. An unregulated exercise of all the faculties, which was to define future philosophy, just as for Rimbaud the disorder of all the senses would define the poetry of the future. A new music as discord, and as discordant accord the source of time.

This is why we have proposed four formulas, which are obviously arbitrary in relation to Kant, but not arbitrary in relation to what Kant has left us for the present and the future. De Quincey's admirable text *The Last Days of Immanuel Kant* said everything, but only the reverse side of things that will find their full development in the four poetic formulas of Kantianism. This is the Shakespearean aspect of Kant, who begins as Hamlet and winds up as Lear, whose daughters would be the post-Kantians.

NOTES

1 Shakespeare, *Hamlet*, Act 1, Scene 5. Shestov often used Shakespeare's formula as the tragic device of his own thought; see "The Ethical Problem in *Julius Caesar*," trans. S. Konovalov, in *The New Adelphi*, June 1928, p. 348, and "Celui qui édifie et détruit des mondes (Tolstoi)," trans. Sylvie Luneau, in *Un homme pris au piège (Pouchkine, Tolstoi, Tchekhov)* (Paris: Union Générale d'Editions, 1966), p. 29 [Deleuze follows Bonnefoy's French translation of this phrase as *le temps est hors de ses gonds*, literally, "time is off its hinges"; see *Hamlet*, trans. Yves Bonnefoy (Paris: Gallimard, Folio, 1992).—Trans.]

2 [This essay was first published as the preface to *Kant's Critical Philosophy: The Doctrine of the Faculties*, trans. Hugh Tomlinson and Barbara Habberjam (Minneapolis: University of Minnesota Press, 1984), pp. vii–xiii. The French text subsequently appeared as "Sur quatre formules qui pourraient résumer la philosophie kantienne," in *Philosophie* 9 (1986): 29–34. The present essay is a revised and expanded version of this earlier text.—Trans.]

3 Eric Alliez, in *Capital Times: Tales from the Conquest of Time,* trans. George van den Abbeele (Minneapolis: University of Minnesota Press, 1996), has analyzed, in ancient thought, this tendency toward the emancipation of time when movement ceases to be circular; for instance, in the "chrematism" and time as a monetary movement in Aristotle.

4 Jorge Luis Borges, "Death and the Compass," trans. Anthony Kerrigan, in *Ficciones* (New York: Knopf, 1993), p. 113, translation modified.

5 Friedrich Hölderlin, "Remarks on 'Oedipus,'" in *Essays and Letters on Theory*, ed. and trans. Thomas Ptau (Albany: State University of New York Press, 1988), pp. 101–8. See also Jean Beaufret's commentary, "Hölderlin et Sophocles," in Hölderlin, *Remarques sur Oedipe* (Paris: Union Générale d'Editions, 10/18, 1965), which analyzes the relation with Kant.

6 [Arthur Rimbaud, *Complete Works*, trans. Paul Schmidt (New York: Harper & Row, 1975), letter to George Izambard, May 13, 1871, p. 101; letter to Paul Demeny, May 15, 1871, p. 103, translation modified.—Trans.]

7 Nietzsche, *The Birth of Tragedy*, trans. Walter Kaufmann (New York: Random House, 1967), p. 9, pp. 67–72.

8 Samuel Beckett, *Murphy* (Paris: Bordas, 1948), chapter 6, p. 85, ["Metabulia" is a neologism coined by Beckett in his French translation of *Murphy; meta* combined with *abulia*, an abnormal lack of ability to act or to make decisions. In the original English version (1938), the term *will-lessness* was used; see *Murphy* (London: Picador, 1973), p. 66.—Trans.]

9 [Franz Kafka, "The Problem of Our Laws," in *The Complete Stories*, ed. Nahum Glatzer (New York: Schocken, 1983), p. 437, translation modified.—Trans.]

10 Franz Kafka, "Advocates," in *The Complete Stories*, ed. Nahum N. Glatzer (New York: Schocken, 1971), pp. 449–51.

11 Sigmund Freud, *Civilization and Its Discontents*, in *The Standard Edition of the Complete Psychological Works*, trans. James Strachey, vol. 21 (London: Hogarth, 1961), pp. 125–26.

12 [Arthur Rimbaud, *Complete Works*, letter to Georges Izambard, May 13, 1871, p. 101; and letter to Paul Demeny, May 15, 1871, p. 103.—Trans.]

CLAUDE IMBERT

For a History of Logic

1999

The cosmological naturalism of the ancients was repudiated shortly after the Renaissance, as everyone knows. A second fact to bear in mind: how philosophers tried to respond with cunning, to retain half of their age-old prerogatives, to perpetuate a phenomenological categorization that mathematics had condemned to irrelevance, and to hide their own discursive capacity in the impenetrability of the transcendental. Such was the nature of Kantian neoclassicism, which was by no means the modernity it is said to be. For the effect of the Copernican turn was to ensure that everything else remained equal; it obtained this from a discursive canon anxious about its completeness. So, between the empirical statement and the license of genius granted to the innocent poetry of Frederick II, nothing was left to rhetorical custom.

In what respect can Kant be called neoclassical? For one thing, he played down the Cartesian option, doubting its concatenations of ideas, which quickly became aleatory outside the realm of a mathematics that scarcely fit the mold. Above all, though, he revived the phenomenology of categorical predications. In a remark included in the second edition of the *Critique of Pure Reason*, he pointed out that the qualitative unity of the diversity of knowledge can be thought of as being "almost like the unity of the theme of a drama, speech, or myth."[1] Called upon to justify his own choice of transcendental concepts, Kant thus supplied new arguments for the epistemological convictions of the ancients. And perhaps the clearest comment he ever made on the transcendental operation, confirming a preface that opened with praise of Aristotle, was this: *o protos euretes . . .*

The philosopher would presumably remain in the game. He allowed himself to place a seal of approval on the conceptual axis that runs from the subject to an experience as self-contained as a world, equipped with a cartography allowing for no exterior. It has been said that this time he found himself alone in that world. There, philosophical language achieved independence, but it did so by accepting the obligation to grammaticalize operations at the limit of its

From *Pour une histoire de la logique: Un héritage platonicien* (Paris: Presses Universitaires de France, 1999), pp. 292–302; trans. Arthur Goldhammer.

capacities—reworking and transforming a syntax already shaped by predication and its tolerable ambiguities. Kant was its conscious organizer. From this came his axiom of completeness and closure. The immediate result was the disturbing vigor of the *chancellery style*, which contemporaries were quick to note. To be sure, he ennobled the German language, as the *Discours de la méthode* and *L'art de penser* had done a century earlier for the French language. He also foreclosed any possible future for it. This style elicited Kleist's enthusiasm and gave rise to the fragmentary writing of German Romanticism and, in reaction, to Hölderlin's poetics.[2] On philosophers it imposed silence in two ways that no dialectic could ever overcome—about the world and about the subject. Thanks to the technique of Kantian deduction, and to this way of grammaticalizing experience within the syntactic space of a propositional canon and capping the whole undertaking with two clauses of completeness and closure, one had entered the age of logics.

The compelling power and uniformity of the philosophical style with which Kant had saddled the *Aufklärung* would come to a quick end once mathematics achieved autonomy of language—a direct consequence of its inventiveness. Critical philosophy allowed a risky hybridization of the dimensions of a Newtonian mathematics with the articulations of a modalized logic, and on transcendental synthesis it had staked a deduction without a future.[3] Since the operation quickly proved useless, people were more willing to overlook its dubious character. To be sure, the identification of two heterogeneous structures, governed on one hand by the principles of the *sensible world* and on the other by those of the *intelligible world* that Kant had so carefully differentiated from it (1770), excluded simple Platonic conjugation.[4] The proposed solution, that of a modal phenomenology, offered a well-tempered formulation of this. For a while longer it was able to conjugate the analogous geometry of sensory apperception and the predication of objects. Yet mathematics, in the time between d'Alembert and Gauss, had already established a direct understanding with physics, in which both conceptualized on the basis of a functional language tailored to their requirements. All subsequent avatars of philosophical logic and its formalist drives were direct consequences of this precarious Kantian accord. Critical philosophy led to either transcendental scholasticism or secession. The former would turn into Brentano's neo-Aristotelianism. The secession, for its part, would take two forms. Either one opted for a functional syntax, which was supposed to impose itself on philosophical language by way of a paraphrase—as Russell insisted at the turn of the twentieth century and as logical positivism would take for its doctrine. Or one opted for a phenomenality of existence in which the clockwork of the pattern was lost. Out of this came two analytics, each incompatible with the other and oblivious of the need for a language appropriate to their operations.

Kant had thus gone as far as possible with an orthology that drew on categorical semantics and predicative syntax for his own purposes. Critical philosophy left as its legacy an exhausted project, one that was rejected by mathematics after Gauss and by physics after Planck. Modal phenomenology was dismissed by a modernity on which experience had no purchase. This present would seek its dimensions in various turns of thought, expression, and representation whose common trait was to have given up on being dimensions of things as well. The situation resulting from this was undeniably confused, faced as it was with the powerful taboos of critical philosophy and the narrow avenue of rationality they delineated. The consequence was the rivalry among logics that marked the beginning of the twentieth century, when everyone claimed the Kantian heritage but argued as if blindfolded. This was the rule as long as functional languages had yet to establish their status within mathematics or give way to unforeseen computational techniques that would sweep away once and for all the mirage of a universal language.

Suppose that these post-Kantian logics can be classified either as *phenomenologies* or *formal languages*. The former were still closely linked to their categorical and Hellenistic prototype, while the latter were dedicated to the algebraic and functional operations of which they were the heirs. When, at the beginning of the twentieth century, each of these logics made contradictory claims to be the repositories of the primary and ultimate authority in regard to all statements, whether of knowledge or of everyday life, conflict was inevitable. It proved ruinous for the philosophical projects that plunged into the fray along with them. The test was crucial in regard to the statement of perception, which refused to line up on one side or the other, in view of its refusal either to renounce its deictic marks of self-referentiality or to assert mathematical extensionality. That was the end of the paradigm of the primal utterance (*premier énoncé*), which in high Greek prose ensured that the epiphany of the world would match up with common sense. The consequence, resisted by some, was the precise identification of the enunciative functions so judiciously explored by Hellenism and committed to the description of the world. Once this singularity was recognized and a closure clearly foreseen by Kant was understood, the adversaries could all be equitably dismissed. The logic of the *Principia mathematica* was projected onto the mathematical future for which the way was being paved by Herbrand, Gödel, Church, and Turing. As for phenomenology after Kant, it knew that it was inextricably associated with an achievement of the Greeks that had not waited for it to arrive and therefore that it was incapable of the extension that it expected yet despaired of achieving. The lesson in this case verged on myth. One learned yet again that it is impossible to eat one's cake and have it too.

Critical philosophy thus left a novel situation in its wake, as everyone continued to invoke its name as a reference without being able to make it new. This dilemma was resolved in the 1930s. Classical Hellenism had by then taken shape, and people would come to understand the precision of its choices, the grounds for them, the prodigious revisions they entailed, and the ways in which its stylistic inventiveness could be put to use. Everything about it was carefully regulated, including the function of language and its role as a cosmic clock. The intersection of two forms of *actio*, that of language and that of the world, distributed the authority of the *perceptio* among any number of events but without atomizing its texture. The Platonic heritage had taken up one after another all the promises associated with the propositional paradigm of the Sophist—a grammatical miracle, if you will. The end of the avenues of intelligibility it had opened up had been reached. Recovering its initial intent now required coming up with a way of philosophizing that would no longer be dedicated to the propositional regime of Hellenism. Greek naturalism had chosen its modes of grasping (*prises*)—categorization, *deixis*, indicative—and its units of meaning. The time had come to change modes and units in order to take philosophical realism in a different direction. I will briefly discuss two examples, which are in fact far more than mere examples. But I will overlook the lengthy history of their meditation so as to bring out certain distinctive features in their expression.

The exposition will be clearer if we stick to two philosophers who went beyond the requisites and risks of the proposition, choosing instead to align their thinking as precisely and closely as possible with their language. The order in which we approach these two thinkers is of little importance, since they were independent yet curiously complementary. Hence I will dive right in.

To begin, why did Merleau-Ponty cast his lot with the *chiasmus*, which became the—quite unusual—key term of his last writings?[5] In what respect did he free himself from perception—the term and the thing? What did he bring out that could serve as an index of the philosophical function and support a new figure of realism while borrowing from the register of figures of speech? Merleau-Ponty drew on all the meanings of chiasmus, together with their histories, in formulating his program. First came the muted evocation of the *optical chiasm*, to which he still referred in his first books.[6] This term from cerebral neurology was welcome as a way of invalidating the prejudice in favor of an affine representation of a hypothetical sensory impression, as well as a way of indicating the location of the dividing line between where expression begins and that which is not yet expression. This also shifted the locus of the whole apparatus of sensory effects, not only the so-called sense data but also their enunciated form—the simple machine about which Wittgenstein waxed ironic. One had to concede that stimuli were distributed among widely separated and unexpected places in the cerebral substrate. This argument, which proved salutary against the apophatic works of a certain version of common sense, reopened the Cartesian question of the union of soul and body. This was the point on which Merleau-Ponty broke with phenomenology in the 1950s. Opting for an analysis of expression (philosophy having no access to that which precedes expression), he cited Valéry—the Valéry of the *Cahiers*, still quite close to *Monsieur Teste* but setting against his absolute solitude a consciousness in chiasmus, always already divided—"chiasma of two destinies." Valéry had freed himself from a substantial *cogito*, tethered to itself and to its boredom. Finally, when Merleau-Ponty substituted this typed figure for perception, for what had been his initial philosophical locus, he simultaneously dispelled any fantasy of adequation, accepting the image of a broken vision, as if constantly oscillating between the seer and the visible.

This substitution might well have hit its target more accurately and effectively than the Copernican inversion, which in any case left everything equal. With the conjunction of three directions—physiological, intersubjective, then resolutely polemical—Merleau-Ponty reached the end of his quest, which had always been the expression of existence. A quest that had revisited all the concepts of the philosophical ancien régime, taken over all the assumptions and arguments of the *Phénoménologie de la perception*, and fluctuated between thought as meaning and thing as exteriority had thus silently fomented its outcome. It would take up this "philosophy of today" that Merleau-Ponty so plainly pursued through all the variety of his texts. First proof: Merleau-Ponty scored by making clear what was unintelligible in the other regime—that is, the broken episodes in *Monsieur Teste*, *Le temps retrouvé* of Proust, and soon the *I-thou* and nonpersons of Claude Simon.[7] Shouldn't philosophical hypotheses be judged by their capacity for intelligibility?

Finally, in a still more strikingly original use of chiasmus, Merleau-Ponty recognized its effective presence in the canvases of Cézanne, which revealed to him the distinctive character of the history of modern painting. Here the operation was materialized in the form of a work, in a painting in which colors and forms exchanged stratagems, faces were painted as objects, and movement was transferred to the map of the visible.[8] Merleau-Ponty thus came to occupy the place of the "painter of modern life" created by Baudelaire, left anonymous, and not very closely associated with the singular and modest Constantin Guys. In this place he set a nonperception where Valéry had placed his double *Teste*, a composite of Degas and Mallarmé. Had we come very far, following the rhythm of a singularly slow-moving history, so refractory to change, so careful to hold on to its past inventions, so wary of losing any of its acquired resources, but which had to be stripped of its postulate of permanence? The rupture involved a rhetorical term, a figure of speech suddenly yanked from the periphery back to the center. By way of challenge and competition, perhaps, it revived the singularity of the prior figure, of the *perceptio*, neutralized by more than twenty centuries of usage. Restored to the family of meaning from which it derives (the Latin *capere* and the Greek *lambanein*, including the *katalepsis* in which the perceptive apprehension ends and initial concepts are elaborated), it found itself responsible for certain troubling implications—such as its overtones of grasping and touching and its psychiatric future of tetanic clutching.

It was enough in any case for Merleau-Ponty to have touched the most protected area of philosophical language to heal it of the drive for immediacy revealed by the act of grasping. For once the initial regime of *actio* and transitivity in which perception entered into the world's gyration was disappointed, all that remained was a hand and its trope of grasping: *manus misit hostis ad omnia desiderabilia ejus*. Frank words, which the organon would be no better able to resist. Such affinities, which had been willed and then assigned to the intemporal implicit in certain types of epistemological naturalism, along with the family of terms that had become the emblem of this philosophical operation, suddenly became worrisome. Whereupon, charged with the burden of lifting the illusion of immediacy, chiasmus confirmed the indirect language that Merleau-Ponty had opposed to the *Voices of Silence* and the Hegelianism of Malraux.[9] By introducing here an allele of indirect discourse, he suggested that all constituted sensory experience inevitably involves (some form of) couching in language and all knowledge is somehow filtered by the intervention of (some type of) symbolism. Self-evident truths actually opened out into their grammatical dimensions, and each of them raised the question of the truth of its configuration.

A similar role would be played by the search for nonpropositional dimensions taught by the late texts of Wittgenstein. This is indeed the primary and fundamental meaning of a *language game*. Following the opening pages of the *Philosophical Investigations*, the first example is that of a word, which is equivalent to an order and is immediately understood. This and other words taken in context suffice without the sentencelike formulation of a statement. Later this type of formulation would be integrated but inserted in a grammar of overlaps and intentions that strips away the regime of statement formation. Was this a negation or completion of the *Tractatus*, or perhaps completion by negation? To pose the question in such terms is pointless. Better to note the abandonment of the illusory logical overview that eliminated all complexity from language—along with everything the philosopher would so desperately need to vary the limits of his silence. To which he was in fact attached far more than he was to analysis.

What the philosopher held to be unsayable offered no hope of a singular experience capable of delivering him from it. Nor did he appeal to an ontological order situated beyond language. Language states nothing but itself—the aphorism makes good sense if you think about it—and the limit of a language lies within that language. It is equivalent to a changing, circumstantial injunction for each occurrence, to put it in a nutshell. But it is also an injunction to speak differently, or to try to do so. The *Philosophical Investigations* were sanctioned in advance by the closing formulation of the *Tractatus*, "Whereof one cannot speak, thereof one must be silent," which at the time marked the outer edge of a discursive choice that Wittgenstein would quickly reconsider, just as Merleau-Ponty would free himself from perception.

Of course Merleau-Ponty went at things from a different angle. The chiasmus between self and exterior is an unstable threshold invariably approached from its "for us" side, as opposed to the hardened naturalism of faculties of the soul. Valéry took this substitution forthrightly to its limit: "Syntax, that faculty of the soul" (*Tel Quel*). Persisting there was an insistence on expression, endlessly attempted and never satisfied, within the dimensions of a language constantly in need of reinvention, without a prioris. This other "faculty" may also put up quite well with logics, whose strength lies not in what they concede in the way of formalism but in their controllable generativity. A logic thematizes a fundamental connection—for instance, predication, later a functional relation—but runs up against its limit in the monotony it imposes even before it explores the entire field of concatenations and deductions of which it is capable. And whenever a logic is obliged to compete with a language, it has to confront the fact that language is eminently open insofar as its capacity for variation is concerned yet even so forfeits nothing of its function of intelligibility. In the analytical abode a door was thus left unsecured. Quine, the most faithful of Russell's disciples, plunged analysis into an endless labor of translation among rival paradigms, because there was no end to learning its language.[10] But Wittgenstein had already given up on unifying logic and language: language is like a city whose various neighborhoods belong to different eras. Expression haltingly follows certain principles of relevance and realism understood retroactively, and always with the help of some language game. Those principles are singular yet capable of bestowing more intelligibility than their initial occurrence promised. In any case that intelligibility will be greater than what a universal language could ever promise, since the process, being intimately linked to a life-form or still enigmatic anthropological base, has in its favor the fact that it gives rationalism a new lease on life.

An abrupt intervention of a fact of nature, if you like, for which experience and words are still lacking, but whose secret requirement makes the simple linguistic turn ridiculous. It illustrates the resurgence of history that Merleau-Ponty recounted in the final pages of an unfinished manuscript, *La prose du monde*:

> To speak is not simply my own initiative, to listen is not to endure the initiative of the other, and in the final analysis this is true because we *continue*, we resume an effort older than we are, upon which both of us have intruded, and which is the manifestation, the unfolding [*devenir*] of truth. (p. 200)

This manuscript was in fact continued under the figure of the chiasmus, which we have briefly described.

The precept was heeded. The proof: it was repeated practically word for word when Michel Foucault said that he submitted to "a voice that said something like, 'I must go on, I can't go on, I must go on'—with these words that have perhaps already said me" (*L'ordre du discours*, p. 8).

Beckett too said the same thing, and it makes no difference who was quoting whom—the important thing being the encounter, which took place in the 1960s. To continue may be, as in a diagonal argument, to reinvent a genre that borrows from everyone yet is none of them at a time when the list seemed to have been exhausted. It may also be in the sense of "a fundamental thought experiment" that Merleau-Ponty borrowed a philosophical function from Cavaillès—or at any rate a response to the obsolete formalisms and phenomenological constraints in which the transmission of Hellenism was caught as in a trap.

Can rhetoric appropriate the philosophical realisms we have touched on, or is its domain the ethics of conviction? To put it more directly, can rhetoric give up its own distinctive form of intervention along with the immediacy of its effects and the moment of emotional transparency on which it thrives? A difference is inevitable, a difference that stems from the tempo at which philosophy unfolds—Wittgenstein said that he wanted to be read as slowly as he wrote, that is, with the slowness of a text begun anew time and time again. This injunction of the real, of doubt, and of truth, which gives the philosopher's argument its distinctiveness, is also the price of its legitimacy. It does not prevent it from having a rhetoric of its own. Here there is nothing of the literalness of mathematics, by virtue of which a theorem is identified with the unbroken series of explicit transformations that lead up to it, starting from a set of axioms and previously established theorems. There is no philosophy that does not quote, no philosophy that does not renew an inheritance, no philosophy that does not revisit previously elaborated experiences, no philosophy that does not continue thanks to the very manner of its discontinuity. It is already a considerable achievement if it recognizes its own progress along with what it adds to the texture of its discursive operation in modifying it.

One man's philosophy may be another man's rhetoric—and vice versa, as we have seen. But if a pronouncement regarding the ineffable can be a rhetorical moment, the sense of incompleteness or limit is the very thing that singularizes, renews, and shifts the focus of the philosophical operation. As for the hypothesis of closure and completeness, which came immediately after the paralogism of a universal character, it was a curious avatar of our history. It is not without interest to note that, in inaugurating the reign of plural logics, it initiated the history of its own refutation.

Notes

[1] "Analytic of Pure Concepts of Understanding," sec. 12, added to second edition of *Critique of Pure Reason*.

[2] See Heinrich Heine, *De l'Allemagne*; Philippe Lacoue-Labarthe and Jean-Luc Nancy, *L'Absolu littéraire*.

[3] The term can be found in the *Opus postumum*.

[4] On the model: Theaetetus, with whom I am currently speaking, is seated. See my introduction, pp. 13–14 [not excerpted here].

[5] See the posthumous text *Le visible et l'invisible*.

[6] *Structure et comportement* and *Phénoménologie de la perception*.

[7] See the last *Notes de cours 1959–1961*, p. 215.

[8] See *L'oeil et l'esprit*, 1961, chap. 1.

[9] See *Signes*, chap. 1.

[10] *Word and Object*, 1960.

PART II

Histories of Truth

Jean Cavaillès and Albert Lautman, the French philosophers and mathematicians who would perish in the Resistance, not only offered different approaches to the debates on the foundations of mathematics of the day, as with the debate that opens this section; they already anticipated a complex theme in French philosophy that would be elaborated after the war and assume a singular and distinctive role—the idea of a history of truth. After the Liberation, the philosophy of mathematics would be taken up again in France at a time when, in Foucault's words, there were "many historians, few logicians." With this turn to history and for Georges Canguilhem in particular, the "philosophy of the concept" would in certain ways free itself from the centrality of logic and mathematics in favor of a larger picture of ideologies and related problematics in the sciences. Following Edmund Husserl and the problems or aporias in his approach, the role of history in mathematics was developed through a study of "sedimentations of sense" in the work of Jean-Toussaint Desanti. At the same time, in Derrida's isolation of the problem of "presence" in his translation of and introduction to Husserl's *Origin of Geometry*, we find an actual explicit reference to "a history of truth," which would lead away from strictly mathematical issues to the question of "writing." As with Imre Lakatos's work in English-speaking philosophy, the introduction of history would change the nature of the larger debate about mathematics along different lines. Michel Serres developed the question of mathematics within the history of philosophy in his great book *Le système de Leibnitz et ses modèles mathématiques* (1968) and then in a wide-ranging series of books and articles. Starting with his 1953 essay on "difference" in Bergson, Deleuze would continue to work on the questions of mathematics. He imagined a "minor" tradition focused not on axioms and deductions but on problems and potentials, of which Proclus rather than Euclid served as ancient precursor and which would be carried on after the war by Ilya Prigogine's metaphysics of chaos and by Whitehead's philosophy of process, in his own departure from his earlier work with Russell on mathematical logic. An axiomatic approach would later be developed by Alain Badiou in his study of "the model" in the 1960s, which would eventually lead him as well to something like a "history of truth," marked, as already with Lautman, by Heidegger as well as by set theory.

But there was also another important discussion, based neither in Husserl nor Heidegger but in the history of science, in relation to which we find a second early explicit reference to a history of truth. The reference appears in an early Foucault essay translated into English for the first time in this volume, in which he succinctly summarizes the debates surrounding the work of the distinguished historian of science Alexandre Koyré, who was widely read at the time. Koyré mattered in particular to the kind of historical epistemology practiced by Gaston Bachelard and Canguilhem, in which Foucault would later see the distinctively French formulation of the "history of reason" opened up by Kant's essay on enlightenment but in a manner freed from any prior founding structures of subjective or even intersubjective experience. In this French style of historical epistemology we can nevertheless trace a departure from the monolithic story of the rise of modern science and philosophy in Europe found not simply in Husserl's "crisis" and Heidegger's "world-picture," but also in Koyré's own study of the turn from a "closed world" to an "open universe." We can distinguish three ways in which there was a departure from the centrality of the paradigm of modern science or "the mathematicization of nature," each important for Foucault himself and his own elaboration of a history of systems of thought within which the idea of a history of truth would assume a new form.

In the first place, the introduction of history into epistemology seemed to show that the history of sciences was not commanded by a single method of inference, whether inductive or deductive, such that it no longer made sense to try to work out a single great scientific logic, method, or line of demarcation. In Canguilhem's own meticulous studies of the concept of life in the vitalism/mechanism debates or in organicist models of society, for example, the "philosophy of the concept" would discover a new purpose, focused not so much on securing correct methods as on the role of scientific ideologies and metaphysical pictures and the vital role of error in the growth of knowledge. Canguilhem would develop an idea of "sciences of truth" and of what it means to be *dans le vrai*, from which Foucault would depart in his own way. In Foucault's idea of a history of *savoirs* underlying the surface debates in various *connaissances*, the law of logical contradiction is no longer central. The critical question would rather lie in the larger bodies of discourse from which knowledge arises and on which its existence depends.

In the second place, there was a departure from the idea that sciences are continuous with common sense, simply refining it through more sophisticated procedures of investigation and inference. On the contrary, sciences were thought to arise from "ruptures" and ensuing "breaks" with ordinary ideas and the practices, habits, discourses—the ideologies—that underlie them, in a process that itself had many starting points and no final end. From this Foucault would draw the consequence that the history of truth is inseparable from the history of how the particular domains of true-or-false discourse emerge, which, in turn, delimit and constrain how knowledge functions.

In the third place, there is then a corresponding turning away from the picture of a unified science, given in one fell swoop in Europe in a grand narrative of modernity, toward a picture of a disunified or plural domain of many different kinds of knowledge, emerging at different moments and overlapping with other practices, only some of which would cross what Foucault would call the "threshold" of mathematical formalization. When the critical questions concern criminology or psychiatry and their role in a history of truth, this threshold matter less. The role not simply of logic but of mathematics itself was then seen in context of this more plural history—for example, with the role of statistical facts and modes of mathematical inference within the larger field of "biopower," which Foucault would later propose. But what model of critique and what conception of truth would then fit with this new picture of a discontinuous, disunified, or plural history of knowledge or science?

As for the question of truth in such a critical history of systems of thought, Foucault would add a new element that he would develop through the successive stages of his long preoccupation with Kant's essay on enlightenment—that of the critical attitude itself and its relationship with governmentality and so with subjectivity. The new problem is sketched out in his lecture course of 1975 in what he called "elements for a history of truth," where he argues for a history of truth as "event" intersecting with the more familiar story of truth as "demonstration" in Western or European philosophy. The idea of truth as event goes back to the work of Jacques Lacan in the 1950s (later to be so influential for Canguilhem's young students), which Foucault now tried to introduce in a new philosophical frame. There were the problems of what he later called "the analytics of truth"—the attempt to substitute warranted assertability for truth, the arguments over the correspondence and coherence theories of truth, or even Heideggerian themes of the disclosure and forgetting of Being. But there was also another series of questions to which the history of the critical attitude belonged, found in Nietzsche's ideas on the will-to-knowledge or the will-to-truth, Max Weber's view of the "vocation of the Scholar," and the changing function of the intellectual in France following the Dreyfus Affair. To include the critical attitude was thus to introduce a new question into the history of truth: how the problem of such events of truth came to be subordinated or "colonized" within the sciences and the problem of demonstration in them, and how conversely they might free themselves from such expertise and pose critical questions *to* knowledge as to power. For such a history, Lacan played a key role when, in the 1950s, he tried to recenter the whole question of psychoanalysis, at once philosophical and institutional, around what he came to call *la vérité freudienne*.

What is the role of psychoanalysis in a history of truth? Lacan suggested it was more than simply the debates about whether or in what sense psychoanalysis is a science or how it is related to phenomenology, hermeneutics, or Kojève's questions of desire and intersubjectivity in Hegel. It was also a question of the peculiar kind of truth that analysts deal with—the "truth" of our unconscious desires as betrayed in the arcana of our symptoms, dreams, and jokes, our neuroses and psychoses, which psychoanalysis tries to unravel in its singular practice. For this truth, Lacan said, there is and can be no total knowledge, no complete mastery. It is never fully said, only always half said, ever yet writing itself in our lives, as if in response to an enigmatic tragic necessity. Yet many of the scientific concepts in psychoanalysis—the very idea of symptom or traumatic event and of their rememorization—presuppose this peculiar kind of truth and the singular practice devised to deal with it. Psychoanalysis is thus a strange kind of science that disturbs the distinction between demonstration and event in the history of truth that Foucault set out to investigate.

For Lacan, almost from the start, the question of *la vérité freudienne* was not only a question of knowledge, but also at the same time an institutional or practical matter, which in turn went back to Freud's brief formative training in Charcot's neurological clinic in Paris. That is what made the problem of transference in Freud's own case studies—especially in the Dora case—such a key question. These studies show that transference (or countertransference) arises precisely when it is supposed that some subject *can* know or master this truth. It is only when it is supposed that the analyst himself is such a subject that the problem of truth is transferred into the analytic setting, where it in turn can be unraveled and so undone. Such would be Freud's way out of the problem that goes back to Charcot's clinic, where the hysterical women patients kept "theatricalizing" symptoms in great games of defying anatomical medicine and its supposed "masters" or "teachers"—their dramatic poses dutifully recorded and analyzed in turn. When Freud associated the notion of symptom instead with the truth of traumatic events in the lives of the hysterics, in effect he freed the notion from any pre-given psychiatric symptomology, inserting it instead into the endless process of analysis itself. He thus created a new practice not simply in psychiatry but in the history of truth itself, in its relation to the university and the kind of master and transference it supposed, and again in the role of desire and knowledge in Socratic ignorance and so in philosophical *agon* or argument. In trying to work out this role of truth and knowledge, central to his own teaching, Lacan would turn to a number of other questions and models important in the philosophical debates of the day. Thus he would refer not simply to Heideggerian ideas about truth and *Dichtung*, but also to the truths of revolutions in politics or history, and especially to the larger question of truth and the law in writing and in the arts. Thus, in a study of Gide, he declared that truth "has the structure of fiction"; and for the endless work of the unconscious, he would draw on Blanchot's notion of "impossibility" in thinking and Bataille's idea of expenditure and transgressive desire. It is then this larger role of truth in the ways we talk about ourselves and one another that Foucault would try to develop in his history of the critical attitude, leading to his last lectures on *parrhesia* and "the courage of truth."

But while Lacan thus helped introduce this question of truth into the history of the concept, he thus also linked it to a series of aesthetic and political debates.

Thus, as Derrida expanded the question of a history of truth he found when he tried to insert literary objects into the kind of origin Husserl had tried to work out for geometry, he would eventually stage a quarrel within Lacan himself, at once aesthetic and institutional, as he did earlier in his questioning of Heidegger. The problem of "truth in fiction" continues in the problem of "truth in painting," an idea from Cézanne's letters that Derrida used in a detailed commentary on the problem of truth in Heidegger's essay on the origin of the work of art, surrounding the undecidability of truth and of institution or history, in the course of which the politics of Heidegger's own conception of instrumentality and of being-in-the-world would be examined. The history of truth would thus be inserted into a larger questioning of presence, not simply in the role of truth (and fiction) in psychoanalysis but also in Heidegger's epochs of Being, where it would be displaced by a messianic sense of what is to come. Derrida would go on to develop the problem of the relation of the law of fiction to truth through his readings of Nietzsche's writings on the "history of the error" and "truth and lie in the extra-moral sense," as well as in his own lecture on "the history of the lie." Thus, the question of writing or literature in the history of truth, first formulated in relation to Husserl, then in terms of the questions of the proper and the decidable, would lead Derrida to question not simply the opposition between fiction and lie or truth but at the same time the very conception of the history of philosophy. But the question of a history of truth that would emerge from the great debates about logic and the foundation of mathematics in the meantime would see another development. Following his own study of those debates in the 1960s, Alain Badiou would take up the question in his 1988 opus *Being and Event* and a series of related writings. The problem of truth remains, but in the new guise of a fidelity to those events that void our usual categories and corresponding sets, to be found, for example, in Beckett's idea of courage in impossible or unspeakable situations. The history of truth becomes the history of such events and ensuing courage and fidelity with respect to them.

For Badiou, it is Deleuze who first formulated the question of event and truth, which he went on to elaborate in his new ontology. But in Deleuze's own writings, the idea of event is associated not with truth or set-theoretical logic, but rather with a kind of "non-sense" in what appears to us, which allows for the creation of new ideas. The kind of events that complicate or differentiate veridical sorts of narratives (with fixed beginnings and endings that allow for fixed distinctions between subjective and objective points of view) introduce such paradoxical possibilities to speak or to see in other ways, or what Deleuze came to call "powers of the false," developing the idea in Kafka as well as Nietzsche, then in Orson Welles and Alain Resnais. If Deleuze was concerned less with truth or fidelity to past events than with the way in which they open up possibilities for the invention of ideas not only in philosophy but also in the arts and sciences, he had from the start himself invented an approach to the history of philosophy not dominated by the question of truth at all. He tried to show that throughout philosophy's history, dramatizations of ideas were always prior to relations of truth; such dramatizations make possible the invention of concepts (such as Descartes's *cogito*, Kant's condition, and Bergson's duration) for which there are no preexisting categories, sets, or fixed stories. More precisely, he tried to show that the question of truth and particular ways of seeking it vary in philosophy according to different "conceptual personae" that bring out the negatives against which the struggle or search for truth, its particular game or *agon*, is directed. Thus the Platonic persona of Socrates was involved in a dialectical contest with his interlocutors to arrive at the kind of truth given through Plato's invention of Forms and the way things participate in them. A very different kind of truth as well as drama is then to be found in Descartes's meditations and the search for indubitable ideas; it involves in particular the new figure of the Idiot, who in this process requires no prior learning. In Kant we find the figure of a Judge at the Court of Reason; later, more obviously dramatic figures and forms appear in Kierkegaard and Nietzsche. What matters is the target or object against which such dramas are conducted—what Marx called "ideology" is different from what Spinoza called "superstition" or Descartes's "error," or again Kant (in this respect already anticipated by Hume), "transcendental illusion." The history of truth in philosophy can then be seen as, in effect, a matter of these various foci of its struggle and drama, the peculiar conditions and presuppositions from which they emerge, the new creations to which they give rise, the peculiar nonnarrative links they have with one another. But what then is the presupposition or condition of this attempt to see truth as only one part of such a *theatricum philosophicum*? Deleuze's answer is that it supposes a new "image of thought" in which the negative is stupidity (and the related inability to see, speak, or act) as a condition of the invention of ideas or concepts—as when Foucault himself talked of "problematizations" making possible a creativity that can't be inferred from a given historical situation. The theme of the history of truth then intersects with another in the French philosophy of the day—that of a constitutive role played, if not by problematizations, then by aporia, question, or paradox in philosophy or in the very idea of what it is to think or to think critically.

JEAN CAVAILLÈS AND ALBERT LAUTMAN

Mathematical Thought

1946

Excerpts from the Remarks of Jean Cavaillès

The philosopher confronting the current development of mathematics can now ask himself what positive conclusions he is in a position to state.

I should point out immediately that I make no pretense of stating these conclusions in a definitive form. This is a very difficult task, and for the moment I am simply presenting my thoughts on the matter, thoughts that are still to a certain extent work in progress, and I shall discuss only those points about which I think I have achieved a maximum degree of certitude.

The first point I wish to make is that the idea of defining mathematics is one that it seems to me should be rejected, not only in light of the results I have just presented to you but also as a result of reflection on the work of the mathematician.

Mathematics constitutes a becoming [*un devenir*], that is, a reality irreducible to anything other than itself. What can the project of "defining mathematics" mean? Either it means to assert that mathematics is X, where X is not mathematics, which would be absurd. Or it means to enumerate the methods used by mathematicians.

I set aside the first solution, even though it has had and still has its defenders. That leaves the second. I do not think that any mathematician would grant that his methods could be enumerated in a definitive and exhaustive way. Methods can be enumerated at a given point in time, but it is absurd to say, "This alone is mathematics, and without the use of these methods we are no longer doing mathematics." This view accords, I think, with the results obtained thus far, for example, the necessarily open-ended character of any mathematical theory, which proves that new rules of reasoning must be introduced whenever a theory is developed. It also accords with the concept of mathematics set forth by the intuitionists. Heiting, for example, wrote recently that mathematics constitutes a developing organic system on which no limits can be imposed.

From "La pensée mathématique," *Bulletin de la Société française de philosophie* 40, no. 1 (1946); trans. Arthur Goldhammer.

Mathematics is a becoming, that is, a developing body of thought. The best we can do is to try to understand its history; in other words, in order to situate mathematics in relation to other intellectual activities, we can try to identify certain characteristics of its development. I shall mention two:

1. Its development is autonomous [*ce devenir est autonome*]. In other words, while it is impossible for us to situate ourselves outside it, we can study the contingent, historical development of mathematics as it presents itself to us and thereby perceive certain necessities underlying the logic of ideas and methods. Here, obviously, the word "necessity" cannot be specified in any other way. We identify problems and observe that those problems required the development of a new idea. This is the best we can do, and clearly the use here of the word "required" is all too facile, since what we can observe are successes that have already been achieved. We can, however, say that the ideas that did emerge did indeed lead to solutions of problems that did in fact arise.

I believe that, by doing this kind of work, it is possible to go beyond the striking contingency in the ways that theories connect with one another. I have tried to do so in the case of set theory. I do not claim to have succeeded in this. Nevertheless, in the development of what might seem to be the prime example of an ingenious theory based on radically unpredictable innovations, it seemed to me possible to detect an internal necessity: certain analytic difficulties gave rise to key notions and led to the development of certain methods by Bolzano and Lejeune-Dirichlet initially and ultimately by Cantor. Autonomy, hence necessity.

2. Mathematics is truly a developing body of thought in the sense that its development is unpredictable. It may not be unpredictable for the working mathematician, whose research is directed by his intuition, but it cannot be predicted at the outset in any authentic way. This might be called the fundamental dialectic of mathematics: if new ideas stem from specific problems that may arise, their novelty is truly complete. In other words, new ideas, including generalizations that lead to new methods, cannot be discovered simply by analyzing ideas that have been used previously.

I can describe this novelty by moving to my next point, namely, that the work of mathematicians is a type of experimental activity.

By "experiment" I mean a system of actions governed by a rule and subject to conditions independent of the actions involved. I recognize the vagueness of this definition, but I don't think that it can be improved very much without delving into actual examples. By that I mean that every mathematical method is defined in terms of a prior mathematical situation. If it is dependent on that situation in part, it is also to a certain extent independent of it, in that the result of applying the method can be determined only after the fact. That is what I mean by a mathematical experiment.

Does this mean that a mathematical experiment is somehow related to what we ordinarily mean by an experiment? It is better, I think, to distinguish between the two meanings of the word. In particular, an experiment in physics is a complex composite of many heterogeneous elements that I do not wish to examine in any detail today: to do so would take us too far afield. Suffice it to say that that the actions involved in a physics experiment do not have the characteristic of being performed in accordance with a rule, nor does the result have meaning within the system itself, as is the case in a mathematical experiment. To put it another way, given a mathematical system, the action of carrying out a mathematical experiment yields a result, and the very derivation of that result places it within a mathematical system which extends the preexisting system (that is, contains it as a special case). . . .

In this respect, I believe I can go farther than Gentzen, who attempts to reconcile mathematics in itself with the constructionist requirement of intuitionism. I believe that a concept of systems of mathematical objects existing in themselves is by no means necessary as a warrant for mathematical reasoning. Take, for example, the concept of the continuous: this conception of mathematical objects is to be rejected for a rather simple reason, namely, that it is completely useless, not only for the development of mathematics itself but also for understanding that development.

Indeed, if it corresponded to anything precise, it would mean that even if the objects to which mathematicians refer cannot be grasped in any kind of intuition, mathematical argument would still at some point require their properties and simultaneous presence. This is not the case, and, more than that, if we try to make what this means precise, we run into difficulties that force us to reject the concept; I am here alluding to the Skolem paradox.

I do not want to go into this paradox in detail, especially since to explain it precisely, a formalization would be required. Roughly speaking, it says the following: if we have a model that we assume satisfies a system of axioms, it is always possible to construct a countable model satisfying the same system of axioms. In particular, one can satisfy the system of axioms of set theory with a countable model.

This paradox, to which Skolem and many others, including Gentzen this summer, have devoted much thought, comes down to the following: it is impossible to give an exhaustive characterization of a model satisfying a system of axioms. If we assume the statement of the axioms, that is, the enumeration of the properties we need for our objects, we cannot require those axioms to engender the objects as well. We are obliged to assume the existence of a field of objects, and then, from the properties of those objects in this field, we can deduce other properties. What we cannot say is that our field of objects can be characterized in a uniform way by our system of axioms.

What is interesting about this is not only that it eliminates the (as it were) idealist concept of the existence of mathematical objects but also that it brings out the intimate connections that exist between different moments in the development of mathematical thought.

There is no absolute beginning. Historically, we see mathematics arise in the group of translations of elementary geometry, but in order to make precise what we mean by this—whether through the activity of numeration, which already implicitly contains what Poincaré called the intuition of pure number, or through the inception of elementary geometry itself—we are in fact forced to develop all of mathematics. We can of course stop at some arbitrary point and say, "This state satisfies us," but if we respect the impulse that gave rise to these notions and presided over their development, we are forced to explore the problems that arise, for instance, when we insist on going beyond circumstances external to a given problem. At that point, new notions emerge, and out of these notions comes not only the entire development of mathematics down to the present time but the need for further development, the need to tackle unsolved problems that has led to the transformation of mathematics which is currently under way.

In conclusion, therefore, I will say that the very notion of the existence of mathematical objects interests us as philosophers because it poses the problem of existence for objects of thought.

What does it mean for an object to exist? Here we find ourselves faced with the fact that the very nature of mathematical knowledge, being rigorous and certain, prevents us from positing objects as existing independently of the system built upon those objects and, indeed, independently of a necessary chain of reasoning going all the way back to the very first human efforts.

Hence we can never posit objects in themselves, nor can we properly say "Here is the world" and then go on to describe that world. In each instance we are forced to say, "These objects correlate with some human activity." Our thought simply discovers the rules of mathematical reasoning required by such problems as may arise. At times our thinking may spill over into new areas, or unsolved problems may require us to go beyond certain limits and once again to posit new objects or to modify the definitions of previously posited objects.

Excerpts from the Remarks of Albert Lautman

I agree with M. Cavaillès that the concept of an immutable universe of ideal mathematical beings is an impossibility. Although this is an extremely appeal-

ing vision, it lacks any real consistency. The properties of a mathematical being depend essentially on the axioms of the theory in which those beings appear, and that dependence deprives them of the immutability that is a necessary characteristic of an intelligible universe. I nevertheless regard numbers and shapes as possessing an objectivity as certain as that which the mind encounters in the observation of physical nature. But this objectivity of mathematical beings, which manifests itself concretely in the complexity of their nature, reveals its true meaning only within the framework of a theory of the participation of mathematics in a higher and more hidden reality, which in my view constitutes a veritable world of Ideas.

In order to make clear how the study of recent developments in mathematics can justify the Platonic interpretation I have proposed, I must first insist on what has been called the structural aspect of contemporary mathematics. We are dealing here with mathematical structures, but we shall see in a moment how easy it is to work back from such mathematical structures to a consideration of dialectical structures embodied in actual mathematical theories.

The structural aspect of contemporary mathematics is evident from the importance of the role played in all branches of mathematics by Cantor's set theory, Galois's group theory, and Dedekind's theory of modules of algebraic numbers. What characterizes these various theories is that they are all *abstract*. They study the possible modes of organization of elements whose precise nature is a matter of indifference. Hence it is possible, for example, to define global properties of order, completeness, division into classes, irreducibility, dimension, closure, and so on, which yield a qualitative characterization of the collections to which they apply. Mathematics is animated by a new spirit: lengthy calculations are giving way to the more intuitive reasoning of topology and algebra. Consider, for instance, what mathematicians call existence theorems, that is, theorems that establish the existence of certain functions or certain solutions without actually constructing them. In a great many cases, the existence of the desired function can be deduced from the global topological properties of a suitably defined surface. In particular, this is the way in which a whole geometric theory of analytic functions has been developed since Riemann, a theory that makes it possible to deduce the existence of new transcendental beings from the almost intuitive consideration of the topological structure of certain Riemann surfaces. In this case, knowledge of the mathematical structure of the surface leads to assertion of the existence of the desired function.

If we reflect on the internal mechanism of the theory just alluded to, we notice that it establishes a connection between the degree of completeness of the internal structure of a certain mathematical being (a surface) and the existence of another mathematical being (a function), or, in other words, between the *essence* of one being and the *existence* of another. These notions of essence and existence, like those of form and substance, whole and part, container and contents, are not mathematical notions, yet reflection on actual mathematical theories leads to them. I call these "dialectical notions" and propose the term "dialectical ideas" for the problem of the possible connections among dialectical notions so defined. The rational relation of dialectics and mathematics then stems from the fact that while the problems of dialectics can be conceived and formulated independently of mathematics, any attempt to solve those problems necessarily relies on some mathematical example chosen to provide concrete support for the dialectical relationship under consideration. . . .

I pointed out earlier that the distinction between an ideal dialectics and an actual mathematics ought to be interpreted primarily in terms of the origin of mathematics in dialectics. By this I mean the following: dialectics in itself is purely problematic, based as it is on a fundamental antithesis between pairs of notions that appear on their face to be opposites yet which give rise to the problem of a possible synthesis or reconciliation. It was in these terms, for instance, that I considered in my thesis the problem of the relations between the local and the global, the extrinsic and the intrinsic, the continuous and the discontinuous, and so forth. It turns out that, exactly as in Plato's *Sophist*, these contraries are not opposed but can be composed to constitute those mixed entities of which mathematics consists. This inevitably gives rise to many complex subtleties, unpredictable innovations, and obstacles that must be overcome or circumvented—in short, to all the contingent historical developments that constitute the life of mathematics yet appear to the metaphysician as necessary extensions of an initial dialectic. One moves imperceptibly from a dialectical problem to the inception of a universe of mathematical notions, and in my view mathematical philosophy should aim at recognition of the moment when the Idea gives rise to the real. In a pamphlet published after my thesis by Librairie Hermann, I tried to show that these concepts are analogous to those of Heidegger. It seems to me that the extension of the dialectic into mathematics corresponds to what Heidegger calls the genesis of ontic reality starting from ontological analysis of the Idea. One thus introduces an ordering of before and after at the level of Ideas that is not a temporal ordering but rather an eternal model of time, the pattern of a continuous, ongoing genesis, a necessary order of creation.

JACQUES LACAN

Intervention on Transference

1952

What happens in an analysis is that the subject is, strictly speaking, constituted through a discourse, to which the mere presence of the psychoanalyst brings, before any intervention, the dimension of dialogue.

Whatever irresponsibility, or even incoherence, the ruling conventions might come to impose on the principle of this discourse, it is clear that these are merely strategies of navigation (see the case of "Dora," p. 16)[1] intended to ensure the crossing of certain barriers, and that this discourse must proceed according to the laws of a gravitation, peculiar to it, which is called truth. For "truth" is the name of that ideal movement which discourse introduces into reality. Briefly, *psychoanalysis is a dialectical experience,* and this notion should predominate when posing the question of the nature of the transference.

In this sense my sole objective will be to show, by means of an example, the kind of propositions to which this line of argument might lead. I will, however, first allow myself a few remarks which strike me as urgent for the present guidance of our work of theoretical elaboration, remarks which concern the responsibilities conferred on us by the moment of history we are living, no less than by the tradition entrusted to our keeping.

The fact that a dialectical conception of psychoanalysis has to be presented as an orientation peculiar to my thinking, must, surely, indicate a failure to recognize an immediate given, that is, the self-evident fact that it deals solely with words. While the privileged attention paid to the function of the mute aspects of behavior in the psychological maneuver merely demonstrates a preference on the part of the analyst for a point of view from which the subject is no more than an object. If, indeed, there be such a mis-recognition, then we must question it according to the methods which we would apply in any similar case.

From *Feminine Sexuality: Jacques Lacan and the Ecole Freudienne*, ed. Juliet Mitchell and Jacqueline Rose and trans. Jacqueline Rose (New York: W.W. Norton, 1985), pp. 62–72 ["Intervention sur le transfert," in *Ecrits* (Paris: Editions du Seuil, 1966); first published in *Revue française de psychanalyse* (1952)].

It is known that I am given to thinking that at the moment when the perspective of psychology, together with that of all the human sciences, was thrown into total upheaval by the conceptions originating from psychoanalysis (even if this was without their consent or even their knowledge), then an inverse movement appeared to take place among analysts which I would express in the following terms.

Whereas Freud took it upon himself to show us that there are illnesses which speak (unlike Hesiod, for whom the illnesses sent by Zeus descended on mankind in silence) and to convey the truth of what they are saying, it seems that as the relationship of this truth to a moment in history and a crisis of institutions becomes clearer, so the greater the fear which it inspires in the practitioners who perpetuate its technique.

Thus, in any number of forms, ranging from pious sentiment to ideals of the crudest efficiency, through the whole gamut of naturalist propaedeutics, they can be seen sheltering under the wing of a psychologism which, in its reification of the human being, could lead to errors besides which those of the physicians scientism would be mere trifles.

For precisely on account of the strength of the forces opened up by analysis, nothing less than a new type of alienation of man is coming into being, as much through the efforts of collective belief as through the selective process of techniques with all the formative weight belonging to rituals: in short, a *homo psychologicus,* which is a danger I would warn you against.

It is in relation to him that I ask you whether we will allow ourselves to be fascinated by his fabrication or whether, by rethinking the work of Freud, we cannot retrieve the authentic meaning of his initiative and the way to maintain its beneficial value.

Let me stress here, should there be any need, that these questions are in no sense directed at the work of someone like our friend Lagache: the prudence of his method, his scrupulous procedure and the openness of his conclusions, are all exemplary of the distance between our *praxis* and psychology. I will base my demonstration on the case of Dora, because of what it stands for in the experience of transference when this experience was still new, this being the first case in which Freud recognized that the analyst[2] played his part.

It is remarkable that up to now nobody has stressed that the case of Dora is set out by Freud in the form of a series of dialectical reversals. This is not a mere contrivance for presenting material whose emergence Freud clearly states here is left to the will of the patient. What is involved is a scansion of structures in which truth is transmuted for the subject, affecting not only her comprehension of things, but her very position as subject of which her "objects" are a function. This means that the conception of the case-history is *identical* to the progress of the subject, that is, to the reality of the treatment.

Now, this is the first time Freud gives the term of transference as the concept for the obstacle on which the analysis broke down. This alone gives at the very least the value of a return to sources to the examination I will be conducting of the dialectical relations which constituted the moment of failure. Through this examination, I will be attempting *to define in terms of pure dialectics the transference*, which we call negative on the part of the subject as being the operation of the analyst who interprets it.

We will, however, have to go through all the phases which led up to this moment, while also tracing through them all the problematic insights which, in the given facts of the case, indicate at what points it might have had a successful outcome. Thus we find:

A first development, which is exemplary in that it carries us straight onto the place where truth asserts itself. Thus, having tested Freud out to see if he will show himself to be as hypocritical as the paternal figure, Dora enters into her indictment, opening up a dossier of memories whose rigor contrasts with the lack of biographical precision which is characteristic of neurosis. Frau K and her father have been lovers for years, concealing the fact with what are at times ridiculous fictions. But what crowns it all is that Dora is thus left defenseless to the attentions of Herr K, to which her father turns a blind eye, thus making her the object of an odious exchange.

Freud is too wise to the consistency of the social lie to have been duped by it, even from the mouth of a man whom he considers owing to him a total confidence. He therefore had no difficulty in removing from the mind of the patient any imputation of complicity over this lie. But at the end of this development he is faced with the question, which is moreover classical in the first stage of a treatment: "This is all perfectly correct and true, isn't it? What do you want to change in it?" To which Freud's reply is:

A first dialectical reversal which wants nothing of the Hegelian analysis of the protest of the "beautiful soul," which rises up against the world in the name of the law of the heart: "Look at your own involvement," he tells her, "in the disorder which you bemoan" (p. 36).[3] What then appears is:

A second development of truth: namely, that it is not only on the basis of her silence, but through the complicity of Dora herself, and, what is more, even under her vigilant protection, that the fiction had been able to continue which allowed the relationship of the two lovers to carry on. What can be seen here is not simply Dora's participation in the courtship of which she is the object on the part of Herr K. New light is thrown on her relationship to the other partners of the quadrille by the fact that it is caught up in a subtle circulation of precious gifts, serving to compensate the deficiency in sexual services, a circulation which starts with her father in relation to Frau K, and then comes back to the patient through the liberality which it releases in Herr K. Not that this stands in the way of the lavish generosity which comes to her directly from the first source, by way of parallel gifts, this being the classic form of honorable redress through which the bourgeois male has managed to combine the reparation due to the legitimate wife with concern for the patrimony (note that the presence of the wife is reduced here to this lateral appendage to the circuit of exchange).

At the same time it is revealed that Dora's Oedipal relation is grounded in an identification with her father, which is favored by the latter's sexual impotence and is, moreover, felt by Dora as a reflection on the weight of his position as a man of fortune. This is betrayed by the unconscious allusion which Dora is allowed by the semantics of the word "fortune" in German: *Vermögen*. As it happens, this identification showed through all the symptoms of conversion presented by Dora, a large number of which were removed by this discovery.

The question then becomes: in the light of this, what is the meaning of the jealousy which Dora suddenly shows towards her father's love affair? The fact that this jealousy presents itself in such a *supervalent* form, calls for an explanation which goes beyond its apparent motives (pp. 54–55).[4] Here takes place:

The second dialectical reversal which Freud brings about by commenting that, far from the alleged object of jealousy providing its true motive, it conceals an interest in the person of the subject-rival, an interest whose nature being much less easily assimilated to common discourse, can only be expressed within it in this inverted form. This gives rise to:

A third development of truth: the fascinated attachment of Dora for Frau K ("her adorable white body," p. 61),[5] the extent to which Dora was confided in, up to a point which will remain unfathomed, on the state of her relations with her husband, the blatant fact of their exchange of friendly services, which they undertook like the joint ambassadoresses of their desires in relation to Dora's father.

Freud spotted the question to which this new development was leading.

If, therefore, it is the loss of this woman that you feel so bitterly, how come you do not resent her for the additional betrayal that it was she who gave rise to those imputations of intrigue and perversity in which they are all now united in accusing you of lying? What is the motive for this loyalty which makes you hold back the last secret of your relationship (that is, the sexual initiation, readily discernable behind the very accusations of Frau K)? It is this secret which brings us:

To the third dialectical reversal, the one which would yield to us the real value of the object which Frau K is for Dora. That is, not an individual, but a mystery, the mystery of her femininity, by which I mean her bodily femininity—as it appears uncovered in the second of the two dreams whose study makes up the second part of Dora's case-history, dreams which I suggest you refer to in order to see how far their interpretation is simplified by my commentary.

The boundary post which we must go round in order to complete the final reversal of our course already appears within reach. It is that most distant of images which Dora retrieves from her early childhood (note that the keys always fall into Freud's hands even in those cases which are broken off like this one). The image is that of Dora, probably still an *infans*, sucking her left thumb, while with her right hand she tugs at the ear of her brother, her elder by a year and a half (p. 51 and p. 21).[6]

What we seem to have here is the imaginary matrix in which all the situations developed by Dora during her life have since come to be cast—a perfect illustration of the theory of repetition compulsion, which was yet to appear in Freud's work. It gives us the measure of what woman and man signify for her now.

Woman is the object which it is impossible to detach from a primitive oral desire, and yet in which she must learn to recognize her own genital nature. (One wonders here why Freud fails to see that the aphonia brought on during the absences of Herr K (pp. 39–40)[7] is an expression of the violent appeal of the oral erotic drive when Dora was left face to face with Frau K, without there being any need for him to invoke her awareness of the *fellatio* undergone by the father (pp. 47–48),[8] when everyone knows that cunnilingus is the artifice most commonly adopted by "men of means" whose powers begin to abandon them.) In order for her to gain access to this recognition of her femininity, she would have to take on this assumption of her own body, failing which she remains open to that functional fragmentation (to refer to the theoretical contribution of the mirror stage), which constitutes conversion symptoms.

Now, if she was to fulfill the condition for this access, the original *imago* shows us that her only opening to the object was through the intermediary of the masculine partner, with whom, because of the slight difference in years, she was able to identify, in that primordial identification through which the subject recognizes itself as *I*. . . .

So Dora had identified with Herr K, just as she is in the process of identifying with Freud himself. (The fact that it was on waking from her "dream of transference" that Dora noticed the smell of smoke belonging to the two men does not indicate, as Freud said (p. 73),[9] a more deeply repressed identification, but much more that this hallucination corresponded to the dawning of her reversion to the *ego*.) And all her dealings with the two men manifest that aggressivity which is the dimension characteristic of narcissistic alienation.

Thus it is the case, as Freud thinks, that the return to a passionate outburst against the father represents a regression as regards the relationship started up with Herr K.

But this homage, whose beneficial value for Dora is sensed by Freud, could be received by her as a manifestation of desire only if she herself could accept herself as an object of desire, that is to say, only once she had worked out the meaning of what she was searching for in Frau K.

As is true for all women, and for reasons which are at the very basis of the most elementary forms of social exchange (the very reasons which Dora gives as the grounds for her revolt), the problem of her condition is fundamentally that of accepting herself as an object of desire for the man, and this is for Dora the mystery which motivates her idolatry for Frau K. Just as in her long meditation before the Madonna, and in her recourse to the role of distant worshipper, Dora is driven towards the solution which Christianity has given to this subjective impasse, by making woman the object of a divine desire, or else, a transcendant object of a desire, which amounts to the same thing.

If, therefore, in a third dialectical reversal, Freud had directed Dora towards a recognition of what Frau K was for her, by getting her to confess the last secrets of their relationship, then what would have been his prestige (this merely touches on the meaning of positive transference)—thereby opening up the path to a recognition of the virile object? This is not my opinion, but that of Freud (p. 120).[10]

But the fact that this failure to do so was fatal to the treatment, is attributed by Freud to the action of the transference (pp. 116–20),[11] to his error in putting off its interpretation (p. 118),[12] when, as he was able to ascertain after the fact, he had only two hours before him in which to avoid its effects (p. 119).[13]

But each time he comes back to invoking this explanation (one whose subsequent development in analytic doctrine is well known), a note at the foot of the page goes and adds an appeal to his insufficient appreciation of the homosexual tie binding Dora to Frau K.

What this must mean is that the second reason only strikes him as the most crucial in 1923, whereas the first bore fruit in his thinking from 1905, the date when Dora's case-study was published.

As for us, which side should we come down on? Surely that of crediting him on both counts by attempting to grasp what can be deduced from their synthesis.

What we then find is this. Freud admits that for a long time he was unable to face this homosexual tendency (which he none the less tells us is so constant in hysterics that its subjective role cannot be overestimated) without falling into a perplexity (p. 120, n. 1)[14] which made him incapable of dealing with it satisfactorily.

We would say that this has to be ascribed to prejudice, exactly the same prejudice which falsifies the conception of the Oedipus complex from the start, by making it define as natural, rather than normative, the predominance of the paternal figure. This is the same prejudice which we hear expressed simply in the well-known refrain "As thread to needle, so girl to boy."

Freud feels a sympathy for Herr K which goes back a long way, since it was Herr K that brought Dora's father to Freud (p. 19),[15] and this comes out in numerous appreciative remarks (p. 29, n. 3).[16] After the breakdown of the treatment, Freud persists in dreaming of a "triumph of love" (pp. 109–10).[17]

As regards Dora, Freud admits his personal involvement in the interest which she inspires in him at many points in the account. The truth of the matter is that it sets the whole case on an edge which, breaking through the theoretical monographs which make up a genre of our literature, to the tone of a Princesse de Clèves trapped by a deadly blocking of utterance.[18]

It is because he put himself rather too much in the place of Herr K that, this time, Freud did not succeed in moving the Acheron.

Due to his counter-transference, Freud keeps reverting to the love which Herr K might have inspired in Dora, and it is odd to see how he always interprets as though they were confessions what are in fact the very varied responses which Dora argues against him. The session when he thinks he has reduced her to "no longer contradicting him" (p. 104)[19] and which he feels able to end by expressing to her his satisfaction, Dora in fact concludes on a very different note. "Why, has anything so very remarkable come out?" she says, and it is at the start of the following session that she takes her leave of him.

What, therefore, happened during the scene of the declaration at the lakeside, the catastrophe upon which Dora entered her illness, leading on everyone to recognize her as ill—this, ironically, being their response to her refusal to carry on as the prop for their common infirmity (not all the "gains" of a neurosis work solely to the advantage of the neurotic)?

As in any valid interpretation, we need only stick to the text in order to understand it. Herr K could only get in a few words, decisive though they were: "My wife is nothing to me." The reward for his effort was instantaneous: a hard slap (whose burning after-effects Dora felt long after the treatment in the form of a transitory neuralgia) gave back to the blunderer—"If she is nothing to you, then what are you to me?"

And after that what will he be for her, this puppet who has none the less just broken the enchantment under which she had been living for years?

The latent pregnancy fantasy which follows on from this scene cannot be argued against our interpretation, since it is a well-known fact that it occurs in hysterics precisely as a function of their virile identification.

It is through the very same trap door that Freud will disappear, in a sliding which is even more insidious. Dora withdraws with the smile of the *Mona Lisa* and even when she reappears, Freud is not so naïve as to believe her intention is to return.

At this moment she has got everyone to recognize the truth which, while it may be truthful, she knows does not constitute the final truth, and she then manages through the mere *mana* of her presence to precipitate the unfortunate Herr K under the wheels of a carriage. The subduing of her symptoms, which had been brought about during the second phase of the treatment, did however last. Thus the arrest of the dialectical process is sealed by an obvious retreat, but the positions reverted to can only be sustained by an assertion of the *ego*, which can be taken as an improvement.

Finally, therefore, what is this transference whose work Freud states somewhere goes on invisibly behind the progress of the treatment, and whose effects, furthermore, are "not susceptible to definite proof" (p. 74)?[20] Surely in this case it can be seen as an entity altogether relative to the counter-transference, defined as the sum total of the prejudices, passions and difficulties of the analyst, or even of his insufficient information, at any given moment of the dialectical process. Doesn't Freud himself tell us (p. 118)[21] that Dora might have transferred onto him the paternal figure, had he been fool enough to believe in the version of things which the father had presented to him?

In other words, the transference is nothing real in the subject other than the appearance, in a moment of stagnation of the analytic dialectic, of the permanent modes according to which it constitutes its objects.

What, therefore, is meant by interpreting the transference? Nothing other than a ruse to fill in the emptiness of this deadlock. But while it may be deceptive, this ruse serves a purpose by setting off the whole process again.

Thus, even though Dora would have denied any suggestion of Freud's that she was imputing to him the same intentions as had been displayed by Herr K, this would in no sense have reduced its effectivity. The very opposition to which it would have given rise would probably, despite Freud, have set Dora off in the favorable direction: that which would have led her to the object of her real interest.

And the fact of setting himself up personally as a substitute for Herr K would have saved Freud from over-insisting on the value of the marriage proposals of the latter.

Thus transference does not arise from any mysterious property of affectivity, and even when it reveals an emotive aspect, this only has meaning as a function of the dialectical moment in which it occurs.

But this moment is of no great significance since it normally translates an error on the part of the analyst, if only that of wishing too much for the good of the patient, a danger Freud warned against on many occasions.

Thus analytic neutrality takes its true meaning from the position of the pure dialectician who, knowing that all that is real is rational (and vice versa), knows that all that exists, including the evil against which he struggles, corresponds as it always will to the level of his own particularity, and that there is no progress for the subject other than through the integration which he arrives at from his position in the universal: technically through the projection of his past into a discourse in the process of becoming.

The case of Dora is especially relevant for this demonstration in that, since it involves an hysteric, the screen of the *ego* is fairly transparent—there being nowhere else, as Freud has said, where the threshold is lower between the unconscious and the conscious, or rather, between the analytic discourse and the *word* of the symptom.

I believe, however, that transference always has this same meaning of indicating the moments where the analyst goes astray, and equally takes his or her bearings, this same value of calling us back to the order of our role—that of a positive non-acting with a view to the ortho-dramatization of the subjectivity of the patient.

Notes

1 *Pelican Freud* (vol. 8), p. 45 (see note 2).

2 So that the reader can check my commentary in its textual detail, wherever I refer to Freud's case study, reference is given to Denoël's edition in the text, and to the 1954 P.U.F. [edition] in a footnote (*Standard Edition* vol. VII, and *Pelican Freud,* vol. 8 (tr.)).

3 *Pelican Freud* (vol. 8), p. 67.

4 Ibid., pp. 88–89.

5 Ibid., p. 96.

6 Ibid., p. 85 and p. 51.

7 Ibid., pp. 71–72.

8 Ibid., pp. 80–81.

9 Ibid., p. 109.

10 Ibid., p. 162.

11 Ibid., pp. 157–62.

12 Ibid., p. 160.

13 Ibid., p. 161.

14 Ibid., p. 162, n. 1.

15 Ibid., p. 49.

16 Ibid., p. 60, n. 2.

17 Ibid., pp. 151–52.

18 *La Princesse de Clèves,* Madame de Lafayette (Paris: Claude Barbin, 1678). This novel has always had in France the status of a classic. What is relevant here is that (a) it is taken up almost entirely with the account of a love which is socially and morally unacceptable; and (b) in the decisive moment of the plot, the heroine confesses to her husband, who, previously a model of moral generosity, is destroyed by the revelation (tr.).

19 *Pelican Freud,* p. 145.

20 Ibid., p. 110.

21 Ibid., p. 160.

MICHEL FOUCAULT

Alexandre Koyré: The Astronomical Revolution, Copernicus, Kepler, Borelli

1961

Some histories of truth are sad: a pall is cast over them by the recounting of so many fabulous and forgotten errors. At best they favor us at times with a kind of solace: the pilot souls that guided Kepler's planets in their definitively elliptical orbits console us for the knowledge that they no longer move in circles. Pride in Copernicus, who made us stars, makes up for the annoyance we feel at no longer being at the center of the world.

Prof. Koyré's book is in every way less sad: in a grave, scholarly voice he recounts the marvelous and uninterrupted nuptials of truth and falsehood. Yet we are the ones who, mired in our shopworn language, speak of truth and error and admire their marriage. The authority of this patient and profound work comes from a place more remote. The rigor in the presentation of these little-known texts and their proper exegesis derives from the application of a philosopher's norms as well as a historian's: ideas are examined only at the chaotic moment before true and false have separated. What is recounted is a joint labor, which takes place at a level below the discriminations that history subsequently introduces. Kepler's ellipses are identified with the rare cosmic numbers that shape the muted music of the spheres.

Koyré shows how the discipline of astronomy, which we think of as having become scientific between Copernicus and Kepler, was sustained by a vast Pythagorean project. Freud held that Copernicus, Darwin, and psychoanalysis marked the three great frustrations visited upon man's narcissism by European science. In regard to Copernicus, at least, he was wrong. When the center of the world departed this earth, the human animal was not abandoned to an anonymous planetary fate: he was made to describe a rigorous circle, the perceptible image of perfection, around a center that was the light of the world, the visible god of Trismegistus, the pupil of the cosmic eye. In this light, earth was liberated from its sublunary weight. Think of Marsilio Ficino's hymn to

From "Alexandre Koyré, "La révolution astronomique, Copernic, Kepler, Borelli," *La nouvelle revue française* 108 (1961), pp. 1123–24; trans. Arthur Goldhammer.

the sun and the whole theory of light to which painters, physicists, and architects subscribed. The philosophy of man was that of Aristotle. Humanism was associated with a sweeping return of Western culture to solar thought. Classicism would establish itself in this luminous world, but once the youthful violence of the sun was quelled, the great throne of fire that enchanted Copernican cosmology became the pure homogeneous space of intelligible forms.

Kepler too was haunted by memories that dated back beyond Aristotle. It took him ten years of calculation, or scruples, to deny planets the perfection of circular orbits, and ten more years to reconstruct an entirely harmonious world around those ellipses. He needed those twenty years to fit the physical problem of planetary movement and its cause into the old smooth vault in which celestial objects moved in accordance with spherical geometry alone. Prof. Koyré has reconstituted Kepler's quest step by step, keeping faith in two ways with the object of his study. Kepler never stated a new truth without indicating the erroneous path he had followed to get there; hence the truth was *his* truth. Montaigne lost the signs marking the path he had followed, and he knew that he had lost them. Descartes, with one stroke, grouped all possible errors, wrapped them up in one big, essential bundle, and dealt with them impatiently as a diabolical repository of every conceivable danger, the better to be rid of them. Between the two came Kepler, who never states the truth without recounting the error. Truth offers itself at the point where a statement and a narrative meet. This marks a crucially important moment in the history of our language: on one hand, narrative was soon to abandon its vocation as mere storytelling or fantasy in order to transmit something that was of the order of the definitive and essential; as for the affirmation of truth, it was about to acquire the ability to convey individual modulations of every kind, to incorporate adventures and idle daydreams. It was at the beginning of the seventeenth century that the birthplace of truth changed its location: no longer ranged with the figures of the world, it lay now in the interior and intersecting forms of language. Truth was written in the curve of a thought that made mistakes and said so. This was the small, human-sized circle that Kepler traced when he erased from the sky the big imaginary circles in which the perfection of the planets had been inscribed.

This luminous new world, whose geometry had every right to be called physical, suddenly bent itself into the shape of a tiny but decisive circle of thought, which constantly reasserted itself. We understand how this became the natural landscape of a philosophy, a language, and a culture more preoccupied with the truth of things than with their being.

JACQUES DERRIDA

Of Grammatology

1967

There has to be a transcendental signified for the difference between signifier and signified to be somewhere absolute and irreducible. It is not by chance that the thought of being, as the thought of this transcendental signified, is manifested above all in the voice: in a language of words [*mots*]. The voice *is heard* (understood)—that undoubtedly is what is called conscience—closest to the self as the absolute effacement of the signifier: pure auto-affection that necessarily has the form of time and which does not borrow from outside of itself, in the world or in "reality," any accessory signifier, any substance of expression foreign to its own spontaneity. It is the unique experience of the signified producing itself spontaneously, from within the self, and nevertheless, as signified concept, in the element of ideality or universality. The unworldly character of this substance of expression is constitutive of this ideality. This experience of the effacement of the signifier in the voice is not merely one illusion among many—since it is the condition of the very idea of truth—but I shall elsewhere show in what it does delude itself. This illusion is the history of truth and it cannot be dissipated so quickly. Within the closure of this experience, the word [*mot*] is lived as the elementary and undecomposable unity of the signified and the voice, of the concept and a transparent substance of expression. This experience is considered in its greatest purity—and at the same time in the condition of its possibility—as the experience of "being." The word "being," or at any rate the words designating the sense of being in different languages, is, with some others, an "originary word" (*"Urwort"*),[1] the transcendental word assuring the possibility of being-word to all other words. As such, it is precomprehended in all language and—this is the opening of *Being and Time*—only this precomprehension would permit the opening of the question of the sense of being in general, beyond all regional ontologies and all metaphysics: a question that broaches philosophy (for example, in the *Sophist*) and lets itself be taken over by philosophy, a question that Heidegger repeats by submitting the history of metaphysics to it. Heidegger reminds us constantly

From *Of Grammatology*, trans. Gayatri C. Spivak (Baltimore: Johns Hopkins University Press, 1976), pp. 20–21 [*De la grammatologie* (Paris: Editions de Minuit, 1967)].

that the sense of being is neither the word "being" nor the concept of being. But as that sense is nothing outside of language and the language of words, it is tied, if not to a particular word or to a particular system of language (*concesso non dato*), at least to the possibility of the word in general. And to the possibility of its irreducible simplicity. One could thus think that it remains only to choose between two possibilities. (1) Does a modern linguistics, a science of signification breaking the unity of the word and breaking with its alleged irreducibility, still have anything to do with "language"? Heidegger would probably doubt it. (2) Conversely, is not all that is profoundly meditated as the thought or the question of being enclosed within an old linguistics of the word which one practices here unknowingly? Unknowingly because such a linguistics, whether spontaneous or systematic, has always had to share the presuppositions of metaphysics. The two operate on the same grounds.

Note

[1] Cf. *Das Wesen der Sprache* ["The Nature of Language"] and *Das Wort* ["Words"], in *Unterwegs zur Sprache* [Pfüllingen], 1959 [*On the Way to Language*, trans. Peter D. Hertz (New York, 1971)].

JACQUES DERRIDA

Edmund Husserl's Origin of Geometry: An Introduction

1962

At the same time, the culture and tradition of the *truth* are characterized by a paradoxical historicity. In one sense, they can appear disengaged from all history, since they are not intrinsically affected by the empirical content of real history and by determined cultural interconnections. This emancipation can be confused with a breaking from history in general. For those who confine themselves to historical factuality, as well as for those who enclose themselves in the ideality of validity, the narration of the truth can only have the historic originality of myth.

But in another sense, one that corresponds to Husserl's intention, the tradition of truth is the most profound and purest history. Only the pure unity of such a tradition's sense is apt to establish this continuity. Indeed, without this no authentic history would be thought or projected as such; there would only be an empirical aggregate of finite and accidental units. As soon as phenomenology breaks from both conventional Platonism and historicist empiricism, the movement of truth that it wishes to describe is really that of a concrete and specific history—the foundations of which are a temporal and creative subjectivity's acts based on the sensible world and the life-world as cultural world.

This progress is brought about by the permanent totalization and repetition of its acquisitions. Geometry is born "out of a *first* acquisition, out of first creative activities. We understand its persisting manner of being: it is not only a mobile forward process from one set of acquisitions to another but a continuous synthesis in which all acquisitions maintain their validity, all make up a totality such that, at every present stage, the total acquisition is, so to speak, the total premise for the acquisitions of the new level. . . . The same thing is true of every science" (p. 159).

Let us understand this as true of every non-descriptive science. These syntheses do not occur in a psychological memory, however collective, but rather

From *Edmund Husserl's Origin of Geometry: An Introduction*, trans. John P. Leavey (Lincoln: University of Nebraska Press, 1989), pp. 59–64 [*Introduction à "L'origine de la géométrie" de Husserl*, rev. ed. (Paris: Presses Universitaires de France, 1962)].

in that "*rational memory*" so profoundly described by Gaston Bachelard, a memory based on a "*recurrent fruitfulness,*" which alone is capable of constituting and retaining the "*events of reason.*"[1] In his *Philosophy of Arithmetic*, Husserl already distinguished between psychological temporality as successiveness (what Hume described) and the temporality of the synthetic interconnections of sense. He continued to explicate this difference, and in the *Origin* (p. 166) he emphasizes that a scientific stage is not only a sense which "in fact comes later," but the integration of the whole earlier sense in a new project.

Egological subjectivity cannot be responsible for this development, which is continually totalized in an absolute Present. Only a communal subjectivity can produce the historical system of truth and be wholly responsible for it. However, this total subjectivity, whose unity must be absolute and *a priori* (otherwise even the slightest truth would be unimaginable), is but the common place of all egological subjectivities, whether actually present or possible, whether past, present, or future, whether known or unknown. "Every science is related to an open chain of the generations of those who work for and with one another, researchers either known or unknown to one another who are the productive subjectivity of the total living science" (p. 159 [modified]).

Since the totality of science is open, the universal community also has the unity of a horizon. Furthermore, the image of the "open chain" does not exhaust the depth of this communal subjectivity. For it not only has the unity of interrelatedness and co-responsibility—each investigator not only feels himself *tied* to all the others by the unity of an object or task—but the investigator's own subjectivity is constituted by the idea or horizon of this total subjectivity which is made responsible in and through him for each of his acts as a scientific investigator. In and through him, that means without being substituted for him, because, at the same time, he remains the absolute origin, the constituting and present source of truth. Phenomenologically, the transcendental *we* is not *something other* than the transcendental *Ego*. The latter's acts, even when they seem mandated by an ideal community, do not cease to be irreducibly those of a monadic "*I think*"—to which it suffices to reduce the empirical egological content of the *ego* in order to discover the dimension of the "*we*" as a moment of the *eidos* "*ego.*"[2] One would indeed be tempted to think that it is the *we* that makes possible the reduction of the empirical *ego* and the emergence of the *eidos* "*ego,*" if such an hypothesis did not lead, against Husserl's most explicit intentions, to placing the egological monad in abstract relation to the total subjectivity. In any case, if there is a history of truth, it can only be this concrete implication and this reciprocal envelopment of totalities and absolutes. This is possible only because we are dealing with ideal and spiritual implications. The description of these two characteristics, ideality and spirituality, so frequently evoked in the *Origin*, does not correspond, as we know, to any metaphysical assertion. In addition to which, they are "*founded*" in the sense of *Fundierung*.

The irreducible historicity of geometrical becoming is characterized by the fact that "the *total* sense of geometry" (and its necessary poetic correlate, total subjectivity) "could not have been present as a project and then as mobile fulfillment at the beginning" (159). If the history of geometry were only the development of a purpose wholly present from the beginning, we would have to deal only with an explication or a quasi-creation. We would have on one side a synchronic or timeless [*uchronique*][3] ground and, on the other side, a purely empirical diachrony with its indicative function but without any proper unity of its own. Neither pure diachrony nor pure synchrony make a history. The rejected hypothesis is once more that of a complicity between "Platonism" and empiricism.

As a matter of fact, even before the possibility of the open project of geometry, "a more primitive formation of sense *(Sinnbildung)* necessarily went before it as a preliminary stage, undoubtedly in such a way that it appeared for the first time in the evidence of successful actualization" (159–60 [modified]).

Having reached this point, Husserl performs a detour which may seem disconcerting. Instead of describing this primitive genesis of sense in itself and in its *Erstmaligkeit*, he tacitly and provisionally considers it to be *already* done, its sense being already evident. He is content to recall that we know the general form of this evidence:[4] the latter must be—it cannot not be—like all evidence (whether perceptive or eidetic), the intuition of a natural reality or of an ideal object, i.e., "grasping an existent in the consciousness of its original being-itself-there" (160 [modified]). This recalls the "*principle of all principles*" defined in *Ideas I.* However little we may know about the first geometrical evidence, we do know *a priori* that it has had to assume this form. But even though applied to a historical origin in this case, this *a priori* knowledge concerning the form of evidence is nothing less than historical. Defining a "*source of authority*" [*Ideas I*, §24, p. 83] for the cognition of any object in general, it is one of those *formal a priori* supposed by every material science; here by geometry and history. Since the first geometrical evidence has had to conform to this pattern, we can have a first certainty about it in the absence of any other material knowledge. Hence the *content* of geometrical evidence (a content which is historical because created for the first time) is not defined for the moment. Husserl considers it already acquired.

This abstention before the content of the primordial act and evidence is provisional. It is a question of a methodological limitation and, once again, of the necessity to take one's starting point in the constituted. But this methodological necessity is only legitimate on the basis of a profound philosophical decision. Having cleared this stage, Husserl in effect continues his meditation (now protected by that formal legitimation) as if his theme were no longer the origin of geometrical sense, but the *genesis of the* absolute (i.e., ideal) Objectivity of sense, this sense being already present for any consciousness whatsoever. Husserl repeatedly and obstinately returns to a question which is at bottom the following: how can the subjective egological evidence of sense become objective and intersubjective? How can it give rise to an ideal and true object, with all the characteristics that we know it to have: omnitemporal validity, universal normativity, intelligibility for "*everyone*," uprootedness out of all "*here and now*" factuality, and so forth? This is the historical repetition of the question of Objectivity so frequently asked in the five lectures of *The Idea of Phenomenology*: how can subjectivity go out of itself in order to encounter or constitute the object?[5]

Husserl has, then, provisionally abstained before the historical content of *Erstmaligkeit* only to ask the question of its objectification [*objectivation*], i.e., of its launching into history and its historicity. For a sense has entered into history only if it has become an absolute object, i.e., an ideal object which, paradoxically, must have broken all the moorings which secured it to the empirical ground of history. The conditions of Objectivity are then the conditions of historicity itself.

Notes

[1] Cf. in particular *Le rationalisme appliqué*, 4th ed. (Paris: Presses Universitaires de France, 1970), pp. 2 and 42–46.

[2] Then begins the formidable difficulties grappled with in the fifth of the *Cartesian Meditations*, and into which we do not want to enter here.

[3] [Derrida wants to suggest by the word *uchronie* a temporality akin to the spatiality of *utopia*. We should also note Derrida's use of the roots "temporalité" and "chronie" in various words: *panchronie* and *uchronie* versus *omnitemporalité* and *intemporalité* (as well as *synchronie, diachronie,* and *anachronie*). When *uchronie* occurs again . . . , it is translated as intemporality.]

[4] This is done in terms which recall those of *Ideas I*, no doubt, but above all those of *FTL*: cf. notably *FTL*, §59, pp. 156–59.

[5] Husserl had posed this question in the same terms but in its most inclusive extension and with a more critical, but less historical, inflexion in *FTL*, §100, pp. 263–64. There, however, it is limited to the egological sphere of Objectivity. Here it is focused on the possibility of objective spirit as the condition for history and in this respect takes the opposite view to Dilthey's question. Dilthey, in effect, starts from the already constituted objective spirit. For him, what matters is knowing how the significations and the values of this objective milieu can be interiorized and assumed as such by individual subjects—first of all in the historian's work on the basis of testimonies which are individual in their origin or object. Moreover, this question led Dilthey to discover, like Husserl, a non-psychological dimension of the subject. Dilthey writes: "Now the following question arises: how a nexus which is not produced as such in a mind [*tête*], which consequently is not directly experienced and can no more be led back to the lived experience of a person, how can it be constituted as such in the historian on the basis of the statements of this person or of statements made about this matter? This presupposes that some logical subjects, who are not psychological subjects, can be constituted" (Part III: "Plan der Fortsetzung zum Aufbau der geschichtlichen Welt in den Geisteswissenschaften. Entwürfe zur Kritik der historischen Vermunft" ["Plan for the Continuation of the Formation of the Historical World in the Human Studies. Sketches for a Critique of

Historical Reason"], in Dilthey's *Der Aufbau der geschichtlichen Welt in den Geisteswissen-schaften*, ed. Bernard Groethuysen, 2nd ed. (Stuttgart: B. G. Teubner and Gottingen: Vandenhoeck and Ruprecht, 1958), Vol. 7 of *Gesammelte Schriften*, p. 282).

This question is "turned over" in the *Origin* in formulas which are strangely similar to those of Dilthey. This "reverse side" of the question concerns the radical origin and the conditions of possibility for the objective spirit itself. After the interconnections of sense and the evidences of a monadic *ego* from which we cannot not start, de facto as well as de jure, how can an objective spirit in general be constituted as the place of truth, tradition, co-responsibility, and so forth? We will see that, according to Husserl, a "logical" subject will no more be able to be responsible for such a possibility than could the psychological subject.

MICHEL FOUCAULT

Elements for a History of Truth

1974

I would like to open a parenthesis here and insert a little history of truth in general. It seems to me that we could say that knowledge of the kind we call scientific basically presupposes that there is truth everywhere, in every place and all the time. More precisely, this means that while there are of course moments for scientific knowledge when the truth is grasped more easily, points of view that allow it to be perceived more easily or certainly, and instruments for discovering it where it is hidden, remote or buried, nonetheless, for scientific practice in general, there is always the truth; the truth is always present, in or under every thing, and the question of truth can be posed about anything and everything. The truth may well be buried and difficult to reach, but this only directs us to our own limits and circumstances. The truth in itself permeates the entire world, without break. There is no black hole in the truth. This means that for a scientific type of knowledge nothing is too small, trivial, ephemeral, or occasional for the question of truth, nothing too distant or close to hand for us to put the question: what are you in truth? The truth dwells in everything and anything, even Plato's famous nail clippings.[1] This means not only that the truth lives everywhere and that the question of truth can be posed at every [moment], but it also means that no one is exclusively qualified to state the truth, if, of course, they have the instruments required to discover it, the categories necessary to think it, and an adequate language for formulating it in propositions. Speaking even more schematically, let's say that we have here a philosophic-scientific standpoint of truth linked to a technology for the construction of truth, or for finding it in principle, a technology of demonstration. Let's say that we have a technology of demonstrative truth joined, in short, to scientific practice.

Now I think there has been a completely different standpoint of truth in our civilization. This completely different standpoint of truth, no doubt more

From "Lecture of 23 January 1974," in *Psychiatric Power: Lectures at the Collège de France, 1973–1974*, ed. Jacques Lagrange and trans. Graham Burchell (New York: Palgrave Macmillan, 2006), pp. 235–40, 246–47 ["Eléments pour une histoire de la vérité," in *Le pouvoir psychiatrique* (Paris: Editions du Seuil/Gallimard, 2003)].

archaic than the one I am talking about, was gradually pushed aside or covered over by the demonstrative technology of truth. This other standpoint of truth, which is, I think absolutely crucial in the history of our civilization by virtue of it being covered over and colonized by the other, is that of a truth which, precisely, will not be everywhere and at all times waiting for us whose task is to watch out for it and grasp it wherever it happens to be. It will be the standpoint of a dispersed, discontinuous, interrupted truth which will only speak or appear from time to time, where it wishes to, in certain places; a truth which does not appear everywhere, at all times, or for everyone; a truth which is not waiting for us, because it is a truth which has its favorable moments, its propitious places, its privileged agents and bearers. It is a truth which has its geography. The oracle who speaks the truth at Delphi[2] does not express it anywhere else, and does not say the same thing as the oracle in another place; the god who cures at Epidaurus,[3] and who tells those who come to consult him what their illness is and what remedy they must apply, only cures and expresses the truth of the illness at Epidaurus and nowhere else. A truth, then, which has its geography, and which has its calendar as well, or, or at least, its own chronology.

Take another example. In the old Greek, Latin and medieval medicine of crises, to which I will come back, there is always a moment for the truth of the illness to appear. This is precisely the moment of the crisis, and there is no other moment at which the truth can be grasped in this way. In alchemical practice, the truth is not lying there waiting to be grasped by us; it passes, and it passes rapidly, like lightning; it is in any case linked to the opportunity, to the *kairos*, and must be seized.[4]

It is not only a truth with its geography and calendar, but also with its messengers or privileged and exclusive agents. The agents of this discontinuous truth are those who possess the secrets of times and places, those who undergo tests of qualification, those who have uttered the required words or performed ritual actions, and those again whom truth has chosen to sweep down on: prophets, seers, innocents, the blind, the mad, the wise, et cetera. This truth, with its geography, its calendars, and its messengers or privileged agents, is not universal. Which does not mean that it is rare, but that it is a dispersed truth, a truth that occurs as an event.

So you have attested truth, the truth of demonstration, and you have the truth-event. We could call this discontinuous truth the truth-thunderbolt, as opposed to the truth-sky that is universally present behind the clouds. We have, then, two series in the Western history of truth. The series of constant, constituted, demonstrated, discovered truth, and then a different series of the truth which does not belong to the order of what is, but to the order of what happens, a truth, therefore, which is not given in the form of discovery, but in the form of the event, a truth which is not found but aroused and hunted down: production rather than apophantic. It is not a truth that is given through the mediation of instruments, but a truth provoked by rituals, captured by ruses, seized according to occasions. This kind of truth does not call for method, but for strategy. The relationship between this truth-event and the person who is seized by it, who grasps it or is struck by it, is not a relationship of subject to object. Consequently it is not a relationship within knowledge but, rather, a relationship of a shock or clash, like that of a thunderbolt or lightning. It is also a hunting kind of relationship, or, at any rate, a risky, reversible, warlike relationship; it is a relationship of domination and victory, and so not a relationship of knowledge, but one of power.

There are those who are in the habit of writing the history of truth in terms of the forgetting of Being,[5] that is to say, when they assert forgetting as the basic category of the history of truth, these people place themselves straightaway within the privileges of established knowledge, that is to say, something like forgetting can only take place on the ground of the assumed knowledge relationship, laid down once and for all. Consequently, I think they only pursue the history of one of the two series I have tried to point out, the series of apophantic truth, of discovered, established, demonstrated truth, and they place themselves within that series.

What I would like to do, what I have tried to do in the last years, is a history of truth starting with the other series,[6] that is to say, I have tried to single out the technology—today, effectively dismissed, brushed aside and supplanted—of the truth-event, truth-ritual, truth-power relationship, as opposed to the truth-discovery, truth-method, truth-knowledge relationship, as opposed, therefore, to truth that is presupposed and placed within the subject-object relationship.

I would like to emphasize the truth-thunderbolt against the truth-sky, that is to say, on the one hand, to show how this truth-demonstration, broadly identified in its technology with scientific practice, the present day extent, force and power of which there is absolutely no point in denying, derives in reality from the truth-ritual, truth-event, truth-aspect, albeit one that has become superabundant and assumed gigantic dimensions, but still an aspect or a modality of truth as event and of the technology of this truth-event.

Showing that scientific demonstration is basically only a ritual, that the supposedly universal subject of knowledge is really only an individual historically qualified according to certain modalities, and that the discovery of truth is really a certain modality of the production of truth; putting what is given as the truth of observation or demonstration back on the basis of rituals, of the qualifications of the knowing individual, of the truth-event system, is what I would call the archeology of knowledge.[7]

And then there is a further move to be made, which would be to show precisely how, in the course of our history, of our civilization, and in an increasingly accelerated way since the Renaissance, truth-knowledge assumed its present, familiar and observable dimensions; to show how it colonized and took over the truth-event and ended up exercising a relationship of power over it, which may be irreversible, but which for the moment anyway is a dominant and tyrannical power, to show how this technology of demonstrative truth colonized and now exercises a relationship of power over this truth whose technology is linked to the event, to strategy, and to the hunt. We could call this the genealogy of knowledge, the indispensable historical other side to the archeology of knowledge, and which I have tried to show you, very schematically, with some dossiers, not what it might consist of, but how it might be sketched out. Opening up the dossier of judicial practice was an attempt to show how, through judicial practice, politico-juridical rules were gradually formed for establishing the truth in which we saw the technology of the truth-test ebbing away and disappearing with the advent of a certain type of political power and the establishment of the technology of a truth of certified observation, of a truth authenticated by witnesses, et cetera.

What I would now like to do with regard to psychiatry is show how in the nineteenth century this event type of truth is gradually hidden by a different technology of truth, or at least, how, with regard to madness, there was an attempt to cover up this technology of the truth-event with a technology of demonstrative truth, of observation. We could also do this, and in the next years I will try to do it with regard to pedagogy and the dossier on childhood.[8]

It could be said that this is all very well historically, but all the same, there is little now that corresponds to the truth-test-event series in our society; we may be able to find this technology of the truth-event in some old practices—say in oracular, prophetic practices, et cetera—but it is a long time since this game was played and there is no point in returning to it. Actually, I think there really is something else here, and that in actual fact, within our civilization, this truth-event, this technology of the truth-thunderbolt, seems to me to have subsisted for a long time and has considerable historical importance.

First, with regard to the judicial forms I have talked about in previous years and to which I have just referred, a very profound and fundamental transformation is involved. You remember what I said to you about archaic medieval justice, of justice before the twelfth century, more or less: the medieval procedure for discovering the guilty person, or rather, for assigning individual culpability, the procedures broadly placed under the rubric of "the judgment of God," were in no way methods for discovering what really happened. There was absolutely no question of reproducing within "God's judgment" something like the *analogon*, the image itself of what really happened at the level of criminal action. "God's judgment" and tests of this kind were procedures for governing how to determine the victor in a confrontation between two individuals in dispute.[9] Even confession was not a sign or a method for discovering a sign of culpability in medieval judicial techniques.[10] When the Inquisitors of the Middle Ages tortured someone, they did not appeal to the kind of argument made by present-day torturers, that someone's acknowledgment of guilt is the best proof, even better, closer, than that of an eyewitness; the torturer of the Middle Ages did not seek to obtain this kind of proof *a fortiori*. In fact, torturing someone in the Middle Ages involved the judge and the person accused or suspected in a real physical struggle—the rules of which, while not rigged, were of course completely unequal and with no reciprocity—to find out whether or not the suspect would stand up to it. When he gave way, this was not so much a demonstrative proof that he was guilty, as quite simply the reality of the fact that he had lost in the game, in the confrontation, and could consequently be sentenced. All this could then be inscribed, secondarily as it were, in a system of significations: God, then, has abandoned him, et cetera. But this was absolutely not the mundane sign of his culpability; it was the final phase, the final episode, the conclusion of a confrontation.[11] And finally to pass from this technique for establishing the truth in the test to the establishment of truth in the certified report, through evidence and demonstration, required the whole process by which penal justice was brought under Senate control.[12]

. . .

I think the transition from a technology of truth-event to truth-demonstration is linked, on the one hand, to the extension of political procedures of the inquiry. The inquiry, the report, the evidence of several people, the cross-checking of information, the circulation of knowledge from the center of power to the points where it ends up and back again, as well as all the agencies of parallel verification, progressively, over a long history, gradually constituted the instrument of the political and economic power of industrial society; hence the refinement, the increasingly fine grid of these techniques of inquiry within the elements where they were usually applied. Broadly speaking, the refinement by which we passed from a basically fiscal kind of inquiry in the Middle Ages—knowing who collects what, who possesses what, so that the necessary deductions are made—to a police kind of investigation into people's behavior, into how they live, think, make love, et cetera, this transition from fiscal inquiry to police investigation, the constitution of a police individuality starting from fiscal individuality, which was the only individuality known by power in the Middle Ages, reveals the tightening of the technique of inquiry in our kind of society.[13]

Moreover, there was not only a local tightening, but also a planetary extension to the entire surface of the globe. There is a double movement of colonization: colonization in depth, which fed on the actions, bodies, and thoughts of individuals, and then colonization at the level of territories and surfaces. We can say that from the end of the Middle Ages we have seen the entire surface of the Earth, down to the finest grain of things, bodies, and actions, subjected to generalized investigation: a sort of grand inquisitorial parasitism. That is to say, at any time, at any place, and with regard to anything in the world, the question of truth can and must be posed. Truth is everywhere and awaits everywhere, at any place and at any time. This, very schematically, is the great process that led to this move from a technology of the truth-event to a technology of truth-findings.

The other process was a sort of opposite process, [. . . *] establishing the rarity of this truth of anywhere and anytime. This rarefaction is not brought to bear on the emergence or production of truth, however, but precisely on who can discover it. In one sense, this universal truth of anywhere and anytime, which any inquiry can and must track down and discover with regard to no matter what, is accessible to anyone; anyone can have access to it, since it is there, everywhere and all the time. However, the necessary circumstances are still required, and we must acquire the forms of thought and techniques that will give us access to this truth that is everywhere, but always deep down, buried, and difficult to reach.

So we will have, of course, a universal subject of this universal truth, but it will be an abstract subject because, concretely, the universal subject able to grasp this truth is rare, since it must be a subject qualified by procedures of pedagogy and selection. Universities, learned societies, canonical teaching, schools, laboratories, the interplay of specialization and professional qualification, are all ways or organizing the rarity of those who can have access to a truth that science posits as universal. It will be the abstract right of every individual to be a universal subject, if you like, but to be one in fact, concretely, will necessarily entail rare individuals being qualified to perform the function of universal subject. In the history of the West since the eighteenth century, the appearance of philosophers, men of science, intellectuals, professors, laboratories, et cetera, is directly correlated with this extension of the standpoint of scientific truth and corresponds precisely to the rarefaction of those who can know a truth that is now present everywhere and at every moment. Fine. That's the little history I wanted to present. What is its relationship to madness? We're just coming to it.

Notes

[1] Foucault is alluding to the debate between Socrates and Parmenides on the problem of the things of which there are Ideas. See, Plato, *Parmenides*, 130c–d.

[2] From the middle of the eighth century B.C. until the end of the fourth century A.D., Delphi, a town of Phocis at the foot of Parnassus, was a favorite site for Apollo to deliver his oracles through the mouth of the Pythia. See, M. Delcourt, *Les grands sanctuaires de la Grèce* (Paris: Presses universitaires de France, 1947) pp. 76–92; M. Delcourt, *L'oracle de Delphes* (Paris: Payot, 1955); R. Flacelière, *Devins et oracles grecs* (Paris: Presses universi-

*(Recording:) we could call it

taires de France, 1972) pp. 49–83; and, G. Roux, *Delphes, son oracle et ses dieux* (Paris: Les Belles Lettres, 1976).

[3] Epidaurus, a town of Argolis on the east Peloponnese, was the site of the sanctuary Apollo's son, Asclepius, where divination through dreams was practiced. See M. Delcourt, *Les grands sanctuaires*, pp. 93–113; R. Flacelière, *Devins et oracles grecs*, pp. 36–37; and, G. Vlastos, "Religion and medicine in the cult of Asclepius: a review article," *Review of Religion*, vol. 13, 1948–1949, pp. 269–290.

[4] The notion of καιρός *(kairos)* defines the occasion, the opportunity to be seized, and consequently the time of possible action. Hippocrates (460–377 B.C.) devotes a chapter of his *Des maladies*, I, to this notion, in (*Oeuvres complètes*, éd. Littré (Paris, J.-B. Baillière, 1849), vol. VI, ch. 5, "Of the opportune and inopportune," pp. 148–151; English translation, "Diseases 1" in *Hippocrates*, vol. V, trans. Paul Potter (Cambridge, Mass.: Harvard University Press, the Loeb Classical Library, 1988). See, P. Joos, "Zufall, Kunst und Natur bei idem Hippokratitkern," *Janus*, no. 46, 1957, pp. 238–252; P. Kucharski, "Sur la notion pythagoricienne de *kairos*," *Revue philosophique de la France et de l'étranger*, vol. CLII, no. 2, 1963, pp. 141–169; and P. Chantraine, "καιρός" in *Dictionnaire étymologique de la langue grècque. Histoire des mots* (Paris: Klincksieck, 1970), vol. II, p. 480.

[5] Foucault is alluding here to the Heideggerian problematic that, in a discussion with G. Preti, he then associated with that of Husserl in the same reproach of calling into "question all our knowledge and its foundations [. . .] on the basis of that which is original [. . .] at the expense of all articulated historical content," M. Foucault, "Les problems de la culture. Un débat Foucault-Preti" (September 1972), *Dits et écrits*, vol. 2, p. 372. So it is the Heideggerian conception of history that is intended here. See especially, M. Heidegger, (1) *Sein und Zeit* (Halle: Nemeyer, 1927); English translation, *Being and Time*, trans. J. Macquarrie and E. Robinson (Oxford: Blackwells, 1967); (2) *Vom Wesen des Grundes* (Halle: Nemeyer, 1929); English translation, *The Essence of Reasons*, trans. Terrence Malick (Evanston: Northwestern University Press, 1969); (3) *Vom Wesen der Wahreit* (Frankfurt: Klostermann, 1943); English translation, *The Essence of Truth, on Plato's parable of the cave allegory and Theaetetus*, trans. T. Sadler (London: Continuum, 2002); (4) *Holzwege* (Frankfurt: Klostermann; 1952); English translation, *Off the Beaten Track*, trans. J. Young and K. Haynes (Cambridge: Cambridge University Press, 2002); (5) *Vorträge und Aufsätze* (Pfullingen: Neske, 1954); (6) *Nietzsche*, vol. 2 (Pfullingen: Neske, 1961); English translation, *Nietzsche, vol. 2: The Eternal Recurrence of the Same*, trans. David Farrell Krell (San Francisco: Harper & Row, 1984). On the relations between Foucault and Heidegger, see M. Foucault, (1) *Les mots et les choses*, ch. 9, "L'homme et ses doubles," § iv and vi; *The Order of Things*, ch. 9, "Man and his doubles," sections 4 and 6; (2) "L'homme est-il mort?" (interview with C. Bonnefoy, June 1966), *Dits et écrits*, vol. 1, p. 542; (3) "Ariane s'est pendue" (April 1969), *Dits et écrits*, vol. 1, p. 768 and p. 770; (4) "Foucault, le philosophe, est en train de parler. Pensez" (29 May 1973), *Dits et écrits*, vol. 2, p. 424; (5) "Prisons et asiles dans le mécanisme du pouvoir" (interview with M. D'Eramo, March 1974), *Dits et écrits*, vol. 2, p. 521; (6) "Structuralisme et poststructuralisme" (interview with G. Raulet, Spring 1983), *Dits et écrits*, vol. 4, p. 455; English translation, "Scruturalism and Post-Structuralism," trans. Jeremy Harding, *Essential Works of Foucault*, 2, p. 456; (7) "Politique et éthique: une interview," *Dits et écrits*, vol. 4, p. 585; "Politics and Ethics: An Interview," trans. P. Rabinow, *The Foucault Reader*, pp. 373–374; (8) "Le retour de la morale" (interview with G. Barbedette and A. Scala, 29 May 1984), *Dits et écrits*, vol. 4, p. 703; English translation, "The Return of Morality," trans. Thomas Levin and Isabelle Lorenz, in Michel Foucault, *Politics, Philosophy, Culture. Interviews and Other Writings, 1977–1984*, ed. Lawrence D. Kritzman (New York and London: Routledge, 1988); (9) "Vérité, pouvoir et soi" (interview with R. Martin, 25 October 1982), *Dits et écrits*, vol. 4, p. 780.

[6] In the third lecture of the 1970–1971 course, "The Will to Knowledge (*savoir*)," Foucault proposed the "opposite view" of a history of the "will to knowledge (*connaître*)," in

which truth has "the immediate, universal and bare form of observation, external to the procedure of judgment," proposing the need to "write a history of the relationships between truth and torture (*supplice*)," in which "truth is not observed but decided in the form of the oath and the invocation prescribed by the ritual of the ordeal." A regime, consequently, in which "truth is not linked to the possible light and gaze brought to bear on things by a subject, but to the obscurity of the future and disturbing event." Other fragments of such a history are put forward in the ninth lecture of the 1971–1972 course, "Penal Theories and Institutions," which deals with the system of proof in procedures of the oath, ordeals, and judicial duel from the tenth to the thirteenth century. Foucault was inspired by M. Detienne, *Les maîtres de vérité dans la Grèce archaïque* (Paris: Maspero, 1967); English translation, *The Masters of Truth in Archaic Greece*, trans. Janet Lloyd (New York: Zone Books, 1999).

7 The thirteenth lecture of the course "Penal Theories and Institutions" dedicated to "the confession, the test" explains the meaning of the detour through what Foucault calls "juridico-political matrices" such as the test, the inquiry, et cetera, and distinguishes three levels of analysis: (a) an "historical description of the sciences," in which "the history of the sciences" consists; (b) an "archeology of knowledge," which takes the relationships of knowledge and power into account; and (c) a "dynastic of knowledge," which, thanks to the freeing of the juridico-political matrices which authorize the archeology, is situated "at the level which combines the most profit, knowledge and power" (course manuscript consulted thanks to the kindness of Daniel Defert). Foucault takes up this distinction between the "archeological" and "dynastic" in an interview with S. Hasumi, September 1972, "De l'archéologie à la dynastique," *Dits et écrits*, vol. 2, p. 406. On "archeology," see the many definitions given by Foucault: (1) in *Dits et écrits*, vol. 1: "Michel Foucault, *Les mots et les choses*," pp. 498–499; "Sur les façons d'écrire l'histoire," p. 595; "Réponse à une question," p. 681, and "Michel Foucault explique son dernier livre," pp. 771–772; (2) in *Dits et Écrits*, vol. 2: "La volonté de savoir," p. 242; "La vérité et les forms juridiques," pp. 643–644; English translation, "Truth and Juridical Forms," trans. Robert Hurley, *Essential Works of Foucault, 3*; (3) in *Dits et écrits*, vol. 3: "Cours du 7 janvier 1976," p. 167; English translation, lecture of 7 January 1976, "*Society Must Be Defended*," ch. 1, pp. 10–11; "Dialogue sur le pouvoir," pp. 468–469; (4) in *Dits et écrits*, vol. 4: "Entretien avec Michel Foucault," p. 57; "Structuralisme et poststructuralisme," p. 443; English translation, "Structuralism and Post-Structuralism," trans. Jeremy Harding, *Essential Works of Foucault*, 2, pp. 444–445.

8 In fact Foucault will not keep to this program apart from some comments on the role of childhood in the generalization of psychiatric knowledge and power in the 1974–1975 Collège de France lectures of 5, 12, and 19 March: *Les anormaux*, pp. 217–301; *Abnormal*, pp. 231–321.

9 From the Old English, *ordal*, judgment, the "judgment of God" or "ordeal," means to settle contentious questions with the idea that God intervenes in the case to judge during tests likes those of "fire," the "branding iron," "cold or boiling water," and the "cross," et cetera. See L. Tanon, *Histoire des tribunaux de l'Inquisition en France* (Paris: L. Larose and Forcel, 1893) on the penalties of "fire" (pp. 464–479) and the "cross" (pp. 490–498). As J.-P. Lévy emphasizes in his *La hiérarchie des preuves dans le droit savant du Moyen Age, depuis la renaissance du droit romain jusqu'à la fin du xive siècle* (Paris: Sirey, 1939), in this procedure "the trial is not an investigation with the aim of finding out the truth [. . .]. It is originally a struggle, and later, an appeal to God; the concern with making the truth come out is left up to Him, but the judge does not seek it himself" (p. 163).

Foucault referred to the question of the ordeal in the third lecture of the 1970–1971 Collège de France lectures, "The Will to Knowledge," in which he noted that in "the treatments to which madness was subjected, we find something like this ordeal test of the truth." The ninth lecture of the 1971–1972 lectures, devoted to accusatory procedure and the system of proof, refers to it (see above note 6). See also, M. Foucault, "La vérité et les forms juridiques"; "Truth and Juridical Forms." See A. Esmein, *Histoire de la procedure criminelle en France, et spécialement de la procedure inquisitoire depuis le xiii*[e] *siècle jusqu'à nos jours* (Paris: Larose et Forcel, 1882), pp. 260–283; E. Vacandard, "L'Eglise et les ordalies," in *Études de critique et d'histoire religieuse*, vol. I (Paris: V. Lecoffre, 1905), pp. 189–214; G. Glotz, *Études socials et juridiques sur l'antiquité grecque*, ch. 2, "L'ordalie" (Paris: Hachette, 1906), pp. 69–97; A. Michel, "Ordalies," in A. Vacant, ed., *Dictionnaire de théologie catholique*, vol. XI (Paris: Letouzey et Ané, 1930), col. 1139–1152; Y. Bongert, *Recherches sur les cours laïques du x*[e] *au xiii*[e] *siècles* (Paris: A. et J. Picard, 1949), pp. 215–228; H. Nottarp, *Gottelsurteilstudien* (Munich: Kosel-Verlag, 1956); and J. Gaudemet, "Les ordalies au Moyen Age: doctrine, legislation et pratique canonique," in *Recueil de la Société Jean Bodin* (Brussels: 1965), vol. XVII, Part 2, *La Preuve*.

[10] In the basically accusatory procedures that involved taking God as witness so that he produces the accuracy or retraction of the accusation, confession was not enough to pronounce sentence. See H.C. Lea, *A History of the Inquisition of the Middle Ages*, vol. 1, pp. 407–408; A. Esmein, *Histoire de la procedure criminelle*, p. 273; and J.-P. Lévy, *La hiérarchie des preuves*, pp. 19–83. On confession, see *Surveiller et punir*, pp. 42–45; *Discipline and Punish*, pp. 37–40.

[11] Torture, unlike the sovereign means of proof by ordeal—the expression of God's testimony—was a way of provoking judicial confession. The inquisitorial procedure was integrated into canon law in 1232 when Pope Gregory IX called upon the Dominicans to establish a tribunal of Inquisition specifically for the search for and punishment of heretics. Recourse to judicial torture was approved by the bull *Ad Extirpanda* of Pope Innovent IV of 15 May 1252, and later, in 1256, by that of Alexander IV, *Ut Negotium Fidei*. Referring to the question of the Inquisition in the third lecture of the 1970–1971 lectures, "The Will to Knowledge," Foucault said that "it is a matter of something other than obtaining a truth, a confession [. . .]. It is a challenge which, within Christian thought and practice, takes up the forms of the ordeal." See *Surveiller et punir*, pp. 43–47; *Discipline and Punish*, pp. 38–42; "Michel Foucault. Les réponses du philosophe," *Dits et écrits*, vol. 2, pp. 810–811. See H.C. Lea, *A History of the Inquisition*, vol. 1, ch. 9, "The Inquisitional Process," pp. 399–429, and on torture, pp. 417–427; L. Tanon, *Histoire des tribunaux de l'Inquisition*, section III, "Procédure des tribunaux de l'Inquisition," pp. 326–440; E. Vacandard, *L'Inquisition. Etude historique et critique sur le pouvoir coercitif de l'Eglise* (Paris: Bloud et Gay, 1907, 3rd ed.), p. 175; H. Leclercq, "Torture," in F. Cabrol, H. Leclercq, H.I. Marrou, eds., *Dictionnaire d'archéologie chrétienne et de liturgie*, vol. XV (Paris: Letouzey et Ané, 1953), col. 2447–2459; P. Fiorelli, *La Tortura giudiziaria nel diritto comune* (Milan: Giuffrè, 1953). On the Inquisition in general, see J. Guiraud, *Histoire de l'Inquisition au Moyen Age*, in two volumes (Paris: A. Picard, 1935–1938); and H. Maisonneuve, *Etudes sur les origins de l'Inquisition* (Paris: J. Vrin, 1960, 2nd ed.).

[12] This question was the topic of the third lecture of the 1971–1972 lectures, "Penal Theories and Institutions," devoted to confession, investigation and proof. See the course summary, "Théories et institutions pénales," *Dits et écrits*, vol. 2, pp. 390–391, English translation, "Penal Theories and Institutions," *Essential Works of Foucault, 1*, pp. 18–20.

[13] This passage echoes a number of treatments by Foucault of "the inquiry": (1) The 1971–1972 lectures at the Collège de France, the first part of which deals with the inquiry and its development in the Middle Ages; see the course summary, "Théories et institutions pénales," *Dits et écrits*, vol. 2, pp. 390–391; "Penal Theories and Institutions," trans. Robert Hurley, *Essential Works of Foucault, 1*, pp. 17–19; (2) The Collège de France lectures of 1972–1973, "The Punitive Society," in which, in the lecture of 28 March 1973, Foucault returns to the constitution of an "inquiry knowledge"; (3) The third lecture (23 May 1973) on "La vérité et les formes juridiques," pp. 581–588; "Truth and Juridical Forms," pp. 44–52. Foucault returns to the process of the colonization of a "truth-test" in the form of the event by a "truth-findings" in the form of a body of knowledge in 1975 in "La maison des fous," *Dits et écrits*, vol. 2, pp. 696–697.

PIERRE-FRANÇOIS MOREAU

Image, Idea

1975

Under this head we may place that which takes the place of a "theory of knowledge" in Spinoza and which is in fact a theory of the production of knowledge, or, rather, knowledge*s*, in the plural, because knowledge is inevitably assorted into a variety of genres. It is a matter not of a greater or lesser degree of approximation but rather of different types of knowledge, which must be attributed to different causes. Production: for universal necessity applies to knowledge, too, and is not less substantial in the production of ideas than in the production of the properties of a triangle. Knowledges are effects and in turn produce other effects of their own. And this assigns them a place in the rigorous order of the *Ethics*: after the ontology of Book I, which analyzes the principle of all things (the potential to act), and before the theory of sentiments and of servitude in the later books. In fact, in order to study how man behaves, we must first see how he understands himself and the world and find out why he labors under illusions and how he can escape from them. The first distinction (between internal and external necessity) will have repercussions at different levels of the system. Depending on whether or not an individual produces effects that follow exclusively from his nature, he will or will not have adequate knowledge of those effects, and this will determine whether he follows the path of the passions or that of reason.

Men of course make mistakes. But not always. To account for this, we must posit (at least) two types of knowledge: imagination and understanding. Their alternation forms the basis of the passage from common illusion to the *other norm of truth*, which is that of objective knowledge. To say simply that there are degrees of knowledge, however, would not have been very original: philosophy had been saying this for centuries, and this is precisely what Spinoza did not do. In the epistemological tradition, in fact, a certain unity of knowledge always obtains, yet different degrees of knowledge are still regularly distinguished. Sometimes these differences are attributed to the separation of two

From *Spinoza* (1975; Paris: Presses Universitaires de France, 2009), pp. 81–85, 88–89; trans. Arthur Goldhammer.

worlds (the sensible and the intelligible), other times to two ways of perceiving the same world. This is of little consequence: whether one goes wrong by yielding to the prestige of the sensible or by allowing the will to exceeds the limits of natural reason, the hierarchical conception of degrees of knowledge remains. Error is a deficiency, a lack of truth, something like the shadow of truth.

To ascribe this status to error is not without consequences. The fact that error is conceptualized only as a falling away from truth prevents analyzing its intrinsic content: traditionally, it is enough to reject false discourse so as to embrace the truth instead of trying to find out why the false discourse exists, much less discover its internal logic. Once unmasked, the false has only to make way for the true, to return to the nothingness it should never have left.

In Spinoza, however, we find nothing of the kind: no falling away from truth and no insistence that the false disappear. There is of course a rupture, but there is equal necessity on both sides. Indeed, it is because Spinozism is the only philosophy in which error is not conceptualized as either a lack or a sin that it is possible to formulate a theory of its production: if it is produced, and by a process different from that which leads to the truth, it is because it is not merely the opposite of truth.

Let us look at the Cartesian model in terms of which Spinoza conceptualized the tradition he opposed. It is probably Book II ("Origin and Nature of the Spirit") that contains the greatest number of allusions to Cartesianism. This model is fairly elaborate. It brings together several faculties: understanding, senses, will. True knowledge of things comes only from the understanding, which can give us nothing else; in the natural light of reason there is no error. Where, then, does the false come from? Strictly speaking, it has no objective causes. No matter how complicated a problem may be, we can always unravel it by reducing it to its simplest elements, which can be grasped by intellectual inspection. It is not enough, however, to see what is the case; I must also adhere to it. What the understanding, which is a kind of gaze, presents to me, I must either accept or reject. As for the other faculties of knowledge, sense and imagination, they, too, are of the order of the gaze. Ultimately it is the will that decides among them: I tell the truth when my will does not venture beyond the limits of my understanding; I err (or, what comes to the same thing, I pronounce the truth only by accident) when my will ventures beyond the strict limits of natural light. Hence error in the final analysis has no causes different from those of the will itself: it is the subject whose radical act turns discourse toward the truth or away from the truth. There is nothing in things or in our nature that forces us to deceive ourselves. Error is therefore nothing in itself. The proof of this is that Descartes, who often denounces "prejudices," never attempts to provide a theory of their structure. They are nothing more than that which stands in the way of knowledge, and as such they must be expunged. For Descartes, then, the privative character of error rests on the acknowledged distance between the understanding and the will and the putative freedom of the latter. Nothing constrains the will, which in the end is responsible for judgment.

Spinoza's theory is a detailed deconstruction of these arguments.

To begin with, the understanding and the will do not exist as faculties of the soul. They are universal terms under which we collect a large number of singular facts while erasing the differences among them. What happens to these notions is the same as what happens to man in general. *So many images of men accumulate in the human body at the same time that they surpass the powers of the imagination—not entirely, to be sure, but sufficiently that the mind cannot imagine the small differences that exist between individual human beings (in color, size, and so on), nor can it determine their precise number. It distinctly imagines only that which is common to all. . . . That is what the mind expresses by the name "man" and what it affirms of an infinity of singular beings.*[1] Like "man," the will and the understanding are "creatures of reason," which is to say, fictions: only individuals exist—men, ideas, volitions.

These faculties and others like them are either absolutely fictitious or else are merely metaphysical beings, or, in other words, universals, which we ordinarily create out of particular things. Hence the understanding and the will bear the same relation to such and such a particular idea or particular volition as "rockness" bears to a given rock or as "man" does to Peter or Paul.[2]

In the end, though, one could accept this absolute nominalism and translate Cartesian language into its terms. Instead of reducing judgment to the understanding and the will in general, it would suffice to decompose each judgment into an idea and an elementary assertion or negation. Each volition is then individualized; it is nevertheless radical. Spinoza, however, marshaled his arguments precisely against such an interpretation:

a) To assume that an idea, in order to be affirmed, needs a volition is to reduce that idea to a sort of mute picture without force of its own. But universal necessity cannot remain separate from what a mode of thought is: there is no such thing as an inert idea. To think otherwise would be to classify thought as a kind of painting.

b) Error presents itself as necessary. We do not acquiesce in it; it imposes itself on us. It is not by force of will that we see the sun as standing at a distance of two hundred paces from us: the structure of our bodies is such that we cannot imagine it any other way.

c) Neither does an idea replace an error by an act of our will. The idea turns back the error because it is stronger: it captures our assent as one captures a citadel. *It is never we who affirm or deny anything*, said the Short Treatise, *but the thing itself which affirms or denies in us something about itself.*[3]

d) In any case, the false idea is not eliminated but *turned aside* by the true idea: the necessity that produced the false idea still obtains, hence the effect is still present. It merely retreats from the front of the stage, where a more powerful idea takes its place.

What follows from this? First, that it is impossible to distinguish between the idea and the volition: if it is true, it asserts itself and has no need of any external force. *Let us therefore conceive a singular volition: for instance, the mode of thought whereby the mind affirms that the three angles of a triangle are equal to two right angles. This assertion contains the concept—that is, the idea—of the triangle, which means that it cannot be conceived without the idea of the triangle. . . . What is more, the idea of the triangle must contain this very assertion, namely, that these three angles are equal to two right angles. . . . This assertion belongs to the essence of the idea of the triangle and is nothing other than that idea itself. Hence there is in the mind no volition, which is to say, no affirmation or negation, other than that which the idea contains as idea.*[4]

Furthermore, the image owes its prestige not to a pure illusion but to its own production. It is not the mere absence of the idea, its lack or anticipation: the image too arises out of natural necessity. That is why it does not vanish when the idea comes; it simply ceases to be mistaken for adequate knowledge. It is image because the disposition of bodies produces it and will continue to produce it; it is error only insofar as it arises in a vacuum of ideas. Contrary to the whole classical tradition, falseness is therefore not mere privation of knowledge: it is a presence whose role has been shifted. *Falseness cannot consist in absolute privation (for it is minds, not bodies, that we say make errors and mistakes), nor can it consist in absolute ignorance, for to ignore and to err are two different things. Hence it consists in a privation of knowledge contained in an inadequate knowledge of things, that is, in inadequate and confused ideas.*[5]

An example will help to make this clearer: *When we look at the sun, we imagine that it is about 200 feet from us. The error, moreover, consists not just in this imagined fact but also in the fact that in imagining the sun in this way, we do not know its true distance from us or the reason why we imagine it as we do. For later, even though we know that the sun is at a distance from us greater than six hundred times the diameter of the earth, we will nevertheless continue to imagine that it is close to us.*[6] The sun of astronomy has indeed shunted the sun of the senses to one side because it is more powerful, yet it cannot make the sun of the senses disappear. By destroying the unity of knowledge, that is, by assigning to each genre of knowledge its proper causes, we both rescue error from nothingness and give ourselves the means to account for it: the groundwork has been laid for a theory of ideology.

. . .

Now we can return to what is at last recognized as the substance of false discourse. It is not absorbed into its opposite; it has its own rules of production and indeed its own rules *tout court*. It is associated with a practice, to which it necessarily corresponds (and which it expresses if it does not engender it). Now we can understand why Spinoza was able to describe his *other* so clearly: the thought of the other is included in the system; it is not extrinsic to the work, nor is it merely a convenient expository device. By way of contrast, consider the attitude of Descartes, who pours scorn on his predecessors without taking the trouble to analyze the content of their discourse. Kant was the same: the preface of the *Metaphysics of Law* goes so far as to state that a doctrine cannot lay claim to the truth unless it indiscriminately rejects all that has gone before it. For classical thought generally, the history of philosophy is meaningless.

For Spinoza, on the other hand, it has a meaning. Not because it is a moment to be integrated (the negative has no power), but because it is the durable (and durably produced) shackle from which we must free ourselves and which we must exhibit if we are to do so. There is necessity in the production of error, necessity in the internal coherence of error, and necessity in the need for analysis in order to destroy error. It is this triple materiality that sets the Spinozist theory of error against the whole tradition of philosophy both before and after Spinoza.

One exception is worth mentioning: Bachelard. In his work, too, the image/sensations complex of "common knowledge" persists as something other than the simple opposite of scientific knowledge: it has its own symbols, its own basic images, its own substantialist mythology. Above all it has its roots in the practices of daily life (and in this connection one might ask if laboratory practice is not the theoretical equivalent of the human body's encountering common notions). And finally, it, too, must be painstakingly annihilated, not for the illusory purpose of making it disappear (for it is constantly reborn as long as the life that necessarily reproduces it lasts) but in order to render it ineffective as an epistemological obstacle. This is the basis of the recourse to a "psychoanalysis of objective knowledge," whose method is in fact to give a minute description of the other of science. Only in this way can its spell be broken.

Another exception can be seen in a few sketchy comments by Marx, which Lenin among others developed in *What Is to Be Done?* What we find there is the opposition between historical materialism and the spontaneous ideology of the proletariat, an ideology conceptualized not as the mere absence of science but as a form of thought with a coherence all its own (reformism, eclectic illusion, blunting of contradictions) as well as a material base, being rooted in class domination, the apparatuses that impose that domination, and the trade union struggle that is carried on within this framework. Once again, a theory of ideology is possibly only after it has been recognized as possessing a certain materiality and only after the line separating it from its other has been traced at a level other than that of mere content.

Bringing together the philosopher of the potential act, the Bolshevik leader, and the epistemologist in this context may seem arbitrary. It is not an accident, however: what we see here is the sign of a common rejection of the dominant ideology of knowledge. In these three perspectives, knowledge is conceptualized without being related to a subject. This clears the way to move beyond classical transparency and to construct a theory of false discourse.

Notes

[1] Baruch Spinoza, *Ethics*, Part II, 40.

[2] Ibid., 48.

[3] Baruch Spinoza, *Short Treatise on God, Man, and His Well-Being*, Part II, chap. XVI.

[4] Spinoza, *Ethics*, Part II, 49.

[5] Ibid., 35.

[6] Ibid.

JULIA KRISTEVA

The True-Real

1979

When we listen to the contemporary forms of discourse that try to expound on its source and development, we recognize that the great disruptive force in present-day speech can be summed up as follows: the *truth* they seek (to say) is the *real*, that is, the "true-real" [*vréel*]. This obsessive fear, which we always possessed, has become today a massive (if not mass) burden, all the more so since no common code exists to justify, and so neutralize, it.

Perhaps the Freudian discovery of the unconscious was merely the cautious start of an epistemological and existential revolution which destroyed the whole rational system installed by the classical age and marked out before it by ancient philosophy. We know (and I shall return briefly to this) how logic and ontology have inscribed the question of *truth* within *judgment* (or sentence structure) and *being*, dismissing as *madness, mysticism or poetry* any attempt to articulate that impossible element which henceforth can only be designated by the Lacanian category of the *real*. After the flowering of mysticism, classical rationality, first by embracing Folly with Erasmus, and then by excluding it with Descartes, attempted to enunciate the real as truth by setting limits on Madness; modernity, on the other hand, opens up this enclosure in a search for other forms capable of transforming or rehabilitating the status of *truth*.

The spectacles of mass terror and terrorism, as well as the inquiry into the "languages" of the unnameable provided by the analysis of psychosis and the new experiences of modern theater, painting and literature, are just some of the indications of how the *true* has lost its former logical and ontological security, and is now expressed instead as the "true-real."

However, this irruption immediately raises the problem of socialization. How can this fear of the true-real be signified and included in a (social) contact, however modified? The old question returns: how can the *true-real* be made *plausible*?

From *The Kristeva Reader*, ed. Toril Moi (New York: Columbia University Press, 1986), pp. 216–17, 219–22, 227–28, 236; trans. Seán Hand ["Le vréel," in *Folle vérité: vérité et vraisemblance du texte psychotique*, ed. Julia Kristeva and Jean-Michel Ribette (Paris: Editions du Seuil, 1979)].

Let us not be fooled by words: our perspective goes well beyond the limits of the old problem of rhetoric. The traditional true [*vrai*] and plausible [*vraisemblable*], which will be considered, will be stretched by the "true-real" [*vréel*] (an area of risk and salvation for the speaking being) and by *semblance* [*semblant*], which is given a social meaning by its own perverse cunning. This gives enunciation a topology constructed by heterogeneous spaces which is completely different from ontological topology.

. . .

To continue, then, let me briefly recall the philosophical tradition from which an analytic concept of enunciation breaks loose.

From Plato on, *Being* is already a *true Being*: *esse verum*, as the scholastics were to put it. The strategy of this formulation gradually becomes clearer: the subject of enunciation has foreclosed his real, "natural" dependence as well as his symbolic debt to the Other. This subject, who is punctual, atomic, put up simply in order to be denied in terms of volume and dynamics (and who will become, with some supplementary constraints, the subject of science), falls within a register of a visionary *representation* that must be sutured in order to preserve it from psychosis. Once the Heraclitean *Logos* has been transformed into visual images, anything that can be considered external to its order takes on the uncomfortable status, not so much of an *object*, as of an object-spoken-in-a-representing-utterance [*énoncé*]: the status of a *complement*. Since the foreclosure of the real and of the Other brings about the fall of the subject of enunciation, the ensuing gap [*béance*] is elaborated through a process of *subtle suture* between different orders: Being, which has become an *object*, now becomes a *complement* in the linguistic chain of a discourse that can speak the *truth* precisely because of this transformation. This shows why the truth in question has nothing to do with the authenticity of real Being, but is synonymous with the *coherence* of the complement-formation, which *is* what this denied subject is saying. It is a truth of the order of syntax (whoever says "complement" says "syntax") that can be linguistic or logical, but that nevertheless governs the conditions of production both of the subject of enunciation and of its potential multiplicity of statements.[1]

Grammar, logic, ontology—sentence, judgment, being—syntax, syllogism, reference: the philosophic-logical debate on truth oscillates between three axes which give rise to different movements and disciplines. Since truth consists of whatever is demonstrable, it either frees itself from the laws of the *sentence* and the order in which elements are given; or it lies in the psychic act of nominating and judging; or else it is to be located in the correspondence between this act and a referent, or to Being in general. The namegiver in Plato's *Cratylus* is undoubtedly the prototype of this master-subject of the law who guarantees the possibility of truth in Platonic discourse, by being presented as complete and untouchable, like a god or a fictional creation.

For all the distinctions I have just recalled are indeed to be found in Plato, with the famous suggestion that there is a "necessary connection" between the truth of the sentence and the truth of the judgment, between the parts of discourse and thought: the Forms (*eide*), that are neither things nor ideas, but which institute the order of "universals." A sentence is true if the arrangement of its parts corresponds to a connection between the eidetic essences: from this we derive the notion of truth as revelation, as the uncovering of its *eide*, as *aletheia* (see the *Theaetetus*, for example, which has been commented on by Heidegger). Aristotle, more formalist, perceives one single class of propositions (*logoi*), that of declaratives which can be true or false, while prayers and orders have only rhetorical value (*On Interpretation*). But the *Metaphysics* is much more Platonic: a statement is true if it states whatever is. Being is formulated in this way, without any explicit relation to the "speaking subject" other than that of the internal dependence (resonance, interdiction) between Being and *Logos* revealed later by phenomenology. However, if no economy or subject of enunciation is conceived of, already it is no longer the sentence which is true, but what is expressed by the sentence, namely the *proposition*. This is the direction which medieval philosophy was to take.

But the ongoing subjectivization of truth, the fact that it depends on the namegiver, inevitably gives rise to uneasiness in the face of another truth which cannot be determined and which does not even operate in its own field of effects, although it is always evoked, like a phantom, by those who wish to understand: that is to say, the *semblance* of truth which is at work in the discourse of art. This widens the field of the *plausible*, making it decidable but uncertain, making homologous with the truth the discourse of another speaking being, who is no longer a namegiver but a ludic accomplice of the law: the subject of art, and the object of rhetoric.[2]

With Abelard, but also with Peter of Ailly and Gregory of Rimini, the Middle Ages essentially returns to the theory of truth as being something peculiar to the *proposition* (but not to the sentence) and therefore to judgment. At the center of its preoccupations, therefore, is the relation between the speaking subject and a universe of things which are divine and true to the extent that they refer to the divine Thing (*Una Res*). Consequently, this theory puts forward the most subjective concept of semantics possible: that of *modi significandi*.

Modernity, in the major philosophical movements, relativizes the notion of truth, and, while maintaining it, often presents it to us in an extremely attractive way. Leibniz thus recognizes that truth cannot be solely an affair of *actual* propositions, but that unformulated prior propositions (the pre-supposition?) must be found. He grants truth to *non-existent* but *possible* propositions (envisaging a plurality of worlds, including a non-human one). This truth of the sole signifier is suggested in a startling way in the dialogue *De connexione inter res et verba et veritatis realitate* (*New Essays*, IV, v): truth is a network of signs which can be classed according to their printing ink (although Leibniz does admit that truth all the same belongs only to *certain* signs). The more somber Hegel stresses the inseparability of truth from falsity in the Spirit's movement as absolute totality, and, alongside assertions about the possibility of attaining truth in ethics, gives this definition, which acknowledges the importance of the "uncanny": "*The truth is thus the bacchanalian revel, where not a member is sober*; and because every member no sooner becomes detached than it *eo ipso* collapses straightaway, the revel is just as much a state of transparent unbroken calm" (my emphasis).[3]

The break between the concept of a truth which we might call theoretical and which acknowledges the place of the real, and a linguistic-logical truth, is from this point on complete. In its rupture with classical philosophy, logical positivism draws out all the consequences of such a break. Thus, for Frege, truth is confused with reference. *Über Sinn und Bedeutung* therefore postulates that the distinction between truth and falsity does not hold for fiction since its sentences have no reference; but that it applies to historical discourse since the latter is referential.[4] Tarski is even more rigorous in his use of this distinction: "true" and "false" apply only to sentences, not to propositions ("The Concept of Truth in Formalized Languages"); but since the use of a sentence to nominate an existing object is the criterion of its truth, and since this use in natural languages depends on circumstance, then truth, in the strict sense of the term, that is, eternal truth, applies only to formal languages.

This brings us to the end of the chain of development which led the philosophy of logic to exclude the question of its *own* truth as it had originally posed it, from "natural" discourse. Since the namegiver and his true utterance are shown to be an artifice, thought is left with only one alternative: either to conserve this term (truth) for formalized languages and metaphoric (strong) usage in religious discourse; or else to move toward another notion of truth for so-called natural discourses, that is, for differentiated subjective structures. It is the latter which is the wager of the Freudian undertaking.

. . .

In hysterical discourse, truth, when not weighed down by the symptom, often assumes the obsessive, unsayable and emotionally charged weft of visual representation. Floating in isolation, this vision of an unnamed real rejects all nomination and any possible narrative. Instead it remains enigmatic, setting the field of speech ablaze only to reduce it to cold ashes, fixing in this way an hallucinatory and untouchable *jouissance*. Without being able to speak of hysterical psychosis (insofar as the term means anything) it is nonetheless necessary to recognize this as a banal immersion of hysterical discourse in the structures of psychosis: a banality seized upon as a historical provocation in the present feminist dissatisfaction with a language reputed to be too abstract and incapable of rendering the truth of the body: or to put it bluntly, with a language that is phallic. In the hysterical hallucination so current in this discourse, we therefore find ourselves in a border zone where the real, in order to burst on the scene as truth, leaves a hole in the subject's discourse, but is nonetheless taken up by that very discourse in a repetitive representation that produces meaning (thus allowing life and *jouissance* to continue), without creating signification (thus, by producing a too flimsy barrier against the symptom, this process opens the door to the manic-depressive states).

. . .

Benveniste said that Artaud was the greatest French linguist.

To be sure: such a practice of truth cannot be carried out with impunity. Since the signifier is the (sole) truth, it is the body and vice versa. In this economy, there are no *images* or *semblances* (any more than in the Eucharist): each element is neither real, nor symbolic, nor imaginary, but true. Thus the truth of the signifier, namely its separability, otherness, death, can be seen to be exerted on the flesh itself—as on words. The mutilation of the hands of a female painter is perhaps no more or less painful than the displacement of the language she writes or draws. In a man, Artaud, the fundamental sign/body of enunciative truth can only be castration. In Artaud's texts, Abelard and Heliogabalus are perhaps not mere fantasies, but rather the necessary culmination of the process of "true" writing. That this is so is corroborated by the *jouissance* of the text describing these bodies, these moments of castration.

Who can prevent this *jouissance*, this truth, and replace it with the plausibility of reasonable discourse? Here medicine and psychoanalysis encounter the old weapon, the proven balm for use against this sort of wound: religion. The latter is a discourse that creates plausibility through fictional devices (projection, introjection, characters, etc.), and economizes on the signifier as truth and/or as death: castration, and rejection or refuse. And apart from these solutions? There still remains that language-practice in which the true is the beautiful. But can one learn to write? And anyway, who can write alone? The mystery remains, but today its backdrop is a void.

Notes

[1] See my "Object or Complement" in *Polylogue* (Paris: Seuil, 1977), pp. 225–62.

[2] I shall not repeat here what I have written elsewhere of the plausible. See "Meaning and fashion" and "The productivity called text," in *Séméiotiké* (Paris: Seuil, 1969), pp. 60–89 and pp. 208–45, respectively.

[3] G. W. F. Hegel, *The Phenomenology of Mind*, tr. J. B. Baillie (London: Allen & Unwin, 1966), p. 105. My emphasis.

[4] I have tackled the undecidable nature of the reference in literary discourse in "Poetry and negativity," in *Séméiotiké*, pp. 246–77. One question: what is the status of reference in psychotic discourse?

GILLES DELEUZE

The Powers of the False

1985

If we take the history of thought, we see that time has always put the notion of truth into crisis. Not that truth varies depending on the epoch. It is not the simple empirical content, it is the form or rather the pure force of time which puts truth into crisis. Since antiquity this crisis has burst out in the paradox of "contingent futures." If it is *true* that a naval battle *may* take place tomorrow, how are we to avoid one of the true following consequences: either the impossible proceeds from the possible (since, if the battle takes place, it is no longer possible that it may not take place), or the past is not necessarily true (since the battle could not have taken place).[1] It is easy to regard this paradox as a sophism. It nonetheless shows the difficulty of conceiving a direct relation between truth and the form of time, and obliges us to keep the true away from the existent, in the eternal or in what imitates the eternal. We have to wait for Leibniz to get the most ingenious, but also the strangest and most convoluted, solution to this paradox. Leibniz says that the naval battle may or may not take place, but that this is not in the same world: it takes place in one world and does not take place in a different world, and these two worlds are possible, but are not "compossible" with each other.[2] He is thus obliged to forge the wonderful notion of incompossibility (very different from contradiction) in order to resolve the paradox while saving truth: according to him, it is not the impossible, but only the incompossible that proceeds from the possible; and the past may be true without being necessarily true. But the crisis of truth thus enjoys a pause rather than a solution. For nothing prevents us from affirming that incompossibles belong to the same world, that incompossible worlds belong to the same universe: "Fang, for example, has a secret; a stranger calls at his door . . . Fang can kill the intruder, the intruder can kill Fang, they can both escape, they can both die, and so forth . . . you arrive at this house, but in one of the possible pasts you are my enemy, in another, my friend . . ."[3] This Borges's reply to Leib-

From *Cinema 2: The Time-Image*, trans. Hugh Tomlinson and Robert Galeta (Minneapolis: University of Minnesota Press, 1989), pp. 130–31 ["Les puissances du faux," in *Cinéma 2: L'image-temps* (Paris: Editions de Minuit, 1985)].

niz: the straight line as force of time, as labyrinth of time, is also the line which forks and keeps on forking, passing through *incompossible presents*, returning to *not-necessarily true pasts*.

A new status of narration follows from this: narration ceases to be truthful, that is, to claim to be true, and becomes fundamentally falsifying. This is not at all a case of "each has its own truth," a variability of content. It is a power of the false which replaces and supersedes the form of the true, because it poses the simultaneity of incompossible presents, or the coexistence of not-necessarily true pasts. Crystalline description was already reaching the indiscernibility of the real and the imaginary, but the falsifying narration which corresponds to it goes a step further and poses inexplicable differences to the present and alternatives which are undecidable between true and false to the past. The truthful man dies, every model of truth collapses, in favor of the new narration. We have not mentioned the author who is essential in this regard: it is Nietzsche, who, under the name of "will to power," substitutes the power of the false for the form of the true, and resolves the crisis of truth, wanting to settle it once and for all, but, in opposition to Leibniz, in favor of the false and its artistic, creative power . . .

Notes

[1] Cf. P. M. Schuhl, *Le dominateur et les possibles*, PUF (on the role of this paradox in Greek philosophy). Jules Vuillemin has taken up the whole question in *Nécessité ou contingence*, Editions de Minuit.

[2] Cf. Leibniz, *Theodicy*, Sections 414–16; in this astonishing text, which we consider a source of all modern literature, Leibniz presents "contingent futures" as so many compartments making up a pyramid of crystal. In one compartment Sextus does not go to Rome and cultivates his garden in Corinth; in another he becomes king in Thrace; but in another, he goes to Rome and takes power . . . It will be noticed that this text is presented in a very complex and inextricable narration, even though it presumes to save the Truth; it is first a dialogue between Valla and Antony, in which is inserted another dialogue between Sextus and the oracle of Apollo, then this is succeeded by a third dialogue, Sextus and Jupiter, which gives way to the Theodorus and Pallas discussion at the end of which Theodorus wakes up.

[3] Borges, "The garden with forking paths," in *Labyrinths*, trans. Donald A. Yates, Harmondsworth: Penguin, 1970.

ALAIN BADIOU

Veracity and Truth from the Standpoint of the Faithful Procedure: Forcing

1988

Since the language with which a subject surrounds itself is separated from its real universe by unlimited chance, what possible sense could there be in declaring a statement pronounced in this language to be veridical? The external witness, the man of knowledge, necessarily declares that these statements are devoid of sense ("the obscurity of a poetic language," "propaganda" for a political procedure, etc.). Signifiers without any signified. Sliding without quilting point. In fact, the meaning of a subject-language is *under condition*. Constrained to refer solely to what the situation presents, and yet bound to the future anterior of the existence of an indiscernible, a statement made up of the names of a subject-language has merely a hypothetical signification. From inside the faithful procedure, it sounds like this: "*If* I suppose that the indiscernible truth contains or presents such or such a term submitted to the enquiry by chance, *then* such a statement in the subject-language will have had such a meaning and will (or won't) have been veridical." I say "will have been" because the veracity in question is relative to that *other* situation, the situation-to-come in which a truth of the first situation (an indiscernible part), will have been presented.

A subject always declares meaning in the future anterior. What is *present* are terms of the situation on the one hand, and names of the subject-language on the other. Yet this distinction is artificial, because the names, being themselves presented (despite being empty), *are* terms of the situation. What exceeds the situation is the referential meaning of the names; such meaning exists solely within the retroaction of the *existence* (thus of the presentation) of an indiscernible part of the situation. One can therefore say: such a statement of the subject-language will have been veridical if the truth is such or such.

But of this "such or such" of a truth, the subject solely controls—because it is such—the finite fragment made up of the present state of the enquiries. All

From *Being and Event*, trans. Oliver Feltham (New York: Continuum, 2006), pp. 400–406 ["Véridicité et vérité du point de vue de la procédure fidèle: le forçage," in *L'être et l'événement* (Paris: Editions du Seuil, 1988)].

the rest is a matter of confidence, or of knowing belief. Is this sufficient for the legitimate formulation of a hypothesis of connection between what a *truth* presents and the *veracity* of a statement that bears upon the names of a subject-language? Doesn't the infinite incompletion of a truth prevent any possible evaluation, *inside* the situation, of the veracity-to-come of a statement whose referential universe is suspended from the chance, itself to-come, of encounters, and thus of enquiries?

When Galileo announced the principle of inertia, he was still separated from the truth of the new physics by all the chance encounters that are named in subjects such as Descartes or Newton. How could he, with the names he fabricated and displaced (because they were at hand—"movement," "equal proportion," etc.), have supposed the veracity of his principle *for* the situation-to-come that was the establishment of modern science; that is, the supplementation of his situation with the indiscernible and unfinishable part that one has to name "rational physics"? In the same manner, when he radically suspended tonal functions, what musical veracity could Schoenberg have assigned to the notes and timbres prescribed in his scores in regard to that—even today—quasi-indiscernible part of the situation named "contemporary music"? If the names are empty, and their system of reference suspended, what are the criteria, from the standpoint of the finite configurations of the generic procedure, of veracity?

What comes into play here is termed, of necessity, a *fundamental law of the subject* (it is also a law of the future anterior). This law is the following: if a statement of the subject-language is such that it will have been veridical for a situation in which a truth has occurred, this is because *a* term of the situation exists which both belongs to that truth (belongs to the generic part which *is* that truth) and maintains a particular relation with the names at stake in the statement. This relation is determined by the encyclopaedic determinants of the situation (of knowledge). This law thus amounts to saying that one can *know*, in a situation in which a post-evental truth is being deployed, whether a statement of the subject-language has a chance of being veridical in the situation which adds to the initial situation a truth of the latter. It suffices to verify the existence of *one* term linked to the statement in question by a relation that is itself discernible in the situation. If such a term exists, then its belonging to the truth (to the indiscernible part which is the multiple-being of a truth) will impose the veracity of the initial statement within the *new* situation.

Of this law, there exists an ontological version, discovered by Cohen. Its lineaments will be revealed in Meditation 36. Its importance, however, is such that its concept must be explained in detail and illustrated with as many examples as possible.

Let's start with a caricature. In the framework of the scientific procedure that is Newtonian astronomy, I can, on the basis of observable perturbations in the trajectory of certain planets, state the following: "An as yet unobserved planet distorts the trajectories by gravitational attraction." The operator of connection here is pure *calculation*, combined with existing observations. It is certain that *if* this planet exists (in the sense in which observation, since it is in the process of being perfected, will end up encountering an object that it does classify amongst the planets), *then* the statement "a supplementary planet exists" will have been veridical in the universe constituted by the solar system supplemented by scientific astronomy. There are two other possible cases:

— that it is impossible to justify the aberrations in the trajectory by the surmise of a supplementary planet belonging to the solar system (this *before* the calculations), and that it is not known what other hypothesis to make concerning their cause;
— or that the supposed planet does not exist.

What happens in these two cases? In the first case, I do not possess the *knowledge* of a fixed (calculable) relation between the statement "something is inflecting the trajectory" (a statement composed of names of science—and "something" indicates that one of these names is empty), and *a* term of the situation, a specifiable term (a planet with a calculable mass) whose scientifically observable existence in the solar system (that is, this system, plus its truth) would give meaning and veracity to my statement. In the second case, the relation exists (expert calculations allow the conclusion that this "something" must be a planet); but I do not *encounter* a term within the situation which validates this relation. It follows that my statement is "not yet" veridical in respect to astronomy.

This image illustrates two features of the fundamental law of the subject:

— Since the knowable relation between *a* term and a statement of the subject-language must exist within the encyclopedia of the situation, it is quite possible that *no* term validates this relation for a given statement. In this case, I have no means of anticipating the latter's veracity, from the standpoint of the generic procedure.
— It is also possible that there does exist a term of the situation which maintains with a statement of the subject-language the knowable relation in question, but that it has not yet been investigated, such that I do not know whether it belongs or not to the indiscernible part that is the truth (the result, in infinity, of the generic procedure). In this case, the veracity of the statement is *suspended*. I remain separated from it by the chance of the enquiries' trajectory. However, what I can anticipate is this: *if* I encounter this term, and it turns out to be connected to the name of the event, that is, to belong to the indiscernible multiple-being of a truth, *then*, in the situation-to-come in which this truth exists, the statement will have been veridical.

Let's decide on the terminology. I will term "forcing" the relation implied in the fundamental law of the subject. That a term of the situation *forces* a statement of the subject-language means that the veracity of this statement in the situation-to-come is equivalent to the belonging of this term to the indiscernible part which results from the generic procedure. It thus means that this term, bound to the statement by the relation of forcing, belongs to the truth. Or rather, this term, encountered by the subject's aleatory trajectory, has been *positively* investigated with respect to its connection to the name of the event. A term forces a statement if its positive connection to the event forces the statement to be veridical in the new situation (the situation supplemented by an indiscernible truth). Forcing is a relation *verifiable by knowledge*, since it bears on a term of the situation (which is thus presented and named in the language of the situation) and a statement of the subject-language (whose names are "cobbled together" from multiples of the situation). What is *not* verifiable by knowledge is whether the term that forces a statement belongs or not to the indiscernible. Its belonging is uniquely down to the chance of the enquiries.

In regard to the statements which can be formulated in the subject-language, and whose referent (thus, the universe of sense) is suspended from infinity (and it is *for* this suspended sense that there is forcing of veracity), three possibilities can be identified, each discernible by knowledge inside the situation, and thus free of any surmise concerning the indiscernible part (the truth):

a. The statement cannot be forced: it does not support the relation of forcing with *any* term of the situation. The possibility of it being veridical is thus ruled out, whatever the truth may be;

b. The statement can be universally forced: it maintains the relation of forcing with *all* the terms of the situation. Since some of these terms (an infinity) will be contained in the truth, whatever it may be, the statement will always be veridical in any situation-to-come;

c. The statement can be forced by certain terms, but not by others. Everything depends, in respect to the future anterior of veracity, on the chance of the enquiries. If and when *a* term which forces the statement will have been positively investigated, the statement will be veridical in the situation-to-come in which the indiscernible (to which this term belongs) supplements the situation for which it is indiscernible. However, this case is neither *factually* guaranteed (since I could still be separated from such an enquiry by innumerable chance encounters), nor guaranteed *in principle* (since the forcing terms could be negatively investigated, and thus not feature in a truth). The statement is thus not forced to be veridical.

A subject is a local evaluator of self-mentioning statements: he or she *knows*—with regard to the situation-to-come, thus from the standpoint of the indiscernible—that these statements are either certainly wrong, or possibly veridical but suspended from the will-have-taken-place of *one* positive enquiry.

Let's try to make forcing and the distribution of evaluations tangible.

Take Mallarmé's statement: "The poetic act consists in suddenly seeing an idea fragment into a number of motifs equal in value, and in grouping them." It is a statement of the subject-language, a self-mentioner of the state of a finite configuration of the poetic generic procedure. The referential universe of this statement—in particular, the signifying value of the words "idea" and "motifs"—is suspended from an indiscernible of the literary situation: a state of poetry that will have been beyond the "crisis in verse." Mallarmé's poems and prose pieces—and those of others—are enquiries whose grouping-together defines this indiscernible as the truth of French poetry after Hugo. A local configuration of this procedure is a subject (for example, whatever is designated in pure presentation by the signifier "Mallarmé"). Forcing is what a knowledge can discern of the relation between the above statement and this or that poem (or collection): the conclusion to be drawn is that if this poem is "representative" of post-Hugo poetic truth, then the statement concerning the poetical act will be verifiable in knowledge—and so veridical—in the situation-to-come in which this truth exists (that is, in a universe in which the "new poetry," posterior to the crisis in verse, is actually presented and no longer merely announced). It is evident that such a poem must be the vector of relationships—discernible in the situation—between itself and, for example, those initially empty words "idea" and "motifs." The existence of this *unique* poem—and what it detains in terms of encounters, evaluated positively, would guarantee the veracity of the statement "The poetic act . . ." in any poetic situation-to-come which contained it—was termed by Mallarmé "the Book." But after all, the savant's study of *Un coup de dés . . .* in Meditation 19 is equivalent to a demonstration that the enquiry—the text—has definitely encountered a term which, at the very least, forces Mallarmé's statement to be veridical; that is, the statement that what is at stake in a modern poem is the motif of an idea (ultimately, the very idea of the event). The relation of forcing is here detained within the analysis of the text.

Now let's consider the statement: "The factory is a political site."[1] This statement is phrased in the subject-language of the post Marxist-Leninist political procedure. The referential universe of this statement requires the occurrence of that indiscernible of the situation which is politics in a non-parliamentary and non-Stalinian mode. The enquiries are the militant interventions and enquiries of the factory. It can be determined *a priori* (we can know) that workers, factory-sites, and sub-situations force the above statement to be veridical in every universe in which the existence of a currently indiscernible mode of politics will have been established. It is possible that the procedure has arrived at a point at which workers have been positively investigated, and at which the veracity-to-come of the statement is guaranteed. It is equally possible that this not be the case, but then the conclusion to be drawn would be solely that the chance of the encounters must be pursued, and the procedure maintained. The veracity is merely suspended.

A contrario, if one examines the neo-classical musical reaction between the two wars, it is noticeable that no term of the musical situation defined in its own language by this tendency can force the veracity of the statement "music is essentially tonal." The enquiries (the neo-classical works) can continue to appear, one after the other, hereafter and evermore. However, Schoenberg having existed, not one of them ever encounters anything which is in a knowable relation of forcing with this statement. Knowledge alone decides the question here; in other words, the neo-classical procedure *is not generic* (as a matter of fact, it is constructivist—see Meditation 29).

Finally, a subject is at the intersection, via its language, of knowledge and truth. Local configuration of a generic procedure, it is suspended from the indiscernible. Capable of conditionally forcing the veracity of a statement of its language for a situation-to-come (the one in which the truth exists) it is the savant of itself. A subject is a knowledge suspended by a truth whose finite moment it is.

Note

[1] On the factory as a political place, cf. *Le perroquet*, nos. 56–57, Nov.–Dec., 1985, in particular Paul Sandevince's article.

PART III

Questions of Difference

Foucault took the vision of uncertainty and indetermination in philosophy that Merleau-Ponty developed in his inaugural lecture of 1953 at the Collège de France, *In Praise of Philosophy*, as an antecedent for his own idea of "problematization," which he elaborated in the 1980s in terms of the critical activity of "getting away from oneself" and one's certainties. In the interval between these two moments of principled uncertainty, we find a long development of the constitutive role of question, problem, aporia, or paradox in philosophy, taken up by many different authors and idioms. There is a sense in which the new kind of critique sought in philosophy was itself primarily a questioning or problematizing activity, one that supposes a responsibility for the uneliminable aporias in all thought or all positions in thought, or one that is given through an unending dissensual space of contestation in all constituted forms of power or social division. For Foucault, the question of enlightenment in Kant's "age of critique" or in relation to the signs of Revolution would itself be taken anew, reformulated in French philosophy in terms of the very idea of questioning itself. As Deleuze would put it, in philosophy the question always persists in the solutions given to it, such that philosophical questions are themselves constantly being reformulated or recast, themselves constantly being declared "false" or, in the words of Wittgenstein, "dissolved." Thus Foucault's skepticism about anthropological universals supposed a constant activity of breaking with the self-evidence (*évidences*), thus opening up or "eventalizing" history itself.

But while Foucault tried to introduce this questioning within the heart of the philosophy of the concept, it was also at the same time elaborated in other ways, as already with Merleau-Ponty's praise. The theme of "difference" in French philosophy is inseparable from the notion of a change in the image of thought based in constitutive paradox, non-sense, or aporia. Thus when Derrida tried to derive the idea from Heidegger in contrast to Husserl, it was only to then rethink the whole idea of "the question" in Heidegger's own thinking. When Deleuze first introduced the idea in a new reading of Bergson, he would extend it not only to the paradoxical element in structuralism but also to the new idea of critique and experimentation in Nietzsche. A notion of questions of difference was thus to be found not only in Merleau-Ponty's phenomenological indeterminations but also in the peculiarities of the idea of structure elaborated through what might be called the paradoxes of identification in it: Lacan's "purloined letter," always "missing-from-its-place," or Lévi-Strauss's "floating signifer," always exceeding the divisions introduced by a given language or symbolic system. It was this idea that Jean-Claude Milner would go on to develop as the "paradoxical sets" within all forms of subjective identification. When Derrida dramatically introduced an *a* into "*différance*," declaring that it was neither a word nor a concept, it was this larger space of questioning he was trying to get at. Deleuze's attempt to free the very idea of difference from its subordination to the identities of contradiction, logical or dialectical, was to give it a larger and paradoxical role in thought, anticipated by Kant's Ideas and paralogisms. Thus, when Foucault himself introduced his idea of the "historical a priori" in 1969, he took as a basic presupposition of those threshold moments of change in discursive systems that "we are differences" and are always becoming-other than who or what we had supposed ourselves to be.

At first, the interconnected notions of difference, paradox, and question were developed mostly as a logical or (negative) ontological matter, part of a new image of thought. But later, in the 1980s, they would be taken up and developed again in terms of the social or political presuppositions of thought or of what it means to think together in community, solidarity, or friendship: what Rancière would call the "community of equals," Nancy "the inoperative community," and Lyotard the peculiar "we" of a *différend*. We then find an engagement not simply with logic or knowledge but with juridical thinking and institutions, and the corresponding ideas of equality and justice as they are in turn reflected in philosophy. How do problematizations interrupt the history of the rule of law? What is the nature of wrongs for which there preexists no agreed means of settlement and which thus confront us with question and dissensus? What notion of justice itself would include the potential for such questions? In what kind of space are they shared or "distributed?" And how would they lead to a rethinking of democratic politics?

The form of such questions is therefore never the old Platonic one, "What is an *x*?" or its transcendental or dialectical variants. Questions of that type presuppose the sort of fixed classifications or taxonomies that the idea of a prior "difference" was precisely thought to undo. As a logical matter, that was in fact the central theme in Deleuze's 1956 essay on Bergson—what kind of question arises when the notion of difference or multiplicity is freed from the laws of contradiction and ontologies of reidentifiable or denumerable entities and worked out instead through "complex repetitions" or paradoxical "disjunctive syntheses?" As in Foucault's elaboration of the "heterotopia" in Borges's Chinese encyclopedia, a kind of paradoxical humor accompanies such philosophical questioning, not to be confused with ironic negations, Socratic or Romantic. It is rather a matter of "sense" or "making sense," and the very idea of sense or institutions of sense must be rethought to include it. Thus the problem of sense or *Sinn* had itself been dislodged from its role both in Frege (associated with public conditions for the "truth-conditions" of propositions or rules of reference or denotation) and in Husserl (as part of a search for intersubjective Urdoxa of the life-world, grounding all experience). Rather, there is no such public or instituted sense of propositional truths or intersubjective conditions of agreement without a prior zone from which new questions arise.

Deleuze's question was then how to put an experience of the question or of difference first in thought, prior to fixed methods or shared common sense, and what this means for the very idea of philosophical questions themselves and the ways they are repeated and can be taken up anew today. It was an early formulation of a question that, accompanying notions of "difference," would have a long life. Deleuze would go on to develop his idea of a paradoxical "disjunctive synthesis" and "heterogenesis of ideas" in terms of a larger picture of the conceptual constructions and dramas within which new questions arise, new concepts invented. What Deleuze developed as a matter of non-sense in the generation or "giving" of sense would become for Derrida a matter of the assumptions of a "proper sense" and a free "dissemination" outside its metaphysical enclosure, leading to a long engagement with the notion of philosophy as questioning in Heidegger, for which he would eventually substitute the term "aporia" and related "chances" of thinking. In both cases we find questions of the untranslatability or foreignness of the language of philosophical concepts or ideas.

If for Deleuze philosophy is paradoxical as such, if the peculiar concepts it invents are always strange or foreign since there preexists no words for them, it is because they come from new problems or questions which, in turn, persist in the solutions given to them, later to be reformulated and taken up from a new angle. Conversely, new questions always introduce differences that don't reduce to distinctions, oppositions, or simple binaries but instead translate a sense of possibility and impossibility in what we can say, see, and do. That is just what makes them, in contrast to resolvable puzzles or problem sets, a philosophical matter. The unruly differential element in all institutions of sense, from which new questions come, is thus not a matter of mere noise, chaos, or absurdity any more than it is a matter of logical contradiction or possibility in discourse, as a persistent dogmatic image of thought in philosophy would have us believe. On the contrary, it and its paradoxical or aporetic experience becomes a peculiar condition of thinking itself, prior not simply to programmatic method but also to community or what it means to think together. For, as Foucault would retort to Richard Rorty's talk of "solidarity," the we never preexists the question; it always comes after as part of the larger experiment to which new questions give rise, such that there are questions posed *to* politics as distinct from particular political questions and their solutions. At the same time, Derrida's attempt to recast the kind of deconstructive questioning he had found in Levinas in terms of an aporetic element in all programmatic thought moved in the direction of a reexamination of the idea of friendship and so of a community and a response-ability, which would allow for the arrival of something "altogether other" yet to come. Questions of difference then became tied up with a larger complex of problems, from which fresh divisions would derive in turn.

CLAUDE LÉVI-STRAUSS

Introduction to the Work of Marcel Mauss

1950

There is nothing to prevent us from continuing Mauss's thinking in the other direction: the direction which the *Essai sur le don* was to define, after overcoming the equivocation that we noted earlier in reference to *hau*. For, luckily, whereas *mana* comes at the end of the *Esquisse*, *hau* only appears at the beginning of the *Essai sur le don*, and it is treated throughout as a point of departure, and not a goal. If we were to project the conception of exchange, which Mauss there invites us to formulate, back on to the notion of *mana*, where would it take us? It has to be admitted that, like *hau*, *mana* is no more than the subjective reflection of the need to supply an unperceived totality. Exchange is not a complex edifice built on the obligations of giving, receiving and returning, with the help of some emotional-mystical cement. It is a synthesis immediately given to, and given by, symbolic thought, which, in exchange as in any other form of communication, surmounts the contradiction inherent in it; that is the contradiction of perceiving things as elements of dialogue, in respect of self and others simultaneously, and destined by nature to pass from the one to the other. The fact that those things may be *the one's* or *the other's* represents a situation which is derivative from the initial relational aspect. But does not the same apply in the case of magic? Magical reasoning, implied in the action of producing smoke to elicit clouds and rain, is not grounded in a primordial distinction between smoke and cloud, with an appeal to *mana* to weld the one to the other, but in the fact that a deeper level of thinking identifies smoke with cloud; that the one is, at least in a certain respect, the same thing as the other: that identification is what justifies the subsequent association, and not the other way round. All magical operations rest on the restoring of a unity; not a lost unity (for nothing is ever lost) but an unconscious one, or one which is less completely conscious than those operations themselves. The notion of *mana* does not belong to the order of the real, but to the order of thinking, which, even when it thinks itself, only ever thinks an object.

From *Introduction to the Work of Marcel Mauss*, trans. Felicity Baker (London: Routledge & Kegan Paul, 1987), pp. 58–64 [*Introduction à l'oeuvre de Marcel Mauss* (Paris: Presses Universitaires de France, 1950)].

It is in that relational aspect of symbolic thinking that we can look for the answer to our problem. Whatever may have been the moment and the circumstances of its appearance in the ascent of animal life, language can only have arisen all at once. Things cannot have begun to signify gradually. In the wake of a transformation which is not a subject of study for the social sciences, but for biology and psychology, a shift occurred from a stage when nothing had a meaning to another stage when everything had meaning. Actually, that apparently banal remark is important, because that radical change has no counterpart in the field of knowledge, which develops slowly and progressively. In other words, at the moment when the entire universe all at once became *significant*, it was none the better *known* for being so, even if it is true that the emergence of language must have hastened the rhythm of the development of knowledge. So there is a fundamental opposition, in the history of the human mind, between symbolism, which is characteristically discontinuous, and knowledge, characterized by continuity. Let us consider what follows from that. It follows that the two categories of the signifier and the signified came to be constituted simultaneously and interdependently, as complementary units; whereas knowledge, that is, the intellectual process which enables us to identify certain aspects of the signifier and certain aspects of the signified, one by reference to the other—we could even say the process which enables us to choose, from the entirety of the signifier and from the entirety of the signified, those parts which present the most satisfying relations of mutual agreement—only got started very slowly. It is as if humankind had suddenly acquired an immense domain and the detailed plan of that domain, along with a notion of the reciprocal relationship of domain and plan; but had spent millennia learning which specific symbols of the plan represented the different aspects of the domain. The universe signified long before people began to know what it signified; no doubt that goes without saying. But, from the foregoing analysis, it also emerges that from the beginning, the universe signified the totality of what humankind can expect to know about it. What people call the process of the human mind and, in any case, the progress of scientific knowledge, could only have been and can only ever be constituted out of processes of correcting and recutting of patterns, regrouping, defining relationships of belonging and discovering new resources, inside a totality which is closed and complementary to itself.

We appear to be far removed from *mana*, but in reality we are extremely close to it. For, although the human race has always possessed an enormous mass of positive knowledge, and although the different societies have devoted more or less effort to maintaining and developing it, it is nonetheless in very recent times that scientific thinking became established as authority and that forms of societies emerged in which the intellectual and moral ideal, at the same time as the practical ends pursued by the social body, became organized around scientific knowledge, elected as the center of reference in an official and deliberate way. The difference is one of degree, not of nature, but it does exist. We can therefore expect the relationship between symbolism and knowledge to conserve common features in the non-industrial societies and in our own, although those features would not be equally pronounced in the two types of society. It does not mean that we are creating a gulf between them, if we acknowledge that the work of equalizing of the signifier to fit the signified has been pursued more methodically and rigorously from the time when modern science was born, and within the boundaries of the spread of science. But everywhere else, and still constantly in our own societies (and no doubt for a long time to come), a fundamental situation perseveres which arises out of the human condition: namely, that man has from the start had at his disposition a signifier-totality which he is at a loss to know how to allocate to a signified, given as such, but no less unknown for being given. There is always a non-equivalence or "inadequation" between the two, a non-fit and overspill which divine understanding alone can soak up; this generates a signifier-surfeit relative to the signifieds to which it can be fitted. So, in man's effort to understand the world, he always disposes of a surplus of signification (which he shares out among things in accordance with the laws of the symbolic thinking which it is the task of ethnologists and linguists to study). That distribution of a supplementary ration—if I can express myself thus—is absolutely necessary to ensure that, in total, the available signifier and the mapped-out signified may remain in the relationship of complementarity which is the very condition of the exercise of symbolic thinking.

I believe that notions of the *mana* type, however diverse they may be, and viewed in terms of their most general function (which, as we have seen, has not vanished from our mentality and our form of society), represent nothing more or less than that *floating signifier* which is the disability of all finite thought (but also the surety of all art, all poetry, every mythic and aesthetic invention), even though scientific knowledge is capable, if not of stanching it, at least of controlling it partially. Moreover, magical thinking offers other, different methods of channeling and containment, with different results, and all these methods can very well coexist. In other words, accepting the inspiration of Mauss's precept that all social phenomena can be assimilated to language, I see in *mana, wakan, orenda*, and other notions of the same type, the conscious expression of a *semantic function*, whose role is to enable symbolic thinking to operate despite the contradiction inherent in it. That explains the apparently insoluble antinomies attaching to the notion of *mana*, which struck ethnographers so forcibly, and on which Mauss shed light: force and action; quality and state; substantive, adjective and verb all at once; abstract and concrete; omnipresent and localized. And, indeed, *mana* is all those things together; but is that not precisely because it is none of those things, but a simple form, or to be more accurate, a symbol in its pure state, therefore liable to take on any symbolic content whatever. In the system of symbols which makes up any cosmology, it would just be a *zero symbolic value*, that is, a sign marking the necessity of a supplementary symbolic content over and above that which the signified already contains, which can be any value at all, provided it is still part of the available reserve, and is not already, as the phonologists say, a term in a set.[1]

Note

[1] Linguists have already been led to formulate hypotheses of this type. For instance: "A zero-phoneme . . . is opposed to all other French phonemes by the absence both of distinctive features and of a constant sound characteristic. On the other hand, the zero-phoneme . . . is opposed to the absence of any phoneme whatsoever" (R. Jakobson and J. Lotz, "Notes on the French phonemic pattern," 1949, p. 155).

MAURICE MERLEAU-PONTY

In Praise of Philosophy

1953

Bergson wanted to be finished with traditional problems, not to eliminate the problematic of philosophy but to revivify it. He saw so clearly that all philosophy must be, in the words of Le Roy, a new philosophy, that it is so little the discovery of a solution inscribed in being which satisfies our curiosity, that he demands of it not only the invention of solutions but the invention of its own problems. In 1935 he wrote: "I call an *amateur* in philosophy anyone who accepts the terms of a usual problem as they are . . . doing philosophy authentically would consist in *creating* the framework of the problem and of *creating* the solution." Thus when he says that well-posed problems are very close to being solved, this does not mean that we have already *found* what we are looking for, but that we have already invented it. It is not that there would be a question in us and a response in things, an exterior being to be discovered by an observing consciousness; the solution is also in us, and being itself is problematic. Something of the nature of the question passes into the answer.

The famous Bergsonian coincidence certainly does not mean, then, that the philosopher loses himself or is absorbed into being. We must say rather that he experiences himself as transcended by being. It is not necessary for him to go outside himself in order to reach the things themselves; he is solicited or haunted by them from within. For an ego which is *durée* cannot grasp another being except in the form of another *durée*. By experiencing my own manner of using up time, I grasp it, says Bergson, as a "choice among an infinity of possible *durées*." There is a "singular nature" of the *durée* which makes it at once my manner of being and a universal dimension for other beings in such a way that what is "superior" and "inferior" to us still remains "in a certain sense, interior to us." What I observe is a concordance and a discordance of things with my *durée*; these are the things with me in a lateral relationship of coexistence. I have the idea of a *durée* of the universe distinct from mine only because it extends the whole length of mine and because it is necessary that something in

From *In Praise of Philosophy*, trans. John Wild and James M. Edie (Evanston, IL: Northwestern University Press, 1963), pp. 14–15, 41–42 [*Eloge de la philosophie* (Paris: Editions Gallimard, 1953)].

the melting sugar respond to my waiting for a glass of sugar water. When we are at the source of the *durée*, we are also at the heart of things because they are the adversity which makes us wait. The relation of the philosopher to being is not the frontal relation of the spectator to the spectacle; it is a kind of complicity, an oblique and clandestine relationship. We understand now how Bergson can say that the absolute is "very close to us and, in a certain measure, in us." It is in the way in which things modulate our *durée*.

. . .

It is possible to fear that our time also is rejecting the philosopher that dwells within it, and that once again philosophy will evaporate into nothing but *clouds*. For to philosophize is to seek, and this is to imply that there are things to see and to say. Well, today we no longer seek. We "return" to one or the other of our traditions and "defend" it. Our convictions are founded less on perceived values and truths than on the vices and errors of those we do not like. We love very few things, though we dislike many. Our thinking is a thought in retreat or in reply. Each of us is expiating for his youth. This decadence is in accord with the course of our history. Having passed a certain point of tension, ideas cease to develop and live. They fall to the level of justifications and pretexts, relics of the past, points of honor; and what one pompously calls the movement of ideas is reduced to the sum of our nostalgias, our grudges, our timidities, and our phobias. In this world, where negation and gloomy passion take the place of certitude, one does not seek above all to see, and, because it seeks to see, philosophy passes for impiety. It would be easy to show this in connection with two absolutes which are at the center of our discussions: God and history.

GILLES DELEUZE

Bergson's Conception of Difference

1956

Duration can be presented as substance itself insofar as duration is simple, indivisible. Alteration must therefore maintain itself and achieve its status without allowing itself to be reduced to plurality, to contradiction, or even to alterity. Internal difference will have to distinguish itself from *contradiction, alterity*, and *negation*. This is precisely where Bergson's method and theory of difference are opposed to the other theory, the other method of difference called dialectic, whether it's Plato's dialectic of alterity or Hegel's dialectic of contradiction, each of which implies the presence and the power of the negative. The originality of Bergson's conception resides in showing that internal difference does not go, and is not required to go as far as contradiction, alterity, and negativity, because these three notions are in fact less profound than itself, or they are viewpoints only from the outside. The real sense of Bergson's endeavor is thinking internal difference as such, as pure internal difference, and raising difference up to the absolute.

Duration is only one of two tendencies, one of two halves. So, if we accept that it differs from itself in all its being, does it not contain the secret of the other half? How could it still leave external to itself *that from which* it differs, namely the other tendency? If duration differs from itself, that from which it differs is still duration in a certain sense. It is not a question of dividing duration in the same way we divided what is composite: duration is simple, indivisible, pure. The simple is not divided, *it differentiates itself*. This is the essence of the simple, or the movement of difference. So, the composite divides into two tendencies, one of which is the indivisible, but the indivisible differentiates itself into two tendencies, the other of which is the principle of the divisible. Space is broken up into matter and duration, but duration differentiates itself into contraction and relaxation; and relaxation is the principle of matter. Organic form is broken up into matter and *élan vital*, but the *élan vital* differentiates itself into instinct

From *Desert Islands and Other Texts, 1953–1974*, ed. David Lapoujade and trans. Michael Taormina (Los Angeles, CA: Semiotext[e], 2004), pp. 38–39, 49–51 ["La conception de la différence chez Bergson," in *L'île déserte et autres textes* (Paris: Editions de Minuit, 2002); first published in *Les études bergsoniennes* 4 (1956), pp. 77–112].

and intelligence; and intelligence is the principle of the transformation of matter into space. Clearly, the composite is not broken up in the same way that the simple differentiates itself: the method of difference takes both these two movements together. But now this power of differentiation must be examined. It is this power which will lead us to the pure concept of internal difference. To determine such a concept, we will have to show *in what way* that which differs from duration, i.e., the other half, can still be duration.

. . .

Bergson can leave many readers with a certain impression of vagueness and incoherence: vagueness, because we learn in the end that difference is the unforeseeable, indetermination itself; and incoherence, because he seems to recycle for his own purposes the same notions he just finished criticizing. We see him attacking degrees, and here they come front and center in duration itself to the point that Bergsonism seems a philosophy of degrees: "One moves by imperceptible degrees from recollections deposited throughout time to movements that outline nascent or possible action in space";[1] "recollection is thus gradually transformed into perception";[2] "similarly, there are degrees of liberty."[3] Bergson especially attacks intensity, and yet relaxation and contraction are invoked as fundamental principles of explanation: "between brute matter and the most reflective mind, are all the possible intensities of memory or, what amounts to the same thing, all the degrees of liberty."[4] Finally, Bergson attacks the negative and opposition, but they slip in the back door with inversion: geometrical order partakes of the negative, it comes from "the inversion of genuine positivity," "from an interruption";[5] and if we compare science and philosophy, we see that science is not relative, but "is about a reality of an inverse order."[6]

This impression of incoherence, however, I believe is unjustified. It is true that Bergson does come back to degrees, but not to differences of degree. His idea is this: there are no differences of degree in nature, only *degrees of difference itself*. Theories that rely on differences of degree mix everything up, because they fail to see differences of nature; they lose themselves in space and in the composites which space gives us. Furthermore, that which differs in nature is in the end that which differs in nature *from itself*; consequently, that from which it differs is only its lowest *degree*; this is duration, defined as difference of nature itself. When the difference of nature between two things has become one of the two things, the other of the two is only the *last* degree of the first. So it is that difference of nature, when it appears in person, is exactly the virtual coexistence of two *extreme* degrees. Since they are extremes, the twofold current passing between them forms intermediate degrees. These constitute the principle of composites and make us believe in differences of degree, but only if we examine them for themselves, forgetting that the extremities which they unite are two things that differ in nature. In fact, the extremities are degrees of difference itself. Therefore, that which differs is relaxation and contraction, matter and duration as the degrees, the intensities of difference. And in general, if Bergson does not thus simply fall back on differences of degree, neither does he come back to differences of intensity in particular. Relaxation and contraction are the degrees of difference itself only because they are opposed, in as much as they are opposed. As extremes, they are the *inverse* of each other. Bergson criticizes metaphysics for not having seen that relaxation and contraction are the inverse of each other; metaphysics believed they were only two more or less intense degrees in the degradation of the same immobile, stable, eternal Being.[7] In fact, just as degrees are explained by difference and not the reverse, so intensities are explained by inversion and presuppose it. There is no immobile and stable Being as principle; *the point of departure* is contraction itself; it is duration, whose relaxation is inversion. Bergson's concern with finding a genuine beginning, a genuine point of departure, shows up again and again, e.g., perception and affection: we will begin with action instead of affection because nothing can be said of affection, since there is no reason for it to be what is rather than something else."[8] But why is relaxation the inverse of contraction, and not contraction the inverse of relaxation? Because *philosophy precisely begins with difference*, and because difference of nature is that duration of which matter is only the lowest degree. Difference is the genuine beginning; it is in this respect that Bergson most diverges from Schelling, at least in appearance. By beginning with something else, on the other hand, some immobile and stable Being, indifference becomes posited as first principle, less is mistaken for more, and a simple view of intensities becomes inevitable. However, when Bergson makes inversion the basis for intensity, he seems to escape this view only to come back to negativity, to opposition. Again, in this instance, such an objection is not entirely exact. Ultimately, the opposition of the two terms that differ in nature is only the positive actualization of a virtuality that contained them both. The role of the intermediate degrees resides precisely in this actualization: they insert one in the other, the recollection in the movement. So, in my view, there is no incoherence in Bergson's philosophy, but there is a profound reconsideration of the concept of difference. Nor do I believe that indetermination is a vague concept. Indetermination, the unforeseeable, contingency, freedom—these all signify a certain independence with respect to causes: in this sense, Bergson honors the *élan vital* with many contingencies.[9] What he means is that the thing is in a certain way *prior* to causes; we must begin with the thing because the causes come after. Indetermination, however, always only means that the thing or the action could have been otherwise. "Could the act have been other?" That is a meaningless question. What Bergson demands of himself is to make us understand why a thing is itself rather than something else. What explains the thing itself is difference, not the causes of the thing. "Freedom must be sought in a particular nuance or quality of the action itself and not in a relation of this act with what it is not or what it could have been."[10] Bergsonism is a philosophy of difference, a philosophy of the actualization of difference: in it we meet difference in person, which actualizes itself as the new.

Notes

[1] Henri Bergson, *Matière et mémoire* (1896), p. 83.

[2] Ibid., p. 139.

[3] Henri Bergson, *Essai sur les données immédiates de la conscience* (1889), p. 180.

[4] Bergson, *Matière et mémoire*, p. 250.

[5] Henri Bergson, *L'évolution créatrice* (1907), p. 220.

[6] Ibid., p. 231.

[7] Ibid., pp. 319–26.

[8] Bergson, *Matière et mémoire*, p. 65.

[9] Bergson, *L'évolution créatrice*, p. 255.

[10] Bergson, *Essai sur les données immédiates de la conscience*, p. 137.

JACQUES DERRIDA

Différance

1968

What am I to do in order to speak of the *a* of *différance*? It goes without saying that it cannot be *exposed*. One can expose only that which at a certain moment can become *present*, manifest, that which can be shown, presented as something present, a being-present[1] in its truth, in the truth of a present or the present of the present. Now if *différance* ~~is~~ (and I also cross out the "~~is~~") what makes possible the presentation of the being-present, it is never presented as such. It is never offered to the present. Or to anyone. Reserving itself, not exposing itself, in regular fashion it exceeds the order of truth at a certain precise point but without dissimulating itself as something, as a mysterious being, in the occult of a nonknowledge or in a hole with indeterminable borders (for example in a topology of castration).[2] In every exposition it would be exposed to disappearing as disappearance. It would risk appearing: disappearing.

So much so that the detours, locutions, and syntax in which I will often have to take recourse will resemble those of negative theology, occasionally even to the point of being indistinguishable from negative theology. Already we have had to delineate *that différance is not*, does not exist, is not a present-being (*or* in any form; and we will be led to delineate also everything *that* it *is not*, that is, *everything*; and consequently that it has neither existence nor essence. It derives from no category of being, whether present or absent. And yet those aspects of *différance* which are thereby delineated are not theological, not even in the order of the most negative of negative theologies, which are always concerned with disengaging a superessentiality beyond the finite categories of essence and existence, that is, of presence, and always hastening to recall that God is refused the predicate of existence, only in order to acknowledge his superior, inconceivable,

Address given before the Société française de philosophie, 27 January 1968, published simultaneously in the *Bulletin de la Société française de philosophie*, July–September 1968, and in *Théorie d'ensemble*, coll. Tel Quel (Paris: Editions du Seuil, 1968). From *Margins of Philosophy*, trans. Alan Bass (Chicago: University of Chicago Press, 1982), pp. 5–6, 11–12, 14–15, 21–22 [*Marges de la philosophie* (Paris: Editions de Minuit, 1972)].

and ineffable mode of being. Such a development is now in question here, and this will be confirmed progressively. *Différance* is not only irreducible to any ontological or theological—ontotheological—reappropriation but as the very opening of the space in which ontotheology—philosophy—produces its system and its history, it includes ontotheology, inscribing it and exceeding it without return.

. . .

Since language, which Saussure says is a classification, has not fallen from the sky, its differences have been produced, are produced effects, but they are effects which do not find their cause in a subject or a substance, in a thing in general, a being that is somewhere present, thereby eluding the play of *différance*. If such a presence were implied in the concept of cause in general, in the most classical fashion, we then would have to speak of an effect without a cause, which very quickly would lead to speaking of no effect at all. I have attempted to indicate a way out of the closure of this framework via the "trace," which is no more an effect than it has a cause, but which in and of itself, outside its text, is not sufficient to operate the necessary transgression.

Since there is no presence before and outside semiological difference, what Saussure has written about language can be extended to the sign in general: "Language is necessary in order for speech to be intelligible and to produce all of its effects; but the latter is necessary in order for language to be established; historically, the fact of speech always comes first."[3]

Retaining at least the framework, if not the content, of this requirement formulated by Saussure, we will designate as *différance* the movement according to which language, or any code, any system of referral in general, is constituted "historically" as a weave of differences. "Is constituted," "is produced," "is created," "movement," "historically," etc., necessarily being understood beyond the metaphysical language in which they are retained, along with all their implications. We ought to demonstrate why concepts like *production*, constitution, and history remain in complicity with what is at issue here. But this would take me too far today—toward the theory of the representation of the "circle" in which we appear to be enclosed—and I utilize such concepts, like many others, only for their strategic convenience and in order to undertake their deconstruction at the currently most decisive point. In any event, it will be understood, by means of the circle in which we appear to be engaged, that as it is written here, *différance* is no more static than it is genetic, no more structural than historical. Or is no less so; and to object to this on the basis of the oldest of metaphysical oppositions (for example, by setting some generative point of view against a structural-taxonomical point of view, or vice versa) would be, above all, not to read what here is missing from orthographical ethics. Such oppositions have not the least pertinence to *différance*, which makes the thinking of it uneasy and uncomfortable.

. . .

What differs? Who differs? What is *différance*?

If we answered these questions before examining them as questions, before turning them back on themselves, and before suspecting their very form, including what seems most natural and necessary about them, we would immediately fall back into what we have just disengaged ourselves from. In effect, if we accepted the form of the question, in its meaning and its syntax ("what is?" "who is?" "who is that?"), we would have to conclude that *différance* has been derived, has happened, is to be mastered and governed on the basis of the point of a present being, which itself could be some thing, a form, a state, a power in the world to which all kinds of names might be given, a *what*, or a present being as a *subject*, a *who*. And in this last case, notably, one would conclude implicitly that this present being, for example a being present to itself, as consciousness, eventually would come to defer or to differ: whether by delaying and turning away from the fulfillment of a "need" or a "desire," or by differing from itself. But in neither of these cases would such a present being be "constituted" by this *différance*.

. . .

Therefore, it is the determination of Being as presence or as beingness that is interrogated by the thought of *différance*. Such a question could not emerge and be understood unless the difference between Being and beings were somewhere to be broached. First consequence: *différance* is not. It is not a present being, however excellent, unique, principal, or transcendent. It governs nothing, reigns over nothing, and nowhere exercises any authority. It is not announced by any capital letter. Not only is there no kingdom of *différance*, but *différance* instigates the subversion of every kingdom. Which makes it obviously threatening and infallibly dreaded by everything within us that desires a kingdom, the past or future presence of a kingdom. And it is always in the name of a kingdom that one may reproach *différance* with wishing to reign, believing that one sees it aggrandize itself with a capital letter.

Can *différance*, for these reasons, settle down into the division of the ontico-ontological difference, such as it is thought, such as its "epoch" in particular is thought, "through," if it may still be expressed such, Heidegger's uncircumventable meditation?

There is no simple answer to such a question.

Notes

[1] TN. As in the past, *être* (*Sein*) will be translated as Being. *Etant* (*Seiendes*) will be either beings or being, depending on the context. Thus, here *étant-présent* is "being-present." For a justification of this translation see Derrida, *Writing and Difference*, trans. Alan Bass's (Chicago: University of Chicago Press, 1978), Translator's Introduction, p. xvii.

[2] TN. ". . . a hole with indeterminable borders (for example, in a topology of castration)." This phrase was added to "La différance" for its publication in the French edition of this volume and refers to the polemic Derrida had already engaged (in *Positions*; elaborated further in *Le facteur de la vérité*) with Jacques Lacan. For Derrida, Lacan's "topology of castration," which assigns the "hole" or lack to a place—"a hole with determinable borders"—repeats the metaphysical gesture (albeit a negative one) of making absence, the lack, the hole, a transcendental principle that can be pinned down as such, and can thereby *govern* a theoretical discourse.

[3] TN. Ferdinand de Saussure, *Course in General Linguistics*, trans. Wade Baskin (New York: Philosophical Library, 1959), p. 18.

JEAN-FRANÇOIS LYOTARD

The Differend: Phrases in Dispute

1983

1. You are informed that human beings endowed with language were placed in a situation such that none of them is now able to tell about it. Most of them disappeared then, and the survivors rarely speak about it. When they do speak about it, their testimony bears only upon a minute part of this situation. How can you know that the situation itself existed? That it is not the fruit of your informant's imagination? Either the situation did not exist as such. Or else it did exist, in which case your informant's testimony is false, either because he or she should have disappeared, or else because he or she should remain silent, or else because, if he or she does speak, he or she can bear witness only to the particular experience he had, it remaining to be established whether this experience was a component of the situation in question.

. . .

7. This is what a wrong [*tort*] would be: a damage [*dommage*] accompanied by the loss of the means to prove the damage. This is the case if the victim is deprived of life, or of all his or her liberties, or of the freedom to make his or her ideas or opinions public, or simply of the right to testify to the damage, or even more simply if the testifying phrase is itself deprived of authority (Nos. 24–27). In all of these cases, to the privation constituted by the damage there is added the impossibility of bringing it to the knowledge of others, and in particular to the knowledge of a tribunal. Should the victim seek to bypass this impossibility and testify anyway to the wrong done to him or to her, he or she comes up against the following argumentation: either the damages you complain about never took place, and your testimony is false; or else they took place, and since you are able to testify to them, it is not a wrong that has been done to you, but merely a damage, and your testimony is still false.

. . .

12. The plaintiff lodges his or her complaint before the tribunal, the accused argues in such a way as to show the inanity of the accusation. Litigation takes

---

From *The Differend: Phrases in Dispute*, trans. Georges Van Den Abbeele (Minneapolis: University of Minnesota Press, 1988), pp. 3, 5, 9–10 [*Le différend* (Paris: Editions de Minuit, 1983)].

place. I would like to call a *differend* [*différend*] the case where the plaintiff is divested of the means to argue and becomes for that reason a victim. If the addressor, the addressee, and the sense of the testimony are neutralized, everything takes place as if there were no damages (No. 9). A case of differend between two parties takes place when the "regulation" of the conflict that opposes them is done in the idiom of one of the parties while the wrong suffered by the others is not signified in that idiom. For example, contracts and agreements between economic partners do not prevent—on the contrary, they presuppose—that the laborer or his or her representative has had to and will have to speak of his or her work as though it were the temporary cession of a commodity, the "service," which he or she putatively owns. This "abstraction," as Marx calls it (but the term is bad, what concreteness does it allege?), is required by the idiom in which the litigation is regulated ("bourgeois" social and economic law). In failing to have recourse to this idiom, the laborer would not exist within its field of reference, he or she would be a slave. In using it, he or she becomes a plaintiff. Does he or she also cease for that matter to be a victim?

13. One remains a victim at the same time that one becomes a plaintiff. Does one have the means to establish that one is a victim? No. How can you know then that one is a victim? What tribunal can pass judgment in this matter? In effect, the differend is not a matter for litigation; economic and social law can regulate the litigation between economic and social partners but not the differend between labor-power and capital. By what well-formed phrase and by means of what establishment procedure can the worker affirm before the labor arbitrator that what one yields to one's boss for so many hours per week in exchange for a salary is *not* a commodity? One is presumed to be the owner of something. One is in the case of the accused who has to establish a non-existent or at least a non-attribute. It is easy to refute him or her. It all happens as if what one is could only be expressed in an idiom other than that of social and economic law. In the latter, one can only express what one has, and if one has nothing, what one does not have either will not be expressed or will be expressed in a certifiable manner as if one had it. If the laborer evokes his or her essence (labor-power), he or she cannot be heard by this tribunal, which is not competent. The differend is signaled by this inability to prove. The one who lodges a complaint is heard, but the one who is a victim, and who is perhaps the same one, is reduced to silence.

JACQUES RANCIÈRE

Disagreement: Politics and Philosophy

1995

Philosophy becomes "political" when it embraces aporia or the quandary proper to politics. Politics, as we will see, is that activity which turns on equality as its principle. And the principle of equality is transformed by the distribution of community shares as defined by a quandary: when is there and when is there not equality in things between who and who else? What are these "things" and who are these whos? How does equality come to consist of equality *and* inequality? That is the quandary proper to politics by which politics becomes a quandary for philosophy, an object of philosophy. We should not take this to mean that pious vision in which philosophy comes to the rescue of the practitioner of politics, science, or art, explaining the reason for his quandary by shedding light on the principle of his practice. Philosophy does not come to anyone's rescue and no one asks it to, even if the rules of etiquette of social demand have established the habit whereby politicians, lawyers, doctors, or any other body getting together to reflect, wheel in the philosopher as specialist of thinking in general. If that invitation is to bear any intellectual fruit, the encounter must identify its point of disagreement.

We should take disagreement to mean a determined kind of speech situation: one in which one of the interlocutors at once understands and does not understand what the other is saying. Disagreement is not the conflict between one who says white and another who says black. It is the conflict between one who says white and another who also says white but does not understand the same thing by it or does not understand that the other is saying the same thing in the name of whiteness. The term is so broad it obviously calls for a certain amount of fine-tuning and obliges us to make certain distinctions. Disagreement is not misconstruction. The concept of misconstruction supposes that one or other or both of the interlocutors do or do not know what they are saying or what the other is saying, either through the effects of simple ignorance, studied

From *Disagreement: Politics and Philosophy*, trans. Julie Rose (Minneapolis: University of Minnesota Press, 1999), pp. ix–xii, 107–8 [*La mésentente: politique et philosophie* (Paris: Editions Galilée, 1995)].

dissimulation, or inherent delusion. Nor is disagreement some kind of misunderstanding stemming from the imprecise nature of words. Ancient received wisdom, very much in vogue again these days, deplores the way people fail to understand each other properly because of the ambiguity of the words exchanged, and requires us always, at all times, or at least wherever truth, justice, and good are at stake, to try and give each word a well-defined meaning, one that distinguishes it from all other words, discarding words that do not designate any defined property or that inevitably lead to homonymic confusion. It sometimes happens that this wisdom goes by the name of philosophy and manages to pass off this rule of linguistic economy as philosophy's privileged exercise. The reverse also happens, whereby philosophy is denounced as the very thing that promotes empty words and irreducible homonyms; every human activity, this wisdom goes, should get clear about itself, purging its vocabulary and conceptual underpinnings of all philosophy's bilge.

The arguments of misconstruction and misunderstanding thereby call for two types of language medicine, both consisting similarly in finding out what speaking means. It is not hard to see their limitations. The first type of treatment constantly has to assume the ignorant misconstruction of which it is the flip side, reserved knowledge. The second imposes a rationality ban on too many areas. Numerous speech situations in which reason is at work can be imagined within a specific structure of disagreement that has neither to do with a misconstruction that would call for additional knowledge nor with a misunderstanding that would call for words to be refined. Disagreement occurs wherever contention over what speaking means constitutes the very rationality of the speech situation. The interlocutors both understand and do not understand the same thing by the same words. There are all sorts of reasons why X both does and does not understand Y: while clearly understanding what Y is saying, X cannot *see* the object Y is talking about; or else, X understands and is bound to understand, sees and attempts to make visible another object using the same name, another reason within the same argument. Thus, in the *Republic*, "political philosophy" comes into existence in the long protocol of disagreement over an argument in which everyone agrees: that justice consists in giving each his due. It would no doubt be convenient if, to say just what he understands by justice, the philosopher had entirely different words at his disposal from those of the poet, the merchant, the orator, or the politician. Divine wisdom apparently did not provide these, and the lover of strict and appropriate languages can furnish them only at the cost of not being understood at all. Where philosophy runs up against poetry, politics, and the wisdom of honest merchants, it has to borrow the others' words in order to say that it is saying something else entirely. It is in this that disagreement lies and not mere misunderstanding, which can be resolved by a simple explanation of what the other's sentence is saying—unbeknownst to this other.

Disagreement clearly is not to do with words alone. It generally bears on the very situation in which speaking parties find themselves. In this, disagreement differs from what Jean-François Lyotard has conceptualized as a differend. Disagreement is not concerned with issues such as the heterogeneity of regimes of sentences and the presence or absence of a rule for assessing different types of heterogeneous discourse. It is less concerned with arguing than with what can be argued, the presence or absence of a common object between X and Y. It concerns the tangible presentation of this common object, the very capacity of the interlocutors to present it. An extreme form of disagreement is where X cannot see the common object Y is presenting because X cannot comprehend that the sounds uttered by Y form words and chains of words similar to X's own. This extreme situation—first and foremost—concerns politics. Where philosophy encounters both politics and poetry at once, disagreement bears on what it means to be a being that uses words to argue. The structures proper to disagreement are those in which discussion of an argument comes down to a dispute over the object of the discussion and over the capacity of those who are making an object of it.

The following pages try to define a few pointers for understanding disagreement whereby the aporia of politics is embraced as a philosophical object. We will be testing the following hypothesis: that what is called "political philosophy" might well be the set of reflective operations whereby philosophy tries to rid itself of politics, to suppress a scandal in thinking proper to the exercise of politics. This theoretical scandal is nothing more than the rationality of disagreement. What makes politics an object of scandal is that it is that activity which has the rationality of disagreement as its very own rationality. The basis of philosophy's dispute with politics is thus the very reduction of the rationality of disagreement. This operation, whereby philosophy automatically expels disagreement from itself, is thereby identified with the project of "really" doing politics, of achieving the true essence of what politics talks about. Philosophy does not become "political" because politics is so crucial it simply must intervene. It becomes political because regulating the rationality situation of politics is a condition for defining what belongs to philosophy.

. . .

So consensus, before becoming the reasonable virtue of individuals and groups who agree to discuss their problems and build up their interests, is a determined regime of the perceptible, a particular mode of visibility of *right* as *arkhê* of the community. Before problems can be settled by well-behaved social partners, the rule of conduct of the dispute has to be settled, as a specific structure of community. The identity of the community with itself must be posited, along with the rule of right as identical to the elimination of wrong. There is a lot of talk about how the extension of the legitimate state and the sphere of law is characteristic of our regimes, but, beyond agreement that the rule is preferable to the arbitrary and liberty to servitude, it remains to be seen precisely what phenomena are indicated by this. Like every word at stake in politics, the word "law" is a homonym for quite different things: the juridical provisions of codes and ways of implementing them, philosophical notions of community and what it is based on, political structures of wrong, modes of police management of the relations between the state and social groups and interests. Simple celebration of the legitimate state then takes convenient shortcuts that allow us, in the face of the nonright of archipolice states, to bundle all these heterogeneous "rights" together in a single unquestioned rule of law, characterized by a happy harmony between the legislative activity of the public authorities, the rights of individuals, and the procedural inventiveness of law offices. But the rule of *the* law is always the rule of *a* law, that is, of a regime of unity among all the different senses of the law posited as a regime of identity of the community. Today, the identification between democracy and the legitimate state is used to produce a regime of the community's identity as itself, to make politics evaporate under a concept of law that identifies it with the spirit of the community.

JACQUES DERRIDA

As If It Were Possible, "Within Such Limits"

2001

Although I never restrict it to the propositional form (in the necessity of which I also believe, of course), I have never thought I had to give up questioning (or that anyone could or should be able to)—give up any form of question, a certain "primacy of questioning" (Michel Meyer), or that which ties the question to the problem, to *problematization*. Is there ever a question pure of any problem, in other words on the one hand pure of any elaboration, any syntax, any articulable differentiality; but also, on the other hand, pure of any self-protection? For problematization is certainly the only *consistent* organization of a question, its grammar and semantics, but also a first *apotropaic* measure to protect oneself against the starkest question, both the most inflexible and the barest, the question of the other when it *puts me in question* at the moment it is addressed to me. I have tried elsewhere to take into account this *shield* of the *problema*. The *problema* also designates "the substitute, the deputy, the prosthesis, whatever or whomever one *puts forward* to protect oneself while concealing oneself, whatever or whoever comes in the place or the name of the other."[1]

Problematization is already an articulated organization of the response. That is true everywhere, particularly in the history of philosophical or scientific configurations. Whatever name you call them by, however you interpret them (paradigm, *episteme, themata*, and so on), these historical configurations that act as a basis for questions are already possibilities of response. They preorganize and render possible the event, the apparent invention, the emergence and elaboration of questions, their problematization, and the reappropriation that makes them for a moment determinable and treatable.

In the inevitability of the question, it seems to me, there is not only an essence of philosophy but an unconditional right and duty, the joint ground of philosophy as science and law. Since this unconditionality is pointed out where

From *Paper Machine*, trans. Rachel Bowlby (Stanford, CA: Stanford University Press, 2005), pp. 85–86, 90–92 ["Comme si c'était possible, 'within such limits,'" in *Papier machine* (Paris: Editions Galilée, 2001)].

it seems to be a matter of course, I must also make the following clear: although I have constantly used everything I have written as a *question of the question*,[2] *this same necessity* is not reducible to the question. A double necessity, double law of the inevitable and the imperative injunction ("It is necessary"), it exceeds the question at the very moment of reaffirming its necessity. In confirming so often that everything begins not with the question but with the response, with a "yes, yes,"[3] that is in origin a response to the other, it is not a matter of again "putting into question," as the phrase goes, this unconditionality, but rather of thinking both its possibility and its impossibility, the one *like* the other.

. . .

When the impossible *makes itself* possible, the event takes place (possibility *of* the impossible). That, indisputably, is the paradoxical form of the event: if an event is only possible, in the classic sense of this word, if it fits in with conditions of possibility, if it only makes explicit, unveils, reveals, or accomplishes that which was already possible, then it is no longer an event. For an event to take place, for it to be possible, it has to be, as event, as invention, the coming of the impossible. That's a meager statement of the obvious, an obviousness that is nothing less than obvious. This is what has always guided me, between the possible and the impossible. This is what has so often prompted me to speak of a *condition of impossibility*.

The issue is thus nothing less than the powerful concept of the *possible* that runs through Western thought, from Aristotle to Kant and Husserl (then differently to Heidegger), with all its meanings, virtual or potential: being-in-potential, in fact; *dynamis*, virtuality (in its classic and modern forms, pretechnological and technological), but also power, capacity, everything that renders skilled, or able, or that formally enables, and so on. The choice of this thematic does of course hold a strategic value, but it also carries with it a movement for going further, beyond any calculable stratagem. It carries what is called deconstruction toward a question that causes trembling, tormenting it from the inside, the most powerful and the most precarious axiomatic—powerless in its very power—of dominant thinking about the possible in philosophy—a philosophy that is thus a slave to the power of its very dominance.

But how is it possible, it will then be asked, that what renders possible renders impossible the very thing that it renders possible, and introduces; but as its chance, a chance that is not negative, a principle of ruin in the very thing that it is promising or promoting?

The *im-* of the im-possible is surely radical, implacable, undeniable. But it is not only negative or simply dialectical: it *introduces* into the possible, it is *its usher today*: it gets it to come, it gets it to move according to an anachronic temporality or an unbelievable filiation—which moreover is also the origin of faith. For it exceeds knowledge, it conditions the address to the other, it puts any theorem in the space and time of a witnessing ("I am speaking to you, believe me"). To put it another way, and this is the introduction to an aporia that has no examples, an aporia of logic rather than a logical aporia: here we have an impasse of the undecidable, by which a decision cannot not get through.

All responsibility has to go by way of this aporia, which, far from paralyzing, sets in motion a new thinking of the possible. It guarantees it its rhythm and respiration: diastole, systole, and syncope, beating of the *im*-possible possible, of the impossible as condition of the possible. From the very heart of the im-possible, one would thus hear the impulse or pulse of a "deconstruction."

The condition of possibility would then give a chance to the possible, but by depriving it of its purity. The law of this spectral contamination, the impure law of this impurity—that is what has to be continually reelaborated. For example: the possibility of failure is not only set down as a prior risk in the condition of the possibility of success of a performative (a promise must *be able not* to be kept; in order to be freely given promise, and even in order to succeed, it must threaten not to be kept or to become a threat:[4] whence the originary inscription of guilt, confession, excuse, and forgiveness in the promise). It must continue to mark the event, even when it succeeds, as the trace of an impossibility, sometimes its memory and always its haunting. This im-possibility is thus not simply the opposite of the possible. It seems only to be opposed but it also supports possibility: it passes through it and leaves in it the trace of its taking away.

An event would not be worthy of its name, it would not make anything happen, if all it did was to deploy, explicate, or actualize what was already possible: which is to say, in short, if it came back down to unfolding a program or applying a general rule to a case. For there to be event, it has to be possible, of course, but also there has to be an interruption that is exceptional, absolutely singular, in the regime of possibility; it must not be reducible to explication, unfolding, or the putting into action of a possibility. The event, if there is such a thing, is not the actualization of a possibility, a straightforward putting into action, a realization, an effectuation, the teleological accomplishment of a capacity, the process of a dynamic dependent on "conditions of possibility." The event has nothing to do with history, if what we understand by history is teleological process. It must in a certain way break off that type of history. These are the premises which led me to speak, particularly in *Specters of Marx*, of messianicity without messianism. Thus *it must be* that the event is also introduced as impossible or that its possibility be threatened.

But then why this "it must be [*il faut*]," it will be asked? What is the status of this necessity, of this law that, all things considered, is apparently contradictory and doubly obligatory? What is this "double bind" on the basis of which it "would be necessary [*il faut*]" again to rethink the possible as *im*-possible?

It is perhaps a necessity that also escapes from the habitual regime of necessity (*ananke, Notwendigkeit*)—from necessity as natural law or as law of freedom. For it is not possible to think the possibility of the impossible *otherwise* without rethinking necessity. We have just been recalling the area of my analyses that concerned the event or the performative, and I have also attempted these analyses, in an analogous way, and particularly over the past fifteen years, in relation to destination, witnessing, invention, the gift, forgiveness, and also that which links hospitality to the im-possible promise, to the pervertibility of the performative in general—and above all, in relation to death, to the aporicity of the aporia in general.

It is not so much that this pervertibility is transcendental as that it affects the classic mode of reflection on the transcendental, on the transcendental "condition of possibility," in all its forms: medieval onto-theology, criticism, or phenomenology.[5] It does not delegitimate transcendental questioning, it de-limits it and interrogates its original historicity. For nothing can discredit the right to the transcendental or ontological question. This is the only force that resists empiricism and relativism. Despite appearances to which philosophers in a hurry often rush, nothing is less empiricist or relativist than a certain attention to the multiplicity of contexts and the discursive strategies they govern; than a certain insistence on the fact that a context is always open and nonsaturable; or than taking into account the *perhaps* and the *quasi* in thinking about the event, and so on.

Notes

[1] Derrida, "Passions: An Oblique Offering" (1993), in *On the Name*, p. 137; cf. p. 10. I also examined the Foucauldian concept of "problematization" in "To Do Justice to Freud: The History of Madness in the Age of Psychoanalysis," in *Resistances of Psychoanalysis* (1996), trans. Peggy Kamuf, Pascale-Anne Brault, and Michael B. Naas (Stanford, Calif.: Stanford University Press, 1996), p. 115.

[2] See especially Derrida, *Of Spirit: Heidegger and the Question* (1987), trans. Geoffrey Bennington and Rachel Bowlby (Chicago: University of Chicago Press, 1989), particularly the section on the promise, the *yes* before any opposition of *yes* and *no*—and most of all that which comes "before any question," pp. 92–94; and *Politics of Friendship*, passim.

[3] On the repetition of this "yes, yes," see also "Ulysses Gramophone: Hear Say Yes in Joyce," trans. Tina Kendall, in Derrida, *Acts of Literature*, ed. Derek Attridge (New York: Routledge, 1992), pp. 256–309; and "Nombre de oui," in *Psyche: Inventions de l'autre* (Paris: Galilée, 1987), 639ff.

[4] On this impossible possibility, this *im*-possibility as pervertibility, as the permanent possibility of the perversion of a promise into a threat, see Derrida, "Avances," preface to Serge Margel, *Le tombeau du Dieu artisan* (Paris: Minuit, 1995).

[5] I did also, a very long time ago, analyze in an analogous way, in the space of Husserlian phenomenology, an *im-possibility*, the impossibility of full and immediate intuition, the "essential possibility of nonintuition," the "possibility of the crisis" as "crisis of the *logos*." This possibility of im-possibility, I said then, is not simply negative: the trap becomes a chance as well: "this possibility [of crisis] remains linked for Husserl with the very movement of truth and the production of ideal objectivity: this has in fact an essential need for writing" (Derrida, *Of Grammatology*, trans. Gayatri Chakravorty Spivak [Baltimore: Johns Hopkins University Press, 1976], p. 40, trans. mod.; and earlier in *Edmund Husserl's "The Origin of Geometry": An Introduction* [1962], trans. John P. Leavey, Jr. [1978; Lincoln: University of Nebraska Press, 1989]).

PART IV

Event

The concept of event is a complex problem within postwar French philosophy and forms part of its search for a new idea of philosophy or of thinking itself. Events are those critical moments when we are forced to think and have a chance of thinking in new ways, when new questions arise, new aporias appear, translating new forces or conjunctures. It is when paradoxes or problematizing new truths appear, disrupting doxa. It is the peculiar time of invention or creation in thought or philosophy. Events are thus not to be confused with simple occurrences in stories or histories, in causal or teleological sequences, or even in states of affairs governed by fixed parameters. Depending on one's logic or ontology, it supposes the "void" in Badiou, the "altogether other" in Derrida, and the "point of complication" in Deleuze, for which there exist no fixed or projectable predicates. An event is thus something that can't be foreseen or mastered and therefore cannot be made part of a fixed program—it redistributes the sense of what came before, what might yet happen, forcing us to behave in new ways. It is the part of what happens to us that we can't immediately grasp or make present, the part of impossibility in what we think is possible for us. An event therefore has a peculiar relation to subjectivity and intersubjectivity, action and agency. As Deleuze says: "Not to predict but to be attentive to new forces knocking at the door." Heidegger's idea of *Ereignis*, Freud's idea of trauma, Marx's idea of revolution, Nietszche's *amor fati*, Holderlin's "caesura points," Mallarmé's new "game" or "play" of chance were all explored, questioned, reread in terms of the idea of the existence, the subsistence or "immanence" of the event.

One cluster of problems concerns the question of event and history—our role in making it and in writing it, the problem of action or agency and the relation of history to theater or to fiction. What Foucault called "actuality" is one formulation of the problem, which in turn goes back to the notion of "conjuncture" in Althusser, though Foucault turns it into a kind of skeptical nominalism. In the 1960s, around the time Althusser was advancing his new conception of history, we can find the problem of event in a series of different readings of Marx's *Eighteenth Brumaire of Louis Bonaparte*. It is then that Deleuze would develop his idea of "time out of joint," which Derrida would later take up in terms of ghosts and messianic themes associated with the "death of Marx." But at the time the contrast was with Sartre, who, in his *Search for the Method*, would turn to Marx's *Eighteenth Brumaire* in his attempt to develop the sense in which it is men and women who make history. What for Sartre was a question of agency and reification was for Deleuze more a matter of difference and repetition, or of history, first as tragedy and then as farce, a peculiar theater of action. It was thus a question of the political and its relation to revolution, and then later, in the 1980s, to the failure or end of revolution.

We thus find an initial contrast between the everyday and the event, or between notions of situation, engagement, and project, on one hand, and those moments or conjunctures where new shifts occur, or new possibilities of action arise, within the larger structure or complexity of historical formations and the corresponding subjective roles or positions that they determine, on the other. It is just such moments, developed by Althusser in terms of Brechtian "theatricality," that mattered to Deleuze at the time. The problem was not engagement but what to do in the face of problematizing events thrown up by history, where new ideas, new ways of acting and speaking arise—what Deleuze would call the times in which we become other, without being sure of quite who or what. It is this idea that Foucault would go on to develop in terms of the time of the political, or of emancipatory or critical acts with respect to the determinations of history. With his analysis of the emergence of discipline and, with biopower, of statistics, the problem would in turn be associated with questions of routinization, standardization, and probability, and the invention of ways one seeks to depart from those—more revolt than revolution.

The concept of event was at the same time associated with the problem of temporality, posed by Kant and Bergson and also central to Heidegger and Husserl. Time was not to be viewed as succession, past to present to future, as with clocks or narratives with fixed beginnings and ends. For Deleuze, Hamlet's "time out of joint" meant not doubt but how to think and act in the peculiar time that never comes back to the same place, in the city or in nature, when the past becomes indeterminate, the future yet to come. We find this problem already in Kant's disciple Hölderlin when he wrote of "caesura points" in the tragic dramas of *Oedipus Rex* and *Antigone*, where beginnings and ends don't rhyme, when new histories are introduced into history, which neither men or the gods can completely control or anticipate. The problem also later became a question of chance and probability. For Deleuze, Hume's substitution of probability in habit and memory for Cartesian certainty opened up a new question of "chance," developed by Nietzsche and Mallarmé. The "game of thought" could then be played in a new way in which new moves could alter the rules or open them to "play," irreducible to the calculations of probability or statistical regularity. The philosophical consequence of this sort of chance, which no throw of the dice can ever abolish, is to be seen in Nietzsche's philosophical game, which Deleuze contrasts with Pascal's Wager, still rooted in probabilities. Derrida also took up these themes of play and chance, not simply in relation to the idea of structure and impossibility, but also in his questioning of Heidegger, with respect to "thrownness" and related "projects" or "projections" as well as the language of Sending and Destiny associated with the idea of Event or *Ereignis* in the History of Being; for Derrida, the problem of chance becomes that of "inventions of the other" in thought. In many ways, in Victor Goldschmidt's study of the idea of event in Stoicism, we already find an alternative to Heidegger, which Deleuze would go on to develop in his *Logic of Sense*, connecting it to a basic question in ethics: how not to be unworthy of what happens to us. The Stoic problem of accepting fate while refusing necessity would then recur in Spinoza's ethics or with the theme of *amor fati* in Nietzsche, or in another way with the problem of *fortuna* and *necessità* in Machiavelli, where it rejoins the issue of chance in political or historical determinations.

But how then did the idea figure in psychoanalysis? In what ways did Freud fit with the larger conceptions of the event in history or with the new ideas of temporality? For Lacan, that was a key question that helped free psychoanalysis from all developmental psychology. It was already formulated by Freud in his elaboration of the idea of the "traumatic event" and its substitute-expression in symptoms or dreams in his study of hysteria, but also, through transference, with the repetition of such events in the theater of analysis itself. The way such events never stop writing themselves in our lives, Lacan tried to show, involved a play of chance and necessity, or *tyche* and *automaton*. In particular, Freud spoke of a *Nachträglichkeit* (deferred action), in the ways such events would later recur under fresh descriptions or new writings. It is this idea of *Nachträglichkeit* which Derrida would go on to develop in relations to his own ideas of presence and memory, then trace and archive, where it rejoined the question of time in machines or technologies, thus forming part of a larger preoccupation with the question of time in technology. With the idea of archive, the notion of event would free itself from fixed sources or final recollections or descriptions, thus rejoining the question of memory in history.

The psychoanalytic elaboration of the unrepresentability of traumatic events and the time through which they are worked out in memory or history resonated with corresponding themes, or structures, in literature. In particular, Blanchot wrote of a "part" in what happens to us that goes beyond our mastery or anticipation, yet engages our thinking. Such events in literature, which undo our ability to say "I" or "we," are shown in "neutral" or "absent" spaces and times, often associated with what he called the "space of death." If in the 1960s we find a division surrounding the idea of revolution, and so of action and engagement in, or critical disengagement from, history, starting in the 1980s, under the influence of the discussion of memory by Pierre Nora and Paul Ricoeur and in relation to World War II and the role of the Shoah in it, we find an extension of the psychoanalytic and literary notion of "traumatic event" to history itself. Events were then associated with ideas of "disaster" or "catastrophe" in history, and in particular mass death and extreme violence and our responses to it after the fact. This side of the question of the event would be developed in particular by Lyotard, in relation to the philosophico-ethical task of bearing witness as well as to aesthetic questions of the sublime. We thus find one starting point for the sort of "ethics of trauma," which Alain Badiou would later see as "depoliticizing" and against which he would then redirect his own notion of event within revolution.

The notion of event leads to an elaboration of different "times" in philosophy. With Badiou, we find a focus on how to remain "faithful" to a past introduced by cuts or voids in history and associated with the universal law announced by St. Paul. For Derrida, on the other hand, what counts is a future, yet to come, given by something other, messianic yet without a messiah, supposing a kind of Judaic ur-law. With Deleuze—and, in another way, with Foucault, each dispensing with the very idea of a prior law—we find the development of a kind of pragmatism that would free the idea of what happens to us from all salvationism or the final judgment of God or even man. Then the event becomes a matter of the present or *l'actuel*, or the time in which we are confronted with the forces of new ways of seeing, saying, and acting, which at once require and make possible an experimentation, an invention of new ways of relating to ourselves and one another.

VICTOR GOLDSCHMIDT

The Stoic System and the Idea of Time

1953

109. I will not attempt to summarize the results of these studies here. As far as Stoic philosophy is concerned, it is enough to note that the theory of time suffuses and clarifies the entire system. Yet the educational requirements of ancient tradition relegated this theory to a chapter of physics, so that exegesis is obliged (by a *legal* obligation, as I hope to have shown) to recover it from other parts of the doctrine and make it accessible. Nevertheless, it may be worthwhile to add a few words here to allusions made in passing about how the Stoic conception of time differs from or is similar to that of other philosophies.

Stoic time is *qualitative*, not *mathematical*.[1] This opposition, which dates back beyond Aristotle,[2] also applies to the astronomical time of the *Timaeus*. There is nevertheless agreement, in the sense that the Stoics, like Plato, taught the existence of a plurality of "proper times" subordinate to a "common time."[3] In both systems, moreover, it is activity and movement (of the planets in one case, of any corporeal agent in the other) that define and delimit time.

The insistence on the autonomy of free agents leads to accentuating the present as the only real mode of time, as the locus of instantaneous freedom and completion. In cosmology as in ethics, perfection is achieved suddenly, without gradual development; it is "present from the outset."[4] This refusal of slow geneses is not without analogy to the contemporary idea of structure, "which must be present at one stroke."[5] The time for maturation, "creative" time, is real only in the eyes of God and on the cosmic scale. Any man who gave himself over to this would sink into servitude of things "not within our power."

110. Stoicism recognized this creative time: "If you now said to me, 'I want a fig,' I would answer, 'It takes time. Let the flowers come first, then let the fruit be born, and finally allow it to ripen. Yet while the fruit of the fig tree does not reach maturity suddenly, in an hour's time, you would harvest the fruit of a human will that quickly and *that easily*.'"[6] The full meaning of this sentence, whose tone is almost Bergsonian, depends, however, on its final phrase. What the metaphor of the ripening fruit is intended to teach is not passive patience

Le système stoïcien et l'idée du temps (Paris: Librairie Philosophique J. Vrin, 1953), pp. 211–18; trans. Arthur Goldhammer.

but continual and constant effort of the moral will. And initiative and its purpose are located solely in the present. The time of waiting is not within their grasp or something they care about. It is true that apprenticeship in initiative and *progress* (προχοπη) imply duration, and it seems that this duration is in a sense at the disposal of the person who makes progress.[7] This is because the apprentice philosopher tends constantly to convert illusory time into the real present, but he succeeds only by dint of a conversion, a sudden transformation that disrupts the preceding progress rather than growing out of it in any sense naturally as the fruit grows out of the flower. A sharp rebuttal of Bergson's use of the image of a glass of sugared water to illustrate "the need for waiting" can be found in another text of Epictetus: "Bound as we are to many things, we are oppressed by them and torn in opposite directions. So when sailing is impossible, we sit anxiously and constantly look out to see what wind is blowing. 'The North Wind . . . When will the Zephyr blow?' When it wants to, my friend, or when Aeolus wants it to. Zeus gave power over the winds not to you but to Aeolus.' What should we do, then? Arrange the things that are in our power as best we can, and for the rest, make use of them as we find them."[8] For the sage, in other words, there is no "need to wait."[9]

111. This depreciation of the future as grounds for *concern* leaves intact the *care* devoted to duties. Duties, as we have seen, are introduced by circumstances, and Stoicism accepts all imperatives inherent in situations; it is a philosophy of action, and, more particularly, of social action.[10] Abstracted from its passionate concerns, however, action in a sense remains external to the sage. The actor does not identify with his role and does not "commit" himself to it entirely. Even in antiquity this sort of detached commitment, which can be found as well in contemporary literature,[11] seems to have antagonized those who insisted on total commitment and unreserved submission.[12] It is clear, in fact, that the Stoic attitude avoids the artificial and oppressive alternative between the ivory tower and deified action. As a result, the Stoic idea of freedom takes on a new appearance. It is still "inner freedom," as is rightly taught, but it is also—and with the submission to duty (which is a submission to Fate), more precisely—a refusal to kneel before action[13] and to worship what one does not refuse to accept. In this sense, and despite numerous differences, Stoicism is related to those philosophies that organize duties without making absolutes of their content, acceptance, or success, such as the probabilism of the New Academy or Cartesian ethics. But for now it is enough to have pointed out this problem, which is so profoundly "uncontemporary."

112. Independence with respect to the future and to success can be illustrated by a distinction that Eugène Dupréel has drawn between two types of technique: technique in the ordinary sense of the word (technique A) and religious practices (technique B) that claim to achieve ends beyond the reach of ordinary techniques. "In order to succeed, what one might call the collabora-

tion of the interval is necessary. The interval is everything that can occur between the project and the outcome which is not due to the action of the agent himself, and which combines with the direct effort of the agent to ensure or prevent success. . . . Technique B claims to influence only that part of the operation which lies beyond the agent's powers and knowledge; it bears only on the interval, and for itself leaves *no interval*."[14]

In Stoic terms: a technique to succeed in realms that are not within our power. If such a technique succeeds in reducing the interval, it does so by dint of being *confatal*.[15] Properly speaking, however, the very idea of interval, or *distance*, makes no sense whatsoever in this system. There is no gap between the intention and the act, between project and realization, between the good desired and the good obtained.[16] The contingency over which technique B must triumph no longer resides in things (which are not within our power), hence it can only reside in us, in our desires and regrets. It manifests itself whenever we respond to a real event (which by definition is a good, and "opportune")[17] with a wish for another, hence a false, good. Philosophy offers itself to us as the only technique capable of reducing this interval and overcoming this contingency in us.

Technique B thus becomes completely useless, or else it becomes indistinguishable from philosophy as a result of a total change of intention: instead of seeking to obtain, it aims to win acceptance. It teaches us not to find a solution to our problems but to pose our problems solely in terms of the solution that has already been given to them here and now.

113. Submission to Fate and internal freedom of attitude, at once active and detached, with regard to the future; the selection of a *goal*, but only "on condition";[18] and achievement of the *end* at every moment—all of these theses make Stoic liberty, seen from outside, indistinguishable from servitude.[19] The happiness of the sage is apprehended in the moment, within a limited temporal instant that seems to deprive it of every appearance of happiness. It does not manifest itself in a long and happy life, displayed for all to see. It does not express itself in *ecstasies* outside of time, in dramatic or solemn raptures whose rare occurrences can be enumerated by respectful students, as in Plotinus. It is everywhere and always, yet no external sign makes it manifest.

Emile Bréhier has shown that the ideal of the sage combined two concepts that were not separated and distinguished from each other until later: decency and sanctity.[20] Similarly, the theory of happiness and virtue, achieved in time and in the quotidian,[21] contains as if in anticipation a seemingly modern religious concept, which finds its exact equivalent in Kierkegaard's description of the knight of faith: "One seeks in vain a fissure through which the infinite can enter. He is solid everywhere. His conduct is firm, entirely given to the finite. . . . Nothing to indicate that superb and alien nature in which one recognizes the knight of the infinite . . . Wherever he intervenes, he does so with a perseverance characteristic of the man of this earth who puts his spirit into such tasks. . . . He lives as carefree as a vagabond, and yet he pays for the favorable weather most dearly, every moment of his life. . . . At every instant this man completes and accomplishes the movement of the infinite."[22]

114. More perhaps than any other doctrine of antiquity, Stoicism has preserved its vitality and through the ages exercised an influence extending well beyond the confines of the schools. It is fair to ask, however, if this victory has not itself succumbed to a counterattack of the vanquished. It is not at all certain that the wisdom of the ages did not profoundly alter the system and undermine its unity when, ceding to an already ancient temptation,[23] it severed the *Fatum stoïcum* from providence[24] and, more generally, separated ethics from physics.[25] And what is more, it was prescient to do so, if Alexandre Koyré is right that Stoic physics is utterly a thing of the past and stands as a prime example of a "scientific" construct that is nothing but dead weight, despite the survival of the philosophy of which it was an integral part.[26] Hence it would not be at all surprising if detailed investigation of the hardiness of Stoic doctrine turned up frequent misunderstandings of its actual content.

Nothing like this is true of the Stoic theory of time. Although this theory was indeed a part of physics, of which it constituted a modest chapter usually neglected even by historians of antique Stoicism, no one would suggest that it exerted an active and direct influence beyond the Portico. Although we have been able to identify certain points that this theory shared in common with more recent doctrines, it seems clear that these commonalities were not the result of either influence of evolution. They are merely *common structures*, from which one could derive arguments in favor of a *perennis philosophia* (in another sense, no doubt, than that of tradition or Leibniz) or, even more significantly, hints of a method that might possibly lead to its discovery.[27]

What would even then remain to be discovered would be not exactly the historical process of causality but the philosophical logic underlying the constitution of these common structures. The most remarkable feature of the Stoic theory was its derivation of the reality of time from the initiative of the agent or agents or Universal Agent. Now, the agent is a real (corporeal) individual endowed with reason. Each of his acts can achieve immediate perfection without pursuing a remote *end*, except in the sense of a *goal*. Being manifests itself in what it does more than in what it projects. The motivating cause, rational and perfect at every moment, makes it possible to overcome the alternative of mechanism and finalism. Time, through this movement of realization, becomes the locus of sudden and immediate completion (αθρως),[28] and this instant can stretch out into present *extent* (διαστημα) for as long (if one can put it this way) as the initiative of the act perseveres. Note that this initiative does not continue because it has acquired velocity but rather as a result of a continually renewed force of the will (παλιν χαι παλιν). By contrast, time is stripped of its power of maturation. Its privilege of keeping us in suspense, of making us wait, is seen as an illusion whose power stems solely from the relinquishing of our freedom. A doctrine of evolution could be true only on the cosmic scale, where all instants are contemporary. The fundamental structure of Stoic time is not before-after but all-at-once. The contemplative gaze cannot apprehend this structure, however; a moral effort is required. Time derives from the act; it is not the image of eternity. Furthermore, this all-at-once retains its temporal character: it is a "part" of time that flows, a part of the flux, the *aion*. As Stoic freedom can be seen only from within, the reality of the present remains, for anyone who is not its active agent and artisan, indistinguishable from the time that passes, from the time of which the first creator of a "system of evolution"[29] would one day be obliged to admit that it was a cause of destruction rather than of generation.[30]

As indicated above, this subtle transfiguration of time can also be seen in the work of Kierkegaard, that is, in an entirely different doctrinal context. The same caveat no doubt applies to most of the other similarities noted above (and the list could be extended). In this respect, the Stoic theory of time is not just a concatenation of dogmas that can be transmitted as such from one school to another but equally a set of intellectual structures the can be applied and put to use in many different ways.[31] This does not answer the question of why it was possible in each individual case not exactly to revive but rather to rediscover these structures; indeed, it makes the question more difficult to answer. Here it is enough simply to formulate the question, the answer to which surely goes well beyond the limits of a study of Stoicism, and whose methodological and perhaps metaphysical implications no doubt extend beyond each of the systems considered.

Notes

[1] See p. 209, n. 1 [references otherwise unidentified are to the books from which this excerpt is taken, not reproduced here].

[2] Sec. 12.

[3] *Ibid.*; A. Rivaud, ed., *Timée*, p. 151, n. 1 (*ad* 38 a).

[4] E. Bréhier, *Chrysippe*, pp. 146, 215; see above p. 203, n. 5.

[5] E. Bréhier, *Transformation de la philosophie française* (Paris, 1950), pp. 128 ff. and chap. 11; *Revue philosophique*, Oct.-Dec. 1949, p. 388.

[6] Epictetus, *Diss.*, I, XV, 7–8.

[7] In reality, the opposition is only between that which is in our power and that which is not, and it seems that the time of moral progress is at our disposal precisely to the extent that it depends on our initiative (Marcus Aurelius, XI, 7). Platonism liberates the philosopher from all external things and circumstances and proclaims that he has no "further need" of anything (*Euthyd.*, 280 b 3; *Lysis*, 268 c i. f.; cf. on the contrary Aristotle, *Nic. Eth.*, I, 9, 1099 a 31–b 8; VII, 14, 1553 b 16 ff., and the texts cited in p. 201, n. 2). Yet "the measure of dialectical conversations is the whole of life" (*Rep.* V, 450 b); the dialectic refuses "to be rushed by the flow of water" from the clepsydra, and the perfection of our moral progress requires a series of reincranations. Compare also, in the

Epistle of Saint James, the opposition between the future as conceived by foolish people who make plans ("You who do not know what will happen tomorrow!") and the patience of those believers who await the coming of the Lord, a patience illustrated by the example of the farmer who waits for fruit to ripen (IV, 13–14; V, 7–8).

[8] Epictetus, *Diss.*, I, 1, 16–17. See the text by Marcus Aurelius (cited in sec. 72).

[9] Recall, however, that the example of the glass of water is useful for interpreting Bergsonism only in the most superficial way and that we have already had occasion to remark on several points that the two systems have in common in other respects.

[10] Cf. p. 179, n. 3; *de fin.*, III, XIX and the formula, in Marcus Aurelius, of the *logikon kal politikon zoon* (e.g., IX, 16). On this point, it is worth recalling what Montesquieu has to say in *De l'esprit des lois* 24.10.

[11] More than one Stoic theme can be found in particular in the literary work of Jean-Paul Sartre. On the point in question, see, e.g., *Les chemins de la liberté*, vol. 1, p. 102: "Not for a second did he cease to be *level-headed*, prepared, in perfect harmony with himself. He was annoyed, but his annoyance stayed outside him. Inside, he was comfortable."

[12] Cf. the text of Epictetus cited on p. 102, n. 7.

[13] Compare what was said about parasitic causality (p. 110) and conditional acceptance (secs. 70, 76). It should be added that it is precisely through the conditional valuation and legalization of duty (secs. 76, 95 beg.), that the freedom of the sage accords with the will of destiny. If he made his acceptance absolute in order to devote himself to it sincerely, with all his soul (that is, all his passions, sec. 93 beg.), a new "impediment" would arise, threatening both his freedom and his obedience (sec. 76).

[14] Eugène Dupréel, *Sociologie générale* (Paris, 1948), pp. 207–209.

[15] Seneca, *Quest. Nat.*, II, XXXVII–XXXVIII (cf. p. 90, n. 4).

[16] See p. 100.

[17] See p. 203, n. 8 and 9.

[18] See p. 145, n. 5; p. 157, n. 4.

[19] See pp. 78, 176.

[20] Emile Bréhier, *Chrysippe*, p. 214.

[21] Secs. 83, 88.

[22] Kierkegaard, *Fear and Trembling*; Marcus Aurelius, X, 12, 2.

[23] Sec. 46.

[24] Cf. Leibniz, *Theodicy*, pref.

[25] See p. 182, n. 7.

[26] See Alexandre Koyré, *Bulletin de la Société française de philosophie*, May–June 1936, p. 139.

[27] See the paper cited on p. 65, n. 3.

[28] Cf. Simpl., in *Arist. de anima*, 217, 36 (S.V.F., II, 393).

[29] The expression, applied to the philosophy of Aristotle, is from W. Windelband, *Lehrb. d. Gesch. d. Phil.*, Tübingen, 1928, sec. 13.

[30] Aristotle, *Phys.*, Δ, 13, 222 b. 18-20.

[31] In *La sagesse de Plotin*, p. 198, M. de Gandillac points out a quite similar phenomenon: "Whether or not he encountered the Christianity of the 'great Church' along his route, no dialogue between him and it was possible. Yet it was indeed Plotinus who . . . would supply early Christian theology as well as a central current of Christian spirituality with their frameworks and forms of expression." Now, the actual influence of the works of Plotinus on Christian thought was diffuse and indirect (see pp. xv–xvi). It is not attributable to certain parallels (e.g., p. 68 on triads), which nevertheless reveal common structures.

JEAN-PAUL SARTRE

Search for a Method

1960

Existentialism, then, can only affirm the specificity of the historical *event*; it seeks to restore to the event its function and its multiple dimensions. Of course, Marxists do not ignore the event; in their eyes it expresses the structure of society, the form which the class struggle has assumed, the relations of force, the ascending movement of the rising class, the contradictions which at the center of each class set particular groups with different interests in opposition to each other. But a Marxist aphorism shows how for almost a hundred years now, Marxists have tended not to attach much importance to the event. The outstanding event of the eighteenth century, they say, would not be the French Revolution but the appearance of the steam engine. Marx did not move in this direction, as is demonstrated very well by his excellent article *The Eighteenth Brumaire of Louis Napoleon Bonaparte*. But today the fact—like the person—tends to become more and more symbolic. The duty of the event is to verify that a priori analyses of the situation—or at least not to contradict them. Thus French Communists tend to describe facts in terms of what can-be or must-be. Here is how one of them—and not one of the least important—explains the Soviet intervention in Hungary.

> Certain workers could be deceived, could commit themselves to a path which they did not believe to be that in which the counter-revolution was involving them, but subsequently these workers *could not help reflecting* on the consequences of this policy . . . [they] *could not do otherwise than be uneasy at seeing* [etc.] . . . . [They] could not (without indignation) see the return of the regent, Horthy. . . . It is *entirely natural* that under such circumstances the formation of the present Hungarian government has answered the prayers and expectation of the working class . . . in Hungary.

From *Search for a Method*, trans. Hazel E. Barnes (New York: Vintage, 1963), pp. 124–30 ["Question de méthode," preface to *Critique de la raison dialectique*, vol. 1 (Paris: Editions Gallimard, 1960)].

In this passage—the purpose of which is more political than theoretical—we are not told what the Hungarian workers did but what they *were unable not to do*. And why were they unable? Because they could not contradict their eternal essence as socialist workers. In a curious way, this Stalinized Marxism assumes an air of immobility; a worker is not a real being who changes with the world; he is a Platonic Idea. Indeed, in Plato, the Ideas are the Eternal, the Universal, the True. Motion and the event, as confused reflections of these static forms, are outside of Truth. Plato seeks to approach them through myths. In the Stalinist world the event is an edifying myth. Here we find what we might call the theoretical foundation for those fake confessions. The man who says, I have committed such and such an offense, such an act of treason, is performing a mythical, stereotyped recital, with no concern for verisimilitude, because he is asked to present his so-called crimes as the symbolic expression of an eternal essence. For example, the 1950 confession of abominable acts was for the purpose of unveiling the "true nature" of the Yugoslav regime. For us the most remarkable thing is the fact that the contradictions and errors in date, with which the confessions of Rajk were crammed full, never awakened in the Communists the vaguest suspicion. The materiality of fact is of no interest to these idealists; only its symbolic implications count in their eyes. In other words, Stalinist Marxists are blind to events. When they have reduced the meaning of them to the universal, they are quite willing to recognize that a residue remains, but they make of this residue the simple effect of chance. Fortuitous circumstances have been the occasional cause of what could not be dissolved (date, development, phases, origin and character of agents, ambiguity, misunderstandings, etc.). Thus, like individuals and particular enterprises, the lived falls over to the side of the irrational, the unutilizable, and the theoretician considers it to be *non-signifying*.

Existentialism reacts by affirming the specificity of the historical event, which it refuses to conceive of as the absurd juxtaposition of a contingent residue and an a priori signification. Its problem is to discover a supple, patient dialectic which espouses movements as they really are and which refuses to consider a priori that all lived conflicts pose contradictories or even contraries.[1] For us, *the interests* which come into play cannot necessarily find a mediation which reconciles them; most of the time they are mutually exclusive, but the fact that they cannot be satisfied at the same time does not necessarily prove that their reality is reduced to a pure contradiction of ideas. The thing stolen is not the contrary of the thief, nor is the exploited the contrary (or the contradictory) of the exploiter. Exploiter and exploited are men in conflict in a system whose principal characteristic is *scarcity*. To be sure, the capitalist owns the instruments of labor, and the worker does not own them: there we have a pure contradiction. But to be precise, this contradiction never succeeds in accounting for each event. It is the framework for the event; it creates a permanent tension in the social environment, a split within the capitalist society; but this fundamental structure of every contemporary event (in our bourgeois societies) does not by any means explain the event in its concrete reality. The day of the tenth of August, of the ninth of Thermidor, that day in the month of June 1848, etc., cannot be reduced to concepts. The relation between groups on each of those days is one of armed struggle, to be sure, and violence. But this struggle reflects *in itself* the structure of enemy groups, the immediate insufficiency of their development, the hidden conflicts which, though never clearly declared, result in an internal disequilibrium, the deviations which the present instruments impose on each one's action, the manner in which their needs and claims are manifested to each one.

Lefebvre has irrefutably established that after 1789, fear was the dominating passion of the revolutionary populace (which does not exclude heroism—quite the contrary) and that all these days of the popular offensive (July 14, June 20, August 10, September 3, etc.) are fundamentally *defensive* days. Military sections took the Tuileries by assault because they feared that an army of counter-revolutionaries might come forth from it some night to massacre Paris. *Today* this simple fact escapes Marxist analysis. The idealist voluntarism of the Stalinists can conceive only of an *offensive* action; it attributes negative sentiments to the class whose power is declining and to this class alone. Furthermore, when one recalls that the *sans-culottes*, mystified by the instruments of thought which they had at their disposal, allowed the immediate violence of their material needs to be transformed into an exclusively political violence, then one's idea of the Terror will be very different from the classical conception.

The event is not the passive resultant of a hesitant, distorted action and of an equally uncertain reaction; it is not even the fleeting, slippery synthesis of reciprocal incomprehensions. But across all the tools of action and thought which falsify *praxis*, each group realizes by its conduct a certain revelation of the other. Each of them is subject insofar as it directs its own action, and each is object insofar as it submits to the action of the other; each tactic foresees the other's tactic, more or less thwarts it, and is thwarted in turn. Inasmuch as each revealed activity of a group surpasses the activity of an opposing group, is modified in its tactics because of the latter and consequently modifies the structures of the group itself, the event in its full concrete reality is the organized unity of a plurality of oppositions reciprocally surpassed. Perpetually surpassed by the initiative of all and of each one, it surges up precisely from these very surpassing, as a double unified organization, the meaning of which is to realize in unity the destruction of each of its terms by the other. Thus constituted, the event reacts upon the men who compose it and imprisons them in its *apparatus*; of course, its being set up as an independent reality and its imposition on individuals are accomplished only by an immediate fetishizing. Already, for example, all the participants in the "day of August 10" know that the seizure of the Tuileries and the fall of the monarchy are at stake; the objective meaning of what they are doing is going to be imposed upon them as a real existence to the same degree that the other's resistance does not allow them to grasp their activity as the pure and simple objectification of themselves. Beginning here and precisely because the fetishizing has as a result the *realization* of fetishes, the event must be considered as a system in motion, drawing men along toward its own annihilation; the result is rarely clear-cut. On the evening of August 10, the King has not been deposed, but he is no longer at the Tuileries; he has been placed under the protection of the Assembly. His person remains just as embarrassing. The more real consequences of August 10 are, first, the appearance of the dual power (classical in Revolutions); second, the convocation of the Convention, which sets to work again at the basic problem, left unresolved by the event; finally, there is the dissatisfaction and growing unrest of the populace of Paris, which does not know whether or not its coup has succeeded. The result of this fear will be the September massacres. Thus it is the *very ambiguity* of the event which often confers upon it its historical efficacy. This is sufficient for us to affirm its specificity. For we do not wish to regard it as the simple unreal signification of molecular bumps and jolts—neither as their specific resultant nor as a schematic symbol of more profound movements. We view it rather as the moving, temporary unity of antagonistic groups which modifies them to the extent that they transform it.[2] As such, the event has its unique characteristics: its date, its speed, its structures, etc. The study of these factors allows us to make History rational even at the level of the concrete.

Notes

[1] If two propositions are contradictory to each other, this means that one cannot be true without the other's being false, and vice versa (e.g., "A is true" and "A is not true"). If they are contrary, then they cannot both be true at once, but it is possible that both are false (e.g., "All S is P" and "No S is P"). H.B.

[2] Obviously the conflict may be manifested here more or less clearly, or it may be veiled by the temporary complicity of the contending groups.

LOUIS ALTHUSSER AND ETIENNE BALIBAR

The Errors of Classical Economics: Outline of a Concept of Historical Time

1968

Let us begin with the last point, for it will make us more sensitive to the consequences of these principles. As a first approximation, we can argue from the specific structure of the Marxist whole that it is no longer possible to think the process of the development of the different levels of the whole *in the same historical time*. Each of these different "levels" does not have the same type of historical existence. On the contrary, we have to assign to each level a *peculiar time*, relatively autonomous and hence relatively independent, even in its dependence, of the "times" of the other levels. We can and must say: for each mode of production there is a peculiar time and history, punctuated in a specific way by the development of the productive forces; the relations of production have their peculiar time and history, punctuated in a specific way; the political superstructure has its own history . . . ; philosophy has its own time and history . . . ; aesthetic productions have their own time and history . . . ; scientific formations have their own time and history, etc. Each of these peculiar histories is punctuated with peculiar rhythms and can only be known on condition that we have defined the *concept* of the specificity of its historical temporality and its punctuations (continuous development, revolutions, breaks, etc.). The fact that each of these times and each of these histories is *relatively autonomous* does not make them so many domains which are *independent* of the whole: the specificity of each of these times and of each of these histories—in other words, their relative autonomy and independence—is based on a certain type of articulation in the whole, and therefore on a certain type of *dependence* with respect to the whole. The history of philosophy, for example, is not an independent history by divine right: the right of this history to exist as a specific history is determined by the articulating relations, i.e., relations of relative effectivity, which exist within the whole. The specificity of these times and

From *Reading Capital*, trans. Ben Brewster (1970; New York: Verso, 2009), pp. 99–103 ["Les défauts de l'économie classique: Esquisse du concept d'histoire," in *Lire le capital* (Paris: Editions Maspero, 1968)].

histories is therefore *differential*, since it is based on the differential relations between the different levels within the whole: the mode and degree of *independence* of each time and history is therefore necessarily determined by the mode and degree of *dependence* of each level within the set of articulations of the whole. The conception of the "relative" independence of a history and of a level can therefore never be reduced to the positive affirmation of an independence *in vacuo*, nor even to the mere negation of a dependence in itself; the conception of this "relative" independence defines its "relativity," i.e., the type of *dependence* that produces and establishes this mode of "relative" independence as its necessary result; at the level of the articulation of component structures in the whole, it defines that type of dependence which produces relative independence and whose effects we can observe in the histories of the different "levels."

This is the principle on which is based the possibility and necessity of different *histories* corresponding respectively to each of the "levels." This principle justifies our speaking of an economic history, a political history, a history of religions, a history of ideologies, a history of philosophy, a history of art and a history of the sciences, without thereby evading, but on the contrary, necessarily accepting, the relative independence of each of these histories in the specific dependence which articulates each of the different levels of the social whole with the others. That is why, if we have the right to constitute these different histories, which are merely differential histories, we cannot be satisfied, as the best historians so often are today, by *observing* the existence of different times and rhythms, without relating them to the concept of their difference, i.e., to the typical dependence which establishes them in the articulation of the levels of the whole. It is not enough, therefore, to say, as modern historians do, that *there are* different periodizations for different times, that each time has its own rhythms, some short, some long; we must also think these differences in rhythm and punctuation in their foundation, in the type of articulation, displacement and torsion which harmonizes these different times with one another. To go even further, I should say that we cannot restrict ourselves to reflecting the existence of *visible* and measurable times in this way; we must, of absolute necessity, pose the question of the mode of existence of *invisible* times, of the invisible rhythms and punctuations concealed beneath the surface of each visible time. Merely reading *Capital* shows that Marx was highly sensitive to this requirement. It shows, for example, that the time of economic production is a specific time (differing according to the mode of production), but also that, as a specific time, it is a complex and non-linear time—a time of times, a complex time that cannot be *read* in the continuity of the time of life or clocks, but has to be *constructed* out of the peculiar structures of production. The time of the capitalist economic production that Marx analyzed must be *constructed* in its concept. The concept of this time must be constructed out of the reality of the different rhythms which punctuate the different operations of production, circulation and distribution: out of the concepts of these different operations, e.g., the difference between production time and labor time, the difference between the different cycles of production (the turnover of fixed capital, of circulating capital, or variable capital, monetary turnover, turnover of commercial capital and of finance capital, etc.). In the capitalist mode of production, therefore, the time of economic production has absolutely nothing to do with the obviousness of everyday practice's ideological time: of course, it is rooted in certain determinate sites, in biological time (certain limits in the alternation of labor and rest for human and animal labor power; certain rhythms for agricultural production) but in essence it is not at all identified with this biological time, and in no sense is it a time that can be *read immediately* in the flow of any given process. It is an invisible time, essentially illegible, as invisible and as opaque as the reality of the total capitalist production process itself. This time, as a complex "intersection" of the different times, rhythms, turnovers, etc., that we have just discussed, is only accessible in *its concept*, which, like every concept is never immediately "given," never *legible* in visible reality: like every concept this concept must be *produced, constructed*.

The same could be said of political and ideological time, of the time of the theoretical (philosophy) and of the time of the scientific, let alone the time of art. Let us take an example. The time of the history of philosophy is not immediately legible either: of course, in historical chronology we do *see* philosophers *following one another*, and it would be possible to take this sequence for the history itself. Here, too, we must renounce the ideological pre-judgment of visible succession, and undertake *to construct the concept of the time of the history of philosophy*, and, in order to understand this concept, it is absolutely essential to define the specific difference of the philosophical as one of the existing cultural formations (the ideological and scientific formations); to define the philosophical as belonging to the level of the *Theoretical* as such; and to establish the differential relation of the Theoretical as such firstly to the different existing practices, secondly to ideology and finally to the scientific. To define these differential relations is to define the peculiar type of articulation of the Theoretical (philosophical) with these other realities, and therefore to define the peculiar articulation of the history of philosophy with the histories of the different practices, with the history of ideologies and the history of sciences. But this is not enough: in order to construct the concept of the history of philosophy it is essential to define in philosophy itself the specific reality which constitutes philosophical formations as such, and to which one must refer in order to think the mere possibility of *philosophical events*. This is one of the essential tasks of any theoretical attempt to produce the concept of history: to give a rigorous definition of the *historical fact* as such. Without anticipating this investigation, I should like to point out that, in its generality, the *historical* fact, as opposed to all the other phenomena that occur in historical existence, can be defined as *a fact which causes a mutation in the existing structural relations*. In the history of philosophy it is also essential, if we are to be able to discuss it as a history, to admit that *philosophical facts, philosophical events of historical scope*, occur in it, i.e., precisely *philosophical facts* which cause real mutations in the *existing philosophical structural relations*, in this case the *existing theoretical problematic*. Obviously, these facts are not always *visible*, rather, they are sometimes the object of a real repression, a real and more or less lasting historical denegation. For example, the mutation of the dogmatic classical problematic by Locke's empiricism is a philosophical event with historical scope, one which still dominates idealist critical philosophy today, just as it dominated the whole of the eighteenth century, Kant, Fichte and even Hegel. This historical fact and above all the length of its range (and in particular its importance for the understanding of German idealism from Kant to Hegel) is often suspected; its real profundity is rarely appreciated. Its role in the interpretation of Marxist philosophy has been absolutely decisive, and we are still largely held prisoner by it. For another example, Spinoza's philosophy introduced an unprecedented theoretical revolution in the history of philosophy, probably the greatest philosophical revolution of all time, insofar as we can regard Spinoza as Marx's only direct ancestor, from the philosophical standpoint. However, this radical revolution was the object of a massive historical repression, and Spinozist philosophy suffered much the same fate as Marxist philosophy used to and still does suffer in some countries: it served as damning evidence for a charge of "atheism." The insistence of the seventeenth- and eighteenth-century establishment's hounding of Spinoza's memory, and the distance every writer had ineluctably to take with respect to Spinoza in order to obtain the right to speak (cf. Montesquieu), are evidence both of the repulsion and the extraordinary attraction of his thought. The history of philosophy's repressed Spinozism thus unfolded as a subterranean history acting at *other sites* (*autres lieux*), in political and religious ideology (deism) and in the sciences, but not on the illuminated stage of visible philosophy. And when Spinoza re-appeared on this stage in German idealism's "*Atheismusstreit*," and then in academic interpretations, it was more or less under the aegis of a *misunderstanding*. I think I have said enough to suggest what direction the construction of the concept of history in its different domains must take; and to show that the construction of this concept incontestably produces a reality which has nothing to do with the visible sequence of events recorded by the chronicler.

We have known, since Freud, that the time of the unconscious cannot be confused with the time of biography. On the contrary, *the concept of the time of the unconscious must be constructed* in order to obtain an understanding of certain biographical traits. In exactly the same way, it is essential to construct the concepts of the different historical times which are never given in the ideological obviousness of the continuity of time (which need only be suitably divided into a good periodization to obtain the time of history), but must be constructed out of the differential nature and differential articulation of their objects in the structure of the whole. Are more examples necessary to convince us of this? Read Michel Foucault's remarkable studies in the "history of madness," or the "birth of clinical medicine," and you will see the distance between the elegant sequences of the official chronicle, in which a discipline or a society merely reflect its good conscience, i.e., the mask of its bad conscience—and the absolutely unexpected temporality that constitutes the essence of the process of constitution and development of those cultural formations: there is nothing in true history which allows it to be read in the ideological continuum of a linear time that need only be punctuated and divided; on the contrary, it has its extremely complex and peculiar temporality which is, of course, utterly paradoxical in comparison with the disarming simplicity of ideological pre-judgment. An understanding of the history of cultural formations such as those of "madness" and of the origins of the "clinical gaze" (*regard clinique*) in medicine presupposes a vast effort not of abstraction but *in* abstraction, in order to construct and identify the object itself, and in order to construct from this *the concept of history*. This is antipodal to the empirically visible history in which the time of all histories is the simple time of continuity and in which the "content" is the vacuity of events that occur in it which one later tries to determine with dividing procedures in order to "periodize" that continuity. Instead of these categories, continuity and discontinuity, which summarize the banal mystery of all history, we are dealing with infinitely more complex categories specific to each type of history, categories in which new logics come into play, in which, naturally, the Hegelian schemata, which are merely the sublimation of the categories of the "logic of movement and time," no longer have more than a highly approximate value, and even this *only on condition that they are used approximately (indicatively) in accordance with their approximate nature*—for if we had to take these Hegelian categories for adequate categories, their use would become theoretically absurd, and practically either vain or disastrous.

GILLES DELEUZE

The Logic of Sense

1969

Either ethics makes no sense at all, or this is what it means and has nothing else to say: not to be unworthy of what happens to us. To grasp whatever happens as unjust and unwarranted (it is always someone else's fault), is, on the contrary, what renders our sores repugnant—veritable *ressentiment*, resentment of the event. There is no other ill will. What is really immoral is the use of moral notions like just or unjust, merit or fault. What does it mean then to will the event? Is it to accept war, wounds, and death when they occur? It is highly probable that resignation is only one more figure of *ressentiment*, since *ressentiment* has many figures. If willing the event is, primarily, to release its eternal truth, like the fire on which it is fed, this will would reach the point at which war is waged against war, the wound would be the living trace and the scar of all wounds, and death turned on itself would be willed against all deaths. We are faced with a volitional intuition and a transmutation. "To my inclination for death," said Bousquet, "which was a failure of the will, I will substitute a longing for death which would be the apotheosis of the will." From this inclination to this longing there is, in a certain respect, no change except a change of the will, a sort of leaping in place (*saut sur place*) of the whole body which exchanges its organic will for a spiritual will. It wills now not exactly what occurs, but something *in* that which occurs, something yet to come which would be consistent with what occurs, in accordance with the laws of an obscure, humorous conformity: the Event. It is in this sense that the *Amor fati* is one with the struggle of free men. My misfortune is present in all events, but also a splendor and brightness which dry up misfortune and which bring about that the event, once willed, is actualized on its most contracted point, on the cutting edge of an operation. All this is the effect of the static genesis and of the immaculate conception. The splendor and the magnificence of the event is sense. The event is not what occurs (an accident), it is rather inside what occurs, the purely expressed. It signals and awaits us. In

From *The Logic of Sense*, ed. Constantin V. Boundas and trans. Mark Lester with Charles Stivale (New York: Columbia University Press, 1990), pp. 149–52, 171–74 [*Logique du sens* (Paris: Editions de Minuit, 1969)].

accordance with the three preceding determinations, it is what must be understood, willed, and represented in that which occurs. Bousquet goes on to say: "Become the man of your misfortunes; learn to embody their perfection and brilliance." Nothing more can be said, and no more has ever been said: to become worthy of what happens to us, and thus to will and release the event, to become the offspring of one's own events, and thereby to be reborn, to have one more birth, and to break with one's carnal birth—to become the offspring of one's events and not of one's actions, for the action is itself produced by the offspring of the event.

The actor is not like a god, but is rather like an "anti-god" (*contredieu*). God and actor are opposed in their readings of time. What men grasp as past and future, God lives it in its eternal present. The God is Chronos: the divine present is the circle in its entirety, whereas past and future are dimensions relative to a particular segment of the circle which leaves the rest outside. The actor's present, on the contrary, is the most narrow, the most contracted, the most instantaneous, and the most punctual. It is the point on a straight line which divides the line endlessly, and is itself divided into past-future. The actor belongs to the Aion: instead of the most profound, the most fully present, the present which spreads out and comprehends the future and the past, an unlimited past-future rises up here reflected in an empty present which has no more thickness than the mirror. The actor or actress represents, but what he or she represents is always still in the future and already in the past, whereas his or her representation is impassible and divided, unfolded without being ruptured, neither acting nor being acted upon. It is in this sense that there is an actor's paradox; the actor maintains himself in the instant in order to act out something perpetually anticipated and delayed, hoped for and recalled. The role played is never that of a character; it is a theme (the complex theme or sense) constituted by the components of the event, that is, by the communicating singularities effectively liberated from the limits of individuals and persons. The actor strains his entire personality in a moment which is always further divisible in order to open himself up to the impersonal and pre-individual role. The actor is always acting out other roles when acting one role. The role has the same relation to the actor as the future and past have to the instantaneous present which corresponds to them on the line of the Aion. The actor thus actualizes the event, but in a way which is entirely different from the actualization of the event in the depth of things. Or rather, the actor redoubles this cosmic, or physical actualization, in his own way, which is singularly superficial—but because of it more distinct, trenchant and pure. Thus, the actor delimits the original, disengages from it an abstract line, and keeps from the event only its contour and its splendor, becoming thereby the actor of one's own events—a *counter-actualization*.

The physical mixture is exact only at the level of the whole, in the full circle of the divine present. But with respect to each part, there are many injustices and ignominies, many parasitic and cannibalistic processes which inspire our terror at what happens to us, and our resentment at what occurs. Humor is inseparable from a selective force: in that which occurs (an accident), it selects the pure event. In eating, it selects speaking. Bousquet listed the characteristics of the humor-actor (*de l'humour-acteur*): to annihilate his or her tracks whenever necessary; "to hold up among men and works *their being before bitterness*," "to assign to plagues, tyrannies, and the most frightful wars the comic possibility of having reigned for nothing"; in short, to liberate for each thing "its immaculate portion," language and will, *Amor Fati*.[1]

Why is every event a kind of plague, war, wound, or death? Is this simply to say that there are more unfortunate than fortunate events? No, this is not the case since the question here is about the double structure of every event. With every event, there is indeed the present moment of its actualization, the moment in which the event is embodied in a state of affairs, an individual, or a person, the moment we designate by saying "*here*, the moment has come." The future and the past of the event are evaluated only with respect to this definitive present, and from the point of view of that which embodies it. But on the other hand, there is the future and the past of the event considered in itself, sidestepping each present, being free of the limitations of a state of affairs, impersonal and pre-individual, neutral, neither general nor particular, *eventum tantum*. . . . It has no other present than that of the mobile instant which represents it, always divided into past-future, and forming what must be called the counter-actualization. In one case, it is my life, which seems too weak for me and slips away at a point which, in a determined relation to me, has become present. In the other case, it is I who am too weak for life, it is life which overwhelms me, scattering its singularities all about, in no relation to me, nor to a moment determinable as the present, except an impersonal instant which is divided into still-future and already-past. No one has shown better than Maurice Blanchot that this ambiguity is essentially that of the wound and of death, of the mortal wound. Death has an extreme and definite relation to me and my body and is grounded in me, but it also has no relation to me at all—it is incorporeal and infinitive, impersonal, grounded only in itself. On one side, there is the part of the event which is realized and accomplished; on the other, there is that "part of the event which cannot realize its accomplishment." There are thus two accomplishments, which are like actualization and counter-actualization. It is in this way that death and its wound are not simply events among other events. Every event is like death, double and impersonal in its double. "It is the abyss of the present, the time without present with which I have no relation, toward which I am unable to project myself. For in it *I* do not die. I forfeit the power of dying. In this abyss they (*on*) die—they never cease to die, and they never succeed in dying."[2]

How different this "they" is from that which we encounter in everyday banality. It is the "they" of impersonal and pre-individual singularities, the "they" of the pure event wherein *it* dies in the same way that *it* rains. The splendor of the "they" is the splendor of the event itself or of the fourth person. This is why there are no private or collective events, no more than there are individuals and universals, particularities and generalities. Everything is singular, and thus both collective and private, particular and general, neither individual nor universal. Which war, for example, is not a private affair? Conversely, which wound is not inflicted by war and derived from society as a whole? Which private event does not have all its coordinates, that is, all its impersonal social singularities? There is, nevertheless, a good deal of ignominy in saying that war concerns everybody, for this is not true. It does not concern those who use it or those who serve it—creatures of *ressentiment*. And there is as much ignominy in saying that everyone has his or her own war or particular wound, for this is not true of those who scratch at their sores—the creatures of bitterness and *ressentiment*. It is true only of the free man, who grasps the event, and does not allow it to be actualized as such without enacting, the actor, its counter-actualization. Only the free man, therefore, can comprehend all violence in a single act of violence, and every mortal event *in a single Event* which no longer makes room for the accident, and which denounces and removes the power of *ressentiment* within the individual as well as the power of oppression within the society. Only by spreading *ressentiment* the tyrant forms allies, namely slaves and servants. The revolutionary alone is free from the *ressentiment*, by means of which one always participates in, and profits by, an oppressive order.

. . .

It seems, however, if we follow the surviving partial and deceiving texts, that the Stoics may not have been able to resist the double temptation of returning to the simple physical causality or to the logical contradiction. The first theoretician of alogical incompatibilities, and for this reason the first important theoretician of the event, was Leibniz. For what Leibniz called "compossible" and "incompossible" cannot be reduced to the identical and the contradictory, which govern only the possible and the impossible. Compossibility does not even presuppose the inherence of predicates in an individual subject or monad. It is rather the inverse; inherent predicates are those which correspond to events from the beginning compossible (the monad of Adam the sinner includes in predicative form only future and past events which are compossible with the sin of Adam). Leibniz was thus extremely conscious of the anteriority and originality of the event in relation to the predicate. Compossibility must be defined in an original manner, at a pre-individual level, by the convergence of series which singularities of events form as they stretch themselves out over lines of ordinary points. Incompossibility must be defined by the divergence of such series: if another Sextus than the one we know is incompossible with our world, it is because he would correspond to a singularity the series of which would diverge from the series of our world, clustered about the Adam, the

Judas, the Christ, and the Leibniz that we know. Two events are compossible when the series which are organized around their singularities extend in all directions; they are incompossible when the series diverge in the vicinity of constitutive singularities. Convergence and divergence are entirely original relations which cover the rich domain of alogical compatibilities and incompatibilities, and therefore form an essential component of the theory of sense.

Leibniz, though, makes use of this rule of incompossibility in order to exclude events from one another. He made a negative use of divergence of disjunction—one of exclusion. This is justified, however, only to the extent that events are already grasped under the hypothesis of a God who calculates and chooses, and from the point of view of their actualization in distinct worlds or individuals. It is no longer justified, however, if we consider the pure events and the ideal play whose principle Leibniz was unable to grasp, hindered as he was by theological exigencies. For, from this other point of view, the divergence of series or the disjunction of members (*membra disjuncta*) cease to be negative rules of exclusion according to which events would be incompossible or incompatible. Divergence and disjunction are, on the contrary, affirmed as such. But what does it mean to make divergence and disjunction the objects of affirmation? As a general rule, two things are simultaneously affirmed only to the extent that their difference is denied, suppressed from within, even if the level of this suppression is supposed to regulate the production of difference as much as its disappearance. To be sure, the identity here is not that of indifference, but it is generally *through identity* that opposites are affirmed at the same time, whether we accentuate one of the opposites in order to find the other, or whether we create a synthesis of the two. We speak, on the contrary, of an operation according to which two things or two determinations are affirmed *through* their difference, that is to say, that they are the objects of simultaneous affirmation only insofar as their difference is itself affirmed and is itself affirmative. We are no longer faced with an identity of contraries, which would still be inseparable as such from a movement of the negative and of exclusion.[3] We are rather faced with a positive distance of different elements: no longer to identify two contraries with the same, but to affirm their distance as that which relates one to the other insofar as they are "different." The idea of a positive distance as distance (and not as an annulled or overcome distance) appears to us essential, since it permits the measuring of contraries through their finite difference instead of equating difference with a measureless contrariety, and contrariety with an identity which is itself infinite. It is not difference which must "go as far as" contradiction, as Hegel thought in his desire to accommodate the negative; it is the contradiction which must reveal the nature of *its* difference as it follows the distance corresponding to it. The idea of positive distance belongs to topology and to the surface. It excludes all depth and all elevation, which would restore the negative and the identity. Nietzsche provides the example for such a procedure, which must not, under any circumstances, be confused with some unknown identity of contraries (as is commonplace in spiritualist and dolorist philosophy). Nietzsche exhorts us to live health and sickness in such a manner that health be a living perspective on sickness and sickness a living perspective on health; to make of sickness an exploration of health, of health an investigation of sickness: "Looking from the perspective of the sick toward *healthier* concepts and values and, conversely, looking again from the fullness and self-assurance of a *rich* life down into the secret work of the instinct of decadence—in this I have had the longest training, my truest experiences; if in anything, I became master in *this*. Now I know how, have the know-how, to *reverse perspectives*. . . ."[4] We cannot identify contraries, nor can we affirm their entire distance, except as that which relates one to the other. Health affirms sickness when it makes its distance from sickness an object of affirmation. Distance is, at arm's length, the affirmation of that which it distances. This procedure which makes of health an evaluation of sickness and sickness an evaluation of health—is this not the Great Health (or the Gay Science)? Is it not this which permits Nietzsche to experience a superior health at the very moment that he is sick? Conversely, Nietzsche does not lose his health when he is sick, but when he can no longer affirm the distance, when he is no longer able, by means of his health, to establish sickness as a point of view on health (then, as the Stoics say, the role is over, the play has ended). "Point of view" does not signify a theoretical judgment; as for "procedure," it is life itself. From Leibniz, we had already learned that there are no points of view on things, but that things, beings, are themselves points of view. Leibniz, however, subjected the points of view to exclusive rules such that each opened itself onto the others only insofar as they converged: the points of view on the same town. With Nietzsche, on the contrary, the point of view is opened onto a divergence which it affirms: another town corresponds to each point of view, each point of view is another town, the towns are linked only by their distance and resonate only through the divergence of their series, their houses and their streets. There is always another town within the town. Each term becomes the means of going all the way to the end of another, by following the entire distance. Nietzsche's perspective—his perspectivism—is a much more profound art than Leibniz's point of view; for divergence is no longer a principle of exclusion, and disjunction no longer a means of separation. Incompossibility is now a means of communication.

Notes

[1] See Joe Bousquet, *Les capitales* (Paris: Le Cercle du Livre, 1955), p. 103.

[2] Maurice Blanchot, *L'espace littéraire* (Paris: Gallimard, 1955), p. 160.

[3] On the role of exclusion and expulsion, see the chapter on "contradiction" in Hegel's *Logic*.

[4] Nietzsche, *Ecce Homo*, trans. Walter Kaufmann, in *On the Genealogy of Morals and Ecce Homo* (New York: Vintage Books, 1969), p. 223.

GILLES DELEUZE

Difference and Repetition

1968

What does this mean: the empty form of time or third synthesis? The Northern Prince says "time is out of joint." Can it be that the Northern philosopher says the same thing: that he should be Hamletian because he is Oedipal? The joint, *cardo*, is what ensures the subordination of time to those properly cardinal points through which pass the periodic movements which it measures (time, number of the movement, for the soul as much as for the world). By contrast, time out of joint means demented time or time outside the curve which gave it a god, liberated from its overly simple circular figure, freed from the events which made up its content, its relation to movement overturned; in short, time presenting itself as an empty and pure form. Time itself unfolds (that is, apparently ceases to be a circle), instead of things unfolding within it (following the overly simple circular figure). It ceases to be cardinal and becomes ordinal, a pure *order* of time. Hölderlin said that it no longer "rhymed," because it was distributed unequally on both sides of a "caesura," as a result of which beginning and end no longer coincided. We may define the order of time as this purely formal distribution of the unequal in the function of a caesura. We can then distinguish a more or less extensive past and a future in inverse proportion, but the future and the past here are not empirical and dynamic determinations of time: they are formal and fixed characteristics which follow *a priori* from the order of time, as though they comprised a static synthesis of time. The synthesis is necessarily static, since time is no longer subordinated to movement; time is the most radical form of change, but the form of change does not change. The caesura, along with the before and after which it ordains once and for all, constitutes the fracture in the I (the caesura is exactly the point at which the fracture appears).

Having abjured its empirical content, having overturned its own ground, time is defined not only by a formal and empty order but also by a totality and a series. In the first place, the idea of a totality of time must be understood as

From *Difference and Repetition*, trans. Paul Patton (New York: Columbia University Press, 1994), pp. 88–92 [*Différence et répétition* (Paris: Presses Universitaires de France, 1968)].

follows: the caesura, of whatever kind, must be determined in the image of a unique and tremendous event, an act which is adequate to time as a whole. The image itself is divided, torn into two unequal parts. Nevertheless, it thereby draws together the totality of time. It must be called a symbol by virtue of the unequal parts which it subsumes and draws together, but draws together as unequal parts. Such a symbol adequate to the totality of time may be expressed in many ways: to throw time out of joint, to make the sun explode, to throw oneself into the volcano, to kill God or the father. This symbolic image constitutes the totality of time to the extent that it draws together the caesura, the before and the after. However, in so far as it carries out their distribution within inequality, it creates the possibility of a temporal series. In effect, there is always a time at which the imagined act is supposed "too big for me." This defines *a priori* the past or the before. It matters little whether or not the event itself occurs, or whether the act has been performed or not: past, present and future are not distributed according to this empirical criterion. Oedipus has already carried out the act, Hamlet has not yet done so, but in either case the first part of the symbol is lived in the past, they are in the past and live themselves as such so long as they experience the image of the act as too big for them. The second time, which relates to the caesura itself, is thus the present of metamorphosis, a becoming-equal to the act and a doubling of the self, and the projection of an ideal self in the image of the act (this is marked by Hamlet's sea voyage and by the outcome of Oedipus's enquiry: the hero becomes "capable" of the act). As for the third time in which the future appears, this signifies that the event and the act possess a secret coherence which excludes that of the self; that they turn back against the self which has become their equal and smash it to pieces, as though the bearer of the new world were carried away and dispersed by the shock of the multiplicity to which it gives birth: what the self has become equal to is the unequal in itself. In this manner, the I which is fractured according to the order of time and the Self which is divided according to the temporal series correspond and find a common descendant in the man without name, without family, without qualities, without self or I, the "plebeian" guardian of a secret, the already-Overman whose scattered members gravitate around the sublime image.

All is repetition in the temporal series, in relation to this symbolic image. The past itself is repetition by default, and it prepares this other repetition constituted by the metamorphosis in the present. Historians sometimes look for empirical correspondences between the present and the past, but however rich it may be, this network of historical correspondences involves repetition only by analogy or similitude. In truth, the past is in itself repetition, as is the present, but they are repetition in two different modes which repeat each other. Repetition is never a historical fact, but rather the historical condition under which something new is effectively produced. It is not the historian's reflection which demonstrates a resemblance between Luther and Paul, between the Revolution of 1789 and the Roman Republic, etc. Rather, it is in the first place for themselves that the revolutionaries are determined to lead their lives as "resuscitated Romans" before becoming capable of the act which they have begun by repeating in the mode of a proper past, therefore under conditions such that they necessarily identify with a figure from the historical past. *Repetition is a condition of action before it is a concept of reflection*. We produce something new only on condition that we repeat—once in the mode which constitutes the past, and once more in the present of metamorphosis. Moreover, what is produced, the absolutely new itself, is in turn nothing but repetition: the third repetition, this time by excess, the repetition of the future as eternal return. For even though the doctrine of eternal return may be expounded as though it affected the whole series or the totality of time, the past and the present no less than the future, such an exposition remains purely introductory. It has no more than a problematic and indeterminate value, no function beyond that of posing the problem of eternal return. Eternal return, in its esoteric truth, concerns—and can concern—only the third time of the series. Only there is it determined. That is why it is properly called a belief of the future, a belief in the future. Eternal return affects only the new, what is produced under the condition of default and by the intermediary of metamorphosis. However, it causes neither the *condition* nor the *agent* to return: on the contrary, it repudiates these and expels them with all its centrifugal force. It constitutes the autonomy of the product, the independence of the work. It is repetition by excess which leaves intact nothing of the default or the becoming-equal. It is itself the new, complete novelty. It is by itself the third time in the series, the future as such. As Klossowski says, it is the secret coherence which establishes itself only by excluding my own coherence, my own identity, the identity of the self, the world and God. It allows only the plebeian to return, the man without a name. It draws into its circle the dead god and the dissolved self. It does not allow the sun to return, since it presupposes its explosion; it concerns only the nebulae, for which alone it moves and from which it becomes indistinguishable. For this reason, as Zarathustra says at one point to the demon, we simplify matters in expounding the doctrine of eternal return as though it affected the totality of time; we make a hurdy-gurdy song of it, as he says at another point to his animals. In other words, we rely upon the overly simple circle which has its content the passing present and as its shape the past of reminiscence. However, the order of time, time as a pure and empty form, has precisely undone that circle. It has undone it in favor of a less simple and much more secret, much more tortuous, more nebulous circle, an eternally excentric circle, the decentred circle of difference which is re-formed uniquely in the third time of the series. The order of time has broken the circle of the Same and arranged time in a series only in order to re-form a circle of the Other at the end of the series. The "once and for all" of the order is there only for the "every time" of the final esoteric circle. The form of time is there only for the revelation of the formless in the eternal return. The extreme formality is there only for an excessive formlessness (Hölderlin's *Unförmliche*). In this manner, the ground has been superseded by a groundlessness, a universal ungrounding which turns upon itself and causes only the yet-to-come to return.

Note on the Three Repetitions

Marx's theory of historical repetition, as it appears notably in *The Eighteenth Brumaire of Louis Bonaparte*, turns on the following principle, which does not seem to have been sufficiently understood by historians: historical repetition is neither a matter of analogy nor a concept produced by the reflection of historians, but above all a condition of historical action itself. Harold Rosenberg illuminates this point in some fine pages: historical actors or agents can create only on condition that they identify themselves with figures from the past. In this sense, history is theater: "their action became a spontaneous repetition of an old role. . . . It is the revolutionary crisis, the compelled striving for 'something entirely new,' that causes history to become veiled in myth . . ." (Harold Rosenberg, *The Tradition of the New*, London: Thames & Hudson, 1962, ch. 12, "The Resurrected Romans," pp. 155–6).

According to Marx, repetition is comic when it falls short—that is, when instead of leading to metamorphosis and the production of something new, it forms a kind of involution, the opposite of an authentic creation. Comic travesty replaces tragic metamorphosis. However, it appears that for Marx this comic or grotesque repetition necessarily comes *after* the tragic, evolutive and creative repetition ("all great events and historical personages occur, as it were, twice . . . the first time as tragedy, the second as farce"). This temporal order does not, however, seem to be absolutely justified. Comic repetition works by means of some defect, in the mode of the past properly so called. The hero necessarily confronts this repetition so long as "the act is too big for him": Polonius's murder by mistake is comic, as is Oedipus's enquiry. The moment of metamorphosis, tragic repetition, follows. It is true that these two moments are not independent, existing as they do only for the third moment beyond the comic and the tragic: the production of something new entails a dramatic repetition which excludes even the hero. However, once the first two elements acquire an abstract independence or become genres, then the comic succeeds the tragic as though the failure of metamorphosis, raised to the absolute, presupposed an earlier metamorphosis already completed.

Note that the three-stage structure of repetition is no less that of Hamlet than that of Oedipus. Hölderlin showed this with incomparable rigor in the case of Oedipus: the before, the caesura and the after. He indicated that the relative dimensions of the before and after could vary according to the position of the caesura (for example, the sudden death of Antigone by contrast with Oedipus's long wandering). The essential point, however, is the persistence of the triadic structure. In this regard, Rosenberg interprets Hamlet in a manner which conforms completely to Hölderlin's schema, the caesura being constituted by the sea voyage: Rosenberg, *The Tradition of the New*, ch. 11, "Character Change and the Drama," pp. 135–53. Hamlet resembles Oedipus by virtue of not only the content but also the dramatic form.

MICHEL FOUCAULT

Eventalization

1978

I am trying to work in the direction of what one might call "eventalization." Even though the "event" has been for some while now a category little esteemed by historians, I wonder whether, understood in a certain sense, "eventalization" may not be a useful procedure of analysis. What do I mean by this term? First of all, a breach of self-evidence. It means making visible a *singularity* at places where there is a temptation to invoke a historical constant, an immediate anthropological trait, or an obviousness that imposes itself uniformly on all. To show that things "weren't as necessary as all that"; it wasn't as a matter of course that mad people came to be regarded as mentally ill; it wasn't self-evident that the only thing to be done with a criminal was to lock him up; it wasn't self-evident that the causes of illness were to be sought through the individual examination of bodies; and so on. A breach of self-evidence, of those self-evidences on which our knowledges, acquiescences, and practices rest: this is the first theoretico-political function of "eventalization."

Second, eventalization means rediscovering the connections, encounters, supports, blockages, plays of forces, strategies, and so on, that at a given moment establish what subsequently counts as being self-evident, universal, and necessary. In this sense, one is indeed effecting a sort of multiplication or pluralization of causes.

Does this mean that one regards the singularity one is analyzing simply as a fact to be registered, a reasonless break in an inert continuum? Clearly not, since that would amount to treating continuity as a self-sufficient reality that carries its own raison d'être within itself.

This procedure of causal multiplication means analyzing an event according to the multiple processes that constitute it. So, to analyze the practice of penal incarceration as an "event" (not as an institutional fact or ideological effect) means to determine the processes of "penalization" (that is, progressive

From "Questions of Method," in *Power*, ed. James D. Faubion and trans. Robert Hurley (New York: The New Press, 2000), pp. 226–29 [*Dits et écrits, tome II: 1976–1988*, ed. Daniel Defert and François Ewald with the assistance of Jacques Lagrange (1994; Paris: Editions Gallimard, 2001)].

insertion into the forms of legal punishment) of already existing practices of internment; the processes of "carceralization" of practices of penal justice (that is, the movement by which imprisonment as a form of punishment and technique of correction becomes a central component of the penal order). And these vast processes need themselves to be further broken down: the penalization of internment comprises a multiplicity of processes such as the formation of closed pedagogical spaces functioning through rewards, punishments, and so on.

As a way of lightening the weight of causality, "eventalization" thus works by constructing around the singular event analyzed as process a "polygon" or, rather "polyhedron" of intelligibility, the number of whose faces is not given in advance and can never properly be taken as finite. One has to proceed by progressive, necessarily incomplete saturation. And one has to bear in mind that the further one breaks down the processes under analysis, the more one is enabled and indeed obliged to construct their external relations of intelligibility. (In concrete terms: the more one analyzes the process of "carceralization" of penal practice down to its smallest details, the more one is led to relate them to such practices as schooling, military discipline, and so on.) The internal analysis of processes goes hand in hand with a multiplication of analytical "salients."

This operation thus leads to an increasing polymorphism as the analysis progresses:

1. A polymorphism of the elements brought into relation: starting from the prison, one introduces the history of pedagogical practices, the formation of professional armies, British empirical philosophy, techniques of use of firearms, new methods of division of labor.

2. A polymorphism of relations described: these may concern the transposition of technical models (such as architectures of surveillance), tactics calculated in response to a particular situation (such as the growth of banditry, the disorder provoked by public tortures and executions, the defects of the practice of penal banishment), or the application of theoretical schemas (such as those representing the genesis of ideas and the formation of signs, the utilitarian conception of behavior, and so on).

3. A polymorphism of domains of reference (varying in their nature, generality, and so on), ranging from technical mutations in matters of detail to the attempted emplacement in a capitalist economy of new techniques of power designed in response to the exigencies of that economy.

Forgive this long detour, but it enables me to better reply to your question about hyper- and hyporationalisms, one that is often put to me.

It has been some time since historians lost their love of events and made "de-eventalization" their principle of historical intelligibility. The way they work is by ascribing the object they analyze to the most unitary, necessary, inevitable, and (ultimately) extrahistorical mechanism or structure available. An economic mechanism, an anthropological structure, or a demographic process that figures the climactic stage in the investigation—these are the goals of de-eventalized history. (Of course, these remarks are only intended as a crude specification of a certain broad tendency.)

Clearly, viewed from the standpoint of this style of analysis, what I am proposing is at once too much and too little. There are too many diverse kinds of relations, too many lines of analysis, yet at the same time there is too little necessary unity. A plethora of intelligibilities, a deficit of necessities.

But for me this is precisely the point at issue, both in historical analysis and in political critique. We aren't, nor do we have to put ourselves, under the sign of a unitary necessity.

JACQUES DERRIDA

Psyche: Inventions of the Other

1987

So, then, the singular structure of an event, for the speech act I am speaking of must be an event. It will be so, on the one hand, insofar as it is singular, and, on the other hand, inasmuch as its very singularity will produce the coming or the coming about of something new. It should make come about or allow the coming of what is new in a "first time ever." The full weight of the enigma is borne in every word used here—"new," "event," "coming," "singularity," "first time" (here the English phrase "first time" marks the temporal aspect that the French *première fois* elides). Never does an invention appear, never does an invention take place, without an inaugural event. Nor is there any invention without an advent, if we take this latter word to mean the inauguration for the future of a *possibility* or of a *power* that will remain at the disposal of everyone. Advent there must be, because the event of an invention, its act of inaugural production, once recognized, legitimized, countersigned by a social consensus according to a system of conventions, must be valid *for the future* [*l'avenir*]. It will only receive its status of invention, furthermore, to the extent that this socialization of the invented thing is protected by a system of conventions that will at the same time ensure its inscription in a common history, its belonging to a culture: to a heritage, a patrimony, a pedagogical tradition, a discipline, a chain of generations. Invention *begins* by being susceptible to repetition, exploitation, reinscription.

While limiting ourselves to a network that is not solely lexical and cannot be reduced to the games of a simple verbal invention, we have already encountered the convergence of several modes of coming or of venue, the enigmatic collusion of *invenire* and *inventio*, of *event* and *advent*, of *future-to-come* [*l'avenir*], of *adventure*, and of *convention*. How could one translate this lexical cluster outside the Romance languages while preserving its unity, the unity linking

From *Psyche: Inventions of the Other, Volume 1*, ed. Peggy Kamuf and Elizabeth G. Rottenberg (Stanford, CA: Stanford University Press, 2007), pp. 5–7, 39, 43–44; first published as "Psyche: Inventions of the Other," trans. Catherine Porter, in *Reading de Man Reading*, ed. Lindsay Waters and Wlad Godzich (Minneapolis: University of Minnesota Press, 1989), pp. 25–65 [*Psyché: Inventions de l'autre, tomes I et II* (Paris: Editions Galilée, 1987)].

the *first time* of invention to the *coming*, to the arrival of the future [*avenir*], of the event, of the advent, of the convention or of the adventure? Of course, for the most part, these words of Latin origin are welcomed, for example, into English (even the term "venue," in its narrow, highly coded judicial sense, and the special sense of "advent" designating the coming of Christ); they are welcome with, however, a notable exception at the center of this home and hearth: the *venir* itself. To be sure, an invention amounts, says the *Oxford English Dictionary*, to "the action of coming upon or finding." But I can already imagine the inventiveness required of the translator of this lecture in those places where it exploits the institution of the Latin-based languages. Even if this verbal collusion appears adventurous or conventional, it makes us think. What does it make us think? What else? Whom else? What do we still have to invent in regard to the coming, the *venire*? What does it mean, *to come*? To come a first time? Every invention supposes that something or someone comes a *first time*, something or someone comes to someone, to someone else. But for an invention to be an invention, in other words, *unique* (even if the uniqueness has to be repeatable), it is also necessary for this first time to be a last time: archaeology and eschatology acknowledge each other here in the irony of the *one and only* instant.

So we are considering the singular structure of an event that seems to produce itself by speaking about itself, *by the act of speaking of itself* once it has begun to invent on the subject of invention, paving the way for it, inaugurating or signing its singularity, bringing it about, as it were; and all the while it is also naming and describing the generality of its genre and the genealogy of its topos: *de inventione*, sustaining our memory of the tradition of a genre and its practitioners. In its claim to be inventing again, such a discourse would be stating the inventive beginning by speaking of itself in a reflexive structure that not only does not produce coincidence with or presence to itself but instead projects forward the advent of the self, of "speaking" or "writing" of itself as other, that is to say, following a *trace*.

. . .

Such is what all governmental policies on modern science and culture attempt when they try—and how could they do otherwise?—to program invention. The aleatory margin that they seek to integrate remains homogeneous with calculation, within the order of the calculable; it devolves from a probabilistic quantification and still resides, we might say, in the same order and in the order of the same. An order where there is no absolute surprise, the order of what I will call the invention of the same. This invention comprises *all* invention, or almost. And I shall not *oppose* it to invention of the other (indeed, I shall oppose nothing to it), for opposition, dialectical or not, still belongs to this regimen of the same. The invention of the other is not opposed to that of the same, its difference beckons toward another coming about, toward this other invention of which we dream, the invention of the entirely other, the one that allows the coming of a still unanticipatable alterity, and for which no horizon of expectation as yet seems ready, in place, available. Yet it is necessary to prepare for it; to allow the coming of the entirely other, passivity, a certain kind of resigned passivity for which everything comes down to the same, is not suitable. Letting the other come is not inertia ready for anything whatever. No doubt the coming of the other, if it has to remain incalculable and in a certain way aleatory (one happens upon the other in the encounter), escapes from all programming. But this aleatory aspect of the other has to be heterogeneous in relation to the integrable aleatory factor of a calculus, and likewise to the form of undecidable that theories of formal systems have to cope with. This invention of the entirely other is beyond any possible status; I still call it invention, because one gets ready for it, one makes this step destined to let the other come, *come in*. The invention of the other, the incoming of the other, is certainly not *constructed* as a subjective genitive, and just as assuredly not as an objective genitive either, even if the invention comes from the other—for this other is thenceforth neither subject nor object, neither a self nor a consciousness nor an unconscious. To get ready for this coming of the other is what can be called deconstruction. It deconstructs precisely this double genitive and, as deconstructive invention, itself comes back in the step [*pas*]—and also as the step—of the other. To invent would then be to "know" how to say "come" and to answer the "come" of the other. Does that ever come about? Of this event one is never sure.

. . .

Invention comes down or back to the same, and this is always possible, as soon as it can receive a status and thereby be legitimized by an institution that it then becomes in its turn. For what is being invented in this way are always institutions. Institutions are inventions and the inventions to which a status is conferred are in turn institutions. How can an invention *come back* to being the same, how can the *invenire*, the advent of the future-to-come, come around to coming back, to folding back toward the past a movement said to be always innovative? For that to happen, it suffices that invention be possible and that it invent what is possible. Then, right from its origin ("Par le mot *par* commence donc ce texte"), it envelops in itself a repetition, it unfolds only the dynamics of what was already *found there*, a set of comprehensible possibilities that come into view as ontological or theological truth, a program of cultural or techno-scientific politics (civil or military), and so forth. By inventing the possible on the basis of the possible, we relate the new—that is, something quite other that can also be quite ancient—to a set of present possibilities, to the present and state of the order of possibility that provides for the new the conditions of its status. This statutory economy of public invention does not break the *psyché*, does not pass beyond the mirror. And yet the logic of supplementarity introduces into the very structure of the psyche a fabulous complication, the complication of a fable that does more than it says and invents something other than what it offers for copyrighting. The very movement of this fabulous repetition can, through a crossing of chance and necessity, produce the new of an event. Not only with the singular invention of a performative, since every performative presupposes conventions and institutional rules—but by bending these rules with respect for the rules themselves in order to allow the other to come or to announce its coming in the opening of this dehiscence. That is perhaps what is called deconstruction.

ALAIN BADIOU

The Event as Trans-Being

1998

Let us assume mathematics to be the thought of Being *qua* Being. Let us suppose that the latter comes into its own thought when the existential decisions prescribed by an orientation are at stake. What then can philosophy's own field be deemed to be?

We have already seen why it is up to philosophy to identify the ontological vocation of mathematics. Save for the rare moments of "crisis," mathematics thinks Being per se. Yet at those moments mathematics is not a thinking of the *thought* that it is. Admittedly, to be historically able to unfold as the thought of Being, and owing to how difficult it is to uproot it from the metaphysical power of the One which is encountered there, it could just as well be said there is no alternative but to identify mathematics as something completely different to ontology. It is up to philosophy to state and legitimize the following equation: mathematics = ontology. That said, philosophy manages on its own to be released from what is apparently its highest responsibility by asserting that it is simply not in charge of thinking Being *qua* Being. In fact, the movement by which philosophy is purified does not lie in its jurisdiction. It is all about identifying what its own conditions are, and this is a pattern scanning philosophy's entire history. Philosophy has been released from, or even relieved of, physics, cosmology, and politics, as well as many other things. It is also important for it to be released from ontology per se. But this task is complex largely owing to the fact that it entails that real mathematics be crossed reflexively—and not epistemologically. For example, in *L'Etre et l' événement*, I simultaneously sought to:

— Examine the ontological efficiency of the axioms of Set Theory through the successive categories of difference, void, excess, infinite, Nature, decision, truth, and Subject;

From *Briefings on Existence: A Short Treatise on Transitory Ontology*, ed. and trans. Norman Madarasz (Albany: State University of New York Press, 2006), pp. 59–62 [*Court traité d'ontologie transitoire* (Paris: Editions du Seuil, 1998)].

— Show how and why ontological thought is accomplished without having to be identified as such;
— Examine, in the non-unified vision I propose of philosophy's destiny, the philosophical connections of axiomatic interpretations: Plato's *Parmenides* on the One and difference, Aristotle on the void, Spinoza on excess, Hegel on the infinite, Pascal on decision, and Rousseau on the being of truths, and so forth.

The way I see it is that the work to do here is still wide open. As Albert Lautman's works especially demonstrated already in the 1930s, every significant and innovative fragment of real mathematics can and ought to prompt its ontological identification in terms of a living condition.[1] I tried my hand at this myself recently with respect to the status of the concept of number in the renewed version John Horton Conway introduced and—more on this anon—with respect to the theory of categories and *toposes*.[2]

On the other hand, a vast question opens up regarding what is subtracted from ontological determination. This is the question confronting what is not Being *qua* Being. For the subtractive law is implacable: if real ontology is set up as mathematics by evading the norm of the One, unless this norm is reestablished globally there also ought to be a point wherein the ontological, hence mathematical field, is de-totalized or remains at a dead end. I have named this point the "*event*." While philosophy is all about identifying what real ontology is in an endlessly reviewed process, it is also the general theory of the event—and it is no doubt the special theory, too. In other words, it is the theory of what is subtracted from ontological subtraction. Philosophy is the theory of what is strictly impossible for mathematics.

Inasmuch as mathematics ensures Being as such in thought, the theory of event aims at determining a trans-being.

The question then becomes the following: granted that the event is that about which all is not mathematicized, do we have to conclude that the multiple is intrinsically heterogeneous? By taking the event as Being's breaking point—something I call the "structure of trans-being"—it does not exempt us from thinking the being of the event itself. The being of trans-being. Does this being of the event require a theory of the multiple which is heterogeneous to the theory explaining Being, that is, Being *qua* Being? I see Deleuze's position as hinting at this. Thinking the event fold originally demands a double-edged manifold theory, one that pursues Bergson's legacy. According to this view, extensive and numerical manifolds must be distinguished from intensive or qualitative multiplicities. An event is always the gap between two heterogeneous multiplicities. What occurs ends up making a fold, as it were, between the extensive spreading out and the intensive continuum.

As for myself, I contend the contrary, namely, that multiplicity is axiomatically homogenous. That's when I have to explain the being of the event both as a breach of the law according to which manifolds spread out as well as something homogenous to this law. This takes place through a defection of axioms: an event is nothing but a set, a manifold. But its emergence and supplementation subtract one of the axioms of the manifold, namely, the axiom of foundation.

Taken literally, this means an event is strictly an un-founded manifold. This defection is in fact a pure chance supplement to the manifold-situation for which it is an event.

This said, the general question of the status of the event in relation to the ontology of the manifold, over which Gilles Deleuze and I argued at length, and on how not to reintroduce the power of the One to such an extent that the manifold law ends up failing, is in my opinion the main question of any contemporary philosophy. Besides, this was all pre-constituted with Heidegger in the slide from *Sein* to *Ereignis*, from Being to his conception of the Event. We might also shift registers and have an altogether opposite glance at the question. Lacan invested it in the thought of the psychoanalytic act. He saw it as an eclipse of truth between presupposed knowledge and transmissible knowledge, or between interpretation and the matheme. This is also a decisive problem for Nietzsche: if the task is to break the history of the world in two, what is the thinkable principle of such a break in the absolute affirmation of life? It also happens to be Wittgenstein's central problem: how does the act open up onto a silent access to the "mystical element," that is, to ethics and aesthetics, if sense is always captive of a proposition?

In each of the aforementioned cases, the latent matrix of the problem is the following: if by "*philosophy*" one must understand both the One's jurisdiction and the conditioned subtraction from this jurisdiction, how can philosophy seize what is happening? Namely, seize what is happening in thought? Philosophy will always be split between recognizing the event as the One's supernumerary coming, and the thought of its being as a simple extension of the manifold. Is truth what comes to Being or what unfolds Being? We remain divided. The whole point is to contend, for as long as possible and under the most innovative conditions for philosophy, the notion that truth itself is but a multiplicity: in the two senses of its coming (a truth makes a typical multiple or generic singularity befall) and of its being (there is not *the* Truth, there are only disparate and untotalized truths that cannot be totalized).

A radical gesture is precisely required here. Besides, this is how modern philosophy is recognized: by subtracting the examination of truths from the simple form of judgment. What this has always meant is to decide upon a single ontology of manifolds. This is all about remaining faithful to Lucretius. It is all about telling ourselves every instant is one in which

From all over an infinite space opens
When atoms, innumerable and boundless,
Flutter about in eternal movement.[3]

Despite his Stoic inflections, was Deleuze not himself faithful to Lucretius? I would like to return to what made Deleuze choose against ontological mathematicity in the end, and what made him choose the word "life" as Being's main name.

Notes

[1] Albert Lautman (1908–1944) worked primarily in the 1930s. After the Nazi invasion of France, he joined the Résistance. In 1944, he was arrested and executed. His main body of work has been collected in *Essai sur l'unité mathématique* (Paris: Hachette, 1977) but has never been translated into English. Save for the most cosmopolitan historians of mathematics, Lautman remains pretty much unknown. Badiou draws a stirring portrayal of his life and work in the introduction to *Abrégé de métapolitique* (Paris: Éditions du Seuil, 1998). See also the special issue devoted to Lautman of *Revue d'histoire des sciences* (Paris: Presses Universitaires de France, 1987), 40.

[2] Alain Badiou, *Le nombre et les nombres* (Paris: Editions du Seuil, the "Des travaux" series, 1990), chap. 12.

[3] Lucretius, *On Nature*, II: 496.

PART V
The Subject

The problem of the event is inseparable from a new idea of the subject, a new way of posing the question of subjectivity and of intersubjectivity, just as problematizations or new or disruptive truths are also subjective matters, requiring new inventions of ourselves. But what then exactly is meant by "the subject," and how does it form part of the larger search for new forms or images of thought in the postwar period? Sometimes the problem is posed as getting rid of or coming after a certain classical notion of subjectivity. Foucault's division between a philosophy of the concept and a philosophy of subject can be read in this way as a search for an analysis of rationality that would be freed from all subjectivity. That is what links it to the critique of psychologism in logic that Frege originally opposed to Husserl, and more generally to the attempt in all formal or structural analysis to eliminate biographical or psychological references. But, as Derrida points out, many authors—notably Lacan, Althusser, and later Badiou—keep the term "subject" and attempt to offer theories of it, and even Foucault would end up trying to analyze what he called "processes of subjectivization" while still maintaining his skepticism about "anthropological universals." The problem might then be posed in another way, in terms of a contrast between the *constitution* of the subject in language, discourse, or social formations and the *constituting* role it would have in philosophies of consciousness. But, with respect to that constituting role, there is a further problem, that of a de-centering of the subject and the peculiar role of the body in it, at first directed against phenomenological ideas of "the Flesh"—Lacan's "body in bits and pieces" or his idea of voice and gaze as objects of desire, Derrida's questioning of the "proper body" centered in "hearing-oneself-speaking," or again with elaborations of Artaud's "body without organs." Thus, already in 1937 with Sartre's *Transcendence of the Ego*, Deleuze would find the start of a search for an "impersonal" transcendental field, such that the problem becomes that of "a life," which, in contrast to "the life of the corresponding individual," would free itself from the two great classical functions of the idea of the subject: individualization and personalized or centered consciousness.

In all these formulations, moreover, the subject is not exactly what in English we call "the self," "the person," "the individual," "the agent," or even "the mind"; even the question of consciousness is posed in another way, related to new conceptions of the unconscious. Here we find an attempt to work out the nature and implications of something in our lives, or in our ways of being and being-together, that can't simply be self-reflected or constituted by continuities of memory, that is im-personal or irreducible to persons of speech or discourse, that can't be individualized any more than collectivized, that can't be centered or made present in a consciousness or a "proper body," with its voice and its gaze. The idea of the subject rather lies at the intersection of a cluster of new problems. For it is not simply a matter of the individual subject but also, as already with Husserl's Fifth Cartesian Mediation, of the intersubjectivity supposed by the notion of an "objective world" or again of the assumptions of the "for us" in Hegel's *Phenomenology of Spirit*. Thus the question of *autrui* is not simply one of the existence of others, but more fundamentally how others figure in the identification of ourselves, as already with Sartre's analysis of others as a form of hell. With Levinas and Derrida, there then arises a more radical alterity—something "altogether other," which precisely undoes identification of self. In Deleuze's Proustian idea of *autrui* as the expression of different possible worlds, the problem becomes one of the universe in which they are composed together. The question of intersubjectivity then becomes one of a *partage*, community, or friendship, which preserves the singularities or alterities in our being and being together.

But along with this problem of alterity, there arises the problem of exteriority and interitority, irreducible to the notion of inner representations of external objects or the external world. In many ways, Jacques Bouveresse's exposure of the "myth of interiority" in Wittgenstein's private-language argument fits with these discussions. When Foucault analyzes what Blanchot called "the outside" in thought, it refers to something that is, as it were, more external than the external world, while involving something closer to us than the internal world—something prior to the distinctions between private and public or individual and collective. It is something outside the institutions and corresponding rules or regularities that determine who speaks and about what upon which such distinctions normally depend.

In his lectures on Nietzsche, influential at the time, Heidegger had credited Descartes with introducing the idea of *sub-jectum*, itself a philosophical translation of the Greek *upo-keimenon*, thus initiating modern philosophy. But, as Canguilhem points out in his essay on the exhaustion of the cogito in Foucault, Descartes in fact didn't use the term "subject"; rather, he was concerned with *la pensée* and *évidence*. It is only in Kant, in his attempt to desubstantialize the idea of the "I think," that the terms "subject" and "object" start to be used as part of a central framework for representation, in which the relation of the subject to the law (moral or legal as well as epistemological) becomes central. Derrida, who sees being "before the Law" as key for the whole question of the subject, went on to question Heidegger's etymology of the subject in another way, isolating the problem of "presence-to-self," "hearing-oneself-speak," and "the proper." He pursues this question in his discussion of the German term *Geist* (and "ghost"), and again when he suggests that there is something symptomatic in Heidegger's failure to engage with Spinoza—a philosopher important for Deleuze's idea of the sub-individual nature of singular essences and the trans-individual character of the Substance or plane on which they are composed, decomposed, recomposed together.

For his part, Canguilhem had posed the question in another way, from the other side of Foucault's fork. In his lecture "What Is Psychology?" first given in 1956, then revived in the context of the 1960s, we find something in some ways closer to the later Wittgenstein, for whom psychology was "empirical methods plus conceptual confusion," although he addressed the problem in a more historical manner. Later French cognitivist philosophers counting neurology as the key psychological science would oppose both philosophers. Canguilhem's essay, which ends with a famous remark about how the road to psychology leads to the police station, is directed against any supervenient notion or determinant unity in the ideas of the psyche developed in different bodies of discourse; and Canguilhem presents a suggestive account of different notions and discourses in the modern period, somewhat different from Heidegger, whom Foucault was reading at the time. It is this dis-unified picture of the various ways the subject comes to figure in bodies of knowledge that Foucault would then go on to elaborate in his own original conception of "discourse," governed by anonymous or impersonal regularities determining who speaks and what gets talked about.

A central way the problem of the subject was posed at the time was in terms of language and the question of "enunciation" in writing as in speech. For Lacan, that was the key question. He thought that we *are* "sexed speaking beings," and that the unconscious is structural in our speech and as such supplies the conditions for the talking cure. Lacan's own ongoing development of this question in turn draws on several important sources. There is the Saussurian distinction between *langue* and *parole*, developed through the analysis of phonology by the Prague School, then extended to culture (and so to society) by Lévi-Strauss: a language as a set of tacit rules, speech as moves in the games these rules define. But, as Jean-Claude Milner stresses, for the question of "the subject" and "the other," Émile Benveniste was perhaps an even more central figure in the structuralist constellation. For what he suggestively called the "apparatus of enunciation" (especially in the Indo-European languages which he studied)—involving verb tenses as well as shifters and other deictic expressions like "here" and "now"—determined the forms of subjectivity in language. The problem of enunciation was important for Lacan, and in particular for the role of what he called *lalangue* in the idiosyncratic singularity of our symptoms, which would free the idea of the subject of the unconscious from any identification with fixed or limited classes or groups. But Foucault, who would keep the term *énoncé* ("statement" or "utterance"), developed the idea in another way. He tried to isolate a "subjectivity in discourse," irreducible to the ones Benveniste had found in language, arguing that subjectivity was a discursive and not simply a logical or linguistic matter, irreducible to speech acts. His essay on the "author-function" is a well-known example. Authorship is an individualizing rule for the organization of "things said," which assumes different forms in different times and places, sometimes acquiring divergent roles in science and in art, sometimes not counting at all, according to the position it assumes within larger kinds of regularities. It is thus a matter of institution, law, and the materiality of discourse rather than simply a matter of language. What it is to be an author can thus be contested or transformed—as, for example, with attempts to undo its individualizing function through collective forms (e.g., Bourbaki in mathematics as well as in artists' groups) or in deliberatively machinic or mechanical practices, removed from subjective impulse or biography, as with automatic writing. The function of authorship is thus linked to the idea of oeuvre (or work) in its relation to "techniques of self," which Foucault would analyze in his own last writings.

Closer to Levinas than Benveniste, Maurice Blanchot developed the sense in which in literary works, in their spaces and times as well as in their narrative voices, there exists a dimension irreducible to first-, second-, or even third-person utterances, tied up with the subsistence of those "events" which dispossess us of our ability to say "I" or "we," introducing a neutral or neutralized space. In particular, Blanchot associated this neutral space with questions of death or dying, speaking of an *on meurt* (as in "one lives, one dies") prior to "I die," "you die," or "we die." The idea of such an anonymous space was then developed in various philosophical ways. Deleuze associated it not simply with Spinoza (whose idea of substance was like the "it" in "it's raining"), but also with the peculiar rhythm Ferlinghetti called the "fourth-person singular" in poetry. Deleuze thought this was the same kind of anonymity to be found in the *on dit* ("it is said") in Foucault, what Foucault called the "anonymous murmur" of discourse, prior to the regularities of who says what. For Deleuze it is a glorious, vital anonymity, not to be confused with the banalizing anonymity of *Das Mann* in Heidegger. But the problem of neutrality and subjectivity in Blanchot was elaborated in another way by Derrida, surrounding themes of impossibility and not-being-at-home; in particular, in his essays on the theme of *Geschlecht*, Derrida raises the whole issue of why Heidegger's *Dasein* is neutral with respect to gender or gender identification. One is not far from Proust's dismissal of the "gross statistical" categories of sexual identification in his search for signs of artistic intelligence, later elaborated by Deleuze.

If Lacan is in many ways a central figure for all these questions of the subject, it is because he connected the idea of the subject to the law and the idea of the law to sexual or Oedipal identification. But his views in fact go back to two figures from the 1930s: Georges Bataille, with his ideas of "sovereignty" and "transgression" associated not simply with Nietzsche but also with the Marquis de Sade, and Alexandre Kojève, whose lectures on Hegel turned *The Phenomenology of Spirit* into the key work for the whole question of subjectivity and identification. In each case, Lacan tried to develop his idea of a constitutive *méconnaisance* ("misrecognition"), irreducible to the mutual recognition Kojève stressed in Hegel, and linked to the violence and crime that would derive from the fragmented body, and its compensation in the jubilations of the mirror image. It was this picture of *méconnaisance* that would impress Althusser in his attempt to work out a non-Hegelian model of ideology and its constitutive role in the apparatuses through which subjects would relate to the formation and reproduction of their roles in a given mode of production. We thus find the question of the state in Althusser and more generally the problem of subjectivity and politics: the problem of the political conceptions of the subject and sovereignty and of subject and recognition in relation to the law, and hence the related political problems posed by class, race, gender, sex, or "abnormality" in the ways we identify ourselves and one another. In what ways are identificatory practices required by the very idea and functioning of the power of governments and states, and in what ways might a kind of "dis-identification" and corresponding processes of subjectivization then form part of all politics of resistance and emancipation?

SIMONE DE BEAUVOIR

The Second Sex

1949

O is not born, but rather becomes, woman. No biological, psychic, or economic destiny defines the figure that the human female takes on in society; it is civilization as a whole that elaborates this intermediary product between the male and the eunuch that is called feminine. Only the mediation of another can constitute an individual as an *Other*. Inasmuch as he exists for himself, the child would not grasp himself as sexually differentiated. For girls and boys, the body is first the radiation of a subjectivity, the instrument that brings about the comprehension of the world: they apprehend the universe through their eyes and hands, and not through their sexual parts. The drama of birth and weaning takes place in the same way for infants of both sexes; they have the same interests and pleasures; sucking is the first source of their most pleasurable sensations; they then go through an anal phase in which they get their greatest satisfactions from excretory functions common to both; their genital development is similar; they explore their bodies with the same curiosity and the same indifference; they derive the same uncertain pleasure from the clitoris and the penis; insofar as their sensibility already needs an object, it turns toward the mother: it is the soft, smooth, supple feminine flesh that arouses sexual desires, and these desires are prehensile; the girl like the boy kisses, touches, and caresses her mother in an aggressive manner; they feel the same jealousy at the birth of a new child; they show it with the same behavior: anger, sulking, urinary problems; they have recourse to the same coquetry to gain the love of adults. Up to twelve, the girl is just as sturdy as her brothers; she shows the same intellectual aptitudes; she is not barred from competing with them in any area. If well before puberty and sometimes even starting from early childhood she already appears sexually specified, it is not because mysterious instincts immediately destine her to passivity, coquetry, or motherhood but because the intervention of others in the infant's life is almost originary, and her vocation is imperiously breathed into her from the first years of her life.

The world is first present to the newborn only in the form of immanent

From *The Second Sex*, trans. Constance Borde and Sheila Malovany-Chevallier (New York: Alfred A. Knopf, 2010), pp. 283–84 [*Le deuxième sexe* (Paris: Editions Gallimard, 1949)].

sensations; he is still immersed within the Whole as he was when he was living in the darkness of a womb; whether raised on the breast or on a bottle, he is invested with the warmth of maternal flesh. Little by little he learns to perceive objects as distinct from himself: he separates himself from them; at the same time, more or less suddenly, he is removed from the nourishing body; sometimes he reacts to this separation with a violent fit;[1] in any case, when it is consummated—around six months—he begins to manifest the desire to seduce others by mimicking, which then turns into a real display. Of course, this attitude is not defined by a reflective choice; but it is not necessary to *think* a situation to *exist* it. In an immediate way the newborn lives the primeval drama of every existent—that is, the drama of one's relation to the Other. Man experiences his abandonment in anguish. Fleeing his freedom and subjectivity, he would like to lose himself within the Whole: here is the origin of his cosmic and pantheistic reveries, of his desire for oblivion, sleep, ecstasy, and death. He never manages to abolish his separated self: at the least he wishes to achieve the solidity of the in-itself, to be petrified in thing; it is uniquely when he is fixed by the gaze of others that he appears to himself as a being. It is in this vein that the child's behavior has to be interpreted: in a bodily form he discovers finitude, solitude, and abandonment in an alien world; he tries to compensate for this catastrophe by alienating his existence in an image whose reality and value will be established by others. It would seem that from the time he recognizes his reflection in a mirror—a time that coincides with weaning—he begins to affirm his identity:[2] his self merges with this reflection in such a way that it is formed only by alienating itself. Whether the mirror as such plays a more or less considerable role, what is sure is that the child at about six months of age begins to understand his parents' miming and to grasp himself under their gaze as an object. He is already an autonomous subject transcending himself toward the world: but it is only in an alienated form that he will encounter himself.

Notes

[1] Judith Gautier says in her accounts of her memories that she cried and wasted away so terribly when she was pulled away from her wet nurse that she had to be reunited with her. She was weaned much later.

[2] This is Dr. Lacan's theory in *Les complexes familiaux dans la formation de l'individu* (*Family Complexes in the Formation of the Individual*). This fundamental fact would explain that during its development "the self keeps the ambiguous form of spectacle."

GEORGES BATAILLE

Sovereignty

1954

1. The Useful Object and the Sovereign Subject

Although I spoke of objective sovereignty, I never lost sight of the fact that sovereignty is never truly objective, that, on the contrary, it denotes profound subjectivity. In any case, the real sovereign is the no doubt objective result of conventions based on subjective reactions. Sovereignty is objective only in consequence of our blunder in this regard, as we have access to the subject only by positing some object which we then either negate or destroy.

The world of things is given to us as a series of appearances which depend on one another. Effect depends on cause, and, in general, every object depends on the totality of other objects, being ultimately the effect of which the totality is the cause. I have no intention of offering more than a glimpse of these relations, but the interdependence of things seems to me in any event so complete that I can never introduce a relation of subordination between one and another. We see power relations (*rapports de forces*), and an isolated element will no doubt be subject to the influence of the mass, but the mass cannot *subordinate* it. Subordination presupposes another kind of relation, that of object to subject.[1] The subject is the being *as it appears to itself from within*. The subject can also appear to us from outside: for instance, the *other* appears to us in the beginning as exterior to us, but at the same time it is given to us, via a complex representation, in the same way that it appears to itself, on the inside, and it is as such that we love it, as such that we strive to make contact with it. Second, we apprehend ourselves from outside, just as we apprehend the *other*, which is an object for us. We live in a world of *subjects* whose *outward, objective* aspect is always inseparable from the *interior*. In ourselves, however, what is given to us of ourselves objectively, such as our body, appears to us as subordinate. My body is subject to my will, which within myself I identify with the presence, perceptible from within, of the being that I am. Thus, in general, the object, or the be-

La souveraineté, in *Oeuvres complètes*, vol. 8, ed. Denis Hollier (Paris: Editions Gallimard, 1976), pp. 283–87, 288–90, 296–98; trans. Arthur Goldhammer.

ing objectively given, appears to me as subordinated to subjects, of which it is the property. In a world in which all things were limited in our eyes to what they are in themselves, where surely nothing could appear to us in the light of subjectivity, relations of objects among themselves would be nothing but power relations. Nothing would ever enjoy preeminence [*précellence*], preeminence being a trait of a subject for which an other is an object.

Indeed, I cannot represent myself, a thing in a world of things. I forget that the existence within me continually obliges me to treat as a thing that which I eat or which serves me and to treat myself and others like me as subjects that eat and serve. What is in the world is reduced in my understanding to a series of interdependent appearances. Theoretically, no subordination is possible in this series. But in fact I neglect the subject that I am, which contemplates this series and mechanically treats what it eats and that which serves it as subordinate. Mechanically, I place on the same footing things that generally appear to me in their mutual interdependence without preeminence and things that I eat or that serve me and which are, in relation to the subject that I am, *servile* objects. Hence mechanically, the totality of things, and, more generally, the totality of beings, appears to me in the guise of *servile* objects.

When value is sovereignly asserted in relation to the subject, things are unambiguously subordinated to it. But nothing changes when, manifest sovereignty having been abolished, attenuated or camouflaged forms take its place.

Traditional sovereignty is underscored in a very visible way. This is the sovereignty of exception (one single subject among many enjoys the prerogatives of the totality of subjects). By contrast, any subject maintaining sovereign value opposed to the subordination of the object shares that value with all men. It is man in general, whose existence necessarily has something of the nature of the subject, who in general is opposed to things, for instance, animals, which he kills and eats. Asserting himself nevertheless as subject, he is sovereign in relation to the thing that the animal is, but man in general works. If he works, he is in relation to the sovereign life what the object that he uses or eats generally is in relation to the subject that he has not ceased to be. In this way a slippage occurs, which tends to limit sovereignty to the exceptional case. I can work for myself; I can even work for others in a community in which each person is assigned an equal share of obligations and benefits, without thereby losing my sovereignty for any longer than it takes to complete my task. But if the sharing is not equal, sovereignty is alienated to the benefit of the person who does not work himself but profits from my work. In traditional sovereignty, a single person enjoys in principle the benefit of being the subject, but this does not mean simply that the masses work while he consumes a substantial part of the products of their labor; it also assumes that the masses see in the sovereign the subject of which they are the object.

2. The Sovereign Who Is Different from Others Differs from Them as the Subject Differs from the Objective Action of Labor

This inevitable play on words is unfortunate. I mean that the individual member of the masses, who works part of the time for the benefit of the sovereign, *recognizes* him; I mean that he *recognizes himself* in the sovereign. The individual member of the masses no longer sees the sovereign as the object that in his eyes he must initially appear to be, but as the *subject*. Indeed, the same is true in general of others like himself, especially those who belong to the same community. But in a special way the sovereign is for him the internal existence—the underlying truth—to which a portion of his effort is given over, that portion that he gives to others than himself. In a sense, the sovereign is the intermediary between the individual and others. In the eyes of the individual he stands for the others. Yet he expects from those others, from those similar to himself, a labor equal to his own. The moment the others acquire a spokesperson to represent them, that person speaks for them insofar as he represents their inward selves and not their laboring appendages, which do work in a manner analogous to inert things, to subordinate instruments. It must be inevitable, humanly speaking, that a man should give others like himself the sense that he is there for the others, in whose place he is able to speak and respond. This is not always associated with language; what matters is that the privileged person must never be placed in relation to *others* in the situation in which the object finds itself in relation to the subject which is its end and which it serves. The individual members of a mass cannot see one of their number as the person who represents the others if he is even for an instant subordinated to any one of them, if he is not what the subject is for the object with respect to others in the group. Thus the sovereign does not work but consumes what others produce with their labor. The portion of the product that is not necessary for the subsistence of the *object* that the producer temporarily is—that is the portion that goes to the *subject*, which is what the sovereign is. The sovereign restores to the primacy of the present the surplus portion of production, whose magnitude depends on the extent to which men submit to the primacy of the future. The sovereign, epitomizing the essence of the *subject*, is the person through and for whom the instant, the *miraculous* instant, is the sea that absorbs all the rivulets of labor. In the feast the sovereign spends indiscriminately on himself and others what was amassed through the labor of all.

3. What the Sovereign Is for the Person Who "Recognizes" Him

What I am saying is perhaps poorly supported, theoretical, and remote from a reality which is never simple or pure. But the *inward* experience that guides me commits me to maintaining the autonomy of this representation with respect to the specific historical data studied, for example, by ethnography. If there is one element that we grasp from within, it is surely sovereignty, even if it happens to be not the sovereignty toward which we personally strive but rather that which we grant to royal personages in a manner that often seems indefensible.[2] Such an experience probably makes no sense apart from the objective facts associated with it, but those data must themselves be understood in light of this experience, without which the facts would not even be *facts*. Such conditions of experience appear to us objectively: like production, there is a surplus share and a share necessary for subsistence—but when the *present time* comes into play, even if I am speaking of the *objects*, of the consumed products, that are involved, those objects are *destroyed* or consumed, and the preference granted to the *instant* corresponds to disdain for the objective world. I can still approach the instant from other angles, but it never refers to anything other than the inner world of the *subject*.

. . .

The man who assumes in the eyes of each participant in a community the value of the *others* can do so, as I said earlier, to the extent that he signifies the *subjectivity* of those others. This assumes communication from *subject* to *subject* as I described it, communication in which *objects* are the intermediaries, but only if they are in the process reduced to insignificance, *if they are destroyed as objects*. In particular, this is the case with the sovereign, who is originally an object distinct from the person who sees in him not only the man but also the sovereign. If I see a passerby in the street, I can think of him as a distinct object in which I take absolutely no interest, but if I choose I can also think of him as a *person like myself*. This is the case if I deny him, at least in part, the objective character of a random passerby, which I do if I suddenly look at him as a brother, now seeing him only as a *subject* with whom I *can* and *must* communicate, and if I cease to regard as alien anything that concerns him subjectively. *Brother* in a sense designates a distinct object, but precisely the object that carries within it the negation of that which defines it as object. It is an object for me, it is not me, it is not the *subject* that I am, but if I say that it is my brother, I do so in order to assure myself that it is *like* the *subject* that I am. Hence I deny the *subject-object* relation that appeared to me initially, and my negation defines a *subject-subject* relation between my brother and me, which transcends but does not eliminate the first relation. Sometimes the word *brother* denotes a blood relationship (objectively definable, carrying within it the negation of that which distinguishes, the affirmation of similarity), sometimes a bond of the same nature apprehended as existing between *every* other person and myself. I insist on this latter sense, since my intention is to oppose it to the sense of the word *sovereign*, which, if *I personally had a sovereign*, would relate to the *subject* that this *sovereign* would be for me. As I said earlier, the *subject* is initially me, and the *sovereign* is initially an *object* for me. But to the extent that I work in the service of others whom the *sovereign* represents, I am not a *subject* but an *object* of the person or persons for whom I work. I am still a subject, but only when my work is done. Furthermore, I treat myself as an object, working as I do on my own behalf. I become a *subject* again when I deny in myself on behalf of the present moment the primacy of the moment to come, but just as I sometimes envisage as an *object* subjected to the service of the *subject* that I then am the person I was when I was working, the sovereign looks at me as an object insofar as I produce that which is his to dispose of as he sees fit. He knows that I have not really ceased to be a *subject*, but, as I am not completely a *subject* since I am working, and not only for myself but for others and therefore for the sovereign who represents them. I am a subject, but the sovereign, who does not work, is a subject in a different sense. I am a subject only in the narrowest sense. I cannot easily recover intact the always unanticipated apparition which is that of subjectivity, and which nothing distorts and the servitude of effort does not weigh down. In principle I would no longer have this capricious and profoundly *sacred* apparition at my disposal if my work had not in any case preserved the *sovereign* from this misery. In principle, by the effect of my labor, the sovereign can, if he wishes, live in the moment: what matters, moreover, is not that he wants to but that he can and that, since he can, he *manifests* this power. The sovereign is from the beginning the locus of this contradiction: incarnating the subject, he is its external aspect. But this is not entirely accurate: essentially, sovereignty is posited inwardly; the only true manifestation of its presence is interior communication. (I would like this scheme not to be strictly dependent on particular realities, but I cannot fail to point out that the person of the king is often so profoundly sacred that it is dangerous to touch what he touches: that which is sacred, which is dangerous, is crudely held to be interior, essentially having no meaning apart from its interiority.)[3]

. . .

6. The Marquis de Sade, or the Sovereign Revolt

I cannot refrain at this point from introducing considerations that relate to the position of a noteworthy individual, the Marquis de Sade, who by dint of his birth partook of sovereign splendor but who nevertheless carried rebellion to an extreme.

I could say about the marquis what Voltaire said about God, that if he had not existed, it would have been necessary to invent him, yet it is difficult to speak of him without misunderstandings. Indeed, it was because of misunderstandings that his whimsical humors became entangled with the revolutionary convulsions of his times. This high-ranking nobleman rightly remarked that unless we have full control of ourselves and our world, we are either dupes or slaves. His error was perhaps to imagine that we can at will hold *others* to be external to ourselves, so that they can never count for us as anything but absurd, or else count for us only in consequence of our fear of them or of the advantage we hope to derive from them. Thus he argued that we can kill or torture those others whenever doing so might result in pleasure for us, since to us they mean nothing. This is a crude error: we can if we so choose look upon one or several or even a great many others in this way, but being (*l'être*) is never *myself alone* but always *myself and others like me*. Even if the group of *others like me* changes, if I exclude from its ranks someone I had previously included or add someone I had previously excluded, I speak and as of that moment I am—the being in me is—outside myself as well as inside. Hence to be in control of ourselves and of the world is subject to at least this limitation: namely, that, if not the world itself, a portion of the beings the world contains is not entirely distinct from us. The world is not, as Sade ultimately represented it, composed of himself and things. But the idea of revolt that he conceived is nevertheless at the ultimate extreme of what is possible. If its implications are contradictory, they cannot erase its significance.

Sade called the abolition of the monarchical order a crime: hence the revolutionary crowd was in on the crime, each revolutionary was the accomplice of all the others, and, since each had a hand in the deed, everyone must persevere. The society of criminals was obliged to dedicate itself to crime, and each citizen could attain the ultimate in pleasure by killing and torturing. Sade of course linked this liberty in crime to the abolition of the death penalty. He argued that only the passion of the criminal and not the coldness of law could justify execution, for the passion of the criminal at least put him outside himself. I can put Sade's singular view of the matter in somewhat different terms. Execution is transgression of the prohibition of murder. In essence, transgression is a sacred act. Legal execution is profane and as such unacceptable.

I shall now use this terminology (which is in a sense my own) to express the whole of Sade's thought. The man who ceased to see his own subjective truth in the king, who wished to find it in himself, found it, as in essence the king had done, only in crime. If he found it, it was through the murder of the king, but if he turned away from crime, he would subject himself not to the king, whom he had killed, but to that power which in the name of the king had limited the liberty of anyone lacking the sovereign prerogative and, now that the king was dead, would limit the liberty of all.

This fundamental truth is schematic; the sovereign liberty of the king has little to do with the limitless crimes of the monsters spawned by the imagination of the author of *Juliette*. Think of the moments of libidinous butchery when those monsters' cries of pleasure mingle with their vomit. The principle is nevertheless the same, sovereignty being the negation of prohibition. Indeed, Sade's cruel monsters have no other meaning: their excess underscores and accentuates this principle. To me the only thing that matters is to mark the point at which revolt falters. The rebel refuses to alienate for the sake of others a sovereignty that is his alone, but as Sade was aware and expressed in paradoxical terms, he could not continue in the direction in which he was headed. He had killed the royal subjectivity that imposed itself on him and deprived him of his own subjectivity, but he was unable to recover for himself that which the king's glory had deprived him of. In monarchical society he had been nothing but an object, but nothing in republican society was different except that he no longer confronted a *subject* whose sovereign character seemed to be the sole cause of his limitation. In a society that has rejected institutional sovereignty, personal sovereignty is not automatically given. The very person who fought to abolish that which oppressed him, which reduced him to the status of a thing, must still somehow regain that which oppression deprived him of. Indeed, he has even lost what monarchical society at least still had, a representation of being complete enough that being could not be confused with things or reduced to objectivity.

Notes

[1] The fact that sovereigns say "my subjects" introduces an ambiguity that I cannot avoid: the *subject* for me is the *sovereign*. The subject I am speaking of is in no sense *subjugated*.

[2] The most rationalist among us can still grasp this to some extent if they consider the emotion that their king (or queen) communicates to foreign crowds.

[3] "Among the Malays," writes H. Webster (*Le tabou*, trans. J. Marty [Paris: Payot, 1952], p. 252), "not only is the person of the king considered sacred, but it is also believed that the sanctity of his body is communicated to the symbols of his royalty and will cause the death of anyone who violates the royal taboos. Thus everyone is firmly convinced that whoever commits a grave offense against the royal person or touches (even for an instant) or imitates (even with the king's permission) the principal symbols of his rank, or misuses one of these objects or one of the royal privileges, will be *Kena daulat*, that is, mortally stricken by an almost electric discharge of the divine power which the Malays believe resides in the person of the king and which they call *daulat*, 'royal sanctity.'" Quoted from W.W. Skeat, *Malay magic* (London, 1900), p. 23. [Here retranslated from the French.—trans.]

GEORGES CANGUILHEM

What Is Psychology?

1958

A psychologist is more likely to be embarrassed by the question "What is psychology?" than a philosopher by the question "What is philosophy?" For philosophy is much more constituted by the question of its sense and its essence than defined by an answer to that question. The fact that the question is posed again and again, for lack of a satisfactory answer, is, for anybody aspiring to call himself a philosopher, a reason for humility and not a cause of humiliation. For psychology, however, the question of its essence, or (more modestly) of its concept, also puts in question the very existence of the psychologist to the extent that, being unable to declare exactly what he is, he finds it extremely difficult to answer for what he does. He is forced to seek in his ever questionable efficacy the sole justification of his importance as a specialist—an importance that would by no means embarrass some practitioners were it to engender an inferiority complex on the part of the philosopher.

To say that the efficacy of the psychologist is questionable is not to say that it is illusory. What should be noted is that this efficacy certainly lacks a firm foundation as long as it cannot be proved to derive from the application of a science—that is to say, as long as the status of psychology fails to be fixed in such a way that it amounts to something more and better than a composite empiricism codified in a literary manner for teaching purposes. It is indeed the case that a lot of work in psychology suggests a mixture of philosophy without rigor, ethics without obligation and medicine without control. Philosophy without rigor—because it is eclectic while claiming to be objective; ethics without obligation—because it uncritically incorporates ethical forms of experience (those of the confessor, the teacher, the boss, the judge, etc.); medicine without control—because out of the three types of illness that are most unintelligible and the least curable—skin disease, nervous disease and mental illness—the study and treatment of the latter two have always served for psychology as a source of observations and hypotheses.

From *I & C.* 7 (1980), pp. 37–50; trans. Howard Davies ["Qu'est-ce que la psychologie?" in *Etudes d'histoire et de philosophie des sciences* (Paris: J. Vrin, 1968); first published in *Revue de métaphysique et de morale* 1 (1958)].

It seems therefore that in asking "What is psychology?" we are posing a question that is neither irrelevant nor futile.

The characteristic unity of the concept of a science has traditionally been taken as deriving from the object of that science: the object has been thought of as itself dictating the method to be used in the study of its properties. But in the last analysis this amounted to limiting science to the study of a given, to the exploration of a domain. When it became apparent that every science more or less gives itself its given, and thereby appropriates what is called its domain, the concept of a science began to place more emphasis on method than on object. Or, to be more precise, the expression "the object of the science" acquired a new meaning. The object of a science is no longer simply the specific field in which problems are to be resolved and obstacles removed, it is also the intentions and ambitions of the subject of the science, the specific project that informs a theoretical consciousness.

A possible way of answering the question "What is psychology?" would be to demonstrate that, despite the multiplicity of its methodological projects, the domain of psychology is none the less a unitary one. To this category of response belongs that given so brilliantly by Daniel Lagache in 1947, in answer to a question posed in 1936 by Edouard Claparède.[1] The unity of psychology is established here through the possibility of its being defined as a general theory of conduct, a synthesis of experimental psychology, clinical psychology, psychoanalysis, social psychology and anthropology.

Closer inspection suggests, however, that this unity resembles more a pact of peaceful coexistence between professionals than a logical essence obtained by the identification of a constant in a variety of cases. Of the two tendencies, naturalist (experimental psychology) and humanist (clinical psychology) [which Lagache seeks to reconcile], the second appears to be allowed greater weight. This is no doubt what explains the absence of animal psychology from this review of the litigants in the case. One can of course see that it is subsumed here within experimental psychology—which is to a great extent a psychology of animals—but there it is restricted to the status of material to which the method may be applied. And indeed, a psychology may be said to be experimental only by virtue of its method and not by virtue of its object. Yet, contrary to appearances, it is in terms more of its object than of its method that a psychology is called clinical, psychoanalytical, social or anthropological. All these adjectives connote a sole and single object of study—man, loquacious or taciturn, sociable or unsociable. Can one then speak with any rigor of a *general* theory of conduct, so long as the question of whether there is continuity or discontinuity between human language and animal language, human society and animal society is left unresolved? It is possible that it is not for philosophy to decide on this point, but for science, for many sciences in fact, psychology being one of them. But in that case psychology cannot, for purposes of self-definition, prejudge that which it is required to judge. Unless it does so, however, it is inevitable that, in presenting itself as a general theory of conduct, psychology will come to embody a certain idea of man. Philosophy will then have to be allowed to ask psychology where this idea comes from and whether, in fact, it does not originate in a particular philosophy.

Not being a psychologist, I would like to try and approach the basic problem posed above from an opposite direction, that is to say, to seek to determine whether or not the unity of a probject could possibly be the factor which might confer unity on the various disciplines which call themselves psychological. This mode of investigation, however, requires a step backwards. The attempt to discover how far the different fields *overlap* may be conducted by exploring them separately and by comparing them in their present state (over a ten-year period, in the case of Lagache's study). The search for the points at which the various programs might *meet* implies isolating the meaning of each, not when it has become lost in the automatic aspects of the program's implementation, but at the precise moment in time when it emerges from the situation that brings it into existence. To look for an answer to the question "What is psychology?" thus imposes on us the necessity of sketching out a brief history of psychology, considered only, of course, in terms of its founding orientations and in relation to the history of philosophy and the sciences: a necessarily teleological history, since its goal is to bring to bear on the question under discussion the presumed original sense of the various disciplines, methods or programs whose present heterogeneity makes the question a legitimate one to pose.

Psychology as a Natural Science

Whereas psychology, etymologically, means science of the soul, it is remarkable that there is no independent psychology to be found, in theory or in fact, in those very philosophical systems of classical antiquity where the *psyche*, the soul, is held to be a natural being. The study of the soul is divided between metaphysics, logic and physics. Aristotle's treatise *De Anima* is actually a work of general biology, one of the texts devoted to physics. Following Aristotle and in the scholastic tradition, philosophy treatises in the early seventeenth century continue to deal with the soul in a chapter of their physics.[2] As the object of study of physics is the natural and organized body capable of life, the soul is regarded by physics as part of the living body and not as a substance distinct from matter. From this point of view, a study of the organs of knowledge, the five external senses and the internal senses (common sense, phantasy, memory), is no different from the study of the organs of respiration or digestion. The soul is a natural object of study, a form located in the hierarchy of forms, even if its essential function is the knowledge of forms. The science of the soul is a branch of physiology in its original, universal, sense—that of theory of nature.

An unbroken line leads from this ancient conception to one aspect of modern psychology, neuro-physiology—long understood as consisting exclusively of psycho-neurology (but today embracing psycho-endocrinology as well)—and to psychopathology as a medical discipline. In this respect it is worth recalling that prior to the two revolutions which led to the rise of modern physiology, those of Harvey and Lavoisier, a revolution of equal importance to the theories of circulation and respiration was accomplished by Galen; it was he who established, clinically and experimentally, following the doctors of the Alexandria school, Herophilus and Erasistratus, against the Aristotelian doctrine but in conformity with the anticipations of Alcmaeon, Hippocrates and Plato—that it is the brain and not the heart that is the organ of sensation and movement, the seat of the soul. Galen stands at the beginning of a long uninterrupted sequence of research in empirical pneumatology which last for centuries; it is based on the theory of animal spirits which is finally supplanted by electro-neurology at the end of the eighteenth century. Gall, although decidedly pluralistic in his conception of the relationship between psychical functions and encephalic organs, is in direct line of descent from Galen and, despite certain extravagances, dominates research on cerebral localizations during the first sixty years of the twentieth century, up to and including Broca.

In its aspect as psycho-physiology and psychopathology, modern psychology thus goes right back to the second century.

Psychology as the Science of Subjectivity

The decline of Aristotelian physics in the seventeenth century marks the end of psychology as a para-physics, as the science of a natural object; correlatively, it marks the birth of psychology as the science of subjectivity.

The people ultimately responsible for the advent of modern psychology, as the science of the thinking subject, are the mechanistic physicists of the seventeenth century.[3]

If the reality of the world is no longer to be identified with the contents of perception, and if reality is reached and posited by a process of reduction of the illusions of normal sensory experience, then, as the possibility of a falsification of the real, the qualitative deficiency of this experience falls to the responsibility of the mind itself, that is to say of the subject of experience, insofar as this subject is not assimilable to the mathematical and mechanistic reason which is the instrument of truth and the measure of reality.

But in the eyes of the physicist, this responsibility is a culpability. Psychology is consequently constituted as an enterprise for the exculpation of the mind. Its project is that of a science which explains, vis-à-vis physics, why it is that the mind is by nature constrained initially to mislead reason in its dealings with reality. Psychology sets itself up as the physics of the external senses in order to account for the distortions for which the exercise of the senses is held responsible, in the function of knowledge, by mechanistic physics.

A—The physics of the external senses

For two reasons, therefore, psychology, the science of subjectivity, begins as a psychophysics. First, because if it is to be taken seriously by physicists it cannot present itself as something less than physics. Secondly, because it has to seek in nature, that is to say in the structure of the human body, the reason for the existence of the unreal residues of human experience.

But we are not dealing here with a return to the ancient idea of a science of the soul as a branch of physics. The new physics is a calculus. Psychology tends to imitate it. It will attempt to identify the quantitative constants of sensation and the relations between these constants.

In this respect, Descartes and Malebranche are the leading figures. In his *Rules for the Direction of the Mind* (XII), Descartes proposes the reduction of the qualitative differences between sensory data to differences between geometrical figures. He is talking about sensory data insofar as they represent, in the proper sense of the term, the informing of one body by other bodies: what is informed by the external sense is an internal sense—"phantasy, which is nothing but a real and figured body." In Rule XIV, Descartes deals specifically with what Kant will later call the intensive magnitude of sensations (*Critique of Pure Reason*, Transcendental Analytic: Anticipation of Perception): comparisons between light, sounds etc., can be converted into exact relationships only by analogy with the extension of a body possessing a figure. Add to this the fact that Descartes, if not exactly the inventor of the term and the concept of reflex, nevertheless affirmed the constancy of the link between stimulus and response, and it is easy to see that a psychology, understood as a mathematical physics of the external senses, begins with him and goes on up to Fechner, with a little help from physiologists such as Hermann Helmholtz—and in spite of, as well as in opposition to, the Kantian reservations which were in turn criticized by Herbart.

The variety of psychology was broadened by Wundt so as to assume the dimensions of an experimental psychology, one that in his work was informed by the desire to discover, in the laws of the "facts of consciousness," an analytic determinism of the same type as that which mechanics and physics were suggesting might have universal scientific validity.

Fechner died in 1887, two years prior to the publication of Bergson's *Essai sur les données immédiates de la conscience* (1889). Wundt died in 1920, having trained many followers, some of whom are still alive, and not before witnessing the first attacks of the Gestalt psychologists on the (experimental and mathematical) analytical physics of the external sense. These attacks were in accordance with Ehrenfel's observations on Gestalt qualities (*Uber Gestaltqualitäten*, 1890), observations which were themselves related to Bergson's analyses of perceived totalities as organic forms transcending their supposed parts (*Essai*, chap. 2).

B—The Science of the Internal Senses

The science of subjectivity, however, is not reducible to the elaboration of a physics of the external senses: it claims to be the science of self-consciousness or the science of the internal senses. The term Psychology, signifying the science of the self (Wolff), dates from the eighteenth century. The whole history of this psychology can be read as the history of the misunderstandings occasioned by Descartes' *Meditations*, although Descartes himself is not to be held responsible for them.

When at the beginning of the third Meditation, Descartes considers his "interior," in order to render himself more known and more familiar to himself, the object of his attention is Thought. The Cartesian interior, the consciousness of the *ego cogito*, is the direct knowledge that the soul has of itself insofar as it is pure understanding. Descartes calls his *Meditations* metaphysical because they are intended to capture the nature and the essence of the *Cogito* in the immediate apprehension of its existence. The Cartesian meditation is not a personal anecdote. The reflexion which endows the knowledge of the self with mathematical rigor and impersonality is not that self-observation which the spiritualists at the beginning of the nineteenth century, made bold to place under the patronage of Socrates—with the result that Monsieur Pierre-Paul Royer-Collard can assure Napoleon that the motto *Know Thyself*, the *Cogito* and *Introspection* afford an unassailable foundation for throne and altar.

The Cartesian interior has nothing in common with the internal sense of the Aristotelians which "conceives its objects internally and inside the head"[4] and which, as we have seen, Descartes holds to be an aspect of the body (*Rule XIII*). It is for this reason that Descartes states that the soul knows itself directly and more easily than the body. The explicity polemical intention of this remark is too often forgotten: the Aristotelians considered that the soul does not know itself directly. "The knowledge of the soul is not direct, but is reached only by reflection. For the soul resembles the eye that sees all and that can see itself only in reflection as in a mirror . . . and the soul likewise sees and knows itself only by reflection and by recognition of its effects."[5] This is a thesis that rouses Descartes to indignation when Gassendi takes it up in his objections to *Meditation III* and to which he replies: "It is not the eye that sees itself, nor the mirror, but the mind which alone knows the eye, the mirror and itself."

Now this decisive answer still does not put an end to this scholastic disputation. Maine de Biran once again turns it against Descartes in his *Mémoire sur la décomposition de la pensée*. Auguste Comte invokes it in his argument against the possibility of introspection, that is to say, against the method of self-knowledge which Royer-Collard borrows from Reid in order to make of psychology the scientific propaedeutic of metaphysics, justifying by experiment the traditional theses of spiritualist substantialism.[6] Even Cournot, in his sagacity, does not disdain to take up the argument once more in support of the idea that psychological observation is more concerned with the conduct of others than with the observer's self, that psychology is more closely related to wisdom than science, and that "it is inherent in psychological facts that they should express themselves as aphorisms rather than as theorems."[7]

Descartes has been the object of a double misunderstanding: by those who, in opposition to him, set up an empirical psychology taking the form of a natural history of the self—from Locke to Ribot, by way of Condillac, the French Ideologues and the English Utilitarians; and by those who, in setting up a rational psychology based on the intuition of a substantial self, thought that they were following his lead.

Kant still today retains the honor of having established that although Wolff was able to baptize these newborn post-Cartesians (*Psychologia empirica*, 1731; *Psychologia rationalis*, 1734), he was unable to provide any basis for their claims to legitimacy. Kant shows on the one hand that phenomenal inner sense is merely a form of empirical intuition, tending to identify itself with time, and on the other hand that the self, subject of all apperceptive judgment, is an organizational function of experience, one which, however, can never constitute the object of a science since it is the transcendental condition of all science. The *Metaphysical Foundations of Natural Science* (1786) refuses to make of psychology a science in the image of either mathematics or physics. There is no possible mathematical psychology in the sense in which there is a mathematical physics. Even if one were to apply to the modifications of the internal senses the mathematics of the continuum, by virtue of the anticipation of perception with respect to intensive magnitudes, the result would be no more interesting than a geometry limited to the study of the properties of the straight line. Neither is there any such thing as an experimental psychology, capable of constituting itself as chemistry does, by use of analysis and synthesis. It is not possible to experiment either on ourselves or on others. And internal observation modifies its object. Trying to catch oneself in the act of self-observation would lead to insanity. Psychology can therefore only be descriptive. Its true place is within an *Anthropology* where it would represent the propaedeutic to a theory of skill and prudence culminating in a theory of wisdom.

C—The Science of the Intimate Senses

If one terms classical psychology that psychology which one is proposing to refute, we must say that in psychology everyone has his classics. The Ideologues, descendants of the Sensationalists, could regard as classical the Scottish psychology which, like them, favored an inductive method only in order to affirm, unlike them, the substantiality of the mind. But the atomistic and analytic psychology of the Ideologues and the Sensationalists, before being rejected as a classical psychology by the theoreticians of Gestalt psychology, had already been dismissed in the same way by the romantic psychologist Maine de Biran. For him, psychology becomes the technique of the *journal intime* and the science of the *sens intime*. Descartes' solitude was the *ascesis* of a mathematician. The solitude of Maine de Biran is the idleness of a Sub-Prefect. The Cartesian *I think* founds thought in itself. The *I wish* of Maine de Biran founds consciousness for itself in opposition to exteriority. Tucked away in his snug office, Maine de Biran discovers that psychological analysis is not a process of simplification but one of complication, that the primitive psychical fact is not an element but already a relationship, and that this relationship is lived in effort. He comes to two conclusions which are unexpected for a man in a function of authority, that is, of command: he finds that consciousness requires the conflict of a power and a resistance, and that man is not, as Bonald thought, an intelligence served by organs, but a living organization served by an intelligence. The soul is necessarily incarnated and there is consequently no psychology without biology. Self-observation does not dispense from recourse to the physiology of voluntary movement nor to the pathology of affectivity. Maine de Biran's situation was unique, coming as he did between the two Royer-Collards. He debated with the doctrinaire and was judged by the psychiatrist. He left us his *Promenade avec M. Royer-Collard dans les jardins du Luxembourg* and we also have an *Examen de la doctrine de Maine de Biran*[8] written by Antoine-Athanase Royer-Collard, the younger brother of the aforementioned. If Maine de Biran had not read and discussed Cabanis (*Rapports du physique et du moral de l'homme*, 1798) and Bichat (*Recherches sur la vie et la mort*, 1800) he would not occupy the important place he does in the history of pathological psychiatry. The second Royer-Collard, following Pinel and with Esquirol, is one of the founders of the French school of psychiatry. Pinel had advocated the idea that the insane were both sick, like other medical patients, neither possessed nor criminal, and also different from other patients and hence needing to be treated separately and segregated into specialized wards or hospitals. Pinel was the founder of mental medicine as an independent discipline, building it up from its beginnings in the therapeutic isolation of the insane at Bicêtre and La Salpetrière. Royer-Collard followed his example in the Maison Nationale de Charenton, where he became head physician in 1805, the same year in which Esquirol submitted his thesis on *Les passions considérées comme causes, symptômes et moyens curatifs de l'aliénation mentale*. In 1816, Royer-Collard became Professor of Legal Medicine at the University of Paris and then in 1821 was the first to hold the chair of mental medicine. Among the students of Royer-Collard and Esquirol was Calmeil, who studied paralysis of the insane, Bayle, who identified and isolated general paralysis and Félix Voisin, who began the study of infantile mental retardation. And it was at La Salpetrière in 1862, that, following Pinel, Esquirol, Lelut, Baillarger and Falret among others, Charcot became the head of a department, the work of which was to be followed by Theodule Ribot, Pierre Janet, Cardinal Mercier and Sigmund Freud.

We have seen the positive beginnings of psycho-pathology with Galen; we see it culminate in Freud, creator of the term *psychoanalysis* in 1896. Psycho-pathology had not developed in isolation from the other psychological disciplines. As a result of the work of Maine de Biran, it forced philosophy for more than a century to ask itself which of the two Royer-Collards it should look to for a definition of psychology. Psycho-pathology is thus both judge and contesting party in the uninterrupted debate, conduct of which has been bequeathed to psychology by metaphysics (continued contribution by the latter notwithstanding), on the relationship of the physical and the psychical. For a long time before it became psycho-somatic, this relationship was described as somato-psychic. This inversion, moreover, is the same as that which has been effected in the signification given to the unconscious. If one assimilates psyche to consciousness—taking Descartes, rightly or wrongly, as one's authority—then the unconscious is of the order of the physical. If, on the other hand, one considers that physical phenomena can be unconscious, then psychology cannot be reduced to the science of consciousness. The physical is no longer that which is hidden, but that which hides itself, that which we hide; it is no longer only the intimate, but also—to use a term that Bossuet borrowed from the mystics—the abyssal. Psychology is no longer only the science of the intimate, it is the science of the depths of the soul.

Psychology as the Science of Reactions and Behavior

By proposing to define man as a living organization served by an intelligence, Maine de Biran mapped out in advance—better, it seems, than Gall, who, according to Lelut, declared that "man is no longer an intelligence, but a will served by organs"[9]—the terrain on which a new psychology would be built in the course of the nineteenth century. At the same time, however, he assigned its limits, situating human life, in his *Anthropologie*, between animal life and spiritual life.

The nineteenth century sees the constitution of a psychology conceived as nervous and mental pathology, as the physics of the external senses and as the science of the internal and intimate senses, of a biology of human behavior. The reasons for this development seem to us to be as follows. First, the scientific reasons, namely, the constitution of a Biology that was a general theory of the relations between organisms and environments and which marked the end of the belief in the existence of a separate human order. Next, the technical and economic reasons: the development of an industrial regime drawing attention to the industrious character of the human species—and this marks the end of the belief in the dignity of speculative thought. And finally, the political reasons: these boil down to the diffusion of egalitarianism and to the end of the belief in the values of social privilege. When conscription and public education are the concern of national government, then the claim for equality in matters of military service and of civic function (to each according to his labor, or his works, or his merits) becomes the real, though often unnoticed, basis of a phenomenon that is characteristic of modern societies—the generalized practice of expertise, in the broad sense, as that which determines competence and exposes simulation.

Now what distinguishes this psychology of behavior in our view from the other types of psychological investigation is its inherent inability to grasp or convey with any degree of clarity the sense of its founding project. If the founding projects of certain earlier types of psychology may be held to have arisen out of philosophical misconceptions, here, on the other hand, because all connection with philosophical theory is denied, the question arises as to whence such a psychological program can derive its meaning. In assuming the status of an objective science of aptitudes, reactions and behavior, modeled on biology, this psychology and their psychologists completely neglect to situate their specific behavior in relation to the historical circumstances and to the social environments in which they are led to propose their methods or techniques and procure acceptance of their services.

Nietzsche, outlining the psychology of the nineteenth-century psychologist, wrote: "We psychologists of the future . . . almost take it for a sign of degeneration when an instrument tries to 'know itself': we are instruments of knowledge and would like to possess all the naiveté and precision of an instrument—consequently, we must not analyze ourselves, 'know ourselves.'"[10] An astonishing, yet also a profoundly revealing misconception. The psychologist wishes only to be an instrument, without seeking to know of whom or of what he is the instrument. Nietzsche seemed to be much more happily inspired when, at the beginning of *The Genealogy of Morals*, he puzzled over the enigma of the English psychologists, the Utilitarians, and their preoccupation with the genesis of moral feelings. He wondered then what had pushed the psychologists towards cynicism and towards the explanation of human conduct in terms of interest, utility and the forgetting of these important motivations. And yet here we have Nietzsche, faced with the behavior of nineteenth-century psychologists, abandoning all provisional cynicism, that is to say, all lucidity!

The idea of utility as a psychological principle is the result of the philosophical emergence of human nature as a faculty of artifice (Hume, Burke) or, to put it more prosaically, it results from the definition of man as a toolmaker (the Encyclopaedists, Adam Smith, Franklin). But the principle of the biological psychology of behavior does not seem to have emerged in this way from an explicit philosophical intuition, no doubt because it could begin to function only by remaining unformulated. The principle is the definition of man himself as a tool. Utilitarianism, implying the idea of utility for man and the idea of man as the judge of utility, was succeeded by instrumentalism, implying the idea of utility for man and the idea of man as a means of utility. Intelligence is no longer that which creates the organs and uses them, but that which serves them. It is no accident that the historical origin of the psychology of reactions is to be found in the work inspired by the discovery of the personal equation for the astronomers using the telescope (Maskelyne, 1796). Man was studied first as an instrument of the scientific instrument before being studied as the instrument of all instruments.

Research into the laws of adaptation and learning, into the relation of adaptation to learning, into the detection and measurement of aptitudes, into the conditions governing output and productivity (whether of individuals or of groups)—research which is inseparable from its application to selection and evaluation—is all based on one implicit postulate: that the nature of man is to be a tool, that his vocation is to be set in his place and to be set to work.

Of course, Nietzsche is right when he says that psychologists want to be the "naive and precise instruments" of this study of man. They have tried to achieve objective knowledge, even if the determinism that they seek to discover in human behavior is no longer the Newtonian type familiar to the first nineteenth-century physicists, but rather a statistical determinism, increasingly based on biometric data. But what in the end is the meaning of this second-order instrumentalism? What is it that urges or inclines psychologists to become the category of men who serve as instruments of the ambition to treat man as an instrument?

As far as the other types of psychology are concerned, the soul or the subject (natural entity or consciousness of interiority) is the principle invoked to legitimize a certain idea of man in his relation to the truth of material objects. For a psychology, on the other hand, which will run a mile from the word "soul" and laugh at the word "consciousness," the truth of man is given in the fact that there is no longer any idea of man which ascribes to him a value other than that of a tool. It has to be recognized, nonetheless, that in order for the idea of tool to exist, there have to be ideas that are not in themselves tools, and that in order to attribute a certain value to a tool, it necessarily follows that not every value is that of a tool limited to the production of others. If the psychologist does not derive his psychological project from an idea of man, does he then think he can legitimize it by his utilizatory conduct towards men? Utilizatory conduct—this formulation is worth insisting upon, despite two possible objections. It might be said, on the one hand, that this type of psychology is not unaware of the distinction between theory and application; on the other hand, that utilization takes place not in the activity of the psychologist but in that of the person or persons who require him to produce his reports and diagnoses. We would say in reply that, unless one confuses the theoretician of psychology with the professor of psychology one is forced to recognize that more often than not the present-day psychologist is a professional practitioner whose "science" derives totally from the search for the "laws" of adaptation to a socio-technical—and not a natural—environment. This, moreover, necessarily gives to his quantifications an evaluative aspect and a significance in terms of expertise. The end result is that the behavior of the psychologist of human behavior almost inevitably carries with it a belief in his own superiority, a good authoritarian conscience and a managerial attitude towards human relations. And this is why we have to come to the cynical question of who it is that designates the psychologists as the instruments of instrumentalism. How does one recognize the men who are worthy of assigning to man-the-instrument his role and his function? Who selects the selectors?

It goes without saying that the comments made here are not concerned with technical competence. The fact that there are good and bad psychologists, some well-trained and capable, and others who are dangerous by reason of a stupidity not proscribed by law—this is not what is at issue. The important question relates to the existence of a science or scientific technique which does not contain within itself any idea capable of endowing it with a scientific sense. In his *Introduction à la psychologie*, Paul Guillame presents a psychological analysis of a man undergoing psychological tests. The man being tested, feeling that he is the object of a certain action, defends himself: Guillaume sees in this state of mind an implicit recognition of the efficacy of the test. But it is equally legitimate to perceive here in embryo a psychology of the psychological tester. The defensive attitude of the man subjected to testing is an index of his repugnance at seeing himself treated like an insect by a man in whom he recognizes no authority to pronounce on what he is and on what he must do. "To treat someone like an insect" is a phrase that Stendhal borrows from Cuvier.[11] And what if we were to treat the psychologist like an insect, if we were to apply Stendhal's suggestion to the bleak and insipid Kinsey, for example?

In other words, behavioral psychology, throughout the nineteenth and twentieth centuries, has tried to achieve autonomy by cutting itself off from philosophy and from the type of speculation that seeks an idea of man by looking beyond what is biologically and sociologically given. But there is no way in which this psychology can avoid the application of its results to the behavior of those who obtain them. The question "What is psychology?", inasmuch as philosophy is no longer permitted to seek the answer, becomes "What do psychologists hope to achieve, doing what they do? In the name of *what* have they set themselves up as psychologists?" When Gideon recruited the Israelite commando force with which he pushed the Midianites back across the Jordan (*Judges*, chap. 7), he used a two-stage set which allowed him first to choose 10,000 men out of 32,000 and then 300 out of 10,000. But this test owed to God both its purpose and its criteria of selection. To select a man capable of selecting it is usually necessary to operate at a level above that of technical selection procedures. In the immanence of scientific psychology the question still stands: who has, not the competence, but the mission to be a psychologist? Psychology is still based on a duality, not that of factual consciousness and the norms entailed by the idea of man, but that of a mass of "subjects" and a corporate elite of specialists equipped with a self-appointed mission.

For Kant and for Maine de Biran psychology was part of an *Anthropology*—that is to say, despite the fashionable ambiguity of the term, part of a philosophy. As far as Kant is concerned, the general theory of human aptitude remains related to the theory of wisdom. Instrumentalist psychology, on the other hand, is a general theory of aptitude making no reference whatever to wisdom. Unless we are able to define this psychology in terms of an idea of man, locating psychology in philosophy, then of course we have no power to prevent anybody from claiming himself to be a psychologist and from claiming what he does to be psychology. But equally, philosophy cannot be prevented from continuing to question the scientifically and technically ill-defined status of psychology. As it does so, philosophy conducts itself with its inherent naiveté (not at all the same as simple-mindedness, and not exclusive of a certain working cynicism) and thus goes back once again onto the side of the people and of the born non-specialists.

Thus it is with a degree of vulgarity that philosophy confronts psychology with the question "Tell me what you are up to and I'll know what you are." But once in a while, at least, the philosopher must be allowed to approach the psychologist as a counselor and to say: if you leave the Sorbonne by the exit in the Rue Saint-Jacques, you can either turn up the hill or go down towards the river; if you go up, you will get to the Pantheon which is the resting place of a few great men, but if you go downhill then you're bound to end up at the Préfecture de Police.

Notes

1 *L'unité de la psychologie*, P.U.F., Paris, 1949.

2 Cf. Scipion du Pleix, *Corps de philosophie contenant la logique, la physique, la métaphysique et l'éthique*, Geneva 1636 (1st edition, Paris 1607).

3 Cf. Aron Gurwitsch, *Développement historique de la Gestalt-Psychologie*, in *Thalès*, 2nd year, 1935, pp. 167–175.

4 Scipion du Pleix, op. cit., *Physique*, p. 439.

5 Ibid., p. 353.

6 *Cours de philosophie positive*, 1st lecture.

7 *Essai sur les fondements de nos connaissances*, 1851, paras. 371–376.

8 Published by his son Hyacinthe Royer-Collard (in the *Annales médico-psychologiques*, 1843, vol. II, p. 1).

9 *Qu'est-ce que la phrénologie? Ou Essai sur la signification et la valeur des systèmes de psychologie en général et de celui de Gall, en particulier*, Paris 1836, p. 401.

10 *The Will to Power*, trans. Kaufmann and Hollingdale, Bk. II, para. 426.

11 "I said to my friend Monsieur de Ranville: 'Instead of hating the bookseller in the neighboring town who sells the *Almanach populaire*, do as the great Cuvier says—treat him like an insect. Find out what his means of subsistence are, try and guess his way of making love'" (Stendhal, *Mémoires d'un touriste*, Calmann-Levy, II, p. 23).

JACQUES LACAN

Responses to Students of Philosophy Concerning the Object of Psychoanalysis

1966

I. Consciousness and the Subject

You have spoken of the mirage engendered by a confusion between consciousness and the subject, a mirage denounced by the experience of psychoanalysis. Now philosophy speaks of consciousness (the Cartesian cogito, transcendental consciousness, Hegelian self-consciousness, Husserl's apodictic cogito, Sartre's prereflexive cogito . . .): how does the psychoanalytic experience account for the misprision engendered within a subject by the fact of identifying with one's consciousness?

What is consciousness for a psychoanalyst?

Is it possible to get someone to "step out" of his consciousness? Is not the subject of (a) consciousness condemned to it?

That concerning which you say I spoke seems to me rather to have been excerpted by you from a text that I wrote in homage to the memory of Maurice Merleau-Ponty, the only one, I hope, to lend to a confusion that I must clarify first in your reading.

I write that "the 'I think' to which presence (according to the preceding: that of the phenomenological subject) would be reduced does not cease implying . . . all the powers or reflection through which subject and consciousness are fused." This does not mean that there is anything in the nature of a confusion involved. At a crucial point of the Cartesian *askesis*, precisely the one I am invoking here, consciousness and the subject coincide. It is holding that privileged moment as exhaustive of the subject which is misleading—making of it the pure category that the presence of a gaze (as a mode of opaqueness within the visible) would come to make flesh with its vision (the context of my sentence).

It is, on the contrary, at that moment of coincidence itself, insofar as it is grasped by reflection, that I intend to mark the site through which psychoana-

From *October* 40 (Spring 1987), pp. 106–13; trans. Jeffrey Mehlman ["Réponse à des étudiants," *Cahier pour l'analyse*, no. 3 (1966), pp. 5–13].

lytic experience makes its entrance. At simply being sustained within time, the subject of the "I think" reveals what it is: the being of a fall. I am that which thinks: "Therefore I am," as I have commented on elsewhere, noting that the "therefore," the causal stroke, divides inaugurally the "I am" of existence from the "I am" of meaning.

That rift or split (*refente*) is precisely that whereof psychoanalysis affords us a daily experience. I have castration anxiety at the same time as I regard it as impossible. Such is the crude example with which Freud illustrates that split, reproduced at all levels of subjective structure.

I say that it ought be be held as primordial and as the first cast of primary repression.

I say that the philosophical "consciousneses" you have lined up on the skewer right up to Sartre at the tip have no other function than to suture that cleavage of the subject, and the analyst recognizes what is at stake in this bolting shut of the truth (for which the perfect instrument would plainly be the ideal promised to us by Hegel as absolute knowledge).

The pretext with which that operation always disguises itself is betrayed by the style of the good apostle, which is illustrated particularly well in the discourse of Leibniz. It is in order to "save the truth" that the door is shut on it.

That is why the question of an initial error in philosophy imposes itself as soon as Freud has produced the unconscious on the stage he assigned to it ("the other stage," as he calls it) and accords it the right to speak.

That is what Lacan comes back to, because the lifting of the seal is so threatening that its very practitioners dream of nothing else than relegating it elsewhere. That right, I say, is held by the unconscious by dint of what it structures as language, and I would clarify the illumination without end with which Freud allows that fact to reverberate if you had asked me the question organized around the terms: the unconscious and the subject.

I would then have been able to add to it this complement: that that very reason is not sufficient to establish that right, and that what is needed, as in the establishment of any right, is a transition to action, and that it is in the presence of that that the psychoanalyst today is in retreat.

That is why what I teach is not addressed in its initial impetus to philosophers. It is not, if I may say so, on your front that I am fighting.

For it is remarkable that you are asking me questions without troubling yourselves about wherein I am authorized to sustain positions that you attribute to me with more or less exactitude. The site of the utterance, be it known, is essential in not being elided from any statement.

Distrust, then, your own precipitousness: for a while yet, nourishment will not be lacking for philosophical grazing. But it is simply that a psychoanalytic acting out—or transition to action—might prompt it to recognize substance on the side of penury.

It is not up to psychoanalysis to account for philosophical error for the benefit of philosophy, as though philosophy thereafter would be able to "realize" or account for it itself. There can be no such thing, since to imagine it is precisely philosophical error itself. The subject is not wrong to identify with his consciousness, as you have me put it, God knows why, but in being compelled to miss the topology which makes a fool of him in that identification.

I have said: topology. For that is what prevails here. I mean that without structure, it is impossible to grasp anything of the *real* of the economy: of the cathexis or investment, as one says, even without knowing what one is saying.

It is for having lacked the elaboration prepared at this juncture by linguistics that Freud hesitated to decide as to the origin of the change, which he distinguished in consciousness, quite perspicacious in recognizing it to be excessive in relation to the epiphenomenal slimness to which a certain physiology was intent on reducing it, and freeing himself therefrom, indicating to his followers the phenomenon of attention in order to cross swords.

An apparently insufficient clue: psychoanalysts have rarely known how to make use of a key when Freud did not teach them how it opens. Perhaps the advance I am making this year toward a certain object called "*petit a*" will permit some progress on this score.

I hope, then, to have restored to its proper place the function of a confusion which was first of all in your question.

The remainder of the text, if it is indeed the one you are referring to, shows precisely that what it is aiming at, at this juncture, is the danger of a reduction of the subject to the *ego*. It is that recentering, during a period of psychoanalytic slumber, of psychoanalytic theory on the ego that I was obliged to denounce at length in order to render possible a return to Freud.

By what trick of fate was that disaffected accessory, to wit: the ego—which served as no more than a label for psychology itself, once that discipline was intent on being a bit more objective—elevated precisely at the time when one would have expected its critique to be taken up anew from the perspective of the subject?

This can be conceived solely by way of the slippage undergone by psychoanalysis at being confronted with the managerial exploitation of psychology, particularly in its use for job recruitment.

The *autonomous ego*, the conflict-free sphere proposed as a new Gospel by Mr. Heinz Hartmann to the New York circle, is no more than the ideology of a class of immigrants preoccupied with the prestigious values prevailing in central European society when with the diaspora of the war they had to settle in a society in which values sediment according to a scale of *income tax*.

I thus anticipated the requisite warning signal by proposing as early as 1936, with the "mirror stage," a model that is already structural in essence, which recalled the true nature of the ego in Freud, namely: an imaginary identification, or more exactly, an enveloping series of such identifications.

Note for your purpose that I recall on this occasion the difference separating the image from the illusory (the "optical illusion" begins only with judgment; prior to that, it is a gaze objectivated in a mirror).

Heinz Hartmann, quite cultivated in such matters, was able to hear that call as early as the Marienbad Congress at which I issued it in 1936. But one is simply helpless against the attraction of diversifying the forms of the concentration camp: psychologizing ideology is one of them.

You philosophers don't seem to me to need this register of my remarks unless Alain has not been sufficient for you.

Are you sufficiently edified to free me from answering as to the way to "get somebody to step out of his consciousness"? I am not Alphonse Allais, who would answer you: flay him.

It is not to his consciousness, that the subject is condemned, but to his body, which in many ways resists actualizing the division of the subject.

That such resistance has served to lodge all kinds of errors (including the soul) does not prevent that division from achieving effects of truth within it, such as what Freud discovered under the name over which his disciples still vacillate in assenting: castration.

II. Psychoanalysis and Society

What is the relation between the subject of a revolutionary praxis aiming at going beyond its alienated labor and the subject of alienated desire?

What is, according to you, the theory of language implied by Marxism?

What do you think of the recent remark by Dr. Mannoni, who, speaking (at a recent meeting of institutional psychotherapists) of psychoanalytic therapy, characterized it as "the intervention of one institution within another institution"?

That raises the question of the social function of "mental illness" and of psychoanalysis. What is the social significance of the fact that the psychoanalyst must be paid by the analysand? Need psychoanalysis take into account the fact that it is a class therapy?

The subject of alienated desire—you mean no doubt what I articulate as: the desire of—is the desire of the Other, which is correct, with the sole modification that there is no subject of desire. There is the subject of the fantasy, that is: a division of the subject caused by an object, that is: stopped up by it, or more exactly, the object for which the category of cause occupies the place in the subject.

The object is the one lacking in philosophical consideration in order to situate itself, that is: in order to know that it is nothing.

That object is the one to which we come in psychoanalysis in that it leaps from its place, like a ball that escapes during the fray in order to score a goal on its own.

That is the object after which we run in psychoanalysis, even as we apply all conceivable awkwardness toward seizing it in theory.

It is only once the status of that object—the one I call "*petit a*," and with which I have entitled my course this year as the object of psychoanalysis—has been acknowledged that we will be able to give a meaning to the alleged impetus you attribute to the subject's revolutionary praxis of going beyond his alienated labor. In what way can one go beyond the alienation of his labor? It is as though you wanted to go beyond the alienation of discourse.

All I can see as transcending that alienation is the object sustaining its value, what Marx, in a homonym singularly anticipatory of psychoanalysis, called the fetish, it being understood that psychoanalysis reveals its biological significance.

Now, that causal object is the one whose regulated exclusion (*coupe*) assumes its ethical shape in the *embourgeoisement* which gives a planetary dimension to the fate of what is called in French, not without reason, *cadres*—white-collar workers.

See there a lineament of what might bring your question to the state of a rough sketch.

But in order to avoid any misunderstanding, note that I maintain that psychoanalysis does not have the slightest right to interpret revolutionary practice—which will be motivated further on—but that on the contrary, revolutionary theory would do well to hold itself responsible for leaving empty the function of truth as cause, when therein lies, nevertheless, the first supposition of its own effectiveness.

It is a matter of calling into question the category of dialectical materialism, and it is a matter of common knowledge that Marxists are not very adept at doing it, even though they are, on the whole, Aristotelians, which is already not too bad.

Only my theory of language as structure of the unconscious can be said to be implied by Marxism, if, that is, you are not more demanding than the material implication with which our most recent logic is satisfied, that is, that my theory of language is true whatever be the adequacy of Marxism, and that it is needed by it, whatever be the defect that it leaves Marxism with.

So much for the theory of language implied logically by Marxism.

As for the one it has implied historically, I have barely but to offer you, given the modest limits of my information as to what goes on beyond a certain doctrinal curtain, thirty pages by Stalin that put an end to the frolics of *Marrism* (from the name of the philologist Marr, who considered language to be a "superstructure").

Statements of rudimentary common sense concerning language and specifically concerning the point that it *is not* a superstructure, whereby the Marxist, on the subject of language, situates himself far above the logical positivist.

The least you can accord me concerning my theory of language is, should it interest you, that it is materialist.

The signifier is matter transcending itself in language. I leave you the choice of attributing that sentence to a Communist Bouvard or a Pecuchet exhilarated by the marvels of DNA.

For you would be wrong to think that I care enough about metaphysics to make a trip to meet it.

I have it at home, that is, in my practice where I entertain it in terms which allow me to answer you in lapidary fashion as to the social function of mental illness: its *social* function, as you in fact put it, is irony. When you have experienced a schizophrenic, you will know the irony that arms him, working at the root of every social relation.

When, however, the illness is neurosis, the irony misses its function, and it is Freud's find to have recognized it there nevertheless, in which manner he restored it therein to its full rights, which is tantamount to a cure of the neurosis.

Psychoanalysis has now taken over the role of neurosis: it has the same social function, but it too misses it. I attempt to reestablish irony with its rights, in which manner perhaps we too will cure the pychoanalysis of today.

That a psychoanalysis must be paid for does not imply that it is a class therapy, but the two things are all that remain of irony in it at present.

That may seem an overly ironic answer. If you reflect on it, it will certainly seem more authentic to you than if I had referred you to what I said above about the function of the fetish.

I see that I have left aside Mannoni, for failure to know exactly what it was that he said. We will find out shortly in *Les temps modernes*.

III. Psychoanalysis and Philosophy

To what extent can psychoanalysis account for philosophy and in what sense is it authorized to say that philosophy is paranoia (in an unpublished text by Freud commented on by Kaufmann)?

If illusion is the endpoint of sublimation, what is its relation to ideology? Is sublimation not a form of alienation?

Within the teaching of philosophy, how do you conceive of that of psychoanalysis?

I have already said enough to be brief, for all this is giving me no pleasure.

That philosophy is a variety of paranoia is a variety of Freud's irony in its savage phase. It is certainly not by chance that Freud consigns it to the unpublished (the Alphonse Allais reference here, too, would not be out of place; we should not be surprised to encounter Kaufmann—who is familiar with irony—here).

I regret that you believe that sublimation is an illusion. The slightest reading of Freud would convince you that he says exactly the opposite.

Religion, yes, an illusion, says Freud, but that's because he sees a neurosis in it.

I don't know what can be expected from within the teaching of philosophy, but I have recently had an experience of it that has left me prey to a doubt: which is that psychoanalysis can contribute to what is called hermeneutics only by restoring philosophy to its links with obscurantism.[1]

For to depend on the economics of the matter, that is, on what is obscure (since at the same time, one prides oneself on not having had any experience of it) at the very moment that, as a philosopher, one should be confronting the stumbling of the subject is of the same order as the celebrated fantasy of the Rat Man, who placed two packets of shit on eyes which, as if by chance, were those of Anna Freud, the daughter of his psychoanalyst.

Thus would the philosopher operate in regard to truth when *it* runs the risk of seeing him in his particular poverty.

But all this is not that serious, and the religious aspirations in this case are sufficiently acknowledged for one to be able to say that psychoanalysis has no interest in it.

IV. Psychoanalysis and Anthropology

Can there be or is there a fundamental discipline that would account for the unity of the human sciences?

Can psychoanalysis serve as the basis for an anthropology?

The best anthropology can go no further than making of man the speaking being. I myself speak of a science defined by its object.

Now the subject of the unconscious is a *spoken* being, and that is the being of man; if psychoanalysis is to be a science, that is not a presentable object.

In point of fact, psychoanalysis refutes every idea heretofore presented of man. It should be said that all of them, however many there were, were no longer in touch with anything, even before psychoanalysis.

The object of psychoanalysis is not man; it is what he lacks—not an absolute lack, but the lack of an object. Even then agreement must be reached as to the lack in question—it is that which excludes the possibility of naming its object.

It is not to scarce bread, but to cake that the Queen sent her peoples in time of famine.

Therein lies the unity of the human sciences, if you like, which is to say that it provokes smiles if one fails to recognize in it the function of a limit.

It provokes smiles at a certain use of interpretation, as the sleight of hand of comprehension. An interpretation whose effects are understood is not a psychoanalystic interpretation. It is enough to have been analyzed or to be an analyst to realize that.

This is why psychoanalysis as a science will be structuralist, to the point of recognizing in science a refusal of the subject.

NOTE

[1] The reference is to Paul Ricoeur, *De l'interprétation: essai sur Freud*, Paris, Seuil, 1965.

MAURICE BLANCHOT

The Absence of the Book

1969

What Kafka teaches us—even if this formulation cannot be directly attributed to him—is that storytelling brings the neutral into play. Narration that is governed by the neutral is kept in the custody of the third-person "he," a "he" that is neither a third person nor the simple cloak of impersonality. The narrative "he" [*il*] in which the neutral speaks is not content to take the place usually occupied by the subject, whether this latter is a stated or an implied "I" or the event that occurs in its impersonal signification.[1] The narrative "he" or "it" unseats every subject just as it disappropriates all transitive action and all objective possibility. This takes two forms: (1) the speech of the narrative always lets us feel that what is being recounted is not being recounted by anyone: it speaks in the neutral; (2) in the neutral space of the narrative, the bearers of speech, the subjects of the action—those who once stood in the place of characters—fall into a relation of self-nonidentification. Something happens to them that they can only recapture by relinquishing their power to say "I." And what happens has always already happened: they can only indirectly account for it as a sort of self-forgetting, the forgetting that introduces them into the present without memory that is the present of narrating speech.

This, of course, does not mean that the narrative necessarily relates a forgotten event, or even the event of forgetting that dominates lives and societies, which, separated—or as one still says, alienated—from what they are, move as though in their sleep seeking to recapture themselves. It is narrative (independently of its content) that is a forgetting, so that to tell a story is to put oneself through the ordeal of this first forgetting that precedes, founds, and ruins all memory. Recounting, in this sense, is the torment of language, the incessant search for its infinity. And narrative would be nothing other than an allusion to the initial detour that is borne by writing and that carries it away, causing us, as we write, to yield to a sort of perpetual turning away.

From *The Infinite Conversation*, trans. Susan Hanson (Minneapolis: University of Minnesota Press, 1992), pp. 384–87 ["L'absence du livre," in *L'entretien infini* (Paris: Editions Gallimard, 1969)].

The act of writing: this relation to life, a deflected relation through which what is of no concern is affirmed.

The narrative "he" [or "it," *il*], whether absent or present, whether it affirms itself or hides itself, and whether or not it alters the conventions of writing—linearity, continuity, readability—thus marks the intrusion of the other—understood as neutral—in its irreducible strangeness and in its wily perversity. The other speaks. But when the other is speaking, no one speaks because the other, which we must refrain from honoring with a capital letter that would determine it by way of a majestic substantive, as though it had some substantial or even unique presence, is precisely never simply the other. The other is neither the one nor the other, and the neutral that indicates it withdraws from both, as it does from unity, always establishing it outside the term, the act, or the subject through which it claims to offer itself. The narrative (I do not say narrating) voice derives from this its aphony. It is a voice that has no place in the work, but neither does it hang over it; far from falling out of some sky under the guarantee of a superior Transcendence, the "he" [*il*] is not the "encompassing" of Jaspers, but rather a kind of void in the work—the absence-word that Marguerite Duras evokes in one of her narratives: "a hole-word, hollowed out in its center by a hole, the hole in which all the other words should have been buried." And the text goes on: "One could not have spoken it but it could have been made to resound—immense, endless, an empty gong."[2] This is the narrative voice, a neutral voice that speaks the work from out of this place without a place, where the work is silent.

The narrative voice is neutral. Let us rapidly consider the traits that characterize it at first approach. For one thing, it says nothing, not only because it adds nothing to what there is to say (it knows nothing), but because the narrative voice subtends this nothing—the "silencing and "keeping silent"—in which speech is here and now already engaged; thus it is not heard in the first place, and everything that gives it a distinct reality begins to betray it. Then again, without its own existence—speaking from nowhere, suspended in the narrative as a whole—neither does it dissipate there in the manner of light, which, though itself invisible, makes things visible: radically exterior, it comes from exteriority itself, from the outside that is the enigma proper to language in writing. But let us consider still other traits, traits that are actually the same. The narrative voice that is inside only inasmuch as it is outside, at a distance without there being any distance, cannot be embodied. Although it may well borrow the voice of a judiciously chosen character, or even create the hybrid function of mediator (the voice that ruins all mediation), it is always different from what utters it: it is the indifferent-difference that alters the personal voice. Let us (on a whim) call it spectral, ghostlike. Not that it comes from beyond the grave, or even because it would once and for all represent some essential absence, but because it always tends to absent itself in its bearer and also efface him as the center: it is thus neutral in the decisive sense that it cannot be central, does not create a center, does not speak from out of a center, but, on the contrary, at the limit, would prevent the work from having one; withdrawing from it every privileged point of interest (even afocal), and also not allowing it to exist as a completed whole, once and forever achieved.

Tacit, the narrative voice attracts language indirectly, obliquely, and, under this attraction of an oblique speech, allows the neutral to speak. What does this indicate? The narrative voice bears the neutral. It bears the neutral insofar as: (1) To speak in the neutral is to speak at a distance, preserving this distance without *mediation* and without *community*, and even in sustaining the infinite distancing of distance—its irreciprocity, its irrectitude of dissymmetry: for the neutral is precisely the greatest distance governed by dissymmetry and without one or another of its terms being privileged (the neutral cannot be neutralized). (2) Neutral speech does not reveal, it does not conceal. This does not mean that it signifies nothing (by claiming to abdicate sense in the form of non-sense); it means that the neutral does not signify in the same way as the visible-invisible does, but rather opens another power in language, one that is alien to the power of illuminating (or obscuring), of comprehension (or misapprehension). It does not signify in the optical manner; it remains outside the light-shadow reference that seems to be the ultimate reference of all knowledge and all communication, to the point of making us forget that it only has the value of a venerable, that is to say inveterate, metaphor. (3) The exigency of the neutral tends to suspend the attributive structure of language: the relation to being, implicit or explicit, that is immediately posed in language as soon as something is said. It has often been remarked—by philosophers, linguists, and political analysts—that nothing can be negated that has not already been posited beforehand. To put this another way, every language begins by declaring and in declaring affirms. But it may be that recounting (writing) draws language into a possibility of saying that would say being without saying it, and yet without denying it either. Or again, to say this more clearly, too clearly: it would establish the center of gravity of speech elsewhere, there where speaking would neither affirm being nor need negation in order to suspend the work of being that is ordinarily accomplished in every form of expression. In this respect, the narrative voice is the most critical voice that, unheard, might give to be heard. That is why, as we listen to it, we tend to confuse it with the oblique voice of misfortune, or of madness.[3]

Notes

[1] The "he" [or "it," *il*] does not simply take the place traditionally occupied by a subject, a mobile fragmentation; it modifies what we mean by place: a fixed location, unique or

determined by its placement. Here we should once again (confusedly) say that the "he," dispersing after the fashion of a lack in the simultaneous plurality—the repetition—of a moving and diversely unoccupied place, designates "its" place as both the place from which it will always be missing and that will thus remain empty, but also as a surplus of place, a place that is always too many: hypertopia.

[2] *Le ravissement de Lol V. Stein* (Paris: Gallimard, 1964). [*The Ravishing of Lol Stein*, trans. Richard Seaver (New York: Grove, 1966) and (New York: Pantheon, 1979, c. 1966).]

[3] It is this voice—the narrative voice—that I hear, perhaps rashly, perhaps rightly, in the narrative by Marguerite Duras that I mentioned a while back. The night forever without dawn—the ballroom where the indescribable event occurred that cannot be recalled and cannot be forgotten, but is retained in forgetting: the nocturnal desire to turn around in order to see what belongs neither to the visible nor to the invisible, that is, to remain for a moment, through one's gaze, as close as possible to strangeness where the rhythm of revealing-concealing has lost its rectifying force; then the need (the eternal human wish) to place in another's charge, to live once again in another, in a third person, the dual relation, the fascinated, indifferent relation that is irreducible to any mediation, a neutral relation, even if it implies the infinite void of desire; finally, the imminent certainty that what has once taken place will always begin again, always give itself away and refuse itself. Such are, it seems to me, the "coordinates" of the narrative space, the circle by which, as we enter it, we incessantly enter the outside. But who is telling the story here? Not the one who is relating it, who formally—and also a little shamefully—does the speaking, actually usurping speech to the point that he seems to be an intruder; it is rather the one who cannot recount because she bears—this is her wisdom, her madness—the torment of the impossible narration, knowing herself (by a closed knowledge anterior to the scission of reason-unreason) to be the measure of this outside where, as we accede to it, we risk falling under the attraction of a speech that is entirely exterior: pure extravagance.

JACQUES BOUVERESSE

The Myth of Interiority

1976

I do not believe that an adequate account of Wittgenstein's position relative to Descartes is given by saying that for him, in contrast to Descartes, the body is easier to know, and better known, than the mind.[1] To say this—as Wittgenstein himself might put it—is to make the difference seem too small, in that it suggests that Wittgenstein accepted in principle a contrast of the type that Descartes posited between the mental and the physical and simply reversed the order of gnoseological priority that is supposed to exist between the two terms of the opposition.

In fact, Wittgenstein in no way accepted the distinction that Descartes makes between my self and my body as a purely physical system or machine, because such a distinction implies a quite exceptional usage of the word "body" (which is never used in our ordinary language games to express a contrast of this sort), a metaphysical usage, the idea for which could only occur to a philosopher.[2] As Wittgenstein says, a person who points out, for instance, that it is not the body but the soul that experiences pain tells us nothing. For he probably means that the body is in the end only a machine, but has anyone ever tried to believe that a machine can suffer (cf. *PI*, secs. 359–360)? The body, in the sense it which it is conceived here, can suffer if a machine can suffer. Now, the philospher who contends that it is in fact the body that suffers does not mean that it is a machine that is suffering but perhaps that it is the being of flesh and blood, the human being who stands before him, and not an ethereal entity about which he knows nothing. And when we say of a being other than man that it suffers, we say so not because it is a body that resembles the body of man but because *it* resembles a man and behaves like a man. To assert that it is not the body that thinks, feels, or wills assumes that the word "body" has been assigned a very special meaning such that the assertion becomes a simple grammatical truth.

To say that the crucial question in this debate is "Could sensory experiences take place in the absence of an organism?" (see Geach, *Mental Acts*; chap. 25; Kenny, *Cartesian Privacy*, pp. 353–353), is not a good way of presenting the prob-

Le mythe de l'intériorité: Expérience, signification et language privé chez Wittgenstein (Paris: Editions de Minuit, 1976), pp. 526–33; trans. Arthur Goldhammer.

lem either. For if one means that Descartes answered this question in the affirmative, the assertion is both true and false. It is true in that, for him, sensation, considered independently of every kind of judgment or inference, and in particular from every kind of speculation as to possible causes, is a strictly mental thing and hence I can know that I have sensations and know what it is to have a sensation without needing to know that I have a body (cf. *Méditation seconde*, VII, p. 29; *Principes*, VIII-1, p. 33). In this sense one can indeed say that "it is the soul that feels and not the body" (VI, p. 109) and that sensation is in the end nothing other than a mode of thought (this aspect of sensation no doubt corresponds fairly well to what Wittgenstein calls "my immediate private sensations"):

> To will, understand, imagine, feel, etc., are merely so many ways of thinking, all of which belong to the soul. (I, p. 366)
>
> There is nothing which is entirely within our power except our thoughts; at least, that is, if we take the word "thought" for all the operations of the soul, so that not only meditation and will but even the functions of seeing, hearing, making one movement rather than another, etc., inasmuch as they depend on thoughts, are thoughts. (II, p. 36)

But it by no means follows from this that I could feel sensations if I had no body. For Descartes said repeatedly that the soul feels only insofar as it is joined to a body, that is to say, only insofar as external objects via the intermediary of the body, or the body itself, exert a certain causal action on it. Sensation, like man himself, is a dual being, which belongs simultaneously to the world of thought and the world of extent. As M. Gueroult has written:

> The sensible, as sensible, is radically excluded from the essence of the soul, while as representation it is no less radically excluded from the essence of the body. At the same time, it must relate to the soul as representation, which presupposes thought, while as sensible it relates to the body, because only the sensible is capable of giving us its existence. The sensible then appears as an in-between excluded from everywhere, for it has its place neither in the soul as such nor the body as such, though at the same time it necessarily relates to both: to the soul, via the faculty of thought which it implies, although it is repugnant to the essence of the soul because of its content; and to the body, as that without which its existence would never be given to us, though it is repugnant in itself to the nature of that body.[3]

A true and important fact, in view of the problem with which we are now concerned, is that insofar as we can judge, the idea of pain, according to

Descartes, does not in itself imply any essential reference to the normal causes and expressions of pain. That the sensation of pain appears "on the occasion of" certain movements of the body—when it is struck by a sword, say—and manifests itself through other movements, such as those that give rise to the natural expressions of pain, is not part of our concept of pain:

> When I examined why sadness in the mind follows I know not what sensation of pain, and why the sensation of pleasure gives rise to joy, or why I know not what emotion of the stomach, which I call hunger, makes us want to eat, and dryness of the throat makes us want to drink, and so on, I can give no reason other than that nature instructs me in this way; for there is certainly no affinity or relation (that I can understand at least) between this emotion of the stomach and the desire to eat, or between the sensation of the thing that causes pain and the thought of sadness to which this sensation gives rise. (VII, p. 76; cf. VIII-1, p. 321)

It follows that, insofar as my strictly rigorous knowledge of pain is concerned, nothing obliges me to assume that it has a cause outside myself or that it normally has causes of a particular kind, and nothing prohibits me from assuming that a sword thrust gives rise in someone else's soul to what I myself would call a keen sensation of pleasure but which manifests itself there as pain does in me, in the form of cries, moans, contortions, etc. For in regard to the question of the relation that exists between the sensation of pain and the characteristic behaviors whereby pain normally expresses itself, Descartes's answer is clearer still. There is no essential connection between the two things, since, for example, animals, which give signs of pain quite comparable to those we observe in our fellow men, are nevertheless nothing more than highly perfected natural automata. And if I can be sure that other humans really feel pain, it is not because they show "obvious" signs of pain or even because they say they feel pain, because no such behavior absolutely rules out the possibility that they are mere talking automata. It is because their pertinent use of language in regard to an infinite number of things unrelated to the passions proves to me that they possess a spiritual soul like my own:

> None of our exterior actions can convince those who examine them that our body is not simply a machine that moves by itself, but in it there is also a soul that has thoughts, apart from words or other signs produced in regard to subjects that arise, unrelated to any passion. (IV, p. 574)

Another sign of the absence of any logical connection between internal processes and their characteristic public expressions is the fact that, according to Descartes, we have no reason to assume that certain animals have thoughts and therefore a soul unless we assume that all do (see IV, p. 576). Whereas for Wittgenstein, because "the human body is the best picture of the human soul" (*PI*, p. 178), and because the body and human behavior serve as a paradigm for the application of psychological terms, it is quite natural (and in a sense indispensable) to attribute a mental life to certain animals yet difficult, strange, or impossible to do so for certain others.

Under these conditions, it is fair to say that the argument by analogy as frequently used by philosophers has a curiously circular aspect. Indeed, on one hand I say that I know what pain is solely on the basis of my personal experience, abstracting of course from the empirical relation that also exists between my sensation and my behavior. On the other hand, the concept of pain is transferred to other beings by analogy, in virtue of the resemblance that exists between their behavior and mine in certain circumstances. But if the relation that exists between pain and its ordinary modes of expression is purely contingent, what prevents me from assuming that beings that have never shown the least sign of pain are constantly suffering in the cruelest possible way, or that, in virtue of the principle that similar effects produce similar causes, a stone struck by a sword feels the same pain as we do in similar circumstances though we know nothing about it?

It is clear that the argument by analogy works only to the extent that pain is something that (only) a living being, or, more precisely, a human being or a being sufficiently like a human being, can feel. To be correct or incorrect, reasonable or dubious, the analogical transposition must first be possible, must first make *sense*. Before asking what might justify it, it is a good idea simply to ask what might prompt it. And the conditions in which we implement it (if any) show precisely that our concept of pain is essentially linked to the human body and human behavior. This is precisely what Wittgenstein means: "What gives us *so much as the idea* that living beings, things, can feel?" (*PI*, sec. 283). The answer is that we did not first have the idea of pain (based on our own case) and then this other idea, but that we initially acquired the concept of pain as the concept of a thing that certain beings and not others could meaningfully be said to have or feel. (We have not necessarily been told what beings those might be.)

What distinguishes Wittgenstein from Descartes is therefore essentially the fundamental importance that the former attaches to language and to the links that exist between properly linguistic activity and other human activities. I can attribute a sensation of pain to someone (myself or someone else) only insofar as I have a concept of what it is to have a sensation of this type. I can be said to possess such a concept only insofar as I can exercise it in a language game that I play with others. And in this language game, the actions and reactions of, and with respect to, the person who is said to suffer play an absolutely essential role. In this sense, contrary to one of the things suggested by the idea of an intrinsically private language, what I can say about my mental life is in no way independent of what others say about it on the basis of what they observe and of the way in which they react to what I say.

From this point of view, Wittgenstein's position seems equally remote from Cartesianism and behaviorism, both of which in fact trace their source to precisely the same error of principle. In fact, they are antithetical answers to a question that Wittgenstein dismisses: What is it that allows us to extend to certain objects outside ourselves understandings that are so exclusively associated with what we know about ourselves and about assertions of which we are absolutely certain only insofar as we are concerned personally? The Cartesian answer is that we have sufficient reason to believe that these objects are not objects but beings endowed as we are with a rational and spiritual soul. The behaviorist response is, broadly speaking, that the generalization does not really take place, because after all it is not necessary to assume that when we say, for instance, that X feels pain (for an X different from ourselves), we are saying anything more than could be expressed with a statement or class of statements of the form "X is behaving (or is disposed to behave) in such and such a way."

Hence we can say that both the Cartesian and the behaviorist do the opposite of what Wittgenstein recommends. Instead of accepting the language game that is actually played as a fundamental given, they try to explain it, and their explanations are inadequate: "What we have rather to do is to *accept* the everyday language-game, and to note *false* accounts of the matter *as* false. The primitive language-game which children are taught needs no justification; attempts at justification need to be rejected" (*PI*, p. 200). This has nothing to do in this instance with conformism or question-begging. As we have seen, Wittgenstein is suggesting that the language game we play with the word "pain" originally rests on a base of instinctive behavior constituted by attitudes and responses that do not derive from a certain more or less legitimate way of seeing but rather *are* a way of seeing. (In this sense, we do not *learn* to treat other men as men, and indeed we must learn many things before we can consider them, even momentarily, as objects [e.g., automata].) It is an erroneous way of presenting the facts that leads Cartesians and behaviorists to the idea that they have to justify (or tolerate or refute) a belief without sufficient foundation, whereas for Wittgenstein what is involved is something which is not a belief and which constitutes a foundation.

Notes

Translator's note: Wittgenstein quotes are from *Philosophical Investigations*, 3d ed., ed. G.E.M. Anscombe (Englewood Cliffs, NJ: Prentice Hall, 1958).

[1] See A. Kenny, "Cartesian Privacy," in WPI, p. 361.

[2] See J. W. Cook, "Human Beings," in P. Winch, ed., *Studies in the Philosophy of Wittgenstein* (London: Routledge & Kegan Paul, 1969), pp. 117–151.

[3] M. Gueroult, *Descartes selon l'ordre des raisons* (Paris: Aubier, 1953), vol. 1, p. 150.

GILLES DELEUZE AND FÉLIX GUATTARI

A Thousand Plateaus

1980

When Virginia Woolf was questioned about a specifically women's writing, she was appalled at the idea of writing "as a woman." Rather, writing should produce a becoming-woman as atoms of womanhood capable of crossing and impregnating an entire social field, and of contaminating men, of sweeping them up in that becoming. Very soft particles—but also very hard and obstinate, irreducible, indomitable. The rise of women in English novel writing has spared no man: even those who pass for the most virile, the most phallocratic, such as Lawrence and Miller, in their turn continually tap into and emit particles that enter the proximity or zone of indiscernibility of women. In writing, they become-women. The question is not, or not only, that of the organism, history, and subject of enunciation that oppose masculine to feminine in the great dualism machines. The question is fundamentally that of the body—the body they *steal* from us in order to fabricate opposable organisms. This body is stolen first from the girl: Stop behaving like that, you're not a little girl anymore, you're not a tomboy, etc. The girl's becoming is stolen first, in order to impose a history, or prehistory, upon her. The boy's turn comes next, but it is by using the girl as an example, by pointing to the girl as the object of his desire, that an opposed organism, a dominant history is fabricated for him too. The girl is the first victim, but she must also serve as an example and a trap. That is why, conversely, the reconstruction of the body as a Body without Organs, the anorganism of the body, is inseparable from a becoming-woman, or the production of a molecular woman. Doubtless, the girl becomes a woman in the molar or organic sense. But conversely, becoming-woman or the molecular woman is the girl herself. The girl is certainly not defined by virginity; she is defined by a relation of movement and rest, speed and slowness, by a combination of atoms, an emission of particles: haecceity. She never ceases to roam upon a body without organs. She is an abstract line, or a line of flight. Thus girls do not belong to an age group, sex, order, or

From *A Thousand Plateaus: Capitalism and Schizophrenia*, trans. Brian Massumi (Minneapolis: University of Minnesota Press, 1987), pp. 276–79 [*Mille plateaux* (Paris: Editions de Minuit, 1980).

kingdom: they slip in everywhere, between orders, acts, ages, sexes; they produce *n* molecular sexes on the line of flight in relation to the dualism machines they cross right through. The only way to get outside the dualisms is to be-between, to pass between, the intermezzo—that is what Virginia Woolf lived with all her energies, in all of her work, never ceasing to become. The girl is like the block of becoming that remains contemporaneous to each opposable term, man, woman, child, adult. It is not the girl who becomes a woman; it is becoming-woman that produces the universal girl. Trost, a mysterious author, painted a portrait of the girl, to whom he linked the fate of the revolution: her speed, her freely machinic body, her intensities, her abstract line or line of flight, her molecular production, her indifference to memory, her nonfigurative character—"the nonfigurative of desire."[1] Joan of Arc? The special role of the girl in Russian terrorism: the girl with the bomb, guardian of dynamite? It is certain that molecular politics proceeds via the girl and the child. But it is also certain that girls and children draw their strength neither from the molar status that subdues them nor from the organism and subjectivity they receive; they draw their strength from the becoming-molecular they cause to pass between sexes and ages, the becoming-child of the adult as well as of the child, the becoming-woman of the man as well as of the woman. The girl and the child do not become; it is becoming itself that is a child or a girl. The child does not become an adult any more than the girl becomes a woman; the girl is the becoming-woman of each sex, just as the child is the becoming-young of every age. Knowing how to age does not mean remaining young; it means extracting from one's age the particles, the speeds and slowness, the flows that constitute the youth of *that* age. Knowing how to love does not mean remaining a man or a woman; it means extracting from one's sex the particles, the speeds and slownesses, the flows, the *n* sexes that constitute the girl of *that* sexuality. It is Age itself that is a becoming-child, just as Sexuality, any sexuality, is a becoming-woman, in other words, a girl. This by way of response to the stupid question, Why did Proust make Albert Albertine?

Although all becomings are already molecular, including becoming-woman, it must be said that all becomings begin with and pass through becoming-woman. It is the key to all the other becomings. When the man of war disguises himself as a woman, flees disguised as a girl, hides as a girl, it is not a shameful, transitory incident in his life. To hide, to camouflage oneself, is a warrior function, and the line of flight attracts the enemy, traverses something and puts what it traverses to flight; the warrior arises in the infinity of a line of flight. Although the femininity of the man of war is not accidental, it should not be thought of as structural, or regulated by a correspondence of relations. It is difficult to see how the correspondence between the two relations "man-war" and "woman-marriage" could entail an equivalence between the warrior and the girl as a woman who refuses to marry.[2] It is just as difficult to see how the general bisexuality, or even homosexuality, of military societies could explain this phenomenon, which is no more imitative than it is structural, representing instead an essential *anomie* of the man of war. This phenomenon can only be understood in terms of becoming. We have seen how the man of war, by virtue of his *furor* and celerity, was swept up in irresistible becomings-animal. These are becomings that have as their necessary condition the becoming-woman of the warrior, or his alliance with the girl, his contagion with her. The man of war is inseparable from the Amazons. The union of the girl and the man of war does not produce animals, but simultaneously produces the becoming-woman of the latter and the becoming-animal of the former, in a single "block" in which the warrior in turn becomes animal by contagion with the girl at the same time as the girl becomes warrior by contagion with the animal. Everything ties together in an asymmetrical block of becoming, an instantaneous zigzag. It is in the vestiges of a double war machine—that of the Greeks, soon to be supplanted by the State, and that of the Amazons, soon to be dissolved—that Achilles and Penthesilea, the last man of war and the last queen of the girls, choose one another, Achilles in a becoming-woman, Penthesilea in a becoming-dog.

The rites of transvestism or female impersonation in primitive societies in which a man becomes a woman are not explainable by a social organization that places the given relations in correspondence, or by a psychic organization that makes the woman desire to become a man just as the man desires to become a woman.[3] Social structure and psychic identification leave too many special factors unaccounted for: the linkage, unleashing, and communication of the becomings triggered by the transvestite; the power (*puissance*) of the resultant becoming-animal; and above all the participation of these becomings in a specific war machine. The same applies for sexuality: it is badly explained by the binary organization of the sexes, and just as badly by a bisexual organization within each sex. Sexuality brings into play too great a diversity of conjugated becomings; these are like *n* sexes, an entire war machine through which love passes. This is not a return to those appalling metaphors of love and war, seduction and conquest, the battle of the sexes and the domestic squabble, or even the Strindberg-war: it is only after love is done with and sexuality has dried up that things appear this way. What counts is that love itself is a war machine endowed with strange and somewhat terrifying powers. Sexuality is the production of a thousand sexes, which are so many uncontrollable becomings. *Sexuality proceeds by way of the becoming-woman of the man and the becoming-animal of the human*: an emission of particles. There is no need for bestialism in this, although it may arise, and many psychiatric anecdotes document it in ways that are interesting, if oversimplified and consequently off the track, too beastly. It is not a question of "playing" the dog, like an elderly gentleman on a postcard; it is not so much a question of making love with animals. Becomings-animal are basically of another power, since their reality resides not in an animal one imitates or to which one corresponds but in themselves, in that which suddenly sweeps us up and makes us become—a *proximity,* an *indiscernibility* that extracts a shared element from the animal far more effectively than any domestication, utilization, or imitation could: "the Beast."

Notes

[1] See Trost, *Visible et invisible* (Paris: Arcanes) and *Librement mécanique* (Paris: Minotaure): "She was simultaneously, in her sensible reality and in the ideal prolongation of her lines, like the projection of a human group yet to come."

[2] See the examples of structural explanation proposed by Jean-Pierre Vernant, in *Problèmes de la guerre en Grèce ancienne*, pp. 15–16.

[3] On transvestism in primitive societies, see Bruno Bettelheim (who offers an identificatory psychological interpretation), *Symbolic Wounds* (Glencoe, Ill.: Free Press, 1954), and especially Gregory Bateson (who proposes an original structural interpretation), *Naven: A Survey of the Problems Suggested by a Composite Picture of the Culture of a New Guinea Tribe Drawn from Three Points of Views*, 2nd ed. (Stanford, Calif.: Stanford University Press, 1958).

MAURICE FLORENCE

Foucault

1984

In the early 1980s, Denis Huisman asked François Ewald, Foucault's assistant at the Collège de France, to reedit the entry on Foucault for a new edition of the Dictionnaire des philosophes. *The text submitted to Huisman was written almost entirely by Foucault himself, and signed pseudonymously "Maurice Florence."*

To the extent that Foucault fits into the philosophical tradition, it is the critical *tradition of Kant*, and his project could be called a *Critical History of Thought*.[1] This should not be taken to mean a history of ideas that would be at the same time an analysis of errors that might be gauged after the fact; or a decipherment of the misinterpretations linked to them and on which what we think today might depend. If what is meant by thought is the act that posits a subject and an object, along with their various possible relations, a critical history of thought would be an analysis of the conditions under which certain relations of subject to object are formed or modified, insofar as those relations constitute a possible knowledge [*savoir*]. It is not a matter of defining the formal conditions of a relationship to the object; nor is it a matter of isolating the empirical conditions that may, at a given moment, have enabled the subject in general to become acquainted with an object already given in reality. The problem is to determine what the subject must be, to what condition he is subject, what status he must have, what position he must occupy in reality or in the imaginary, in order to become a legitimate subject of this or that type of knowledge [*connaissance*]. In short, it is a matter of determining its mode of "subjectivation," for the latter is obviously not the same, according to whether the knowledge involved has the form of an exegesis of a sacred text, a natural

From *Aesthetics, Method, and Epistemology*, ed. James D. Faubion and trans. Robert Hurley (New York: The New Press, 1998), pp. 459–63 [*Dits et écrits, tome II: 1976–1988*, ed. Daniel Defert and François Ewald with the assistance of Jacques Lagrange (1994; Paris: Editions Gallimard, 2001); first published in *Dictionnaire des philosophes*, ed. Denis Huisman (Paris: Presses Universitaires de France, 1984), pp. 942–44].

history observation, or the analysis of a mental patient's behavior. But it is also and at the same time a question of determining under what conditions something can become an object for a possible knowledge [*connaissance*], how it may have been problematized as an object to be known, to what selective procedure [*procédure de découpage*] it may have been subjected, the part of it that is regarded as pertinent. So it is a matter of determining its mode of objectivation, which is not the same either, depending on the type of knowledge [*savoir*] that is involved.

This objectivation and this subjectivation are not independent of each other. From their mutual development and their interconnection, what could be called the "games of truth" come into being—that is, not the discovery of true things but the rules according to which what a subject can say about certain things depends on the question of true and false. In sum, the critical history of thought is neither a history of acquisitions nor a history of concealments of truth; it is the history of "veridictions," understood as the forms according to which discourses capable of being declared true or false are articulated concerning a domain of things. What the conditions of this emergence were, the price that was paid for it, so to speak, its effects on reality and the way in which, linking a certain type of object to certain modalities of the subject, it constituted the historical a priori of a possible experience for a period of time, an area and for given individuals.

Now, Michel Foucault did not pose this question—or this series of questions, which are those of an "archaeology of knowledge"—and does not wish to pose it concerning just any game of truth, but concerning only those in which the subject himself is posited as an object of possible knowledge: What are the processes of subjectivation and objectivation that make it possible for the subject qua subject to become an object of knowledge [*connaissance*], as a subject? Of course, it is a matter not of ascertaining how a "psychological knowledge" was constituted in the course of history but of discovering how various truth games were formed through which the subject became an object of knowledge. Michel Foucault attempted to conduct his analysis in two ways. First, in connection with the appearance and insertion of the question of the speaking, laboring, and living subject, in domains and according to the form of a scientific type of knowledge. This had to do with the formation of certain "human sciences," studied in reference to the practice of the empirical sciences, and of their characteristic discourse in the seventeenth and eighteenth centuries (*The Order of Things*). Foucault also tried to analyze the formation of the subject as he may appear on the other side of a normative division, becoming an object of knowledge—as a madman, a patient, or a delinquent, through practices such as those of psychiatry, clinical medicine, and penality (*Madness and Civilization, Birth of the Clinic, Discipline and Punish*).

Foucault has now undertaken, still within the same general project, to study the constitution of the subject as an object for himself: the formation of procedures by which the subject is led to observe himself, analyze himself, interpret himself, recognize himself as a domain of possible knowledge. In short, this concerns the history of "subjectivity," if what is meant by the term is the way in which the subject experiences himself in a game of truth where he relates to himself. The question of sex and sexuality appeared, in Foucault's view, to constitute not the only possible example, certainly, but at least a rather privileged case. Indeed, it was in this connection that through the whole of Christianity, and perhaps beyond, individuals were all called on to recognize themselves as subjects of pleasure, of desire, of lust, of temptation and were urged to deploy, by various means (self-examination, spiritual exercises, admission, confession), the game of true and false in regard to themselves and what constitutes the most secret, the most individual part of their subjectivity.

In sum, this history of sexuality is meant to constitute a third segment, added to the analyses of relations between the subject and truth or, to be exact, to the study of the modes according to which the subject was able to be inserted as an object in the games of truth.

Taking the question of relations between the subject and truth as the guiding thread for all these analyses implies certain choices of method. And, first, a systematic skepticism toward all anthropological universals—which does not mean rejecting them all from the start, outright and once and for all, but that nothing of that order must be accepted that is not strictly indispensable. In regard to human nature or the categories that may be applied to the subject, everything in our knowledge which is suggested to us as being universally valid must be tested and analyzed. Refusing the universal of "madness," "delinquency," or "sexuality" does not imply that what these notions refer to is nothing, or that they are only chimeras invented for the sake of a dubious cause. Something more is involved, however, than the simple observation that their content varies with time and circumstances: It means that one must investigate the conditions that enable people, according to the rules of true and false statements, to recognize a subject as mentally ill or to arrange that a subject recognize the most essential part of himself in the modality of his sexual desire. So the first rule of method for this kind of work is this: Insofar as possible, circumvent the anthropological universals (and, of course, those of a humanism that would assert the rights, the privileges, and the nature of a human being as an immediate and timeless truth of the subject) in order to examine them as historical constructs. One must also reverse the philosophical way of proceeding upward to the constituent subject which is asked to account for every possible object of knowledge in general. On the contrary, it is a matter of proceeding back down to the study of the concrete practices by which the subject is constituted in the immanence of a domain of knowledge. There too, one must be careful: Refusing the philosophical recourse to a constituent subject does not amount to acting as if the subject did not exist, making an abstraction of it on behalf of a pure objectivity. This refusal has the aim of eliciting the processes that are peculiar to an experience in which the subject and the object "are formed and transformed" in relation to and in terms of one another. The discourses of mental illness, delinquency, or sexuality say what the subject is only in a certain, quite particular game of truth; but these games are not imposed on the subject from the outside according to a necessary causality or structural determination. They open up a field of experience in which the subject and the object are both constituted only under certain simultaneous conditions, but in which they are constantly modified in relation to each other, and so they modify this field of experience itself.

Hence a third principle of method: Address "practices" as a domain of analysis, approach the study from the angle of what "was done." For example, what was done with madmen, delinquents, or sick people? On course, one can try to infer the institutions in which they were placed and the treatments to which they were subjected from the ideas that people had about them, or knowledge that people believed they had about them. One can also look for the form of "true" mental illnesses and the modalities of real delinquency in a given period in order to explain what was thought about them at the time. Michel Foucault approaches things in an altogether different way. He first studies the ensemble of more or less regulated, more or less deliberate, more or less finalized ways of doing things, through which can be seen both what was constituted as real for those who sought to think it and manage it and the way in which the latter constituted themselves as subjects capable of knowing, analyzing, and ultimately altering reality. These are the "practices," understood as a way of acting and thinking at once, that provide the intelligibility key for the correlative constitution of the subject and the object.

Now, since it is a matter of studying the different modes of objectivation of the subject that appear through these practices, one understands how important it is to analyze power relations. But it is essential to clearly define what such an analysis can be and can hope to accomplish. Obviously, it is a matter not of examining "power" with regard to its origin, its principles, or its legitimate limits, but of studying the methods and techniques used in different institutional contexts to act upon the behavior of individuals taken separately or in a group, so as to shape, direct, modify their way of conducting themselves, to impose ends on their inaction or fit it into overall strategies, these being multiple consequently, in their form and their place of exercise; diverse, too, in the procedures and techniques they bring into play. These power relations characterize the manner in which men are "governed" by one another; and their analysis shows how, through certain forms of "government," of madmen, sick people, criminals, and so on, the mad, the sick, the delinquent subject is objectified. So an analysis of this kind implies not that the abuse of this or that power has created madmen, sick people, or criminals, there where there was nothing, but that the various and particular forms of "government" of individuals were determinant in the different modes of objectivation of the subject.

One sees how the theme of a "history of sexuality" can fit within Michel Foucault's general project. It is a matter of analyzing "sexuality" as a historically singular mode of experience in which the subject is objectified for himself and for others through certain specific procedures of "government."

Note

[1] The italicized phrase is by François Ewald, who wrote the first part of this statement.—Ed.

EMMANUEL LEVINAS

Outside the Subject

1987

1. From Subject to Object

Psychologism in logic—a product of late nineteenth-century naturalistic empiricism—attempted to reduce the ideality of the logical and mathematical forms of scientific thought, the thought of an intelligence, of a thinking I, to the psychological phenomenon—individual but anonymous—of thinking itself. Reduction of the *ideal* and of the *I* to a thinking that is not the thinking of an I—to anonymous thinking taking place in time and subjected to the laws, the empirical constants, that regulate the psychism's changes of state as manifested in the form of thought. Laws or constants visible to consciousness reflecting upon itself. Empirical psychological laws, more coercive than the intellectual act of an *I* who would think freely—an *I* that might be illusory within a universal determinism. Hence the temptation to reduce the universality and the ideality of ideas and concepts, as well as the unity of the "I think" (which not very long ago had seemed to dominate the *res cogitans* and the *res extensa*), to the order of nature and the anonymity of the particular (which, since Aristotle, is supposedly the "only thing that exists"), to the unfolding of mental reality, *to the subjective, which thus becomes the matrix of all the thinkable.*

Edmund Husserl's *Logical Investigations*, inaugurating phenomenology and already availing itself of it, questioned, from the beginning of the century, that naturalistic interpretation of consciousness and the reduction of thought to a psychological mechanism. Husserl not only showed the radical skepticism implied by that doctrine, which immediately compromised its own claim to truth; he insisted upon what was termed the *intentional* character of consciousness, thereby destroying the image of a monolithic consciousness and an interpretation of psychic phenomena according to a matter-based model. All consciousness is conscious of that consciousness itself, but also and especially of something other than itself, of its intentional correlate, of its *thought-of.* A thought [*pensée*] that is conscious of a thought-of [*pensé*], which, as object, is inherent in thought,

From *Outside the Subject*, trans. Michael B. Smith (Stanford, CA: Stanford University Press, 1994), pp. 151–58 [*Hors sujet* (Saint Clement: Editions Fata Morgana, 1987)].

without being cut from the same cloth, so to speak. An opening of thought onto something present to thought and quite distinct from the lived experience of that thought. Husserl stressed the irreducibility of intentionality: a being-open-to that is neither a principle of contiguity, resemblance or causality, nor one of a deducible consequence, nor yet again the relation of sign to signified or of the whole to the part. Intentionality—from thought to thought-of, from subjective to objective—is not the equivalent of any of those relations that can be read off the object or between objects. Openness of thought onto the thought-of. "Openness onto": a thinking that is not, however, a blind shiver [*frisson*] of the mental, but that, precisely as intention, is a project: "project" of a thought-of, which, though not cut out from the mental fabric of thought, is "unreally" inherent in it, and presents itself in thought as in-itself. It shows itself within—manifests itself in the in-itself or is in-itself in manifestation.

In opposition to the natural temporal flow of mental or subjective reality and the empirical constants in which psychologism sought an empirical rationality, Husserl's phenomenology, in its analysis of subjectivity, preserved the objectivity or the in-itself, or the presence, or the being of the object, sheltering it from all confusion with the lived psychism of thought; and it supported that objectivity in its independence, by the invariable objectivity of logical, mathematical forms, and by the rational necessity of the *eidetic*. Visible, and therefore true forms. All consciousness is consciousness of something. Consciousness is not only the lived experience of the psychism, of the cogitations assured of their subjective existence: it is meaningfulness [*du sensé*], thoughts casting themselves toward something that shows itself in them. For a whole generation of students and readers of *Logical Investigations*, phenomenology, heralding a new atmosphere in European philosophy, meant mainly thought's access to being, a thought stripped of subjectivist encumbrances, a return to ontology without criticist problems, without relativism's fears—the flowering of the eidetic sciences, the contemplation of essences, the method of the disciplines named regional ontologies. Logic itself, enlarged to form a *mathesis universalis* and entitled "formal ontology," invites subjective thought to espouse its forms. "The return to the things themselves," the rallying cry of phenomenology, is most often understood as that priority of being over the consciousness in which it shows itself, dictating its Law to the acts of consciousness and their synthesis.

2. From Object to Subject

And yet the ultimate lesson of Husserl's phenomenology—which distinguishes within the subjective, thanks to the notion of intentionality, between the subjective of the lived psychism and the objective that, through that subjective, is projected or shows itself—does not consist in turning its back on the element of that projection that is purely act, in order to lose itself in the objective theme and thereby become worthy of scientific dignity. Phenomenology does not want to be *naive realism*. It tells us, according to Husserl, that thought absorbed by the object is precisely naive; it teaches that, separated from its intentional birth in consciousness, the objective remains an abstraction exposed to inevitable misunderstandings, to be prevented by focusing on the emergence of the objective from the subjective. It should of course not be said, as the psychologists would have it, that the objective is always already subjective. But it should be said that the objective, separated from the subjective that carries it, or constitutes it "intentionally," is abstract, hiding its own perspectives, the work of a naive thought. Husserl's phenomenology tells us that the scientific or philosophical manner of understanding is to study the constitution of the objective articulations of being—things, values, correlates of affectivity and will—*in* the concreteness of thought and the noetic-noematic life of consciousness, cleared of all prior contamination by the prematurely affirmed objective—in a mode of thought, sought after or attained, called pure or transcendental consciousness, by an operation termed *phenomenological reduction*. An operation that brings out, in the phenomenon, all the dimensions of meaning, all the "horizons" that would escape the notice of a naive thought, one that neglected to reflect upon its own functioning. Naive thought: as if the thinking subject need not beware of what he or she can posit otherwise than by thinking, or as if, outside the thinking subject, there were still meaning.[1]

3. The Pure Ego

But what seems primordial in that transcendental phenomenology, stressing the concreteness of the phenomenon as noetic-noematic intentionality, is the origination of the "phenomenon" in what Husserl's *Ideas* introduced as early as 1913 under the name *pure ego* (and to which the 1901 *Logical Investigations* still objected as being a product of the influence of a lingering psychologism)—a notion to which great importance would henceforth attach. Phenomenology is not to be conceived of as the discourse of an anonymous psychism; the intention of noetic-noematic thought is the intention of an ego that is no more drawn "from the body" of the psychism of consciousness than is the object; an ego that, "transcendent in immanence," according to Husserl's paradoxical expression, remains unique, and, thus, absolute, unrelated to anything else, in itself, although living in actuality or actively in the acts of consciousness that "proceed from it." No reduction has any hold on it. . . . It is absolutely devoid of explicit components, an indescribable in-itself and for-itself, pure I and nothing further.[2]

The I, absolute and pure, to which the noetic-noematic life goes back and whence it springs, undergoes and doubtless withstands the supreme methodological test, the *Transcendental Reduction*, through which Husserl returns to thought, untainted by the "things of the world," which have only to "keep quiet," so to speak, to be and to appear, to show themselves plainly and directly without even the shadows that might be projected by them onto the pure and impassible Me or I. The ego remains untarnished, not worn or marked by phenomena, preserved from any unnoticed or secret commerce with the object, free of any premature complicity with the true, in a domain in which appearing [*l'apparaître*] is all that counts. Identity and impartiality of the pure I who does not subject unveiled being—the phenomenon, constituting itself or showing itself in the intentions—to the risk of being anachronistically enlisted, as soon as it appears, in the service of presuppositions. Identity of the pure I and possibility of a temporality in the phenomenon thanks to a subtle intentionality of *retentions* and *protentions* having entered into the initial presence of the proto-impression. Time related thus to its unique *exstasis* (which is rather *authority* [*instance*] of the present), authority that will return in *representation*. A thought in which the being of beings will in the final analysis be *presence* in the synthetic truth of a theory. Identity of the I—identity of uniqueness already exempt from all membership that, as in the case of the simple individual, would have brought it to the promiscuity of individuals contained within the extension of a genus in which they are placed and are the equivalent of one another. Uniqueness, identity of uniqueness, precisely *me* or *I* who is not just a metaphor for the identical, but its original meaning in its self-awakening—an awakening to self that is not reflective consciousness, an awakening predestinating identity to transcendental purity. The transcendental I, who does not arise out of any thematizing operation and does not claim for itself the identity of the *same* that reveals itself in the diverse, in the name of a "common" difference. A logically unjustifiable identity, showing itself in the *I* of the said, in the saying [*dire*] that belongs in some way to the constitution of the I it expresses. Vigilance of a continual reawakening, *I* that, Rimbaud notwithstanding, is not an *other*. Identity of the *I*, protected from all surprise of an "already," from any *fait accompli* and outside all kinship. Identity of the unique, brilliantly named *monad* by Leibniz, unchanging identity—the wonder of which should astonish us more than it does.

4. A Subject Outside the Subject

We should be more astonished at that monadic identity, that identity of uniqueness in the *I* that has no need of justifying itself logically as the individuation of a kind by the addition of an attribute differing from the one possessed by other individuals of the same kind, or by an irreducible position of the individual in space and time—the famous material individuation. The *I* is different because of its uniqueness, not unique because of its difference.

What is the source of that uniqueness, which cannot be understood as the residue of an abstraction, of a return of the individual to the ideal unity of the kind, to which the individual belonged? Its meaning is certainly not constituted, in turn, in a subject more absolute, so to speak, than the constituted absolute, moment of the "bad infinity," moment of an iteration. The pure I, the subject of the transcendental consciousness in which the world is constituted, is itself *outside the subject*: self without reflection—uniqueness identifying itself as incessant awakening. It has been distinguished, ever since the *Critique of Pure Reason*, from any datum presented to knowledge in the *a priori* forms of experience, and "rational psychology" has even been condemned for having taken it as the sublime but legitimate object of knowledge. It is by setting out from the implications of the *Critique of Practical Reason* that the transcendental I will be postulated beyond its formative function for knowledge [*forme dans le connaître*]. And Husserl, in his critique of the Cartesian *cogito*, the reflective turn of which he admires, is critical of the fact that in Descartes' *Meditations* the *I* is uncovered and certain, at the horizon of the world. The *pure I*, which the Cartesian ego becomes in the *phenomenological reduction*, takes on, from that point on, the exceptional status of a transcendent I in the very immanence of intentionality, "indescribable pure Ego and nothing more."[3]

5. Before Truth

And nothing more? Objectivation, the projection of intentionality—are these the ultimate secret of thought that the phenomenological vocation of philosophy has to clarify? Does the light that is at the beginning of thought manifest itself only in the form of a light shining on the forms that bring together in presence, and allow one to think together, the chaotic thickness of the *hylē*, which Husserl's texts refuse to omit, even in their polemics against empiricist sensualism and the affirmation of intentionality? Is the light of thought destined only to help us see the synthetic forms that—through the jumbled content of the elements, the structureless elements of the sensible—have already tied (at the deepest possible level) the knot of simultaneity—the morphology of which it would then be phenomenology's calling to establish? It is no doubt because of that light—belonging to the intentional act, belonging to the noesis whose role it is to illuminate the forms of the noemata, modalities of the meaningful and rational—that Husserl's magnificent discovery of affective and axiological intentionality (without which the entire non-theoretical, lived experience of consciousness would lapse into "hyletic" content) contains the affirmation of a "doxic element that resides within all positionality."[4] This would also indicate, for the meaning of being, the priority of presence and representation, that is, simultaneity maintained in the guise of a theoretical system.

But the positing of the transcendental I in its absolute uniqueness, ensuring the truth of being in the realm of appearance—is it not ordered, in its uniqueness, in a different light than the one illuminating the structures of the phenomenon? Does it not hark back to the ethical intrigue prior to knowledge? Face-to-face with the other man that a man can indeed approach as presence, and that he does approach as such in the sciences of man, had not the thinking one [*le pensant*] already been exposed—beyond the presence of the other, plainly visible in the light—to the defenseless nakedness of the face, the lot or misery of the human? Had he not already been exposed to the misery of nakedness, but also to the loneliness of the face and hence to the categorical imperative of assuming responsibility for that misery? The Word of God in that misery committing him to a responsibility impossible to gainsay. A uniqueness of the irreplaceable and chosen. From unique to unique, beyond any kinship and any prior commonality of kind—a closeness and a transcendence outside all subject, outside all synthesis of a mediator. But an awakening to the indescribable "pure I" of transcendental constitution, recovered by the phenomenological reduction.

Notes

[1] [Translator's note: This rather cryptic formulation appears to define "naive thought" according to Husserl. It would be a thought unaware of what may be posited "otherwise than by thinking," i.e., by affectivity and will, and prone to becoming overly absorbed in the "object," to the point of believing itself to be merely reading off meanings from a "reality" existing independently of its own subjectivity.]

[2] E. Husserl, *Ideas Pertaining to a Pure Phenomenological Philosophy*, book 1 (The Hague: Martinus Nijhoff, 1982), p. 191.

[3] Ibid.

[4] Ibid, p. 301.

LUCE IRIGARAY

Love Between Us

1989

Marx defined the origin of the exploitation of man by man as the exploitation of woman by man, and he affirmed that the first human exploitation stems from the division of labor between man and woman. Why did he not devote his life to resolving this exploitation? He perceived the root of the evil but he did not treat it as such. Why? The answer is to be found partly in the writings of Hegel, in particular in those chapters where he addresses love, Hegel being the only Western philosopher to have broached the question of love as labor.

To ask a woman philosopher [*une philosophe*] to speak to you of love is thus an entirely pertinent request. It corresponds to the necessity for you and for me to think and to practice that which Marxist theories and practices have left in the shadows up until now, giving rise to partial economic and cultural revolutions with which we cannot today be satisfied. I will give three examples or symptoms: the fate of the earth as a natural resource; the problems concerning the liberation of women; and the worldwide crisis of culture exemplified by the student revolts that have been born and reborn here and elsewhere since 1968. Moreover, it is in the same melting pot of revolution that the struggles of students, of the feminism of difference, and of ecological movements have repeatedly found their impulse in our countries. The stakes of these programs persist, stakes often subjected to repression, even among us, by powers blind to their objectives or by militants who misunderstand the profundity and radicalism of what is involved in these struggles. Indeed, it is not a matter of changing such and such a thing within a horizon already defined as human culture, it is a matter of changing the horizon itself. It is a matter of understanding that our interpretation of human identity is theoretically and practically incorrect.

It is the analysis of the relations between women and men that can help us

From *Who Comes After the Subject*, ed. Eduardo Cadava, Peter Connor, and Jean-Luc Nancy (New York: Routledge, 1991), pp. 167–70; trans. Jeffrey Lomonaco ["L'amour entre nous," given in Italian, September 3, 1989, at the national festival of *l'Unitá*, the daily of the Italian Communist Party; "Pour introduire: l'amour entre nous," in *J'aime àtoi* (Paris: Editions Grasset & Fasquelle, 1992), pp. 37–40].

change this situation. Unless we pose the questions there where they are posed most radically, we fall or relapse into an infinity of secondary ethical tasks, as Hegel writes in Chapter 6 of *The Phenomenology of Spirit* while treating the flaw tainting our entire culture. This flaw concerns the lack of ethical relations between the sexes. And the countless ethical tasks, which are multiplied in proportion to the complexity of our civilizations, do not accomplish the work that imposes itself today: to remove the exploitation existing between the sexes in order to allow humanity to continue the development of its History.

I will thus start out from Hegel again in order to explain the motives for this exploitation and to indicate some remedies for it.

At several points in his work, at several moments of his life, Hegel reflects on the question of the love between the sexes, which he analyzes notably as labor. How does Hegel define the love between men and women? He defines it as it is most often practiced in our epoch, but also as it is defined by patriarchal, monotheistic religions or, apparently at another extreme, by theories of sexuality, the Freudian one being an example. He defines it as it is still for the most part our custom and our duty to live it, in private and in public. He defines it as that which exists within a culture of the patriarchal type, without managing to resolve the lack of spirit and ethics that he perceives. He also defines it in accordance with his method. This means that in order to resolve what he calls natural immediacy within the family, Hegel has recourse to pairs of opposites. He is therefore obliged to define man and woman as opposed and not as different. But is it not still most often in this way that the masculine and feminine genders are interpreted?

Man and woman are in opposition, then, in the labor of love, according to Hegel. This labor is defined within the family that they form, insofar as they are a couple (of opposites). Outside the context of the family, Hegel is preoccupied little with endowing each gender with an identity, in particular a juridical one, even though he affirms that the status of a human person is tributary of this recognition by civil law. A sexed/gendered [*sexué*] law would therefore be solely familial in his perspective. There would not be a sexed/gendered [*sexuée*] identity for the citizen.

It is still so for us today. There are still no civil rights proper to women and men.[1] This is particularly evident as it concerns women, since the existing law is adapted more to men than to women insofar as the former have for centuries been the model for citizenship, the woman citizen being abusively defined by an equality of rights that do not satisfy her needs. In all rigor, even today there is no civil law that makes human persons of men and women. Inasmuch as they are sexed/gendered, they remain in natural immediacy. Furthermore, this means that there still are no rights of real persons because only women and men exist—not neuter individuals. The rights of these abstract citizens are more or less copied or deduced from religious, and above all patriarchal, duties or rights. Whence the difficulty in distinguishing between these domains. We still lack a civil law concerning real persons, and first and foremost women and men. In the absence of such rights, our sexuality relapses to a level of barbarity at times worse than that of animal societies.

How then, for Hegel, are the relations between woman and man in the family organized? The woman is wife and mother. But this function, for her, corresponds to an abstract duty. She is therefore not *this* particular woman, irreducible in her singularity, wife of *this* particular man, himself irreducible, and she is no more *this* particular woman, mother of *this* particular child or *these* particular children. This singularity is left to her only from the point of view of the man, for whom she remains bound to natural immediacy. For her, it is a matter of being wife and mother insofar as these functions represent a task vis-à-vis the universal that she performs by renouncing her singular desires.

Love is therefore not possible on the part of woman, Hegel writes, for love is labor of the universal, in the sense that she must love man and child without loving *this* particular man or *this* particular child. She must love man and child as generic members of the human species dominated by mankind. She must love them as the ones who are able to achieve the infinite of humankind, unconsciously assimilated to the masculine, in disregard of her gender and her relationship to the infinite. In other words, the woman's love is defined as familial and civil duty. She does not have the right to singular love nor to love for herself. She is therefore not able to love but is rather subjected to love and to reproduction. She must be sacrificed and must sacrifice herself to this task, disappearing within it as this particular woman alive right now. She must also disappear in terms of desire, unless it be as abstract desire: desire to be wife and mother. This effacement of herself in a function tied to the family is her civil task. For the man, on the contrary, the love of the woman represents the repose of the citizen in the singularity of a home. He must thus love this particular woman insofar as she is singular nature, on the condition that she remain bound to this singularity and he can therefore exchange her while remaining faithful to his relationship to the universal.

The universal for the woman is therefore reduced to a practical labor included within the horizon of the universal defined by the man. Deprived of the relation to the singularity of love, the woman is also deprived of the possibility of a universal for herself. Love, for her, corresponds to a duty—and not a right—that defines her role within humankind, where she appears as the servant of the man.

As for the man, he surrenders himself to the singularity of love as a regression to natural immediacy. Love with a woman in his home represents the repose that complements his labor as a citizen. Insofar as he is a citizen, he is supposed to renounce his sexed/gendered singularity in order to accomplish a universal task in the service of the community. In the name of this supposed universality, he would therefore have the right and the duty to represent all of humankind [*l'espèce humaine*] in the city.

Love, for the man, is thus a permissible lapse into natural immediacy. His wife or another woman must devote herself to granting him this regression on account of the difficult labor of the universal that he assures in other ways. But she must also send him back to this task, distance him from her, unceasingly engender him as the craftsman of universal spirit. The redemption of the man's fall into singularity is found in his consequent capacity to resume his labor as citizen, in the child who, once conceived, deprives the man of the possession of his *jouissance* as his own, and also in the acquired goods supposedly possessed in equality by the two sexes, goods that represent the *for itself* of the union of the man and the woman in the family. The finality of love for the two spouses is finally to acquire a familial capital. The family would thus be a privileged birthplace of capitalism.

Clearly, the self-renunciation demanded of the woman is coupled with the loss of identity of the man as citizen. The woman is made to bend to the lack of forms and norms of the masculine desire that perhaps defines itself *against* incest, *against* the mother, that other who is unpossessable in her singularity—but nevertheless does not define itself *as* masculine desire, unless one were to think that this desire wants only enslavement to death.

In fact, for centuries in the West, marriage has been an institution that chains the woman to a universal duty—the becoming of the spirit of the man in the community—and that chains the man to a regression to the natural in order to assure, in other ways, the service of the State. Insofar as there are no two juridical, sexed/gendered persons, there are, in fact, no nuptials. They are both enslaved to the State, to religion, and to the acquisition of goods. Furthermore, this absence of two in the couple necessitates the intervention of other limits tributary of the work of the negative in accordance with the culture of the man: death as the assembling-place of sensible desires; the real or symbolic dissolution of the citizen in the community; the enslavement to capital or property.

This division of tasks between home and city cannot be perpetuated without depriving the woman both of her relationship to the singular in love and the necessary singularity in her relationship to the universal. The home—couple or family—must be a place of the singular *and* of the universal for each sex, as must be the life of the citizen, be it man or woman. This signifies that the order of cultural identity, and not only natural identity, must be realized for both sexes within the couple, the family, the State. Without a cultural identity adequate to the natural identity of each sex, nature and universal are separate, like earth and sky—infinitely distant from each other and no longer married to one another. The division of tasks between earth and sky—suffering and labor here below, reward and felicity beyond—begins during an epoch of our culture described by mythology and inscribed in philosophy and theology, themselves separated from then onwards, something that is often not the case, as in most far Eastern traditions, for example.

JACQUES DERRIDA

"Eating Well," or the Calculation of the Subject: An Interview with Jacques Derrida

1989

The question "Who comes *after* the subject?" (this time I emphasize the "after") implies that for a certain philosophical opinion today, in its most visible configuration, something named "subject" can be identified, as its alleged passing might also be identified in certain identifiable thoughts or discourses. This "opinion" is confused. The confusion consists at least in a clumsy mixing up of a number of discursive strategies. If over the last twenty-five years in France the most notorious of these strategies have in fact led to a kind of discussion around "the question of the subject," none of them has sought to "liquidate" anything (I don't know moreover to what philosophical concept this word might correspond, a word that I understand more readily in other codes: finance, crime, terrorism, civil or political criminality; one only speaks of "liquidation" therefore from the position of the law, indeed, the police). The diagnostic of "liquidation" exposes in general an illusion and an offence. It accuses: they tried to "liquidate," they thought they could do it, we will not let them do it. The diagnostic implies therefore a promise: we will do justice, we will save or rehabilitate the subject. A slogan therefore: a return to the subject, the return of the subject. Furthermore, one would have to ask, to put it very briefly, if the structure of every subject is not constituted in the possibility of this kind of repetition one calls a return, and more important, if this structure is not essentially *before the law*, the relation to law and the experience, if there *is* any, of the law, but let's leave this. Let's take some examples of this confusion, and also some proper names that might serve as indices to help us along. Did Lacan "liquidate" the subject? No. The decentered "subject" of

From *Who Comes After the Subject?* ed. Eduardo Cadava, Peter Connor, and Jean-Luc Nancy (New York: Routledge, 1991), pp. 96–99, 102–7; trans. Peter Connor and Avital Ronell ["'Il faut bien manger' ou le calcul du sujet: Entretien (avec J.-L. Nancy)," *Cahiers Confrontations*, no. 20 (Winter 1989)].

which he speaks certainly doesn't have the traits of the classical subject (thought even here, we'd have to take a closer look . . .), though it remains indispensable to the economy of the Lacanian theory. It is also a correlate of the law.

Jean-Luc Nancy: Lacan is perhaps the only one to insist on keeping the name . . .

JD: Perhaps not the only one in fact. We will speak later on about Philippe Lacoue-Labarthe, but we might note already that Althusser's theory, for example, seeks to discredit a certain authority of the subject only by acknowledging for the instance of the "subject" an irreducible place in a theory of ideology, an ideology that, *mutatis mutandis*, is just as irreducible as the transcendental illusion in the Kantian dialectic. This place is that of a subject constituted by interpellation, by its being-interpellated (again being-before-the-law, the subject as a subject subjected to the law and held responsible before it). As for Foucault's discourse, there would be different things to say according to the stages of its development. In his case, we would appear to have a history of subjectivity that, in spite of certain massive declarations about the effacement of the figure of man, certainly never consisted in "liquidating" the Subject. And in his last phase, there again, a return of mortality and a certain ethical subject. For these three discourses (Lacan, Althusser, Foucault) and for some of the thinkers they privilege (Freud, Marx, Nietzsche), the subject can be re-interpreted, restored, re-inscribed, it certainly isn't "liquidated." The question "who," notably in Nietzsche, strongly reinforces this point. This is also true of Heidegger, the principal reference or target of the *doxa* we are talking about. The ontological question that deals with the *subjectum*, in its Cartesian and post-Cartesian forms, is anything but a liquidation.

J-LN: For Heidegger, nevertheless, the epoch that comes to a close as the epoch of metaphysics, and that perhaps closes epochality as such, is the epoch of the metaphysics of subjectivity, and the end of philosophy is then the exiting of the metaphysics of subjectivity . . .

JD: But this "exiting" is not an exit, it cannot be compared to a passage beyond or a lapsing, even to a "liquidation."

J-LN: No, but I can't see in Heidegger what thread in the thematic or the problematic of the subject still remains to be drawn out, positively or affirmatively, whereas I can see it if it's a question of truth, if it's a question of manifestation, a question of the phenomenon . . .

JD: Yes. But two things: The very summary exposition that I have just ventured was a quick response, precisely, to whatever summariness there might be in this *doxa* that doesn't go to the trouble of analyzing, up close, in a differentiated manner, the differential strategies of all these treatments of the "subject." We could have chosen examples closer to us, but let's move on.

The effect of the *doxa* consists in saying: all these philosophers think they have put the subject behind them . . .

J-LN: So it would now be a matter of going back to it, and that's the slogan.

JD: It's the effect of the slogan I was getting at. Second thing: what you called the "thread to be drawn" in Heidegger, perhaps follows, among other paths, that of an *analogy* (to be treated very cautiously) between the function of the *Dasein* in *Being and Time* and the function of the subject in an ontological-transcendental, indeed, ethico-juridical setting. *Dasein* cannot be reduced to a subjectivity, certainly, but the existential analytic still retains the formal traits of every transcendental analytics. *Dasein*, and what there is in it that answers to the question "Who?" comes to occupy, no doubt displacing lots of other things, the place of the "subject," the *cogito* or the classical "*Ich denke*." From these, it retains certain essential traits (freedom, resolute-decision, to take up this old translation again, a relation or presence to self, the "call" [*Ruf*] toward a moral conscience, responsibility, primordial imputability or guilt [*Schuldigsein*], etc.). And whatever the movements of Heideggerian thought "after" *Being and Time* and "after" the existential analytic, they left nothing "behind," "liquidated."

J-LN: What you are aiming at in my question then is the "coming after" as leading to something false, dangerous . . .

JD: Your question echoes, for legitimate strategic reasons, a discourse of "opinion" that, it seems to me, one must begin by critiquing or deconstructing. I wouldn't agree to enter into a discussion where it was imagined that one knew what the subject is, where it would go without saying that this "character" is the same for Marx, Nietzsche, Freud, Heidegger, Lacan, Foucault, Althusser, and others, who would somehow all be in agreement to "liquidate" it. For me, the discussion would begin to get interesting when, beyond the vested confusion of this *doxa*, one gets to a more serious, more essential question. For example, if throughout all these different strategies the "subject," without having been "liquidated," has been re-interpreted, displaced, decentered, re-inscribed, then, first: what becomes of those problematics that seemed to presuppose a classical determination of the subject (objectivity, be it scientific or other—ethical, legal, political, etc.), and second: who or what "answers" to the question "who"?

J-LN: For me, "who" designated a *place*, that place "of the subject" that appears precisely through deconstruction itself. What is the place that *Dasein*, for example, comes to occupy?

JD: To elaborate this question along topological lines ("What is the place of the subject?"), it would perhaps be necessary to give up before the impossible, that is to say, before the attempt to reconstitute or reconstruct that which has already been deconstructed (and which, moreover, has deconstructed "itself," an expression that encapsulates the whole difficulty) and ask ourselves, rather: What are we designating, in a tradition that one would have to identify in a rigorous way (let's say for the moment the one that runs from Descartes to Kant and to Husserl) under the concept of subject, in such a way that once certain predicates have been deconstructed, the unity of the concept and the name are radically affected? These predicates would be, for example, the sub-jective structure as the being-thrown—or under-lying—of the substance or of the *substratum*, of the *hypokeimenon*, with its qualities of stance or stability, of permanent presence, of sustained relation to self, everything that links the "subject" to conscience, to humanity, to history . . . and above all to the law, as subject subjected to the law, subject to the law in its very autonomy, to ethical or juridical law, to political law or power, to order (symbolic or not) . . . There is, therefore, at the heart of what passes for and presents itself as a transcendential idealism, a horizon of questioning that is no longer dictated by the egological form of subjectivity or intersubjectivity. On the French philosophical scene, the moment when a certain central hegemony of the subject was being put into question again in the 1960s was also the moment when, phenomenology still being very present, people began to become interested in those places in Husserl's discourse where the egological and more generally the subjective form of the transcendental experience appeared to be more *constituted* than *constitutive*—in sum, as much grounded as precarious. The question of time and of the other became linked to this transcendental passive genesis . . .

J-LN: Still, it was by penetrating *into* this Husserlian constitution, by "forcing" it, that you began your own work . . .

JD: It is within, one might say (but it is precisely a question of the effraction of the within) the living present, that *Urform* of the transcendental experience, that the subject conjoins with nonsubject or that the *ego* is marked, without being able to have the originary and presentative experience of it, by the non-*ego* and especially by the *alter ego*. The *alter ego* cannot present itself, cannot become an originary presence for the *ego*. There is only an analogical a-presentation [*apprésentation*] of the *alter ego*. The *alter ego* can never be given "in person," it resists in principle the principles of phenomenology—namely, the intuitive given of originary presence. This dislocation of the absolute subject from the other and from time neither comes about, nor leads *beyond* phenomenology, but, rather, if not in it, then at least on its border, on the very line of its possibility. It was in the 1950s and 1960s, at the moment when an interest in these difficulties developed in a very different way Levinas, Tran Duc Tao, myself)[1] and following moreover other trajectories (Marx, Nietzsche, Freud, Heidegger), that the centrality of the subject began to be displaced and this discourse of "suspicion," as some were saying then, began to be elaborated in its place. But if certain premises are to be found "in" Husserl, I'm sure that one could make a similar demonstration in Descartes, Kant, and Hegel. Concerning Descartes, one could discover, following the directions of your own work,[2] similar aporia, fictions, and fabrications. Not identical ones, but similar ones. This would have at least the virtue of de-simplifying, of "de-homogenizing" the reference to something like The Subject. There has never been The Subject for anyone, that's what I wanted to begin by saying. The subject is a fable, as you have shown, but to concentrate on the elements of speech and *conventional* fiction that such a fable presupposes is not to stop taking it seriously (it is the serious itself) . . .

J-LN: Everything you have recalled here comes down to emphasizing that there is not, nor has there ever been any presence-to-self that would not call into question the *distance* from self that this presence demands. "To deconstruct," here, comes down to showing this distance at the very heart of presence, and, in so doing, prevents us from simply separating an outdated "metaphysics of the subject" from another thinking that would be, altogether, elsewhere. However, *something has happened*, there has been a *history* both of the thinking of the subject and of its deconstruction. What Heidegger determined as the "epoch" of subjectivity, has this taken place, or has the "subject" always been only a surface effect, a fallout that one cannot impute to the thinkers? But in that case, what is Heidegger talking about when he talks about subjectivity?

JD: An enormous question. I'm not sure that I can approach it head on. To the degree I can subscribe to the Heideggerian discourse on the subject, I have always been a little troubled by the Heideggerian delimitation of the epoch of subjectivity. His questions about the ontological inadequacy of the Cartesian view of subjectivity seem to me no doubt necessary but inadequate, notably in regard to what would link subjectivity to *representation*, and the subject-object couple to the presuppositions of the principle of reason in its Leibnizian formulation. I have tried to explain this elsewhere. The repudiation of Spinoza seems to me to be significant. Here is a great rationalism that does not rest on the principle of reason (inasmuch as in Leibniz this principle privileges both the final cause and representation). Spinoza's substantialist rationalism is a radical critique of both finalism and the (Cartesian) representative determination of the idea; it is not a metaphysics of the cogito or of absolute subjectivity. The import of this repudiation is all the greater and more significant in that the epoch of subjectivity determined by Heidegger is also the epoch of the rationality or the techno-scientific rationalism of modern metaphysics . . .

J-LN: But if the repudiation of Spinoza stems precisely from his having distanced himself from what was dominant elsewhere, does that not confirm this domination?

JD: It's not Spinoza's case that is most important to me. Heidegger defines a modern hegemony of the subject of representation or of the principle of reason. Now if his delimitation is effected through an unjustified repudiation, it is the interpretation of the epoch that risks becoming problematic. And so everything becomes problematic in this discourse. And I would graft on another remark at this point. We were speaking of dehiscence, of intrinsic dislocation, of *différance*, of destinerrance, etc. Some might say: but what we call "subject" is not the absolute origin, pure will, identity to self, or presence to self of consciousness but precisely this noncoincidence with self. This is a riposte to which we'll have to return. By what right do we call this "subject"? I am thinking of those today who would try to reconstruct a discourse around a subject that would not be predeconstructive, around a subject that would no longer include the figure of mastery of self, of adequation to self, center and origin of the world, etc. . . . but which would define the subject rather as the finite experience of nonidentity to self, as the underivable interprellation inasmuch as it comes from the other, from the trace of the other, with all the paradoxes or the aporia of being-before-the-law, etc. Perhaps we'll pick this up again later on. For the moment, since we're speaking of Heidegger, let me add this. I believe in the force and the necessity (and therefore in a certain irreversibility) of the act by which Heidegger *substitutes* a certain concept of *Dasein* for a concept of subject still too marked by the traits of being as *vorhanden, and hence by an interpretation of time*, and insufficiently questioned in its ontological structure. The consequences of this displacement are immense, no doubt we have not yet measured their extent. There's no question of laying these out here in an improvised manner, but I simply wanted to note this: the time and space of this displacement opened up a gap, marked a gap, they left fragile, or recalled the essential ontological fragility of the ethical, juridical, and political foundations of democracy and of every discourse that one can oppose to national socialism in all its forms (the "worst" ones, or those that Heidegger and others might have thought of opposing). These foundations were and remain essentially sealed within a philosophy of the subject. One can quickly perceive the question, which might also be the task: can one take into account the necessity of the existential analytic and what it shatters in the subject and turn towards an ethics, a politics (are these words still appropriate?), indeed an "other" democracy (would it still be a democracy?), in any case towards another type of responsibility that safeguards against what a moment ago I very quickly called the "worst?" Don't expect from me an answer in the way of a formula. I think there are a certain number of us who are working for just this, and it can only take place by way of a long and slow trajectory. It cannot depend on a speculative decree, even less on an opinion. Perhaps not even on philosophical discursivity.

Having said this, whatever the force, the necessity, or the irreversibility of the Heideggerian gesture, the point of departure for the existential analytic remains tributary of precisely what it puts into question. Tributary in this respect—I am picking this out of the network of difficulties that I have associated with it at the beginning of *Of Spirit* (on the question of the question, technology, animality, and epochality)—which is intimately linked to the axiom of the subject: the chosen point of departure, the entity exemplary for a reading of the meaning of Being, is the entity that *we* are, we the *questioning* entities, we who, in that we are open to the question of Being and of the being of the entity we are, have this relation to self that is lacking in everything that is not *Dasein*. Even if *Dasein* is not the subject, this point of departure (which is moreover assumed by Heidegger as ontologico-phenomenological) remains analogous, in its "logic," to what he inherits in undertaking to deconstruct it. This isn't a mistake, it's no doubt an indispensable phase, but now . . .

J-LN: I'd like to point something out to you: a moment ago you were doing everything to dismiss, to disperse the idea of *a* "classic" problematic of the subject. Now you are targeting in Heidegger that which would remain tributary of the classical thinking or position of the subject. That seems a bit contradictory . . .

JD: I didn't say "there is no problematic of the subject," but rather that it cannot be reduced to a homogeneity. This does not preclude, on the contrary, seeking to define certain analogies or common sources, provided that one takes into account the differences. For example, the point of departure in a structure of *relation to self as such and of reappropriation* seems to me to be common just as much to transcendental idealism, to speculative idealism as the thinking of absolute subjectivity, as it is to the existential analytic that proposes its deconstruction. *Being and Time* always concerns those possibilities most proper to *Dasein* in its *Eigentlichkeit*, whatever the singularity may be of this "propriation" that is not, in fact, a subjectivation. Moreover, that the point of departure of the existential analytic is the *Dasein* privileges not only the rapport to self but also the power to ask questions. Now I have tried to show (*Of Spirit*, p. 129, n. 5, sq) what this presupposed and what could come about, even in Heidegger, when this privilege of the question was complicated or displaced. To be brief, I would say that it is in the relation to the "yes" or to the *Zusage* presupposed in every question that one must seek a new (postdeconstructive) determination of the responsibility of the "subject." But it always seems to me to be more worthwhile, once this path has been laid down, to forget the word to some extent. Not to forget it, it is unforgettable, but to rearrange it, to subject it to the laws of a context that it no longer dominates from the center. In other words, no longer to speak about it, but to write it, to write "on" it as on the "subjectile," for example.[3]

In insisting on the *as such*, I am pointing from afar to the inevitable return of a distinction between the *human* relation to self, that is to say, that of an entity capable of conscience, of language, of a relation to death as such, etc., and a *nonhuman* relation to self, incapable of the phenomenological *as such*—and once again we are back to the question of the animal.[4] The distinction between the animal (which has no or is not a *Dasein*) and man has nowhere been more radical nor more rigorous than in Heidegger. The animal will never be either a subject or a *Dasein*. It doesn't have an unconscious either (Freud), nor a rapport to the other as other, no more than there is an animal face (Levinas). It is from the standpoint of *Dasein* that Heidegger defines the humanity of man.

Why have I rarely spoken of the "subject" or of "subjectivity," but rather, here and there, only of "an effect" of "subjectivity"? Because the discourse on the subject, even if it locates difference, inadequation, the dehiscence within auto-affection, etc., continues to link subjectivity with man. Even if it acknowledges that the "animal" is capable of auto-affection (etc.), this discourse nevertheless does not grant it subjectivity—and this concept thus remains marked by all the presuppositions that I have just recalled. Also at stake here of course is responsibility, freedom, truth, ethics, and law.

The "logic" of the trace or of *différance* determines this re-appropriation as an ex-appropriation. Re-appropriation necessarily produces the opposite of what it apparently aims for. Ex-appropriation is not what is proper to man. One can recognize its differential figures as soon as there is a relation to self in its most elementary form (but for this very reason there is no such thing as elementary).

J-LN: When you decide not to limit a potential "subjectivity" to man, why do you then limit yourself simply to the animal?

JD: Nothing should be excluded. I said "animal" for the sake of convenience and to use a reference that is as classical as it is dogmatic. The difference between "animal" and "vegetal" also remains problematic. Of course the relation to self in ex-appropriation is radically different (and that's why it requires a thinking of *différance* and not of opposition) in the case of what one calls the "nonliving," the "vegetal," the "animal," "man," or "God." The question also comes back to the difference between the living and the nonliving. I have tried to indicate the difficulty of this difference in Hegel and Husserl, as well as in Freud and Heidegger.

J-LN: For my part, in my work on freedom, I was compelled to ask myself if the Heideggerian partition between *Dasein*, on the one side, and, on the other side, *Vor-* or *Zuhandensein* would not reconstitute a kind of distinction between subject and object.

JD: The categories of *Vorhandenheit* and *Zuhandenheit* are also intended to avoid those of object (correlated of the subject) and instrument. *Dasein* is first of all thrown. What would link the analytic of *Dasein* with the heritage of the subject would perhaps be more the determination of *Dasein* as *Gewor-*

fenheit, its primordial being-thrown, rather than the determination of a *subject* that would come to be *thrown*, but a being-thrown that would be more primordial than subjectivity and therefore [more primordial] than objectivity as well. A passivity that would be more primordial than traditional passivity and than *Gegenstand* (*Gegenwurf*, the old German word for object, keeps this reference to throwing, without stabilizing it into the stance of a *stehen*). I refer you to what I have said about the "*dé-sistance*"[5] of the subject in Philippe Lacoue-Labarthe. I am trying to think through this experience of the throwing/being-thrown of the subjectile beyond the Heideggerian protocols about which I was just speaking and to link it to another thinking of destination, of chance and of destinerrance (see again "My Chances,"[6] where I situate a (repudiated) relationship between Heidegger and a thinking of the Democritean type).

Starting at "birth," and possibly even prior to it, being-thrown reappropriates itself or rather ex-appropriates itself in forms that are not yet those of the *subject* or the *project*. The question "who" then becomes: "Who (is) thrown?" "Who becomes—'who' from out of the destinerrance of the being-thrown?" That it is still a matter here of the trace, but also of iterability (cf. my "Limited Inc."[7]) means that this ex-appropriation cannot be absolutely stabilized in the form of the subject. The subject assumes presence, that is to say sub-stance, stasis, stance. Not to be able to stabilize itself *absolutely* would mean to be able *only* to be stabilizing itself. Ex-appropriation no longer closes itself; it never totalizes itself. One should not take these figures for metaphors (metaphoricity implies ex-appropriation), nor determine them according to the grammatical opposition of active/passive. Between the thrown and the falling (*Verfallen*) there is also a possible point of passage. Why is *Geworfenheit*, while never put into question, subsequently given to marginalization in Heidegger's thinking? This is what, it seems to me, we must continue to ask. And ex-appropriation does not form a boundary, if one understands by this word a closure or a negativity. It implies the irreducibility of the relation to the other. The other resists all subjectivation, even to the point of the interiorization-idealization of what one calls the work of mourning. The non-subjectivable in the experience of mourning is what I tried to describe in *Glas* and in *Mémoires* (*for Paul de Man*). There is, in what you describe in your recent book[8] as an experience of freedom, an opening that also resists subjectivation, that is to say, it resists the modern concept of freedom as subjective freedom.

J-LN: In what you are calling ex-appropriation, inasmuch as it does not close in on itself and *although* it does not close in on itself (let us say in and in spite of its "passivity") is there not also necessarily something on the order of *singularity*? It is in any case something on the order of the singular that I was getting at with my question *who*.

JD: Under the heading of *Jemeinigkeit*, beyond or behind the subjective "self" or person, there is for Heidegger a singularity, an irreplaceability of that which remains nonsubstitutable in the structure of *Dasein*. This amounts to an irreducible singularity or solitude in *Mitsein* (which is also a condition of *Mitsein*), but it is not that of the individual. This last concept always risks pointing towards both the ego and an organic or atomic indivisibility. The *Da* of *Dasein* singularizes itself without being reducible to any of the categories of human subjectivity (self, reasonable being, consciousness, person), precisely because it is presupposed by all of these.

J-LN: You are getting around to the question "Who comes after the subject?" reversing its form: "Who comes before the subject? . . .

JD: Yes, but "before" no longer retains any chronological, logical, nor even ontologico-transcendental meaning, if one takes into account, as I have tried to do, that which resists the traditional schema of ontologico-transcendental questions.

Notes

[1] Cf. for example *La voix et le phénomène* (Paris, PUF, 1967), p. 94, n. 1—*Speech, and Phenomena*, trans. David B. Allison (Northwestern University Press, 1973), p. 84, n. 1. This note develops the implications of Husserl's sentence: "We can only say that this flux is something which we name in conformity with what is constituted, but is nothing temporally 'objective.' It is absolute subjectivity and has the absolute properties of something to be denoted metaphorically as 'flux,' as a point of actuality, primal source-point, that from which springs the 'now,' and so on. In the lived experience of actuality, we have the primal source-point and a continuity of moments of reverberation [*Nachhallmomenten*]. For all this, names are lacking." The note ends with: "There is no constituting subjectivity. The very concept of constitution must be deconstructed."

[2] Cf. *Ego Sum* (Paris, Flammarion, 1975).

[3] Cf. "Forcener le subjectile" in *Antonin Artaud: Portraits et dessins* (Paris, Gallimard, 1986).

[4] Cf. *Of Spirit*, pp. 27–75, sq. and *Psyché*, p. 415 sq.

[5] Cf. "*Desistance*," preface to the American translation of Philippe Lacoue-Labarthe's *Typography*, ed. C. Fynsk (Harvard University Press, 1989).

[6] Cf. "My Chances" in *Taking Chances*, trans. A. Ronell and I. Harvey (Johns Hopkins University Press, 1984).

[7] Cf. *Limited Inc.*, trans. Samuel Weber (Northwestern University Press, 1988).

[8] *L'expérience de la liberté* (Paris, Galilee, 1988).

GILLES DELEUZE

Immanence: A Life

1995

What is a transcendental field? It can be distinguished from experience in that it doesn't refer to an object or belong to a subject (empirical representation). It appears therefore as a pure stream of a-subjective consciousness, a pre-reflexive impersonal consciousness, a qualitative duration of consciousness without a self. It may seem curious that the transcendental be defined by such immediate givens: we will speak of a transcendental empiricism in contrast to everything that makes up the world of the subject and the object. There is something wild and powerful in this transcendental empiricism that is of course not the element of sensation (simple empiricism), for sensation is only a break within the flow of absolute consciousness. It is, rather, however close two sensations may be, the passage from one to the other as becoming, as increase or decrease in power (virtual quantity). Must we then define the transcendental field by a pure immediate consciousness with neither object nor self, as a movement that neither begins nor ends? (Even Spinoza's conception of this passage or quantity of power still appeals to consciousness.)

But the relation of the transcendental field to consciousness is only a conceptual one. Consciousness becomes a fact only when a subject is produced at the same time as its object, both being outside the field and appearing as "transcendents." Conversely, as long as consciousness traverses the transcendental field at an infinite speed everywhere diffused, nothing is able to reveal it.[1] It is expressed, in fact, only when it is reflected on a subject that refers it to objects. That is why the transcendental field cannot be defined by the consciousness that is coextensive with it, but removed from any revelation.

The transcendent is not the transcendental. Were it not for consciousness, the transcendental field would be defined as a pure plane of immanence, because it eludes all transcendence of the subject and of the object.[2] Absolute immanence is in itself: it is not in something, *to* something; it does not depend on an object or belong to a subject. In Spinoza, immanence is not immanence *to*

From *Pure Immanence*, trans. Anne Boyman (New York: Zone Books, 2001), pp. 25–33 ["Immanence: une vie," *Philosophie* 47 © 1995 Editions de Minuit].

substance; rather, substance and modes are in immanence. When the subject or the object falling outside the plane of immanence is taken as a universal subject or as any object *to which* immanence is attributed, the transcendental is entirely denatured, for it then simply redoubles the empirical (as with Kant), and immanence is distorted, for it then finds itself enclosed in the transcendent. Immanence is not related to Some Thing as a unity superior to all things or to a Subject as an act that brings about a synthesis of things: it is only when immanence is no longer immanence to anything other than itself that we can speak of a plane of immanence. No more than the transcendental field is defined by consciousness can the plane of immanence be defined by a subject or an object that is able to contain it.

We will say of pure immanence that it is A LIFE, and nothing else. It is not immanence to life, but the immanent that is in nothing is itself a life. A life is the immanence of immanence, absolute immanence: it is complete power, complete bliss. It is to the degree that he goes beyond the aporias of the subject and the object that Johann Fichte, in his last philosophy, presents the transcendental field as *a life*, no longer dependent on a Being or submitted to an Act—it is an absolute immediate consciousness whose very activity no longer refers to a being but is ceaselessly posed in a life.[3] The transcendental field then becomes a genuine plane of immanence that reintroduces Spinozism into the heart of the philosophical process. Did Maine de Biran not go through something similar in his "last philosophy" (the one he was too tired to bring to fruition) when he discovered, beneath the transcendence of effort, an absolute immanent life? The transcendental field is defined by a plane of immanence, and the plane of immanence by a life.

What is immanence? A life . . . No one has described what *a* life is better than Charles Dickens, if we take the indefinite article as an index of the transcendental. A disreputable man, a rogue, held in contempt by everyone, is found as he lies dying. Suddenly, those taking care of him manifest an eagerness, respect, even love, for his slightest sign of life. Everybody bustles about to save him, to the point where, in his deepest coma, this wicked man himself senses something soft and sweet penetrating him. But to the degree that he comes back to life, his saviors turn colder, and he becomes once again mean and crude. Between his life and his death, there is a moment that is only that of *a* life playing with death.[4] The life of the individual gives way to an impersonal and yet singular life that releases a pure event freed from the accidents of internal and external life, that is, from the subjectivity and objectivity of what happens: a "Homo tantum" with whom everyone empathizes and who attains a sort of beatitude. It is a haecceity no longer of individuation but of singularization: a life of pure immanence, neutral, beyond good and evil, for it was only the subject that incarnated it in the midst of things that made it good or bad. The life of such individuality fades away in favor of the singular life immanent to a man who no longer has a name, though he can be mistaken for no other. A singular essence, a life . . .

But we shouldn't enclose life in the single moment when individual life confronts universal death. *A* life is everywhere, in all the moments that a given living subject goes through and that are measured by given lived objects: an immanent life carrying with it the events or singularities that are merely actualized in subjects and objects. This indefinite life does not itself have moments, close as they may be one to another, but only between-times, between-moments; it doesn't just come about or come after but offers the immensity of an empty time where one sees the event yet to come and already happened, in the absolute of an immediate consciousness. In his novels, Alexander Lernet-Holenia places the event in an in-between time that could engulf entire armies. The singularities and the events that constitute *a* life coexist with the accidents of *the* life that corresponds to it, but they are neither grouped nor divided in the same way. They connect with one another in a manner entirely different from how individuals connect. It even seems that a singular life might do without any individuality, without any other concomitant that individualizes it. For example, very small children all resemble one another and have hardly any individuality, but they have singularities: a smile, a gesture, a funny face—not subjective qualities. Small children, through all their sufferings and weaknesses, are infused with an immanent life that is pure power and even bliss. The indefinite aspects in a life lose all indetermination to the degree that they fill out a plane of immanence or, what amounts to the same thing, to the degree that they constitute the elements of a transcendental field (individual life, on the other hand, remains inseparable from empirical determinations). The indefinite as such is the mark not of an empirical indetermination but of a determination by immanence or a transcendental determinability. The indefinite article is the indetermination of the person only because it is determination of the singular. The One is not the transcendent that might contain immanence but the immanent contained within a transcendental field. One is always the index of a multiplicity: an event, a singularity, a life . . . Although it is always possible to invoke a transcendent that falls outside the plane of immanence, or that attributes immanence to itself, all transcendence is constituted solely in the flow of immanent consciousness that belongs to this plane.[5] Transcendence is always a product of immanence.

A life contains only virtuals. It is made up of virtualities, events, singularities. What we call virtual is not something that lacks reality but something that is engaged in a process of actualization following the plane that gives it its particular reality. The immanent event is actualized in a state of things and of the lived that make it happen. The plane of immanence is itself actualized in an object and a subject to which it attributes itself. But however inseparable an object and a subject may be from their actualization, the plane of immanence is itself virtual, so long as the events that populate it are virtualities. Events or singularities give to the plane all their virtuality, just as the plane of immanence gives virtual events their full reality. The event considered as non-actualized (indefinite) is lacking in nothing. It suffices to put it in relation to its concomitants: a transcendental field, a plane of immanence, a life, singularities. A wound is incarnated or actualized in a state of things or of life; but it is itself a pure virtuality on the plane of immanence that leads us into a life. My wound existed before me: not a transcendence of the wound as higher actuality, but its immanence as a virtuality always within a milieu (plane or field).[6] There is a big difference between the virtuals that define the immanence of the transcendental field and the possible forms that actualize them and transform them into something transcendent.

Notes

[1] "As though we reflected back to surfaces the light which emanates from them, the light which, had it passed unopposed, would never have been revealed" (Henri Bergson, *Matter and Memory* [New York: Zone Books, 1988], p. 36).

[2] Cf. Jean-Paul Sartre, who posits a transcendental field without a subject that refers to a consciousness that is impersonal, absolute, immanent: with respect to it, the subject and the object are "transcendents" (*La transcendance de l'ego* [Paris: Vrin, 1966], pp. 74–87). On James, see David Lapoujade's analysis, "Le flux intensif de la conscience chez William James," *Philosophie* 46 (June 1995).

[3] Already in the second introduction to *La doctrine de la science*: "The intuition of pure activity which is nothing fixed, but progress, not a being, but a life" (*Oeuvres choisies de la philosophie première* [Paris: Vrin, 1964], p. 274). On the concept of life according to Fichte, see *Initiation à la vie bienheureuse* (Paris: Aubier, 1944), and Martial Guéroult's commentary (p. 9).

[4] Dickens, *Our Mutual Friend* (New York: Oxford University Press, 1989), p. 443.

[5] Even Edmund Husserl admits this: "The being of the world is necessarily transcendent to consciousness, even within the originary evidence, and remains necessarily transcendent to it. But this doesn't change the fact that all transcendence is constituted solely in the *life of consciousness*, as inseparably linked to that life . . ." (*Méditations cartésiennes* [Paris: Vrin, 1947], p. 52). This will be the starting point of Sartre's text.

[6] Cf. Joë Bousquet, *Les capitales* (Paris: Le Cercle du Livre, 1955).

PART VI

Institution and Insurrection

Processes of subjectivization and moments of dis-identification led in particular to a rethinking of the idea of politics in contrast to the policies of states or governments, and with it, an attempt to imagine a politics outside these constituted powers, their apparatuses, modes of legitimization, claims to sovereignty, administrative capacities, and forms of knowledge. The existence of such an outside becomes itself inseparable from the potential of resistance and its variants—disobedience, in-servitude, refusal, withdrawal or *re-trait* ("step back")—or again with what Deleuze called resistance to the "intolerable" or the "shameful" as an aesthetico-political function of thought. For Foucault, "We don't want to be governed like that anymore" is the great cry of all critical acts of emancipation. The very idea of "the political" is then to be found in acts of resistance, withdrawal, or emancipation for which there preexists no we or I, no unifying identification, no social knowledge or program, not even in "civil society" or "public space," which no constituted power can ever completely eliminate or absorb. There thus exists what we might call an "im-political" element in all constituted power, the existence and nature of which becomes a complex theme in postwar French philosophy, and forms part of its search for a new role of the political in philosophy and of philosophy in the political, leading to the transformation of the two great modern philosophical figures: the intellectual and the professor. "Sartre was our outside," Deleuze would say.

But what is the function of philosophy outside the role of the university professor, traditional since Kant? This question became part of a new philosophical critique of institutions—the school, the church, and the party—to which Foucault would soon add the cluster of normalizing institutions: psychiatric, medical, and penal. One might then speak of the question of institution and insurrection: institutions as ways of producing and reproducing identities or identifications and insurrections as involving not simply revolts, strikes, demonstrations, and upheavals, but also the element within such events that serves to suspend, neutralize, break with such instituted relations, opening up new questions—dissensual *différends* or "disagreements," unforeseen problematizations, new aporia for responsibility. It was just in this way that the new questions of sexuality, femininity, or ecology that emerged with the insurrection of May 1968 became political and not simply cultural or ethical. The question then became how to avoid the two extremes of an insurrection-proof idea of government or state and an institution-free idea of conflict or struggle. Thus the element of insurrection had to be isolated from the ideals of a prior Republic, as with the idea in ancient philosophy of an *arche*, foundation or first principle. Politics is then always in this sense "an-archical," without foundation, based in no higher republic, guided by no final utopia, not even governed by a socialist or social-democratic regulative ideal. There is no end to it; it always comes first. It has no guarantee other than its own activity, no necessity other than its own responsibility.

To elaborate such an idea of the political thus required a long rethinking of the dreams and conceptions within which it had been enclosed in the nineteenth century—the promises of communism, the assurances of nationalism, or the dreams of a universalized cosmopolitanism. It was as if one were no longer in possession of such pictures and so could no longer rely on the great historical schemes or narratives that underlay them—modernity and tradition, *Gemeinschaft* and *Gesellschaft*. To rethink or reinvent politics was thus to imagine new forms and rethink older ones not simply through new critical readings in political philosophy, but also through the formulation of a series of new themes: force and law, justice and violence, and the relation between war and politics. The problem of freedom and equality, territory and geography, rights and powers were all reexamined in this light. In all these cases, we find the intimation of an ambiguous or indeterminate universal in which the "we" always follows the unforeseen questions and forms of struggle that translate the impolitical potential in all constituted powers.

A central question in these debates was the concept of revolution that had haunted the political thought of the nineteenth century and returned in 1968. But in the 1980s the problem became rather the theme of the failure or the end of revolution or the way it had ended in totalitarianism in the twentieth century. The historian François Furet would argue that the French Revolution is over, and with it the very idea of a division between right and left. The focus then was on reinventing the political in democratic politics. There was thus a search for an idea of democracy that was not, or not in the first place, a given form of government so much as an endless potential for resistance and questioning in all forms of government, even ones with parliaments and legal rights.

When Foucault declared in 1976 that "we have not cut off the King's head in political theory," he helped articulate this sense of a demos that is never reducible to popular sovereignty, emerging rather through insurrection and struggle. His own attempt to substitute biopower and governmentality for the traditional distinction between state and society, and so to see power in terms of resistance, formed part of a larger debate that was developed through belated readings of Hannah Arendt (and the question of the rights of those who have no rights) and Carl Schmidt (with his ideas of sovereignty and exception). One aspect of the debate centered around new translations and discussions of La Boétie on voluntary servitude and "the One," which were in turn taken up by Pierre Clastres in terms of violence and by Claude Lefort in terms of his idea of the "empty space" of political agon. In a certain sense this problem of those outside power returned to the question Merleau-Ponty had raised in 1947 of the "force of those with no force." For it is no good for those without force to "speak" if the identificatory mechanisms remain the same; one needs to change the very space in which force appears or is heard, posing questions *to* politics as well as simply taking sides on political issues. A democratic politics worth its name must include this space of resistance and questioning.

In a certain sense, then, postwar French philosophy elevated the idea of resistance into a veritable meta-political principle. No doubt the word, used after what in France is called "the Liberation," derives from the experience of the German occupation and the division between resistance and collaboration. One found out who was willing to do what in concrete situations of power, and Foucault would attribute his own preoccupation with subject and history to this determinant experience. The war brought not simply new divisions and geographies in philosophy (notably the relation to Heidegger on both sides of the Rhine) but also new concepts and problems as well as a series of questions about the shameful status of Vichy France, its legitimacy, its popular support, and the ways in which the individual and collective memories left in its wake were at odds with official narratives and academic histories. The problem of resistance would then recur with questions of violence and decolonization in the Algerian War and the response of intellectuals to it, then with the student revolts of May 1968, and later with the dissident movements of Eastern Europe before the fall of the Berlin Wall.

It is not surprising that the problem of war and politics should occupy such an important place in postwar political thought—the nature of World War II itself as a biopolitical war of populations and mass death and destruction, as well as the new wars of insurrection and liberation afterward. When Foucault tried to reverse Clausewitz's famous idea that war continues politics with other means, he drew on a substantial literature on Clausewitz, notably by Raymond Aron and later André Glucksmann. There would be Deleuze and Guattari on the "war-machine," territory and city in arts and philosophy, Paul Virilio on war and media, and later uses of Carl Schmidt on the violence of exception and the role of nonpartisan wars. In these different reflections on the relations of war and politics, one finds the notion that the alternative to war is not perpetual peace (or related pacifism) but a new idea of politics itself, the role of violence or force in it, and the nature of struggle and conflict in its agonistic or polemical expressions. We find the problem not simply in Lefort and the empty space of democracy, but also in Derrida's reading of the term "violence" (*Gewalt*) as it occurs in Walter Benjamin's critique of it, or in the various developments of the theme of "force" in Machiavelli or in Nietzsche and Spinoza. In such ideas of force or violence, we are confronted with something that can neither be completely monopolized by a state (as with Hobbes) nor resolved and absorbed into history (as with Hegel), yet is inseparable from the very nature of politics But the problem of violence outside history or the state had also already been developed in anthropology by Pierre Clastres and, earlier, by Georges Dumézil; it is also to be found in the new questions introduced by Lévi-Strauss after the war in relation to the idea of structure.

Lévi-Strauss in effect substituted for the socio-philosophical or Durkheimian problem of anomie and social cohesion in modernity the anthropologico-philosophical question of inclusion and exclusion in the order of culture—what Lacan would later call "the Symbolic Order." Who or what must be excluded (or remain outside) for a culture to exist or for its constitutive codes of kinship or economics to function? Lévi-Strauss's early distinction between anthropophagic and anthropoemic societies was already a way of posing the problem of violence and exclusion. Thus in his discussions of the subject in relation to the law of a culture, the focus is not on the identities of excluded groups or communities, but on the violence inherent in them or in their potential to expose, undo, or question the order of constituted practices of identification for us all.

The notion of a violence that is inherent in the very process of identification requires us to rethink the problem of community or intersubjectivity. The political question then becomes how to make room for "non-identical" spaces, "non-essentialized" communities, or how to create the singular, non-denumerable "multiplicities" that would populate or compose them. The paradox of identification—that there exists no inclusive "we" without excluding someone or something, no constituted intersubjectivity without an outside or other space—is a problem not only in and for politics but also, at the same time, in arts and letters. Blanchot's idea of *désoeuvrement* and the attempt to see in the space and force of literature a neutrality and corresponding sense of "impossibility" in thought and action would gradually assume a political dimension, breaking with his own earlier writings. In relation to the war—and, in particular, Shoah in the war—Blanchot would write of a kind of disaster that would befall the very idea of friendship or *philia* in philosophy and, in particular, the idea of community in communism, leading to an effort to put politics back into play. Instead of the traditional narrative of an "essential community" lost in a mythical past prior to the modern onslaught of rationalization and division, in the 1980s, there arose different voices coming from different quarters in an attempt to imagine a singular community, always yet to come, whose peculiar nature must be at once rethought and reinvented. Along with what Rancière was calling the "community of equals," there then arose the various formulations of what Jean-Luc Nancy called *la communauté désoeuvrée*, "the inoperative community." This space of nonidentification was expressed through a series of paradoxical expressions: in Rancière's commentary on the phrase of 1968, "we are all German Jews" and then more directly in his idea of "the part of those with no part" (as earlier with Merleau-Ponty's "force of those with no force"); in Jean-Luc Nancy's recasting of Bataille's "community of all those without community"; or Derrida's disquisitions on Montesquieu's "O my friend, there is no friend." In each case, the very nature of politics and of the political was at issue. For the part or force of those without part or community is not—or is not only—that of an excluded group awaiting recognition, but rather that of a recalcitrant or problematizing element in the very identificatory mechanisms and divisions of us all. At the same time, Deleuze would elaborate his search for a pre- and trans-individual space in terms of the questions of territory and deterritorialization and so of the "plane of composition" of the other spaces of a "people yet to come."

But what exactly is the politics of this other space, this singular community, this non-identifiable force, mass, or multiplicity in our ways of being and being-together? What sort of organization or institution can a community or group have when the usual identificatory mechanisms are suspended, when the "we" and "I" are up for grabs? The question was in part an institutional one: how to invent groups (movements, associations, or communities) outside the great apparatuses of the school, the party, or the church and their administrative or ideological structures, as with the extra-territoriality of Lacan's Freudian School and the many splits or scissions to which it would give rise, in which we see the pattern of the avant-garde group. Jean-Luc Nancy and Philippe Lacoue-Labarthe would associate the very idea of the avant-garde group (born of German Romanticism, but later developed by Bataille and Blanchot) with the question of a literary community. But the "groupuscules," inspired by Mao, to which many of Lacan's philosophy students would in fact turn, would look rather to a revolutionary truth and justice. In the Group for Information on Prisons created by Foucault and Daniel Defert, in which Deleuze would see the only really new kind of group, there was a move away from an initial Maoism toward a new kind of critical thinking. There was an attempt to introduce this "outside" into the nature and function of the teaching of philosophy, at first in the radical campus at Vincennes, and then in another way with the creation of the Collège international de philosophie and Derrida's analyses with the Groupe de recherche sur l'enseignement philosophique.

These extra-institutional groups were in turn related to others outside France, in other regimes or economic systems, also affected by the insurrections of 1968. There thus arose the question of a transnational or extraterritorial critical philosophy. When Deleuze advanced "absolute deterritorialization" as a condition of thought, it was in terms of a new geo-philosophy of "peoples yet to come"; and Derrida's ideas of idiomaticity and monolinguism, of "hospitality" for the foreign or the uncanny, formed part of his questioning of the traditional utopian or cosmopolitan alternatives to nationalism in philosophy. The political problem of dis-identification thus acquired a more global dimension.

MAURICE MERLEAU-PONTY

A Note on Machiavelli

1960

How could he have been understood? He writes against good feelings in politics, but he is also against violence. Since he has the nerve to speak of *virtue* at the very moment he is sorely wounding ordinary morality, he disconcerts the believers in Law as he does those who believe that the State is the Law. For he describes that knot of collective life in which pure morality can be cruel and pure politics requires something like a morality. We would put up with a cynic who denies values or an innocent who sacrifices action. We do not like this difficult thinker without idols.

He was certainly tempted by cynicism: he had, he says, "much difficulty in shielding himself" from the opinion of those who believe the world is "ruled by chance."[1] Now if humanity is an accident, it is not immediately evident what would uphold collective life if it were not the sheer coercion of political power. Thus the entire role of a government is to hold its subjects in check.[2] The whole art of governing is reduced to the art of war,[3] and "good troops make good laws."[4] Between those in power and their subjects, between the self and the other person, there is no area where rivalry ceases. We must either undergo or exercise coercion. At each instant Machiavelli speaks of oppression and aggression. Collective life is hell.

But what is original about Machiavelli is that, having laid down the source of struggle, he goes beyond it without ever forgetting it. He finds something other than antagonism in struggle itself. "While men are trying not to be afraid, they begin to make themselves feared by others; and they transfer to others the aggression that they push back from themselves, as if it were absolutely necessary to offend or be offended." It is in the same moment that I am about to be afraid that I make others afraid; it is the same aggression that I repel and send back upon others; it is the same terror which threatens me that I spread abroad—I live my fear in the fear I inspire. But by a counter-shock, the suffering that I cause rends me along with my victim; and so cruelty is no solution but must always begin again. There is a circuit between the self and others, a

From *Signs*, trans. Richard C. McCleary (Evanston, IL: Northwestern University Press, 1964), pp. 211–13, 222–23 ["Note sur Machiavel," in *Signes* (Paris: Editions Gallimard, 1960)].

Communion of Black Saints. The evil that I do I do to myself, and in struggling against others I struggle equally against myself. After all, a face is only shadows, lights, and colors; yet suddenly the executioner, because this face has grimaced in a certain way, mysteriously experiences a slackening—*another anguish* has relayed his own. A sentence is never anything but a statement, a collection of significations which as a matter of principle could not possibly be equivalent to the unique savor that each person has for himself. And yet when the victim admits defeat, the cruel man perceives another life beating through those words; he finds himself before *another himself*. We are far from the relationships of sheer force that hold between objects. To use Machiavelli's words, we have gone from "beasts" to "man."[5]

More exactly, we have gone from one way of fighting to another, from "fighting with force" to "fighting with laws."[6] Human combat is different from animal combat, but it is a fight. Power is not naked force, but neither is it the honest delegation of individual wills, as if the latter were able to set aside their differences. Whether new or hereditary, power is always described in *The Prince* as questionable and threatened. One of the duties of the prince is to settle questions before they have *become insoluble* as a result of the subjects' emotion.[7] It would seem to be a matter of keeping the citizens from becoming aroused. There is no power which has an absolute basis. There is only a crystallization of opinion, which tolerates power, accepting it as acquired. The problem is to avoid the dissolution of this consensus, which can occur in no time at all, no matter what the means of coercion, once a certain point of crisis has been passed. Power is of the order of the tacit. Men let themselves live within the horizon of the State and the Law as long as injustice does not make them conscious of what is unjustifiable in the two. The power which is called legitimate is that which succeeds in avoiding *contempt* and *hatred*.[8] "The prince must make himself feared in such a way that, if he is not loved, he is at least not hated."[9] It makes little difference that those in power are blamed in a particular instance; they are established in the interval which separates criticism from repudiation, discussion from disrepute. Relationships between the subject and those in power, like those between the self and others, are cemented at a level deeper than judgment. As long as it is not a matter of contempt's radical challenge, they survive challenge.

Neither pure fact nor absolute right, power does not coerce or persuade; it thwarts—and we are better able to thwart by appealing to freedom than by terrorizing. Machiavelli formulates with precision that alternation of tension and relaxation, of repression and legality, whose secret is held by authoritarian régimes, but which is a sugar-coated form that constitutes the essence of all diplomacy. We sometimes *prize* more highly those to whom we give credit: "A new prince has never disarmed his subjects; far from it, he hastens to arm them if he finds them without arms; and nothing is shrewder, for henceforth the arms are his. . . . But a prince who disarms his subjects offends them by leading them to believe that he mistrusts them, and nothing is more likely to arouse their hatred."[10] "A city accustomed to freedom is more easily preserved by being governed through its own citizens."[11] In a society in which each man mysteriously resembles every other, mistrusting if he is mistrustful and trusting if he is trustful, there is no pure coercion. Despotism calls forth scorn; oppression would call forth rebellion. The best upholders of authority are not even those who created it; they believe they have a right to it, or at least feel secure in their power. A new power will make an appeal to its adversaries, provided that they rally around it.[12] If they are not retrievable, then authority will lose half its force: "Men must either be won over or gotten rid of; they can avenge themselves for slight offenses, but not for serious ones."[13] Thus the conqueror may hesitate between seducing and annihilating the vanquished, and sometimes Machiavelli is cruel: "the only way to preserve is to lay waste. Whoever becomes master of a town which has begun to enjoy freedom and does not destroy it should expect to be destroyed by it."[14] Yet pure violence can only be episodic.

. . .

To be just we must also add that the task was a difficult one. For Machiavelli's contemporaries the political problem was first of all one of knowing if Italians would long be prevented from farming and living by French and Spanish incursions, when they were not those of the Papacy. What could he reasonably hope for, if not for an Italian nation and soldiers to create it? It was necessary to begin by creating this bit of human life in order to create the human community. Where in the discordancy of a Europe unaware of itself, of a world which had not taken stock of itself and in which the eyes of scattered lands and men had not yet met, was the universal people which could be made the accomplice of an Italian city-state? How could the peoples of all lands have recognized, acted in concert with, and rejoined each other? There is no serious humanism except the one which looks for man's effective recognition by his fellow man throughout the world. Consequently, it could not possibly precede the moment when humanity gives itself its means of communication and communion.

Today these means exist, and the problem of a real humanism that Machiavelli set was taken up again by Marx a hundred years ago. Can we say the problem is solved? What Marx intended to do to create a human community was precisely to find a different base than the always equivocal one of principles. In the situation and vital movement of the most exploited, oppressed, and powerless of men he sought the basis for a revolutionary power, that is, a power capable of suppressing exploitation and oppression. But it became apparent that the whole problem was to constitute a power of the powerless. For those in power either had to follow the fluctuations of mass consciousness in order to remain a proletarian power, and then they would be brought down swiftly; or, if they wanted to avoid this consequence, they had to make themselves the judge of proletarian interests, and then they were setting themselves up in power in the traditional sense—they were the outline of a new ruling class. The solution could be found only in an absolutely new relationship between those in power and those subject to it. It was necessary to invent political forms capable of holding power in check without annulling it. It was necessary to have leaders capable of explaining the reasons for their politics to those subject to power, and to obtain from themselves, if necessary, the sacrifices power ordinarily imposes upon subjects.

These political forms were roughed out and these leaders appeared in the revolution of 1917; but from the time of the Commune of Kronstadt on, the revolutionary power lost contact with a fraction of the proletariat (which was nevertheless tried and true), and in order to conceal the conflict, it begins to lie. It proclaims that the insurgents' headquarters is in the hands of the White Guards, as Bonaparte's troops treat Toussaint-L'Ouverture as a foreign agent. Already difference of opinion is faked up as sabotage, opposition as espionage. We see reappearing within the revolution the very struggles it was supposed to move beyond. And as if to prove Machiavelli right, while the revolutionary government resorts to the classic tricks of power, the opposition does not even lack sympathizers among the enemies of the Revolution. Does all power tend to "autonomize" itself, and is this tendency an inevitable destiny in all human society? Or is it a matter of the contingent development which was tied to the particular conditions of the Russian Revolution (the clandestine nature of the revolutionary movement prior to 1917, the weakness of the Russian proletariat) and which would not have occurred in a Western revolution? This is clearly the essential problem. In any case, now that the expedient of Kronstadt has become a system and the revolutionary power has definitely been substituted for the proletariat as the ruling class, with the attributes of power of an unchecked élite, we can conclude that, one hundred years after Marx, the problem of a real humanism remains intact—and so we can show indulgence toward Machiavelli, who could only glimpse the problem.

If by humanism we mean a philosophy of the inner man which finds no difficulty in the principle in his relationships with others, no opacity whatsoever in the functioning of society, and which replaces political cultivation by moral exhortation, Machiavelli is not a humanist. But if by humanism we mean a philosophy which confronts the relationship of man to man and the constitution of a common situation and a common history between men as a problem, then we have to say that Machiavelli formulated some of the conditions of any serious humanism. And in this perspective the repudiation of Machiavelli which is so common today takes on a disturbing significance: it is the decision not to know the tasks of a true humanism. There is a way of repudiating Machiavelli which is Machiavellian; it is the pious dodge of those who turn their eyes and ours toward the heaven of principles in order to turn them away from what they are doing. And there is a way of praising Machiavelli which is just the opposite of Machiavellianism, since it honors in his works a contribution to political clarity.

Notes

[1] *The Prince*, Chap. XXV.

[2] *Discourses*, II, 23, quoted by A. Renaudet, *Machiavel*, p. 305.

[3] *The Prince*, Chap. XIV.

[4] Chap. XVII.

[5] Chap. XVIII.

[6] *Ibid.*

[7] Chap. III.

[8] Chap. XVI.

[9] Chap. XVII.

[10] Chap. XIV.

[11] Chap. V.

[12] Chap. XV.

[13] Chap. V.

[14] Chap. III.

MICHEL FOUCAULT

The History of Sexuality: An Introduction

1976

Hence the objective is to analyze a certain form of knowledge regarding sex, not in terms of repression or law, but in terms of power. But the word *power* is apt to lead to a number of misunderstandings—misunderstandings with respect to its nature, its form, and its unity. By power, I do not mean "Power" as a group of institutions and mechanisms that ensure the subservience of the citizens of a given state. By power, I do not mean, either, a mode of subjugation which, in contrast to violence, has the form of the rule. Finally, I do not have in mind a general system of domination exerted by one group over another, a system whose effects, through successive derivations, pervade the entire social body. The analysis, made in terms of power, must not assume that the sovereignty of the state, the form of the law, or the overall unity of a domination are given at the outset; rather, these are only the terminal forms power takes. It seems to me that power must be understood in the first instance as the multiplicity of force relations immanent in the sphere in which they operate and which constitute their own organization; as the process which, through ceaseless struggles and confrontations, transforms, strengthens, or reverses them; as the support which these force relations find in one another, thus forming a chain or a system, or on the contrary, the disjunctions and contradictions which isolate them from one another; and lastly, as the strategies in which they take effect, whose general design or institutional crystallization is embodied in the state apparatus, in the formulation of the law, in the various social hegemonies. Power's condition of possibility, or in any case the viewpoint which permits one to understand its exercise, even in its more "peripheral" effects, and which also makes it possible to use its mechanisms as a grid of intelligibility of the social order, must not be sought in the primary existence of a central point, in a unique source of sovereignty from which secondary and descendent forms would emanate; it is the moving substrate of force relations which, by virtue of their inequality, constantly engender states of power, but

From *The History of Sexuality, Volume I: An Introduction*, trans. Robert Hurley (New York: Vintage Books, 1980), pp. 92–97 [*Histoire de la sexualité, 1: La volonté de savoir* (Paris: Editions Gallimard, 1976)].

the latter are always local and unstable. The omnipresence of power: not because it has the privilege of consolidating everything under its invincible unity, but because it is produced from one moment to the next, at every point, or rather in every relation from one point to another. Power is everywhere; not because it embraces everything, but because it comes from everywhere. And "Power," insofar as it is permanent, repetitious, inert, and self-reproducing, is simply the overall effect that emerges from all these mobilities, the concatenation that rests on each of them and seeks in turn to arrest their movement. One needs to be nominalistic, no doubt: power is not an institution, and not a structure; neither is it a certain strength we are endowed with; it is the name that one attributes to a complex strategical situation in a particular society.

Should we turn the expression around, then, and say that politics is war pursued by other means? If we still wish to maintain a separation between war and politics, perhaps we should postulate rather that this multiplicity of force relations can be coded—in part but never totally—either in the form of "war," or in the form of "politics"; this would imply two different strategies (but the one always liable to switch into the other) for integrating these unbalanced, heterogeneous, unstable, and tense force relations.

Continuing this line of discussion, we can advance a certain number of propositions:

— Power is not something that is acquired, seized, or shared, something that one holds on to or allows to slip away; power is exercised from innumerable points, in the interplay of nonegalitarian and mobile relations.
— Relations of power are not in a position of exteriority with respect to other types of relationships (economic processes, knowledge relationships, sexual relations), but are immanent in the latter; they are the immediate effects of the divisions, inequalities, and disequilibriums which occur in the latter, and conversely they are the internal conditions of these differentiations; relations of power are not in superstructural positions, with merely a role of prohibition or accompaniment; they have a directly productive role, wherever they come into play.
— Power comes from below; that is, there is no binary and all-encompassing opposition between rulers and ruled at the root of power relations, and serving as a general matrix—no such duality extending from the top down and reacting on more and more limited groups to the very depths of the social body. One must suppose rather that the manifold relationships of force that take shape and come into play in the machinery of production, in families, limited groups, and institutions, are the basis for wide-ranging effects of cleavage that run through the social body as a whole. These then form a general line of force that traverses the local op-

positions and links them together; to be sure, they also bring about redistributions, realignments, homogenizations, serial arrangements, and convergences of the force relations. Major dominations are the hegemonic effects that are sustained by all these confrontations.

— Power relations are both intentional and nonsubjective. If in fact they are intelligible, this is not because they are the effect of another instance that "explains" them, but rather because they are imbued, through and through, with calculation: there is no power that is exercised without a series of aims and objectives. But this does not mean that it results from the choice or decision of an individual subject; let us not look for the headquarters that presides over its rationality; neither the caste which governs, nor the groups which control the state apparatus, nor those who make the most important economic decisions direct the entire network of power that functions in a society (and makes *it* function); the rationality of power is characterized by tactics that are often quite explicit at the restricted level where they are inscribed (the local cynicism of power), tactics which, becoming connected to one another, attracting and propagating one another, but finding their base of support and their condition elsewhere, end by forming comprehensive systems: the logic is perfectly clear, the aims decipherable, and yet it is often the case that no one is there to have invented them, and few who can be said to have formulated them: an implicit characteristic of the great anonymous, almost unspoken strategies which coordinate the loquacious tactics whose "inventors" or decision makers are often without hypocrisy.

— Where there is power, there is resistance, and yet, or rather consequently, this resistance is never in a position of exteriority in relation to power. Should it be said that one is always "inside" power, there is no "escaping" it, there is no absolute outside where it is concerned, because one is subject to the law in any case? Or that, history being the ruse of reason, power is the ruse of history, always emerging the winner? This would be to misunderstand the strictly relational character of power relationships. Their existence depends on a multiplicity of points of resistance: these play the role of adversary, target, support, or handle in power relations. These points of resistance are present everywhere in the power network. Hence there is no single locus of great Refusal, no soul of revolt, source of all rebellions, or pure law of the revolutionary. Instead there is a plurality of resistances, each of them a special case: resistances that are possible, necessary, improbable; others that are spontaneous, savage, solitary, concerted, rampant, or violent; still others that are quick to compromise, interested, or sacrificial; by definition, they can only exist in the strategic field of power relations. But this does not mean that they are only a reaction or rebound, forming with respect to the basic domination an underside that is in the end always passive, doomed to perpetual defeat. Resistances do not derive from a few heterogeneous principles; but neither are they a lure or a promise that is of necessity betrayed. They are the odd term in relations of power; they are inscribed in the latter as an irreducible opposite. Hence they too are distributed in irregular fashion: the points, knots, or focuses of resistance are spread over time and space at varying densities, at times mobilizing groups or individuals in a definitive way, inflaming certain points of the body, certain moments in life, certain types of behavior. Are there no great radical ruptures, massive binary divisions, then? Occasionally, yes. But more often one is dealing with mobile and transitory points of resistance, producing cleavages in a society that shift about, fracturing unities and effecting regroupings, furrowing across individuals themselves, cutting them up and remolding them, marking off irreducible regions in them, in their bodies and minds. Just as the network of power relations ends by forming a dense web that passes through apparatuses and institutions, without being exactly localized in them, so too the swarm of points of resistance traverses social stratifications and individual unities. And it is doubtless the strategic codification of these points of resistance that makes a revolution possible, somewhat similar to the way in which the state relies on the institutional integration of power relationships.

It is in this sphere of force relations that we must try to analyze the mechanisms of power. In this way we will escape from the system of Law-and-Sovereign which has captivated political thought for such a long time. And if it is true that Machiavelli was among the few—and this no doubt was the scandal of his "cynicism"—who conceived the power of the Prince in terms of force relationships, perhaps we need to go one step further, do without the persona of the Prince, and decipher power mechanisms on the basis of a strategy that is immanent in force relationships.

SARAH KOFMAN

Respect for Women

1982

Preliminary Respect, or the Side Benefit of Non-Seduction

If we turn to the *Anthropology* (to the addendum or appendix to "The Doctrine of Virtue"), we find that the description that Kant gives there of the relation between the sexes is not a moral relation in which each should respect the other as a representative of the sublimity of the moral law but rather a martial relation in which each struggles to dominate the other, where domination is defined as the utilization of others for a personal end motivated by the fear of being dominated.[1] In this war, it is the so-called weaker sex that wins, precisely because of its weakness. This disarms men and compels them to show respect and offer a whole range of compensations: woman's right to respect is thus ostensibly acquired as a result of her weakness, as a measure of protection granted to the weaker by the stronger.

As always, a veritable inversion ensues: the weakness of women and all the traits characteristic of it[2] become so many levers with which to steer men and use them as women will. If women cannot dominate by force, they dominate by indirect means, by the oblique path of ruse, by the art, which they possess, of using men for their own purposes. Thanks to their attractions and to the love they inspire, women shackle their victims and rule them through their own predilections. Citing Pope (though he might just as well have cited Rousseau, the author of *Emile*, which he knew well), Kant says that two traits characterize the female sex: a propensity to dominate and a propensity to please essentially in public (and the second trait can be reduced to the first, since in seeking to please, we are told, a woman always seeks to defeat a potential rival). If women are thus naturally predisposed to dominate, men are naturally predisposed to be dominated. In the final analysis, these reciprocal tendencies explain the particular nature of the masculine sex's respect for the feminine. It cannot be reduced simply to a right granted to the weak by the strong: woman's will to

From *Le respect des femmes* (Paris: Editions Galilée, 1982), pp. 29–40; trans. Arthur Goldhammer.

dominate enlists her pride, her desire to reject the pleadings of man. Women demand consideration on behalf of their sex even if they do not deserve it: that is what respect is. This allows women to economize on virtue and both sexes to create a sexual economy, a kind of respite: the woman refuses, the man insists. When she gives in, it is a favor, and if the tables were to be turned, it would debase the value of her sex, even in the man's eyes. The woman must appear to be cold, must never give in too quickly to the request, lest she be dishonored. In short, what gives value to the female sex and makes woman as such respectable is, as a vast tradition makes clear, her reserve, her modesty: "The woman must be pursued, as the attitude of reserve necessary to her sex requires." Thanks to modesty, woman protects herself and protects man: she avoids being diminished in stature, being reduced to nothing more than a means of satisfying the opposite sex. As she satisfies her will to dominate, she teaches man a lesson in morality by teaching him a lesson in chastity. By preventing him from wallowing in sensuality, "the vice that stems from love of the flesh,"[3] by sparing him the risk of shamelessness, that disgusting vice whereby man makes "use of his person in a way that makes him lower than the beasts" (for he cedes entirely to his animal penchants and reduces himself to a mere object of pleasure), woman prevents man from becoming disgusting in his own eyes, from transforming himself into a thing against nature, no longer worthy of respect—in other words, from defiling himself and all of humanity in his person.

This transgression of morality, which so utterly violates a man's duty to himself, arouses such disgust, Kant tells us, that we consider it immoral even to call such a vice by its name, as if to name it were to expose its full horror to the eyes of all, to copulate in public, or at any rate to exhibit woman's sex without reserve, to exhibit without a veil of any kind that which cannot be contemplated as such without provoking disgust—hence, that which cannot be unveiled, cannot be properly named, without defilement. "It is as if man generally feels ashamed that he is capable of using his person in such a way as to make himself lower than the beasts, ashamed to such a degree that the carnal union of the two sexes in marriage, which is permitted (though in itself it is clearly purely animal), when spoken of in polite society, demands and requires a great deal of finesse to hide it from view as beneath a veil."[4]

Defilement, disgust: even if a simple transgression of man's duty to himself justifies moral condemnation, it does not justify condemnation in such violent terms. Kant himself remarks that no other transgression of one's duty toward oneself—suicide, for example—provokes disgust to this degree. Is this not a tacit avowal that the vice that stems from the coupling of the sexes, voluptuousness or shamelessness, engenders more than just disgust and moral defilement? If feminine modesty makes woman respectable, keeps man from becoming disgusted with himself, and allows him to remain a moral person, it also saves man from quite another sort of disgust, namely, disgust with the female sex, which would be the inevitable consequence of full and complete satisfaction of his predilections. It enables him to remain a man, to remain virile, without succumbing to inconsistency.[5]

The ardor aroused by man's sexual proclivities must therefore be inhibited and restrained by restrictive conditions imposed by practical reason (respect for oneself and others as moral persons) and pragmatic reason (calculation of self-interest within the sexual economy imposed by modesty and respect for women: man must respect women and steer clear of them, woman must protect her sex from man's importunings and thereby dominate him).[6]

These restrictive conditions are best realized in marriage, toward which we must not be skeptical, Kant tells us, because through it "woman becomes free," though it is also true that "man there loses his freedom."[7] Perhaps this is why in "The Conflict of Faculties" celibacy figures among the fundamental principles of dietetics for anyone who seeks to ensure himself a long and happy life, because "it would be difficult to prove that most people who live to a ripe old age were married."

In this economy of respect there is thus no profit without loss, and the profits and losses are not of the same nature for both sexes.

On one hand, respect enables woman to rule like a queen despite her weakness. Yet she, who represents natural predisposition, does not govern. It is man, the minister, who governs through his understanding: "The husband's behavior must show that his most heartfelt concern is for the good of his wife. But he shall be as a minister is to a king when he arranges a celebration for his master's pleasure. He begins by explaining to the king all the deference that is due him but that, for example, there is no money in the treasury, so that the all-powerful master may do whatever he wants so long as it his minister who suggests to him what it is he wants."[8]

On the other hand, all the characteristics of the female sex—its weakness as well as its (more or less illusory) mastery—are to be situated, Kant says, in a more general economy of nature and conceptualized in terms of nature's purposes: by way of the war between the sexes for domination, hence by way of what Kant calls human folly, nature is said to seek man's moral education. This, presumably, is nature's ultimate goal. Seen in this light, respect for women is in a sense a preliminary, a side benefit of non-seduction supposedly leading to ultimate respect, moral respect, which it prefigures and recommends. Respect for women in this sense would be the law of laws, a law more sacred than any other, the sine qua non of moral law, or at any rate an essential lesson for learning to submit to it. Woman ought not to provoke disgust because she "is an object of every man's taste" and offers an education in good taste, in propriety, in fine style, and in the use of the veil—the veil that hides her sex and the veil of language. The lesson in morality necessarily involves a prior lesson in decency, the corollary of which is the passage from "vulgar words" to finesse in expression that casts a veil over all that is repugnant, disgusting, and defiling. Woman's veil—the prohibition of her sex—leads, one might say, to the veil or mask of words, to superfluity of language, to the opening of the endless chain of supplements, to a supplementarity effacing all "proper"—improper—meaning as always already defiled.

In "Conjectures on the Beginnings of Human History," Kant insisted on the importance of decency (symbolized by the fig leaf of the Bible) as the basis of man's emergence as a moral creature, which oriented thought in a new direction and proved more important than "the whole interminable series of subsequent cultural developments." Decency, defined as a "penchant for encouraging others to show us consideration on account of our good manners (while concealing that which might invite contempt)," is not only the real foundation of all true sociability but also the first *sign* of morality in man, of his capacity to respect others: if "preliminary" respect is a "modest beginning," it nevertheless marks an epoch because it prefigures moral respect. It is an index not of arbitrary conventions but of man's reasonable nature, just as woman's *refusal*, which makes the sexual object unavailable to the senses, is a "clever artifice" that teaches man to use reason even as it exhibits the use of reason: "To strengthen and prolong an inclination by withdrawing its objects from the senses already denotes a certain conscious supremacy of reason over predisposition." Owing to this refusal, to modesty, and to decency, man is led from purely sensual stimuli toward ideal stimuli and thus, little by little, from animal desire to love and morality. Furthermore, this transition is also described, as it would be later by Bachofen and Freud, as separation from the mother, from the maternal breast of nature, which man, by way of his imagination, represents to himself after the fact as a paradise.[9]

Man's education in reason and morality therefore culminates in an emancipation from nature, from women, and from his own inclinations, yet all education must necessarily include experience of all three. Man cannot dispense with such a transition. Nature's ruse is to use women and their characteristic nature to end their reign and bring about the reign of man, while leaving women with the illusion of continuing to reign.[10]

In fact, it was nature, alarmed by threats to the continuation of the human race, that planted in woman's nature the fear of physical assault and timidity in the face of physical danger—weaknesses that would authorize her to seek the protection of men. Seeking to inspire in men refined sentiments arising out of culture, sociability, and good manners, nature, Kant argues, also blessed the female sex with mastery of language and expression and with a desire to be treated gently and politely by men, thereby giving woman a mastery over the opposite sex for the purpose of moral education. Men thus found themselves "bound to a child by their own generosity without being aware of it and thereby led if not to morality then at least to its outward trappings in the good manners that are the preface to and recommendation of morality."[11] By way of human folly—and of women—the natural order is thus said to prefigure the moral order, and respect for women is said to herald and lay the groundwork for respect for man.

If the ultimate end of nature is moral, if its purpose is to safeguard humanity, and if, to that end, it seems to privilege neither sex, it nevertheless remains true that in this general economy woman seems to be the loser, since in the final analysis she does not hide her wish to be a man (in order to give greater scope and freer rein to her inclinations), whereas no man would wish to be a woman.[12] This rejection of femininity by both sexes raises the suspicion that the benefits of this whole "natural" enterprise, of this economy of respect, redound essentially to men, and that behind nature's ends lurk the ends of man (*Vir*). Behind the professed respect for women the goal is quite simply to keep women at a respectful distance because they represent risks of two kinds:

— A risk of sensual indulgence, that is, of abuse of the sexual faculty, and therefore an excessive expenditure of energy leading possibly to death. This explains why celibacy is a fundamental dietetic rule.
— A risk of allowing inclination to triumph over reason, that is, of allowing the "feminine" to trump the "masculine." In other words, a risk of emasculation through loss of reason, a risk of forgetting the sublimity of human nature, and a risk of being reduced to the status of a natural object, to animal nature, and thereby to an object of horror and disgust: *horribile visu*.

The risk of femininity is therefore on one hand a risk of death and on the other hand a risk, against which respect offers protection, of exceeding the bounds of the human, of losing one's masculine dignity and virility, and of regressing to mother nature's breast.

Notes

1 Cf., in *The Didactic*, the paragraph "The mania of domination."

2 See "Characteristic," in B: "The Character of Sex."

3 "The Doctrine of Virtue," sec. 7 of part 1: "On defiling oneself through voluptuousness."

4 Ibid.

5 Cf. "Conjectures on the beginnings of human history": "Man found . . . that sexual arousal, which in animals stems from a fleeting and usually periodic impulse, could in his case be prolonged and even increased by the effects of the imagination, which causes its effects to be felt in a more measured way, to be sure, but also more durably and uniformly the more the object is removed from his senses, which avoids the satiety that comes of the satisfaction of a purely animal desire." See also *L'anthropologie, les conséquences pragmatiques* (Paris: Vrin, 2008), p. 152.

6 See also "Doctrine of virtue," sec. 46, in which affection and friendship are subject to

fixed principles and rules that prevent too much familiarity and set standards of respect limiting reciprocal love to ward off the threat of constant interruption, such as that often seen among the ill-bred. "When a person exhibits too much ardor in love, does he not forfeit something of the other person's respect, and once respect is damaged, it is irretrievably lost internally, even if its external (ceremonial) signs continue as before."

[7] *Anthropology*, "The pragmatic consequences."

[8] Ibid.

[9] "Progress is . . . associated with the *emancipation* which exiled man from the maternal breast of nature. . . . In the future, he will often respond to life's difficulties by wishing for paradise, a creation of his imagination in which he might pass his time in tranquil idleness and perpetual peace dreaming and frolicking. But inexorable reason stands between him and this imaginary pleasure dome; reason impels him to develop faculties within himself and does not allow him to return to the state of rustic simplicity from which it wrenched him. . . . Man's departure from the paradise that reason portrays as the first dwelling place of the human race was merely the transition from the rustic state of a purely animal creature to a state of humanity, from the forests in which instinct held him captive to the government of reason, in a word, from the protecton of nature to the state of freedom."

[10] See my article "Ça cloche" in *Les fins de l'homme* (Paris: Galilée, 1981), which develops the work of Jacques Derrida.

[11] *Anthropology*, p. 150.

[12] Ibid., p. 151.

GILLES DELEUZE

Preface to *The Savage Anomaly*

1982

Negri's book on Spinoza, written in prison, is a major book that in many ways renews our understanding of Spinozism. I would like to concentrate on two of the main arguments he develops.

1. Spinoza's Anti-Legalism

Spinoza's fundamental idea is the spontaneous development of forces, at least virtually. In other words, there is no need for mediation in principle to establish the relationships that correspond to forces.

On the contrary, the idea of a necessary mediation belongs essentially to the legal conception of the world found in Hobbes, Rousseau and Hegel. This conception implies: (1) that forces have an individual or private origin; (2) that they must be socialized to bring about adequate relationships corresponding to them; (3) that there is thus mediation of a Power ("Potestas"); and (4) that the horizon is inseparable from crisis, war or antagonism that Power proposes to solve, though an "antagonist solution."

Spinoza is often presented as belonging to this legal lineage between Hobbes and Rousseau. Not according to Negri. For Spinoza, forces are inseparable from a spontaneity and productivity that make possible their development without mediation or their *composition*. They are elements of socialization in themselves. Spinoza immediately thinks in terms of "multitudes" and not individuals. His entire philosophy is a philosophy of "potentia" against "potestas." It takes its place in an anti-legalist tradition that includes Machiavelli and leads to Marx. It is a conception of ontological "constitution" or of a physical and dynamic "composition" that conflicts with the legal *contract*.[1] In Spinoza, the ontological perspective of an immediate production conflicts with any call to a

From *Two Regimes of Madness: Texts and Interviews 1975–1995*, ed. David Lapoujade and trans. Ames Hodges and Mike Taormina (Los Angeles, CA: Semiotext[e], 2006), pp. 25–28 ["Préface à *L'anomalie sauvage*," in *Deux régimes de fous et autres textes (1975–1995)* (Paris: Editions de Minuit, 2003); first published as the preface to Antonio Negri, *L'anomalie sauvage: Puissance et pouvoir chez Spinoza* (Paris: Presses Universitaires de France, 1982)].

Should-Be, a mediation or a finality ("with Hobbes the crisis connotes the ontological horizon and subsumes it; with Spinoza the crisis is subsumed under the ontological horizon").

Although one can sense the importance and newness of Negri's argument, the reader might shrink from the utopian atmosphere it exudes. Thus Negri is careful to point out the special character of the Dutch milieu that made Spinoza's position possible. Against the Orange family that represented a "potestas" in accordance with European monarchy, the Holland of the De Witt brothers could attempt to promote the market as a spontaneity of productive forces, or capitalism as an immediate form of the socialization of forces. Spinozist anomalies and Dutch anomalies . . . But in each case, isn't it the same *utopia*? This is where the strong second point of Negri's analysis comes into play.

2. Spinoza's Evolution

The first Spinoza, the Spinoza of the *Short Treatise* and of the beginning of the *Ethics*, retains the utopian perspective. He renews them, however, by ensuring that forces have maximum expansion by attaining an *ontological constitution* of substance and of modes through substance (pantheism). Yet precisely because of the spontaneity of the operation or the absence of mediation, the *material composition* of concrete reality is not made manifest as a power as such, and knowledge and thought still must turn back into themselves, subjected to a solely ideal productivity of Being instead of opening to the world.

That is why the second Spinoza as he appears in the *Theological-Political Treatise* and as he asserts himself in the *Ethics* is recognizable in two fundamental themes: on the one hand, the power of substance is reduced to the modes for which it serves as horizon; on the other hand, thought opens to the world and establishes itself as material imagination. Utopia then comes to an end in favor of the premises of revolutionary materialism. Not that antagonism and mediation are restored. The horizon of Being subsists immediately but as the *place* of political constitution and not as the *utopia* of ideal and substantial constitution.

Bodies (and souls) are forces. As such they are not only defined by their chance encounters and collisions (state of crisis). They are defined by relationships between an infinite number of parts that compose each body and that already characterize it as a "multitude." There are therefore *processes* of composition and decomposition of bodies, depending on whether their characteristic relationships suit them or not. Two or several bodies will form a whole, in other words, another body, if they compose their respective relationships in concrete circumstances. And it is the highest exercise of the imagination, the point where it inspires understanding, to have bodies (and souls) meet according to composable relationships. Thus the importance of the Spinoza's theory of *common notions* which is the cornerstone of the *Ethics*, from Book II to Book V. The material imagination seals its alliance with the understanding by ensuring, under the horizon of Being, both the physical composition of bodies and the political constitution of humans.

What Negri did so profoundly for Marx in terms of the *Grundrisse*, he now does for Spinoza: a complete reevaluation of the respective place of the *Short Treatise*, and the *Theological-Political Treatise*, in Spinoza's work. Negri does this to suggest an evolution in Spinoza: from *progressive utopia* to *revolutionary materialism*. Negri is certainly the first to give a full, philosophical meaning to the anecdote that tells of how Spinoza drew himself as Masaniello, the Neapolitan revolutionary (cf. what Nietzsche says on the importance of "anecdotes" fitting "thought, in the life of a thinker").

I have given an extremely rudimentary presentation of Negri's two arguments. I do not think that it is appropriate to discuss these arguments and to reject or confirm them too hastily. These arguments have the obvious merit of accounting for the exceptional situation of Spinoza in the history of thought. The theses are profoundly new, but what they make us see are, first of all, the newness of Spinoza himself, in the sense of a "future philosophy." They show the central role of politics in Spinoza's philosophy. Our first task should be to appreciate the scope of these arguments and understand what Negri found in Spinoza, how he is authentically and profoundly Spinozist.

JEAN-CLAUDE MILNER

Indistinct Names

1983

Collections

There exist collections, that is, multiplicities that make One. From the multiplicity to the One there are multiple passages. To collect several terms in a single class on the basis of a property can be done only by the ways of the Same and the Other: all members of the class must have a common property and pass for identical with respect to that property. Conversely, they must also be perceived as different from one another, so that the class does not reduce to a single member. Finally, regardless of whether the class is finite or infinite, it is always possible to construct a (potentially empty) figure of that which does not possess the property: call it an Other, which is the necessary Limit in the Whole. In short, there are no classes but of I.

The essential moment is the judgment of attribution, which can be projected in its entirety onto a linear time scale without reversals or loops: begin by assuming the existence of an identifiable *x*, then associate it with a property P by saying "*x* is P." By the same token, *x* is linked to all other terms having the property (this is the moment of synthesis) and opposed to some term that does not have the property (this is the moment of antithesis) in such a way that the affirmative judgment is set apart from the negative judgment "*y* is not P." The judgment is assumed not to be circular: in other words, it must be possible to identify *x* independent of P, and, reciprocally, it must be possible to posit P independently of its attribution to *x*. Hence merely positing *x* must not determine whether or not it will be called P. Judgment accordingly carries with it not merely the possibility of negative judgment in general but also the possibility of the diametrically opposed negative judgment, the exclusion of which, once decided upon, accomplishes the assertion: one says "*x* is P" but at the same time one says, and erases, "*x* is not P." Furthermore, if only the property P is posited, nothing should depend on the statement that links it as attribute to a singular *x*. The property therefore subsists in reality independent of the enunciation of

From *Les noms indistincts* (Paris: Editions du Seuil, 1983), pp. 105–12, 116, 118–23; trans. Arthur Goldhammer.

the judgment: in other words, the property is definable and can in turn become the subject of an attributive judgment, which analyzes it. From this comes a hierarchy running from the individual *x* to the property, from the property to the property of the property, and so on. Proceeding similarly, we thus obtain metalanguages and types. Step by step, a world is built up, a world in which the judgment considered is true, as are all judgments that it presupposes or entails, and in which the class that it determines is posited along with the limits that circumscribe it. Simultaneously, we have rejected any world that differs from this one by the simple fact that, in it, *x* is not P: this yields the matrix of the possible and "compossible."

Such a procedure is the basis of all representation as well as the possibility that representation can be stated as proposition. Reality as such, insofar as it is coextensive with all that can be represented and stated, is woven entirely of classes, properties, and attributions. Therein lies the solid bedrock to which the realist belief in the statable clings: the assumption that multiplicities are built up out of properties, and that attributive judgments linking a One to a property can at the same time collect Ones into a multiplicity that is also One. Communication is thereby established between the One and the all.

This is nothing other than the *dictum de omni et nullo*, which states that what is said of all is also said of each one. It is worth noting that such an assertion can only be made as an axiom, which warrants any logic of attribution but cannot itself be warranted by such a logic.

In reality, therefore, one is allowed to speak of multiplicities only to the extent that they form classes, and they form classes only to the extent that they are based on an attributable property. Aristotle is here the reference to which one invariably returns for the assertion that there is no science but of the general, or, put differently, that there can be knowledge only of that which constitutes a genus. Such is the truth of this statement that even if no class could be defined, one could as a last resort in dealing with any multiplicity whatsoever save its class character by reference to the property of *being*, which is always available except in the case of Nothingness, and about Nothingness there is no need to speak and nothing to know.

Yet there exist multiplicities whose ground lies elsewhere. Specifically, there are multiplicities that originate not with a representable property of any kind but entirely with the signifier that names them as multiplicities. Accordingly, these multiplicities cannot possibly exist prior to the utterance of the signifier itself. The property reduces to the naming of the property, and the subject receives the property only at the moment the relation is stated. If one then wants to speak of a class, one has to add that it collects its members only in a constantly shifting manner, continually affected by the statements that are produced. These statements may themselves resemble attributions, but only in a purely homonymic sense: this is the case, for example, with insulting utterances, in which the subject named is instantly burdened with the name contained in the statement: "pig," "filth," "garbage." The subject is thus invited to bear a name whose content in terms of properties is entirely summed up in the utterance. Anyone who asked for an Aristotelian definition of the property so designated would be quite embarrassed, since circularity is unavoidable: only the subject so named has that property, and it has that property only at the instant it is named. The property does not subsist apart from the naming; even an omniscient God would be incapable of enumerating the class supposedly constructed in this fashion unless he subscribed to the insulting utterance. Indeed, some theologies structure the damnation of the predestined in precisely this way.

It is convenient here to speak of a performative utterance, but in doing so we dissimulate the essential determination, because the point is obviously that the insult inserts the subject into a multiplicity. Instead of pointing toward the singularity of the subject as such, it is apprehended only at the point at which it is subsumed by a multiplicity, which effaces it. Indeed, the only logical motive for the effect of the insult may be to subsume a singularity in this way, for the multiplicity always looms in the background, so that the signifier by itself seems to create a collection. It is as if linking S to a One were enough to determine a *collection*, that is, a multiplicity whose members belong together only because they count together as One, independent of any prior resemblance.

Insults, however, are only one example among others—a particularly clear example, to be sure, since the language sets them apart. The same structure occurs elsewhere, indeed anywhere that the subject, in order to link itself to S, consents to choose for the real and singular One of its dissimilar desire the symbolic One of a name, which immediately inserts it into a multiplicity. This is what one calls alienation, which at one stroke accomplishes the subsumption of a name and the construction of a class that will henceforth be referred to as symbolic. Symbolic classes and collections are similar in every respect to imaginary classes, except for one radical distinction: no property here exists prior to the name. Indeed, membership cannot be guaranteed by any judgment of attribution. In this procedure, the grammar of which Newman analyzed some time ago, and which Sartre, following Barrès, vulgarized under the rubric of "commitment," deduction has no place, any more than it has a justification. It is accomplished in the moment, in the form of evidence, while the subject thereby alienates and empties itself into the signifier that names it from that point on.

Now, it is quite possible to believe that history knows nothing else. Do peoples, races, nations, and classes have any basis other than their name? The Frenchman, Jew, or proletarian is anyone said to be a Frenchman, Jew, or proletarian. Hence those who believe only in representables are quite prepared to say that the names of history are fictions and that the disputes to which they give rise are always pointless. Cosmopolitans and reconcilers, they focus attention on properties and the classes based on them: cling to the representable and thereby preserve the peace. Yet the point is that no one ever entirely believes them, and reality asserts itself: multiplicities determined solely by names have effects on speaking beings.

This is all the more true because of the fact that these symbolic multiplicities sometimes become realities. Then they are nothing other than crowds. Doctrine of course speaks of them in terms of a unary trait, thus granting that there exist multitudes whose constitutive unifying principle is a trait whose substance matters little because it is merely a contingent value of the signifying function. Alienations, symbolic classes, historical names: anyone who asks for examples of these in representation inevitably encounters dramatizations of crowds. It should come as no surprise, moreover, that crowds and their movements constitute the favorite iconography of those who cannot think beyond assemblies, by which I mean proponents of the political worldview.

At this point one is tempted to speak of pure multiplicity, because there is no avoiding the conclusion that the crowd or symbolic class has more than one member even if one cannot count them. Furthermore, adding or removing a member has no effect, since there is no "one" unless included in the collection: a term ceases to count as "one" the moment it is envisaged as separate from the collecting signifier—regardless of whether this occurs as an effect of aggregation or dispersion. The signifier thus exerts "One" as its major effect: it is that by which the multiplicity accedes to the One and, there being no metalanguage, that which assures that the One of the multiplicity is none other than the One of its members. Comprising One collectively and distributively guaranteeing the One of each individual one, it is, within multiplicity, the signifier of the fact that One exists. In other words, whatever its own intrinsic form, it has but one function that one can name, namely, to be the Signifier One. As a result, it gathers together, but not by way of the imaginary Same: each member of the multiplicity is, as such, indistinguishable from all the others yet non-similar to any of them. This is so much the case that multiplicity can even be combined with unicity: provided that the Signifier One exerts itself, the contingent unicity of that which it gathers together is of little moment. That is why a symbolic class requires only a representable substrate to attach itself to reality.

Such is the function of the One at least, an index sometimes necessary in the face of doubt, so that a given symbolic class will not perish, a given signifier will not cease to assemble. The passion that corresponds to this function in the soul is well known: it is named honor, a repeated and persistent assent to a given value of the Signifier One regardless of the configuration of reality. Respected examples of this exist, but so do terrifying ones. For the "at least one" is also attested in the violent form of extermination to the very last one—*ad unum*—out of which history is woven as the integral of symbolic classes. This is because symbolic classes are, despite appearances, not eternal: their members can be dispersed, and the signifying One can lose its powers.

A symbolic class collected by a signifier: what do we find therein if not the Masterword as such? At the same time one question becomes unavoidable: where are the various names uttered? Some voice is necessary, to be sure, but it is only too clear that the voice is nothing but the detached double of the Masterword itself. For us realists, it is therefore Reality that speaks and names us as it names everything else. Depending on whether a pronouncement takes on the traits of the supreme God or some more secular agency, its style may vary. Many speak at this point of History—*Geschichte*—but it is always a voice emanating from one knows not where to judge the living and the dead: Tribunal or Last Judgment, it issues decrees in which the multiple subject recognizes itself. "You are this," it says in praise or insult, and History—*Historie*—consists solely in hearing its call in order to reconstitute it through documentary traces. This, moreover, is the locus of what one might call the modern experience: each subject has some anecdote to narrate in which a Name—that is, a signifier that places it in a symbolic class—has been given it for the first time. We are familiar with this *topos*, whose resources the novel endlessly explores. It seems intrinsically related to the supposition of Judgment, which today has become, more plainly with each passing day, History and thus Politics. There the proposition that the Name can state the subject as One only by collecting it as multiple is constantly repeated.

Paradoxical Classes

There are real multiplicities. That is, multiplicities that are based on neither an assimilating and binding property nor an accepted signifier. To be inserted into such a multiplicity is not to receive from it a representation of any kind or the One of a discerning name. We may assume at most that a scattered One collects in a cluster in which the imagination recognizes a form to which language gives a name: thus the reality of the north star is aggregated into constellations. But the cluster exists prior to the forms and names, which are only accidentally connected with it. To say more one would have to make the stars themselves speak and question them as to what it means to be a member of a constellation.

Now, consider the names used by psychoanalysis. Stenograms of a cluster of cases, they seem to classify these cases in terms of their common properties, but in return they are supposed to pick out from the cluster precisely that which makes a case, or, in other words, that which resists any commonality. When one says "the neurotic," "the pervert," "the hysteric," "the obsessive," one suggests the uniqueness of a subject in the form of a generic singular that is its homonym. Literally no one can say if these denote a genus or an individual or an archetype. Within this characteristic vacillation multiplicities are spelled out, multiplicities whose mode is dispersion and whose principle is the reality of a desire. Does anyone in fact believe that these are classes based on properties, that neurotics resemble one another and are opposed to some complementary type? Or in any case does anyone believe that this is the point of the name when it is articulated as the object of the analysis? To be sure, psychiatry can construct nosographies, which are classifications of similarities and differences, and it can enumerate symptoms, treated as characteristic properties. But the moment psychoanalysis resorts to homonymy to make use of the names it receives in this way, it knows or ought to know that it is resorting to a sham: something else subsists that is not exhausted in the representable class. Something that does not say that neurotics are interchangeable but rather articulates that which is irreplaceable in each of them. This is because the bond that appears to be constructed by the common name has no substance other than that which forever separates the linked terms. And if one apprehends those terms through that which causes them to resemble each other, one can be sure of missing that real quality to which the name pointed. The names "neurotic," "pervert," "and "obsessive" name or pretend to name the neurotic, perverse, or obsessive way in which one subject differs radically from all others.

But isn't this structurally identical to the myth of the prisoners, which intervenes the moment a multiplicity has to be constituted out of a real object, in particular a desire? Hence one must contend both that the myth is the myth of multiplicities of desiring subjects and that the names of psychoanalysis are valid only by way of such procedures.

Hence just as the statement "I am lying" cannot be uttered without initiating the incessant back-and-forth between truth and falsehood characteristic of paradox, so, too, does the judgment "So-and-so is neurotic" define a class that is nothing other than paradoxical: the property that seems to be its principle and connection is the name of that which plucks it out of the round of properties and connections. It is easy to see that such a judgment cannot be Aristotelian: the predicate in fact points to nothing but a subjectivity, and this can come only from the subject. As for the subject, designated by a proper name—and how else could it be designated?—it is true that, reduced to itself, it would remain in suspense, but the content that it receives from the predicate only repeats what is inherently subjective in itself. Thus the temporality of the judgment is always intricate: the subject anticipates the predicate, since the former already posits the One of the real whose singularity the latter is supposed to name. This One was therefore already named when the utterance was initiated, yet at the same time it was not named because, by sticking to the subject, one would remain in suspense, simply scanning the sentence, which does not name. The predicate also feeds back onto the subject: it is at the moment the statement is complete that it emerges that what was named in the subject was precisely that which constitutes it as a real One, namely, its position with respect to its desire.

Except that no one seriously utters such a judgment. Or, rather, no one ever utters such a judgment without at the same time transforming it into an ordinary and shallow psychological attribution. Indeed, a statement that would properly state what is at issue here would be a sentence of a quite different sort, utterable only outside human language altogether in the extralinguistic form of an interjection, slip, rhythmic expression, silence, or joke (*Witz*). The articulable nominations that substitute for these are therefore pure shams: as such, they are all equivalent in that they effect interpretation, and this effect is their sole value. There is no real virtue in using psychiatric names other than to string together a discourse.

Thus we see that the paradoxical class to which these names point does not originate with them. In other words, it is not a symbolic class. Uttering the signifier "neurotic" does not call a collection into being: contrary to what intelligent nominalists believe, the case here is not a consequence of the utterance. No voice from who knows where needs to be restored in order to call the subjects to their positions and say to them, "You are such-and-such."

If such a voice existed, the most it would say would be: "Do not give up on your desire whatever it may be." In this way it would summon the subject to resist the real and to construct a paradoxical class on the basis of its singularity. Any maxim justified in these terms will have the form of a thetic judgment, no matter what the nouns that support it might be. What is then ruled out is first of all the imaginary class: the subject is bound never to convert the thesis into synthesis or antithesis and never to respond to the incessant demands that all, as delimited Whole, make upon it to act as Connection: the question of whether one should or should not consent to a given representable property in order to belong or not to belong to a given realist class is futility itself, even if it is also the locus of circumstances and conjectures.

Choosing one's camp, as the saying goes, is therefore never anything other than a problem of imaginary conduct, assuming that one believes it to be a matter of calculating properties and determining oneself on the basis thereof. In general, however, we know that nothing of the sort is the case and that, under the colors of historical realism, a very different commodity is on offer: the categorical imperative for some, and openness to every variety of obedience for others. Here there is only one recourse: strive to grasp more than just the conjunctural aspects of the case and to hear between the lines of what is said the name of that which one is being asked to give up on.

What is also ruled out is symbolic ethics, that is, formal universality, and the requirement that no maxim is valid unless it can be formulated as a universal law. On the contrary, the vanishing of all universes is ostensibly the sign of desire—vanishing in a moment of blankness in which, if the right conditions are met, clarity is combined with contentment. Cartesian terms are probably more suitable than any other to spell out the inevitable assertion of anticipated certitude. It would then be tempting to say that Kant, who sets such store by symbolic ethics, must be set aside if one weren't also aware that his language is sometimes necessary and alone capable of yielding truth effects.

This is because it is sometimes necessary to have recourse to homonyms to allow the signifiers of one ethical system to be used to prevent the subject from becoming caught in the toils of another. Thus we see that the vocabulary of symbolic ethics, which lends itself to the stripping of the Universal, severs realist ethics from real ethics—to prevent the subject from concluding, in the guise of not giving in, that obstinacy is always to be preferred. Conversely, it may be that requirements couched in the language of conjuncture and circumstance aim to restore the incisiveness of the case and illustrate why it should be preferred to universalist and formalist platitude. Thus, here as always, interpretation is a must: one needs to hear the accent of truth—or, by contrast, of humiliation—now in the voice of the abstract *dictamen*, now in that of egoism.

Interpretation must at any rate be permitted. The discourse of psychoanalysis bears witness to this and approaches the shores where interpretation is born: it is permissible to interpret, it says, that is, to link the real One of a desire to the symbolic One of a signifier, which allows itself to be heard in the connected fabric of a seeming Imaginary. People also say: truth speaks. Or again: a linguistic signifier can have truth effects. Or again: there are encounters. Or again: there are real nominations. Or again: *scilicet*, it is permitted that, in a second stage, truth array itself among the sayable signifiers.

JACQUES RANCIÈRE

The Community of Equals

1992

The theme of the community of equals nowadays generally gives rise to two kinds of brooding. The first is a grudging relief. There is an entire literature that invites us to shudder retrospectively at the thought of the danger we were in (or would have been in if we had not been so smart) from the combined threat of real leveling on the one hand and the great Whole which swallows up individual will and reason on the other. A somewhat degenerate form of catharsis is the justification given for such literary endeavors, which see fit to set continually before our eyes the fantasy of that great entity whose fascination for us so clearly spelled our doom. The second kind of brooding is a "reasonable" nostalgia. Though only too well aware of what the abovementioned threat made possible, we still take it to represent something we would not want to lose, namely a particular configuration of being-together without which thought and action are bereft of the virtue of generosity which distinguishes the political from mere business management. By some inverse exorcism, it is the very *passé* and superseded character of this figure, which is no longer the object of either fear or hope, that serves to maintain that barely perceptible gap and allows a shimmering cloud of egalitarian and communal honor to continue hovering above the banal administration of financial indexes and corporate reorganizations.

Both these feelings gauge a conceptual figure by the balance sheet of history. If we want to avoid this, perhaps we need to alter the terms of the question slightly; perhaps, instead of settling our accounts with the community of equals, we ought to consider how the community of equals does its own accounting, or rather what kind of accounting gives rise to this figure in the first place. What I have in mind here is a twofold line of inquiry. The more fundamental aspect—which I shall leave aside for now—has to do with the relationship of the idea of community to the idea of loss itself, to what we retain of a loss or to what takes shape around it. In this connection, I am put in mind of a quatrain of Rilke's which reminds us that "Losing too is ours" (*Auch noch verlieren ist*

From *On the Shores of Politics*, trans. Liz Heron (New York: Verso, 1995), pp. 63–65, 83–84, 87–91 [*Aux bords du politique* (Paris: Editions Osiris, 1992)].

unser), thus linking the notion of loss to the notion of common property. Even more simply, we might well recall the link between the idea of community and the judgment of the Gospel according to which "He that findeth his life shall lose it"—a pronouncement which may readily be coupled with the Platonic motif of the inversion of life, and which has the following remarkable implication: the collapse of the representation of another life does not nullify that life but instead lends it a vertiginous reality. And at the core of this vertiginousness is equality, the desire to partake of equality.

I shall leave aside this basic or overarching question, however, and concentrate on an issue that arises from it. The fact is that the great accounting between the Whole and loss breaks down into a series of smaller calculations, into ways of measuring equality that do not allow themselves to be reduced to rules and standards without putting up a fight. Ways of counting, of counting oneself, of getting oneself to count. Ways of defining interests that cannot be reduced even to the simple calculation of pleasure versus pain; forms of profit that are also ways of being-together (of resembling one another or being distinct from one another) and of defining those gaps which Hannah Arendt saw as the very principle of political *inter esse*. And ways of defining interests entered on more lines and in more ledgers than can be covered by the double bookkeeping of reality/utopia and science/ideology. Our inquiry needs therefore to go into a lower gear: whenever equality or community is the issue, we need to ask what is in a position to win or lose a particular interest on such and such a line. In how many ways may equals be reckoned equal? How indeed are they to be counted in order for this calculation to be made? And so on.

If we pursue a few of these accountings, we shall be led to reconsider the notion that the standard of equality is the law (whether celestial or infernal) of the communitarian body. For it may well be that relations of community and equality are themselves but a never-ending settling of accounts. By taking a closer look at the accounts presented by equality to community we shall see the image of the single great body crumble, and encounter all the deficit and discord which ensure that the community of equals can never materialize without some cement plugging the cracks in the image, without some obligation to keep tallying members and ranks and retranslating the terms of the formula.

. . .

What binds us together prior to all community, prior to any equality of intelligence, is the link that runs through all those points where the weight of things in us becomes consent, all those points where acquiescence comes to be loved as inequality and is reflected in the activities of comparing, setting up and explaining ranks. Tradition readily calls this passion; Jacotot preferred to call it inequality, belief in the inequality of intelligences. Existing without reason, inequality has an even greater need to rationalize itself at every moment and in every place. Jacotot gives such rationalization the generic name of "explanation." Explanation in this sense is rooted in the necessity to attribute reason to something that has none, to things whose lack of reason is intolerable. In this way, simple non-reason, the contingency of things, is turned into active unreason. And this "origin of inequality" is reiterated in every explanation; every explanation is a fiction of inequality. I explain a sentence to someone because I assume that he would not understand it if I did not explain it to him. That is to say, I explain to him that if I did not explain he would not understand. I explain to him, in short, that he is less intelligent than I am, and that that is why he deserves to be where he is and I deserve to be where I am. The social bond is maintained by this endless manufacture of acquiescence, which in schools is called explanation and in public assemblies and courts goes by the name of persuasion. Explanation turns all *wishing to say* into a scholar's secret; rhetoric turns all *wishing to hear* into knowing how to hear.

Even before Cabet and the Icarians came to blows over the principles of community—over work versus fraternity—Jacotot conveyed to them the disconcerting message that there was no principle of the community of equals which was also a principle of social organization. There was no *ratio cognoscendi* that was at the same time a *ratio essendi*. There were but two ways of grasping hold of arbitrariness, the primary non-reason of things and of language: the egalitarian reason of the community of equals or the inegalitarian unreason of social bodies. The community of equals can always be realized, but only on two conditions. First, it is not a goal to be reached but a supposition to be posited from the outset and endlessly reposited. All that strategies or pedagogies of the community of equals can do is cause that community to fall into the arena of active unreason, of explanatory/explained inequality ever seeking to pass itself off as the slow road to reconciled futures. The second condition, which is much like the first, may be expressed as follows: the community of equals can never achieve substantial form as a social institution. It is tied to the act of its own verification, which is forever in need of reiteration. No matter how many individuals become emancipated, society can never be emancipated. Equality may be the law of the community, but society inevitably remains in thrall to inequality. Attempting to set up the community of labor or the community of fraternity amounts to casting the imaginary veil of the One over the radical division of the two orders and their inextricable entwinement. A community of equals can never become coextensive with a society of the unequal, nor can either exist without the other. They are as mutually exclusive in their principles as they are mutually reinforcing in their existence. Anyone proposing to put the principle of their union into practice, to make society equal, should be confronted by the following dilemma: a choice must be made between being equal in an unequal society and being unequal in an "equal" society, a society which transforms equality into its opposite. A community of equals is an insubstantial community of individuals engaged in the ongoing creation of equality. Anything else paraded under this banner is either a trick, a school or a military unit.[1]

. . .

So the egalitarian polemic invents an insubstantial community completely determined by the contingency and resolve of its enactment. This egalitarian invention of community refuses the terms of the dilemma that forces a choice between the immateriality of egalitarian communication and the inegalitarian weight of social bodies. Social materiality is not just that weight of bodies to which only the discourse of inegalitarian rationalization applies. For it too may be traversed by a wish-to-say which posits community by presupposing concord in a specific form, the form of an obligation to hear. The *there is* of the event brings out the facticity of *being-there-together*. In the movement of the event replayed, of the text restaged, the community of equals occasionally finds the wherewithal to imprint the surface of the social body with the traces of its actual effects.

The communist passion cannot therefore be reduced to a misinterpretation either of Plato's *Republic* or of the Christians' mystical body; nor can it be reduced to the inability of a youthful workers' democracy to deal with the indeterminacy and boundlessness of its desire. The original source of the communitarian miscalculation lies in a singular experience of transgression. I characterized this transgression earlier, in Platonic terms, as the revolt of cardinal against ordinal, but the revolt in question was a far cry from the Platonic opposition between the arithmetical multiplicity of desires and the geometrical proportionality of the well-ordered community. It was grounded in a logical experience, that of a common measure applied to incommensurables. Equality and inequality are incommensurate with each other, and yet, when the egalitarian event and the invention of community connect, they do indeed become commensurable. The experience of this common measure is an extreme experience. Equality is an exception. Its necessity is governed by the contingency and the resolve which inscribe its presupposition in transgressive strokes lending themselves to the invention of community, to the invention of demonstrations of effective community. It is not hard, then, to understand the attraction, the continually renewed dream, of community as a body united by some principle of life (love, fraternity or work) having currency among the members of that body or serving as a yardstick in the distribution of functions within it. The accepted measuring rod of the egalitarian exception is the violence which is repeatedly reproduced in response to the tension generated by the vain attempt to suppress it. The practice of the community of sharing in itself nourishes the passion for sharing without dividing, the passion for an equality with substance in a social body which is measured by it. The communist passion yearns to release equality from its exceptionalism, to suppress the ambivalence of sharing, to transform the polemical space of shared meaning into a space of consensus. Beyond any misunderstanding about the idea of the communitarian body, the communist dream of the nineteenth century held firm to the egalitarian experience, to the measurement of the incommensurable, just as Kantian transcendental appearance held firm to the experience of a specific destiny for reason.

Consequently, the satisfaction of having overcome the dead ends and follies of community was in danger of meaning only that the exceptionalism of equality had been forgotten. Beyond communitarian miscalculations lay the appeal of that simple equation which reduces equality to the rule of the principle of unification of the multitude under the common law of the One. With the time of reverence for rhetoric and the glorification of new beginnings safely past, a return would at last be made to that terra firma where justice comes down to the common measure of the *jus*. Yet such a return quickly encounters the necessity that allows the established state to underwrite any kind of communitarian equality only if that state backs it up by projecting all legal-political authority behind it, in the form of the metalegality of the Rights of Man, so that the unresolvable question whether equality is the foundation of community or vice versa has to be addressed at this level. The unresolvable question gives rise to endless argument between the partisans of equality based on the common measure of the universal and the partisans of equality based on respect for the tiniest of differences. This endless argument would be of no consequence were it not for the fact that its very unresolvability serves to justify the practice of submitting every case of the application of equality, as inscribed in the legal-political text, to the wisdom of the legal experts. The trouble is that experts in law exist whereas experts in equality do not—or, more exactly, that equality begins only when the power of the experts ceases to hold sway. Wherever the vaunted triumph of law and of the legal state takes the form of recourse to experts, democracy has been reduced to a caricature of itself—to nothing more than government by wise men.

The memory of the communitarian miscalculation is thus the memory of the fact that equality may be inscribed upon the social body only through the experience of the measurement of incommensurables, through the recollecting of an event that constituted the inscription of the presupposition of equality and through the restaging of that event. Such restaging has no foundation and is justified by a "there was" which always refers back to yet an earlier "there was." The communitarian obligation is bound to the violent contingency of the event and to the facticity of being-there-together. The way in which facticity becomes a principle of obligation is indeed one of the oldest (yet ever fresh) scandals for political thinking, which has never ceased battling with it, whether as enactment or as community. Here we are put in mind, on the one hand, of the way in which Hannah Arendt, in *On Revolution*, confronts the monstrousness whereby some population or other, by virtue merely of geographical chance, is described as a free and equal people, so that qualities which can properly be applied only to an acting subject are ascribed to a state or body. On the other hand, one recalls Aristotle's reflections as he grapples with another aspect of the problem: who should govern? Logic suggests that the best should hold power and exercise it for as long as possible. But Aristotle finds that this ideal cannot always be realized. Specifically, in the case of a city made up of men who are all free and of like nature, the golden rule must give way to facticity. We are confronted by the fact of a city that is a *plethos*—"a lot of people," all possessing the attribute of freedom. Here, in short, the politician is helpless and can only go along with things as they are until he can somehow find a way to have the justice of proportion prevail amidst the confusion entailed by the rule of the many. Now the characteristic thing about the modern way of founding equality is that it worsens the scandal of facticity and heightens the contingency of the being-there-together of the *plethos* by means of an egalitarian act which is the inscription of the unfoundable right of the multitude.

The invention of community—the ever-to-be-recommenced invention of the community of equals—is kindled in the disjointed and random relationship between what is there and what forces change; in the facticity of the process of sharing; and in what it is that causes this process to refer back to an earlier coming together of egalitarian event and egalitarian text. In this way, a particular relationship is established between the invention of community and the state of the social realm. From the invention of community flow a number of effects which eventually come to be inscribed in the social fabric in the shape of hybrid forms that may equally well be described as conquests for the workers, as new means of tightening the bonds of domination or as aspects of the consensual self-regulation of a social machine now going merrily on its way without asking itself any more questions. Such profit-and-loss calculations leave out the essential thing, however, which is that these aspects of the social inscription of invented community constitute a topography, an aleatory distribution of places and cases, of sites and situations, which in their very dispersal are so many opportunities for a resurgence of the egalitarian signifier, for a fresh corroborative delineation of the community of equals. Democracy is not the simple dominion of the common law as inscribed in legal-political texts, nor is it the plural dominion of the passions. It is first and foremost the space of all those locations the facticity of which tallies with the contingency and resolve of the egalitarian inscription in the making. Thus, the street, the factory or the university can become the locus of a resurgence of this kind in response to the chance passage of some apparently insignificant political measure, to a word out of place or an ill-judged assertion, any of which may open the door to a fresh testing of community, to a reinscription of the egalitarian signifier, to the recollection of the earlier event that inscribed itself forcibly in this place. In the autumn of 1986, for instance, we saw how the single word "selection" had the power to establish a new communication between the egalitarian signifier and the factual situation, existing in France, of a university open to all regardless of economic considerations. Those who at the time contrasted the success of this movement, so circumscribed in its goals and organization, with the vain revolutionary dream of 1968 evidently forgot that the victorious calm of the moment was only possible thanks to the violence of those earlier events which had put the university in question and used the streets to effect communication between the university as a place and society as a whole.

There can therefore be moments of community—not those festive moments that are sometimes described, but dialogic moments, moments when the rule laid down by Gregory of Nazianzus is contravened, when an impertinent dialectic is created by those who have no rights in the matter, but who nevertheless assert such rights in the junction between the violence of a new beginning and the invocation of something already said, something already inscribed. There are moments when the community of equals appears as the ultimate underpinning of the distribution of the institutions and obligations that constitute a society; moments when equals declare themselves as such, though aware that they have no fundamental right to do so save the appeal to what has been inscribed earlier, which their action raises behind it as a banner. They thus experience the *artificial* aspect of their power—in the sense that "artifice" may mean both something that is not necessary and something that is to be created.

Note

[1] For further thoughts on this, perhaps I may be permitted to direct the reader to my *Le maître ignorant*, Paris 1987; English translation by Kristin Ross, *The Ignorant Schoolmaster*, Stanford, Calif., 1991.

MARCEL GAUCHET

The Revolution of the Rights of Man

1989

The point I would like to explore more fully, however, concerns not only the political content of the Declaration but also the image and logic of the power that was established thanks to the situation just described. Now, at one level, the cluster of demands that defined that power allows us to examine the Revolution's encounter with Rousseau. And "encounter" is the proper term to use, rather than speak of the development of a previously formed influence that would somehow have exerted itself through the events. Had Rousseauist thought not existed, it would have been necessary to invent it, for it offered the most adequate response to the problem of dual power with which the members of the Constituent Assembly were faced. More than any other philosophy, in fact, it ensured the plenitude and preeminence of legislative power while leaving open the possibility of a monarchical executive. The theoretical model was perfectly adapted to the practical difficulty. The signal and seductive virtue of the "general will" is to carve out a place for a king while offering the most radical version of the genesis of collective legitimacy based strictly on individual rights. In this respect, revolutionary Rousseauism represents the archetype of the radicalism of moderation that was implicit in the historical configuration before it won the mind of the people. The rule of law would provide a reassuring figure of reconciliation between old and new, between the primacy of the nation and the dynastic legacy. This became the focal point of a view of power granting absolute priority to the legislative and minimizing the needs of the executive, a view of which Necker would provide a remarkably perceptive analysis even if he did not accord sufficient weight to the pressure of events in bringing it about. A more sophisticated assessment of this Rousseauism needs, however, to take fuller account of the terms and effects of the initial situation. Two other aspects need to be taken into consideration: what it implied about relations between representatives and represented and what it produced in the way of alienation of the new power with respect to the categories of the old. To return for a moment to a comparative perspective,

From *La révolution des droits de l'homme* (Paris: Editions Gallimard, 1989), pp. xii–xix; trans. Arthur Goldhammer.

the Americans, spurred by their tax dispute with the British Parliament, began by insisting on good representation in order to assure constituents that their interests would be taken into account and that they would exercise control over their representatives.[1] By contrast, the representatives to the French Constituent Assembly started from the opposite extreme, being tightly constrained by the wishes of their constituents under the terms of the archaic "imperative mandate." In order to complete their task of liberation, they had to free themselves from these substantive ties by invoking an ideal country truer than the real one, a country upon which was bestowed the magic of the word *nation*—the nation that emerged when the bonds of the old society were dissolved. Vis-à-vis the power of the monarchy they had to assert themselves as the nation proper, the direct expression of the individuals of which it was composed, while at the same time eschewing any reference to the actual country whose message they were initially charged with delivering. This led to a twofold process of *identification* and *substitution*, which was reflected, on one hand, in the repeated references to direct democracy that can be found in drafts of the Declaration and even in the final version and, on the other hand, in the assertion that the nation has no voice other than that of its representatives. Here we touch on the quintessential blind spot of the revolutionary political imagination: its inability to formulate an adequate concept of representation. The idea of representation therefore had to be squared with one version or another of parliamentary usurpation, and this was the root of the ultimate failure of revolutionary political thought. The blindness at issue here is apparent in the heresy of "representative Rousseauism," which has been the butt of a good deal of ridicule. It is more interesting, however, to try to understand the workings of the illusion that prevented any number of good minds from recognizing such a blatant contradiction or finding ways of dealing with it. In this respect the most enlightening comment is perhaps to be found in Rabaut Saint-Etienne's September 4 speech on the royal veto. His peculiar argument was intended to prove that despite the existence of an Assembly, the "nation is not letting go of legislative power." To be sure, he concedes, the size of the population makes it necessary to resort to mandataries [*mandataires*], but this is merely a technical device that in no way affects the outcome. For "these mandataries, bearing the wills of others, combine those wills into a single will. But their particular wills are merely the Representation of particular wills, and their general will is merely the representation of the general will. These representatives [*représentants*] represent these wills by what they say, just as they represent citizens with their persons. They represent everything and are substitutes in nothing. It is not really the representatives who make the law, it is the people, of whom the representatives are only the organ. Hence it is the people who hold legislative power; the General Assembly does not."[2] It is clear how the identification of the *mandataire* with the people, for which a powerful impulse is provided by the confrontation with the rival *représentant*, made it possible in good faith to couple reverence for the social contract with the fact of deputation. The contradiction is not ignored but is presented as having been overcome. It is worth noting at once how unstable this formulation is. It is open to two quite different expressions, one oligarchic, the other popular, depending on whether the emphasis is placed on the ability of representatives to act as substitutes, to speak and will for the nation, or on the demonstration of the solidarity of the people with its mandataries. And in fact the Revolution would veer from one of these two extremes to the other, from parliamentary regime to ultrademocratic excess, without ever finding equilibrium in acknowledgment of the difference between the people and the power that makes possible its control.

The portrait would not be complete, however, without one additional factor that added an element of substance and credibility to this most unusual doctrine of representation. To counterbalance the prerogatives of its opposition, the revolutionary government attributed to itself prerogatives that committed it to a course of appropriating and emulating the powers of the monarchy. It set itself up as the heir to the accumulation of public power that the monarchical state had established as its goal. The confrontation led to a transfer of authority in which the discontinuity on the level of social forms was coupled with continuity on the level of the political imagination. Rather than give rise to a dynamic of limitation of power, as an elementary physics of government might lead one to believe, the duality of legitimacy led to a reinforcement of power in the emergent instance, which claimed the *national sovereignty* forfeited by the declining instance. Indeed, the graft was effected essentially by means of those two words, "nation" and "sovereignty." It is impossible to sum up in a few sentences the implications of terms that condense everything distinctive about the political history of western Europe, from its theological and political roots in the Middle Ages to the revolution of absolutism. I shall limit myself to a few remarks on the role of the legacy they represent in reinforcing the ideal of unity of power, meaning both intrinsic unity and unity with the collectivity expressed through the unified power itself. Thus far we have encountered the nation *as people*, the nation born with the reduction of the body politic to its initial terms. Now we are discovering the other face of the nation, the nation *as history*, a product of the work of centuries, a mystical entity defining the changeless identity of the collective being across time and despite the continual replacement of its constituent elements—and therefore as the true bearer of the claim to sovereignty. It was this latter nation that ultimately justified the claim on the part of the members of the Constituent Assembly to speak in the name of a collectivity of higher rank than the orders and communities of which they were, in a concrete sense, the delegates. Even more important, it was this latter nation that ultimately persuaded them that the will they had to discern and represent was the will of this transcendent individual, which stood above particular interests of every kind. It encouraged them in their tendency to usurp authority by persuading them that without representation collective expression was meaningless and that by speaking for everyone they were not cutting themselves off from society but rather allowing the mystical union encompassing all citizens to make itself manifest.

The role of sovereignty would prove even more decisive in accrediting the image of a power entitled to rule over and act on behalf of society as a whole. Here again there was on one hand the abstract notion of sovereignty taken from the theoreticians and on the other hand the diffuse, unconscious, but ubiquitous legacy of the history of sovereignty in action. Briefly, we try to show that this was in fact the history of the revolution in government that came after the break with the supernatural, when power ceased to communicate with the celestial order and took up the task of expressing the completeness of the terrestrial order itself. Its absolute eminence then made it the focal point of the operation whereby the community of men discovered its own constitutive principle. Out of this came the figure of the political subject and of society in charge of itself through its government. This meant extending to all things the power issuing from the will of all men as well as joining together in intimate wedlock the collectivity that wills and the power that acts. This idea was most fully expressed in the anthropomorphic identification of society with an individual. For example, Robespierre, in his speech against the royal veto, said, "Every man has by his nature the faculty to govern himself through his will. Men joined in a political body, or Nation, therefore have the same right. This faculty of common will, composed of faculties of particular wills, or legislative power, is inalienable, sovereign, and independent in the whole society as it was in each man taken in isolation from his fellow men."[3] Whence the indispensable unity of the organ of that power, as against any system of distribution and equilibrium—even after the Thermidorians were converted to the division of power, they would adjust its functions so as to continue to see it as embodying a unity of purpose all the more effective as a result. Whence an unshakable faith in the positivity of its acts and the extent of its prerogatives and a deep-seated refusal to think in terms of the people as separate from the government, including extreme suspicion of those who wielded power of any kind. Thus the same Robespierre could write that "the principal object of constitutional laws should be to defend public liberty against the usurpations of those who govern." This was a quite pertinent critique of the Constitution of 1791 and its "bizarre system of absolute representative government, without any counterbalancing system of popular sovereignty." "Such a government," he said, "is the most unbearable of all despotisms."[4] But what remedy could there be? The elimination of usurpers and corrupt officials in order to restore the authentic reign of the people, for the people are good and their power cannot be anything but holy. To the end, the logic remained one of establishing an immediate correspondence between the sovereign and its political instrument by way of endless proscription and preemptive flight into dictatorship by assembly and popular mobilization. The permanent exclusion of the wicked segment of the people and its unworthy representatives took the place of reducing the entire people to silence for the benefit of its representatives as a group. Later there would be a return to the earlier solution but in a new form. Nothing is more striking than the inability of the Thermidorians to free themselves from the attraction of the model in spite of what they had learned about rule by popular societies acting in the place of the people, by a convention acting in the place of the nation, or by a faction acting in the place of a whole assembly or even a committee acting in the name of that faction. Although they believed they had learned the lesson of past errors and navigated around them, all they accomplished was to produce a new version of the substitution of representatives for the people. Once again, it would be impossible to overstate the deep kinship that existed between such oligarchic concentration of power and ultrademocratic tyranny. Despite the antagonism between their sources of inspiration, both derived from the same organizational scheme. Both reflected the same identification of the body politic with the power charged with expressing sovereignty. This could either assume the peaceful but untenable visage of embodiment in an exclusive organ, or it could take the virulent form of a simultaneous and contradictory assertion of omnipotence of both the people and its representatives. These two regimes were fundamentally different, yet the political logic of both was the same. Immediately after Brumaire, Sieyès gave an astonishing formulation of the oligarchic version: "The people in its political activity is nothing but the national representation; only there does it constitute a body."[5] Probably without noticing he had hit upon one of the basic maxims of the old public law: "The nation does not constitute a body in France; it resides entirely in the person of the king."

The legacy was not fatal, any more than the conversion to a Rousseauist mode of thought (whose limited diffusion before 1789 can be granted) or the exploration of radical ways of returning to the foundation. It was only thanks to a very unusual situation that these could come into play or gain traction. Once they had been tied together, however, they formed an extraordinarily cohesive and psychologically inexpugnable system. Henceforth there would be no question of abandoning the intangibly established correspondence between a way of appealing to the primordial independence of each individual and a manner of conceptualizing the power of all, with the nature of representation, the role of the law, and the place of the executive—all ideas whose influence would extend well beyond their incandescent period over more than a century and half of republican tradition, and against which it would be necessary to relearn with much effort the rules of democratic practicability. If there is a mystery in the Revolution, it surely lies in the crucible of that summer of 1789 and in the intricate relationship that was then forged between the initial establishment of the rights of man and the failure to translate them into a viable political form.

Notes

[1] This point is strongly emphasized by Philippe Raynaud in his article "Révolution américaine" in the *Dictionnaire critique de la Révolution française* (Paris: Flammarion, 1988) [trans. into English by Arthur Goldhammer as François Furet and Mona Ozouf, eds., *The Critical Dictionary of the French Revolution* (Cambridge, Mass.: Harvard University Press, 1989)].

[2] *Archives parlementaires*, vol. IX, p. 570. Similar views can be found in *Lettres sur les débats de l'Assemblée nationale relatifs à la Constitution*, by Robinet, who in October 1789 wrote (p. 7): "The nation does not delegate its legislative power to its deputies as it delegates its executive power to the monarch. It can indeed commission someone to execute its will; it cannot commission anyone to exercise it. It must exercise its will itself." He goes on to make astonishing claims about what I dare say might be called the "real presence" of the will of the constituents in their representatives, despite the absence of the former from the debates.

[3] *Oeuvres complètes* (Paris, 1950), vol. 6, p. 86.

[4] *Ibid.* (Paris, 1961), vol. 5, pp. 18–19.

[5] Archives Nationales, 284 AP 5 (2), "Observations constitutionnelles dictées au citoyen Boylay de la Meurthe, membre de la Commission législative des Cinq-Cents dans les derniers jours de brumaire de l'an VIII." The interest of this statement did not escape the notice of Jean-Denis Bredin in his recent biography of the abbé: *Sieyès, la clé de la Révolution française* (Paris: Editions de Fallois, 1988).

JACQUES DERRIDA

Politics of Friendship

1994

The remaining question—about which it can be asked what is left once these questions have finished ringing out—is one whose novelty we will keep in the very form which Plato gave it in *Lysis*, at the moment of his leavetaking following his failure: not "what is friendship?" but who is the friend? Who is it? Who is he? Who is she? *Who*, from the moment when, as we shall see, all the categories and all the axioms which have constituted the concept of friendship in its history have let themselves be threatened with ruin: the subject, the person, the ego, presence, the family and familiarity, affinity, suitability (*oikeiōtés*) or proximity, hence a certain truth and a certain memory, the parent, the citizen and politics (*polítēs* and *politeía*), man himself—and, of course, the brother who capitalizes everything?

The stake of this question is, of course, *also* political. The political belongs to this series, even if it is sometimes placed in the position of the series' *transcendental*. Is it possible, without setting off loud protests on the part of militants of an edifying or dogmatic humanism, to think and to live the gentle rigor of friendship, the law of friendship *qua* the experience of a certain ahumanity, in absolute separation, beyond or below the commerce of gods and men? And what politics could still be founded on this friendship which exceeds the measure of man, without becoming a theologem? Would it still be a politics?

What happens politically when the "who" of friendship then distances itself from all these determinations? In its "infinite imminence"—let us listen to Blanchot—the "who" exceeds even the interest in knowledge, all forms of knowledge, truth, proximity, and even as far as life itself, and the memory of life. It is not yet an identifiable, public or private "I." Above all, as we are going to hear, it is some "one" to whom one speaks (if only to tell him or her that there is no friend), but of whom one does not speak. This, no doubt, is why Blanchot must prefer the vocative and canonical version to the recoil version:

From *Politics of Friendship*, trans. George Collins (New York: Verso, 1997), pp. 293–99, 304–6 [*Politiques de l'amitié* (Paris: Editions Galilée, 1994)].

> We have to renounce knowing those to whom we are bound by something essential; I want to say, we should welcome them in the relation to the unknown in which they welcome us, us too, in our remoteness. Friendship, this relation without dependence, without episode, into which, however, the utter simplicity of life enters, implies the recognition of a common strangeness which *does not allow us to speak of our friends, but only to speak to them*, not to make of them a theme of conversations (or articles), but the movement of understanding in which, speaking to us, they reserve, even in the greatest familiarity, an infinite distance, this fundamental separation from out of which that which separates becomes relation. Here, discretion is not in the simple refusal to report confidences (how gross that would be, even to think of), but it is the interval, the pure interval which, from me to this other who is a friend, measures everything there is between us, the interruption of being which never authorizes me to have him at my disposition, nor my knowledge of him (if only to praise him) and which, far from curtailing all communication, relates us one to the other in the difference and sometimes in the silence of speech.[1]

Consequently, if the testament or the epitaph remains the place of a *De Amicitia* for our time, all the signs of orison find themselves—if not negated or inversed, then at least suspended in a non-negative neutrality. Such a neutrality calls into question not only our memory of the friend, our thought of fidelity, but our memory of what "friendship" has always meant. And yet we do sense that this discreet violence accomplishes an injunction which was already working away at the legacy of this tradition, and was being demanded from within our very memory. On the death of the friend, the "measurelessness of the movement of dying," the "event" of death reveals and effaces at the same time this "truth" of friendship, if only the truth of the far-off places of which Zarathustra spoke. Oblivion is necessary:

> . . . not the deepening of the separation, but its effacement, not an enlarging of the caesura, but its leveling, and the dissipation of this void between us where once developed the frankness of a relation without history. In such a way that at the present time that which was close to us has not only ceased its approach, but has lost even the truth of extreme remoteness. We are able, in a word, to remember. But thought knows that one does not remember: without memory, without thought, it already struggles in the invisible where all falls back into oblivion. This is the place of profound pain. It must accompany friendship into oblivion. (p. 329)

Oblivion must [*Faut l'oubli*]. Friendship without memory itself, by fidelity, by the gentleness and rigor of fidelity, bondless friendship, out of friendship, out of friendship for the solitary one on the past of the solitary. Nietzsche already demanded this "community without community," this bondless bond. And death is the supreme ordeal of this unbinding without which no friendship has ever seen the light of day. The book has as its epigraph these words of Georges Bataille:

> . . . friends to the point of this state of profound friendship in which a forsaken man, forsaken by all his friends, meets in life he who will accompany him beyond life, himself lifeless, capable of free friendship, detached from all bonds.

The moment when the hyperbole seems to engage with the greatest risk, with respect to the inherited concept of friendship and all the politics that have ever spun out of it (Greco-democratic or Christiano-revolutionary) is when the "without sharing" and the "without reciprocity" come to sign friendship, the response or the responsibility of friendship. Without sharing and without reciprocity, could one still speak of equality and fraternity? We are again quite close to Nietzsche, although we are already invited to think a proximity of the distant to which Zarathustra called us (he must have had to suppose it too, teleiopoetically) and always under the neutral and non-dialectizable law of the "*pas*" ["step" or "not"] and the "X without X."

> And yet, to the proximity of the most distant, to the pressure of the most weightless, to the contact of what does not reach us—it is in *friendship* that I can respond, a friendship unshared, without reciprocity, friendship of that which has passed leaving no trace. This is passivity's response to the un-presence of the unknown.[2]

How could such a "response" ever translate into ethical or political responsibility, the one which, in the philosophical and Christian West, has always been associated with friendship? The preceding pages respond (admirably and from within the same "logic") to this question of responsibility. As in the passage we have just quoted, they are written to and inspired by the figure of Levinas, the other great friend, the other unique friend, in a friendship of thought which is not exclusively one of thought. If this language seems "impossible" or untenable with regard to the common sense of friendship, where it has commanded all the canonical discourses we have mentioned thus far, it is also because it is written in terms of *a writing of the disaster*. The disaster is less friendship's (for friendship) than one without which there is no friendship, the disaster at the heart of friendship, the disaster of friendship or disaster *qua* friendship. Star friendship (*Stemen-Freundschaft*).

Without being able to do justice here to these immense books, in particular *L'amitié* or *The Writing of the Disaster*, let us fall back, under the sign of friendship, admiration and unmitigated gratitude, to several passages in which what is most enigmatic, if not most problematic, in friendship receives the keenest attention:

Let us do so in three steps, taking up three questions: (1) the question of the *community*; (2) the "*Greek* question"; (3) the question of *fraternity*.

1. *The question of the community*. It will be asked what "common" can still mean as soon as friendship goes beyond all *living* community. What is being *in common* when it comes to friends only in dying? And what is it that renders this very value of the common valueless, valueless for thinking friendship, if not, fundamentally, this testamentary structure that we have constantly seen at work in all the great discourses on friendship? In order to think this "call to dying in common through separation," Blanchot decides he must undo or suspend the gift, the very generosity of the promise which, according to Nietzsche, remained the essential feature of the friend to come. Here, we are no longer in affinity with Nietzsche—with one Nietzsche, in any case (for there is always more than one):

> Friendship is not a gift, or a promise; it is not generic generosity. Rather, this incommensurable relation of one to the other is the outside drawing near in its separateness and inaccessibility. Desire, pure impure desire, is the call to bridge the distance, to die in common through separation. (p. 50)

Whatever can be thought of the gift or the promise from which such a friendship would free itself, from which it should indeed abstain, whatever can be thought of this duty or this possibility, it is true that in translating gift and promise by "generic generosity," in associating them so closely—nothing could be less self-evident[3]—risks are avoided, notably the political risks which, as we have pointed out, return incessantly: naturalization, the genericity of genre, race, *gens*, the family or the nation; and return, more precisely, with the features of fraternity. But once the necessity of all these neutralizations has been honored ("the outside drawing near in its separateness," "pure impure desire"), once it has been clearly pointed out that the common is not the common of a given community but the pole or the end of a *call* ("the *call* to bridge the distance, to die in common through separation"), the whole question remains: what is being called the *call*, and what is being called "common"? Why these words again, when they no longer mean what they were always thought to mean? When they still mean what they were believed not to mean—a meaning to which a memory, another memory, another friendship, ought to awaken them again? The question is not only the one which brings on semantic vertigo, but the one which asks "what is to be done?": What is to be done today, politically, with this vertigo and its necessity? What is to be done with the "what is to be done?"? And what other politics—which would nevertheless still be a politics, supposing the word could still resist this very vertigo—can this other communality of the "common" dictate to us?

This type of question envelops another. If, through "the call to die in common through separation," *this* friendship is borne beyond being-in-common, beyond being-common or sharing, beyond all common appurtenance (familial, neighborhood, national, political, linguistic and finally generic appurtenance), beyond the social bond itself—if that is possible—then why elect, if only passively, this other with whom I have no relation of this type rather than some other with whom I have none of the sort either? Why would I call this foreigner my friend (for we are speaking of this absolute foreigner, if only the neighborhood foreigner, the foreigner within my family) and not the other? Why am I not the friend of just anyone? Am I not, moreover, just that, in subscribing to such a strong and at the same time disarming and disarmed proposition? There could never be any appeasing response to this question, of course. But the hypothesis can come up that, if this is the way things are, it is because the friendship announced in this language, the one promised or promising without promising anything, is perhaps of the order neither of the common nor of its opposite, neither appurtenance nor non-appurtenance, sharing or non-sharing, proximity or distance, the outside or the inside, etc. Nor therefore, in a word, that of the community. Not because it would be a community without community, "unavowable" or "inoperative," etc., but simply because it would have nothing to do, with regard to what is essential in that which is called friendship, with the slightest reference to community, whether positive, negative, or neutral. This would (perhaps) mean that the aporia requiring the unceasing neutralization of one predicate by another (relation without relation, community without community, sharing without sharing, etc.) calls on significations altogether different from those of the part shared or held in common, regardless of the sign—positive, negative or neutral—assigned to them. This desire ("pure, impure desire") which, in lovence—friendship or love—engages me with a particular him or her rather than with *anybody* or with all hims and all hers, which engages me with these men and these women (and not with all of either and not with just anyone), which engages me with a singular "who," be it a certain number of them, a number that is always small, whichever it is, with regard to "all the others," this desire of the call to bridge the distance (necessarily unbridgeable) is (perhaps) no longer of the order of the common or the community, the share taken up or given, participation or sharing. Whatever the sentence constructed with these words (affirmative, negative, neutral or suspensive), it would never be related to what we persist in naming with these well-worn words: lovence, friendship, love, desire. Consequently, if there were a politics of this lovence, it would no longer imply the motifs of community, appurtenance or sharing, whatever the sign assigned to them. Affirmed, negated or neutralized, these "communitarian" or "communal" values always risk bringing a brother back. Perhaps this risk must be assumed in order to keep the question of the "who" from being politically enframed by the schema of being-common or being-in-common, even when it is neutralized, in a question of identity (individual, subjective, ethnic, national, state, etc.). The law of number and of the "more than one" which goes all through this book would not be any less crucial and ineluctable but it would, then, call for an altogether other language.

. . .

3. Lastly, *fraternity*. What can the name "brother" or the call to fraternity still mean when one or the other arises in the speech of friendship which, like that of Blanchot—at least in his *L'amitié* or *The Writing of the Disaster*—has so radically delivered itself from the hold of all determined communities, all filiation or affiliation, all alliances—families or peoples—and even all given generality, if only by a "gift, a promise, a generic generosity"? We have already noted that allusions to fraternity are rare in Blanchot. But for this very reason, for this reason as well, these allusions are worth dwelling upon. Besides the brief, obviously affirmative, connotations we have already examined in *The Unavowable Community*,[4] a particular generous declaration of friendship addressed to the Jews and to Judaism requires us to question what it says or does not say of the friendship of which *L'amitié* speaks:

> It is obviously the Nazi persecution (which was in operation from the beginning, unlike what certain professors of philosophy would wish to convince us of—to have us believe that in 1933, when Heidegger joined, national socialism was still a proper, suitable doctrine, not deserving of condemnation) which made us feel that *the Jews were our brothers* and that Judaism was more than a culture and even more than a religion, but, rather, the foundation of our relationships with the other [*autrui*].[5]

I shall not hazard an interpretation of this definition of Judaism, although I sense both its highly problematic character and its imposing necessity (which is of course unquestionable, from the moment one decides to call Judaism the very thing one thus defines: a question of a circle with which we cannot here engage again). Putting aside, then, what is most difficult in this definition, but supposing, precisely, that Judaism is "the foundation of our relationships with others," then—and this will be my only question—what does "brothers" mean in this context? Why would *autrui* be in the first place a brother? And especially, why "*our* brothers"? Whose brothers? Who, then, are *we*? Who is this "we"?

(Reading this sentence, and always in view of the admiring and grateful friendship which binds me to the author, I was wondering, among other questions (more than one): why could I never have written that, nor subscribed to it, whereas, relying on other criteria, this declaration would be easier for me to subscribe to than several others? In the same vein, I was wondering why the word "community" (avowable or unavowable, inoperative or not)—why I have never been able to write it, on my own initiative and in my name, as it were. Why? Whence my reticence? And is it not fundamentally the essential part of the disquiet which inspires this book? Is this reserve, with respect to the above definition of Judaism, insufficiently Jewish, or, on the contrary, hyperbolically Jewish, more than Jewish? What, then, once again, does "Judaism" mean? I add that the language of fraternity seems to me just as problematic when, reciprocally, Levinas uses it to extend humanity to the Christian, in this case to Abbot Pierre: "the fraternal humanity of the stalag's confidential agent who, by each of his movements, restored in us the consciousness of our dignity. The man was called Abbot Pierre, I never learned his family name.")[6]

It is rather late in the day now to issue a warning. Despite the appearances that this book has multiplied, nothing in it says anything *against* the brother or against fraternity. No protest, no contestation. Maligning and cursing, as we have seen often enough, still appertain to the inside of the history of brothers (friends or enemies, be they false or true). This history will not be thought, it will not be recalled, by taking up *this* side. In my own special way, like everyone else, I believe, I no doubt love, yes, in my own way, my brother, my only brother. And my brothers, dead or alive, where the letter no longer counts and never has, in my "family" and in my "families"—I have more than one, and more than one "brother" of more than one sex, and I love having more than one, each time unique, of whom and to whom, in more than one language, across quite a few boundaries, I am bound by a conjuration and so many unuttered oaths.

Where, then, is the question? Here it is: I have never stopped asking myself, I request that it be asked, what is meant when one says "brother," when someone is called "brother." And when the humanity of man, as much as the alterity of the other, is thus resumed and subsumed. And the infinite price of friendship. I have wondered, and I ask, what one wants to say whereas one *does not want* to say, one knows that one should not say, because one knows, through so much obscurity, whence it comes and where this profoundly obscure language has led in the past. *Up until now*. I am wondering, that's all, and request that it be asked, what the implicit politics of this language is. For always, and today more than ever. What is the political impact and range of this chosen word, among other possible words, even—and especially—if the choice is not deliberate?

Just a question, but one which supposes an affirmation. If my hypothesis must remain a hypothesis, it cannot be undone with a pledge. The pledge of a testimony irreducible to proof or certitude, as well as to all theoretical determination. If one wishes to retranslate this pledge into a hypothesis or a question, it would, then, perhaps—by way of a temporary conclusion—take the following form: is it possible to think and to implement democracy, that which would keep the old name "democracy," while uprooting from it all these figures of friendship (philosophical and religious) which prescribe fraternity: the family and the androcentric ethnic group? Is it possible, in assuming a certain faithful memory of democratic reason and reason *tout court*—I would even say the Enlightenment of a certain *Aufklärung* (thus leaving open the abyss which is again opening today under these words)—not to found, where it is not longer a matter of *founding*, but to open out to the future, or rather, to the "come," of a certain democracy?

For democracy remains to come; this is its essence in so far as it remains: not only will it remain indefinitely perfectible, hence always insufficient and future, but, belonging to the time of the promise, it will always remain, in each of its future times, to come: even when there is democracy, it never exists, it is never present, it remains the theme of a non-presentable concept. Is it possible to open up to the "come" of a certain democracy which is no longer an insult to the friendship we have striven to think beyond the homo-fraternal and phallogocentric schema?

When will we be ready for an experience of freedom and equality that is capable of respectfully experiencing that friendship, which would at last be just, just beyond the law, and measured up against its measurelessness?

O my democratic friends . . .

Notes

[1] *L'amitié* (Gallimard, 1971), pp. 328–29. Emphasis added.

[2] Maurice Blanchot, *The Writing of the Disaster* [trans. Ann Smock (Bison Book Edition, University of Nebraska Press, 1995)], p. 27.

[3] Elsewhere I have suggested the opposite: that the gift ought to exclude the too natural value of generosity. See *Donner le temps* (Galilee, 1991), p. 205 [trans. Peggy Kamuf, *Given Time, 1. Counterfeit Money* (University of Chicago Press, 1992)], p. 162.

[4] ". . . the heart of fraternity, the heart of the law," p. 47.

The problem of being committees of action without action, or circles of friends which would disown their former friendships in the name of an appeal to friendship (comradeship without preconditions) which would carry the exigency of being there, not as a person or subject, but as the demonstration of a brotherly, anonymous, and impersonal movement.

The presence of the "people" in its limitless power which, so as not to limit itself, accepts *to do nothing* (p. 55).

[5] A letter to Salomon Malka, *L'Arche*, no. 373 (May 1988). Emphasis added, obviously.

[6] Emmanual Levinas, "Qui êtes-vous?" interview with F. Poirié (La Manufacture, 1987), pp. 84–85, cited in M.A. Lescourret, *Emmanuel Levinas* (Flammarion, 1994), p. 121.

JEAN-LUC NANCY

Being Singular Plural

1996

When addressing the fact that philosophy is contemporaneous with the Greek city, one ends up losing sight of what is in question—and rightly so. As is only fitting, however, losing sight of what is in question returns us to the problem in all its acuity after these twenty-eight centuries.

It returns us to the question of the origin of our history. There is no sense of reconstituting a teleology here, and it is not a matter of retracing a process directed toward an end. To the contrary, history clearly appears here as the movement sparked by a singular circumstance, a movement that does not reabsorb this singularity in a universality (or "universal history," as Marx and Nietzsche understood it), but instead reflects the impact of this singularity in renewed singular events. Thus, we have a "future" [*avenir*] and a "to come" [*à venir*]; we have this "future" as a "past," which is not past in the sense of being the starting point of a directed process, but past in the sense of being a "curiosity" ["bizarrerie"] (the "Greek miracle") that is itself intriguing and, as such, remains still "to come." This dis-position of history indeed makes there be *a* history and not a *processus* (here as elsewhere, the Hegelian model reveals itself as uncovering the truth by way of its exact opposite). One can understand, then, Heidegger's "history of Being," and understand that our relation to this history is necessarily that of its *Destruktion*, or deconstruction. In other words, it is a matter of bringing to light this history's singularity as the disassembling law of its unity and understanding that this law itself is the law of meaning.

This clearly supposes that such a task is as demanding and urgent as it is impossible to measure. The task is to understand how history—as a singular, Western accident—"became" what one might call "global" or "planetary" without, at the same time, engendering itself as "universal." Consequently, it is the task of understanding how the West disappeared, not by reciting the for-

From *Being Singular Plural*, trans. Robert D. Richardson and Anne E. O'Byrne (Stanford, CA: Stanford University Press, 2000), pp. 21–26, 34–37 [*Etre singulier pluriel* (Paris: Editions Galilée, 1996)].

mulas of its generalized uniformity, but by understanding the expansion, by and through this "uniformity," of a plural singularity that is and is not, at the same time, "proper" to this "o/accident." And one must understand that this formidable question is none other than the question of "capital" (or of "capitalism"). If one wants to give a full account of "capital"—starting from the very first moments of history that began in the merchant cities—then it is necessary to remove it, far more radically than Marx could have, from its own representation in linear and cumulative history, *as well as* from the representation of a teleological history of its overcoming or rejection. This would appear to be the—problematic—lesson of history. But we cannot understand this task unless we first understand what is most at stake in our history, that is, what is most at stake in philosophy.

According to different versions, but in a predominantly uniform manner, the tradition put forward a representation according to which philosophy and the city would be (would have been, must have been) related to one another as subjects. Accordingly, philosophy, as the articulation of *logos*, is the subject of the city, where the city is the space of this articulation. Likewise, the city, as the gathering of the *logikoi*, is the subject of philosophy, where philosophy is the production of their common *logos*. *Logos* itself, then, contains the essence or meaning of this reciprocity: it is the common foundation of community, where community, in turn, is the foundation of Being.

It is within this uniform horizon, according to different versions (whether strong or weak, happy or unhappy) of this predominant mode of inquiry, that we still understand the famous "political animal" of Aristotle: it is to presume that *logos* is the condition of community, which, in turn, is the condition of humanity; and/or it is to presume that each of these three terms draws its unity and consistency from [its sharing] a communication of essence with the other two (where the world as such remains relatively exterior to the whole affair, presuming that nature of *physis* accomplishes itself in humanity understood as *logos politikos*, whereas *technē* subordinates itself to both).

But this horizon—that of political philosophy in the fullest sense (not as the "philosophy of politics," but philosophy as politics)—might very well be what points to the singular situation where our history gets under way and, at the same time, blocks access to this situation. Or instead, this horizon might be that which, in the course of its history, gives an indication of its own deconstruction and exposes this situation anew in another way.[1] "Philosophy and politics" is the exposition [*énoncé*] of this situation. But it is a disjunctive exposition, because the situation itself is disjunctive. The city is not primarily "community," any more than it is primarily "public space." The city is at least as much the bringing to light of being-in-common *as the dis-position* (dispersal and disparity) of the community represented as founded in interiority or transcendence. It is "community" without common origin. That being the case, and as long as philosophy is an appeal to the origin, the city, far from being philosophy's subject or space, is its problem. Or else, it is its subject or space in the mode of being its problem, its aporia. Philosophy, for its part, can appeal to the origin only on the condition of the dis-position of *logos* (that is, of the origin as justified and set into discourse): *logos* is the spacing at the very place of the origin. Consequently, philosophy is the problem of the city; philosophy covers over the subject that is expected as "community."

This is why philosophical politics and political philosophy regularly run aground on the essence of community or community as origin. Rousseau and Marx are exemplary in their struggle with these obstacles. Rousseau revealed the aporia of a community that would have to precede itself in order to constitute itself: in its very concept, the "social contract" is the denial or foreclosure of the originary division [*déliaison*] between those singularities that would have to agree to the contract and, thereby, "draw it to a close." Although assuredly more radical in his demand for the dissolution of politics in all spheres of existence (which is the "realization of philosophy"), Marx ignores that the separation between singularities overcome and suppressed in this way is not, in fact, an accidental separation imposed by "political" authority, but rather the constitutive separation of dis-position. However powerful it is for thinking the "real relation" and what we call the "individual," "communism" was still not able to think being-in-common as distinct from community.

In this sense, philosophical politics regularly proceeds according to the surreptitious appeal to a metaphysics of the one-origin, where, at the same time, it nevertheless exposes, *volens nolens*, the situation of the dis-position of origins. Often the result is that the dis-position is turned into a matter of exclusion, included as excluded, and that all philosophical politics is a politics of exclusivity and the correlative exclusion—of a class, of an order, of a "community"—the point of which is to end up with a "people," in the "base" sense of the term. The demand for equality, then, is the necessary, ultimate, and absolute gesture; in fact, it is almost indicative of dis-position as such. However, as long as this continues to be a matter of an "egalitarian demand founded upon some generic identity,"[2] equality will never do justice [*ne fait encore pas droit*] to singularity or even recognize the considerable difficulties of wanting to do so. It is here that the critique of abstract rights comes to the fore. However, the "concrete" that must oppose such abstraction is not made up primarily of empirical determinations, which, in the capitalist regime, exhaust even the most egalitarian will: rather, *concrete* here primarily signifies the real object of a thinking of being-in-common, and this real object is, in turn, the singular plural of the origin, the singular plural of the origin of "community" itself (if one still wants to call this "community"). All of this is undoubtedly what is indicated by the word that follows "equality" in the French republican slogan: "fraternity" is supposed to be the solution to equality (or to "equiliberty" ["égaliberté"])[3] by evoking or invoking a "generic identity." What is lacking there is exactly the common origin of the common.[4]

It is "lacking" insofar as one attempts to take account of it within the horizon of philosophical politics. Once this horizon is deconstructed, however, the necessity of the plural singular of the origin comes into play—and this is already under way. But I do not plan to propose an "other politics" under this heading. I am no longer sure that this term (or the term "political philosophy") can continue to have any consistency beyond this opening up of the horizon which comes to us both at the end of the long history of our Western situation *and* as the reopening of this situation. I only want to help to bring out that the combination philosophy-politics, in all the force of its being joined together, *simultaneously exposes and hides the dis-position of the origin* and co-appearance, which is its correlate.

The philosophico-political horizon is what links the dis-position to a continuity and to a community of essence. In order to be effective, such a relation requires an essentializing procedure: sacrifice. If one looks carefully, one can find the place of sacrifice in all political philosophy (or rather, one will find the challenge of the *abstract*, which makes a sacrifice of concrete singularity). But as singular origin, existence is unsacrificable.[5]

In this respect, then, the urgent demand named above is not another political abstraction. Instead, it is a reconsideration of the very meaning of "politics"—and, therefore, of "philosophy"—in light of the originary situation: the bare exposition of singular origins. This is the necessary "first philosophy" (in the canonical sense of the expression). It is an ontology. Philosophy needs to recommence, to restart itself from itself against itself, against political philosophy and philosophical politics. In order to do this, philosophy needs to think in principle about how we are "us" among us, that is, how the consistency of our Being is in being-in-common, and how this consists precisely in the "in" or in the "between" of its spacing.

The last "first philosophy," if one dare say anything about it, is given to us in Heidegger's fundamental ontology. It is that which has put us on the way [*chemin*] to where we are, together, whether we know it or not. But it is also why its author was able to, in a sort of return of *Destruktion* itself, compromise himself, in an unpardonable way, with his involvement in a philosophical politics that became criminal. This very point, then, indicates to us that place from which first philosophy must recommence: it is necessary to refigure fundamental ontology (as well as the existential analytic, the history of Being, and the thinking of *Ereignis* that goes along with it) with a thorough resolve that *starts from the plural singular of origins*, from *being-with*.

. . .

What is known as "society," therefore, in the broadest and most diffuse sense of the word, is the figure [*chiffre*] of an ontology yet to be put into play. Rousseau presented [a glimpse of] it by making the poorly named "contract" the very event that "made a creature of intelligence and a man . . . from a stupid, limited animal,"[6] and not simply an arrangement between individuals. (Nietzsche confirms this presentation in a paradoxical way when Zarathustra says, "human society: that is an experiment . . . a long search . . . and *not* a 'contract.'"[7] Marx saw it when he qualified humanity as social in its very origin, production, and destination, and when the entire movement and posture of his thinking assigned Being itself to this social being. Heidegger designated it in positing being-with as constitutive of being-there. No one, however, has radically thematized the "with" as the essential trait of Being and as its proper plural singular coessence. But they have brought us, together and individually, to the point where we can no longer avoid thinking about this in favor of that to which all of contemporary experience testifies. In other words, what is at stake is no longer thinking:

— beginning from the one, or from the other,
— beginning from their togetherness, understood now as the One, now as the Other,
— but thinking, absolutely and without reserve, beginning from the "with," *as the proper essence of one whose Being is nothing other than with-one-another* [l'un-avec-l'autre].

The one/the other is neither "by," nor "for," nor "in," nor "despite," but rather "with." This "with" is at once both more and less than "relation" or "bond," especially if such relation or bond presupposes the preexistence of the terms upon which it relies; the "with" is the exact contemporary of its terms; it is, in fact, their contemporaneity. "With" is the sharing of time-space; it is the at-the-same-time-in-the-same-place as itself, in itself, shattered. It is the instant scaling back of the principle of identity: Being is at the same time in the same place only on the condition of the spacing of an indefinite plurality of singularities. Being is with Being; it does not ever recover itself, but it is near to itself, beside itself, in touch with itself, its very self, in the paradox of that proximity where distancing [*éloignement*] and strangeness are revealed. We are each time an other, each time with others. "With" does not indicate the sharing of a common situation any more than the juxtaposition of pure exteriorities does (for example, a bench with a tree with a dog with a passerby).

The question of Being and the meaning of Being has become the question of being-with and of being-together (in the sense of the world). This is what is signified by [our] modern sense of anxiety, which does not so much reveal a "crisis of society" but, instead, reveals that the "sociality" or "association" of humans is an injunction that humanity places on itself, or that it receives from the world: to have to be only what it is and to have to, itself, be Being as such.

This sort of formula is primarily a desperate tautological abstraction—and this is why we are all worried. Our task is to break the hard shell of this tautology. What is the being-with of Being?

In one sense, this is the original situation of the West that is always repeating itself; it is always the problem of the city, the repetition of which, for better or worse, has already punctuated our history. Today, this repetition produces itself as a situation in which the two major elements [*données*] compose a sort of antinomy: on the one hand, there is the exposure of the world and, on the other, the end of representations of the world. This means nothing short of a transformation in the relation [that we name] "politico-philosophy": it can no longer be a matter of a single community, of its essence, closure, and sovereignty; by contrast, it can no longer be a matter of organizing community according to the decrees of a sovereign Other, or according to the *telos* [fins] of a history. It can no longer be a matter of treating sociability as a regrettable and inevitable accident, as a constraint that has to be managed in some way or another. Community is bare, but it is imperative.

On the one side, the concept of community or the city is, in every sense, diffracted. It is that which signifies the chaotic and multiform appearance of the infranational, supranational, para-national and, moreover, the dis-location of the "national" in general. On the other side, the concept of community appears to have its own prefix as its only content: the *cum*, the *with* deprived of substance and connection, stripped of interiority, subjectivity, and personality. Either way, sovereignty is nothing.[8] Sovereignty is nothing but the *com-*; as such, it is always and indefinitely "to be completed," as in com-munism or com-passion.

This is not a matter of thinking the annihilation of sovereignty. It is a matter of thinking through the following question: If sovereignty is the grand, political term for defining community (its leader or its essence) that has nothing beyond itself, with no foundation or end but itself, what becomes of sovereignty when it is revealed that it is nothing but a singularly plural spacing? How is one to think sovereignty as the "nothing" of the "with" that is laid bare? At the same time, if political sovereignty has always signified the refusal of domination (of a state by another or by a church, of a people by something other than itself), how is one to think the bare sovereignty of the "with" and against domination, whether this is the domination of being-together by some other means or the domination of togetherness by itself (by the regulation of its "automatic" control)? In fact, one could begin to describe the present transformation of "political space"[9] as a transition toward "empire," where empire signifies two things: (1) domination without sovereignty (without the elaboration of such a concept); and (2) the distancing, spacing, and plurality opposed to the concentration of interiority required by political sovereignty. The question then becomes: How is one to think the spacing of empire against its domination?

In one way or another, bare sovereignty (which is, in a way, to transcribe Bataille's notion of sovereignty) presupposes that one take a certain distance from the politico-philosophical order and from the realm of "political philosophy." This distance is not taken in order to engage in a depoliticized thinking, but in order to engage in a thinking, the site of which is the very constitution, imagination, and signification of the political, which allows this thinking to retrace its path in its retreat and beginning from this retreat. The retreat of the political does not signify the disappearance of the political. It only signifies the disappearance of the philosophical presupposition of the whole politico-philosophical order, which is always an ontological presupposition. This presupposition has various forms; it can consist in thinking Being as community and community as destination, or, on the contrary, thinking Being as anterior and outside the order of society and, as such, thinking Being as the accidental exteriority of commerce and power. But, in this way, being-together is never properly [brought to the fore as an explicit] theme and as the ontological problem. The retreat of the political[10] is the uncovering, the ontological laying bare of being-with.

Notes

[1] In certain regards, what follows pursues the dialogue proposed by Jacques Rancière in his book *Disagreement: Politics and Philosophy*, trans. Julie Rose (Minneapolis: University of Minnesota Press, 1999).

[2] André Tosel, *Démocratie et libéralismes* (Paris: Kimé, 1995), 203. See also the chapter entitled "L'égalité, difficile et nécessaire."

[3] Etienne Balibar, "La proposition de l'égaliberté" (paper delivered at Les conférences du Perroquet, no. 22, Paris, November 1989).

[4] I agree, then, with Jacques Derrida's critique of fraternity in his *Politics of Friendship*, trans. George Collins (London: Verso, 1997). But I must point out that I have also, on occasion, raised the question of Christian fraternity. Moreover, I have reversed my position again and again on the possibility of looking into whether fraternity is necessarily generic or congenital. . . .

[5] See "L'insacrifiable," in Jean-Luc Nancy, *Une pensée finie* (Paris: Galilée, 1990).

[6] Jean-Jacques Rousseau, *The Social Contract*, trans. Maurice Cranston (New York: Penguin Books, 1968), 65.

[7] Friedrich Nietzsche, *Thus Spake Zarathustra*, trans. R. J. Hollingdale (New York: Penguin Books, 1969), 229.

[8] This is, of course, an expression that is dear to Bataille. One could even say that this constituted his expression, absolutely.

[9] See Antonio Negri's "La crise de l'espace politique," and the rest of the articles gathered in number 27, "En attendant l'empire," of *Futur Antérieur* (Paris: l'Harmattan, January 1995).

[10] See the work gathered together not long ago in *Retreating the Political*, ed. Simon Sparks (London: Routledge, 1997), and in *Rejouer le politique* (Paris: Galilée, 1983).

CLAUDE LEFORT

Disincorporation and Reincorporation of Power *and* Voluntary Servitude

1999

Disincorporation and Reincorporation of Power

Historians who do not hesitate to recognize Communism as a totalitarian system nevertheless tend to view it as the result of political will. Yet this system eludes all purely political (in the strict sense of the term) analysis, just as it escapes purely economic or sociological analysis. How, indeed, would one delimit the element of political action where political boundaries were obliterated together with the boundaries of law, economy, social organization, and mores? To speak of politics' encroachment on all areas of existence is still to give in to the idea of a hypertyranny, a hyperdictatorship, or a hyperdespotism, even if these references are ultimately found wanting. Yet it is necessary to recall that the power of the tyrant does not undermine society in its depths. It looms over and threatens, being exercised in an arbitrary fashion. The power of the dictator in modern societies is established as a result of exceptional circumstances: when the interests of the dominant strata can no longer be maintained by peaceful means. The dictator thus secures from his intervention the semblance of legitimacy (usually the army, the alleged guarantor of the nation's integrity, secures this legitimacy). The power of the despot is placed beneath the higher rule of God or the gods. In Russia, the tsar had heaven above him; whereas the earth, of which he was the sovereign possessor, gave his subjects the feeling of a perennial natural order. Communist power was entirely different. It was anchored in a collective organ on which all institutions and bonds among individuals and groups depended. Or, more exactly, that organ was supposed to

From *Complications: Communism and the Dilemmas of Democracy*, trans. Julian Bourg (New York: Columbia University Press, 1999), pp. 139–45, 168–71 ["Désincorporation et réincorporation du pouvoir" and "Servitude volontaire," in *La complication: Retour sur le communisme* (Paris: Librairie Arthème Fayard, 1999)].

bring those institutions and bonds to life and, by the same token (to use a term completely foreign to Communist vocabulary), be their soul.

It is tempting to contrast appearance and reality. We might observe that, far from being abolished, the distance separating those who command from those who obey was evident inside the party itself and throughout the reach of society. The ruling organ, with an entirely new species of master at its helm, monopolized public speech as well as the means of decision, coercion, and information. Furthermore, the position of the leader was exhibited at all the echelons of the hierarchy. However, merely opposing the regime's effective truth to its appearance risks underestimating the effectiveness of representation and not seeing how it shapes behavior. We touch here one of the most difficult points in reflection on Communism. In one sense, we can speak of a symbolic effectiveness; in another sense, of an expropriation of or a hold on the imaginary. These two terms—*symbolic* and *imaginary*—seem to contradict each other. However, the symbolic makes us recognize the instauration of a system in which settled relations among groups and individuals are articulated, and in which shared notions of the real, true, and normal are established. The imaginary makes us understand that the vision of the One is supported by a frantic denial of social division and depends on a phantasm. If language fails us in characterizing the totalitarian phenomenon, is it not because that phenomenon leads to the limit of the nameable? How, indeed, can one be satisfied with the notion of a phantasm when faced with a system of institutions through which men discover the terms of their insertion into a shared life framework? And how can one hold on to the notion of a symbolic order when access to a language allowing each person to name the distance separating him from others and to form an idea of the law beyond the factual constraints to which he is submitted—when access to such a language is blocked? The enigma of the Communist totalitarian system that confronts us certainly does not disappear, but it at least becomes more specific if one sees in it a new mode of domination that blurs the opposition between the dominating and the dominated or, more generally, between *top* and *bottom* and that simultaneously effaces the principle of a separation among the *sites* where action, knowledge, and imagination are practiced in testing limits. Such domination tended toward a petrification of the social in its depths or toward a kind of closing [*bouclage*] of the social around itself, even though that domination was accompanied by a discourse on the creation of a new world and a new man (notably thanks to the demonstration of record industrial production) and by incessant calls for the mobilization of collective energies.

To some extent, the phenomenon escapes the perspective of the historian, sociologist, or economist. Its causes are not precisely localizable. Neither the scope of changes nor the recasting of social relations can be gauged only by examining either government methods—the scale of its coercive means and the doctrine it professes—or the system of property or even new forms of social discrimination. It is inadequate to speak of a turning point in history or a detour in the path pursued by modern society—for as much as we can reconstruct the past over the long term, that past included many other digressions. After all, wanting to define the new model according to several well-chosen criteria, in order to situate it within a typology of the modern world's characteristic regimes, runs the risk of concealing the profundity of the rupture it introduced.

At one point in *Democracy and Totalitarianism*, Raymond Aron gave in briefly to the temptation of typology and even of relativism. Nonetheless, he estimated that the difference between the regime of the monopolistic party and the constitutional-pluralist regime was "essential." That difference pertained not only to lifestyle and modes of governing but also to "the very modality of community."[1] Perhaps one should go further and ask if the totalitarian regime did not undermine what had previously appeared as the very foundation of political society. It is indisputable that one of the distinctive characteristics of the totalitarian regime was the party's monopolization of the means of coercion, information, and indoctrination. Be that as it may, to stop with this characteristic is once again to avoid a question: Was this not the very first time that the dimension of the Other found itself, if not abolished (how could it be?), then at least effaced? The question deserves to be asked as soon as one considers the power the directing organ and its leader had at their disposal. Still, in order to address it, we must acknowledge that, no matter the society considered, there is no power that comes down to domination and the control of a state whose distinctive trait would be the monopoly on legitimate violence (to borrow Weber's formula). Pole of authority, agent of society's cohesion, reducer of its real or virtual conflicts—power is simultaneously guarantor of a law that surpasses communally respected rules and of a permanence that does not derive from the simple factual coexistence of groups sharing the same territory, usually the same language, and linked by reciprocal obligations stemming from the imperatives of a common life. The delimitation of a site of power bears witness to and represents an asymmetry in social space, whether that site exerts a coercive force or even if such force is forbidden it (as we see in the case of many so-called primitive societies). Thus, even if we attribute power a predominant function, we cannot conceptualize it as an institution among others and situate it *in* society. No doubt it appears in society through the visible presence of someone or several persons who are supposed to incarnate it or be its stewards. Yet the signs of power and its distance are always rendered visible and open to all by means of myths, rituals, ceremonies, or a religious elaboration. This is the paradox: from the interior of society, power points to a site that surpasses the limit of society. It signals toward a *beyond*, while it makes clear that it communicates with itself through the variety of its institutions, and possible internal antagonisms. Put differently, we could say that there is no power durably anchored in a community that does not have a symbolic function, in the same way that there is no political society whose constitution does not have a symbolic signification.

Political society does not in itself provide standards of agreement as a consequence of kinship rules or rules that stem from an organization of the production and distribution of goods. Those standards depend on the way in which power is presented, and they bear the trace of an incommensurable, no matter the name used to describe it or the form it takes. Even in the case of an extreme despotism in which the monarch has the status of a demigod, the image of the tremendous power concentrated in his person does not erase this trace of incommensurability. Actually, it is often in his very status that he is seen to be subject to the strictest obligations and, notably, the object of taboos that must be followed as a condition of the maintenance of the social order. The European monarchy's dramatic art since the Middle Ages, whose transformations Ernst Kantorowicz so astutely analyzed, drew from Christianity and, more specifically, from the representation of God's prince-vicar entirely new resources for a spiritual foundation of temporal sovereignty.[2] But such a dramatic art did not move beyond the ancient forms of sacred kingship in which the supernatural and mundane worlds were at once separated from and imbricated in each other. To recognize the many instances of representations through which the dimension of the Other appears is thus to admit a heteronomy of the social. Bearing witness to that heteronomy are both the impossibility of a reabsorption of power in and by society and, at the same time, the impossibility for power to assert itself at a distance from the ensemble of subjects or citizens without gesturing, beyond the scene where it occurs, toward an unrepresentable.

Are we therefore to believe that modern democracy opened the era of autonomy? The disincorporation of power—the fact that those who are entrusted with it depend on popular suffrage and enjoy only a legitimacy granted to them—does not mean that the site of power is limited to the interior of society.[3] If it becomes forbidden to occupy that site, it is always from it that society acquires a representation of itself, as differentiated as that society may be and as manifold the oppositions that shape it. In a sense, as I have repeatedly emphasized, democracy requires that the site of power remain empty.[4] The result of this imperative is that the distinction between the symbolic and the real finds itself tacitly acknowledged, whereas it remained obscured as long as belief in the power, will, and wisdom of a suprahuman being was vested in the image of the monarch. Contrary to a widespread interpretation, power does not become mundane. In fact, those delegated the exercise of public authority (or those who participate in or claim to participate in that authority; that is, those whose calling or career is political action) run the risk of making it appear. One can even observe that once belief in a natural foundation of social inequalities disappears, power both feeds on the unprecedented expectations of citizens with conflicting interests and comes to be regarded simultaneously as an arbiter and instigator of social change.

I therefore speak of the *disincorporation* of power, whereas the sociologist might prefer to restrict himself to the notion of a limitation of politics. This is because politics is not only the result of a juridicofunctional apparatus. In order for it to become institutionalized, for the distinction between political authority and state administration to be precisely defined, and also for the space of civil liberties on which that authority should not encroach to be delimited, it is necessary that the sovereign have ceased to incarnate the community and that he no longer appear above the law. In this respect, the phenomenon of the monarchy under the Old Regime is significant. It would be careless of me to let stand the impression that the monarchy was only a version of sacred kingship, for it already involved a certain limitation of and on political power, even if it ended up violating that limit. If the sovereign had the advantage of a divine election, and if he arrogated to himself the status of a mediator between humans and God, consequently finding himself above the laws of the land, he nevertheless possessed temporal power by being subject to a higher law. It was by recognizing this law that the sovereign's authority was recognized by the community of his subjects. The division between the terrestrial and the celestial was so radical that it checked the sovereign's pretension to monopolize spiritual omnipotence. He was denied this possibility as much as the pope was denied temporal omnipotence. On the one hand, the monarch occupied himself with concentrating in his hands the means of dominating the ensemble of his subjects; on the other, the image of a *singularity* [*un seul*] imposing itself on all provided a model of order according to which each person was inserted into a network of dependences and gradually into a substantial community. Only the dissipation of this image gave birth to a new conception of the political.

The disincorporation of power did not only have the effect of undermining the representation of an organic society. By the same token, the source of the law became unlocalizable. To some extent, the law made itself known in the interdiction confronting anyone who attempted to possess it. We would thus be mistaken to conclude that it sank to the level of an artifice or that it fell into the orbit of a society dominated by a class whose representatives had the means of government at their disposal. No doubt the law was thereafter expressed in the work of legislators mandated by the people, and it thereby bore the mark of capricious opinions and conflicting interests. Yet that legislative work still had to distinguish between the legitimate and the illegitimate. For what is the criterion of legitimacy, however formal, if not the obligation to free oneself from the arbitrary and contingent? Similarly, the fact that none could present themselves as having a monopoly on knowledge of the social order and the ends of human conduct resulted in the disintrication of the theological and the political. This was a significant event, since it led to admitting the legitimacy of diverse and even conflicting beliefs, opinions, and interests, provided such conflict did not imperil public safety. Rather than effacing the dimension of the Other in the experience of life, democracy unveiled it. In reducing dogmatic beliefs, whether theological or philosophical, to the status of particular beliefs, democracy lent a kind of visibility to discord within the framework of a common world. Lastly, the disentanglement [*disintrication*] of power and knowledge precipitated a new legitimacy to the process of the differentiation of modes of understanding. It was always in the particular field where it was exercised that the activity of consciousness grappled with the principles according to which it guided itself, finding the impetus to return to its presuppositions. Far from being reducible to the exclusive effects of the division of labor characteristic of economic systems, the constraint that makes a rule out of taking a *route* [*passage*] in order to face the question of the true and false, or even of the imaginary and the real, testifies to the apprehension of a world that escapes a bird's-eye view or perfunctory glance [*survol*]. On the contrary, access to that world supposes that one learn from it the very means of orienting oneself in it.

Voluntary Servitude

One could say that Communist law allowed taking one step further the phenomenon of *voluntary servitude* that Etienne de La Boétie had described in the sixteenth century. According to the celebrated author of the *Discourse on Voluntary Servitude* (1552–1553), subjects of a monarch or a tyrant (the two terms designating the power of the One [*d'Un seul*]) appeared ready to hand over their property, their parents, and themselves, captivated as they were by the image of the Prince or the very name of the One [*le seul nom d'Un*]. Addressing himself to these subjects, La Boétie declared, "This ruin descends upon you not from alien foes, but from the one enemy whom you yourselves render as powerful as he is, for whom you go bravely to war, for whose greatness you do not refuse to offer your own bodies unto death."[5] Party militants accepted an even stranger condition: they consented, for the party, to be condemned by the party. They gave and denounced themselves to the point of passing themselves off as its enemies out of fear of losing their bond with it. La Boétie had already suggested that men were caught in the phantasm of a body of which they were members:

> He who thus domineers over you has only two eyes, only two hands, only one body, no more than is possessed by the least man among the infinite numbers dwelling in your cities; he indeed has nothing more than the power that you confer upon him to destroy you. Where has he acquired enough eyes to spy upon you, if you do not provide them yourselves? How can he have so many arms to beat you with, if he does not borrow

> them for you? The feet that trample down your cities, where does he get them if they are not your own? How does he have any power over you except through you? How would he dare assail you if he had no cooperation from you?[6]

Although one is tempted to assign to Stalin the power of this faith, as I have insisted, he appeared as the incarnation of the party. One cannot say that the party itself was a tyrant, for its body did not offer itself for view. It had the extraordinary new property of giving consistency to the One in the guise of a collective individual.

I am not brushing aside La Boétie's argument. It prompts one to break with a traditional representation of tyranny that Hannah Arendt continued to share. In the regime La Boétie described, something appeared besides the will of a master unconstrained by any law and to whom the people submitted out of fear. The tyrant awakened or precipitated the people's desire to appear to themselves as united [*tout un*]. Furthermore, not content to show, like Xenophon, that the tyrant installed in the position of the One had no friends, the author of the *Discourse on Voluntary Servitude* described a system that destroyed *friendship*—the capacity of citizens to connect to one another by mutually recognizing one another as equals—throughout the entire society. Indeed, he detected a mechanism of identification with the tyrant that was practiced by degrees from top to bottom on the social hierarchy. This observation was so important in his eyes that he introduced it with these words: "I come now to a point which is, in my opinion, the source and secret of domination, the support and foundation of tyranny."[7] How, indeed, would the tyrant govern a country if he did not have means of relay at his disposal? So, close to him, some five or six people eager to serve him oppressed the masses in his name. Below them one finds innumerable servants behaving in the image of those who dominated them. La Boétie added, "The consequence of all this is fatal indeed. And whoever is pleased to unwind the skein will observe that not . . . six thousand but a hundred thousand, and even millions, cling to the tyrant by this cord to which they are tied."[8] Probably the traits of the schema of domination sketched here could be found in different times and places, but it is noteworthy that La Boétie revealed a mode of the structuration of social relationships such that, to repeat a formula by Solzhenitsyn, *the people become their own enemy*.[9]

There is no doubt that Stalin was the object of a cult, that in turn some of his close associates—Genrikh Yagoda, for example—gave rise to subsidiary cults, and that countless petty tyrants were devoted to him. Merle Fainsod found in the Smolensk archives "whole galleries of Soviet provincial types—the little Stalins who ruled the oblasts [provinces] or the raions [districts]" and who benefited from the servility of functionaries, officers, kolkhoz (collective farm) directors, local aristocrats, professors, students, and even workers recently arrived in the countryside.[10] Nevertheless, Solzhenitsyn was convinced that Communist-style domination involved a new driving force. He found it in ideology when he described the commissar-investigators who in good conscience sent innocents to the camps. "Thanks to *ideology*," he wrote, "the twentieth century was fated to experience evildoing on a scale calculated in the millions."[11] However, the argument does not live down the fact that the agents of terror were—as he himself showed so well—embedded in an institution and incorporated into an *organ*, itself incorporated into the party. More important than their convictions was their submission to the law from which they drew the certainty of being within their rights.

It would be fruitless, not to define what law is, but to delimit features of a conception of law separated from the conception of the party. If it is agreed that law as such—that is, beyond formulated laws likely to be modified—appears as that which cannot be violated and as that which imposes itself absolutely—barring a revolution and a destruction of the foundations of the social order—how would one dissociate it from the framework of the party that exists *absolutely*, that is, does not exist in the way that all things are subject to space and time? No doubt the party could change its policies, and its ranks could vary according to circumstances, growing inordinately or being scaled down. No doubt it could become the scene for rivalries among leaders or even replace those in charge. But the party always expressed the power that society is supposed to exercise over itself, without which society would fall apart. In order to qualify the shock introduced by the totalitarian regime, Arendt used a gripping formula: the regime turned on an "identification of man with the law."[12] But would it not be better to speak of an identification of the Communist body with the law, under whose effect each person felt himself summoned to want, think, and act in the same way?

This last remark returns us to the Arendtian characterization of ideology as a "stringent logicality as a guide to action" or "compulsory processes of deduction."[13] These formulas emphasized both the pretension to possess a total explanation of history and, furthermore, the separation of thought and experience. In spite of their relevance, though, they risk misconstruing the fact that the supposed logic (which, after all, adapted to the theoretical line's sometimes considerable oscillations according to circumstances) was supported only by the injunction for everyone *not to think* anything that contradicted or betrayed official theses—an injunction whose efficacy presupposed that, since it was a matter of thought, it would be interiorized by a subject [*Sujet*]. *Do not think* implies an extreme command, in a sense even more worrisome than the directive to confess crimes one has not committed, since such a confession can at least come with the consciousness of not having had guilty intentions. Thus in the very exercise of thought (in which Arendt saw the fulfillment of the reign of logic), the imprint of the law was found again.

For the party member, "do not think" signified *wanting not to think*, and this wanting resulted in a duty. Acknowledging this allows us immediately to discern the relationship maintained between obedience to the law and voluntary servitude. We return to La Boétie's subtle descriptions of the benefits that *some people*, and then a great number of them, draw from their enslavement. Among these benefits, one must count the power won by self-righteous minds to pose as master thinkers facing a mass of ignorant or irresolute people. And, by the same token, we return to the image concealed by the supposed tyranny of logic advanced by Arendt: a party to which everyone was fettered. In short, one must always return to the interweaving [*intrication*] of power, law, and knowledge in the party. Yet, I must insist, the party is only the concretion of the social, the motor element of the exclusion of plurality and division. One can no more delimit what depends on ideology than one can delimit what depends on law. Both are inseparable from a model of organization and incorporation. Law becomes immobile while, simultaneously, imprinting itself in a network of rules that places everyone squarely under its guillotine blade. Thought is compressed within the limits of a faultless knowledge. Power accepts nothing outside itself.

Notes

[1] [Raymond Aron, *Démocratie et totalitarianisme* (Paris: Gallimard, 1965, 1970), originally published as *Sociologie des sociétés industrielles: Esquisse d'une théorie des régimes politiques* (Paris: Centre de documentation universitaire, 1958), 267; *Democracy and Totalitarianism*, ed. and intro. Roy Pierce, trans. Valence Ionescu (Ann Arbor: University of Michigan Press, 1990), 179 (translation modified).]

[2] Ernst Kantorowicz, *The King's Two Bodies: A Study in Medieval Political Theory* (Princeton, N.J.: Princeton University Press, 1957); *Les deux corps du roi: Essai sur la théologie politique au Moyen Âge*, trans. Jean-Philippe Genet and Nicole Genet (Paris: Gallimard, 1989).

[3] [Claude Lefort discusses the disincorporation of power in "L'image du corps et le totalitarisme" (1974), *Confrontation* 2 (1979), in *L'invention démocratique: Les limites de la domination totalitaire* (Paris: Fayard, 1981); "The Image of the Body and Totalitarianism," trans. Alan Sheridan, in *The Political Forms of Modern Society: Bureaucracy, Democracy, Totalitarianism*, ed. and intro. John B. Thomspon (Cambridge, Mass.: MIT Press, 1986).]

[4] [See, for instance, Claude Lefort, "La logique totalitaire," *Kontinent Skandinavia* 3–4 (1980), in *L'invention démocratique*; "The Logic of Totalitarianism," trans. Alan Sheridan, in *Political Forms of Modern Society*; "Démocratie et avènement d'un 'lieu vide,'" *Psychanalystes: Bulletin du Collège de Psychanalystes* 2 (1982); and "Permanence du théologico-politique?" *Le temps de la réflexion* 2 (1981), in *Essais sur le politique (XIXè–XXè siècles)* (Paris: Seuil, 1986); "The Permanence of the Theologico-Political?" in *Democracy and Political Theory*, trans. David Macey (Minneapolis: University of Minnesota Press, 1988).]

[5] Etienne de La Boétie, *Le discours de la servitude volontaire*, ed. Miguel Abensour, intro. Miguel Abensour and Marcel Gauchet, commentary by Pierre Clastres et al. (Paris: Payot, 1976, 1993), 114–15; [*The Politics of Obedience: The Discourse on Voluntary*

Servitude, intro. Murray N. Rothbard, trans. Harry Kurz (Montreal: Black Rose, 1997), 52].

6 [La Boétie, *Le discours de la servitude volontaire*, 115; *Politics of Obedience*, 52.]

7 La Boétie, *Le discours de la servitude volontaire*, 150; [*Politics of Obedience*, 77 (translation modified)].

8 [La Boétie, *Le discours de la servitude volontaire*, 152; *Politics of Obedience*, 78.]

9 [Claude Lefort discusses this phrase in *Un homme en trop: Réflexions sur "L'archipel du Goulag"* (Paris: Seuil, 1976), chap. 2.]

10 [Merle Fainsod, *Smolensk Under Soviet Rule* (Cambridge, Mass.: Harvard University Press, 1958), 12]; *Smolensk à l'heure de Staline*, trans. Gisèle Bernier (Paris: Fayard, 1967), 28.

11 Aleksandr Solzhenitsyn, *L'archipel du Goulag, 1918–1956: Essai d'investigation littéraire, première et deuxième parties*, 2 vols., trans. Jacqueline Lafond et al. (Paris: Seuil, 1974), 1:131; [*The Gulag Archipelago, 1918–1956: An Experiment in Literary Investigations: I–II*, trans. Thomas P. Whitney (New York: Harper & Row, 1975), 174].

12 [Hannah Arendt, *The Origins of Totalitarianism* (New York: Harcourt Brace, 1951, 1973), 462]; *Le système totalitaire* [part III of *The Origins of Totalitarianism*], trans. Jean-Loup Bourget, Robert Davreau, and Patrick Lévy (Paris: Seuil, 1972), 207.

13 [Arendt, *Origins of Totalitarianism*, 472–73]; *Le système totalitaire*, 221, 223–24.

PART VII

Thinking in Art

The search for a new critique, a fourth critique no longer based in the infinite understanding of God nor the finite existence of Man, was carried on not simply in relation to questions of institution, community, and violence but also, at the same time, in and through arts and letters. The very activity of philosophy became inseparable from a whole series of changes in the basic models in the humanities and social sciences, inherited from the nineteenth century. What it means to write philosophy became a new question, leading to new zones of interaction and exchange with the arts; at the same time, the idea of oeuvre or work of art was correspondingly rethought in its relations with knowledge, technology, and politics. Thus the new novel, the new cinema, and the new criticism that served to challenge the Sartrean *engagement* in the late 1950s seemed to harbor the secret of a new picture of thinking itself, and it fell to philosophy to elaborate and develop it; conversely, the new idea of structure that philosophers found in the social sciences or the humanities became inseparable from new kinds of art or writing, which took over from earlier kinds of formalism, introducing new questions.

The relationship between thinking and art—and so what it means "to think in art"—was thus conceived along new lines that departed from and transformed the discipline called aesthetics, which Kant, in his last *Critique*, had bequeathed to the nineteenth century. For in recasting the questions of oeuvre, genius, and sensibility, what mattered was not simply art and its criticism or judgment, but also the very idea of what art is or what philosophy does or means, going back to Plato's great agon with the poets and tragedians, and so with the entire history of philosophy. Indeed, the question of thinking in art would accompany all the new questions of the period, and all the moments through which they themselves would be taken up or reformulated in turn, in the process generating a whole series of debates about image and text, work and authorship, and, more generally, the very idea of representation and mimesis. Aesthetics became a great laboratory for the inventions, problems, and movements of the day. The relations that writing, art, and philosophy thereby discovered with one another would then serve to dislodge the grand edifice of the history of philosophy, which had been built up on the philological or hermeneutic methods of the nineteenth century and then elaborated philosophically in the great aesthetics of Hegel and later Heidegger, culminating in the theme of "the end of art." The very idea of an intrinsic narrative or a world destiny that would link Europe or Germany to antiquity was questioned and its implications or presuppositions exposed. Thus the picture of a single idea or question that would be transmitted—starting from Athens and passing through developmental stages or epochs from Latin and Christianity to modernity, revolution, and critique—would be disrupted in favor of a "stratigraphic" time, without fixed beginnings or ends, with different layers of times or events, superimposed on one another, taken up again from fresh angles and in new circumstances, as if in an ever-evolving collage or disjointed montage, leading up to a new critical present and appealing to a still-indeterminate community or people. There then arose a new conception of thinking at the borders or within the interstices of constituted ways of talking or seeing, crossing their lines, and in the process discovering new relations with writing or art.

Thus Lyotard's talk of an end to the grand narratives of revolution and emancipation, which had haunted nineteenth-century aesthetics, and the corresponding rise of avant-gardes was inseparable from a new idea of writing, art, and thinking as witness to unrepresentable events, to be rediscovered in turn in the themes of the sublime or enthusiasm in Kant, and anticipating the intractable violence that the disaster of the war would introduce into our very ideas of memory and history. At the same time, the breakup in grand narrative would lead to questions of extra-European or non-Western traditions in thought or in art, as with Levinas's attempt to rethink or reintroduce the question of ethics from the Judaic tradition. When Derrida would question the "white mythology" involved in Benveniste's attempt to derive the categories of Greek philosophy from Greek and Indo-European languages more generally, it was in terms of a sense of "untranslatability," interrupting "proper sense," involving another kind of dissemination, which in turn Derrida would associate with Mallarmé, Bataille, and Artaud. Philosophy would discover a new heterotopian or extraterritorial space, as if speaking a foreign language within whatever languages it uses or whatever image-regimes govern what it can see or do, thereby disrupting the national or modern European languages, which, following the dissolution of the Latin *universitas*, Descartes had associated with rational thought itself. Thus the monolinguistic assumptions of the very idea of a national language were exposed, introducing a new sense of "minor" languages within dominant or hegemonic ones, as with Kafka's literary German in multilingual Prague. In the arts, as in philosophy, the idea of heterotopia tended to replace that of utopia, and with it, a kind of transnationalism replaced the republican cosmopolitan ideals that philosophy had opposed to national geophilosophies that took form in the nineteenth century. The problem became how to reintroduce into the modern idea of the universality of thought this heterodox and stubbornly foreign space and time.

But if arts and letters thus played a key role in the invention of this new space, it was not because they illustrated or applied philosophical ideas or doctrines, which in turn were developed as if in the absence of any aesthetic or sensory forms. More than a meta-discipline for fixed norms of judgment in the appraisal of works of art (for what such system of appraisal applies to the work to come?), aesthetics would shift toward a new zone of invention and creation in which art and philosophy commingle and overlap, sometimes to the point of indistinction, a zone from which new ideas come and new questions arise. The game of philosophical aesthetics would be played in a way that sought to avoid two dangers: didacticism, in which art simply illustrates philosophy, and a romanticism that looks to the work of art for an irrational point outside any possibility of thought. Rather, one imagined the existence of a kind of prephilosophical space in the activity of thought, in which art and philosophy are not yet strictly separated and which supplies new aesthetic or sensible conditions for thought. There would thus exist a nonphilosophical understanding of philosophy in the arts of which philosophy has a need and to which it is addressed. It is precisely through such vital zones of invention that philosophy would then pass from Kant's idea of an "age" of critique, enlightenment, and modernity to times of invention that recast what has come before and open up what is yet to come. The problem of style in philosophy translates into this larger search for a heterodox foreign zone in thought, and in this period, we find the invention of many new styles of writing outside the traditional forms of papers, lectures, or colloquia of professional academic philosophy, embodying a new picture of the relation of thinking to knowledge itself. Philosophy would be read almost as a new art form in its own right, appealing to a kind of creative ignorance within all forms of constituted knowledge or technique. When arts and letters moved outside of the great nineteenth-century institutions of the museum and the library, they sought a "stupidity" of the sort Flaubert had posed against the image of the grand inclusive encyclopedia, which still haunted Hegel. Thus, in contrast to the great humanist ideal of an emancipatory *Wissenschaft* and what Max Weber called the vocation of the scholar, Foucault would elaborate his picture of multiple *savoirs*, things of this world, tied up in larger *dispositifs* of power and requiring a new model of critique and emancipation that would free us to speak and see in other ways.

The result recast the institutional role philosophy plays or the function to which it aspires. In contrast to an academic discipline in the manner of Kant, addressed to a literate or learned public, or participating in the "aesthetic education" of mankind, philosophy seemed to have need of the fresh air of an outside, addressed, in Artaud's terms, to "illiterates" and involving a Flaubertian *bêtise*. The notion of an illiterate public then served to recast the idea of a universal common sense that Descartes had invoked in freeing philosophy from Scholasticism, associating it instead with his method and his meditative exercises. Irreducible to such method or meditations, and perhaps to any other prior ordering, philosophy became associated with processes or practices of writing that proceed in fits and starts through encounters with unsettling events or objects. Nietzsche would become a key precursor of these new styles; he broke not only with philology but also with a professional academic existence, preferring a nomadic activity, wandering through Europe and across the ages, with an untimely sense of what is to come, and leading to the composition of the great anti-Wagnerian philosophical opera called Zarathustra and to new ways of philosophizing with the "hammer" of aphorism and wit. Thus Nietzsche would appear together with Mallarmé as the new heroes of the nineteenth century, pushing the whole discipline of aesthetics toward new forms, new practices. Even the themes of communism in Marx and the related notions of avant-gardes or collectives would be reformulated in terms of the sort of "we" brought together by the violence of disruptive events.

Robert Antelme's phrase "such an upheaval in the general sensibility couldn't but lead to new dispositions of thought" captures a larger postwar shift beyond his own circle of Blanchot and Duras. The phrase applies not simply to literature and criticism but also to theater and painting, in which philosophers looked for new models or "dispositions" of thought. Thus in Beckett, or through the legacies of Brecht and Artaud, there seemed to lie renewed visions of what it is to think: the violent humor of a neutral space in talking and seeing, the cruel role of the body outside the "closure" of representation, or the consequences of "dis-identificatory" acts of emancipation in the theater of historical antagonisms. At the same time, starting already in "Cézanne's Doubt," Merleau-Ponty would elaborate a philosophical picture of what it is "to think in painting," grounded in an embodied relation of "eye and mind" in which the departure from the *dispositif* of Renaissance perspective would match with the construction of an a priori phenomenological orientation capable of answering the unresolved difficulties introduced by Descartes and his optics. The problem of the relation of painting to the larger questions of perspective and modern science posed by Panofksy and Husserl, respectively, would then be taken up and reformulated by Lacan, Foucault, Lyotard, and Deleuze, leading to new concepts of "gaze" or "face" and to the relation between figure and discourse, word and image, sensibility and intelligibility. In painting. as in theater, it was thus a matter of rethinking the relations between general sensibility and dispositions of thought. Starting on either side of the larger dividing line Foucault drew in postwar French critical thought, we find not simply new formulations of the problem of the body but, with them, a larger shift in the constitutive forms of sensibility and the peculiar role they play in thinking in art.

In his "transcendental aesthetic," Kant had seen space and time as a priori forms of intuition. The search for a new role of the sensible body in thought was a search for new kinds of determinations of space and time outside Kant's centering of sensibility into a cognition of distinct objects for a transcendental "I think"; in the exploration of these other, disparate, decentered spaces and times, the arts would play a critical role. In particular, we find the isolation and elaboration of a kind of "aesthetic violence," tied up with an insistent, obtuse, paradoxical sense that the arts would serve to make visible and thinkable—a violence or cruelty of sensation itself as distinct from the "sensational violence" given in representations. How then was such a violence in the arts and of the arts to be related to the kind of clinical or traumatic violence developed by psychoanalysis, or the kind of historical or political violence that disrupts institutional arrangements? Aesthetics would thus play a crucial role in the search for a new critique. Art would be seen as a kind of endless war machine directed against controlled sensibilities and their role in the reigning and increasingly techno-scientific doxa, carried on in an experimental vein, without the assurances of a higher ur-doxa or republic. Art would thus become a clinical as well as a political matter; and politics and clinical practices would correspondingly find new relations with aesthetics. It was thus as if, following the war, the general sense of a loss of humanistic or essentialist-anthropological determinations of sensibility was experienced not with melancholy or nostalgia for tradition and its "community" but, on the contrary, as a kind of liberation, a chance, a source of a new kind of experimentation and critique, and a new sense of community or friendship in thought. To think in art, as in philosophy, one had to encounter the violence of something "unthought"; one had to pass through a sense of impossibility of continuing to speak, or see, or act in the same old ways. Conversely, the problem with Kant's a priori was precisely its ties to a pregiven "I think," a constituted or transcendental common sense in judgment as in cognition. In dispensing with this assumption, in turning rather to dissensus or questioning, critique became inseparable from creation or invention, just as real invention or creation was thought always to contain a violent, critical element.

The crucial and peculiar role of psychoanalysis in postwar French thought that took off from the work of Lacan can be understood in this light. With the development of the new critical aesthetic came the elaboration of a "French Freud," worked out through new translations and readings, in which the very idea of the "work" of the unconscious was understood in terms of the new idea of "oeuvre" and the idea of "oeuvre" in turn was understood in terms of the work of the unconscious. Thus, in his seminar on ethics of 1959–60, Lacan developed an original approach to the relation between art and trauma, as announced by Oedipus's daughter Antigone and then further refined by the Marquis de Sade with Kant. In relation to "the voice" and "the gaze" as objects and causes of desire, Lacan would go on to develop a notion of sublimation as the space in which our perverse desires gain social acceptability through the creation of objects that we then overvalue to the point of fetishization. For his part, Derrida would prefer to see Freud's "speculations" in terms of an ur-law of mystical responsibility, supposed by the act of writing and complicating Lacan's sense that the truth of unconscious desire always has "the structure of fiction." Deleuze and Foucault would each reject the very idea of "the Law" of desire and would look instead to the sort of vital possibilities Nietzsche had called "higher health" or to a kind of vital experimentation and subjectivization, going back to cynical free speech and requiring a peculiar courage and truth.

At the same time, across these divergences, another question arose concerning the larger relations of art and philosophy, or the problem of what it is to think in art. What kind of philosophical construction or work, what kind of philosophical universality, would be capable of including this singular critical violence and the necessarily extraterritorial space in which art and philosophy would mix along new lines? Without the advent of new questions and inventions, can there be a real philosophical heritage or inheritance? Can we therefore say that a foreign, untranslatable, dissensual element exists in all thinking and the kinds of critical history that preserve or transmit it? Does there not then exist an "absolute deterritorialization" in sensibility as a condition of thought itself and thus of its relation to the "relative deterritorializations" and displacements brought on by history? If so, one is never quite "at home" in philosophy as in art, and the question of nationality must be posed in new ways. Perhaps it is through such questions of problems, concepts, and inventions that the great ferment of French philosophy after World War II may live on, outside the peculiar and extraordinary postwar literary and artistic context within which it emerged. Perhaps there is no tradition, no civilization, without this strange, unruly, critical potential that philosophy shares with the arts and that each civilization has contended with in its own way. And so it may be that this kind of critical thinking will find new paths in a global context whose history Europe can no longer claim to monopolize and in which postwar French philosophy may be taken up in unforeseen ways—such that one can say of its future only that it is too early to tell.

MAURICE MERLEAU-PONTY

Eye and Mind

1964

The painter "takes his body with him," says Valéry. Indeed, we cannot imagine how a *mind* could paint. It is by lending his body to the world that the artist changes the world into paintings. To understand these transubstantiations we must go back to the working, actual body—not the body as a chunk of space or a bundle of functions but that body which is an intertwining of vision and movement.

I have only to see something to know how to reach it and deal with it, even if I do not know how this happens in the nervous machine. My mobile body makes a difference in the visible world, being a part of it; that is why I can steer it through the visible. Conversely, it is just as true that vision is attached to movement. We see only what we look at. What would vision be without eye movement? And how could the movement of the eyes bring things together if the movement were blind? If it were only a reflex? If it did not have its antennae, its clairvoyance? If vision were not prefigured in it?

In principle all my changes of place figure in a corner of my landscape; they are recorded on the map of the visible. Everything I see is in principle within my reach, at least within reach of my sight, and is marked upon the map of the "I can." Each of the two maps is complete. The visible world and the world of my motor projects are each total parts of the same Being.

This extraordinary overlapping, which we never think about sufficiently, forbids us to conceive of vision as an operation of thought that would set up before the mind a picture or a representation of the world, a world of immanence and of ideality. Immersed in the visible by his body, itself visible, the see-er does not appropriate what he sees; he merely approaches it by looking, he opens himself to the world. And on its side, this world of which he is a part is not *in itself*, or matter. My movement is not a decision made by the mind, an absolute doing which would decree, from the depths of a subjective retreat,

From *The Primacy of Perception and Other Essays on Phenomenological Psychology, the Philosophy of Art, History and Politics*, ed. James M. Edie (Evanston, IL: Northwestern University Press, 1964), pp. 162–65, 169–70, 172–73, 174–75, 189–90 [*L'oeil et l'esprit* (Paris: Editions Gallimard, 1964)].

some change of place miraculously executed in extended space. It is the natural consequence and the maturation of my vision. I say of a thing that it is moved; but my body moves itself, my movement deploys itself. It is not ignorant of itself; it is not blind for itself; it radiates from a self.

The enigma is that my body simultaneously sees and is seen. That which looks at all things can also look at itself and recognize, in what it sees, the "other side" of its power of looking. It sees itself seeing; it touches itself touching; it is visible and sensitive for itself. It is not a self through transparence, like thought, which only thinks its object by assimilating it, by constituting it, by transforming it into thought. It is a self through confusion, narcissism, through inherence of the one who sees in that which he sees, and through inherence of sensing in the sensed—a self, therefore, that is caught up in things, that has a front and a back, a past and a future. . . .

This initial paradox cannot but produce others. Visible and mobile, my body is a thing among things; it is caught in the fabric of the world, and its cohesion is that of a thing. But because it moves itself and sees, it holds things in a circle around itself.[1] Things are an annex or prolongation of itself; they are incrusted into its flesh, they are part of its full definition; the world is made of the same stuff as the body. This way of turning things around [*ces renversements*], these antinomies,[2] are different ways of saying that vision happens among, or is caught in, things—in that place where something visible undertakes to see, becomes visible for itself by virtue of the sight of things; in that place where there persists, like the mother water in crystal, the undividedness [*l'indivision*] of the sensing and the sensed.

This interiority no more precedes the material arrangement of the human body than it results from it. What if our eyes were made in such a way as to prevent our seeing any part of our body, or if some baneful arrangement of the body were to let us move our hands over things, while preventing us from touching our own body? Or what if, like certain animals, we had lateral eyes with no cross blending of visual fields? Such a body would not reflect itself; it would be an almost adamantine body, not really flesh, not really the body of a human being. There would be no humanity.

But humanity is not produced as the effect of our articulations or by the way our eyes are implanted in us (still less by the existence of mirrors that could make our entire body visible to us). These contingencies and others like them, without which mankind would not exist, do not by simple summation bring it about that there *is* a single man.

The body's animation is not the assemblage or juxtaposition of its parts. Nor is it a question of a mind or spirit coming down from somewhere else into an automaton; this would still suppose that the body itself is without an inside and without a "self." There is a human body when, between the seeing and the seen, between touching and the touched, between one eye and the other, between hand and hand, a blending of some sort takes place—when the spark is lit between sensing and sensible, lighting the fire that will not stop burning until some accident of the body will undo what no accident would have sufficed to do. . . .

Once this strange system of exchanges is given, we find before us all the problems of painting. These exchanges illustrate the enigma of the body, and this enigma justifies them. Since things and my body are made of the same stuff, vision must somehow take place in them; their manifest visibility must be repeated in the body by a secret visibility. "Nature is on the inside," says Cézanne. Quality, light, color, depth, which are there before us, are there only because they awaken an echo in our body and because the body welcomes them.

Things have an internal equivalent in me; they arouse in me a carnal formula of their presence. Why shouldn't these [correspondences] in turn give rise to some [external] visible shape in which anyone else would recognize those motifs which support his own inspection of the world?[3] Thus there appears a "visible" of the second power, a carnal essence or icon of the first. It is not a faded copy, a trompe l'oeil, or another *thing*. The animals painted on the walls of Lascaux are not there in the same way as the fissures and limestone formations. But they are not *elsewhere*. Pushed forward here, held back there, held up by the wall's mass they use so adroitly, they spread around the wall without ever breaking from their elusive moorings in it. I would be at great pains to say *where* is the painting I am looking at. For I do not look at it as I do at a thing; I do not fix it in its place. My gaze wanders in it as in the halos of Being. It is more accurate to say that I see according to it, or with it, than I *see it*.

The word "image" is in bad repute because we have thoughtlessly believed that a design was a tracing, a copy, a second thing, and that the mental image was such a design, belonging among our private bric-a-brac. But if in fact it is nothing of the kind, then neither the design nor the painting belongs to the in-itself any more than the image does. They are the inside of the outside and the outside of the inside, which the duplicity of feeling [*le sentir*] makes possible and without which we would never understand the quasi presence and imminent visibility which make up the whole problem of the imaginary. The picture and the actor's mimicry are not devices to be borrowed from the real world in order to signify prosaic things which are absent. For the imaginary is much nearer to, and much farther away from, the actual—nearer because it is in my body as a diagram of the life of the actual, with all its pulp and carnal obverse [*son envers charnel*] exposed to view for the first time. In this sense, Giacometti[4] says energetically, "What interests me in all paintings is resemblance—that is, what is resemblance for me: something which makes me discover more of the world." And the imaginary is much farther away from the actual because the painting is an analogue or likeness only according to the body; because it does not present the mind with an occasion to rethink the constitutive relations of things; because, rather, it offers our sight [*regard*], so that it might join with them, the inward traces of vision, and because it offers to vision its inward tapestries, the imaginary texture of the real.[5] [. . .]

How crystal clear everything would be in our philosophy if only we could exorcise these specters, make illusions or objectless perceptions out of them, keep them on the edge of a world that doesn't equivocate!

Descartes's *Dioptric* is an attempt to do just that. It is the breviary of a thought that wants no longer to abide in the visible and so decides to construct the visible according to a model-in-thought. It is worthwhile to remember this attempt and its failure.

Here there is no concern to cling to vision. The problem is to know "how it happens," but only so far as it is necessary to invent, whenever the need arises, certain "artificial organs"[6] that correct it. We are to reason not so much upon the light we see as upon the light that, from outside, enters our eyes and commands our vision. And for that we are to rely upon "two or three comparisons which help us to conceive it [light]" in such a way as to explain its known properties and to deduce others.[7] The question being so formulated, it is best to think of light as an action by contact—not unlike the action of things upon the blind man's cane. The blind, says Descartes, "see with their hands."[8] The Cartesian concept of vision is modeled after the sense of touch.

At one swoop, then, he removes action at a distance and relieves us of that ubiquity which is the whole problem of vision (as well as its peculiar virtue). Why should we henceforth puzzle over reflections and mirrors? These unreal duplications are a class of things; they are real effects like a ball's bouncing. If the reflection resembles the thing itself, it is because this reflection acts upon the eyes more or less as a thing would. It deceives the eye by engendering a perception which has no object but which does not affect our idea of the world. In the world there is the thing itself, and outside this thing itself there is that other thing which is only reflected light rays and which happens to have an ordered correspondence with the real thing; there are two individuals, then, bound together externally by causality. As far as the thing and its mirror image are concerned, their resemblance belongs to thought. [What for us is] the "cross-eyed" [*louche*] relationship of resemblance is—in the things—a clear relationship of projection.

A Cartesian does not see *himself* in the mirror; he sees a dummy, an "outside," which, he has every reason to believe, other people see in the very same way but which, no more for himself than for others, is not a body in the flesh. His "image" in the mirror is an effect of the mechanics of things. If he recognizes himself in it, if he thinks it "looks like him," it is his thought that weaves this connection. The mirror image is nothing that belongs to him.

. . .

For Descartes it is unarguably evident that one can paint only existing things, that their existence consists in being extended, and that design, or line drawing, alone makes painting possible by making the representation of extension possible. Thus painting is only an artifice which presents to our eyes a projection similar to that which the things themselves in ordinary perception would and do inscribe in our eyes. A painting makes us see in the same way in which we actually see the thing itself, even though the thing is absent. Especially it makes us see a space where there is none.[9]

The picture is a flat thing contriving to give us what we would see in the [actual] presence of "diversely contoured" things, by offering sufficient diacritical signs of the missing dimension, according to height and width.[10] Depth is a third dimension derived from the other two.

It will pay us to dwell for a moment upon this third dimension. It has, first of all, something paradoxical about it. I see objects which hide each other and which consequently I do not see; each one stands behind the other. I see it [the third dimension] and it is not visible, since it goes toward things from, as a starting point, this body to which I myself am fastened. But the mystery here is a false one. I don't really see it [the third dimension], or if I do, it is only another *size* [measured by height and width]. On the line that lies between my eyes and the horizon, the first [vertical] plane forever hides all the others, and if from side to side I think I see things spread out in order before me, it is because they do not completely hide each other. Thus I see each thing to be outside the others, according to some measure otherwise reckoned [*autrement compté*].[11] We are always on this side of space or beyond it entirely. It is never the case that things really *are* one behind the other. The fact that things overlap or are hidden does not enter into their definition, and expresses only my incomprehensible solidarity with one of them—my body. And whatever might be positive in these facts, they are only thoughts that I formulate and not attributes of the things. I know that at this very moment another man, situated elsewhere—or better, God, who is everywhere—could penetrate their "hiding place" and see them openly deployed. Either what I call depth is nothing, or else it is my participation in a Being without restriction, a participation primarily in the being of space beyond every [particular] point of view. Things encroach upon one another *because each is outside of the others*. The proof of this is that I can see depth in a painting which everyone agrees has none and which organizes for me an illusion of an illusion. . . . This two-dimensional being,[12] which makes me see another [dimension], is a being that is opened up [*troué*]—as the men of the Renaissance said, a window . . .

But in the last analysis, the window opens only upon those *partes extra partes*, upon height and width seen merely from another angle—upon the absolute positivity of Being.

It is this identity of Being, or this space without hiding places that in each of its points is only what it is, neither more nor less, that underlies the analysis of copper engravings. Space is in-itself; rather, it is the in-itself par excellence. Its definition is *to be* in itself. Every point of space is and is thought to be right where it is—one here, another there; space is the evidence of the "where." Orientation, polarity, envelopment are, in space, derived phenomena inextricably bound to my presence. Space remains absolutely in itself, everywhere equal to itself, homogenous; its dimensions, for example, are interchangeable.

He was right also in taking his inspiration from the perspectival techniques of the Renaissance; they encouraged painting to freely produce experiences of depth and, in general, presentations of Being. These techniques were false only insofar as they pretended to bring an end to painting's quest and history, to found once and for all an exact and infallible art of painting. As Panofsky has shown concerning the men of the Renaissance,[13] this enthusiasm was not without bad faith. The theoreticians tried to forget the spherical visual field of the ancients, their angular perspective which relates the apparent size not to distance but to the angle form which we see the object. They wanted to forget what they disdainfully called the *perspective naturalis*, or *communis*, in favor of a *perspective artificialis* capable in principle of founding an exact construction. To accredit this myth, they went so far as to expurgate Euclid, omitting from their translations that eighth theorem, which bothered them so much. But the painters, on the other hand, knew from experience that no technique of perspective is an exact solution and that there is no projection of the existing world that respects it in all aspects and deserves to become the fundamental law of painting. They knew too that linear perspective was so far from being an ultimate breakthrough that, on the contrary, it opens several pathways for painting. For example, the Italians took the way of representing the object, but the northern painters discovered and worked out the formal technique of *Hochraum*, *Nahraum*, and *Schrägraum*. Thus plane projection does not always provoke our thought to reach the true form of things, as Descartes believed. Beyond a certain degree of deformation, it refers back, on the contrary, to our own vantage point. And the painted objects are left to retreat into a remoteness out of reach of all thought. Something in space escapes our attempts to look at it from "above."

Panofsky shows that the "problems" of painting that magnetize its history are often solved obliquely, not in the course of inquiries instigated to solve them but, on the contrary, at some point when the painters, having reached an impasse, apparently forgot those problems and permit themselves to be attracted by other things. Then suddenly, altogether off guard, they turn up the old problems and surmount the obstacle. This unhearing [*sourde*] historicity, advancing through the labyrinth by detours, transgression, slow encroachments, and sudden drives, does not imply that the painter does not know what he wants. It does imply that what he wants is beyond the means and goals at hand and commands from afar all our *useful* activity.

We are so fascinated by the classical idea of intellectual adequation that painting's mute "thinking" sometimes leaves us with the impression of a vain swirl of significations, a paralyzed or miscarried utterance. Suppose, then, that one answers that no thought ever detaches itself completely from a sustaining support; that the only privilege of speaking-thought is to have rendered its own support manageable; that the figurations of literature and philosophy are no more settled than those of painting and are no more capable of being accumulated into a stable treasure; that even science learns to recognize a zone of the "fundamental," peopled with dense, open, rent [*déchirés*] beings of which an exhaustive treatment is out of the question—like the cyberneticians' "aesthetic information" or mathematical-physical "groups of operations"; that, in the end, we are never in a position to take stock of everything objectively or to think of progress in itself; and that the whole of human history is, in a certain sense, stationary. *What*, says the understanding, like [Stendhal's] Lamiel, is it only that?

Is this the highest point of reason, to realize that the soil beneath our feet is shifting, to pompously name "interrogation" what is only a persistent state of stupor, to call "research" or "quest" what is only trudging in a circle, to call "Being" that which never fully *is*?

But this disappointment issues from the spurious fantasy[14] that claims for itself a positivity capable of making up for its own emptiness. It is the regret of not being everything, and a rather groundless regret at that. For if we cannot establish a hierarchy of civilizations or speak of progress—neither in painting nor in anything else that matters—it is not because some fate holds us back; it is, rather, because the very first painting in some sense went to the farthest reach of the future. If no painting comes to be *the* painting, if no work is ever absolutely completed and done with, still each creation changes, alters, enlightens, deepens, confirms, exalts, re-creates, or creates in advance all the others. If creations are not a possession, it is not only that, like all things, they pass away; it is also that they have almost all their life still before them.

NOTES

[1] Cf. *Le visible et l'invisible* (Paris, 1964), pp. 273, 308–11.—*Trans.*

[2] See *Signes* (Paris, 1960), pp. 210, 222–23, especially the footnotes, for a clarification of the "circularity" at issue here.—*Trans.*

[3] Cet equivalent interne, cette formule charnelle de leur presence que les choses suscitent en moi, pourquoi à leur tour ne susciteraient-ils pas un trace, visible encore, où tout autre regard retrouvera les motifs qui soutiennent son inspection du monde?

[4] G. Charbonnier, *Le monologue du peintre* (Paris, 1959), p. 172.

[5] Beaucoup plus loin, puisque le tableau n'est un analogue que selon le corps qu'il n'offre pas à l'esprit une occasion de repenser les rapports constitutifs des choses, mais au regard, pour qu'il les épouse, les traces de la vision du dedans, à la vision ce qui la tapisse intérieurement, la texture imaginaire du réel.

[6] Descartes, *La dioptrique*, Discours VII [conclusion]. Edition Adam et Tannery, VI, p. 165.

[7] Ibid., Discours I, Adam et Tannery, p. 83. [*Oeuvres et lettres de Descartes*, ed. André Bridoux, Edition Pléiade, p. 181. Page references from the Bridoux selections have been added in the belief that this volume is more widely accessible today than the Adam and Tannery complete edition.]

[8] Ibid., Adam et Tannery, p. 84. [Bridoux, p. 182.]

[9] The system of means by which painting makes us see is a scientific matter. Why, then, do we not methodically produce perfect images of the world, arriving at a universal art purged of personal art, just as the universal language would free us of all the confused relationships that lurk in existent languages?

[10] *Dioptrique*, Discours IV, Adam et Tannery, pp. 112–14. [Bridoux, pp. 203–4, in English, *Descartes: Philosophical Writings*, ed. and trans. N. Kemp Smith, Modern Library Edition, pp. 145–47.]

[11] Discours V of the *Dioptrique*, especially Descartes's diagrams, helps considerably to clarify the compressed diagrams.—*Trans.*

[12] That is, the painting.—*Trans.*

[13] E. Panofsky, *Die Perspektive als symbolische Form*, in *Vorträge der Bibliotek Warburg*, IV (1924–25).

[14] "Mais cette deception est celle du faux imaginaire, qui . . ."

MICHEL FOUCAULT

Of Other Spaces

1967

This text, entitled "Des espaces autres" and published by the French journal Architecture-Mouvement-Continuité *in October 1984, was the basis of a lecture given by Michel Foucault in March 1967. Although not reviewed for publication by the author and thus not part of the official corpus of his work, the manuscript was released into the public domain for an exhibition in Berlin shortly before Michel Foucault's death. Attentive readers will note that that the text retains the quality of lecture notes.* Diacritics *wishes to thank Jay Miskowiec for securing permission to translate the text and for furnishing his translation to us.* [Ed.]

The great obsession of the nineteenth century was, as we know, history: with its themes of development and of suspension, of crisis and cycle, themes of the ever-accumulating past, with its great preponderance of dead men and the menacing glaciation of the world. The nineteenth century found its essential mythological resources in the second principle of thermodynamics. The present epoch will perhaps be above all the epoch of space. We are in the epoch of simultaneity: we are in the epoch of juxtaposition, the epoch of the near and far, of the side-by-side, of the dispersed. We are at a moment, I believe, when our experience of the world is less that of a long life developing through time than that of a network that connects points and intersects with its own skein. One could perhaps say that certain ideological conflicts animating present-day polemics oppose the pious descendents of time and the determined inhabitants of space. Structuralism, or at least that which is grouped under this slightly too general name, is the effort to establish, between elements that could have been connected on a temporal axis, an ensemble of relations that makes them appear as juxtaposed, set off against one another, implicated by each other—that makes them appear, in short, as a sort of configuration. Actually,

From *Diacritics* 16, no. 1 (Spring 1986), pp. 22–27; trans. Jay Miskowiec ["Des espaces autres," *Architecture-Mouvement-Continuité*, October 1984].

structuralism does not entail a denial of time; it does involve a certain manner of dealing with what we call time and what we call history.

Yet it is necessary to notice that the space which today appears to form the horizon of our concerns, our theory, our systems, is not an innovation; space itself has a history in Western experience and it is not possible to disregard the fatal intersection of time with space. One could say, by way of retracing this history of space very roughly, that in the Middle Ages there was a hierarchic ensemble of places: sacred places and profane places; protected places and open, exposed places; urban places and rural places (all these concern the real life of men). In cosmological theory, there were the supercelestial places, as opposed to the celestial, and the celestial place was in turn opposed to the terrestrial place. There were places where things had been put because they had been violently displaced, and then on the contrary places where things found their natural ground and stability. It was this complete hierarchy, this opposition, this intersection of places that constituted what could very roughly be called medieval space: the space of emplacement.

This space of emplacement was opened up by Galileo. For the real scandal of Galileo's work lay not so much in his discovery, or rediscovery, that the earth revolved around the sun, but in his constitution of an infinite, and infinitely open space. In such a space the place of the Middle Ages turned out to be dissolved, as it were; a thing's place was no longer anything but a point in its movement, just as the stability of a thing was only its movement indefinitely slowed down. In other words, starting with Galileo and the seventeenth century, extension was substituted for localization.

Today the site has been substituted for extension which itself has replaced emplacement. The site is defined by relations of proximity between points or elements; formally, we can describe these relations as series, trees, or grids. Moreover, the importance of the site as a problem in contemporary technical work is well known: the storage of data or of the intermediate results of a calculation in the memory of a machine; the circulation of discrete elements with a random output (automobile traffic is a simple case, or indeed the sounds on a telephone line); the identification of marked or coded elements inside a set that may be randomly distributed, or may be arranged according to single or to multiple classifications.

In a still more concrete manner, the problem of siting or placement arises for mankind in terms of demography. This problem of the human site or living space is not simply that of knowing whether there will be enough space for men in the world—a problem that is certainly quite important—but also that of knowing what relations of propinquity, what type of storage, circulation, marking, and classification of human elements should be adopted in a given situation in order to achieve a given end. Our epoch is one in which space takes for us the form of relations among sites.

In any case I believe that the anxiety of our era has to do fundamentally with space, no doubt a great deal more than with time. Time probably appears to us only as one of the various distributive operations that are possible for the elements that are spread out in space.

Now, despite all the techniques for appropriating space, despite the whole network of knowledge that enables us to delimit or to formalize it, contemporary space is perhaps still not entirely desanctified (apparently unlike time, it would seem, which was detached from the sacred in the nineteenth century). To be sure a certain theoretical desanctification of space (the one signaled by Galileo's work) has occurred, but we may still not have reached the point of a practical desanctification of space. And perhaps our life is still governed by a certain number of oppositions that remain inviolable, that our institutions and practices have not yet dared to break down. These are oppositions that we regard as simple givens: for example between private space and public space, between family space and social space, between cultural space and useful space, between the space of leisure and that of work. All these are still nurtured by the hidden presence of the sacred.

Bachelard's monumental work and the descriptions of phenomenologists have taught us that we do not live in a homogeneous and empty space, but on the contrary in a space thoroughly imbued with quantities and perhaps thoroughly fantasmatic as well. The space of our primary perception, the space of our dreams and that of our passions hold within themselves qualities that seem intrinsic: there is a light, ethereal, transparent space, or again a dark, rough, encumbered space; a space from above, of summits, or on the contrary a space from below, of mud; or again a space that can be flowing like sparkling water, or a space that is fixed, congealed, like stone or crystal. Yet these analyses, while fundamental for reflection in our time, primarily concern internal space. I should like to speak now of external space.

The space in which we live, which draws us out of ourselves, in which the erosion of our lives, our time and our history occurs, the space that claws and gnaws at us, is also, in itself, a heterogeneous space. In other words, we do not live in a kind of void, inside of which we could place individuals and things. We do not live inside a void that could be colored with diverse shades of light, we live inside a set of relations that delineates sites which are irreducible to one another and absolutely not superimposable on one another.

Of course one might attempt to describe these different sites by looking for the set of relations by which a given site can be defined. For example, describing the set of relations that define the sites of transportation, streets, trains (a train is an extraordinary bundle of relations because it is something through which one goes, it is also something by means of which one can go from one point to another, and then it is also something that goes by). One could describe, via the cluster of relations that allows them to be defined, the sites of temporary relaxation—cafes, cinemas, beaches. Likewise one could describe, via its network of relations, the closed or semi-closed sites of rest—the house, the bedroom, the bed, et cetera. But among all these sites, I am interested in certain ones that have the curious property of being in relation with all the other sites, but in such a way as to suspect, neutralize, or invert the set of relations that they happen to designate, mirror, or reflect. These spaces, as it were, which are linked with all the others, which however contradict all the other sites, are of two main types.

First there are the utopias. Utopias are sites with no real place. They are sites that have a general relation of direct or inverted analogy with the real space of Society. They present society itself in a perfected form, or else society turned upside down, but in any case these utopias are fundamentally unreal spaces.

There are also, probably in every culture, in every civilization, real places—places that do exist and that are formed in the very founding society—which are something like counter-sites, a kind of effectively enacted utopia in which the real sites, all the other real sites that can be found within the culture, are simultaneously represented, contested, and inverted. Places of this kind are outside of all places, even though it may be possible to indicate their location in reality. Because these places are absolutely different from all the sites that they reflect and speak about, I shall call them, by way of contrast to utopias, heterotopias. I believe that between utopias and these quite other sites, these heterotopias, there might be a sort of mixed, joint experience, which would be the mirror. The mirror is, after all, a utopia, since it is a placeless place. In the mirror, I see myself there where I am not, in an unreal, virtual space that opens up behind the surface; I am over there, there where I am not, a sort of shadow that gives my own visibility to myself, that enables me to see myself there where I am absent: such is the utopia of the mirror. But it is also a heterotopia in so far as the mirror does exist in reality, where it exerts a sort of counteraction on the position that I occupy. From the standpoint of the mirror I discover my absence from the place where I am since I see myself over there. Starting from this gaze that is, as it were, directed toward me, from the ground of this virtual space that is on the other side of the glass, I come back toward myself; I begin again to direct my eyes toward myself and to reconstitute myself there where I am. The mirror functions as a heterotopia in this respect: it makes this place that I occupy at the moment when I look at myself in the glass at once absolutely real, connected with all the space that surrounds it, and absolutely unreal, since in order to be perceived it has to pass through this virtual point which is over there.

As for the heterotopias as such, how can they be descried, what meaning do they have? We might imagine a sort of systematic description—I do not say a science because the term is too galvanized now—that would, in a given society, take as its object the study, analysis, description, and "reading" (as some like to say nowadays) of these different spaces, of these other places. As a sort of simultaneously mythic and real contestation of the space in which we live, this description could be called heterotopology. Its *first principle* is that there is probably not a single culture in the world that fails to constitute heterotopias. That is a constant of every human group. But the heterotopias obviously take quite varied forms, and perhaps no one absolutely universal form of heterotopia would be found. We can however classify them in two main categories.

In the so-called primitive societies, there is a certain form of heterotopia that I would call crisis heterotopias, i.e., there are privileged or sacred or forbidden places, reserved for individuals who are, in relation to society and to the human environment in which they live, in a state of crisis: adolescents, menstruating women, pregnant women, the elderly, etc. In our society, these crisis heterotopias are persistently disappearing, though a few remnants can still be found. For example, the boarding school, in its nineteenth-century form, or military service for young men, have certainly played such a role, as the first manifestations of sexual virility were in fact supposed to take place "elsewhere" than at home. For girls, there was, until the middle of the twentieth century, a tradition called the "honeymoon trip" which was an ancestral theme. The young woman's deflowering could take place "nowhere" and, at the moment of its occurrence the train or honeymoon hotel was indeed the place of this nowhere, this heterotopia without geographical markers.

But these heterotopias of crisis are disappearing today and are being replaced, I believe, by what we might call heterotopias of deviation: those in which individuals whose behavior is deviant in relation to the required mean or norm are placed. Cases of this are rest homes and psychiatric hospitals, and of course prisons; and one should perhaps add retirement homes that are, as it were, on the borderline between the heterotopia of crisis and the heterotopia of deviation since, after all, old age is a crisis, but is also a deviation since, in our society where leisure is the rule, idleness is a sort of deviation.

The *second principle* of this description of heterotopias is that a society, as its history unfolds, can make an existing heterotopia function in a very different fashion; for each heterotopia has a precise and determined function within a society and the same heterotopia can, according to the synchrony of the culture in which it occurs, have on function or another.

As an example I shall take the strange heterotopia of the cemetery. The cemetery is certainly a place unlike ordinary cultural spaces. It is a space that is however connected with all the sites of the city-state or society or village, etc., since each individual, each family has relatives in the cemetery. In western culture the cemetery has practically always existed. But it has undergone important changes. Until the end of the eighteenth century, the cemetery was placed at the heart of the city, next to the church. In it there was a hierarchy of possible tombs. There was the charnel house in which bodies lost the last traces of individuality, there were a few individual tombs and then there were the tombs inside the church. These latter tombs were themselves of two types, either simply tombstones with an inscription, or mausoleums with statues. This cemetery housed inside the sacred space of the church has taken on a quite different cast in modern civilizations, and curiously, it is in a time when civilization has become "atheistic," as one says very crudely, that western culture has established what is termed the cult of the dead.

Basically it was quite natural that, in a time of real belief in the resurrection of bodies and the immortality of the soul, overriding importance was not accorded to the body's remains. On the contrary, from the moment when people are no longer sure that they have a soul or that the body will regain life, it is perhaps necessary to give much more attention to the dead body, which is ultimately the only trace of our existence in the world and in language. In any case, it is from the beginning of the nineteenth century that everyone has a right to her or his own little box for her or his own little personal decay; but on the other hand, it is only from that start of the nineteenth century that cemeteries began to be located at the outside border of cities. In correlation with the individualization of death and the bourgeois appropriation of the cemetery, there arises an obsession with death as an "illness." The dead, it is supposed, bring illnesses to the living, and it is the presence and proximity of the dead right beside the houses, next to the church, almost in the middle of the street, it is this proximity that propagates death itself. This major theme of illness spread by the contagion in the cemeteries persisted until the end of the eighteenth century, until, during the nineteenth century, the shift of cemeteries toward the suburbs was initiated. The cemeteries then came to constitute, no longer the sacred and immortal heart of the city, but "the other city," where each family possesses its dark resting place.

Third principle. The heterotopia is capable of juxtaposing in a single real place several spaces, several sites that are in themselves incompatible. Thus it is that the theater brings onto the rectangle of the stage, one after the other, a whole series of places that are foreign to one another; thus it is that the cinema is a very odd rectangular room, at the end of which, on a two-dimensional screen, one sees the projection of a three-dimensional space; but perhaps the oldest example of these heterotopias that take the form of contradictory sites is the garden. We must not forget that in the Orient the garden, an astonishing creation that is now a thousand years old, had very deep and seemingly superimposed meanings. The traditional garden of the Persians was a sacred space that was supposed to bring together inside its rectangle four parts representing the four parts of the world, with a space still more sacred than the others that were like an umbilicus, the navel of the world at its center (the basin and water fountain were there); and all the vegetation of the garden was supposed to come together in this space, in this sort of microcosm. As for carpets, they were originally reproductions of gardens (the garden is a rug onto which the whole world comes to enact its symbolic perfection, and the rug is a sort of garden that can move across space). The garden is the smallest parcel of the world and then it is the totality of the world. The garden has been a sort of happy, universalizing heterotopia since the beginnings of antiquity (our modern zoological gardens spring from that source).

Fourth principle. Heterotopias are most often linked to slices in time—which is to say that they open onto what might be termed, for the sake of symmetry, heterochronies. The heterotopia begins to function at full capacity when men arrive at a sort of absolute break with their traditional time. This situation shows us that the cemetery is indeed a highly heterotopic place since, for the individual, the cemetery begins with this strange heterochrony, the loss of life, and with this quasi-eternity in which her permanent lot is dissolution and disappearance.

From a general standpoint, in a society like ours heterotopias and heterochronies are structured and distributed in a relatively complex fashion. First of all, there are heterotopias of indefinitely accumulating time, for example museums and libraries. Museums and libraries have become heterotopias in which time never stops building up and topping its own summit, whereas in the seventeenth century, even at the end of the century, museums and libraries were the expression of an individual choice. By contrast, the idea of accumulating everything, of establishing a sort of general archive, the will to enclose in one place all times, all epochs, all forms, all tastes, the idea of constituting a place of all times that is itself outside of time and inaccessible to its ravages, the project of organizing in this way a sort of perpetual and indefinite accumulation of time in an immobile place, this whole idea belongs to our modernity. The museum and the library are heterotopias that are proper to western culture of the nineteenth century.

Opposite these heterotopias that are linked to the accumulation of time, there are those linked, on the contrary, to time in its most fleeting, transitory, precarious aspect, to time in the mode of the festival. These heterotopias are not oriented toward the eternal, they are rather absolutely temporal [*chroniques*]. Such, for example, are the fairgrounds, these marvelous empty sites on the outskirts of cities that teem once or twice a year with stands, displays, heteroclite objects, wrestlers, snakewomen, fortune-tellers, and so forth. Quite recently, a new kind of temporal heterotopia has been invented: vacation villages, such as those Polynesian villages that offer a compact three weeks of primitive and eternal nudity to the inhabitants of the cities. You see, moreover, that through the two forms of heterotopias that come together here, the heterotopia of the festival and that of the eternity of accumulating time, the huts of Djerba are in a sense relatives of libraries and museums. For the rediscovery of Polynesian life abolishes time; yet the experience is just as much the rediscovery of time, it is as if the entire history of humanity reaching back to its origin were accessible in a sort of immediate knowledge.

Fifth principle. Heterotopias always presuppose a system of opening and closing that both isolates them and makes them penetrable. In general, the heterotopic site is not freely accessible like a public place. Either the entry is compulsory, as in the case of entering a barracks or a prison, or else the individual has to submit to rites and purifications. To get in one must have a certain permission and make certain gestures. Moreover, there are even heterotopias that are entirely consecrated to these activities of purification—purification that is partly religious and partly hygienic, such as the hamman of the Moslems, or else purification that appears to be purely hygienic, as in Scandinavian saunas.

There are others, on the contrary, that seem to be pure and simple openings, but that generally hide curious exclusions. Everyone can enter into these heterotopic sites, but in fact that is only an illusion: we think we enter where we are, by the very fact that we enter, excluded. I am thinking, for example, of the famous bedrooms that existed on the great farms of Brazil and elsewhere in South America. The entry door did not lead into the central room where the family lived, and every individual or traveler who came by had the right to open this door, to enter into the bedroom and to sleep there for a night. Now these bedrooms were such that the individual who went into them never had access to the family's quarters; the visitor was absolutely the guest in transit, was not really the invited guest. This type of heterotopia, which has practically disappeared from our civilizations, could perhaps be found in the famous American motel rooms where a man goes with his car and his mistress and where illicit sex is both absolutely sheltered and absolutely hidden, kept isolated without however being allowed out in the open.

The last trait of heterotopias is that they have a function in relation to all the space that remains. This function unfolds between two extreme poles. Either their role is to create a space of illusion that exposes every real space, all the sites inside of which human life is partitioned, as still more illusory (perhaps that is the role that was played by those famous brothels of which we are now deprived). Or else, on the contrary, their role is to create a space that is other, another real space, as perfect, as meticulous, as well arranged as ours is messy, ill constructed, and jumbled. This latter type would be the heterotopia, not of illusion, but of compensation, and I wonder if certain colonies have not functioned somewhat in this manner. In certain cases, they have played, on the level of the general organization of terrestrial space, the role of heterotopias. I am thinking, for example, of the first wave of colonization in the seventeenth century, of the Puritan societies that the English had founded in America and that were absolutely perfect other places. I am also thinking of those extraordinary Jesuit colonies that were founded in South America: marvelous, absolutely regulated colonies in which human perfection was effectively achieved. The Jesuits of Paraguay established colonies in which existence was regulated at every turn. The village was laid out according to a rigorous plan around a rectangular place at the foot of which was the church; on one side, there was the school; on the other, the cemetery; and then, in front of the church, an avenue set out that another crossed at right angles; each family had its little cabin along these two axes and thus the sign of Christ was exactly reproduced. Christianity marked the space and geography of the American world with its fundamental sign. The daily life of individuals was regulated, not by the whistle, but by the bell. Everyone was awakened at the same time, everyone began work at the same time; meals were at noon and five o'clock; then came bedtime, and at midnight came what was called the marital wake-up, that is, at the chime of the churchbell, each person carried out her/his duty.

Brothels and colonies are two extreme types of heterotopia, and if we think, after all, that the boat is a floating piece of space, a place without a place, that exists by itself, that is closed in on itself and at the same time is given over to the infinity of the sea and that, from port to port, from tack to tack, from brothel to brothel, it goes as far as the colonies in search of the most precious treasures they conceal in their gardens, you will understand why the boat has not only been for our civilization, from the sixteenth century until the present, the great instrument of economic development (I have not been speaking of that today), but has been simultaneously the greatest reserve of the imagination. The ship is the heterotopia *par excellence*. In civilizations without boats, dreams dry up, espionage takes the place of adventure, and the police take the place of pirates.

MICHEL FOUCAULT

Words and Images

1967

Forgive my lack of competence. I am not an art historian. Until last month I had read nothing by Panofsky. Two [French] translations appeared simultaneously: the famous *Studies in Iconology*, now almost thirty years old (including five essays on the Renaissance, preceded by a lengthy reflection on method which links them all together, along with a preface to the French edition by Bernard Teyssèdre), and two studies of the Gothic Middle Ages with a commentary by Pierre Bourdieu.

After such a lengthy period of time, this simultaneity is striking. I am not in a good position to say what benefit specialists are likely to derive from this long-awaited publication. As a neophyte Panofskyan, and of course an enthusiast, I will use the master's own words to explain his fate, and I will venture to say that the benefit will be great: these translations are going to transform what to us is the remote and alien field of *iconology* into a *habitus*. For apprentice historians, these concepts and methods will cease to be what they must learn and become the basis of the way they see, read, interpret, and understand.

But I won't speculate. I would rather just say what I found new in these texts, which for others are already classics: namely, the dislocation they invite us to share, a dislocation that we may and I hope will find disorienting.

Let me begin with an example: the analysis of the relations between discourse and the visible.

We are convinced, we *know*, that in a culture everything speaks: the structures of language impose their form on the order of things. This is merely another version (a fruitful one, to be sure) of the axiom of the sovereignty of discourse, which classical iconography already took for granted. For Emile Müle, plastic forms were texts invested in stone, line, or color. To analyze a

From "Les mots et les images," review of Erwin Panofsky, *Essais d'iconologie*, in *Dits et écrits, tome I: 1954–1975*, ed. Daniel Defert and François Ewald with the assistance of Jacques Lagrange (1994; Paris: Editions Gallimard, 2001), and *Architecture gothique et pensée scolastique* (Paris: Editions de Minuit, 1967), first published in *Le Nouvel Observateur*, no. 154 (October 25, 1967), pp. 49–50; trans. Arthur Goldhammer.

capital or an illumination was to reveal "what it meant," to restore language where in order to speak more directly language had stripped itself of its words. Not to insist on the autonomy of the plastic universe but to describe the complexity of relationships: intersection, isomorphism, transformation, translation—in short, the whole panoply of the *visible* and the *sayable* that characterizes a culture at a particular point in its history.

Sometimes elements of discourse remain as *themes* across texts, copied manuscripts, or works translated, commented on, and imitated; yet they take shape in plastic *motifs*, which are subject to change (the abduction of Europa, taken from a text of Ovid, is depicted as a scene of bathing in a fourteenth-century miniature but as a violent kidnapping by Dürer). Sometimes the plastic form remains frozen yet accommodates a succession of different themes (the naked woman who represents Vice in the Middle Ages becomes in the sixteenth century Eros stripped and therefore pure, true, and sacred). Discourse and form move with respect to one another, but they are not independent: when the Nativity is represented no longer by a woman giving birth but by a kneeling Virgin, not only is the thematic emphasis shifted to the Mother of the Living God but a triangular and vertical scheme replaces a rectangular one. Finally, it sometimes happens that discourse and plastic form are both subject to changes of the same kind, to reconfiguration as a single, unified whole. In the twelfth century scholastic discourse ceased to present itself as an unbroken flow of proof and discussion. "Summas" displayed their logical architecture by spatializing writing as well as thought: division into paragraphs, visible subordination of parts, and homogeneity of elements at the same level. Taken together, these bestowed visibility on the overall structure of the argument. In the same period, the ogival arch made the structure of churches perceptible; it replaced the uninterrupted continuity of the barrel vault with the compartmentalization of bays; it gave the same structure to all elements of a building with identical function. In both cases the same principle was at work: to make *manifest*.

Hence discourse is not the interpretive basis common to all the phenomena of a culture. Revealing a form is not a roundabout (and more or less subtle or naive) way of *saying* something. In the final analysis, not everything that human beings do is a murmur open to decipherment. Discourse and image have their own modes of being, but complex and intricate relations exist between them. The problem is to describe their reciprocal operation.

Another example: the analysis of the representative function of painting in *Studies in Iconology*.

Until the end of the twentieth century, Western painting "represented": a painting always had a relation to some object through its formal configuration. A perennial problem was to ask whether the form of the work or the meaning determined its essence. Panofsky went beyond this simple opposition to analyze the representative function in all its complexity, in its relation with one value or another to each of the formal levels of the painting.

What a sixteenth-century painting represented was present in the work in four different modes, according to Panofsky. The lines and colors portrayed objects—men, animals, objects, gods—but always in accordance with formal rules of style. In the paintings of a given period there are ritual emplacements that indicate whether one is dealing with a man or an angel, an apparition or a reality. They also indicate expressive values—anger in a face, melancholy in a forest—but in accordance with the formal rules of a convention (the passions in a Le Brun do not have the same characteristic signs as the passions in a Dürer). In turn, these characters, scenes, mimes, and gestures embody themes, episodes, and concepts (fall of Vulcan, origins of the world, inconstancy of Love), but according to the rules of a typology (in the sixteenth century, the sword belonged to Judith, not Salomé). Finally, these themes give *place* (in the strict sense of the word) to a sensibility, a system of values, but in accordance with the rules of a sort of cultural symptomatology.

Representation is not external or indifferent to form. It is linked to it through an operation that can be described provided we identify its levels and prescribe a specific mode of analysis for each. Then the work appears in its articulated unity.

The importance of thinking about forms is today plain to everyone, and its origins can be traced back to the art history of the nineteenth century. Some forty years ago it emigrated to the realm of language and linguistic structures. Numerous problems, quite difficult to resolve, crop up when one tries to go beyond the limits of language, the moment one attempts to deal with actual discourse. Panofsky's work may provide a clue or perhaps a model: it teaches us to analyze not just elements and the laws that govern their combinations but the reciprocal functioning of different systems within the reality of a culture.

JEAN-FRANÇOIS LYOTARD

Discourse, Figure

1971

This book is a defense of the eye, its localization. Shadow is its prey. The penumbra that language after Plato threw like a veil of gray over the sensible, that it thematized repeatedly as a lesser being, and whose side no one ever really took, no one took for real, because it was understood that it was the side of falsity, of skepticism, of the rhetorician, the painter, the condottiere, the libertine, the materialist—that penumbra is the focus of this book. "The eye," said André Breton, "exists in the savage state."[1] The perceptible, said Merleau-Ponty, is the locus of the chiasmus, or, rather, the chiasmus itself, wherein the locus lies. There is no absolute Other, but there is the element that divides, that inverts itself, that sets itself over against itself and thereby becomes perceptible. There is "there is," which is not at first heard speech but the result of tearing two sides from the element, leaving them in that disequilibrium of which the ethical life speaks but which is that of the seeing and the visible, which is language unheard.

It was at any rate Maurice Merleau-Ponty's resolve to delve down into that chiasmus of origin without crushing the disequilbrium by way of the phenomenological reduction, without surmounting the exteriority by way of the immanence of the transcendental sphere, and, to that end, finding a language to signify that which is the root of signifying. This required nothing less than turning language into an act in order to make it consubstantial with the space of the chiasmus it was charged with expressing. But we know what happens when we mix speech and act without further ado, when we dissolve saying in seeing: either speech falls silent, or the seen must already resemble a said. Didn't Hegel challenge the sensible certitude of self-saying without succumbing to the anxiety of incertitude? And even when, looking over his shoulder, condescending to his silence, he strove to follow his index finger designating the Here, didn't he quickly isolate from the supposed faith in the mediate the mediation of pointing, the journey that he called discourse, the same negativity as that of

---

From *Discours, figure* (Paris: Klincksieck, 1971), pp. 11–15, 18–19, 211; trans. Arthur Goldhammer.

language? All in all, then, depth seems empty, in its shadow all cows are black, and the truth is that one has to begin where one is: in the midst of words.

Let us therefore begin there, let us take up a similar challenge, let us enter into the place. Let us attack the self-sufficiency of discourse. It is easy enough to dispel the present prestige of the system, of the enclosure within which men of language believe they can confine everything that makes sense. This brings us back to the text, now written by no one and read by itself. Mediocre advantages. The impertinence remains in the form of a neglect of the perceptible so grave that it is as if men had become two-dimensional beings with nothing palpable about them, two-dimensional beings moving along gaps in the network. Can one smash the prison house by claiming an absolute excess of meaning in primal speech and the need for finitude in order to interpret endlessly (*sans fin*)? The infinity, the openness, that one finds in the hermeneutics of Paul Ricoeur is indicative of doubts about Hegelianism, but heremeneutics remains within the Hegelian sphere. For Hegel was the very first to conceive of the symbol as nothing other than an invitation to think, the very first to see it above all as a moment to be transcended; at bottom he neglected simply to see it. He wanted to hear the voice of his silence. Once that is in hand, hermeneutics is content to leave consciousness's route toward listening open. It thus seems to respect the symbol's transcendence of all commentary, and the infinity of the task. Yet its kinship with dialectic is beyond doubt; it consists in this, that the symbol, the point of departure, is taken not as thing but as confused speech. The transcendence of the symbol is that of a discourse emanating from an Other. It is not Creation as a thick object that marks, that accumulates, otherness; it is being deaf to revelation. The visible is not that which manifests *itself* by reserving *itself* in its verso, it is merely a screen of appearances. It is not appearance, but noise concealing a voice.

What is savage is art as silence. The position of art is a contradiction of the position of discourse. The position of art indicates a function of the figure, which is not signified, and which functions around and even in discourse. It indicates that the transcendence of the symbol is the figure, that is, a spatial manifestation that linguistic space cannot incorporate without being shaken, an exteriority that it cannot internalize as *signification*. Art is posited in otherness as plasticity and desire, curved extent, against invariability and reason, diacritical space. Art seeks the figure; "beauty" is figural, unbound, rhythmic. The true symbol invites thought, but before that it offers itself as an invitation to "see." And the astonishing thing is not that it invites thought, if indeed it is true that once language exists, every object exists to be signified, to be incorporated into a discourse, to fall into the hopper in which thought shakes everything up and sorts everything out; the enigma is that it remains to be "seen," that it maintains itself as continually perceptible, that there exists a world that is a repository of "views," or an interworld that is a repository of "visions," and that all discourse exhausts itself before coming to the end. The absolutely-other would be this beauty or difference.

Must one therefore fall silent in order to make that world manifest? The silence of the beautiful, of feeling, the silence that is prior to speech, the silence of the heart, is impossible; it is not a matter of moving beyond discourse, to its other side. Only from within discourse can we move to and into the figure. We can move to the figure by showing that all discourse has its vis-à-vis, the object of which it speaks, which is over there, as that which it designates on some horizon, some view on the edge of discourse. And one can move into the figure without abandoning language because the figure is lodged in language; it is enough to allow oneself to slip into the pit of discourse to find the eye that lurks at its center, the eye of discourse, in the sense which in the middle of a hurricane there lurks an eye of calm. The figure is outside and inside; that is why even as it holds the secret of "connaturality" it shows this to be a trap. Language is not a homogeneous milieu. It cleaves because it externalizes the perceptible into a vis-à-vis, an object, and is cloven because it internalizes the figural in the articulate. The eye is in speech because there is no articulated language without externalization of a "visible," but it is also there because there is an externality that is at least gestural, "visible," within discourse, which is its expression. By pursuing this double externality, one can perhaps meet the challenge that language makes to the visible, the ear to the eye; one can perhaps show that the gestural extent that gives depth or representation, far from being signifiable in words, lies on the periphery of language as the power of words to designate, and also that it is the birthplace of their power to express; that as such it accompanies them, it is their shadow, in a sense their end, in a sense their beginning. For one need not be immersed in language in order to speak; the "absolute" object, language, does not speak. What speaks is something that must be outside language and not cease to stand there even when it speaks. Silence is the opposite of discourse; it is violence at the same time as beauty; but it is the condition of beauty since it is on the side of the things that are to be spoken *about* and must be expressed. There is no discourse without this opacity to attempt to undo and restore, this inexhaustible thickness. Silence results from the rip whereby a discourse and its object find themselves face-to-face, and it begins the work of signifying; it also results from the rip incorporated into speech, where the work of expression is carried out.

Such violence is inherent in language, is its point of departure, because one speaks in separation, and the object must be constituted-lost in order to need to be signified. It thus records the birth of the problem of knowledge; it compels us to desire truth as the internalization (the completed signification) of externality (of the object). The cognitive function includes within itself the death that creates the vis-à-vis, the desire that creates the thickness of reference. But the expressive function also includes this, only in a different way; it imports it into discourse itself, for the violence of the wrenching does not place a perfectly pure object on one side and a perfectly pure subject on the other, all of it giving rise to any number of cherished exercises on the possibility of truth. This violence turns the object into a sign, but, symmetrically, it turns discourse into a thing, it deposits thickness, it arranges a scene in the articulation and limpidity of signification, while in the meantime, on the side of the object, it is hollowing out its other face, its behind-the-scenes.

The eye is force. To turn the unconscious into a discourse is to omit the energetics. It is to make oneself an accomplice to the whole of Western *ratio*, which kills art at the same time it kills dreams. By putting language everywhere one does not break with metaphysics at all, one completes it. One completes the repression of the perceptible and the ecstatic. The opposition is not between form and force, or perhaps it is that form is being confused with structure. Force is never anything other than the energy that folds and wrinkles the text and turns it into a work, a difference, that is, a form. Painting is not to be read, as semiologists say nowadays. Klee used to say that it was to be *browsed*. It makes us see, it offers itself to the eye as an exemplary thing, a "naturing nature," Klee also used to say, since it makes us see what it is to see. It makes us see that seeing is a dance. To look at painting is to trace paths, or at any rate to co-trace paths, since in making the work the painter imperiously (albeit laterally) mapped out paths to be followed, and his work is a motion contained within four pieces of wood that an eye can set back into motion, into life. "Explosive-fixed" beauty lucidly required by *mad love*.

And what do you think discourse is? Cold prose is virtually nonexistent, except at the lowest level of communication. A discourse is thick. It does not merely signify, it expresses. And if it expresses, it is because it, too, contains motion, movement, and force enough to lift up the table of significations through an earthquake that creates meaning. It, too, is an invitation to browse and not merely to understand. It, too, calls upon the eye; it, too, is energetic. Let us trace the eye's route through the field of language, let us grasp the fixed motion, let us wed the undulations of metaphor, which is the fulfillment of desire, and then we will see how exteriority, force, and shaped space can be present in interiority, in closed signification. [. . .]

In the Freudian utopia we live within limits set by the so-called death instinct, whose rule is that unification of the diverse, even in the unity of a discourse (or of Freudian theory), is always rejected or forbidden. In consideration of this rule, we must abandon the Ego as a constituted unitary agency. By the same token it is time for philosophers to abandon the idea of producing a unitary theory as the last word about things. There is no *arche*, but neither does the Good exist as a unitary horizon. We never touch the thing itself other than metaphorically, but this laterality is not, as Merleau-Ponty believed, that of existence, which is far too close to the unity of the subject, as he himself recognized at the end; it is rather that of the unconscious or of expression, which at one stroke offers and holds back all content. This laterality is difference or depth. But while Merleau-Ponty posited it as the possibility of going over there while remaining right here, as ubiquitous openness, as continuous mobility, and saw its model in the chiasmus of the perceptible, thus succumbing to the illusion of unitary discourse, we are about to rearm figural space with Cézanne and Mallarmé, with Freud, with Frege: depth still greatly exceeds the power of a reflection that would like to signify it, to place it in language, not as a thing but as a definition. Meaning is present as absence of signification. Yet that absence takes hold of it (and it can do so, one can say anything), and meaning exiles itself to the periphery of the new speech act. Therein lies the death instinct, always intimately intertwined with Eros-Logos. To construct meaning is never anything other than to deconstruct signification. No model can be adduced for this elusive configuration. One might say that in the beginning there is violence as castration and that the silence or death that our words seek to ferret out is the offspring of the initial terror that gave rise to desire. Perhaps, but since the locus of this desire is utopia, we must be aware of the need to forgo assigning it a place.

This is of great importance for practice, for the practical critique of ideology. This book itself is only a roundabout way of getting at such a critique, and if it took a long time to overcome my own resistance to writing it, one reason (among others) is surely the fear of being seduced, diverted from this goal, paralyzed by language. What its practical function might be, what parts of it may still be alive and warm, is not for me to judge. [. . .]

Between opposition and difference there is the difference between the space of the text and the space of the figure. This difference is not one of degree; it is constitutive of an ontological gap. The two spaces are two orders of meaning, which communicate but which are therefore separate. One should say *textual* space rather than space of the text and *figural* space rather than space of the figure. This is to indicate that text and figure each engender a distinctive organization of the space they inhabit. This space is not the container of an extrinsic content, and even when it presents itself as such, as is the case for textual space, what is involved is a property that specifies the space in question and not a universal trait. By textual space I therefore mean the space in which the *graphic* signifier is inscribed. As for the space of the figure, "figural" characterizes it better than "figurative." In the lexicon of contemporary painting and criticizing, "figurative" is opposed to "nonfigurative" or "abstract." The pertinent feature of this opposition lies in the analogy between the representing and the represented, in the possibility made available to the spectator of recognizing the latter in the former. This trait is not germane to our problem. The figurative is merely a special case of the figural. We see it in the window that Renaissance painting opened up for us. The term "figurative" indicates the possibility of deriving the pictural object from its "real" model by way of a continuous translation. The trace on the figurative canvas is a non-arbitrary trace. Figurativity is therefore a property relative to the relation between the plastic object and that which it *represents*. It vanishes if the function of the canvas is no longer to represent, if it is itself the object. The value of that object then depends solely on the organization of the signifier. That organization varies between two extremes.

Note

[1] André Breton, *Le surréalisme et la peinture* (Paris: Gallimard, 1965), p. 1.

HENRI MALDINEY

Gaze, Speech, Space

1973

To abstract is to extract from the arrhythmic world of action elements capable of becoming excited and moving rhythmically.

Abstraction is not a modern prejudice. It is the vital act of Art. It represents that power of interiority and transcendence of the visual plane without which art does not exist. Jean Bazaine was quite right to say that abstraction "is a function of a greater or lesser degree of resemblance, not between the work and external reality, but between the work and an interior world that encompasses it and opens out until it reaches the pure rhythmic motifs of being."[1] If our era, for reasons stated earlier, has turned away from everyday appearances and domestic life, it was not to flee the world but to rediscover it at another level, where we demonstrated our distinctive coexistence and "co-birth" [*co-naissance*; cf. *connaissance*, knowledge—Trans.].

What, then, is this abstraction in the end? It is transfigurative action, action that reveals rhythm in the forms that embody it. Those forms gradually lose the qualities that originally characterized them in practical vision only to reappear (reborn) with more essential qualities bestowed on them by rhythm. More than that, the purifying effects of rhythm adapt those forms to the transcendent world they are charged with expressing, the world that is present as style in the initial sensation.

To choose some number of active focal points of the real, whether located in the curve of a shoulder or the curve of a hill, and to rediscover their profound communication—not in the "already seen, already known" composition of their domestic economy but in a drive or instinct (*pulsion*) of the world as a whole, and in the only effective manner, the rhythmic mode. That is the essential task of Abstraction: to render each thing unto itself by transcending it in the direction of its style.[2]

Reality is not the sum of the objects that surround us. It is situated at a more elemental level, and it is the irruption of that elemental level into the quotidian that produces the surprise of Reality. The Real is always that which we did not

Regard, parole, espace (Lausanne: Editions L'Age d'Homme, 1973), pp. 1, 18–20, 124–25, 183–85, 152–64; trans. Arthur Goldhammer.

expect.[3] Hence abstraction is not a matter of eliminating or, as one says, distorting the world without changing it; it consists in transforming, in transposing, forms that recount into forms that speak. There are forms like old gossips that recount all the incidents and accidents of the everyday world. The forms we must create are those that speak of that transcendent reality toward which we and the world proceed together, into our depths.[4] Abstraction is another name for creation. And the abstraction of modern art is one attempt to use rhythm to wrench us away from the intellectualization and mechanization of modern man and his world. It is true that in the process rhythm itself sometimes becomes mechanized and bogged down in spiritual algebra. But the fall of a swallow does not prevent the return of spring.

. . .

There is no aesthetic except of rhythm.

There is no rhythm that is not aesthetic.

These two propositions are not converses of each other, because the word "aesthetic" does not have the same meaning in both.

In the second proposition, where the word is used in a broader and more primitive sense, "aesthetic" refers to the Greek αισθησιξ (= sensation) and covers the whole field of sensory receptivity. To say that every rhythm is aesthetic is to say that the experience of rhythm—in which we encounter it where and as it "takes place"—is of the order of feeling (and of communication within feeling). But an aesthetic of rhythm or rhythms relates only to the dimension of art and beauty, and its field is limited to artistic perception. Is this shift from broad to narrow gradual and continuous? Or is there rupture and leap (consisting of one or more jumps) from one domain to the other, that is, discontinuity and mutation between the sensory aesthetic and the artistic aesthetic?

Our thesis is: "Art is the truth of the perceptible because rhythm is the truth of αισθησιξ."

. . .

What is rhythm, rigorously speaking?

One can and should determine scientifically the physiological, physical, and psychological conditions of its appearance, variations, and disappearance, but these will not tell us what it is *in itself*. Many will think the question is metaphysical and the answer futile: anyone who experiences it won't care about its essence. But that is precisely the point: rhythm is strictly speaking metaphysical; it takes place beyond the physical phenomena that are its fundamental elements. Because it is "produced," concept and act are one. The essence of rhythm gives rise to certain ambiguities, which are invariably also misunderstandings of experience, the most common of which is the confusion of rhythm with cadence. Classical, almost official, it dates from Aristotle, who defined rhythm as order in time.

Contemporary musicians find it hard to liberate themselves from the meaning that to them seems to correspond to the discontinuous, and with it they try to explain rhythm's two antithetical dimensions, continuity and discontinuity. Pierre Boulez, like Karl Stockhausen before him, speaks of rhythmic units that can be multiplied and divided, of rhythmic systems based on objectively measurable durations and tempi. Now, if rhythm assumes (as anything other than an obstacle to be removed) proportionality or even merely commensurability of durations as well as tempi, the unit in which it is measured is no longer time aesthetically experienced but its projection onto an objective spatial image. Even Stockhausen, who highlights the time of experience (*Erlebniszeit*), derives it from objective universal time.

In fact, rhythm involves the whole destiny of sonic space, which is determined by pitches as well as durations, intensities as well as tempi, textures as well as timbres. Rhythm imposes itself on this complex whole: it is the genesis of the plenitude of time right out of the auto-movement of that space. To define it precisely, I shall begin with a study by Hönigswald, the only philosophical work (except for a brief note by L. Klages) to take rhythm as the central theme of a crucial reflection.

Hönigswald defines rhythm as the articulation of time by time, a temporal articulation of time, as it were, in which Living and Lived are one. It is not enough for the articulating moments to constitute an order; that order must also comprise a temporal dimension. Since other writers have dealt or will deal with rhythm in poetry and music, I shall limit myself to the plastic arts. Thus I want to define rhythm where time is least apparent, in sculpture and painting. I do so in the following terms: *The rhythm of a form is the articulation of its implied time*. [. . .]

So? So we must free ourselves from the theoretical illusion, *the* theoretical illusion, that all human experience is structured by the subject-object polarity. There is no denying the relation of *a subject that makes the world an object for itself* and thereby distinguishes itself from the world. But this situation is secondary to the situation of perception. The relation Self-World in Feeling is not reducible to the relation Subject-Object. "Feeling is to perceiving what the cry is to the word."[5] Now, the word is not the truth of the cry. Neither is perception the truth of sensation. Sensation is fundamentally a mode of communication, and in feeling we live our being-*with*-the-world in a "pathic" mode. The basic elements of rhythm belong to a world of this sort, given in relation to communication (rather than objectification). They are not objectively posited as universal facts or phenomena. Nor are they simply material experiences reflected in consciousness. They belong to that primal and primordial world in which we deal with *reality* for the first time and in each of our acts, for the dimension of the real is the communicative dimension of experience.

At this point we confront a crucial question involving the contradictory relations of art and Feeling. Sensation is a certitude that experiences its truth without casting doubt on the reality of the world with which we communicate through it. Now, we posit something as real only after having considered and resolved in a positive sense the possibility that it does not exist. This is the skeptical path of doubt, of critique, and of the mobilization of evidence that can confirm or deny the initial certainty. It is the passage from certitude to truth.

Sensory certitude ignores the casting of doubt. The Self-World relationship is not subjected to the ordeal of the possibility of No. The basic elements of rhythm are not posited in the strict sense of the word. *They are*—with no account being taken of the possibility of *not being*. There is. This is. This *yes* does not refute any *no*. The point is precisely this: these elements are posited in rhythm. Rhythm is the milieu in which their being is freed from the possibility of non-being, and of being-otherwise. Rhythm, because it is a form of presence, an existential, is by itself a warrant of reality. In it, real and possible coincide. Through it art is not—as one says—an imaginary.

Here one ought to point out how we communicate in intimate contact with feeling, in a pathic mode, not with this or that object but with the world as a whole—but time is short. When Van Gogh speaks of "the high yellow note" he "achieved this summer" (in 1888),[6] or when Cézanne, grabbing his coachman by the shoulder in the wagon in which he was riding out to his "theme," cried out in a sort of ecstasy that made an impression on his companion, "Look! The blues . . . those blues over there . . . under the pines,"[7] neither that yellow nor those blues were colors of objects; they were rather introductions to the world, encounters with the worlds of Van Gogh and Cézanne. They number among "those confused sensations that we carry at birth." And for painters the problem is to make of those sensations a work in which the world functions. They can simultaneously put them "to work" and bring them "into the world" only by putting them in rhythm. Whence the question: Is the relation between sensation and rhythm one of continuity or discontinuity? We already sense that there is discontinuity, a jump, because there is a transition from a certitude to a truth.

Notes

[1] Jean Bazaine, *Notes sur la peinture*, p. 37.

[2] The style of a thing is the style of the world of which it is the point of contact with us. It is incompatible with isolation of the thing or object. "To join the women's curves to the shoulders of hills," said Cézanne.

[3] What is the universal index of the real? Its singular unpredictability. Think of the way in which commonplace things suddenly appear real to us once again when we rediscover them. A new light, never before seen, illuminates a familiar landscape. You are surprised to see that the landscape exists—other than as image. Or prepare for a journey in the

most detailed possible way. You think you know it. But when you see the things themselves, the sensation is always different from that occasioned by the most minute imagination of the scene. The real is what you did not foresee. What is *given* to you. It is what the Japanese call the "Ah!" of things.

[4] ". . . to re-create that transcendent reality toward which the individual evolves. Only the living matters" (Tal Coat). "To know [*connaître*] is to be born with [*naître avec*]" (Paul Claudel).

[5] E. Straus, *Vom Sinn der Sinne*, p. 329.

[6] Letter from Vincent Van Gogh to his brother Theo, 24 March 1889.

[7] J. Gasquet, *Cézanne*, p. 121.

JACQUES DERRIDA

Economimesis

1975

Under the cover of a controlled indeterminacy, pure morality and empirical culturalism are allied in the Kantian critique of pure judgments of taste.[1] A politics, therefore, although it never occupies the center of the stage, acts upon this discourse. It ought to be possible to read it. Politics and political economy, to be sure, are implicated in every discourse on art and on the beautiful. But how does one discern the most pointed specificity of such an implication? Certain of its motifs belong to a long sequence, to a powerful traditional chain going back to Plato and to Aristotle. Very tightly interlaced with these, though at first indistinguishable, are other narrower sequences that would be inadmissible within an Aristotelian or Platonic politics of art. But sorting out and measuring lengths will not suffice. Folded into a new system, the long sequences are displaced; their sense and their function change. Once inserted into another network, the "same" philosopheme is no longer the same, and besides it never had an identity external to its functioning. Simultaneously, "unique and original" ["*inédits*"] philosophemes, if there are any, as soon as they enter into articulated composition with inherited philosophemes, are affected by that composition over the whole of their surface and under every angle. We are nowhere near disposing of rigorous criteria for judging philosophical specificity, the precise limits framing a corpus or what properly belongs [*le propre*] to a system. The very project of such a delimitation itself already belongs to a set of conditions [*un ensemble*] that remains to be thought. In turn, even the concept of belonging [to a set] is open to elaboration, that is dislocation, by the structure of the *parergon* [cf. "Le parergon," *La vérité en peinture* (Paris: Champs Flammarion, 1978)].

. . .

What is art? Kant seems to begin by replying: art is not nature, thus subscribing to the inherited, ossified, simplified opposition between *tekhnè* and *physis*. On the side of nature is mechanical necessity; on the side of art, the play of freedom. In between them is a whole series of secondary determinations.

From *Diacritics* 11, no. 2 (June 1981), pp. 3, 4–12, 19–21; trans. Richard Klein [*Mimesis des articulations* (Paris: Aubier-Flammarion, 1975)].

But analogy annuls this opposition. It places under Nature's dictate what is most wildly free in the production of art. Genius is the locus of such a dictation—the means by which art receives its rules from nature. All propositions of an anti-mimetic cast, all condemnations leveled against imitation are undermined at this point. One must not imitate nature; but nature, assigning its rules to genius, folds itself, returns to itself, reflects itself through art. This specular flexion provides both the principle of reflexive judgments—nature guaranteeing legality in a movement that proceeds from the particular—and the secret resource of *mimesis*—understood not, in the first place, as an imitation of nature by art, but as a flexion of the *physis*, nature's relation to itself. There is no longer here any opposition between *physis* and *mimesis*, nor consequently between *physis* and *tekhnè*; or that, at least, is what now needs to be verified.

Section 43 begins: "Art is distinguished from nature as doing (*Thun*) (*facere*) is distinguished from acting (*Handeln*) or working (*Wirken*) generally (*agere*), and as the product (*Produkt*) or result of the former is distinguished as work (*Werk*) (opus), from the working (*Wirkung*) (effectus) of the latter" [*Critique of Judgment*, trans. J.H. Bernard (New York: Hafner Press, 1974)].

These proportional analogies are constructed on a certain number of apparently irreducible oppositions. How are they finally, as they always do, going to dissolve? And to the advantage of what political economy?

In order to dissolve, as they always do, the oppositions must be produced, must be propagated and multiplied. The process is one that has to be followed.

Within art in general (one of the two terms of the preceding opposition) another split engenders a series of distinctions. Their logical structure is not insignificant: there is no symmetry between the terms, but rather a regular hierarchy such that any attempt to distinguish between the two is also to classify one as being more and the other less. The attempt is to define two distinct sorts of art, but in order to display two phenomena of which one is more properly "art" than the other.

Immediately after having distinguished art from nature, Kant specifies that the only thing one ought to call "art" is the production of freedom by means of freedom [*Hervorbringung durch Freiheit*]. Art properly speaking puts free will (*Wilkur*) to work and places reason at the root of its acts. There is therefore no art, in a strict sense, except that of a being who is free and *logon ekon* [has speech]: the product of bees ["cells of wax regularly constructed"] is not a work of art. What can be glimpsed in this inexhaustible reiteration of the humanist theme, of the ontology bound up with it as well, in this obscurantist buzzing that always treats animality *in general*, under the purview of one or two scholastic examples, as if there were only a single "animal" structure that could be opposed to the human (inalienably endowed with reason, freedom, sociality, laughter, language, law, the symbolic, with consciousness, or an unconscious, etc.), is that the concept of art is also constructed with just such a guarantee in view. It is there to raise man up [*ériger l'homme*], that is, always, to erect a man-god, to avoid contamination from "below," and to mark an incontrovertible limit of anthropological domesticity. The whole of economimesis (Aristotle: only man is capable of *mimesis*) is represented in this gesture. Its ruse and its naiveté—the logic of man—lie in the necessity, in order to save the absolute privilege of emergence (art, freedom, language, etc.), of grounding it in an absolute naturalism and in an absolute indifferentialism; somewhere human production has to be renaturalized, and differentiation must get effaced into opposition.

Thus bees have no art. And if one were to name their production a "work of art," it would be "only by analogy" [*nur wegen der Analogie*]. The work of art is always that of man [*ein Werk der Menschen*].

A power, aptitude, property, destiny of man [*Geschicklichkeit des Menschen*], art is distinguished in its turn from science. Scientific knowledge is a power [*un pouvoir*]; art is what it does not suffice to know, in order to know how to do it [*savoir faire*], in order to be able to do it [*pouvoir faire*]. In the region that Kant comes from, the common man is rarely wrong. Solving the problem of the egg of Columbus, that is science: it suffices to know in order to know how. The same may be said of prestidigitation. As for high-wire dancing, that is something else: you have to do it [*faut le faire*] and it does not suffice to know about it (there is a very brief passage of a tightrope walker in a confidential note, "*In meinen Gegenden . . .*" For anyone who would like to take the plunge and put in something of himself: Kant, Nietzsche, Genet).

Distinct from science, art in general (the question of the Fine-Arts has not yet arisen) cannot be reduced to craft [*Handwerk*]. The latter exchanges the value of its work against a salary; it is a mercenary art [*Lohnkunst*]. Art, strictly speaking, is liberal or free [*freie*], its production must not enter into the economic circle of commerce, of offer and demand; it must not be exchanged. Liberal art and mercenary art therefore do not form a couple of opposite terms. One is higher than the other, more "art" than the other; it has more value for not having any economic value. If art, in the literal sense, is "production of freedom," liberal art better conforms to its essence. Mercenary art belongs to art only by analogy. And if one follows this play of analogy, mercenary productivity also resembles that of bees: lack of freedom, a determined purpose or finality, utility, finitude of the code, fixity of the program without reason and without the play of the imagination. The craftsman, the worker, like the bee, does not play. And indeed, the hierarchical opposition of liberal art and mercenary art is that of play and work. "We regard the first as if it could only prove purposive as play, i.e. as occupation that is pleasant in itself. But the second is regarded as work, i.e. as occupation which is unpleasant (a trouble) in itself and which is only attractive on account of its effect (for example salary) and which can consequently only be imposed on us by constraint (*zwangmässig*)" [§ 43].

Let us follow the law of analogy:

1. If art is the distinguishing property of man as freedom, free art is more human than remunerated work, just as it is more human than the so-called instinctual activity of bees. The free man, the artist in this sense, is no *homo oeconomicus*.

2. Just as everything in nature prescribes the utilization of animal organization by man [§ 63], in the same way free man should be able to utilize, were it by constraint, the work of man insofar as it is not free. Liberal art ought thus to be able to use mercenary art (without touching it, that is without implicating itself); an economy must be able to utilize (render useful) the economy of work.

3. The value of play defines pure productivity. With the beautiful and art both proceeding from the imagination, it was still necessary to distinguish between the reproductive imagination and the productive imagination that is spontaneous, free, and playful: "If we seek the result of the preceding analysis, we find that everything runs up into this concept of taste—that it is a faculty for judging an object in reference to the imagination's *free conformity to law*. Now, if in the judgment of taste the imagination must be considered in its freedom, it is in the first place not regarded as reproductive [*reproductiv*], as subject to the laws of association, but as productive [*productiv*] and spontaneous [*selbstthätig*] (as the author of arbitrary forms of possible intuitions): and although in the apprehension of a given object of sense it is tied [*gebunden*] to a definite form of this object and so far has no free play [*freies Spiel*] (such as that of poetry), yet it may be readily conceived that the object can furnish it with such a form containing a collection of the manifold as the imagination itself, if it were let free, would project [*entwerfen*], in accordance with the *conformity to law of the understanding* in general." [*General Remark on the First Section of the Analytic*]

Poetry, the summit of fine art considered as a species of art, carries the freedom of play announced in the productive imagination to its extreme, to the top of the hierarchy. *Mimesis* intervenes, however, not only as one would expect in reproductive operations, but in the free and pure productivity of the imagination as well. The latter deploys the brute power of its invention only by *listening* to nature, to its dictation, its edict. And the concept of nature here itself functions in the service of that ontotheological humanism, of that obscurantism of the economy one could call liberal in its era of *Aufklärung*. Genius, as an instance of the Fine-Arts ("Fine-Arts must necessarily be considered arts of *genius*," § 46) carries freedom of play and the pure productivity of the imagination to its highest point. It gives rules or at least examples but it has its own rules dictated to it by nature: so that the whole distinction between liberal and mercenary art, with the whole machinery of hierarchical subordination that it commands, reproduces nature in its production, breaks with *mimesis*, understood as imitation of what is, only to identify itself with the free unfolding-refolding of the *physis*.

One ought to analyze closely the paragraph that exploits the false opposition between liberal art and crafts. Liberal art is an occupation that is agreeable in itself. The liberal artist—the one who does not work for a salary—enjoys and gives enjoyment. Immediately. The mercenary, insofar as he is practicing his art, does not enjoy. But since we are dealing here with a hierarchy inside of a general organization governed by the universal law of nature, the non-enjoyment of the mercenary artist (his work) serves the cause of liberal enjoyment. And what imposes mercenary art by force, in the last analysis, is nature, which commands genius and which, through all sorts of mediations, commands everything. Speaking immediately after of a "hierarchy" [*Rangliste*] in the grade of the professions, Kant asks whether we ought to consider an occupation such as watchmaking a (free) art or a (mercenary) handicraft. A difficult question that is immediately put aside: it would require "another point of view," that of the "proportion of talents." The rigorous criterion is lacking. Similarly, Kant "does not want to discuss here" the question whether, among the seven liberal arts, some could be classed as sciences and others as handicrafts. The liberal arts taught in the arts faculties of the Middle Ages (*trivium*: grammar, dialectic, rhetoric; *quadrivium*: arithmetic, geometry, astronomy, music) are the disciplines that depend the most on the mind's work—by contrast with the mechanical arts, which above all require manual labor. And yet in the exercise of a liberal art (of the free spirit) a certain constraint must be at work. Something compulsory ("*zwangmässiges*" is also the word used to designate the constraint imposed on handicraft) must intervene as a "mechanism" [*Mechanismus*]. Without this coercive constriction, this tight corset [*corsage*], the spirit which must be free in art, "would have no body and would evaporate altogether." The body, constraint, or mechanism, for example, of poetry, the highest of the liberal arts, would be lexical accuracy or richness [*Sprachnichtigkeit*, *Sprachreichtum*], prosody or metrics. The freedom of a liberal art relates to the system of coercions or constraints, to its own mechanism, as the spirit does to the body or the living body to its corset, which as always, as its name indicates, gives body to things. Attention is required here to seize the organic linchpin of the system: the two arts (liberal and mercenary) are not two totalities independent of or indifferent to one another. Liberal art relates to mercenary art as the mind does to the body, and it cannot produce itself, in its freedom, without the very thing that it subordinates to itself, without the force of mechanical structure which in every sense of the word it *supposes*—the mechanical agency, mercenary, laborious, deprived of pleasure. Hence we hear already the well-known reaction against any non-directive pedagogy: "many modern educators believe that the best way to produce a free art is to remove it from all constraint [*Zwang*] and thus to change it from work into mere play" [Ibid].

It was just said that the free play of liberal art, unlike mercenary art, offers enjoyment [*donne à jouir*]. This is still vague. One needs to distinguish pleasure [*plaisir*] from enjoyment [*jouissance*]. In this context and in a slightly conventional fashion, in order to mark two different concepts, Kant opposes *Lust and Genuss*. And that precisely at the moment when he defines the Fine-Arts [*Beaux-Arts*], fine art [*schöne Kunst*]. Once again, this definition does not proceed by symmetrical opposition, by classification of gender and species. Fine-Arts are free arts certainly, but they do not all belong to the liberal arts. Certain among these belong to the Fine-Arts, others to the Sciences.

What then characterizes the "Fine-Arts"?[1]

This locution, despite being so familiar, is not self-evident. Is there a reason for terming "fine" or "beautiful" an art that produces the beautiful? The beautiful is the object, the *opus*, the form produced. Why then would art be fine or beautiful? Kant never asks this question. It seems called for by his critique. If one transfers to art a predicate which, in all rigor, seems to belong to its product, it is because the relation to the product cannot, structurally, be cut off from the relation to a productive subjectivity, however indeterminate, even anonymous it may be: we have here the implication of signature which should not be confused with the extrinsic demands of some empiricism (whether psychological, sociological, historical, etc.). The beautiful would always be the work [*l'oeuvre*] (as much the act as the object), the art whose signature remains marked at the limit of the work, neither in nor out, out and in, in the parergonal thickness of the frame. If the beautiful is never ascribed simply to the product or to the producing act, but to a certain passage to the limit between them, then it depends, provided with another elaboration, on some parergonal effect: the Fine-Arts are always of the frame and the signature. Kant doubtless would not endorse these propositions which nevertheless do not appear to be entirely incompatible with his problematic of aesthetic subjectivity.

When one says that an art is fine or beautiful, one is not referring to a singularity, to some productive act or to some unique production. The generality (music is a fine art, the art of some composer) implies, within the totality of the operation's subjective powers, a repetition, a possibility of beginning again. This iterability belongs to the very concept of the "Fine-Arts."

The repetition is of a pleasure. Whence the answer to the question: can a science be beautiful? No, says Kant. "A beautiful science" would be an absurdity, a non-sense, a nonentity [*Unding*]: nothing. One can certainly find beautiful things around scientific activity; an artist can also put scientific knowledge to work. But as such, an act or an object of science, for example a scientific statement, could not be called beautiful—any more than one could speak of the scientific value of an art. That would just be idle talk [*bavardage*]. The beauty of a scientific statement would be of the order of the *Bonmot*: "tasteful witticisms" [*geschmacksvolle Ausspruche (Bonmots)*].

If *Witz* as such can have no scientific value, science must do without it in order to be what it is. It must therefore do without art, without beauty, and indissolubly, without pleasure. It must not proceed from (in view of) pleasure, must neither take nor give any.

A remark in passing, in the *Introduction*, nevertheless recognizes pleasure at the distant origin of knowledge: "but this pleasure has certainly been present at one time, and it is only because the commonest experience would be impossible without it that it is gradually confounded with mere cognition and no longer arrests particular attention."

If in an immemorial time, which cannot be a time of consciousness, pleasure does not allow itself to be separated from knowledge, one can no longer exclude science from all relation to beauty, to *Witz*, as well as to the whole economy of pleasure (return to the self-same, reduction of the heterogeneous, recognition of the law, etc.) [Cf. "Le parergon" (II) (*Le sans de la coupure pure*), p. 27]. Moreover, one has to admit that in the *bon mot*, the force of *Witz* leads back into the buried or repressed origin of science, that is to the science of science, to the point where all the distinctions, oppositions, limits remarked by the Kantian critique lose their pertinence. It is important to take note of the sweeping consequences [*enjeu*] of this problem in the place where the Kantian text itself allows the effacement of that pertinence to be announced.

Let us return to the point where the limits are firmly inscribed, even if this inscription remains derived. The Fine-Arts are not at all scientific, sciences are not at all beautiful or artistic. The Fine-Arts proceed from and give pleasure, not enjoyment [*jouissance*], science, neither pleasure or enjoyment; fine art, pleasure without enjoyment. Nevertheless, not every art procures pleasure. A new series of distinctions intervenes.

An art that conforms to the knowledge of a possible object, which executes the operations necessary to bring it into being, which knows in advance that it must produce and consequently does produce it, such a *mechanical art* neither seeks nor gives pleasure. One knows how to print a book, build a machine, one avails oneself of a model and a purpose. To mechanical art Kant opposes aesthetic art. The latter has its immediate end in pleasure.

But aesthetic art in turn splits into two hierarchic species. Not every aesthetic art is a fine or beautiful art. There is thus aesthetic art that has no relation to the beautiful. Among aesthetic arts, certain of them, the agreeable arts, have enjoyment [*jouissance, Genuss*] as their aim. The Fine Arts seek pleasure [*Lust*] without enjoyment. Kant defines them first in two stringent lines without parentheses after having leisurely described the art of enjoyment (fourteen lines including a long parenthesis), the art of conversation, jest, laughter, gaiety, simple-minded entertainment, irresponsible gossip around the table, the art of serving, the management of music during the meal, party games, etc. All these are directed to enjoyment. "On the other hand, fine or beautiful art is a mode of representation which is purposive for itself and which, although devoid of purposes [*ohne Zweck*], yet furthers the culture of the mental powers in reference to social communication" [§ 44].

Sociality, universal communicability: that can only be pleasure, not enjoyment. The latter involves an empirical sensibility, includes a kernel of incommunicable sensation. Pure pleasure, without empirical enjoyment, therefore belongs to judgment and reflection. But the pleasure of judgment and reflection must be *without* concept, for the reasons already recognized.

This pleasure dispenses with [*faire son deuil de*] both concept and enjoyment. It can only be given in reflective judgment. And according to the order of a certain *socius*, of a certain reflective intersubjectivity.

So what is the relation with *economimesis*? To be able to take pleasure in a reflective pronouncement [*prédication*] without enjoying and without conceiving, belongs, of course, to the essence [*le propre*] of man, of free man—capable of pure, that is non-exchangeable productivity. Non-exchangeable in terms of sensible objects or signs of sensible objects (money for example), non-exchangeable in terms of enjoyment—neither as a use value nor as exchange value.

And nevertheless this pure productivity of the inexchangeable liberates a sort of immaculate commerce. Being a reflective exchange, universal communicability between free subjects opens up space for the play of the Fine-Arts. There is in this a sort of pure economy in which the *oikos*, what belongs essentially to the definition [*le propre*] of man, is reflected in his pure freedom and his pure productivity.

Why then *mimesis* here? The productions of the Fine-Arts are not productions of nature, that, as Kant repeatedly recalls, goes without saying. *Facere* and not *agere*. But a certain *quasi*, a certain *als ob* re-establishes analogical *mimesis* at the point where it appears detached. The works of the Fine-Arts must have the appearance of nature and precisely in so far as they are productions (fashionings) of freedom. They must resemble *effects* of natural *action* at the very moment when they, most purely, are works [*opera*] of artistic confection. "In a product of the Fine-Arts, we must become conscious that it is art and not nature; but yet the purposiveness in its form must seem [*scheinen*] to be as free from all constraint [*Zwang*] of arbitrary rules as if [*als ob*] it were a product of pure nature. On this feeling of freedom in the play of our cognitive faculties, which must at the same time be purposive, rests that pleasure [*Lust*] which alone is universally communicable, without being based on concepts" [§ 45].

What is the scope of the *as if*?

Pure and free productivity must resemble that of nature. And it does so precisely because, free and pure, it does not depend on natural laws. The less it depends on nature, the more it resembles nature. *Mimesis* here is not the representation of one thing by another, the relation of resemblance or of identification between two beings, the reproduction of a product of nature by a product of art. It is not the relation of two products but of two productions. And of two freedoms. The artist does not imitate things in nature, or, if you will, in *natura naturata*, but the acts of *natura naturans*, the operations of the *physis*. But since an analogy has already made *natura naturans* the art of an author-subject, and, one could even say, of an artist-god, *mimesis* displays the identification of human action with divine action—of one freedom with another. The communicability of pure judgments of taste, the (universal, infinite, limitless) exchange between subjects who have free hands in the exercise or the appreciation of fine art, all that presupposes a commerce between the divine artist and the human one. And indeed this commerce is a *mimesis*, in the strict sense, a play, a mask, an identification with the other on stage, and not the imitation of an object by its copy. "True" *mimesis* is between two producing subjects and not between two produced things. Implied by the whole third *Critique*, even though the explicit theme, even less the word itself, never appears, this kind of *mimesis* inevitably entails the condemnation of imitation, which is always characterized as being servile.

As the first effect of this anthropo-theological *mimesis*, a divine teleology secures the political economy of the Fine-Arts, the hierarchical opposition of free art and mercenary art. *Economimesis* puts everything in its place, starting with the instinctual work of animals without language and ending with God, passing by way of the mechanical arts, mercenary art, liberal arts, aesthetic arts and the Fine-Arts.

We are now at the point where the structure of *mimesis* effaces the opposition between nature and art, *agere* and *facere*. And perhaps we rediscover here the root of that pleasure which, before having been reserved for art and for the beautiful, used to belong to knowledge. As for Aristotle, *mimesis* is that which belongs to the essential definition [*le propre*] of man. Kant speaks of imitation as "aping" (*singerie*) [§ 49]; the ape knows how to imitate, but he does not know how to mime in the sense in which only the freedom of a subject mimes itself. The ape is not a subject and has no relation—not even that of subjection—to the other as such. And the *Poetics* places *mimesis* at the conjoined origin of knowledge and pleasure: "Poetry does seem to owe its origin to two causes, and two natural causes [*physikai*]. To imitate [*mimeisthai*] is natural [*symphyton*: innate, congenital] for men and shows itself from infancy—man differs from other animals in that he is very apt at imitation [*mimetikôtaton*] and it is by means of this that he acquires his first knowledge [*mathesis protas*], and secondly in that all men take pleasure in imitations [*khairein tois mimemasi pantas*]" [1448 b].

It must still be explained, in order to carry the analysis of a traditional link as far as possible, why the *Poetics* associates pleasure and knowledge while, in the same space of *mimesis*, the third *Critique* appears to disassociate them. In the first place it is because here, as we have seen, the unity of pleasure and knowledge was not excluded but merely re-assigned to the unconsciousness of some immemorial time. And in the second, because nature, the object of knowledge, will turn out to have been an art, an object of pleasure; and natural beauty will have been the production of a natural art. A strange imperfect tense signals it, referring either to an "above-in-the-text" or to some originary production. Following an *als ob*: "On this feeling of freedom in the play of our faculties of knowledge, which must at the same time be purposive, rests that pleasure which alone is universally communicable, without however being based on concepts. Nature was beautiful when it simultaneously was seen as art [*Die Natur war schön, wenn sie zugleich als Kunst aussah*] and art cannot be called beautiful unless we are conscious that it is art while yet it is seen, by us, as nature" [45].

The only beauty therefore remains that of productive nature. Art is beautiful to the degree that it is productive *like* productive nature, that it reproduces the production and not the product of nature, to the degree that nature may once have been (was), before the critical disassociation and before a still to be determined forgetfulness, beautiful. The analogy leads back to this precritical time, anterior to all the disassociations, oppositions, and delimitations of critical discourse, "older" even than the time of the transcendental aesthetic.

The beautiful brings productive nature back to itself, it qualifies a spectacle that artist-nature has given itself. God has given himself to be seen in a spectacle, just as if he had masked—had shown—himself: a theomime, a physiomime, for the pleasure of God—an immense liberality which however can only give itself to itself to be consumed.

If *economimesis* institutes a specular relation between two liberties, readable in reflective judgment and in *gustus reflectans*, how can man's freedom be said to resemble the freedom of God? Do we know what freedom is, what *freedom* means before having conceived of *physis* as *mimesis*? Before the fold God gives himself in a miroir? How can man's freedom (in a liberal economy) resemble God's freedom which resembles itself and reassembles itself in it. It resembles it precisely by not imitating it, the only way one freedom can resemble another.

The passage of *mimesis* cannot proceed by concepts but only—between freedoms—by exemplars with reflective value, quasi-natural productions which will institute the non-conceptual rules of art.

The original agency here is the figure of genius. It capitalizes freedom but in the same gesture naturalizes the whole of *economimesis*. "Fine art is the art of genius" [§ 46]. *Ingenium* is natural, it is a natural talent, a gift of Nature [*Naturgabe*]. A productive and donative instance, genius is itself produced and given by nature. Without this gift of nature, without this present of a productive freedom, there would not be any fine art. Nature produces what produces, it produces freedom [for] itself [*elle se produit la liberté*] and gives it to itself. In giving non-conceptual rules to art (rules "abstracted from the act, that is from the product"), in producing "exemplars," genius does nothing more than reflect nature, represent it: both as its legacy or its delegate and as its faithful image. "Genius is the innate disposition of the spirit [*ingenium*], *by which* nature gives rules to art" [§ 46].

The non-conceptual role, readable in the act and off the exemplar, does not derive from imitation (genius is incompatible with "the spirit of imitation"). Genius is not learned. "To learn is nothing other than to imitate." Beyond the fact that with this last proposition (§ 47), one returns to the language of the *Poetics*, the affinity is confirmed by the fact that the originality of genius and the exemplarity of its products must incite a certain imitation. A good imitation: one which is not a servile repetition, which does not reproduce, which avoids counterfeiting and plagiarism. This free imitation of a freedom (that of genius) which freely imitates divine freedom is a point that is "difficult to explain." The ideas "awaken," stir up, excite "similar ideas," neighboring, related, analogical [*ähnliche*] ones. The difficult nuance which relates good to bad imitation, good to bad repetition, is fixed briefly in the opposition between *imitation* and *copy* [*contrefaçon*], between *Nachahmung* and *Nachtmachung*. The indiscernibility of that distinction, which nevertheless pervades everything, is repeated, imitated, counterfeited in the signifier: a perfect anagrammatical inversion, except for a single letter.

Once nature has detached genius in order to represent it and to give its rules to art, everything turns out to be naturalized, immediately or not, everything is interpreted as a structure of naturality: the content of empirical culturalism, the political economy of art, its very particular propositions, going from the verse of Frederick the Great to assertions about salary scales.

The second remark on salary belongs to the chapter "On the Divisions of the Fine-Arts" [§ 51]: "Everything which is studied and painful must therefore be avoided [in the Fine-Arts]; for fine art must be free art in a double sense: it is not, of course, in the form of some salaried activity [*Lohngeschäft*], work whose quantity can be evaluated according to a determined measure, which can be imposed [*erzwingen*] or paid for [*bezahlen*]: but at the same time the mind must feel itself occupied, although appeased and excited without looking to any other purpose (independent, that is, of any salary).

"The orator therefore gives something that he does not promise, namely an attractive play of the imagination; but he also cheats a little on what he promises and on what he announces as being properly his business, namely the purposive occupation of the understanding. The poet conversely promises little and announces a mere play with ideas, but he supplies something which has the value of a serious occupation, because he provides in this play food for the understanding and gives life to his concepts by the aid of the imagination: on the whole, the poet thus gives more, and the orator less than he promises."

At the summit is the poet, analogous (and that precisely by a return of *logos*) to God: he gives more than he promises, he submits to no exchange contract, his overabundance generously breaks the circular economy. The hierarchy of the Fine-Arts therefore signifies that some power supersedes the (circular) economy, governs and places itself above (restricted) political economy. The naturalization of political economy subordinates the production and the commerce of art to a transeconomy.

Economimesis is not impaired by it, on the contrary. It unfolds itself there to infinity. It suffers that transeconomy in order to pass to infinity as "Kantism" passes into "Hegelianism." An infinite circle plays [with] itself and uses human play to reappropriate the gift for itself. The poet or genius receives from nature what he gives, of course, but first he receives from nature (from God), besides the given, the giving, the power to produce and to give more than he promises to men. The poetic gift, content and power, wealth and action, is an add-on [*un en-plus*] given as a [power] to give [*un donner*] by God to the poet, who transmits it in order to permit this supplementary surplus value to make its return to the infinite source—this source which can never be lost (by definition, if one can say that of the infinite). All that must pass through the voice. The genius poet is the voice of God who gives him voice, who gives himself and by giving gives to himself, gives himself what he gives, gives himself the [power] to give (*Gabe* and *es gibt*), plays freely with himself, only breaks the finite circle or contractual exchange in order to strike an infinite accord with himself. As soon as the infinite gives itself (to be thought), the *opposition* tends to be effaced between restricted and general economy, circulation and expendiary productivity. That is even, if we can still use such terms, the *function* of the passage to the infinite: the passage of the infinity between gift and debt.

Being what he is, the poet gives more than he promises. More than anyone asks of him. And this more belongs to the understanding: it announces a game and it gives something conceptual. Doubtless it is a plus-law [a more/no-more law] [*un plus-de-loi*], but one produced by a faculty whose essential character is *spontaneity*. Giving more than he promises or than is asked of him, the genius poet is paid for this more by no one, at least within the political economy of man. But God supports him. He supports him with speech and in return for gratitude He furnishes him his capital, produces and reproduces his labor force, gives him surplus value and the means of giving surplus value.

This is a poetic commerce, because God is a poet. There is a relation of hierarchical analogy between the poetic action of the speaking art, at the summit, and the action of God who dictates *Dichtung* to the poet.

This structure of *economimesis* necessarily has its *analogon* in the city. The poet, when he is neither writing nor singing, is just a man among men, must also eat. He must sustain the (mechanical) labor force which poetry, Kant shows, *cannot* forgo. So that he may not forget that his essential wealth comes to him from on high, and that his true commerce links him to the loftiness of free, not mercenary art, he receives subsides from the sun-king or from the enlightened-and-enlightening monarch, from the king-poet, the analogue of the poet-god: from Frederick the Great, a sort of national fund for letters which serves to lessen the rigors of supply and demand in a liberal economy. But this powerful scheme does not necessarily carry over into another organization of the restricted economy. *Economimesis* itself can still find a way to make a profit [*peut s'y retrouver dans ses comptes*].

Frederick the Great, the "great king," is almost the only poet quoted by the third *Critique*—a sign of the servile precaution and bad taste on the part of the philosopher, it is often ironically noted. But these poetic lines, like the commentary that surrounds them, very rigorously describe the generous overabundance of a solar source. God, King, Sun, Poet, Genius, etc. give of themselves without counting. And if the relation of alterity between a restricted economy and a general economy is above all not a relation of opposition, then the various helio-poetics—Platonic, Kantian, Hegelian, Nietzschean (up to and including Bataille's)—form an apparently *analogical* chain. No oppositional logic seems fitted to disassociate its *themes*.

. . .

Hearing holds a certain privilege among the five senses. The classification of the *Anthropology* places it among the *objective* senses (touch, sight, and hearing) which gives a *mediate* perception of the object (sight and hearing). Objective senses put us in relation to an outside—which is not what taste and smell do. Here the sensible gets mixed in, with saliva for example, and penetrates the organ without preserving its objective subsistance. Mediate objective perception is reserved for sight and hearing which require the mediation of light or air. As for touch, it is objective and immediate.

There are thus two mediate objective senses, hearing and sight. In what respect does hearing prevail over sight? By virtue of its relation to air, that is to vocal production which can cause it to vibrate. A look is incapable of that. "It is precisely by this element, moved by the organ of voice, the mouth, that men, more easily and more completely, enter with others in a community of thought and sensations, especially if the sounds that each gives the other to hear are articulated and if, linked together by understanding according to laws, they constitute a language. The form of an object is not given by hearing, and linguistic sounds [*Sprachlaute*] do not immediately lead to the representation of the object, but by that very fact and because they signify nothing in themselves, at least no object, only, at most, interior feelings, they are the most appropriate means for characterizing concepts, and those who are born deaf, who consequently must also remain mute (without language) can never accede to anything more than an *analogon* of reason" [*Anthropology*, § 18].

"More easily and more completely": no exterior means is necessary, nothing exterior poses an obstacle. Communication here is closer to freedom and spontaneity. It is also more complete, since interiority expresses itself here directly. It is more universal for all these reasons. Speaking now of tone and modulation, the third *Critique* discovers in hearing a sort of "universal tongue." And once sounds no longer have any relation of natural representation with external sensible things, they are more easily linked to the spontaneity of the understanding. Articulated, they furnish a language in agreement with its laws. Here indeed we have the arbitrary nature of the vocal signifier. It belongs to the element of freedom and can only have interior or ideal signifieds, that is, conceptual ones. Between the concept and the system of hearing-oneself-speak, between the intelligible and speech, the link is privileged. One must use the term hearing-oneself-speak [*le s'entendre-parler*] because this structure is autoaffective; in it the mouth and the ear cannot be disassociated. And the proof of it, at the juncture of the empirical and the metempirical, is that the deaf are dumb. They have no access to the *logos itself*. With other senses and other organs they can *imitate* the *logos*, establish with it a sort of empty or purely external relation. They can only become *analogons* of that which regulates all analogy and which itself is not analogical, since it forms the ground of analogy, the *logos* of analogy towards which everything flows back but which itself remains without system, outside of the system that it orients as its end and its origin, its embouchure and its source. That is why the mouth may have analogues in the body at each of the orifices, higher or lower than itself, but is not simply exchangeable with them. If there is a vicariousness of all the senses it is *less true* of the sense of hearing; that is, of hearing-oneself-speak. The latter has a unique place in the system of the senses. It is not the "noblest" of senses. The greatest nobility accrues to sight which achieves the greatest remove from touch, allows itself to be less affected by the object. In this sense, the beautiful has an essential relation with vision in so far as it consumes less. Mourning presupposes sight. *Pulchritudo vaga* gives itself above all to be seen: and by suspending consumption on behalf of the *theorein*, it forms an object of pure taste in nature. Poetry, as a fine art, presupposes a preliminary concept and occasions a more adherent beauty on a more immediately present horizon of morality.

But if hearing is not the most noble of the senses, it takes its absolute privilege from its status as the least replaceable. It tolerates substitution badly and almost succeeds in resisting all vicariousness.

> *Is there anything* vicarious in the senses [Vicariat der Sinne], *that is, can one sense be used as a substitute for another? There may be. One can evoke by gesture the usual speech from a deaf person, granted that he has once been able to hear. In this, the eyes serve/ in place of ears/. The same thing may happen through observing the movements of his teacher's lips, indeed by his own speech muscles. But he will never attain real concepts* [wirklichen Begriffen], *since the signs necessary to him are not capable of universality, seeing the movements of another's organs of speech must convert the sounds, which his teacher has coaxed from him, into a feeling of the movement of his*

> *own speech muscles. But he will never attain real concepts* [wirklichen Begriffen], *since the signs necessary to him are not capable of universality. (. . .) Which deficiency* [Mangel] *or loss of sense is more serious, that of hearing or sight? When it is inborn, deficiency of hearing is the least reparable* [ersetzlich]. [Ibid. § 22]

Hence hearing, by its unique position, by its allergy to prosthesis, by the auto-affective structure that distinguishes it from sight, by its proximity to the inside and to the concept, by the constitutive process of hearing-oneself-speak is not merely one of the senses among others. It is not even, in spite of the conventional classifications, an external sense. It has a relation of evident affinity with what Kant calls internal sense. Now the latter is unique and its element, its "form" is time. Like hearing-oneself-speak. It does not properly belong, as the other senses do, to anthropology but to psychology. Thus hearing-oneself-speak, in its singular relation to the unique internal sense and by the eminent place it occupies in the third *Critique*, tears the problematic away from its anthropological space in order to make it pass, with all the consequences that can entail, into a psychological space.

> *The inner sense is not pure apperception, a consciousness of what man does (for the latter belongs to the power of thought) but of what man feels, to the extent he is affected by his own play of thought. Inner intuition, and consequently the relation between representations in time (whether simultaneous or successive), is at the basis of this consciousness. Its perceptions, and the (true or apparent) inner experience resulting from the combination of the perceptions does not simply belong to anthropology, in which one neglects the question of knowing whether or not man has a soul (as a special incorporal substance), but to psychology in which we believe that we perceive such a sense within ourselves, and in which the mind, represented in its quality as a pure faculty of feeling and thinking, is considered as a substance especially inhabiting man. —As a result there is but one inner sense, for there are not various organs by which man receives an inner sensation of himself . . .* [Ibid. § 24]

If hearing-oneself-speak, insofar as it also passes through a certain mouth, transforms everything into auto-affection, assimilates everything to itself by idealizing it within interiority, masters everything by mourning its passing, refusing to touch it, to digest it naturally, but digests it ideally, consumes what it does not consume and *vice versa*, produces disinterestedness in the possibility of pronouncing judgments, if that mouth governs a space of analogy into which it does not let itself be drawn, if it is from the irreplaceable place of this enormous "phantasm" (but one does not know what a phantasm is prior to the system of these effects) that it orders pleasure, what is the border or the absolute over-board [*le bord ou le débord absolu*] of this problematic? What is the (internal and external) border which traces its limit and the frame of its *parergon*? In other words, what is it that does not enter into this theory thus framed, hierarchised, regulated? What is excluded from it and what, proceeding from this exclusion, gives if form, limit, and contour? And what about this over-board with respect to what one calls the mouth? Since the mouth orders a pleasure dependant on assimilation, to ideal auto-affection, what is it that does not allow itself to be transformed into oral auto-affection, taking the *os* for a *telos*? What is it that does not let itself be regulated by exemplorality?

There is no answer to such a question. One cannot say, it is this or that, this or that thing. We will see why. And the impossibility of finding examples in this case, Kant's inability to furnish any at a certain moment will be very noticeable. In the same way that we have often had to treat examples preceding the law in a reflective manner, we are now about to discover a sort of law without example; and first of all we shall state our answer in a tautological form, as the inverted duplication of the question.

What this logo-phonocentric system excludes is not even a negative. The negative is its business and its work. What it excludes, what this very work excludes, is what does not allow itself to be digested, or represented, or stated—does not allow itself to be transformed into auto-affection by exemplorality. It is an irreducible heterogeneity which cannot be eaten either sensibly or ideally and which—this is the tautology—by never letting itself be swallowed must therefore *cause itself to be vomited*.

Vomit lends its form to this whole system, beginning with its specific parergonal overflow. It must therefore be shown that the scheme of vomiting, as the experience of disgust, is not merely one excluded term among others.

What then is the relation between disgust and vomit? It is indeed vomit that interests us rather than the act or process of vomiting, which are less disgusting than vomit insofar as they imply an activity, some initiative whereby the subject an at least still mimic mastery or dream it in auto-affection, believing that he *makes himself vomit*. Here, hetero-affection no longer even allows itself to be pre-digested in an act of making-oneself-vomit.

Why vomit then, as a parergon of the third *Critique* considered as a general synthesis of transcendental idealism?

Note

[1] *Fine-Arts* has been used throughout to translate *Beaux-Arts*, which translates *schöne Kunst*.

GILLES DELEUZE

What Is a *Dispositif*?

1988

Foucault's philosophy is often presented as an analysis of concrete "*dispositifs*" or apparatuses. But what is an apparatus? First of all, it is a skein, a multilinear whole. It is composed of lines of different natures. The lines in the apparatus do not encircle or surround systems that are each homogenous in themselves, the object, the subject, language, etc., but follow directions, trace processes that are always out of balance, that sometimes move closer together and sometimes farther away. Each line is broken, subject to *changes in direction*, bifurcating and forked, and subjected to *derivations*. Visible objects, articulable utterances, forces in use, subjects in position are like vectors or tensors. Thus the three main instances Foucault successively distinguishes—Knowledge, Power and Subjectivity—by no means have contours that are defined once and for all but are chains of variables that are torn from each other. Foucault always finds a new dimension or a new line in a crisis. Great thinkers are somewhat seismic; they do not evolve but proceed by crises or quakes. Thinking in terms of moving lines was Herman Melville's operation: fishing lines, diving lines, dangerous, even deadly lines. These are lines of sedimentation, Foucault says, but also lines of "fissure" and "fracture." Untangling the lines of an apparatus means, in each case, preparing a map, a cartography, a survey of unexplored lands—this is what he calls "field work." One has to be positioned on the lines themselves; and these lines do not merely compose an apparatus but pass through it and carry it north to south, east to west or diagonally.

The first two dimensions of an apparatus or the ones that Foucault first extracted are the curves of visibility and the curves of utterance. Because apparatuses are like Raymond Roussel's machines, which Foucault also analyzed; they are machines that make one see and talk. Visibility does not refer to a general

From *Two Regimes of Madness: Texts and Interviews 1975–1995*, ed. David Lapoujade and trans. Ames Hodges and Mike Taormina (Los Angeles, CA: Semiotext[e], 2006), pp. 338–48 ["Qu'est-ce qu'un dispositif?" in *Deux régimes de fous et autres textes (1975–1995)* (Paris: Editions de Minuit, 2003); first published in *Michel Foucault, philosophe: Rencontre internationale, Paris, 9, 10, 11 Janvier 1988* (Paris: Editions du Seuil, 1989)].

light that would illuminate preexisting objects; it is made up of lines of light that form variable figures inseparable from an apparatus. Each apparatus has its regimen of light, the way it falls, softens and spreads, distributing the visible and the invisible, generating or eliminating an object, which cannot exist without it. This is not only true of painting but of architecture as well: the "prison apparatus" as an optical machine for seeing without being seen. If there is a historicity of apparatuses, it is the historicity of regimes of light but also of regimes of utterances. Utterances in turn refer to the lines of enunciation where the differential positions of the elements of an utterance are distributed. And the curves themselves are utterances because enunciations are curves that distribute variables and a science at a given moment, or a literary genre or a state of laws or a social movement are precisely defined by the regimes of utterances they engender. They are neither subjects nor objects but regimes that must be defined for the visible and the utterable with their derivations, transformations, mutations. In each apparatus, the lines cross thresholds that make them either aesthetic, scientific, political, etc.

Thirdly, an apparatus contains lines of force. One might say that they move from one single point to another on the previous lines. In a way, they "rectify" the previous curves, draw tangents, surround the paths from one line to another, operate a to-and-fro from seeing to speaking and vice versa, acting like arrows that constantly mix words and things without ceasing to carry out their battles. A line of forces is produced "in every relationship between one point and another" and moves through every place in an apparatus. Invisible and unspeakable, this line is closely combined with the others but can be untangled. Foucault pulls this line and finds its trajectory in Roussel, Brisset and the painters Magritte and Rebeyrolle. It is the "dimension of power" and power is the third dimension of space, interior to the apparatus and variable with the apparatuses. Like power, it is composed with knowledge.

And finally, Foucault discovered lines of subjectivation. This new dimension has already given rise to so much misunderstanding that it is hard to specify its conditions. More than any other, this discovery came from a crisis in Foucault's thought, as if he needed to rework the map of apparatuses, find a new orientation for them to prevent them from closing up behind impenetrable lines of force imposing definitive contours. Leibniz expressed in exemplary fashion this state of crisis that restarts thought when it seems that everything is almost resolved: you think you have reached shore but are cast back out to sea. And as for Foucault, he sensed that the apparatuses he analyzed could not be circumscribed by an enveloping line without other vectors passing above and below: "crossing the line," he said, like "going to the other side"?[1] This going beyond the line of force is what happens when it bends back, starts meandering, goes underground or rather when force, instead of entering into a linear relationship with another force, turns back on itself, acts on itself or affects itself. This dimension of the Self is not a preexisting determination that can be found ready-made. Here again, a line of subjectivation is a process, a production of subjectivity in an apparatus: it must be made to the extent that the apparatus allows it or makes it possible. It is a line of flight. It escapes the previous lines; it escapes *from them*. The Self is not knowledge or power. It is a process of individuation that affects groups or people and eludes both established lines of force and constituted knowledge. It is a kind of surplus value. Not every apparatus necessarily has it.

Foucault designates the apparatus of the Athenian city-state as the first place of creation of a subjectivation: according to his original definition, the city-state invents a line of forces that moves through the *rivalry between free men*. From this line on which a free man can have command over others, a very different line separates itself according to which the one who commands free men must also be master of himself. These optional rules for self-mastery constitute a subjectivation, an autonomous subjectivation, even if it is later called on to furnish new knowledge and inspire new powers. One might wonder whether lines of subjectivation are the extreme edge of an apparatus and whether they trace the passage from one apparatus to another: in this sense, they would prepare "lines of fracture." And no more than other lines, lines of subjectivation have no general formula. Cruelly interrupted, Foucault's research was going to show that processes of subjectivation eventually took on other modes than the Greek mode, for example in Christian apparatuses, modern societies, etc. Couldn't we cite apparatuses where subjectivation no longer goes through aristocratic life or the aestheticized existence of free men but through the marginalized existence of the "excluded"? The sinologist Tokei explains how freed slaves in a way lost their social status and found themselves relegated to an isolated, plaintive, *elegiac* existence from which they had to draw new forms of power and knowledge. The study of the variations in the processes of subjectivation seems to be one of the tasks Foucault left those who came after him. I believe this research will be extremely fruitful and the current endeavors towards a history of private life only partially overlap it. Sometimes the ones subjectivized are the nobles, the ones who say "we the good . . ." according to Nietzsche, but under other conditions the excluded, the bad, the sinners, or the hermits, or monastic communities, or heretics are subjectivized: an entire typology of subjective formations in changing apparatuses. And with combinations to be untangled everywhere: productions of subjectivity escaping the powers and knowledge of one apparatus to reinvest themselves in another through other forms to be created.

Apparatuses are therefore composed of lines of visibility, utterance, lines of force, lines of subjectivation, lines of cracking, breaking and ruptures that all intertwine and mix together and where some augment the others or elicit others through variations and even mutations of the assemblage. Two important consequences ensue for a philosophy of apparatuses. The first is the repudiation of universals. A universal explains nothing; it, on the other hand, must be explained. All of the lines are lines of variation that do not even have constant coordinates. The One, the Whole, the True, the object, the subject are not universals but singular processes of unification, totalization, verification, objectification, subjectivation immanent to an apparatus. Each apparatus is therefore a multiplicity where certain processes in becoming are operative and are distinct from those operating in another apparatus. This is how Foucault's philosophy is a pragmatism, a functionalism, a positivism, a pluralism. Reason may cause the greatest problem because processes of rationalization can operate on segments or regions of all the lines discussed so far. Foucault pays homage to Nietzsche for a historicity of reason. And he notes all of the importance of epistemological research on the various forms of rationality in knowledge (Koyré, Bachelard, Canguilhem), of socio-political research into the modes of rationality in power (Max Weber). Maybe he kept the third line for himself, the study of the types of "reasonable" in potential subjects. But he refused essentially to identify these processes in a Reason *par excellence*. He rejected any restoration of universals of reflection, communication or consensus. In this sense, one could say that his relationship with the Frankfurt School and the successors to this school are a long series of misunderstandings for which he is not responsible. And no more than there are universals of a founding subject or exemplary Reason that would allow judgment of apparatuses, there are no universals of the disaster of reason being alienated or collapsing once and for all. As Foucault told Gérard Raulet, there is not one bifurcation of reason; it constantly bifurcates, there are as many bifurcations and branches as instaurations, as many collapses as constructions following the cuts carried out by the apparatuses and "there is no meaning to the statement that reason is a long story that is now over."[2] From this point of view, the objection raised with Foucault of knowing how to assess the relative value of an apparatus if no transcendental values can be called on as universal coordinates is a question that could lead us backward and lose its meaning itself. Should one say that all apparatuses are equal (nihilism)? Thinkers like Spinoza and Nietzsche showed long ago that modes of existence had to be weighed according to immanent criteria, according to their content in "possibilities," freedom, creativity with no call to transcendental values. Foucault even alluded to "aesthetic" criteria, understood as life criteria, that substitute an immanent evaluation for a transcendental judgment every time. When we read Foucault's last books, we must do our best to understand the program he is offering his readers. An intrinsic aesthetics of modes of existence as the final dimension of apparatuses?

The second result of a philosophy of apparatuses is a change in orientation, turning away from the Eternal to apprehend the new. The new is not supposed to designate fashion, but on the contrary the variable creativity for the apparatuses: in conformance with the question that began to appear in the 20th century of how the production of something new in the world is possible. It is true that Foucault explicitly rejected the "originality" of an utterance as a non-pertinent, negligible criterion. He only wanted to consider the "regularity" of utterances. But what he meant by regularity was the slope of the curve passing through the singular points or the differential values of the group of utterances (he also defined the relationship of forces as distributions of singularities in a social field). By rejecting the originality of utterances, he meant that the potential contradiction of two utterances is not enough to distinguish them or to indicate the newness of one in relation to the other. What counts is the newness of the regime of enunciation itself in that it can include contradictory utterances. For example, we could ask what regime of utterances appeared with the French Revolution or the Russian Revolution: the newness of the regime counts more than the originality of the utterance. Each apparatus is thus defined by its content of newness and creativity, which at the same time indicates its ability to change or even to break for the sake of a future apparatus unless, on the contrary, there is an increase of force to the hardest, most rigid and solid lines. Since they escape the dimensions of knowledge and power, lines of subjectivation seem particularly apt to trace paths of creation, which are constantly aborted but also taken up again and modified until the old apparatus breaks. Foucault's as yet unpublished studies on the various Christian processes will certainly open many directions in this regard. One should not believe, however, that the production of subjectivity is left only to religion; anti-religious struggles are also creative, just as the regimes of light, enunciation and domination move through very diverse domains. Modern subjectivations resemble the Greek subjectivations no more than Christian ones; the same is true of light, utterances and powers.

We belong to these apparatuses and act in them. The newness of an apparatus in relation to those preceding it is what we call its currency, our currency. The new is the current. The current is not what we are but rather what we become, what we are in the process of becoming, in other words the Other, our becoming-other. In every apparatus, we have to distinguish between what we are (what we already no longer are) and what we are becoming: *the part of history, the part of currentness*. History is the archive, the design of what we are and cease being while the current is the sketch of what we will become. Thus history or the archive is also what separates us from ourselves, while the current is the Other with which we already coincide. Some have thought that Foucault was painting the portrait of modern societies as disciplinary apparatuses in opposition to the old apparatuses of sovereignty. This is not the case: the disciplines Foucault described are the history of what we are slowly ceasing to be and our current apparatus is taking shape in attitudes of open and constant *control* that are very different from the recent closed disciplines. Foucault agrees with Burroughs, who announced that our future would be more controlled than disciplined. The question is not which is worse. Because we also call on productions of subjectivity capable of resisting this new domination and that are very different from the ones used in the past against the disciplines. A new light, new utterances, new power, new forms of subjectivation? In every apparatus we must untangle the lines of the recent past from the lines of the near future: the archive from the current, the part of history and the part of becoming, *the part of analysis and the part of diagnosis*. If Foucault is a great philosopher, it is because he used history for something else: like Nietzsche said, to act against time and thus on time in favor, I hope, of a time to come. What Foucault saw as the current or the new was what Nietzsche called the untimely, the "non-current," the becoming that splits away from history, the diagnosis that relays analysis on different paths. Not predicting, but being attentive to the unknown knocking at the door. Nothing reveals this better than a fundamental passage from *The Archeology of Knowledge* (II, 5) that applies to all his work:

> Analysis of the archive therefore includes a privileged area: it is both close to us and different from our current time. It is the edge of time that surrounds our present, overlooks it and indicates its alterity; the archive is what, outside of us, delimits us. The description of the archive unfolds its possibilities (and the mastery of its possibilities) starting with discourses that have just stopped being ours; its threshold of existence begins with the break that separates us from what we can no longer say and what falls outside our discursive practices; it begins with the outside of our own language; its place is the distance from our own discursive practices. In this sense it can serve as our diagnosis. Not because it would allow us to draw a portrait of our distinctive traits and sketch out in advance the aspect we will have in the future. But it releases us from our continuities; it dissipates the temporal identity where we like to look at ourselves to avoid the ruptures of history; it breaks the thread of transcendental teleologies; and while anthropological thought would examine the being of humans or their subjectivity, it exposes the other, the outside. Diagnosis in this sense does not establish the recognition of our identity through the play of distinctions. It establishes that we are difference, that our reason is the difference between discourses, our history the difference between times, our self the difference between masks.

The different lines of an apparatus are divided into two groups: lines of stratification or sedimentation, lines of actualization or creativity. The final result of this method concerns Foucault's entire work. In most of his books, he determines a specific archive with extremely new historical means, the General Hospital in the 17th century, the clinic in the 18th, prison in the 19th, subjectivity in ancient Greece and then in Christianity. But that is only half of his task. Out of a sense of rigor, to avoid confusing things and trusting in his readers, he does not formulate the other half. He only formulates it explicitly in the interviews given alongside the publication of his major works: What are madness, prison, sexuality today? What new modes of subjectivation do we see appearing today that are certainly not Greek or Christian? This last question haunted Foucault until the end (we who are no longer Greek nor even Christian . . .). Foucault attached so much importance to his interviews in France and even more so abroad, not because he liked interviews, but because in them he traced lines of actualization that required another mode of expression than the assimilable lines in his major books. The interviews are diagnoses. It is like for Nietzsche, whose works are difficult to read without the *Nachlass* that is contemporary to each. Foucault's complete works, as Defert and Ewald imagine them, cannot separate the books that have left such an impression on us from the interviews that lead us toward a future, toward a becoming: strata and currentness.

Notes

[1] In "The Lives of Infamous Men," *Power: The Essential Works of Michel Foucault*, vol. 3 (New York: The New Press, 2000).

[2] In "Structuralism and Post-Structuralism," *Telos* 55, Spring 1983, pp. 195–211.

JACQUES RANCIÈRE

The Politics of Aesthetics: The Distribution of the Sensible

2000

I call the distribution of the sensible the system of self-evident facts of sense perception that simultaneously discloses the existence of something in common and the delimitations that define the respective parts and positions within it.[1] A distribution of the sensible therefore establishes at one and the same time something common that is shared and exclusive parts. This apportionment of parts and positions is based on a distribution of spaces, times, and forms of activity that determines the very manner in which something in common lends itself to participation and in what way various individuals have a part in this distribution. Aristotle states that a citizen is someone who *has a part* in the act of governing and being governed. However, another form of distribution precedes this act of partaking in government: the distribution that determines those who have a part in the community of citizens. A speaking being, according to Aristotle, is a political being. If a slave understands the language of its rulers, however, he does not "possess" it. Plato states that artisans cannot be put in charge of the shared or common elements of the community because they do *not have the time* to devote themselves to anything other than their work. They cannot be *somewhere else* because *work will not wait*. The distribution of the sensible reveals who can have a share in what is common to the community based on what they do and on the time and space in which this activity is performed. Having a particular "occupation" thereby determines the ability or inability to take charge of what is common to the community; it defines what is visible or not in a common space, endowed with a common language, etc. There is thus an "aesthetics" at the core of politics that has nothing to do with Benjamin's discussion of the "aestheticization of politics" specific to the "age of the masses." This aesthetics should not be understood as the perverse commandeering of politics by a will to art, by a consideration of the

From *The Politics of Aesthetics: The Distribution of the Sensible*, trans. Gabriel Rockhill (New York: Continuum, 2004), pp. 12–15, 24, 28–30, 42–45 [*Le partage du sensible: Esthétique et politique* (Paris: Editions La Fabrique, 2000)].

people qua work of art. If the reader is fond of analogy, aesthetics can be understood in a Kantian sense—re-examined perhaps by Foucault—as the system of *a priori* forms determining what presents itself to sense experience. It is a delimitation of spaces and times, of the visible and the invisible, of speech and noise, that simultaneously determines the place and the stakes of politics as a form of experience. Politics revolves around what is seen and what can be said about it, around who has the ability to see and the talent to speak, around the properties of spaces and the possibilities of time.

It is on the basis of this primary aesthetics that it is possible to raise the question of "aesthetic practices" as I understand them, that is, forms of visibility that disclose artistic practices, the place they occupy, what they "do" or "make" from the standpoint of what is common to the community. Artistic practices are "ways of doing and making" that intervene in the general distribution of ways of doing and making as well as in the relationships they maintain to modes of being and forms of visibility. The Platonic proscription of the poets is based on the impossibility of doing two things at once prior to being based on the immoral content of fables. The question of fiction is first a question regarding the distribution of places. From the Platonic point of view, the stage, which is simultaneously a locus of public activity and the exhibition-space for "fantasies," disturbs the clear partition of identities, activities, and spaces. The same is true of writing. By stealing away to wander aimlessly without knowing who to speak to or who not to speak to, writing destroys every legitimate foundation for the circulation of words, for the relationship between the effects of language and the positions of bodies in shared space. Plato thereby singles out two main models, two major forms of existence and of the sensible effectivity of language—writing and the theater—which are also structure-giving forms for the regime of the arts in general. However, these forms turn out to be prejudicially linked from the outset to a certain regime of politics, a regime based on the indetermination of identities, the delegitimation of positions of speech, the deregulation of partitions of space and time. This aesthetic regime of politics is strictly identical with the regime of democracy, the regime based on the assembly of artisans, inviolable written laws, and the theater as institution. Plato contrasts a third, good *form of art* with writing and the theater, the *choreographic* form of the community that sings and dances its own proper unity. In sum, Plato singles out three ways in which discursive and bodily practices suggest forms of community: the surface of mute signs that are, he says, like paintings, and the space of bodily movement that divides itself into two antagonistic models (the movement of simulacra on the stage that is offered as material for the audience's identifications and, on the other hand, the authentic movement characteristic of communal bodies).

Here we have three ways of distributing the sensible that structure the manner in which the arts can be perceived and thought of as forms of art *and* as forms that inscribe a sense of community: the surface of "depicted" signs, the split reality of the theater, the rhythm of a dancing chorus. These forms define the way in which works of art or performances are "involved in politics," whatever may otherwise be the guiding intentions, artists' social modes of integration, or the manner in which artistic forms reflect social structures or movements. When *Madame Bovary* was published, or *Sentimental Education*, these works were immediately perceived as "democracy in literature" despite Flaubert's aristocratic situation and political conformism. His very refusal to entrust literature with any message whatsoever was considered to be evidence of democratic equality. His adversaries claimed that he was democratic due to his decision to depict and portray instead of instruct. This equality of indifference is the result of a poetic bias: the equality of all subject matter is the negation of any relationship of necessity between a determined form and a determined content. Yet what is this indifference after all if not the very equality of everything that comes to pass on a written page, available as it is to everyone's eyes? This equality destroys all of the hierarchies of representation and also establishes a community of readers as a community without legitimacy, a community formed only by the random circulation of the written word.

In this way, a sensible politicity exists that is immediately attributed to the major forms of aesthetic distribution such as the theater, the page, or the chorus. These "politics" obey their own proper logic, and they offer their services in very different contexts and time periods. Consider the way these paradigms functioned in the connection between art and politics at the end of the nineteenth century and the beginning of the twentieth. Consider, for example, the role taken on by the paradigm of the page in all its different forms, which exceed the materiality of a written sheet of paper. Novelistic democracy, on the one hand, is the indifferent democracy of writing such as it is symbolized by the novel and its readership. There is also, however, the knowledge concerning typography and iconography, the intertwining of graphic and pictorial capabilities, that played such an important role in the Renaissance and was revived by Romantic typography through its use of vignettes, culs-de-lampe, and various innovations. This model disturbs the clear-cut rules of representative logic that establish a relationship of correspondence at a distance between the sayable and the visible. It also disturbs the clear partition between works of pure art and the ornaments made by the decorative arts. This is why it played such an important—and generally underestimated—role in the upheaval of the representative paradigm and of its political implications. I am thinking in particular of its role in the Arts and Crafts movement and all of its derivatives (Art Deco, Bauhaus, Constructivism). These movements developed an idea of furniture—in the broad sense of the term—for a new community, which also inspired a new idea of pictorial surface as a surface of shared writing.

[. . .]

From this perspective, it is possible to understand the functions served by the notion of modernity. The aesthetic regime of the arts, it can be said, is the true name for what is designated by the incoherent label "modernity." However, "modernity" is more than an incoherent label. It is, in its different versions, the concept that diligently works at [34] masking the specificity of this regime of the arts and the very meaning of the specificity of regimes of art. It traces, in order either to exalt or deplore it, a simple line of transition or rupture between the old and the new, the representative and the non-representative or the anti-representative. The basis for this simplistic historical account was the transition to non-figurative representation in painting. This transition was theorized by being cursorily assimilated into artistic "modernity's" overall anti-mimetic destiny. When the eulogists of this form of modernity saw the exhibition-spaces for the well-behaved destiny of modernity invaded by all kinds of objects, machines, and unidentified devices, they began denouncing the "tradition of the new," a desire for innovation that would reduce artistic modernity to the emptiness of its self-declaration. However, it is the starting point that is erroneous. The leap outside of *mimēsis* is by no means the refusal of figurative representation. Furthermore, its inaugural moment has often been called *realism*, which does not in any way mean the valorization of resemblance but rather the destruction of the structures within which it functioned. Thus, novelistic realism is first of all the reversal of the hierarchies of representation (the primacy of the narrative over the descriptive [35] or the hierarchy of subject matter) and the adoption of a fragmented or proximate mode of focalization, which imposes raw presence to the detriment of the rational sequences of the story. The aesthetic regime of the arts does not contrast the old with the new. It contrasts, more profoundly, two regimes of historicity. It is within the mimetic regime that the old stands in contrast with the new. In the aesthetic regime of art, the future of art, its separation from the present of non-art, incessantly restages the past. [. . .]

What is called *postmodernism* is really the process of this reversal. At first, postmodernism brought to light everything in the recent evolution of the arts and possible ways of thinking the arts that destroyed modernism's theoretical edifice: the crossing-over and mixture between the arts that destroyed Lessing's conventional set of principles concerning the separation of the arts; the collapse of the paradigm of functionalist architecture and the return of the curved line and embellishment; the breakdown of the pictorial/two-dimensional/abstract model through the return of figurative representation and signification as well as the slow invasion of painting's exhibition-space by three-dimensional and narrative forms, from Pop Art to installation art and "rooms" for video art;[2] the new combinations of painting and language as well as of monumental sculpture and the projection of shadows and lights; the breakup of the serial tradition through new mixtures between musical systems, genres, and epochs. The teleological model of modernity became untenable at the same time as its divisions between the "distinctive features" of the different arts, or the separation of a pure domain of art. Postmodernism, in a sense, was simply the name under whose guise certain artists and thinkers realized what modernism had been: a desperate attempt to establish a "distinctive feature of art" by linking it to a simple teleology of historical evolution and rupture. There was not really a need, moreover, to make this late recognition of a fundamental fact of the aesthetic regime of the arts into an actual temporal break, the real end of a historical period.

However, it was precisely the next episode that showed that postmodernism was more than this. The joyful, postmodern artistic license, its exaltation of the carnival of simulacra, all sorts of interbreeding and hybridization, transformed very quickly and came to challenge the freedom or autonomy that the modernatist principle conferred—or would have conferred—upon art the mission of accomplishing. There was thus a return from the carnival to the primal scene. However, the primal scene can be taken in two senses, either as the starting point of a process or as an original separation. Modernist faith had latched on to the idea of the "aesthetic education of man" that Schiller had extracted from the Kantian analytic of the beautiful. The postmodern reversal had as its theoretical foundation Lyotard's analysis of the Kantian sublime, which was reinterpreted as the scene of a founding distance separating the idea from any sensible presentation. From this moment onward, postmodernism came into harmony with the mourning and repenting of modernist thought, and the scene of sublime distance came to epitomize all sorts of scenes of original distance or original sin: the Heideggerian flight of the gods, the irreducible aspect of the unsymbolizable object and the death drive as analyzed by Freud, the voice of the Absolutely Other declaring a ban on representation, the revolutionary murder of the Father. Postmodernism thus became the grand threnody of the unrepresentable/intractable/irredeemable, denouncing the modern madness of the idea of a self-emancipation of mankind's humanity and its inevitable and interminable culmination in the death camps.

The notion of the avant-garde defines the type of subject suitable to the modernist vision and appropriate, according to this vision, for connecting the aesthetic to the political. Its success is due less to the convenient connection it proposes between the artistic idea of innovation and the idea of politically guided change, than to the more covert connection it establishes between two ideas of the "avant-garde." On the one hand, there is the topographical and military notion of the force that marches in the lead, that has a clear understanding of the movement, embodies its forces, determines the direction of historical evolution, and chooses subjective political orientations.[3] In short, there is the idea that links political subjectivity to a certain form: the party, an advanced detachment that derives its ability to lead from its ability to read and interpret the signs of history. On the other hand, there is another idea of the avant-garde that, in accordance with Schiller's model, is rooted in the aesthetic anticipation of the future. If the concept of the avant-garde has any meaning in the aesthetic regime of the arts, it is on this side of things, not on the side of the advanced detachments of artistic innovation but on the side of the invention of sensible forms, and material structures for a life to come. This is what the "aesthetic" avant-garde brought to the "political" avant-garde, or what it wanted to bring to it—and what it believed to have brought to it—by transforming politics into a total life program. The history of the relations between political parties and aesthetic movements is first of all the history of a confusion, sometimes complacently maintained, at other times violently denounced, between these two ideas of the avant-garde, which are in fact two different ideas of political subjectivity: the archi-political idea of a party, that is to say the idea of a form of political intelligence that sums up the essential conditions for change, and the meta-political idea of global political subjectivity, the idea of the potentiality inherent in the innovative sensible modes of experience that anticipate a community to come. There is, however, nothing accidental about this confusion. It is not the case, as today's doxa would have us believe, that artists' ambitious claims to a total revolution of the sensible paved the way for totalitarianism. It is rather that the very idea of a political avant-garde is divided between the strategic conception and the aesthetic conception of the avant-garde.

On Art and Work[4]

The first possible meaning of the notion of a "factory of the sensible" is the formation of a shared sensible world, a common habitat, by the weaving together of a plurality of human activities. However, the idea of a "distribution of the sensible" implies something more. A "common" world is never simply an *ethos*, a shared abode, that results from the sedimentation of a certain number of intertwined acts. It is always a polemical distribution of modes of being and "occupations" in [67] a space of possibilities. It is from this perspective that it is possible to raise the question of the relationship between the "ordinariness" of work and artistic "exceptionality." Here again referencing Plato can help lay down the terms of the problem. In the third book of the *Republic*, the mimetician is no longer condemned simply for the falsity and the pernicious nature of the images he presents, but he is condemned in accordance with a principle of division of labor that was already used to exclude artisans from any shared political space: the mimetician is, by definition, a double being. He does two things at once, whereas the principle of a well-organized community is that each person only does the one thing that they were destined to do by their "nature." In one sense, this statement says everything: the idea of work is not initially the idea of a determined activity, a process of material transformation. It is the idea of a distribution of the sensible: an impossibility of doing "something else" based on an "absence of time." This "impossibility" is part of the incorporated conception of the community. It establishes work as the necessary relegation of the worker to the private space-time of his occupation, his exclusion from participation in what is common to the community.[5] The mimetician brings confusion to [68] this distribution: he is a man of duplication, a worker who does two things at once. Perhaps the correlate to this principle is the most important thing: the mimetician provides a public stage for the "private" principle of work. He sets up a stage for what is common to the community with what should determine the confinement of each person to his or her place. It is this redistribution of the sensible that constitutes his noxiousness, even more than the danger of simulacra weakening souls. Hence, artistic practice is not the outside of work but its displaced form of visibility. The democratic distribution of the sensible makes the worker into a double being. It removes the artisan from "his" place, the domestic space of work, and gives him "time" to occupy the space of public discussions and take on the identity of a deliberative citizen. The mimetic act of splitting in two, which is at work in theatrical space, consecrates this duality and makes it visible. The exclusion of the mimetician, from the Platonic point of view, goes hand in hand with the formation of a community where work is in "its" place.

The principle of fiction that governs the representative regime of art is a way of stabilizing the artistic exception, of assigning it to a *technē*, which means two things: the art of imitations is a technique and not a lie. It ceases to be [69] a simulacrum, but at the same time it ceases to be the displaced visibility of work, as a distribution of the sensible. The imitator is no longer the double being against whom it is necessary to posit the city where each person only does a single thing. The art of imitations is able to inscribe its specific hierarchies and exclusions in the major distribution of the liberal arts and the mechanical arts.

The aesthetic regime of the arts disrupts this apportionment of spaces. It does not simply call into question mimetic division—i.e., the mimetic act of splitting in two—in favor of an immanence of thought in sensible matter. It also calls into question the neutralized status of *technē*, the idea of technique as the imposition of a form of thought on inert matter. That is to say that it brings to light, once again, the distribution of *occupations* that upholds the apportionment of domains of activity. This theoretical and political operation is at the heart of Schiller's *On the Aesthetic Education of Man*. Behind the Kantian definition of aesthetic judgment as a judgment without concepts—without the submission of the intuitive given to conceptual determination—Schiller indicates the political distribution that is the matter at stake: the division between those who act and those who are acted upon, between the cultivated classes that have access to a totalization of lived experience and the uncivilized classes immersed in the parceling out of work and of sensory experience. Schiller's "aesthetic" state, by suspending the opposition between active understanding and passive sensibility, aims at breaking down—with an idea of art—an idea of society based on the opposition between those who think and decide and those who are doomed to material tasks.

In the nineteenth century, this *suspension* of work's negative value became the assertion of its positive value as the very form of the shared effectivity of thought and community. This mutation occurred via the transformation of the suspension inherent in the "aesthetic state" into the positive assertion of the aesthetic *will*. Romanticism declared that the becoming-sensible of all thought and the becoming-thought of all sensible materiality was the very goal of the activity of thought in general. In this way, art once again became a symbol of work. It anticipates the end—the elimination of oppositions—that work is not yet in a position to attain by and for itself. However, it does this insofar as it is a *production*, the identification of a process of material execution with a community's self-presentation of its meaning. Production asserts itself as the principle behind a new distribution of the sensible insofar as it unites, in one and the same concept, terms that are traditionally opposed: the activity of manufacturing and visibility. Manufacturing meant inhabiting the private and lowly space-time of labor for sustenance. Producing unites the act of manufacturing with the act of bringing to light, the act of defining a new relationship between *making* and *seeing*. Art anticipates work because it carries out its principle: the transformation of sensible matter into the community's self-presentation. The texts written by the young Marx that confer upon work the status of the generic essence of mankind were only possible on the basis of German Idealism's aesthetic program, i.e., art as the transformation of thought into the sensory experience of the community. It is this initial program, moreover, that laid the foundation for the thought and practice of the "avant-gardes" in the 1920s: abolish art as a separate activity, put it back to work, that is to say, gave it back to life and its activity of working out its own proper meaning.

I do not mean by this that the modern valorization of work is only the result of the new way for thinking about art. On the one hand, the *aesthetic* mode of thought is much more than a way of thinking about art. It is an idea of thought, linked to an idea of the distribution of the sensible. On the other hand, it is also necessary to think about the way in which artists' art found itself defined on the basis of a twofold promotion of work: the economic promotion of work as the name for the fundamental human activity, but also the struggles of the proletariat to bring labor out of the night surrounding it, out of its exclusion from shared visibility and speech. It is necessary to abandon the lazy and absurd schema that contrasts the aesthetic cult of art for art's sake with the rising power of industrial labor. Art can show signs of being an exclusive activity insofar as it is work. Better informed than the demystifiers of the twentieth century, the critics in Flaubert's time indicated what links the cult of the sentence to the valorization of work, said to be wordless: the Flaubertian aesthete is a pebble breaker. At the time of the Russian Revolution, art and production would be identified because they came under one and the same principle concerning the redistribution of the sensible, they came under one and the same virtue of action that opens up a form of visibility at the same time as it manufactures objects. The cult of art presupposes a revalorization of the abilities attached to the very idea of work. However, this idea is less the discovery of the essence of human activity than a recomposition of the landscape of the visible, a recomposition of the relationship between doing, making, being, seeing, and saying. Whatever might be the specific type of economic circuits they lie within, artistic practices are not "exceptions" to other practices. They represent and reconfigure the distribution of these activities.

Notes

[1] *Le commun*—alternately translated as "something in common," "something common," "what is common," or "what is common to the community"—is strictly speaking what makes or produces a community and not simply an attribute shared by all of its members. The adjectival form of the same word, *commun*, is translated as "common," "shared," or "communal" depending on the context.—Trans.

[2] Cf. Raymond Bellour. "La chambre." *L'entre-images 2.* Paris: P.O.L., 1999. 281–317.

[3] "Subjective" here refers to the political process of "subjectivization" as it is explained in Appendix 1.—Trans.

[4] Rancière is concerned with the relationship between *l'art* et *le travail* in this chapter. The general term "work" was appropriate in most cases as a translation of *le travail*. However, certain contexts and expressions required using "labor" to translate the same term in French.—Trans.

[5] On Rancière's notion of *le commun*, see note 1.—Trans.

A Chronology of Works and Events

The chronology has two different goals: to locate texts that are either excerpted or referred to as particularly significant in the anthology in their context(s), and to sketch a more comprehensive bibliography of French philosophy in the postwar period. Accordingly, it is organized as a table that can be read horizontally and vertically. The rows correspond to years of publication of works and simultaneous events and are grouped into six "moments" that embody an interpretation of the "conversations" (debates, complementarities, and oppositions, even quarrels) and the "inventions" that we consider typical of the philosophical life in France in this period. The columns distinguish as much as possible the primary and secondary references within French philosophy, the French works and some significant contemporary philosophical works from other countries that represent virtual or actual interlocutors in the "Republic of Letters," the philosophical writings and some landmarks in other disciplines (scientific, artistic, literary), and finally the French and the global cultural and political events that form their general background or account for their reception. (We naturally recognize that these selections are of necessity somewhat arbitrary and questionable.)

We distinguish six successive "moments," whose boundaries are of course permeable. They are indeed linked to the identification of the typical categories in the history of ideas: "generations," "schools," "tendencies." But above all, in relation to the interpretive patterns that we have singled out in the construction of the anthology itself (confronting works and texts around such themes as "critique," "history of truth," "the subject," "event," etc.), they delineate crystallizations of problems in one common sense or common perception of philosophical questions and the movements of transition from one to another. The obvious difficulty here is, of course, that the actual intellectual effort never exactly coincides with the publication of books (which can be delayed, posthumous, etc.); it also takes place, sometimes above all, in teachings, conferences, correspondences, articles . . . We have tried to compensate for this distortion by sometimes referring to essays that would later appear in books or to seminar work. But a chronology can only indicate the possibility of a genuine history of the philosophical institution, not replace it.

In the establishment of correspondences between works of philosophy and their historical context, we try to suggest that there are phenomena both of *contemporaneity* and *non-contemporaneity* (or "untimely-ness" in the Nietzschean sense). It is often impossible—again, before an interpretive work, for which we provide only some materials in this anthology—to clearly delineate the two, as in the case of the effects of May 1968, which largely came as a surprise for all protagonists but was quasi-unanimously seen as a philosophical event as much as a political one. Thus while the final crisis of historical communism could be anticipated by many, given the importance of engagement in the practice of philosophy in the French context, its consequences led in the most opposite of directions. Similarly, we are not trying to abstractly oppose tradition and innovation. We insist on the reality of the *theoretical invention* in French philosophy during this period, but we are aware that inventions are inseparable from retroactive interpretations of the philosophical past (e.g., the Bergsonian legacy in the work of Deleuze, the Spinozistic turn of French structuralism, the lasting influence of Comtian biosociological positivism—very different from what is called positivism in other traditions—on French historical epistemology). We try to emphasize idiomatic reiterations without falling into national stereotypes (French "rationalism"—or "irrationalism"). We are especially interested in two kinds of temporal-intellectual schemes: one has to do with certain *aftereffects* of intellectual and/or historical events (examples are the "discovery" of German phenomenology and mathematical logic in the 1930s by Sartre, Merleau-Ponty, Levinas, Cavaillès, and Lautman, whose complete consequences are not seen before the 1950s or even the 1960s, or again the postponed opposite readings of Wittgenstein and Austin in Derrida, Bouveresse, Lyotard, and Descombes); the second concerns the *immediate shiftings* in the philosophical battlefield (as in Kant's notion of philosophy as a *Kampfplatz*, calling for a critical decision) which result from *public conversations* or *interventions*. Thus Heidegger's *Letter to Jean Beaufret* on humanism in 1946 may have changed the philosophical effects of liberation from the German occupation; the Bonneval Conference on the unconscious in 1960 revealed the novelty of the Lacanian reading of Freud to the philosophical community; the Althusser seminars at the Ecole Nationale Supérieure between 1961 and 1965 brought together, even if ephemerally, the various components of structuralism; the Nietzsche conference ("Décade de Cerisy") in 1972, which really launched the post-1968 moment or created what will be perceived inside France as *la pensée 68* and outside France as "anti-enlightenment philosophy" (notably by Habermas). It is only against the background of this phenomenological complexity that we believe it to be possible to read historical determinations of philosophical moments. Our presentation thus offers a picture of philosophy that is at once highly original in its styles yet never isolated from other discourses and practices—much less protected from their contamination by academic codes and rules.

Moment 1: The Legacy of the 1930s

The war period is one of constrained academic and intellectual activity under the German occupation. Prominent philosophical figures join the armed Resistance (Cavaillès, Lautman, Politzer, Canguilhem) and some die. No important philosophical figure, with the possible exception of Bertrand Jouvenel, joins the collaboration (in contrast to the case of literature). A significant group emigrates to the United States, contributing to the creation of the New School for Social Research in New York City (Lévi-Strauss, Koyré). The deportation and extermination of Jews also changes the worldview of eminent nationalist thinkers (Blanchot). It is also a period of remarkable artistic and philosophical innovation, where the new generation born around 1905—partially breaking with a "French" tradition and building on the lessons learned across the border in the 1930s (phenomenology, mathematical logic, behaviorism and Gestalt psychology, structural linguistics)—renovates French philosophy and publishes its masterpieces. This is one sense in which Sartre's disturbing formula (in "La République du silence" in 1944) could be interpreted: "Never have we been so free as under the occupation."

Date	French Works of Philosophy	Other Works of Philosophy (World)	Works of Literature, Art, and Science	Events in France	World Events
1937	**Jean-Paul Sartre** (1905–80), *La transcendance de l'ego*				
1938	**Raymond Aron** (1905–83), *Introduction à la philosophie de l'histoire* **Gaston Bachelard** (1884–1962), *La formation de l'esprit scientifique; La psychanalyse du feu* **Jean Cavaillès** (1903–44), *Méthode axiomatique et formalisme* **Jacques Lacan** (1901–81), *Les complexes familiaux dans la formation de l'individu* **Albert Lautman** (1908–44), *Essai sur les notions de structure et d'existence en mathématique*		**Antonin Artaud** (1896–1948), *Le théâtre et son double* **Sartre**, *La nausée* **Virginia Woolf** (1882–1941), *Three Guineas*		After the Munich agreement, Nazi Germany invades Czechoslovakia
1939	**Cavaillès** and **Lautman**, "La pensée mathématique" **Alexandre Koyré** (1892–1964), *Etudes galiléennes* **Henri Lefebvre** (1901–91), *Le matérialisme dialectique*	**Ludwig Wittgenstein** (1889–1951) becomes a teaching fellow at Cambridge	**Bourbaki**, *Elements de mathématiques*, vol. 1 **Georges Dumézil** (1898–1986), *Mythes et dieux des Germains* **Sigmund Freud** (1856–1939), *Der Mann Moses und die Monotheistische Religion*		Nazi Germany invades Poland after German-Soviet pact
1940	**Bachelard**, *La philosophie du non*			Nazi Germany invades France	

1941		**Roman Jakobson** (1896–1982), *Kindersprache, Aphasie, und allgemeine Lautgesetze*	Nazi Germany invades the USSR After Pearl Harbor, the United States enters the war **Woolf** commits suicide **James Joyce** (1882–1941) dies
1942	In prison, **Cavaillès** writes *Sur la logique et la théorie de la science* (published posthumously in 1947) **Maurice Merleau-Ponty** (1908–61), *La structure du comportement*	**Albert Camus** (1913–60), *L'étranger* **Lucien Febvre** (1878–1956), *Le problème de l'incroyance au XVIe siècle* **Jean Genet** (1910–86), "Le condamné à mort"	Battle of Stalingrad (until 1943)
1943	**Georges Bataille** (1897–1962), *L'expérience intérieure* **Georges Canguilhem** (1904–95), *Le normal et le pathologique* **Sartre**, *L'être et le néant*		

Date	French Works of Philosophy	Other Works of Philosophy (World)	Works of Literature, Art, and Science	Events in France	World Events
1944		**Theodor Adorno** (1903–69) and **Max Horkheimer** (1895–1973), *Dialektik der Aufklärung* **Alfred Tarski** (1902–83), "The Semantic Conception of Truth and the Foundations of Semantics"	**Louis Aragon** (1897–1982), *Aurélien* **Henri de Lubac** (1896–91), *Le drame de l'humanisme athée* **Sartre**, *Huis-Clos*	**Cavaillès** and **Lautman** captured and killed France liberated by Allied forces with help from the Resistance Communist leader Maurice Thorez returns to France from the USSR and joins the government	Bretton Woods monetary agreement
1945	**Merleau-Ponty**, *Phénoménologie de la perception* **Henri Wallon** (1879–1962), *Les origines de la pensée chez l'enfant*	**Karl Popper** (1902–94), *The Open Society and Its Enemies*	**Bertolt Brecht** (1898–1956), *Der kaukasische Kridekreis* **André Breton** (1896–1966), *Arcane 17* **Paul Celan** (1920–70), *Die Todesfuge* Founding of the journal *Les Temps Modernes*, publishing Sartre, Aron, Beauvoir, and Merleau-Ponty)	Marshal Pétain sentenced to death, later commuted to life in prison **Paul Valéry** (1871–1945) dies	Yalta Conference Hiroshima and Nagasaki bombings Victory of Allied forces Nuremberg trial Founding of the United Nations

Moment 2: The Aftermath of the War: 1946–60

Politically, the period is dominated by the emergence and the consequences of the Cold War, which are felt in every cultural and intellectual field, both arising from and contributing to Sartre's notion of *engagement*, but also central for Aron (the great liberal-conservative figure), for communists (whether orthodox or dissidents), and for Gaullists (who cultivate the myth of the savior after General de Gaulle's first resignation from power in 1946). Increasingly, the tension of dramatic colonial wars (Indochina, Algeria) polarizes the moral and political debates, contributing to the delegitimization of reformist socialists who wage them, and progressively accrediting on the left various combinations of anti-imperialist and Third World ideologies. The creative combination of *engagement* and literature is especially noticeable in theater. Philosophically, the dominant current is *existential phenomenology*, with Sartre as a powerful spokesman and Merleau-Ponty as a more lasting theoretical influence, well into the apparently incompatible currents of structuralism and anthropology. Other decisive contributions to the nascent debate over humanism and antihumanism are Heidegger's "French reception" (which surprises many Germans); Gueroult's and Goldschmidt's "structural method" in the history of philosophy; Kojèvian Hegelianism and Marxism; major contributions to the historical epistemology of Bachelard, Koyré, and Canguilhem; and Blanchot's and Bataille's theorization of writing as transgressive interruption of discourse. On the humanist side, the essential divide is between atheist philosophies (Camus) and Christian *personnalisme* (Mounier, even Teilhard).

Date	French Works of Philosophy	Other Works of Philosophy (World)	Works of Literature, Art, and Science	Events in France	World Events
1946	**Sartre**, *Réflexions sur la question juive*	**Martin Heidegger** (1889–1976), *Brief über den Humanismus*	**Bataille** creates the journal *Critique* **Le Corbusier** (1887–1965) builds the *Cité radieuse* in Marseilles **Sergei Eisenstein** (1898–1948), *Ivan the Terrible* **Paul Eluard** (1895–1952), *Poésie ininterrompue* **Célestin Freinet** (1896–1966) creates his libertarian experimental school	Charles de Gaulle quits office and creates a new political party Beginning of the War in Indochina	
1947	**Victor Goldschmidt** (1914–1981), *Les dialogues de Platon: Structure et méthode dialectique* **Lefebvre**, *Critique de la vie quotidienne I* **Alexandre Kojève** (1902–68), *Introduction à la lecture de Hegel* (ed. Queneau) **Merleau-Ponty**, *Humanisme et terreur*	**Rudolf Carnap** (1891–1970), *Meaning and Necessity*	**Robert Antelme** (1917–1990), *L'espèce humaine* **Breton**, *Ode à Charles Fourier* **Charlie Chaplin** (1889–1977), *Monsieur Verdoux* **Fernand Deligny** (1913–96), *Les vagabonds efficaces* **Genet**, *Les bonnes* **Thomas Mann** (1875–1955), *Doktor Faustus* **Arnold Schoenberg** (1874–1951), *A Survivor from Warsaw*	Communist ministers expelled from the government after strikes by automobile workers Plan Langevin Wallon, draft reform of the educational system	Marshall Plan Beginning of the Cold War Founding of Kominform Independence of India and partition war with Pakistan

1948	**Sartre**, "Qu'est-ce que la littérature?" (*Situations, II*)	**György Lukacs** (1885–1971), *Der junge Hegel* **José Ortega y Gasset** (1883–1955), *Une interprétation de l'histoire universelle* **Bertrand Russell** (1872–1970), *Human Knowledge*	**Artaud**, *Pour en finir avec le jugement de Dieu* **Maurice Blanchot** (1907–2003), *Le Très-Haut* **René Char** (1907–88), *Fureur et mystère* **Antonio Gramsci** (1891–1937), *Quaderni del carcere* (1st ed., posthumous) **Michel Leiris** (1901–90), *Biffures (La règle du jeu—I)* **Nathalie Sarraute** (1900–1999), *Portrait d'un inconnu* **Norbert Wiener** (1894–1964), *Cybernetics: or, Control and Communication in the Animal and the Machine*		Universal Declaration of Human Rights Communist coup in Prague Independence of Israel and first Arab-Israeli War

Date	French Works of Philosophy	Other Works of Philosophy (World)	Works of Literature, Art, and Science	Events in France	World Events
1949	**Bataille**, *La part maudite* **Simone de Beauvoir** (1908–86), *Le deuxième sexe* **Bachelard**, *Le rationalisme appliqué* **Vladimir Jankélévitch** (1903–85), *Traité des vertus*; *Debussy et le mystère* **Claude Lévi-Strauss** (1908–2001), *Les structures élémentaires de la parenté* **Emmanuel Levinas** (1906–96). *En découvrant l'existence avec Husserl et Heidegger* **Merleau-Ponty**, "Note sur Machiavel" **Emmanuel Mounier** (1905–50), *Le personnalisme* **Simone Weil** (1909–43), *L'enracinement*	**Karl Löwith** (1897–1973), *Meaning and History* (*Weltgeschichte und Heilgeschehen*)	**Fernand Braudel** (1902–85), *La méditerranée* **Blanchot**, *Lautréamont et Sade* **Ortega y Gasset**, *Meditación de Europa* **George Orwell** (1903–50), *1984* **William Faulkner** (1894–1962) awarded Nobel Prize in Literature	**Cornelius Castoriadis** (1922–97), **Claude Lefort** (1924–), and **Jean-François Lyotard** (1924–98) create Socialisme ou Barbarie Victor Kravchenko's lawsuit against *Les Lettres Françaises* and revelations about Soviet camps	Foundation of NATO Creation of Federal Republic of Germany and German Democratic Republic Creation of the People's Republic of China László Rajk trial in Hungary First Soviet nuclear bomb test
1950	**Lévi-Strauss**, *Introduction à l'oeuvre de Marcel Mauss* **Jean Piaget** (1896–1980), *Introduction à l'épistémologie génétique (I)* **Paul Ricoeur** (1913–2005) translates Husserl's *Ideen I* **Eric Weil** (1904–1977), *Hegel et l'Etat*: *Logique de la philosophie*	**Heidegger**, *Holzwege* **Carl Schmitt** (1888–1985), *Der Nomos der Erde* **Strauss** (1899–1973), *De la tyrannie* (discussion with Kojève) **Alan Turing** (1912–54), *Computing Machinery and Intelligence*	**Aimé Césaire** (1913–2008), *Discours sur le colonialisme* **Marguerite Duras** (1914–96), *Un barrage contre le pacifique*		Beginning of Korean War and McCarthyism in the United States "Stockholm Appeal" of the peace movement

1951	**Bataille** writes *Histoire de l'érotisme (La part maudite, II)* (posthumous) **Camus**, *L'homme révolté* **Gabriel Marcel** (1889–1973), *Les hommes contre l'humain* **Tran Duc Thao** (1917–93), *Phénoménologie et matérialisme dialectique*	**Hannah Arendt** (1906–75), *Origins of Totalitarianism*	UNESCO publishes *Le racisme devant la science* **Samuel Beckett** (1906–89), *Molloy* **André Malraux** (1901–76), *Les voix du silence* **Pierre Schaeffer** (1910–95) creates the Groupe de recherche de musique concrete **Jean Vilar** (1912–71) becomes director of the Théâtre National Populaire	Marshal Pétain dies **Alain (Émile Chartier)** (1868–1951) dies **André Gide** (1869–1951) dies	**Wittgenstein** dies
1952	**Canguilhem**, *La connaissance de la vie* **Frantz Fanon** (1925–61), *Peau noire, masques blancs* **Lacan**, "Intervention sur le transfert" **Lévi-Strauss**, *Race et Histoire*		**Beckett**, *En attendant Godot* Complete posthumous publication of **Robert Musil** (1880–1942)'s *Der Mann Ohne Eigenschaften* **Sartre**, *Saint-Genet, comédien et martyr*	Resistance leaders (André Marty, Charles Tillon) expelled from the Communist Party Sartre clashes over communism with Merleau-Ponty, who leaves *Les Temps Modernes*	Dwight D. Eisenhower elected president of the United States United States tests first hydrogen bomb

Date	French Works of Philosophy	Other Works of Philosophy (World)	Works of Literature, Art, and Science	Events in France	World Events
1953	**Gilles Deleuze** (1925–95), *Empirisme et subjectivité* **Goldschmidt**, *Le système stoïcien et l'idée de temps* **Martial Gueroult** (1891–1976), *Descartes selon l'ordre des raisons* **Jean Hyppolite** (1907–68), *Logique et existence* **Lacan**, "Le mythe individuel du névrosé" **Merleau-Ponty**, *Eloge de la philosophie* **Alphonse de Waelhens** (1911–81), *Phénoménologie et vérité*	**Heidegger**, *Die Frage nach der Technik*; *Einführung in die Metaphysik* **W.V.O. Quine** (1908–2000), *From a Logical Point of View* **Leo Strauss** (1899–1973), *Natural Right and History* **Wittgenstein**, *Philosophical Investigations* (posthumous)	**Breton**, *La clé des champs*	Massive strikes in France **Lacan** (with Daniel Lagache and Françoise Dolto), creates the Société Française de Psychanalyse, which is banned from the International Psychoanalytical Association Fernand Oury (later joined by Fernand Deligny and Félix Guattari) develops "institutional psychotherapy"	Joseph Stalin dies Korean War ends Backed by the CIA, Shah Pahlavi of Iran overthrows communist prime minister Mohammed Mossadeq Egyptian revolution led by Muhammad Naguib and Gamal Abdel Nasser Popular riot in East Berlin against the Communist regime The USSR tests its first hydrogen bomb
1954	**Bataille**, *Somme athéologique (I)* **Bataille**, *La souveraineté* **Lyotard**, *La phénoménologie* **Raymond Ruyer** (1902–87), *La cybernétique et l'origine de l'information* **Jules Vuillemin** (1920–2001), *L'héritage kantien et la révolution copernicienne* **Jean Wahl** (1888–1974), *Les philosophies de l'existence*	**Lukacs**, *Die Zerstörung der Vernunft*	**Pierre Boulez** (1925–), *Le marteau sans maître* (on poems by René Char); Boulez creates the Domaine musical concerts in Renaud-Barrault Theater **Brecht**'s Berliner Ensemble perform *Mutter Courage* in Paris **Françoise Sagan** (1935–2004), *Bonjour tristesse*	Pierre Mendès-France becomes prime minister French defeat in Indochina Independence of Tunisia and Morocco Beginning of Algerian war of independence Interdiction of "Prêtres ouvriers" by Pope Eugenio Pacelli (Pius XII)	

1955	**Jean Beaufret** (1907–82), *Le poème de Parménide* **Gabriel Marcel** (1889–73), *L'homme problématique* **Merleau-Ponty**, *Les aventures de la dialectique* **Ricoeur**, *Histoire et vérité* **Pierre Teilhard de Chardin** (1881–1955), *Le phénomène humain* **Vuillemin**, *Physique et méta-physique kantienne*	**J.L. Austin** (1911–60), W. James Lectures at Harvard; *How to Do Things with Words* (posthumously published in 1962) **Ernst Bloch** (1885–1977), *Das Prinzip Hoffnung* **Herbert Marcuse** (1898–1979), *Eros and Civilization*	**Aron**, *L'opium des intellectuels* **Bataille**, *Lascaux ou la naissance de l'art* **Blanchot**, *L'espace littéraire* **Lévi-Strauss**, *Tristes tropiques* **Vladimir Nabokov** (1899–1977), *Lolita* (refused by U.S. publishers; published in Paris) **Nicolas de Stael** (1914–55), *Le grand concert* (painting)	**Paul Claudel** (1868–1955) dies	Bandung Conference (emergence of the Third World) **Albert Einstein** dies **Mann** dies
1956	**Canguilhem**, "Qu'est-ce que la psychologie?" **Jean-Toussaint Desanti** (1914–2002), *Introduction à l'histoire de la philosophie (Spinoza)* **Deleuze**, "La conception de la différence chez Bergson" **Lacan**, "Fonction et champ de la parole et du langage" **Wahl**, *Vers la fin de l'ontologie* **Eric Weil**, *Philosophie politique*	**Gregory Bateson** (1904–80) invents the "double bind" theory **Wilfrid Sellars** (1912–89), "The Myth of the Given: Three Lectures on Empiricism and the Philosophy of Mind" **Jakobson** and **Morris Halle** (1923–), *Fundamentals of Language*	**Camus**, *La chute* **Sarraute**, *L'ère du soupçon* **Francastel**, *Peinture de société*	A new edition of Marquis de Sade by Jean-Jacques Pauvert is censored Morocco and Tunisia regain their independence from the French Protectorate	Budapest insurrection Suez blockade Failed French-English expedition in Egypt Beginning of de-stalinization and "peaceful coexistence" **Jackson Pollock** dies

Date	French Works of Philosophy	Other Works of Philosophy (World)	Works of Literature, Art, and Science	Events in France	World Events
1957	**Aron**, "La notion du sens de l'histoire" in *Dimensions de la conscience historique* **Roland Barthes** (1915–80), *Mythologies* **Vladimir Jankélévitch** (1903–85), *Le je-ne-sais-quoi et le presque-rien* **Pierre Naville** (1904–93), *De l'aliénation à la jouissance* (on Marx's early philosophy) **Michel Villey** (1914–88), *Leçons d'histoire de la philosophie du droit*	**Noam Chomsky** (1928–), *Syntactic Structures* **Heidegger**, *Der Satz vom Grund* **Ernst Kantorowicz** (1895–1963), *The King's Two Bodies* **Koyré**, *From the Closed World to the Infinite Universe* **Russell**, *Why I Am Not a Christian*	**Antonioni** (1912–2007), *Il Grido* **Aron**, *La tragédie algérienne* **Bataille**, *La littérature et le mal*: *L'érotisme* Final version of **Brecht**'s *Leben des Galilei* performed in Berlin **Camus**, *Réflexions sur la peine capitale* (with Koestler) **Malraux**, *La métamorphose des dieux* **Sartre**, *Le fantôme de Staline* **Starobinski** (1920–), *Rousseau: La transparence et l'obstacle*	**Guy Debord** (1931–94) and others create *Internationale situationniste* **Camus** is awarded the Nobel Prize in Literature	Rome Treatise creates the European Economic Community
1958	**Lévi-Strauss**, *Anthropologie structurale* **Gilbert Simondon** (1924–89), *Du mode d'existence des objets techniques*	**Arendt**, *The Human Condition* **Isaiah Berlin** (1909–97), *Two Concepts of Liberty* **Norberto Bobbio** (1909–2004), *Teoria della norma giuridica* **Heidegger**, *Unterwegs zur Sprache* **Marcuse**, *Eros and Civilization*	**Beauvoir**, *Mémoires d'une jeune fille rangée* **Braudel**, *La longue durée* **Boris Pasternak** (1890–1960), *Doctor Zhivago*	Military coup in Algiers and return of de Gaulle to power, leading to the Fifth Republic	

1959	**Louis Althusser** (1918–90), *Montesquieu, la politique et l'histoire* **Stanislas Breton** (1912–2005), *Approches phénoménologiques de l'idée d'être*	**Strauss**, *What Is Political Philosophy?* **P.F. Strawson** (1919–2006), *Individuals: An Essay in Descriptive Metaphysics*	**Goldmann**, *Le dieu caché* **Queneau** (1903–76), *Zazie dans le métro* **Blanchot**, *Le livre à venir* **Genet**, *Les nègres* **Alain Resnais** (1922–) and **Duras**, *Hiroshima mon amour*	André Malraux becomes minister of culture	Victory of revolution in Cuba (Castro, Guevara) John XXIII (Angelo Roncalli) elected pope
1960	**Gilles Gaston Granger** (1920–), *Pensée formelle et sciences de l'homme* **Lacan**, *L'éthique de la psychanalyse (1959–1960): Séminaires de Jacques Lacan, Livre VII* **Merleau-Ponty**, *L'oeil et l'esprit* **Merleau-Ponty**, *Signes* **Ricoeur**, *La symbolique du mal (Finitude et culpabilité, I)* **Sartre**, *Critique de la raison dialectique (I)* **Sartre**, *Question de méthode*	**Hans-Georg Gadamer** (1900–2002), *Wahrheit und Methode* **Friedrich Hayek** (1899–1992), *The Constitution of Liberty* **Jakobson**, "Linguistics and Poetics" **Quine**, *Word and Object*	**Bachelard**, *La poétique de la rêverie* **Maurice Béjart** (1927–2007) creates "Ballet du XXe siècle" **Alberto Giacometti** (1901–66), "Homme qui marche" **Claude Simon** (1913–2005), *La route des Flandres* Conference at Bonneval on "The Unconscious" (Henri Ey, Lacan, Hyppolite, Merleau-Ponty, Deleuze, Laplanche) Foundation of OULIPO literary group by Queneau, Calvino, Perec, Roubaud	First French nuclear bomb test Failed coup in Algiers ("Semaine des Barricades") Blanchot, Sartre, Breton, Boulez, Beauvoir, Duras, François Maspero, Jean-Pierre Vernant, et al. publish the "Manifeste des 121" supporting the refuseniks in the Algerian War	John F. Kennedy elected president of the United States Creation of the OECD

Moment 3: The Breakaway 1960s

With hindsight, the decade of the 1960s emerges as an exceptional philosophical moment (it has been compared to the founding years of German idealism in the post-Kantian period). This results from the simultaneous coming to intellectual maturity of a new generation of philosophers born in the 1920s (Althusser, Deleuze, Foucault, Derrida, Barthes, Serres, Laplanche, Vernant, etc.), most of them students of Merleau-Ponty, Guerolt, Hyppolite, and Canguilhem, and their production of a remarkable series of seminal works in which a new language is invented and new questions formulated with respect to discourse and knowledge. The category "structuralism" is adapted to name it, provided three caveats are taken into account: (1) the concept of the "structure" is more what is sought or looked for than what is given or taken for granted by them; (2) all the "structuralists" (with the exception of Lévi-Strauss and Dumézil) in the end reject the label because they are essentially elaborating *differences* rather than *theories*; (3) what would later be described as "post-structuralism" is not so much a refutation as an attempt to work out the incomplete, contradictory, or aporetic character of structures in their very definition. Structuralism also connotes a permanent interaction between philosophy and its others, which makes fixed disciplinary delimitations irrelevant (in a striking contrast with analytic philosophy in the English-speaking world or hermeneutics in the German post-Heideggerian tradition). Hence the decisive influence of social anthropology (as redefined by Lévi-Strauss), psychoanalysis (with or against Lacan), and Marxism (with or against Althusser). The polemical expression *la pensée 68*, coined by neoclassical thinkers to identify structuralism as antihumanist thinking with disastrous ethical and political consequences, is grossly simplifying, but it draws attention to the crucial issue of a critique, genealogy, or deconstruction of the metaphysical subject, which certainly polarizes all the reflections on the ambivalent relationship between philosophy and anthropology.

Date	French Works of Philosophy	Other Works of Philosophy (World)	Works of Literature, Art, and Science	Events in France	World Events
1961	**Axelos** (1924–), *Marx penseur de la technique* **Aron**, *Paix et guerre entre les nations* **Althusser**, "Sur le jeune Marx" (and beginning of his seminar at Ecole Normale Supérieure) **Fanon**, *Les damnés de la terre* (preface by **Sartre**) **Foucault**, "Alexandre Koyré, La révolution astronomique, Copernic, Kepler, Borelli" **Foucault**, *Histoire de la folie à l'âge classique* **Foucault**, *Introduction à l'anthropologie de Kant* **Koyré**, *La révolution astronomique* **Lacan**, "Maurice Merleau-Ponty" **Levinas**, *Totalité et infini* **Lefebvre**, *Critique de la vie quotidienne II (Fondement d'une sociologie de la quotidienneté)*	**Heidegger**, *Nietzsche* (lectures, 1936–46)	**Bataille**, *Les larmes d'Eros* **Genet**, *Les paravents* **Jean-Luc Godard** (1930–), *Une femme est une femme* **Henri Michaux** (1899–1984), *Connaissance par les gouffres* **Starobinski**, *L'œil vivant*	French referendum on Algerian self-determination Murderous repression of Algerian nationalist demonstration in Paris on October 17 **Merleau-Ponty** dies	Berlin crisis and construction of the Wall Bay of Pigs, the failed U.S. invasion of Cuba Patrice Lumumba murdered in Congo

Date	French Works of Philosophy	Other Works of Philosophy (World)	Works of Literature, Art, and Science	Events in France	World Events
1962	**Jacques Derrida** (1930–2004), *Introduction à "L'origine de la géométrie" de Husserl* **Deleuze**, *Nietzsche et la philosophie* **Lévi-Strauss**, *La pensée sauvage* **Jean-Pierre Vernant** (1914–2007), *Les origines de la pensée grecque* **Vuillemin**, *La philosophie de l'algèbre*	**Jürgen Habermas** (1929–), *Strukturwandel der Öffentlichkeit* **Heidegger**, *Der Satz vom Grund*; *Annäherung zu Hölderlin* **Thomas Kuhn** (1922–96), *The Structure of Scientific Revolutions* **C.B. Macpherson** (1911–87), *The Political Theory of Possessive Individualism* **Popper**, *Conjectures and Refutations*	**Umberto Eco**, *Opera aperta* **Vasily Grossman** (1905–64) finishes *Life and Fate* (posthumously published in 1989) **Aleksandr Solzhenitsyn** (1918–2008), *One Day in the Life of Ivan Denisovich* **Giorgio Strehler** (1921–97) performs Bertolazzi's *El Nost Milan* in Paris (reviewed by Althusser)	French-Algerian peace agreement Rebellion of OAS terrorist group **Bataille** dies **Bachelard** dies	Cuban missile crisis Beginning of the Vatican II (lasts until 1965) Nelson Mandela arrested and sentenced to life in prison
1963	**Barthes**, "L'activité structuraliste" **Deleuze**, *La philosophie critique de Kant* **Jean-Toussaint Desanti** (1914–2002), *Phénoménologie et praxis* **Foucault**, *Naissance de la clinique*; *Raymond Roussel* **Michel Henry** (1922–2002), *L'essence de la manifestation*	**Arendt**, *On Revolution* **Donald Davidson** (1917–2003), "Actions, Reasons, and Causes" **Schmitt**, *Theorie des Partisanen* **Russell**, *Essays in Skepticism*	**Aragon**, *Le fou d'Elsa* **Joseph Losey** (1909–84), *The Servant* **Alain Robbe-Grillet** (1922–2008), *Pour un nouveau roman* **Sarraute**, *Les fruits d'or*		Civil rights campaign in the United States Assassination of John F. Kennedy Death of Pope John XXIII Death of W.E.B. Du Bois in Accra, Ghana

1964	**Althusser**, "Freud et Lacan" **Deleuze**, *Proust et les signes* **Derrida**, "Violence et métaphysique: Essai sur la pensée d'Emmanuel Levinas" **André Leroi-Gourhan** (1911–86), *Le geste et la parole* **Lévi-Strauss**, *Les mythologiques (I) (Le cru et le cuit)* **Merleau-Ponty**, *Le visible et l'invisible* (posthumous) **Lucien Sebag** (1934–65), *Marxisme et structuralisme* **Simondon**, *L'individu et sa genèse physico-biologique*	**Marcuse**, *One-Dimensional Man*	**Pierre Bourdieu** (1930–2002) and **Jean-Claude Passeron** (1930–), *Les héritiers* **Lacan** moves his seminar to the Ecole Normale Supérieure and creates the Ecole française de psychanalyse ("Ecole freudienne de Paris") **Ariane Mnouchkine** (1939–), creates Théâtre du Soleil **Sartre**, *Les mots*	**Koyré** dies	Beginning of the Vietnam War Nobel Peace Prize awarded to Martin Luther King Jr. Internal coup dismisses Nikita Khrushchev and brings Leonid Brezhnev to power in the USSR
1965	**Althusser**, *Marxisme et humanisme* **Althusser** and **Etienne Balibar** (1942–), "Les défauts de l'économie classique: Esquisse du concept d'histoire" **Aron**, *Démocratie et totalitarisme* **Barthes**, *Eléments de sémiologie* **Henry**, *Philosophie et phénoménologie du corps* **Lefebvre**, *Métaphilosophie* **Leroi-Gourhan**, *Préhistoire de l'art occidental* **Ricoeur**, *De l'interprétation. Essai sur Freud* **Jean-Pierre Vernant** (1914–2007), *Mythe et pensée chez les Grecs*	**Koyré**, *Newtonian Studies* **Marcuse**, *Repressive Tolerance*	Molecular biologists **Lwoff**, **Monod**, and **Jacob** awarded the Nobel Prize in medicine **Régis Debray** (1940–), *Révolution dans la révolution* (written after discussions with Fidel Castro) **Félix Guattari** (1930–92) creates the CERFI and the journal *Recherches* **Georges Perec** (1936–82), *Les choses*		U.S. intervention in Vietnam Malcolm X murdered in New York Military coup of Colonel Boumediène in Algeria, ending the revolutionary internationalist phase of the independence

Date	French Works of Philosophy	Other Works of Philosophy (World)	Works of Literature, Art, and Science	Events in France	World Events
1966	**Barthes**, *Critique et vérité* **Emile Benveniste** (1902–76), *Problèmes de linguistique générale (I)* **Canguilhem**, *Le normal et le pathologique* (expanded edition) **Deleuze**, "Gilbert Simondon, L'individu et sa genèse physico-biologique" **Foucault**, *Les mots et les choses*; *La pensée du dehors* **A.J. Greimas** (1917–92), *Sémantique structurale* **Lacan**, *Ecrits* **Lacan**, "Réponse à des étudiants" **Macherey**, *Pour une théorie de la production littéraire* **Sartre**, "L'universel singulier"	**Adorno**, *Negative Dialectics* **Chomsky**, *Cartesian Linguistics* **Mary Douglas** (1921–2007), *Purity and Danger*	**Heidegger**'s seminars with **Char** in Le Thor **Schaeffer**, *Traité des objets musicaux*	France withdraws from NATO military command **Breton** dies	Cultural Revolution in China

1967	**Barthes**, *Système de la mode* **Canguilhem**, "Mort de l'homme ou épuisement du cogito?" **Deleuze**, "La loi, l'humour et l'ironie" **Derrida**, *De la grammatologie* **Derrida**, *La voix et le phénomène*; *L'écriture et la différence* **Foucault**, "Des espaces autres" **Foucault**, "Les mots et les images" **Jankélévitch**, *Le pardon* **Piaget**, *Biologie et connaissance*	**Bruno Bettelheim** (1903–90), *The Empty Fortress*	**Godard**, *La chinoise* **Celan**, "Todtnauberg" **René Magritte** (1898–1967) retrospective exhibition **Debord**, *La société du spectacle* **Braudel**, *Civilisation matérielle et capitalisme (I)*		Six-Day War and occupation of Palestine by Israel Che Guevara killed in Bolivia Anti-imperialist student's movement in Germany
1968	**Althusser**, "Lénine et la philosophie" **Jean Baudrillard** (1929–2007), *Système des objets* **Canguilhem**, *Etudes d'histoire et de philosophie des sciences* **Deleuze**, *Différence et répétition* **Deleuze**, *Spinoza et le problème de l'expression* **Derrida**, "Différance" **Desanti**, *Les idéalités mathématiques* **Gueroult**, *Spinoza (I and II)* **Levinas**, *Quatre lectures talmudiques* **Nicos Poulantzas** (1938–79), *Pouvoir politique et classes sociales* **Michel Serres** (1930–), *Le système de Leibniz*	**Arendt**, *Men in Dark Times* **Ernst Bloch** (1885–1977), *Atheismus im Christentum* **Habermas**, *Erkenntnis und Interesse*; *Technik und Wissenschaft als „Ideologie"* **Heidegger**, *Das Ende der Philosophie und die Aufgabe des Denkens* **Niklas Luhmann** (1927–98), *Zweckbegriff und Systemrationalität*	**Dumézil**, *L'idéologie des trois fonctions dans les épopées des peuples indo-européens* **Eco**, *La struttura assente*	Student uprisings and general strike (May '68) **Marcel Duchamp** (1887–1968) dies **Kojève** dies	Student uprisings in the United States, Mexico, etc. The Prague Spring and Soviet invasion of Czechoslovakia Assassination of Martin Luther King Jr. Foundation of CELAM in Medellin (inspired by liberation theology)

Date	French Works of Philosophy	Other Works of Philosophy (World)	Works of Literature, Art, and Science	Events in France	World Events
1969	**Aron**, *D'une sainte famille à l'autre: Essai sur les marxismes imaginaires* **Blanchot**, *L'entretien infini* **Canguilhem**, "Qu'est-ce qu'une idéologie scientifique?" **Deleuze**, *Logique du sens* **Foucault**, *L'archéologie du savoir* **Granger**, *Essai d'une philosophie du style*; *Wittgenstein* **Alexandre Matheron** (1926), *Individu et communauté chez Spinoza* **Brice Parain** (1897–1971), *Petite métaphysique du langage* **Ricoeur**, *Le conflit des interprétations. Essais d'herméneutique* **Serres**, *Hermès (I) La communication* **Lucien Sève** (1926–), *Marxisme et théorie de la personnalité*	**John Searle** (1932–), *Speech Acts*	**Benveniste**, *Vocabulaire des institutions indo-européennes* **Boulez** creates IRCAM **Hélène Cixous** (1937–), *Dedans* **Dumézil**, *Mythe et épopée (I)* **Lacan**'s seminar on "L'envers de la psychanalyse"	After losing referendum, de Gaulle quits office; Pompidou elected president	Willy Brandt appointed chancellor of West Germany and starts the "Ostpolitik" of détente

1970	**Althusser**, "Idéologie et appareils idéologiques d'Etat" **Barthes**, *L'empire des signes* **Bataille**, *Oeuvres complètes*, vol. 1 (preface by Foucault) **Goldschmidt**, *Platonisme et pensée contemporaine* **François Jacob** (1920–), *La logique du vivant* **Sarah Kofman** (1934–94), *L'enfance de l'art* **Jacques Monod** (1910–76), *Le hasard et la nécessité* **Poulantzas**, *Fascisme et dictature* **Ricoeur**, *De l'interprétation: Essai sur Freud*		**Beauvoir**, *La vieillesse* **Starobinski**, *La relation critique*	De Gaulle dies Foundation of Organisation Internationale de la Francophonie with **Léopold Sédar Senghor** (1906–2001) as first secretary general	Solzhenitsyn awarded Nobel Prize in Literature Salvador Allende elected president in Chile Beginning of leftist terrorism in Germany (Red Army Faction)
1971	**Jacques Bouveresse** (1940–), *La parole malheureuse* **Stanislas Breton**, *Du principe* **Corbin**, *En Islam iranien: Aspects spirituels et philosophiques* **Louis Dumont** (1911–98), *Homo hierarchicus* **Foucault**, *L'ordre du discours* **Lefort**, *Eléments d'une critique de la bureaucratie* **Lévi-Strauss**, *L'homme nu (Les mythologiques, IV)* **Lyotard**, *Discours, figure* **Rosset** (1939–), *Logique du pire: Eléments pour une philosophie tragique*	**John Rawls** (1921–2002), *A Theory of Justice* **D.W. Winnicott** (1896–1971), *Playing and Reality*	**Francis Bacon** (1909–92) exhibit at the Grand Palais Museum **Blanchot**, *L'amitié* **Sartre**, *L'idiot de la famille (I)*	Peasant upsurge against the military installations of Larzac Foundation of the Groupe d'information sur les prisons by Foucault, Deleuze, Jean-Marie Domenach, Pierre Vidal-Naquet	Communist China admitted to the United Nations

Moment 4: The Limits of Structure: The 1970s

To describe this new, post-1968 moment as a transition is not to minimize its interest. The new generation, which incarnates the structuralist moment, is active in teaching and writing, with younger protagonists emerging (Rancière, Nancy, and Lacoue-Labarthe) and established masters facing the challenge or even contributing to the renewal of the ethical and hermeneutic discourses through major works (Levinas, Ricoeur). But the limits of the structure are now decidedly seen as the defining feature, expressed through a renewed tension between the categories of desire and power, life and text. With a blossoming of philosophical feminist essays, this tension particularly determines a shift from the deconstruction of the subject to the construction of sexual difference (or *différend*) as a new figure of subjectivation. As an international event (including student revolts across the world, antiauthoritarian movements, irreversible cracks in the socialist system), May 1968 has the paradoxical effect of enhancing the critique of state structures (more generally, institutionalized forms of domination, apparatuses, power machines) and devalorizing utopias inasmuch as they embody a notion of a univocal sense of history. A corresponding epistemological effect can be observed in the generalized procedure of reading intellectual works through the prism of their contradictory historical aftereffects (Lefort on Machiavelli, Aron on Clausewitz, Lyotard on Marx and Freud).

Date	French Works of Philosophy	Other Works of Philosophy (World)	Works of Literature, Art, and Science	Events in France	World Events
1972	**Althusser**, *Machiavel et nous* (published posthumously in 1995) **Baudrillard**, *Pour une critique de l'économie politique du signe* **Bourdieu**, *Esquisse d'une théorie de la pratique* **Deleuze** and **Guattari** *Anti-Œdipe (capitalisme et schizophrénie I)* **Derrida**, "Les fins de l'homme" **Gérard Granel** (1930–2000), *Traditionis traditio* **Gérard Lebrun** (1930–1999), *La patience du concept. Essai sur le discours hégélien* **Lefort**, *Le travail de l'oeuvre, Machiavel* **Levinas**, *Humanisme de l'autre homme* **René Thom** (1923–2002), *Stabilité structurelle et morphogenèse*	**Saul Kripke** (1940–), *Naming and Necessity* **Lukacs**, *Ontologie—Marx (Zur Ontologie des gesellschaftlichen Seins I)* (posthumous) **Popper**, *Objective Knowledge*	Conference on Nietzsche at Cerisy with Deleuze, Derrida, and Lyotard	French left signs "Common Programme" Beginning of "Eurocommunism"	Nixon visits China First UN conference on the environment in Stockholm Terrorist killing of Israeli athletes in Munich IRA starts military operations in Ulster The UK, Ireland, and Denmark join the EEC

Date	French Works of Philosophy	Other Works of Philosophy (World)	Works of Literature, Art, and Science	Events in France	World Events
1973	**Aron**, *Histoire et dialectique de la violence* **Dagognet**, *Des révolutions vertes* **Lacan**, *Télévision* **Lyotard**, *Dérive à partir de Marx et Freud* **Henri Maldiney** (1912–), *Regard, parole, espace* **Louis Marin** (1931–92), *Utopiques: Jeux d'espaces*	**Clifford Geertz** (1926–2006), *The Interpretation of Cultures* **Bernard Williams** (1929–2003), *Problems of the Self* **Manfredo Tafuri** (1935–94), *Progetto e utopia: Architettura e sviluppo capitalistico*	**Antoine Vitez** (1930–90) performs Tournier's *Vendredi ou la vie sauvage* **Barthes**, *Le plaisir du texte* **Antoinette Fouque** (1937–), **Cixous,** and others create Editions des Femmes	Beginning of LIP strike in Besançon	Military coup in Chile **Pablo Picasso** (1881–1973) dies
1974	**Althusser**, *Eléments d'autocritique* **Pierre Clastres** (1934–77), *La société contre l'Etat. Recherches d'anthropologie politique* **Derrida**, *Glas* **Foucault**, "La vérité et les formes juridiques" **Foucault**, "Vérité et pouvoir" **Luce Irigaray** (1930–), *Speculum de l'autre femme* **Julia Kristeva** (1941–), *La révolution du langage poétique* **Lacan**, *Encore* (séminaire 72–73) **Lefebvre**, *La production de l'espace* **Levinas**, *Autrement qu'être ou au-delà de l'essence* **Lyotard**, *Economie libidinale* **Jacques Rancière** (1940–), *La leçon d'Althusser* **Serres**, *Hermès (III) La traduction*	**Robert Nozick** (1938–2002), *Anarchy, State, and Utopia* **Francisco Varela** (1946–2001) and **Humberto Maturana** (1928–), *Autopoièsis: The Organization of Living Systems*	**Aragon**, *Théâtre/Roman* **Benveniste**, *Problèmes de linguistique générale (II)* Derrida founds the Groupe de recherche sur l'enseignement de la philosophie (GREPH) **Henri Gouhier** (1898–1994), *Antonin Artaud et l'essence du théâtre* **Perec**, *Espèces d'espaces* Foundation of the Tanztheater Pina Bausch in Wuppertal	Valéry Giscard d'Estaing elected president	Revolution in Portugal **Solzhenitsyn** expelled from the USSR International campaign of intellectuals protesting the warehousing of Soviet dissidents in psychiatric hospitals

1975	**Alain Badiou** (1937–), *Théorie de la contradiction* **Castoriadis**, *L'institution imaginaire de la société* **Michel De Certeau** (1925–86), *L'écriture de l'histoire* **Derrida**, "Economimesis" **Desanti**, *La philosophie silencieuse ou critique des philosophies de la science* **Foucault**, *Surveiller et punir* **Lévi-Strauss**, *La voie des masques* **Moreau**, *Spinoza* **Michel Pêcheux** (1938–83), *Les vérités de La Palice* **Ricoeur**, *La métaphore vive*	**Paul Feyerabend** (1924–94), *Against Method* **J.G.A. Pocock** (1924–), *The Machiavellian Moment*	Ecole des Hautes Etudes en Sciences Sociales created by **Braudel** **Michaux**, *Idéogrammes en Chine*	Abortion depenalized in France (Loi Veil)	Helsinki Treaty between East and West U.S. defeat in Vietnam
1976	**Aron**, *Penser la guerre, Clausewitz* **Miguel Abensour** (1939–) and **Marcel Gauchet** (1946–), Introduction to *Discours de la servitude volontaire de* La Boétie **Baudrillard**, *L'échange symbolique et la mort* **Bouveresse**, *Le mythe de l'intériorité* **Foucault**, *"Il faut defendre la société"* **Foucault**, *Histoire de la sexualité, 1: La volonté de savoir* **François Laruelle** (1937–), *Machines textuelles*; *Nietzsche contre Heidegger* **Foucault** (ed.), *Les machines à guérir*	**Imre Lakatos** (1922–74), *Proofs and Refutations* (posthumous)	**Saul Bellow** (1915–2005) awarded the Nobel Prize in Literature **Boulez** and **Patrice Chéreau** (1944–) stage the centenary *Ring* in Bayreuth	Malraux dies	Beginning of Eurocommunism in France, Italy, and Spain Milton Friedman awarded Nobel Prize in Economics Soweto uprising in South Africa **Heidegger** dies

Date	French Works of Philosophy	Other Works of Philosophy (World)	Works of Literature, Art, and Science	Events in France	World Events
1977	**Stanislas Breton**, *Spinoza, théologie et politique* **Canguilhem**, *Idéologie et rationalité dans l'histoire des sciences de la vie* **Dumont**, *Homo aequalis* **Irigaray**, *Ce sexe qui n'en est pas un* **Levinas**, *Du sacré au saint: Nouvelles lectures talmudiques* **Jean-Luc Marion** (1946–), *L'idole et la distance* **Serres**, *La naissance de la physique dans le texte de Lucrèce*	**Popper** and **John Eccles** (1903–97), *The Self and Its Brain*	**Barthes**, *Fragments d'un discours amoureux* **Renzo Piano** (1937–) builds the Centre Pompidou	Gauchet, Lefort, Castoriadis, Abensour, and Clastres create the journal *Libre* Klaus Croissant (lawyer of Andreas Baader) surrendered by French government to Germany in spite of campaign sponsored by Foucault, Deleuze, etc.	Thousands killed by Argentinian dictatorship Deng Hsiao Ping returns to power in China Anwar El Sadat visits Jerusalem and gives historic speech advocating reconciliation Vaclav Havel and other Czech dissidents draft Charter 77 Terrorist attacks in Spain (ETA), Germany Red Army Faction, and Italy (left and right)
1978	**Derrida**, *La vérité en peinture; Eperons. Les styles de Nietzsche* **Foucault**, "De la gouvernementalité" **Foucault**, "Qu'est-ce que la critique?" **Philippe Lacoue-Labarthe** (1940–2007) and **Jean-Luc Nancy** (1940–), *L'absolu littéraire* **Lefort**, *Les formes de l'histoire* **Jean-Claude Milner** (1941–), *L'amour de la langue* **Poulantzas**, *L'état, le pouvoir, le socialisme*	**Michael Dummett** (1925–), *Truth and Other Enigmas* **Quentin Skinner** (1940–), *The Foundations of the Modern Political Thought* **Edward Said** (1935–2003), *Orientalism*	**François Furet** (1927–97), *Penser la révolution française*	Breakup of the Left Union and electoral defeat; crisis in the Communist Party	John Paul II (Karol Wojtyla) elected pope Aldo Moro assassinated by the Red Brigades Camp David peace agreement (Egypt-Israel) Wei Jinsheng posts "Fifth Modernization" in Beijing poster on Democracy Wall

1979	**Bourdieu**, *La distinction* **Vincent Descombes** (1943–), *Le même et l'autre* **Foucault**, "Omnes et singulatim" **Gueroult**, *Dianoématique (Philosophie de l'histoire de la philosophie)* (posthumous) **Lacoue-Labarthe**, *Le sujet de la philosophie (Typographies I)* **Lyotard**, *La condition post-moderne* **Pierre Macherey** (1938–), *Hegel ou Spinoza* **Nancy**, *Ego sum* **Piaget** and **Chomsky**, *Théories du langage, théories de l'apprentissage*	**Stanley Cavell** (1926–), *The Claim of Reason* **Richard Rorty** (1931–2007), *Philosophy and the Mirror of Nature*	GREPH organizes Etats-Généraux de la Philosophie **Braudel**, *Civilisation matérielle, économie et capitalisme (II et III)* **Paul de Man** (1919–1983), *Allegories of Reading* **Rainer Werner Fassbinder** (1945–82), *Die Ehe der Maria Braun*		Beginning of missile crisis in Europe Iranian revolution led by Ayatollah Khomeini Thatcher elected prime minister of the UK USSR invades Afghanistan

Moment 5: The Im-political 1980s

The im-political 1980s appear as a third determining moment after existentialism and structuralism, signaled by the remarkable concentration of essays and books addressing the ethical-political dilemmas of community and alterity in relationship to the excess of the masses (or multitudes) with respect to institutions, the transcendental illusions involved in collective representations and "we-utterances," and the corresponding search for new experiences and concepts of being-in-common. The strong accent on the essence—or concept or fiction—of the political (and its reverse, the im-political) accompanies a shift in larger world-political interests: from the struggle between the camps of the Cold War to the discontents of globalization and the debate about differences (or even incompatibilities) between classical liberalism and neoliberalism (even before the fall of the Soviet system in 1989), with their dramatic consequences for citizenship and nationality. The key speculative issue becomes then the *relation* (intersubjectivity, transindividuality, correspondence, communication, commerce, gift, becoming-other, etc.) rather than the subject, even better *within* the dilemmas of subjectivization.

Date	French Works of Philosophy	Other Works of Philosophy (World)	Works of Literature, Art, and Science	Events in France	World Events
1980	**Bourdieu**, *Le sens pratique* **Canguilhem**, "Le cerveau et la pensée" (his last public lecture at the Sorbonne) **Deleuze** and **Guattari**, *Mille plateaux* **Derrida**, *La carte postale* **Gauchet** and **Gladys Swain** (1945–93), *La pratique de l'esprit humain* **Kofman**, *L'énigme de la femme: La femme dans les textes de Freud* **Michèle Le Doeuff** (1948–), *L'imaginaire philosophique*		**Barthes**, *La chambre claire* **Deligny**, *Singulière ethnie* **Blanchot**, *L'écriture du désastre* **Beauvoir**, *La cérémonie des adieux*	**Sartre** dies **Barthes** dies **Piaget** dies **Althusser** murders his wife, Hélène **Pierre Nora** (1931–), **Gauchet**, and **Krzysztof Pomian** (1934–) create the journal *Le débat*	Foundation of Solidarity in Poland Beginning of Iran-Iraq War (until 1988)
1981	**Baudrillard**, *Simulacres et simulations* **Stanislas Breton**, *Unicité et monothéisme* **Debray**, *Critique de la raison politique* **Deleuze**, *Logique de la sensation* **Didier Franck** (1947–), *Chair et corps* **Pierre Hadot** (1922–), *Exercices spirituels et philosophie antique* **Kojève**, *Esquisse d'une phénoménologie du droit* (posthumous) **Laruelle**, *Le principe de minorité* **Lefort**, *L'invention démocratique* **Rancière** *La nuit des prolétaires*	Foundation of the Naples political philosophy review *Il Centauro* (Giorgio Agamben, Roberto Esposito, Remo Bodei, Massimo Cacciari, Giacomo Marramao, etc.) **Habermas**, *Theorie des kommunikativen Handelns* **Fredric Jameson** (1934–), *The Political Unconscious* **Alasdair McIntyre** (1929–), *After Virtue* **Hilary Putnam** (1926–), *Reason, Truth, and History*	**Duras**, *La maladie de la mort* **Nadine Gordimer** (1923–), *July's People* **Simon**, *Les géorgiques*	**Lacan** dies François Mitterrand elected president of the Republic The death penalty is abolished	Ronald Reagan elected president of the United States Military coup in Poland against Solidarity

Date	French Works of Philosophy	Other Works of Philosophy (World)	Works of Literature, Art, and Science	Events in France	World Events
1982	**Badiou**, *Théorie du sujet* **Bourdieu**, *Ce que parler veut dire* **de Certeau**, *La fable mystique* **Desanti**, *Un destin philosophique* **Kofman**, *Le respect des femmes* **Marion**, *Dieu sans l'être* **Antonio Negri** (1933–), *L'anomalie sauvage* (French ed., preface by **Deleuze**)	**Popper**, *The Postscript*			Anglo-Argentinian war of Falklands (Malvinas) Worst economic recession since World War II Israeli intervention in Lebanon; massacres of Palestinian refugees in Sabra and Chatila; PLO leader Yasir Arafat takes refuge in Tunisia Leaders of Autonomia operaia (Negri, Oreste Scalzone) convicted in Italy Solidarity advances in Poland; Lech Walesa freed

1983	**Blanchot**, *La communauté inavouable* **Deleuze**, *Cinéma 1: L'image-mouvement* **Descombes**, *Grammaire d'objets en tous genres* **Foucault**, *Fearless Speech* **Kristeva**, *Pouvoirs de l'horreur* **Lévi-Strauss**, *Le regard éloigné* **Levinas**, *Transcendance et intelligibilité* **Lyotard**, *Le différend* **Milner**, *Les noms indistincts* **Nancy**, *L'impératif catégorique* **Rancière**, *Le philosophe et ses pauvres* **Ricoeur**, *Temps et récit (I)*	**John Elster** (1940–), *Sour Grapes: Studies in the Subversion of Rationality*	Foundation of the Collège International de Philosophie by Châtelet, Derrida, Faye, and Lecourt Banlieues 89 urban project launched **Benedict Anderson** (1936–), *Imagined Communities* **Genet,** "Quatre heures à Chatila" **Thom**, *Paraboles et catastrophes*	**Aron** dies Senghor elected to the Académie française	Antinuclear armament marches in the UK, Italy, and Germany
1984	**Florence** (aka **Foucault**), "Foucault" **Foucault**, *Histoire de la sexualité, II: L'usage des plaisirs; Histoire de la sexualité, III: Le souci de soi* **Irigaray**, *Ethique de la différence sexuelle*	**Davidson**, *Inquiries into Truth and Interpretation* **Luhmann**, *Soziale Systeme* **Derek Parfit** (1942–), *Reasons and Persons*		**Foucault** dies	U.S. embargo against Nicaragua

Date	French Works of Philosophy	Other Works of Philosophy (World)	Works of Literature, Art, and Science	Events in France	World Events
1985	**Badiou**, *Peut-on penser la politique?* **Deleuze**, *Cinéma II: L'image-temps* **Deleuze**, "Les puissances du faux" **Luc Ferry** (1951–) and **Alain Renaut** (1948–), *La pensée 68: Essai sur l'antihumanisme contemporain* **Foucault**, "La vie: L'expérience et la science" **Henry**, *Généalogie de la psychanalyse* **Dominique Janicaud** (1937–2002), *La puissance du rationnel* **Kofman**, *Mélancolie de l'art* **Jean Petitot** (1944–), *Morphogenèse du sens* **Ricoeur**, *Temps et récit (III)* **Sartre**, *Critique de la raison dialectique (II)* (posthumous) **Vuillemin**, *Nécessité ou contingence*	**Elster**, *Making Sense of Marx: Studies in Marxism and Social Theory*	**Claude Lanzmann** (1925–), *Shoah* **Simon** awarded Nobel Prize in Literature	**Marc Chagall** (1887–1985) dies	Gorbachev starts Perestroika Black townships revolt in South Africa End of military dictatorship in Brazil and Uruguay Schengen system of border control in Europe Pope John Paul II represses liberation theology
1986	**Deleuze**, *Foucault* **Derrida**, *Parages* (on Blanchot) **Le Doeuff**, *L'étude et le rouet: Des femmes, de la philosophie* **Lacoue-Labarthe**, *L'imitation des modernes* **Lefort**, *Essais sur le politique* **Nancy**, *La communauté désoeuvrée*	**Ilya Prigogine** (1917–2003) and **Isabelle Stengers** (1949–), *La nouvelle alliance*	**Derrida**, *Schibboleth. Pour Paul Celan* *Historikerstreit* on the RFA between **Habermas** and **Ernst Nolte** (1923–)	**Beauvoir** dies **Genet** dies	State of exception and international sanctions in South Africa Nuclear power explosion in Chernobyl

1987	**Derrida**, *De l'esprit* **Derrida**, *Psyché: Inventions de l'autre* **Hubert Damisch** (1928–), *L'origine de la perspective* **Freund**, *Politique et impolitique* **Gouhier**, *L'anti-humanisme au XVIIe siècle* **Levinas**, *Hors sujet* **Rancière**, *Le maître ignorant* **Serres**, *Le contrat naturel*		**Toni Morrison** (1931–), *Beloved* **Jean Nouvel** (1945–) builds Institut du Monde Arabe		First Intifada in Palestinian Territories Gorbachev visits the United States; end of missile crisis Amnesty law for militaries in Argentina (protested by Madres de Mayo) Democratic uprisings in China
1988	**Badiou**, *L'être et l'événement* **Deleuze**, "Qu'est-ce qu'un dispositif?" **Derrida**, *Limited Inc.* **Granger**, *Pour la connaissance philosophique* **Lacoue-Labarthe**, *La fiction du politique* **Nancy**, *L'expérience de la liberté* **Rosset**, *Le principe de cruauté*	**Althusser**, *Filosofia y marxismo* (interview with Fernanda Navarro, published in Mexico) **Karl-Otto Apel** (1922–), *Diskurs und Verantwortung* **Roberto Esposito** (1950–), *Categorie dell'impolitico* **Habermas**, *Der philosophische Diskurs der Modernie* **Gayatri Spivak** (1942–), "Can the Subaltern Speak?"	**Godard**, *Histoire(s) du cinéma*	The National Front gains and the Communist Party loses votes in general elections	Salman Rushdie publishes *The Satanic Verses* and Ayatollah Khomeini calls for deadly *fatwa* against him Soviet retreat from Afghanistan End of Iran-Iraq War The PLO recognizes Israel's existence at the Geneva conference

Date	French Works of Philosophy	Other Works of Philosophy (World)	Works of Literature, Art, and Science	Events in France	World Events
1989	**Dagognet**, *Eloge de l'objet: Pour une philosophie de la marchandise* **Deleuze**, "A Philosophical Concept" **Derrida**, "'Il faut bien manger' ou le calcul du sujet: Entretien (avec J.-L. Nancy)" **Gauchet**, *La Révolution des droits de l'homme* **Irigaray**, "L'amour entre nous" **Simondon**, *L'individuation psychique et collective*		**Sarraute**, *Enfance*	Bicentenary of the French Revolution First "Islamic veil" controversy **Simondon** dies	End of socialist regimes in Eastern Europe Reunification of Germany Demonstration for democracy repressed in Tiananmen Square in Beijing Soviet defeat in Afghanistan
1990	**Badiou**, *Le nombre et les nombres* **Deleuze**, "Post-scriptum sur les sociétés de contrôle" **Derrida**, *Du droit à la philosophie* **Macherey**, *A quoi pense la littérature?* **Ricoeur**, *Soi-même comme un autre*	**Giorgio Agamben** (1942–), *La comunità che viene*		**Althusser** dies	Nobel Peace Prize awarded to Gorbachev Liberation of Mandela and end of apartheid End of dictatorship in Chile First Gulf War in Iraq

1991	**Luc Boltanski** (1940–) and **Laurent Thévenot** (1948–), "De la justification" **Derrida**, "Donner le temps (la fausse monnaie)"; "L'autre cap" **Bruno Latour** (1947–), "Nous n'avons jamais été modernes" **Maldiney**, "Penser l'homme et la folie"		**Alain de Libera** (1948–), *Penser au Moyen-Age*	Resignation of Gorbachev, collapse of the USSR Wars and ethnic cleansing begin in Yugoslavia
1992	**Rémi Brague** (1947–), "Europe la voie romaine" **Claude Imbert** (1933–), "Phénoménologies et langues formulaires" **Janicaud**, "Le tournant théologique de la phénoménologie française"	**Amartya Sen** (1933–), *Inequality Reexamined* **Negri**, *Il potere costituente. Saggio sulle alternative del moderno* **Jameson**, *Postmodernism, Or, the Cultural Logic of Late Capitalism*	*Manufacturing Consent: Noam Chomsky and the Media* (documentary) **Francis Fukuyama** (1952–), *The End of History and the Last Man*	Beginning of "civil war" in Algeria against the Islamic Front Adoption of NAFTA Rodney King beating and riots in south central Los Angeles Maastricht Treatise signed
1993	**Bouveresse**, *L'homme probable (sur Robert Musil)* **Châtelet** (1945–99), *Les enjeux du mobile* **Deleuze**, "Sur quatre formules poétiques" **Derrida**, *Passions*; *Sauf le nom*; *Khôra*; *Spectres de Marx* **Fernando Gil** (1937–2006), *Traité de l'évidence*		**Frank Gehry** (1929–) builds the American Center in Paris	Bill Clinton elected U.S. president Oslo Accords (Israeli-Palestinian) F.W. De Klerk and Mandela awarded Nobel Peace Prize

Date	French Works of Philosophy	Other Works of Philosophy (World)	Works of Literature, Art, and Science	Events in France	World Events
1994	**Françoise Dastur** (1942–), *La Mort: Essai sur la finitude* **Derrida**, *Politiques de l'amitié* **Gauchet** and **Swain**, *Dialogue avec l'insensé—A la recherche d'une autre histoire de la folie* **Bernard Stiegler** (1952–), *La technique et le temps, I*	**Massimo Cacciari** (1944–), *Geo-filosofia dell'Europa*		**Kofman** commits suicide	Genocide in Rwanda
1995	**Deleuze**, "Immanence: une vie" **Descombes**, *La denrée mentale* **Laruelle**, *Théorie des étrangers* **Levinas**, *Altérité et transcendence* **Rancière**, *La mésentente*	**Agamben**, *Homo sacer: il potere sovrano e la nuda vita* **Gerald Cohen** (1941–), *Self-Ownership, Freedom and Equality*		Conservative Jacques Chirac elected president **Canguilhem** dies **Deleuze** dies **Levinas** dies	Israeli Prime Minister Yitzhak Rabin murdered

Moment 6: After 1995: Toward a New Century

Is it possible to define one or several synthetic characters of the philosophical work in this final period of our survey, even in the form of points of heresy (or shared disagreements)? As Zhou Enlai quipped when asked for his assessment of the French Revolution, "It's too soon to tell." Nevertheless, it can be observed that—after the deaths of many protagonists of the previous moments (notable exceptions being Derrida and Lefort) and the affirmation of the generation born in the late 1930s and 1940s (Badiou, Nancy, Rancière, and Bouveresse)—the period is not lacking in strong contributions. They are often produced in an intellectual and institutional space (for teaching and publishing) that is much more transnational, testifying not exactly to a blurring of geophilosophical styles (this is only the most banal effect of globalization), but to a migration of the influence of French philosophy toward other continents (where it is no longer the privilege of French nationals, if it ever was) and the growing interest on the part of the French for various others (Wittgensteinian ordinary-language philosophy or non-Western cosmologies, for example). Hence the strategic importance of new attempts to rethink universalism (a question that, in many ways, replaces humanism as a focus of debates linking theory and practice), attempts that range from the problematization of the sensible to the relativization of the nature/culture distinction.

Date	French Works of Philosophy	Other Works of Philosophy (World)	Works of Literature, Art, and Science	Events in France	World Events
1996	**Derrida**, *Le monolinguisme de l'autre* **Descombes**, *Les institutions du sens* **Laruelle**, *Principes de la non-philosophie* **Nancy**, *Etre singulier pluriel*		**Samuel Huntington** (1927–2008), *The Clash of Civilizations and the Remaking of World Order*		
1997	**Derrida**, *Adieu à Emmanuel Levinas* **Badiou**, *Deleuze*; *Saint-Paul, la fondation de l'universalisme* **Marion**, *Etant donné: Essai d'une phénoménologie de la donation*	**Judith Butler** (1956–), *The Psychic Life of Power*	**Gehry** builds the Guggenheim Museum in Bilbao	Socialist Lionel Jospin elected prime minister ("cohabitation")	UK Prime Minister Tony Blair inaugurates the "Third Way" Kofi Annan becomes UN secretary-general (until 2006) Aslan Maskhadov inaugurated president of autonomous Chechnya
1998	**Badiou**, "L'événement comme trans-être" **Franck**, *Nietzsche et l'ombre de Dieu* **François Jullien** (1951–), *Un sage est sans idée ou l'autre de la philosophie* **Le Doeuff**, *Le sexe du savoir*	**Esposito**, *Communitas* **Habermas**, *Die postnationale Konstellation*		**Lyotard** dies	India's first nuclear bomb test, soon followed by Pakistan's

1999	**Latour**, *Politiques de la nature* **Lefort**, *La complication* **Ferry** and **Renaut**, *Des droits de l'homme à l'idée républicaine*	**Spivak**, *A Critique of Postcolonial Reason*	**J.M. Coetzee** (1940–), *Disgrace*	Putin elected president of Russia
2000	**Gil**, *La conviction* **Rancière**, *Le partage du sensible: Esthétique et politique*		**Dipesh Chakrabarty**, *Provincializing Europe: Postcolonial Thought and Historical Difference*	Second Intifada in Palestinian Territories
2001	**Jocelyn Benoist** (1968–), *Représentations sans objet* **Derrida**, "Comme si c'était possible, 'within such limits'"			George W. Bush elected U.S. president September 11 terrorist attack on World Trade Center and the Pentagon United States invades Afghanistan
2002	**Lacoue-Labarthe** *Poétique de l'histoire*; *Heidegger: La politique du poème* **Nancy**, *La création du monde ou la mondialisation*			

Date	French Works of Philosophy	Other Works of Philosophy (World)	Works of Literature, Art, and Science	Events in France	World Events
2003	**Derrida**, *Voyous*			New controversy on "Islamic veils" in schools **Blanchot** dies	United States invades Iraq **Habermas** and **Derrida** call for the "Rebirth of Europe"
2004				Legislation bans religious symbols from public schools **Derrida** dies	
2005	**Rancière**, *La haine de la démocratie* **Philippe Descola** (1949–), *Par delà nature et culture*			**Ricoeur** dies	Referendum on the EU constitution